A Various Language

*Perspectives on
American Dialects*

A Various Language

Perspectives on American Dialects

Edited by

Juanita V. Williamson
LeMoyne-Owen College

Virginia M. Burke
University of Wisconsin-Milwaukee

HOLT, RINEHART AND WINSTON, INC.
New York   Chicago   San Francisco   Atlanta
Dallas   Montreal   Toronto   London   Sydney

To A.E.W.
and J.M.W.

To the Reader

A Various Language: Perspectives on American Dialects spans over seventy-five years of dialect study in the United States by several generations of scholars. The first generation, which closed with the publication in 1925 of *The English Language in America,* by George Philip Krapp, included phoneticians, philologists, and rhetoricians whose keen ear and feeling for language provided many a sound intuition and insight and a few serious linguistic studies.

A new era began in 1930 with the launching of the Project of *The Linguistic Atlas of the United States and Canada* under the directorship of Hans Kurath. While the Project was patterned to some extent upon earlier European models, it took into account features peculiar to American culture, such as population movement, upward mobility, plurality of standard dialects, and the relationship of history and education to speech. Through the 1930s and 1940s scholars set about gathering, analyzing, and publishing *Atlas* materials and carrying on autonomous *Atlas* projects in the North Central States, the Upper Midwest, the Pacific Coast, and elsewhere. The current generation of scholars, whose initial studies have appeared within the decade, are now guiding the work of younger students in pioneering directions.

It is true that there has as yet been no complete analysis of American English. We do not as yet have enough information about its various dialects to provide a complete description. Our studies remain partial; and there are some areas where no studies have been made. But the work which has been done constitutes an impressive corpus of scholarly materials.

Yet for the most part, students, teachers, and writers of textbooks have had to depend on brief generalized descriptions of American dialects. While some of these descriptions serve well as introductions, they have obvious limitations, especially in recent years when the increasingly multi-dialectal character of school populations, and the desire among educators to understand the impact of population movement upon language, have added fresh impetus to the continuing interest in American dialects. At such a time it is especially necessary for all those working in education, communication, and literature to be familiar with the history and principles, procedures and findings of American dialect study. Only with an adequate scholarly background can teaching materials, teaching methods, and articles on pedagogy be properly evaluated.

It seemed important, therefore, to make available to readers some evidence of the historical sweep and the scope of dialect studies, to go behind the generalized textbook summaries to some of the work on which they have been based. Hence *A Various Language,* a collection of scholarly papers—many of them currently neglected, little known or not readily accessible.

The design of this volume has special significance. Part 1 is at once both overview and introduction. Its six classic articles look back to the earliest work in American dialect study as well as forward to work still needing to be done. As introduction, the articles, singly and severally, touch upon the perspectives treated in more depth in subsequent parts of the collection: historical, literary, regional and social, social and urban. Part 2, using some material rarely anthologized, intensifies the historical perspective, with special attention to the origin of American English. Building on the early article by Krapp, Part 3 presents both in theory and in practice the representation of dialects from early to modern American literature.

Parts 4, 5 and 6 include descriptions of the speech found in various parts of the United States. Most of them deal with phonological features; one or two discuss only grammatical features. A few deal with lexical features.

Part 4 includes articles which are regional in nature. Two deal with relic areas. Articles treating fewer than five features appear in Part 5. These two sections include articles touching most of the areas where studies have been made.

Part 6 opens with an overview of the speech of the city and continues with selected studies of urban speech. In the rapid urbanization of the past few decades, millions of Americans have moved into urban centers, many of them from the rural South; and all have carried with them their own variety of English. Since some of the urban studies are quite long, only portions could be included.

Our long process of search, selection, and design has produced a collection we believe should prove instructive, even exciting, to serious students of American dialects. Clearly, not all articles gathered could be included and very probably some distinguished articles have been overlooked. But we hope that this volume does convey the sweep, depth, scope, and character of American dialect study and that its papers present American English as the various language it is and always has been.

ix

MARCH 1971

J. V. W.   *Memphis, Tennessee*
V. M. B.   *Milwaukee, Wisconsin*

By Way of Introduction
Hans Kurath

Although we do not have a nationwide standard of cultivated speech comparable to that of England or France, the regional differences between the speechways of well-educated Easterners, Westerners, Northerners, and Southerners rarely interfere with effective communication among members of this social group. Nevertheless, a Bostonian can be spotted by the way he pronounces *aunt* and *half,* a New Yorker by the way he sounds *law and order,* a Virginian by the way he says *down and out,* and a South Carolinian by his pronunciation of the vowels in such phrases as *take it away* and *row the boat.* Other regional features in cultivated speech are current in extensive areas. Midwesterners and Up-country Southerners are known for their stable *r* in such words as *here, fair, far, four, poor, fur, father.* Southerners rime *poor* with *four* and start the diphthong in *down* with the vowel of *Dan.* Pennsylvanians have the same vowel in *four* and *forty,* and again in *fair* and *ferry.* Northerners rime *creek* with *kick,* Southerners with *peak.* And so on.

In popular speech—*folk speech,* as I prefer to call it—the regional differences are considerably greater in matters of pronunciation, and there are some marked differences in the rustic vocabulary and in verb forms. But these differences do not seriously interfere with communication when a Midwestern farmer meets his like in the Lower South, or a fisherman from Maine talks with his peer on Puget Sound.

Such differences in our English, whether regional or social, are not a matter of chance. They reflect the history of the American people: the way they settled the country, developed communication routes within and between settlement areas, created cultural institutions such as schools and the press, and maintained cultural relations with the Mother Country across the Atlantic, both in Colonial times and after the War for Independence.

The chief regional types of American English developed in Colonial times along the Atlantic Seaboard. Strung out along the coast for a thousand miles from New England to South Carolina, the several colonies grew rather slowly and had little contact with each other. Under these circumstances each colony, settled by Englishmen speaking various dialects along with Standard English, developed its own variety of English in the course of several generations, largely under the influence of those who spoke a variety of Standard English—Colonial leaders as well as English officials.

During the Westward Movement these regional types of English were carried as far west as the Rocky Mountains in hardly more than half a century. The Western–New England type spread into the basin of the Great Lakes, creating the present *Northern* speech area. The Pennsylvania type was carried across the Allegheny Mountains into the Ohio Valley and into the southern Appalachians, the present *North* and *South Midland* dialect areas. The Virginian and South Carolinian varieties became established in the Cotton Belt along the Gulf of Mexico and in the lower valley of the Mississippi to form the present *Southern* speech area. Farther west—in the Plains and the Rocky Mountains and on the Pacific Coast—the settlement belt overlapped, which led to the development of new blends, especially in California and the Northwest with their teeming population.

So much for a broad view of the origin and the spreading of the chief regional varieties of our English.

Each regional type of American English has a configuration of usages shared by most of the people living in the area. But there are also more or less marked differences between the speech of the upper and lower classes. Such differences are greater in the old population centers along the Atlantic Coast than in the more recently settled Western areas, and they are greater in the South than in the North, with its social mobility of the population. The survival of speech differences between social groups also reflects the effect of schooling. Wherever schooling at public expense was established early and made compulsory, the lower classes have to a large extent abandoned folk forms in grammar, vocabulary, and pronunciation.

Regional differences in our English are not infrequently mistaken as social markers, when large numbers migrate from one dialect area to another, especially when the migrants are Negroes. The sampling of Southern speech for the *Linguistic Atlas* in the 1930s revealed a situation that I summarized as follows in *A Word Geography of the Eastern United States* (1949), page 6:

> By and large the Southern Negro speaks the language of the white man of his locality or area and of his level of education. But in some respects his speech is more archaic or old-fashioned; not un-English, but retarded because of less schooling.

The majority of the Negroes who came to the Northern manufacturing cities during the two World Wars spoke—and many still speak—the dialect of the lower classes of their Southern homes.

Since the use of folk speech often proves to be a handicap in the effort to achieve a decent living, as in a profession or a trade, it is the task of the schools to familiarize our youth with the usage of educated speakers and to train them to such an extent that they can speak and write this class dialect to their advantage whenever the situation calls for it. Mastery of a socially superior dialect should therefore be the objective of instruction, not the elimination of the family dialect.

A teacher who knows how his students talk in their homes and among themselves and has some understanding of the way in which regional and social differences in our English came into being has obvious advantages. Knowing the socially marked differences between "higher" and "lower" usage, he is in a position to focus his efforts on important matters. Understanding that every regional and social dialect has its unique system of forms and sounds, he will not waste his efforts on trying to replace the student's native speech instead of teaching him a "second" dialect that he can use to his advantage.

Interest in American English as a distinctive descendant of British English arose very early in our history. Words peculiar to the United States, later called *Americanisms*, were pointed out with patriotic pride by Noah Webster as early as 1806. Now the *Historical Dictionary of American English* (1938–1944) presents that part of the vocabulary which diverges from British English. New American words as well as old words with new meanings are included in its four stately volumes. Before long we may also have a *Dictionary of American Regional English*, which will display the many words whose currency is restricted to the several regions of our vast country. Northern, Southern, and Western expressions of English stock, as well as the contributions of American Indian languages, Dutch, German, and Spanish, to our regional vocabulary will come to light and help us visualize the complicated sociocultural forces that have shaped American word usage.

With the foundation of the American Dialect Society 80 years ago, studies in regional pronunciation and grammar first make their appearance, and in recent years the *Publications of the American Dialect Society* have presented us with numerous articles and monographs on these aspects of our language. Since 1926, the periodical *American Speech* has vastly increased our information and understanding of the way Americans speak and write.

Forty years ago the first systematic survey of the dialects of the Eastern United States was undertaken under the sponsorship of the American Council of Learned Societies, soon to be followed by similar investigations in the Midwest and the Far West. These surveys, known as the *Linguistic Atlas*, have enabled us to outline the linguistic structure of the Eastern States, where the chief dialectal types of our English had their origin, and to trace their Westward expansion. Since these investigations include the speech of the folk, the middle class, and the cultured, we are now in a position to deal with social as well as regional dialects in better perspective. Moreover, we can safely correlate these varieties of our English with the history of the American people, and thus account for them in socio-cultural terms.

This collection of essays and articles by well-qualified scholars—the only one of its kind—will appeal not only to the specialist in the field of English, but also to the layman with an interest in American history. To the teacher of English it offers a wealth of information on our English in its regional and social manifestations and a sound point of view that should prove helpful in the classroom. It should also encourage him to seek further information in the basic scholarly books published in recent years, and to consult them when specific problems arise in the performance of his task.

JANUARY 1971   **Hans Kurath**
Professor of English, Emeritus
University of Michigan

Contents

Part 4　ASPECTS OF REGIONAL AND SOCIAL DIALECTS

Appendices

part **1**

A VARIOUS
LANGUAGE

The Standard of American Speech

Fred Newton Scott

During the first quarter of the twentieth century many American scholars engaged in a lively dialogue on standards of American speech. It was a dialogue often marked more by predilections and easy assumptions than by painstaking investigation. Fred Newton Scott, always a perceptive listener and careful observer, was in the vanguard of this discussion. As president of the Modern Language Association of America (1907–08), first president of the National Council of Teachers of English (1911–13) and Head of the Department of Rhetoric at the University of Michigan, Scott was in a position of considerable influence in the years before the development of linguistic geography in the United States.

Scott's point of view on American English was remarkably compatible with the linguistic scholarship that was to come after his time. Borrowing a phrase from Bryant's "Thanatopsis," Scott maintains in this essay that American English is "a various language." He rejects a single fixed standard

in pronunciation, idiom, or syntax as untenable both in theory
and in practice. Instead, he advances the idea that several
major regional dialects might come to share the status of
standard speech.

Mr. Henry James somewhere remarks that the reason why English
society is so superior to American society is that in England there is
always something to go on to. By this cryptic phrase he means—if I
understand him—that, whereas an American is limited in his social contacts to the dull round of democratic equality, an Englishman has the
opportunity of passing from a lower social stage to a higher, going on
in the course of a single evening from gatherings of his despised equals
to functions that are quite obviously superior—functions graced by
aristocracy and perhaps even by royalty.

This peculiar view of the inferiority of American society is not, I imagine, shared by any great number of Americans; but, curiously enough,
a view of American speech exactly parallel to it is, both in this country
and in England, well-nigh universal. I mean that almost everyone who
touches upon American speech assumes that it is inferior to British
speech. Just as the Englishman, having endured for a time the society
of his equals, goes on to bask in the sunshine of aristocracy, so the American, when he has used the American language for business or for familiar
intercourse, may then, for higher or more serious purposes, go on to the
aristocratic or royal language of Great Britain.

Thus, to take the first example that comes to hand, when Mr. Rudyard
Kipling, in one of his minor poems, speaks of the American as "a brother
hedged with alien speech," he means us to understand that linguistically
the American is on the wrong side of the hedge. In other words, American
English, in Mr. Kipling's view, is not only an alien speech but a degraded
speech. English is spoken as it should be spoken only in Great Britain.
American English is a provincial or barbarous English which some day,
when we are more civilized, we shall be compelled to unlearn.

That an Englishman should take this view of his native speech is only
natural, and if we regard it merely as an article of the British constitution
we need pay no further attention to it. But, unfortunately, our English
brothers sometimes attempt to support their dogmas by reasons, and
these reasons are often too absurd or too irritating to be passed by in
silence. A characteristic illustration of such an attempt may be found in
a paper by a Mr. H. Thurston, which appeared some little time ago in
the *Nineteenth Century*. Mr. Thurston's point is, that whereas in England
all educated Englishmen speak alike, in America we speak all sorts of

From *The English Journal* 6:1–15 (January, 1917).

tongues. In one of Mr. Howells's novels, for example, he finds a heroine from New York who says "moybid" for "morbid," and a hero from Virginia who says "toned" for "turned." From Henry James's *Bostonians* he takes the following passage[1]: "He came from Mississippi and he spoke very perceptibly with the accent of that country. He prolonged his conso nants and swallowed his vowels. He was guilty of elisions and interpolations which were equally unexpected." Differences in speech such as these, Mr. Thurston goes on to say, are unknown in the United Kingdom among cultivated people. "A novelist on this side of the water having told us that his heroine is English, has practically nothing more to say about the way she talks. She talks—English."

In brief, according to this writer, since there is but one standard of speech in England as against no standard in America, an American who wishes to speak the best English must take his pronunciation from the mother-country.

Deferring for a moment the question of a single, standard speech in America, let us ask whether it is true that all cultured Englishmen speak alike. I think I may appeal to the experience of everyone who has ever been in England, or has ever listened to the speech of Englishmen, to hear me out in saying that they do not. What one finds if one examines impartially the English of the United Kingdom is, first, a large number of dialects, many of them unintelligible to Americans, and, I suspect, to Englishmen also; and secondly, four or five leading types of expression which rise to the dignity of national speech. Of the latter, some are easily understood by Americans; some are not.

At a meeting in London University several years ago I had the pleasure of listening to speeches by eight well-known Englishmen. All used English, and good English too, but, phonetically regarded, there was as great a difference between the speech, say, of Mr. W. T. Stead and that of Sir John Cockburn, as could be heard on any university platform in America. Mr. Stead spoke precisely like an American from the Middle West—he might have been born in Chicago. The others spoke an unmistakable British, though all were easily intelligible.

To illustrate the more difficult types of British speech, I will give one or two personal experiences. I remember once sitting by the side of an eagerly conversing couple in the Dresden Art Gallery for full twenty minutes without guessing their nationality until the exclamation, "Just fahncy!" revealed that they were speaking English, or at least Londonese. A more recent experience was with a young Dutch girl in one of the schools of The Hague, who had acquired a correct and fluent English by several years' residence in a British boarding-school. It is no exaggeration

[1] Here somewhat condensed.

6   to say until I got the hang of her pronunciation, if I may put it so, I understood her Dutch better than her English. I recall one phrase which completely baffled me. It was "mawxstrawnry." After she had repeated it several times at my request, I had her write it down, whereupon it resolved itself into "more extraordinary," as I should pronounce it. I may add that she found my American equally difficult.

If I may trust my own ears, the differences in English speech are as great as the differences in American speech. True, the items of difference are not the same, and they may be subtler, but they exist none the less, and, as Mr. Bernard Shaw has intimated in his *Pygmalion,* they are patent to anyone who will train himself to appreciate them. If they have not as yet been commented on by British novelists, the fault is with the novelists themselves, not in the lack of material offered by their characters. Setting aside purely dialectical differences, one may hear in the speech of educated Londoners such variants as the following: "which, wich; excursion, ixcursion, ixcushion; for, faw; here, he'uh, hyah; idea, idear; office, orfice; porter, pawtuh; yourself, youself, yeh'self; stop, stawp; round, rah'oond, reh'oond; door, dawr, daw, doh'uh"; and many more besides, some of which, if spelled in phonetic symbols, would be quite as ridiculous as the "moybid" of New Yorkers or the "toned" of Virginians.

It may be said, as Mr. Thurston implies, that these are vagaries of the individual, whereas the differences in American speech are generic. So be it. But in this connection one may recall that Scotland, Ireland, and Wales are essential parts of the United Kingdom and as such are entitled to a voice, both literally and figuratively, in deciding questions of the King's English. To draw the suggested parallel, does not our Southern speech (or Northern speech, if the South prefers) have its counterpart in the pleasing and unmistakable accent of Scotchmen or Irishmen, and is not one just as good English as the other?

In fine, the idea that somewhere, in some linguistic Utopia, there exists a standard English which all cultured Englishmen use alike and cannot help using and to which distracted Americans may resort for chastening and absolution, is a pleasing hallucination, which a single glance into Mr. Henry Sweet's *Primer of Spoken English* should have dissipated forever. Not only does good English vary in different parts of the United Kingdom, but, as I shall point out later, it owes no small part of its goodness, that is, its interest and charm, to these same variations.

Turning now to our own country, we may concede at once that Americans, like Englishmen, speak a various language. Perhaps I can best introduce this phase of my subject by quoting from a letter that I received not long ago from a Western businessman:

I have noticed in traveling about the country a good many differences in the pronunciation of common words. The word I call "hot," the New Englander pronounces "hawt" or something like that. On the other hand, what I term a "hog," or perhaps I ought to spell it "hawg," some persons speak of as a "hahg." Once I was fond of the word isolate and used it whenever I had a chance, but so many persons nowadays say "ice-olate" that I have dropped it. What I refer to as a *com*bine some of my customers, who are pretty well educated men, call a com*bine*. Then there is "Chicago." Half the people I meet in the cars are going to "Chicawgo" and the other half to "Chicahgo." Now what I want to know is whether there is any right or wrong about this matter of pronunciation. If one way is right, why don't we all pronounce that way and compel the other fellow to do the same? If there isn't any right or wrong, why do some persons make so much fuss about it?

And he adds in a postscript, "Which do you say—neether or nither?"

To the last question one would prefer to reply as the Irishman did, "nayther," and so escape the troublesome question altogether. However, the general principles involved are too interesting and too important to be lightly put aside. If American speech has a wrong and a right, we ought to find them out, and, having done so, shun the one and cleave to the other.

Time was when the pronunciation of New England was thought to be superior to that of the rest of the country. The man who said "Dawchestuh" and "idear" was felt to belong to a higher intellectual stratum than the man who said "Dorchester" and "idea." A great many persons in the West, feeling a little ashamed of their provincial speech, cultivated the New England pronunciation and learned in course of time to give a pretty fair imitation of it. But speech habits acquired thus late in life are somewhat difficult to maintain, and so persons who put on these false ornaments are very likely to drop them in moments of excitement. There is a well-known public speaker, born in the Middle West, who at the beginning of his speech, when he is on his dignity and a trifle self-conscious, always says "pleasuh" and "feachah" and "chahming," but, as soon as he has warmed up, sounds his *r*'s as plainly as he does his *p*'s and *q*'s.

This superstition, however, is virtually dead. The persons who use the New England pronunciation are relatively so few in number that they may almost be said to speak a special dialect. The aristocratic period has passed and we are now on a thoroughly democratic basis. Hoosier and Wolverine and Badger and Sucker may hold up their heads when they use their native vowels, and the Southerners, who have always been justly proud of their beautiful speech, need no longer take the trouble even to defend it.

8   Speaking at large, we may say that in this country, as in England, there is no standard of pronunciation that is universally recognized, the dictionaries to the contrary notwithstanding. If any considerable body of educated Americans in any part of the country is using seriously a peculiar form of English for transacting the business of life, that form of English is good American and has a chance of becoming our national speech. Its chances are specially good if it is racy, rich in vocabulary, and is used by a large number of representative and gifted citizens.

Which of the various pronunciations cited by my correspondent will, in the fulness of time, drive out the others it is now impossible to say. Perhaps neither "hahg" nor "hawg" will win in the contest, but something half-way between the two. Meanwhile, all are alike good. The Missourian has a perfect right to tell the caviling critics of his pronunciation that they "gotta quit kickin' his dawg aroun'." Whatever may be said of "gotta," "kickin'," and "aroun'," the "dawg" in the democratic aristocracy of American speech is entitled to an honorable place.

The situation in this country, we may conclude, is not very different from that in Great Britain. We have here, as they have there, a variety of dialects, no one of which rises to the dignity of a universal medium. We have here, as they have there, several types of national speech, akin to the dialects, struggling for ascendency; but we have no means of knowing which will ultimately prevail, if any one of them ever does prevail.

It may seem to some persons who have always thought of language as governed by rather rigorous laws, that a doctrine of this sort tends to a condition, not of democracy, but of anarchy, that it throws the doors open to all manner of degraded pronunciations and leads ultimately to linguistic chaos. It must be remembered, however, that what are called the laws of good English are after all only the observed uniformities in the serious speech of large bodies of intelligent and cultured users of the language. The purpose of dictionaries is to record such uniformities. As soon as a degraded pronunciation is used seriously by a sufficiently large number of educated persons it ceases to be degraded and becomes one of the nobility —if a democracy may be said to admit of a nobility.

An interesting example of this elevation of a word is seen in the expression, "an apron." Originally, this was written "a napron," but through carelessness the sound of the *n* was transferred from the noun to the article, and the word "napron" was thus, in popular speech, transformed into "apron." Here was a distinct case of carelessness and degradation. Nevertheless the word passed into common use and in course of time actually drove the older word out of the vocabulary.

But in other similar cases a degraded form, although apparently as fit for survival as the word "apron," has failed to establish itself. Every year, for example, hundreds of thousands of American children create for themselves the words "napple" and "nour." There is a period in the life of almost every American child, I suppose, when he says "Ain't these napples good?" or, "Teacher kept me in for two nours." Nevertheless these terms have not as yet risen above the childish vocabulary.

Are we forced then to abandon the idea of a standard of American speech? Yes and no. The idea of a fixed standard to be settled arbitrarily once and for all by some authority or set of authorities may be abandoned summarily. It is untenable, both in theory and practice. To be sure, some of our expansive orators look forward to a time when all the people of the world shall speak the same language in the same way, and perhaps they are true prophets. But, for my part, if this simplification is ever to come, I am glad that it has not come in my day. A world in which everybody used the same words and language forms would be a much more monotonous, a much less interesting world than the one we live in. There are adventures of the spirit and of the intellect as well as of the body, and one of the most fascinating as well as the most invigorating of them is the tackling of a foreign language. Fortunately such adventures are likely to be open to posterity long after the fastnesses of the earth have become commonplaces of travel. It is of the essence of language to change. No power can stay it. If by some miraculous intervention all the inhabitants of the world could at four o'clock tomorrow afternoon be made to speak exactly alike, it would not be twenty-four hours before differences would begin to make themselves apparent. Variations in types of character, in daily needs, in attitudes toward life and nature and society would bring about rapid variations in the mode of expression, and unless we are to conceive of the whole world as drowned in sloth or in brotherly love, competition and rivalry would soon give one set of variations precedence over the others, so that after a few generations the one language would break up into divergent dialects and ultimately into diverging languages.

What is true of different races and countries is true also, though in a milder way, of different sections of the same country. There is no nation, so far as I am aware, in which all the citizens or even all the educated citizens use precisely the same speech. Compare the German of Berlin with the German of Munich, the Italian of Naples with the Italian of Florence, the Russian of Odessa with the Russian of Petrograd. And just as the world is more interesting and more intellectually alluring because of the existence of foreign languages, so our national life is more interesting, more livable, and more amusing because of the sectional differences of American speech. . . .

But to say this is not to abandon entirely the quest for a standard. If the idea of a fixed standard is put aside, there still remains a touchstone of a wholly different kind to which we may turn with full confidence. Perhaps

10   the clearest and simplest formulation of it is that of Walt Whitman in his
American Primer. Says Whitman:

> The subtle charm of the beautiful pronunciation is not in dictionaries,
> grammars, marks of accent, formulas of a language, or in any laws or
> rules. The charm of the beautiful pronunciation of all words, of all
> tongues, is in perfect flexible vocal organs and in a developed harmo-
> nious soul. All words spoken from these have deeper, sweeter sounds,
> new meanings, impossible on any less terms. Such meanings, such
> sounds, continually wait in every word that exists—in these words—
> perhaps slumbering through years, closed from all tympans of temples,
> lips, brains, until that comes which has the quality patiently waiting in
> the words.

If this doctrine is sound, the stuff out of which a great national language is created is the simple, homely expression of sincere feeling and
sturdy thinking. Live nobly, think good thoughts, have right feelings, be
genuine, do not scream or strain or make pretense, cultivate a harmo-
nious soul—follow these injunctions, and you are laying the foundation
of a standard American speech. Whence the speech comes does not
matter. It may be the language of Potash and Perlmutter. It may be composed of all the dialects spoken in Chicago or in San Francisco. It may be
the speech of Boston, of Texas, or of Montana. No matter. If it is the
voice of high wisdom, of moderation, of human nature at its best, the
words will take on that power and charm which is the test of a great national speech. . . .

But while there is no dialect form, nor, indeed, any kind or combination of vocal sounds which may not conceivably become an element of
our national speech, we may yet distinguish between an unkempt speech
and what may be called a "tidy" speech. There is a kind of ungainly utterance which goes with slovenly thinking and ill-regulated feeling, that
offends, and properly offends, those whom Plato calls "lovers of discourse." Against this we must set our faces like iron. It would be a mistake, however, to suppose that the sense for tidiness of speech is confined
to the educated. A feeling for the nice organization of verbal utterance
may frequently be detected among the unlettered. I have recently heard
an anecdote which aptly illustrates one phase of this inherent language-
sense. A city man who was traveling in the Kentucky mountain region
stopped at a farmhouse and asked for food. The woman of the house
hesitated a moment, and then replied that she had nothing fit to eat. "Oh,
I can eat anything," responded the traveler; "haven't you some corn-
bread?" The woman's face lighted up. "Oh, if cawnbread's all you want,
come right in. Why, cawnbread's just what I ain't got nuthin else on hand
but." Not even the German, pursuing relentlessly his separable particle,
has a stronger grip on syntax than had that unlettered woman. I believe

that such a language-sense is widely distributed throughout the elements which compose our motley population. On this alone one might build the structure of a cogent, logical, well-knit language.

Whatever impression these remarks may have created, I trust I have made one point clear, and that is that when we deal with American speech we shall do well to cultivate the virtue of tolerance. It is clearly not our business to force upon the younger generation the speech of any particular section of the country, or to do them to death for want of well pronouncing shibboleth. The speech of one's own community, the speech which one hears day by day at home and on the street, is the speech which, in modified form, one will probably use all one's life long. If, as a child, I say "glăss" and "păst," I shall in all likelihood continue to do so in old age. And why not? The vowel sound in "glăss" is just as good as that in "glahss," or as the intermediate sound which, in my boyhood, teachers vainly attempted to acquire and to impose on their pupils.

But, on the other hand, such speech as the child uses he must be helped to use effectively. To this end the influences that lead to cheap thinking and disorderly feeling, and to slovenly or bombastic or affected speaking, must be traced to their sources and, as far as possible, counteracted. Thus may be brought about in the pupil that harmony of soul of which Whitman speaks, without which, flexibility of the vocal organs is a sham and a nuisance. In this, as in all other kinds of education, the letter means nothing unless the spirit gives it life.

Finally, American speech is not a degraded or plebeian form of British speech—it is a vigorous, hardy offshoot that is gradually assuming a form appropriate to our character and daily needs. It will grow as the nation grows, and its divergence from British English will correspond to the divergence of this nation from the mother-country in character, modes of thought, and social custom. We need not expect that all Americans will ever speak alike; probably there will always be at least three main types of speech which, by the extent and distinction of their use, will rise above the grade of dialects. If they become standard or prevailing types, it will be because they are found to express better than other modes of speech the thoughts and feelings of the entire nation, especially as these are voiced by men of genius and leaders of thought. The best American speech of any period will be that which, with least strain or affectation or waste of effort, gives adequate utterance to the best that is in the American character.

The Origin of the Dialectal Differences in Spoken American English

Hans Kurath

This article, written just before the launching of the project of the *Linguistic Atlas of the United States and Canada,* is now of great historical value to serious students of the history of American English because it reviews forty years of research on dialects by pre-*Atlas* scholars. At the time it was written, it was programmatic in delineating the kind of research needed to correlate regional differences with the history of the population. After questioning the belief, commonly held in the early years of this century, that American English is a modified variety of seventeenth- and eighteenth-century Southern British Standard, Dr. Kurath offers a tentative alternative. Now emeritus, he was for many years Professor of English at the University of Michigan and Director of the Atlas project. From 1952 to 1963 he edited the *Middle English Dictionary.*

The publication of J. S. Kenyon's *American Pronunciation* in 1924 and of G. P. Krapp's *The English Language in America* in 1925 bears witness to a new interest in spoken American English and its history. In the period intervening between these recent books and the nineties, when Grandgent, Sheldon, Emerson, and Hempl were engaged in ascertaining usage in the various parts of this country, both by personal observation and by carefully prepared questions submitted to competent observers, the pronunciation of English in America received little attention. Even less thought was given to the history of our pronunciation, to which these scholars had also devoted themselves, without, however, pushing their studies very far. As a result we are today not much better informed on these questions than thirty years ago, although W. Read's recent papers on Southern pronunciation[1] have materially increased our knowledge of that area.

And yet, a thorough survey of actual usage in the various sections of the country is as necessary to the historical study of our pronunciation as for the question of a standard of pronunciation. Until we shall possess such a survey, all historical investigation must proceed largely by "safe guesses," and all arguments for a standard will be swayed by local or personal preference.

In undertaking a discussion of the origin of our regional differences in pronunciation, I am not unaware of the fact that pitfalls must lie hidden in this scantily explored field, and I fully realize that my views are of a tentative nature.

It is generally assumed—if one may judge by the statements that appeared in print before the publication of Krapp's work[2]—that American English, apparently also in its spoken form, is essentially the Southern English Standard of the seventeenth and eighteenth centuries as modified locally in the course of the last century or two. This is the view advanced by Whitney, presumably for American English as a whole;[3] by Ellis, for "the eastern United States, New York and Massachusetts";[4] accepted by Emerson for the speech of Ithaca, New York;[5] and defended by Sheldon.[6]

From *Modern Philology*, 25, No. 4 (May, 1928), 385–395. Reprinted with the permission of the University of Chicago Press and Hans Kurath.

[1] "The Vowel System of the United States," *Englische Studien,* XLI, 70 ff.; "Some Phases of American Pronunciation," *JEGP,* XXII, 217 ff.

[2] See the present writer's review in *Language,* III, 131–139.

[3] W. D. Whitney, *Language and the Study of Language* (1868), pp. 171 ff.

[4] A. J. Ellis, *Early English Pronunciation,* V, 236.

[5] O. F. Emerson, "The Ithaca Dialect," *Dialect Notes,* I, 169–73.

[6] F. S. Sheldon, "What is a Dialect?" *Dialect Notes,* I, 293.

14   That such retardation of change in languages cut off from their mother-country does take place nobody can doubt who knows of the history of Icelandic; and that American English preserves words, phrases, constructions, as well as articulations of the seventeenth and eighteenth centuries, that were lost in the Southern English Standard is no less evident. Among the retarded sounds one might mention the vowel in *cut*, which has been lowered to low-central position in Southern English, but is still pronounced with considerable elevation of the back of the tongue in America; the first consonant in *wheat* [ʍiːt], which with us is still generally pronounced as a voiceless labial fricative followed by a voiced glide (except in parts of the South); elsewhere rather commonly in unstressed *whenever, whatever, wherever,* and the exclamatory *why!,*[7] while it became fully voiced in Southern English;[8] the vowel in *get*, which still has a more open pronunciation with us than in Southern English. All of these sounds are common to all of the United States, although the Seaboard of New England is somewhat closer to Southern English.

But not all the deviations of American educated pronunciation from the Southern English Standard can be explained as owing to the conservation of an earlier stage of that Standard, and even the retarded sounds just mentioned can without exception be derived from the Northern English pronunciation of the Southern Standard. To my mind, most of the dialectal differences existing at present between New England, the South, and the North-and-West did not develop out of a uniform Southern English Standard, but have their bases partly in the regional varieties of the Standard and partly in the strongly dialectal speech which the earlier settlers of these regions brought with them from England and Scotland. This conclusion seems to me unavoidable to one tracing the treatment of the *r*, and the vowels preceding an original *r* in the three sections mentioned.

The New Englanders, except those in the northwestern section, and the Southerners, especially those on the Atlantic Coast and in the lower South, pronounce the *r* only before vowels, as in *ready, hurry, far off* (and even in that position it is frequently slighted before an unstressed vowel, as in *carry, Maryland* [kæ(ə)ɪ, mæələnd]); they have no *r*-sound before consonants and finally, as in *large, heard, fair, far cry* [laːdʒ, hɜːd, fɛ·ə, faːkraɪ]. With a considerable minority in the upper South, the tip of the tongue does rise more or less toward the *r*-position in the latter cases (especially in the vowel of *heard,* rarely after the low vowels of *large* and

---

[7] G. Hempl, *Mod. Lang. Notes,* VI, 310–11; and C. H. Grandgent, *ibid.,* VIII, 277. But S. Primer (*Phon. Stud.,* I, 239) claims that in Charleston, S.C., "in the combination *wh* the *h* is always silent."

[8] D. Jones, *An Outline of English Phonetics* (2d ed.), p. 65.

order), but not far enough to produce a distinct *r*-sound; the impression on the ear is rather that of a muffled vowel.[9]

In the rest of the United States, holding two-thirds of the entire population, the *r* is pronounced in all positions. Before vowels it is a voiced fricative formed by narrowing the air-passage at the upper gums with the front edge of the tongue, or even in the region of the palate by tilting it back, as in parts of the Middle West. Before consonants and in final position the tongue is somewhat lower and the *r* has here a more vocalic ring. The former short high-front vowel [ɪ] and the short mid-vowels [ɛ, ʌ, ə] have been encroached upon by the *r* to such an extent that they have entirely disappeared.[10] In words like *first, fern, fur,* a long strong vocalic *r* follows immediately upon the initial consonant. The short of this *r* is heard in the unstressed syllable of *father*.

Adherents of the principle of conservatism should find it hard to reconcile these facts to their theory. For the preconsonantal and final *r* should in that case be preserved, if anywhere . . . in the oldest colonies: eastern Massachusetts, where only the recently immigrated Irish have this *r*, and the tidewater region of Virginia, where it is wholly unknown. The suggestion that the closer personal relations of the maritime colonies with England caused the loss of the *r* in these sections does not bear scrutiny. There is no indication that this peculiarity was confined to the small group that studied and traveled in England and to the rather small groups whose pronunciation they could influence. This *r* was lost by all, as far as we know; by the large rural population as well as by the inhabitants of the few cities. Nor is Sheldon's view that this *r* was reintroduced "in some parts of the country, particularly Ohio and vicinity," as a spelling pronunciation or as an analogical extension of the double pronunciation of words with final *r* (like that of *hear* in *hear it* [hɪərɪt] and in *hear them* [hɪ·əðɛm], respectively) at all probable.[11]

Grandgent[12] inclines to the belief "that the school-master, the spelling-book, and the dictionary, whose authority is wellnigh absolute in sparsely settled and comparatively uncultivated communities, have been largely

[9] Grandgent, *op. cit.,* VII, 276.

[10] R. M. Pierce, *Dictionary of Hard Words* (New York, 1910); G. P. Krapp, *The English Language in America,* II, 167; and H. E. Palmer, *A Dictionary of English Pronunciation with American Variants* (New York, 1927), regularly write a vowel before the *r,* but I have heard that pronunciation only from Scotchmen and Irishmen.

[11] An opinion expressed in the 1892 meeting of the Dialect Society, and reported in *Dialect Notes,* I, 173.

[12] *Op. cit.,* VII, 275. Both the speech of the home and that of the school have a share in forming the speech-habits of the child. But if the speech of the schoolmaster (or his school pronunciation) is at variance with that of the majority of the homes of the community his influence can be but slight.

16   responsible for the prevalence of *r* in the North and West." But he also
hesitatingly concedes that "perhaps, the influence of the Scotch and Irish
immigrants has made itself felt" on this point.

In my opinion, the dialectal basis is the primary factor in the treatment
of the *r*. On this point the kinship of the speech of Eastern New England
and the pronunciation of Standard English in the south of England is
obvious, and no less so the similarity of the speech of our North-and-
West and the pronunciation of Standard English in the north of England
as described by R. J. Lloyd.[13]

Such parallelism in the treatment of only one sound, which, to be sure,
entails an extensive modification of all vowels preceding it,[14] would in
itself be no proof of common origin. But there are other points of similarity and resemblance between the two pairs.

In our North-and-West the vowels represented in *made* and *mode* are
only slightly diphthongal, the upglide of the tongue never passing beyond
the mid-region, and the same seems to be the case in Northern English.[15]
In eastern New England and Virginia, however, the upglide is much
longer, the tongue passing into high position, especially when these
sounds are at the end of a phrase, as in *Is he leaving today?* [tədɛɪ] and in
That is not so! [sɔU], following the tendency that has produced the
strongly diphthongal vowels in Southern English.[16]

Agreement between our North-and-West[17] and the English North is
also found on the following points: (*a*) the preservation of the distinction
between the mid-open long vowel [o̞:] of *four, hoarse, mourning,* and the
low short [ɔ] of *forty, horse, morning* (see Kenyon, *Am. Pron.,* p. 120);
(*b*) the qualitatively identical vowels in *hat* and in *half;* (*c*) perhaps also
a preference for the voiceless *s*-sound in *transition, discern,* and *greasy,*
etc.;[18] (*d*) the peculiar monotonous intonation of the sentence. G. P.

[13] *Northern English* (2d ed., 1908], pars. 100–103 and 113.

[14] In general, the varieties of English in which the post-vocalic and the final *r* are lost have
more open vowels, as in *more, fair* [mɔ·ə, fæ·ə], and also in *poor, here;* but in our South these
vowels are even closer than in the *r*-pronouncing North (see W. Read, *JEGP,* XXII, 220 ff.).

[15] R. Lloyd, *op. cit.,* pars. 89 and 94.

[16] S. Primer, "Charleston Provincialisms," *Phon. Stud.,* I, 232, claims for Charleston, S.C.,
that "the long (e) is equivalent to (ee'j)," i.e. [e:j]. But H. R. Lang, *Phon. Stud.,* II, 185, objects
to this observation, saying that *no* and *may* have [o:] and [e:], respectively. For the history of
these "slow" diphthongs see Jespersen, *Mod. Engl. Gram.,* Vol. I, sec. 11.4.

[17] The North-and-West extends westward from the Hudson River, in some respects even from
the Connecticut River, and southward to the Potomac and the Ohio, although southern traits
are found for a considerable distance to the north of these rivers.

[18] G. Hempl, *Dialect Notes,* I, 438; and R. Lloyd, *op. cit.,* par. 140. Hempl gives a different
interpretation of the facts (p. 443).

Krapp's statement in his *English Language in America,* II, 23, that "in this matter of cadences, it is quite obvious to one familiar with various types of British speech, that the cadences of speech in the north of England are on the whole much closer to those of American speech than are the cadences of the speech of the south of England," certainly does not apply to the speech of New England and our South.

On the other hand, the speech of Seaboard New England agrees with, or resembles, that of the south of England in the following respects: (*a*) The vowel of *hot, lock,* and *stop* has lip-rounding, which, to be sure, is not as pronounced in New England as in the south of England. (*b*) The vowel of *four* and *mourning* is lowered to the level of the vowel in *all* and identical in quality with the vowel of *forty* and *morning,* less widely in New England than in the south of England; in turn, the vowel of *all* is closer in these two varieties of English than in the other two. (*c*) The preference for the high unstressed vowel [ɪ] in *darkness, houses, wicked.* (*d*) The shortened vowel of *coat, whole,* and *home* is recorded for East Anglia (Norfolk) (see Ellis, *Early English Pronunciation,* pp. 1211 ff.). (*e*) The palatalization of the velar stops of *garden* and *cow* in New England (and the South), now considered vulgar and passing out of use, has its parallel in Southern English dialects.[19] (*f*) Although the low-central vowel in New England *half, dance* [ha:f, da:ns], and the low-back vowel in the Southern English pronunciation of these words did not become fashionable before the eighties of the eighteenth century, it is probable that the new sounds are the result of a common preliminary step, namely, the lengthening of the older [æ] before fricatives and the nasal dental consonant groups. (*g*) Certain phases of intonation.

When these resemblances between the several groups are considered together, the case for the dialectal bases becomes a strong one.

Fortunately, the linguistic evidence for a historical connection between American speech of the North-and-West and that of Northern England, on the one hand, and between the speech of eastern New England (and, in part, that of our South) and the pronunciation of the south of England,

---

[19] Grandgent, *op. cit.,* VI, 458–59, and *Old and New* (1920), pp. 127–28. In the earlier article he writes in part: "I am told, however, that it is still prevalent in eastern Virginia [i.e., in 1891]."

S. Primer, "The Pronunciation of Fredericksburg, Va.," *PMLA,* V, 199, says: "This pronunciation is of course not general. Some consider it vulgar and avoid it, but it can be heard in the best families [i.e., in 1890]." And in *Phon. Stud.,* I, 240, he claims that it is heard in Virginia, South Carolina, Boston, and Cambridge, and adds that there is "no doubt that it is an individual peculiarity all over the country. Here [Charleston, S.C.] it is the prevailing pronunciation." Geographically, the statement seems rather too sweeping, but forty years ago this pronunciation was certainly much more common than now.

on the other, is well supported by the history of American colonization, of the westward movement, and of later immigration.

Before the Irish immigration, which began about 1840, the population of the Seaboard of New England had come for the most part from the southeastern counties of England (especially in the earlier period),[20] the home of the Southern English Standard. It is not surprising then that the speech of the seaboard of New England should resemble that Standard in its treatment of the *r* and the other points mentioned. The settlers simply brought with them the speech-habits of their native counties. The earliest of them probably pronounced a weak *r* before consonants and, finally, the later ones not;[21] and even the earliest of them possessed the Southern English tendency to diphthongize the close mid and high vowels.[22]

Western New England, however, received a considerable admixture of Scotch-Irish in the half-century preceding the Revolution,[23] and is therefore in certain respects "Western" in speech. It is the speech of the west of New England that became established in New York State and in the Western Reserve of Ohio.

Like the seaboard of New England, the tidewater region of Virginia received most of its early population from Southeastern England, and therefore has Southern English speech habits. But the Piedmont of Virginia and the Carolinas, and the Great Valley, were largely settled, during the half-century preceding the Revolution, by the Scotch-Irish, who spoke a quite different dialect, namely, the English of the Lowlands of Scotland or the north of England as modified by the Southern English Standard.[24] They neither dropped their *r*'s nor did they pronounce their long mid-vowels diphthongal fashion. The large German element from Pennsylvania ultimately acquired this type of English.

In the Old Southwest these two stocks became intimately mixed, the Scotch-Irish element being, however, much larger in the northern part.

---

[20] E. Channing, *The United States of America* (1765–1865), pp. 1–2.

[21] H. C. Wyld, *History of Modern Colloquial English,* pp. 298–99. G. P. Krapp gives examples of unintentionally phonetic spellings in the New England town records of the latter part of the seventeenth century which are unmistakable evidence that the post-vocalic *r* had been lost by that time, at least with some persons (see *The English Language in America,* II, 229).

[22] Recent investigators have brought forward evidence to show that the Southern English tendency to diphthongal articulation of long vowels was already active in the seventeenth century (Jespersen, *e.g.;* I, 325 ff.

[23] H. J. Ford, *The Scotch-Irish in America,* pp. 225 ff.; F. J. Turner, *The Frontier in American History,* p. 71.

[24] H. J. Ford, *op. cit.,* pp. 90 ff. and 378 ff.

For Kentucky, Tennessee, as well as the southern portions of Ohio, Indiana, and Illinois, and much of Missouri received most of their early population from the Valley of Virginia and the Piedmont, where the Scotch-Irish predominated; while the Cotton Belt of western Georgia, Alabama, Louisiana, Mississippi, and eastern Tennessee was settled very largely by the cotton-growers of the tidewater of Virginia and the Carolinas.[25] The differences in the speech of the two elements were in part leveled out. The Scotch-Irish softened their trilled *r*'s to the present more or less pronounced inversion of the tip of the tongue; the tidewater emigrants gave up their pronounced diphthongization of the long mid-vowels and some other peculiarities. But many purely dialectal articulations remain in the South, especially in secluded mountain districts and among the Negroes.

The population of the Middle Atlantic states was mixed. The religious tolerance of the Quakers attracted immigrants from all parts of the British Isles and of Western Europe. Although we have little definite information regarding the exact provenience of the Quakers themselves, it is nevertheless clear that a considerable majority of the population of the Middle Colonies did not have Southern English speech habits. It is estimated that at the time of the Revolution the population of this region was one-third Quaker, one-third Scotch-Irish, and one-third German.[26] Of these elements the Scotch-Irish certainly did not speak in the manner of the south of England; and, as regards the Quakers, the fact that this religious movement was organized in the north of England and the northern Midlands (1644–54) and found its most numerous and most fervent adherents and apostles in these sections and the west of England,[27] i.e., outside the area in which the Standard arose and was most widely accepted,[28] would seem to warrant the inference that a good portion of them came from those regions. That very many of them knew spoken Southern English intimately is more than doubtful, as nearly all of them belonged to the middle class and had not been at the southern universities or in intimate contact with the nobility. They might use the vocabulary and the idiom of the Southern English Standard, as their leaders undoubtedly

[25] W. E. Dodd, *The Cotton Kingdom*, pp. 9 ff.

[26] "In 1774 Benjamin Franklin computed the proportion [of Scotch-Irish in Pennsylvania] as one-third in a total of 350,000" (Ford, *op. cit.*, p. 265).

[27] The influence of the speech of the west of England on American English is hard to discern. Krapp points out a number of rather doubtful cases of such an influence in his *English Language in America*, II, 121, 125, 142.

[28] W. C. Braithwaite, *The Beginnings of Quakerism* (1912), pp. 127, 130, 153, 164–65, 375, 381–83; *The Second Period of Quakerism* (1919), pp. 408–9.

20   did;[29] but their pronunciation must have had considerable local color, at least as much as the educated speech of the north and the west of England has at the present time (except for those that receive their education in the schools of Southeastern England). Besides, their natural Northern or Western English speech habits would be encouraged in contact with the Scotch. The Scotch, in turn, probably reduced their trilled *r* [r] to the fricative *r* [ɹ] in contact with the Quakers. The German element eventually adopted the resulting local pronunciation of English.

Thus the English of the Middle states was probably not very uniform, but it had as a general feature the strong *r* in all positions, the only slightly diphthongal long mid-vowels, and the other peculiarities enumerated above for our present North-and-West. This form of speech was carried westward and triumphantly crossed the continent, being reinforced in various points by the speech of the Irish, who came in imposing numbers from 1840 onward.[30] The non-English immigrants favored the *r* and nondiphthongal vowels, but their influence probably counted for little.

The New Englanders of the Seaboard who migrated westward to western New England, New York State, the Western Reserve of Ohio, and the Farther West—first through Pennsylvania or the Shenandoah Valley and Kentucky, and, after the opening of the Erie Canal, by the new route—were sooner or later assimilated in speech to the locally prevalent type. They acquired the postvocalic *r*, restrained their inclination to diphthongize the close mid-vowels, and gave up the "Italian *a*" [a:] in *half, pass, dance,* etc., and the short vowel in *stone, whole,* etc.[31]

The dialectal differences in the pronunciation of educated Americans from various sections of the country have their origin largely in the British regional differences in the pronunciation of Standard English.

The Seaboard of New England, drawing for two centuries most of its population from Southeastern England, is in speech akin to the counties whose speech contributed most to the Southern English Standard of

[29] Despite the remoteness of the dignified style of the King James Version (1611) of the Bible, it must have influenced the colloquial language of the Bible-reading Quakers a great deal, thus eliminating dialect words, idioms, and grammatical forms.

[30] For the history of the Westward movement consult F. C. Turner, *The Rise of the New West* (1907), pp. 28–44; and his *Frontier in American History* (1920), pp. 27–28, 164, 215–16, and esp. 223–24.

[31] In an interesting letter in *Dialect Notes,* I, 17, written in 1889, P. Seymour, of Hudson, Ohio, says: "Most men are gone who brought from Connecticut the pronunciation of *stone, coat* with the short *o*; and from New Hampshire of *bone* with the same short *o* . . . and from Massachusetts (I think), *hoarse* and *coarse* pronounced very nearly like *horse* and *course.*"

pronunciation. But the recent Irish influx has undermined the earlier uniformity.[32]

The South is divided and uneven in speech. Tidewater Virginia is strongly Southern English in speech, the Piedmont and the mountain country of the Atlantic states strongly Scotch, Georgia, and the Old Southwest mixed of the two in stock and speech—the latter type predominating in the upper South, the former in the lower South. Besides, there are in this section of the country numerous secluded communities of pronounced dialectal speech.

The North-and-West has, at all events, a Northern English (including Lowland Scotch) basis in stock and speech. This section is surprisingly uniform in speech over its entire vast area, the speech of the Seaboard New Englanders having been assimilated to the "Western" type.

All of the three types of spoken American English are conservative as compared with the pronunciation of the Southern English Standard in the Southeast and the southern Midlands of England. But what they conserve is not the various stages of that Standard, as seems to have been so generally assumed, but certain features—phonetic as well as lexical—of the several basic British regional varieties of Standard English.

---

[32] G. Hempl, *Dialect Notes*, II, 254, put it this way: "However unwilling some New Englanders may be to acknowledge it, the present large immigration of peoples from other parts of the English-speaking world is introducing in New England a more general form of English; and that the Irish have a part in this movement, there can be no doubt. This may be observed in the matter of pronunciation as well as in that of vocabulary."

See also Grandgent's observation, *Old and New*, p. 139, that "the 'Italian *a*' is most constant among farmers, less stable among city people, whose convictions have been shaken by contact with the Irish and also by the school teacher, who has often insisted on a compromise vowel."

The Psychology of Dialect Writing

George Philip Krapp

Professor Krapp was the first American linguist to give
serious attention to American literary dialects. This article,
a classic in the literature, and George Krapp's book *The
English Language in America* (1925) have served as reference
points for all students who, in the past fifty years, have
undertaken analyses of spoken American English and its
representations in literary dialects.

Whether or not there is such a thing as a genuine American dialect,
no one can doubt the interest which readers today take in literature
written in dialect. A race of dialect enthusiasts has sprung up. Dialect
fans cultivate all sorts of exotic lingos, sometimes as earnest philologers,
sometimes as anecdotal humorists, and sometimes as professional literary
artists. These latter have standardized a number of different dialect patterns by industrious repetition. The devices of language employed by
Ring Lardner have acquired a kind of classic dialect quality; and definite

From *The Bookman* 62:522–527 (December, 1926).

Yiddish, Irish, Italian, Negro, and other dialect styles have established themselves so firmly in the public consciousness as to be immediately recognizable when they are seen. All these dialects appear to be immensely interesting to the readers of today. Certainly they lend a variety to writing in America which cannot be paralleled in England. Something in our American circumstances renders us peculiarly susceptible to the dialect character, to the wit, the pathos, even the poetry which is sometimes concealed beneath the garb of uncouth speech.

The first question that occurs to one looking at this exuberant dialect literature is whether it comes up from below, that is, whether it is a reflection and echo of an authentic folk interest in literary expression, or is imposed from above as an ingenious invention of sophisticated literary artists. Undoubtedly the second is the right explanation of its origins. The sporting English of baseball, football, and the ring, the Irish English of Mr. Dooley, the cloak-and-suit brand of English in *Potash and Perlmutter,* the chorus girl and movie English of *Gentlemen Prefer Blondes,* the young-man-in-the-street English of Mr. Weaver's idyls, all these are no doubt based upon a certain degree of observation. They have some foundation in reality. But none of them is a reflection of a folk movement in literature. Nor has there ever been any such folk movement in the whole history of American letters. The poems of Burns were written in dialect because the Scottish folk from whom Burns sprang possessed a traditional literature of song and tale composed in an unconventionalized traditional vernacular. Burns did not merely put the dialect into his poems. The dialect impulse and the poetic impulse came to him together as two things already united. On the contrary, Burns's task was to put enough conventional English into his poems to secure their acceptance by a public accustomed to measure all literature by the established literary standards. Very often the conventional phrase strikes a jarring note, and one feels that Burns would have done better if he had avoided more completely the proprieties of eighteenth-century diction.

Our modern American dialect writers are exposed to exactly the opposite danger. Their tendency is to season the dish too strongly, to put in the dialect flavoring with too liberal a hand. As inventors and recorders it is always easy for them to discover a great many more dialect traits than as artists they should use. The result is a kind of dialect style that seems sometimes to bear no relation to reality, as in Percy MacKaye's representation of the Southern mountain speech. And sometimes the record may be true enough; but it is so elaborate that it becomes work for the painstaking student, not a pleasure to the general reader. The dialect of the Uncle Remus stories was very carefully thought out by Joel Chandler Harris, but it is a question whether it was not too fully thought out and administered from the point of view of the tales regarded

24   as literature. It was not as literature, however, that Harris in the first
place conceived his stories. He thought of them as a scientific record of
the folklore of an interesting people, in language as well as in plot, and
it was a surprise to him to find that the world at large valued them more
highly as literature than as science. The stories have lived, not because
but in spite of their elaborate dialect. Yet so intimate is the relation between language and content in these tales, like that of twins brought up
under the same vine and fig tree, that anyone who attempts to translate
them into a simpler and more conventional idiom, as various persons
have done, soon finds that in the process of translation a great deal of
their charm is destroyed. But the happy accident of the literary success
of the Uncle Remus stories should not mislead prospective writers of
dialect. For it may safely be put down as a general rule that the more
faithful a dialect is to folklore, the more completely it represents the
actual speech of a group of people, the less effective it will be from the
literary point of view. A genuinely adequate representation of a living
dialect could be made only with the help of a phonetic alphabet, and
such a record would contain an enormous amount of detail which would
merely distract and often puzzle the literary reader. The writer of a literary dialect is not concerned with giving an exact picture of the folklore
of speech. As an artist he must always keep his eye on the effect, and
must select and reject what the scientific observation of his material
reveals to him according as it suits or does not suit his purpose.

The writer of literary dialect for this reason may use certain devices
which have no significance whatever to the scientific student of speech.
One of these is eye dialect. This is an ancient trick, practised by Sam
Slick, Major Jack Downing, Hosea Biglow, Moses Adams, Josh Billings,
and all along the line to the Jack Keefes of today. It consists merely in
respelling familiar words to accord with the pronunciation, the pronunciation being the same, however, in the speech of the cultivated as in the
speech of the uncultivated. Thus to spell "is" as "iz," or "dear" as "dere,"
or "once" as "wunce," means nothing to the ear, though it may mean
something to the eye. It would seem as though dialect writing should have
outgrown this simple trick, yet it flourishes as luxuriantly as ever. And
in fact there is some justification for it in literary dialect. To the scientific
student of speech, these misspellings of words universally pronounced
in the same way have no significance, but in the literary dialect they serve
a useful purpose as providing obvious hints that the general tone of the
speech is to be felt as something different from the tone of conventional
speech. For this purpose they are often better than strange or striking
dialect terms would be, even when the dialect terms are true, because
the unfamiliar term frequently seems merely outlandish. But the purpose
of the literary dialect is not so much to arouse wonder as to secure sym-

pathetic attention. When someone writes the word "dear" as "dere," we know it is our own word "dear," but "dear" with a difference. Our loves, we are subtly given to understand, are not as other people's loves.

The two most elaborate of the literary dialects used today are Yiddish English—or, as Mr. Brody has aptly called some brands of it, Yidgin English, after the analogy of pidgin English—and Negro English. Yiddish English is of fairly recent origin as a literary dialect, but Negro English has an ancient history. Among the first of the practitioners of Yiddish English was Myra Kelly, whose Yiddish, however, has always been regarded with an eye of suspicion by those to the manner born. Yet even those who by race and inheritance ought to know more about this peculiar speech have not escaped criticism when they have used it for literary purposes. The number of language perversions and of adaptations from Yiddish which one might record, if one went about with pencil and notebook in hand and listened with an attentive ear to what one heard on Delancey or Orchard Street, is limitless. But when all these observations are assembled and fused into the speech of one person, the result is something that never existed in nature. A person who knows Yiddish has an inexhaustible mine in which to dig for linguistic eccentricities. It takes a kind of inventive genius to write a language as astonishing, and withal as persuasive, as that which Milt Gross puts into the mouths of the Feitlebaums and their neighbors. Here language has become a highly ingenious game, played for its own sake. For as Mr. Brody shrewdly remarks, "Ghetto psychology is well-handled in inverse proportion to the amount of Yidgin a story contains. When a writer uses such crude means of laying on local color, he can afford to stop at the surface, but if he deprives himself of their aid he has to prove his points."

It would be an interesting speculation to inquire to what extent Yiddish English enjoys its literary popularity, not because of its truth to the facts, but because it is so grotesquely contrary to the facts. Certainly it must be granted that the children of Yiddish parentage often learn to speak English with a marvelous propriety. Often they speak English better than the children of American descent because they make more effort to speak well. Perhaps, like a great many jokes, Yiddish English is a joke only because it isn't true. In time it may even come to pass that the most faithful conservers of the pure English idiom will be found among those who have reacted against the environment which the Feitlebaums and the Potashes and Perlmutters are supposed to represent. When that time comes, just as the best English is supposed to be spoken in Dublin, the best French by the cultivated stranger in Paris, so the best American will find its home in Delancey and Orchard Streets.

Like Yiddish English, Negro English is also a disappearing speech;

26   and as it vanishes in reality, it becomes all the more suited for literary purposes. Except in remoter regions of the South, all Negroes of the present generation have passed through the normalizing educational machine through which all other citizens of the republic have passed. The language of the average Negro now differs from the standards of cultivated speech to no greater degree than that of the average white man. But the dialect-speaking Negro has a long literary history. The attempts to record Negro speech go back almost to the beginnings of American literature. Negro personages speaking in character appear in the eighteenth century in some of the earliest plays written in America. But these earliest efforts were not followed at once by any extensive experiments in Negro dialect. In fact, it was not until after the Civil War that the Negro and his speech, regarded as literary material, came into their own. Undoubtedly the diffusion of the Negroes among the general social body, and consequently the increase of direct contacts with them, have greatly contributed to the growth of interest in them. But as these contacts have increased, so also the sense that the Negro is a strange and alien creature has diminished. People still have Negroes in their kitchens, but the old-fashioned colored mammy is as extinct as the auk, and even Southern gentlemen now sigh in vain for the devoted body servant of the old legend. In a word, Negro dialect, like most of our dialect literature, is highly romantic and rhetorical. It pictures a remote and vanishing life in strong colors, replacing to large extent direct observation by inventive fancy. For this reason it is beside the point to apply the test of truth to reality too stringently to it. Many of the features of Negro dialect as it is written today are merely survivals from earlier periods in which they appeared also in the speech of white people. Who ever hears a Negro say "gwine" now for "going"? No doubt it can be heard in some remote rustic region, but in a lifetime of fairly continuous acquaintance with Negroes of many sorts, I have never heard the pronunciation "gwine" from the lips of a Negro speaking naturally. Such pronunciations are philologically interesting, and for the dialect artist they are as symbolical as a bandana handkerchief; but it would be fatal to look at them too critically from the point of view of truth to reality.

Some of the Negro dialects as they have been reported in literature are marvels of ingenuity, such for example as that found in the stories of the Carolina coast narrated by Mr. Gonzalez. These are fascinating tales, not only for the glimpses into primitive folk psychology that they give, but for their illustration of what strange things can happen to English without changing the language into something which is not English. The English of Mr. Gonzalez's stories calls for a new name, however, and perhaps we might call it Nidgin English, after the analogy of Mr. Brody's Yidgin English. The reader who ventures into it will probably soon find that this highly elaborated Nidgin English interferes a good deal with his enjoyment of the stories as literature. There is too much of it. DuBose Heyward in his very artistic and poetic *Porgy*—a book which describes the same kind of life and characters as Mr. Gonzalez's *Black Border*—wisely restricts himself to comparatively few dialect characteristics. (And by the way, how would Mr. Heyward have us pronounce the name of his hero, with a hard or a soft *g*? The word looks like the well-known New England name of a fish called by the natives "pogies," caught from "pogie boats," though the only spelling the dictionaries seem to know for this word is "porgy, porgies"). Which is the truer record of Gullah English, that of Mr. Gonzalez or that of Mr. Heyward? But this is a vain question to ask if the authors, as presumably both of them did, intended their books to be regarded as examples of literature, not as philological treatises. Much more relevant is the question: Which of the two books is the more successful as a work of art?

If our contemporary American dialect literature does not rest on the same kind of foundation as the poetry of Burns, still less is it like the older popular literature of the ballads. The ballads were the compositions of a singing and storytelling folk. They reveal the engaging simplicity and naturalness of a people frankly expressive but not painfully aware of themselves. In America we have a few ballads—cowboy ballads of the Southwest, survivals of older ballads in the Kentucky and Tennessee mountains, and occasional versified narratives of murders, robberies, and executions. But when one examines this ballad literature, one discovers that there is very little that is popular in the language of it—except perhaps in the sense that the poems are written with that elaborate propriety of expression which the simple-minded writer is likely to assume when he submits himself to the perils of taking his pen in hand.

The truth is that our dialect literature is not a popular literature at all, and that it never has been. It is in reality a highbrow literature, the work of persons who stand superiorly aloof from popular life and picture it amusedly, patronizingly, photographically, satirically, sentimentally, as their tastes incline them. It seems indeed that the gap between high life and low life is so narrow in America and so frequently bridged, that everyone is constantly aware of this stimulating or dangerous propinquity. The immigrant of today becomes the millionaire of tomorrow. Indians in their wigwams become oil kings overnight. And probably the opposite happens just as often, the rich and cultivated of one generation becoming the horny-handed sons of toil in the next. The bringing together of different types from various geographical communities, but above all from different social levels, during . . . World War [I], also increased the reflecting man's awareness of his esteemed but ungrammatical neighbors. The high wages and prosperity of the past few years have like-

28   wise undoubtedly helped to provide a favorable atmosphere for the
growth of a dialect literature.

The popular dialect characters today are not country bumpkins and
hayseeds. Swallows do not nest in their whiskers. Farmer Corntassel and
Senator Sorghum are still alive, but they belong to an older generation.
The modern dialect character may be a person who comes from the cultural backwoods, but he does not know it. He—or she—is altogether up
and coming. He wears just as good clothes, as expensive shoes, as fancy
silk shirts as anyone else. Merely by looking at him one may not be able
to tell him from the product of seven generations of culture. It is only
when he opens his mouth that he reveals himself. To the outward eye we
are all alike nowadays. But it is exactly this outward similarity which
makes speech the more significant. The jewels of grammatical impro-
priety which fall from the lips of those who seem to be traveling in our
own class are treasured because they are found in such unexpected settings. Miss Ferber's salesladies are very perfect gentlewomen, until they
begin to talk. They speak then with the tongues not of angels, but of very
fallible human beings.

These rearrangements of types and classes in America keep the whole
social body agitated and make it extremely difficult to fix social attitudes.
Literary dialects do not flourish in England as they do here because in
England a popular dialect bears so little relation to the lives of the cultivated readers—who after all must be the readers of works written in a dialect. In spite of the far-reaching adjustments that have taken place in English life in recent years, class distinctions are still maintained firmly in
England.

It would be a mistake, however, to assume that the attitude of our
American dialect writers toward their characters and the life they describe
is altogether kindly and sympathetic. The hilarity of dialect writing is
often only camouflage from the protection of which the writer shoots the
arrows of a hard and bitter satire. It serves somewhat the same purpose
as the animal fable of Reynard the Fox and of the later fabulists. The best
known of Ring Lardner's characters, for example, is an amusing enough
person, but if one looks beneath the surface, he is much more than that.
He provides many occasions for laughing at him, but very few for laughing with him. He is a two-fisted, self-satisfied, thick-witted creature, with
a hide like an elephant's. His conversation in the intimate social relations
is incredibly brutal and direct. He has been exposed to the elementary
cultural influences of the democratic American surrounding, though they
have taken only in the most superficial way. But he is by no means everybody's fool. His perceptions are not fine, but direct action with him takes
the place of delicacy. He is "not so dumb" but that he will always get
along. He is as hard as nails, and when it comes to the point, as blunt as a

nail. If one were compelled to live with him, one could not escape treating him like a nail and hammering him over the head. But he is amazingly true and typical. He might almost be taken as our most representative citizen. Yet if this is what evolution, democracy, and prosperity have presented to us, what shall we think of evolution, democracy, and prosperity? Mr. Lardner is not an explicit satirist after the fashion of the old school, but implied in all his humor there is a serious criticism of life. Perhaps it is always so with humor that penetrates beneath the surface. Humorists have always been reported to be at bottom serious and even melancholy persons, and certainly the dregs of Mr. Lardner's cup of laughter are bitter.

Whether dialect writing will flourish as abundantly in the future as it does today is a question. But as long as society presents violently contrasting social groups in intimate contact it will continue to provide abundant material for the dialect humorist. The types, however, will change. The rustic Yankee of the earlier periods of American literature is already a thing of the past. So also the day of Hans Breitmann and the comic German is gone because the Germans have disappeared in the general conglomerate. The literary Irishman still has a spark of life in him, but he also is moribund. In another generation the dialect Negro will fade further and further away into the dim haze of romance, and with our present quota restrictions of immigration, the Yiddish of today will soon become legendary and archaic. The last of our dialect characters to disappear will probably be the coarse-grained American citizen whose mental machinery is not adequate to enable him to assimilate the civilities of custom in the midst of which he lives. The only way to get rid of him is to breed him out of the race, but that takes time. Meanwhile new generations of illiterate bounders, climbers, and gold-diggers will continue to enliven our American scene, offering a rich harvest of mirth for the heedless and of philosophical reflection for the thoughtful.

Cultural Levels and Functional Varieties of English

John S. Kenyon

In 1924 John S. Kenyon first published his *American Pronunciation,* which has gone through almost a dozen editions. His description of Midwestern English in this volume and his invaluable work in the Kenyon-Knott *A Pronouncing Dictionary of American English* (1944) are still among the best sources of information on American English. He was among the first to explore the relationship between social status and speech and to recognize that a speaker has a variety of linguistic styles from which he selects, often unconsciously, the style he feels is appropriate to a particular situation and purpose. The important distinction between cultural levels and functional varieties, a distinction which Kenyon was the first to elaborate, is poorly understood even today and is one of the areas of language study now being reexamined by linguists. Though their work has gone beyond Kenyon's, his point of view remains sound. Dr. Kenyon was for almost thirty years Professor of the English Language at Hiram College.

The word *level*, when used to indicate different styles of language, is a metaphor, suggesting higher or lower position and, like the terms *higher* and *lower*, figuratively implies "better" or "worse," "more desirable" or "less desirable," and similar comparative degrees of excellence or inferiority in language.

The application of the term *level* to those different styles of language that are not properly distinguished as better or worse, desirable or undesirable, creates a false impression. I confess myself guilty of this error along with some other writers. What are frequently grouped together in one class as different levels of language are often in reality false combinations of two distinct and incommensurable categories, namely, *cultural levels* and *functional varieties*.

Among *cultural levels* may be included, on the lower levels, illiterate speech, narrowly local dialect, ungrammatical speech and writing, excessive and unskillful slang, slovenly and careless vocabulary and construction, exceptional pronunciation, and, on the higher level, language used generally by the cultivated, clear, grammatical writing, and pronunciations used by the cultivated over wide areas. The different cultural levels may be summarized in the two general classes *substandard* and *standard*.

Among *functional varieties* not depending on cultural levels may be mentioned colloquial language, itself existing in different degrees of familiarity or formality, as, for example, familiar conversation, private correspondence, formal conversation, familiar public address; formal platform or pulpit speech, public reading, public worship; legal, scientific, and other expository writing; prose and poetic belles-lettres. The different functional varieties may roughly be grouped together in the two classes *familiar* and *formal* writing or speaking.

The term *level*, then, does not properly belong at all to functional varieties of speech—colloquial, familiar, formal, scientific, literary language. They are equally "good" for their respective functions, and as classifications do not depend on the cultural status of the users.

The two groupings *cultural levels* and *functional varieties* are not mutually exclusive categories. They are based on entirely separate principles of classification: *culture* and *function*. Although we are here principally concerned with the functional varieties of standard English (the highest cultural level), yet substandard English likewise has its functional varieties for its different occasions and purposes. Thus the functional variety colloquial English may occur on a substandard cultural level, but the term *colloquial* does not itself indicate a cultural level. So the functional variety formal writing or speaking may occur on a lower or on a higher

From *College English* 10:31–36 (October, 1948). Reprinted with the permission of the National Council of Teachers of English.

32   cultural level according to the social status of writer or speaker, and sometimes of reader or audience. It follows, for instance, that the colloquial language of cultivated people is on a higher cultural level than the formal speech of the semiliterate or than some inept literary writing.

Semiliterate formal speech is sometimes heard from radio speakers. I recently heard one such speaker solemnly announce, "Sun day will be Mother's Day." Because the speaker, in his ignorance of good English, thought he was making himself plainer by using the distorted pronunciation *sun day* instead of the standard pronunciation *sundy*, he actually was misunderstood by some listeners to be saying, "Some day will be Mother's Day." About forty years ago the great English phonetician Henry Sweet used this very example to show that "we cannot make words more distinct by disguising them."[1] He was referring to the use, in this instance, of the full sound of vowels in unaccented syllables where standard English has obscure vowels. On the same page Sweet gives another example of the same blunder: "Thus in the sentence *I shall be at home from one to three* the substitution of tuw for tə [ə = the last sound in *sofa*] at once suggests a confusion between the preposition and the numeral." This was also verified on the radio. Not long ago I heard a radio speaker announce carefully, "This program will be heard again tomorrow from one two three." I have also recorded (among many others) the following such substandard forms from the radio: *presidEnt* for the standard form *presidənt*, the days of the week ending in the full word *day* instead of the standard English syllable *-dy, ay man,* for the correct *man, cahnsider* for *cənsider, tooday* for *təday, too go* for *tə go, Coalumbia* for *Cəlumbia,* etc. This is merely one sort among many of substandard features in the formal speech of the semiliterate.[2]

To begin my strictures at home, in *American Pronunciation* (9th ed., 4th printing, p. 17), I use the page heading "Levels of Speech." This should be "Functional Varieties of Standard Speech," for the reference is solely to the different uses of speech on the one cultivated level. Similarly, in the Kenyon-Knott *Pronouncing Dictionary of American English* (p. xvi, §2), I carelessly speak of "levels of the colloquial" where I mean "styles of the colloquial," as three lines above. For though there are different cultural levels of colloquial English, the reference here is only to standard colloquial.

S. A. Leonard and H. Y. Moffett, in their study, "Current Definition of Levels in English Usage,"[3] say (p. 348): "The levels of English usage have

---

[1] Henry Sweet, *The Sounds of English* (Oxford, 1910), p. 78.

[2] See further *American Speech*, VI, No. 5 (June, 1931), 368–372.

[3] *English Journal*, XVI, No. 5 (May, 1927), 345–59.

been most clearly described in Dr. Murray's Preface ["General Explanations," p. xvii] to the *New English Dictionary*. I have varied his diagram a little in order to illustrate better the overlapping between the categories." It appears to me that Leonard and Moffett have so varied the diagram as to obscure Murray's intention. For he is not here primarily exhibiting levels of speech but is showing the "Anglicity," or limits of the English vocabulary for the purposes of his dictionary.[4] The only topical divisions of his diagram that imply a cultural level are "slang" and "dialectal," and the only statement in his explanation of the diagram that could imply it is, "Slang words ascend through colloquial use." This may imply that slang is on a lower cultural level than "colloquial, literary, technical, scientific, foreign." We may also safely infer that Murray would place "Dialectal" on a lower level than colloquial and literary if he were here concerned with cultural levels. Murray's diagram rests consistently on the same basis of classification throughout ("Anglicity"), and he emphasizes that "there is absolutely no defining line in any direction [from the central nucleus of colloquial and literary]." Moreover, Murray's exposition here concerns only vocabulary, with no consideration of the other features that enter so largely into "levels" of language—grammatical form and structure, pronunciation, spelling, and meaning—of styles, in short, only so far as they are affected by vocabulary. These he treats of elsewhere but without reference to levels.

It is not quite clear just how far Leonard and Moffet intend their grouping "literary English," "standard, cultivated, colloquial English," and "naïf, popular, or uncultivated English" to be identical with what they call Murray's "levels," his description of which they commend. But it is clear that they call their own grouping "three levels of usage" (p. 357) and classify them together as a single descending scale (cf. "the low end of the scale," p. 358). The inevitable impression that the average reader receives from such an arrangement of the scale is: Highest level, literary English; next lower level, colloquial English; lowest level, illiterate English; whereas, in fact, the first two "levels" are functional varieties of the one cultural level standard English, while the third ("illiterate or uncultivated," p. 358) is a cultural level.

Krapp has a chapter on "The Levels of English Speech,"[5] in which he reveals some awareness of the confusion of cultural levels with functional varieties. He says:

---

[4] The word *Anglicity* is a coinage of the *Oxford Dictionary*. They define it as "English quality, as of speech or style; English idiom."

[5] George Philip Krapp, *The Knowledge of English* (New York, 1927), pp. 55–76.

34   Among those who pay any heed at all to convention in social relationships, a difference of degree is implicit in all use of English. This
difference of degree is usually thought of in terms of higher and lower,
of upper levels of speech appropriate to certain occasions of more
formal character, of lower levels existing, if not necessarily appropriate,
among less elevated circumstances. These popular distinctions of level
may be accepted without weighing them too heavily with significance
in respect of good, better, and best in speech. A disputatious person
might very well raise the question whether literary English, ordinarily
regarded as being on a high level, is really any better than the spoken
word, is really as good as the spoken word, warm with the breath of the
living moment.

At the risk of having to own the hard impeachment of being disputatious, I must express the fear that the logical fallacy in treating of levels,
which Krapp rather lightly waves aside, is having a serious effect on general ideas of speech levels, and especially of the significance of colloquial
English in good usage. Krapp's grouping, frankly on a scale of "levels"
throughout, constitutes a descending scale from the highest, "Literary
English," through "Formal Colloquial," "General Colloquial," "Popular
English," to the lowest, "Vulgar English." Here the fallacy is obvious:
Literary English, Formal Colloquial, and General Colloquial are not
cultural levels but only functional varieties of English all on the one cul-
tural level of standard English. The last two, Popular English and Vulgar
English, belong in a different order of classification, cultural levels, with-
out regard to function.

So in his succeeding discussion *level* sometimes means the one, sometimes the other; now a functional variety of standard English, and now a
cultural level of substandard or of standard English. It is functional on
page 58 ("a choice between two levels") and on page 60 ("level of general
colloquial"), cultural on page 62 ("popular level" and "cultivated level")
and on pages 63–64 ("popular level," "level of popular speech"), functional on page 64 ("general colloquial level"), cultural again on the same
page ("popular level," "still lower level"), cultural on page 67 ("vulgar
. . . level of speech," "applying the term 'vulgar' to it at certain levels"),
cultural on page 68 ("its own [popular] level"), cultural and functional
in the same phrase on page 68 ("speakers from the popular and the
general colloquial level meet and mix"), and so on most confusingly to
page 75.

The same kind of mixture of cultural levels and functional varieties is
thrown into one apparently continuous scale by Kennedy: "There is the
formal and dignified language of the scholarly or scientific address or paper. . . . The precision and stateliness of this uppermost level . . . is a

necessary accompaniment of thinking on a high plane."[6] Next in order he mentions colloquial speech, which he refers to as "the second level, . . . generally acceptable to people of education and refinement." Clearly this is not a cultural level but a functional variety of standard English, like the "uppermost level." The third level is, however, a cultural one: "the latest slang," workmen's "technical slang and colloquialisms which other persons cannot comprehend," "grammatical solecisms." "The speech of this third level can fairly be ranked as lower in the social scale." His fourth level is also cultural: "At the bottom of the scale is the lingo, or cant, of criminals, hobos, and others of the lowest social level."

Finally, Kennedy fixes the false mental image of a continuous and logically consistent descent from "the cold and lonely heights of formal and highly specialized scientific and scholarly language" to "the stupid and slovenly level of grammatical abuses and insane slang." In reality there is no cultural descent until we reach his third "level," since "formal and dignified language" and "colloquial speech" are only functional varieties of English on the one cultural level of standard English.

In Perrin's excellent and useful *Index*,[7] under the heading "Levels of Usage," he names "three principal levels": "Formal English (likened to formal dress), "Informal English" (described as "the typical language of an educated person going about his everyday affairs"), and "Vulgate English." From his descriptions it appears clearly that Formal and Informal English are functional varieties of standard English, while Vulgate is a substandard cultural level. A similar classification appears in his table on page 365.

On page 19 Perrin uses "level" apparently in the sense of functional variety, not of cultural level: "Fundamentally, good English is speaking or writing in the level of English that is appropriate to the particular situation that faces the speaker or writer. It means making a right choice among the levels of usage." His advice, however, involves two choices: (1) choice of a standard cultural level and (2) choice of the appropriate functional variety of that level.

A clear instance of the inconsistent use of the term *level* is found in Robert C. Pooley's *Teaching English Usage* (New York, 1946), Chapter iii, "Levels in English Usage." He names five levels: (1) the illiterate level; (2) the homely level; (3) standard English, informal level; (4) standard English, formal level; and (5) the literary level. In (1) and (2) *level* has an altogether different meaning from that in (3), (4), and (5). In the first two *level* plainly means "cultural level"; in the last three it just as plainly

---

[6] Arthur G. Kennedy, *Current English* (Boston, 1935), pp. 15–17: "Speech Levels."

[7] Porter G. Perrin, *An Index to English* (Chicago, 1939), pp. 364–65.

means "functional variety of standard English," all three varieties being therefore on the one cultural level of standard English. So *level* in the two groups belongs to different orders of classification. All misunderstanding and wrong implications would be removed from this otherwise excellent treatment of levels if the last three groups were labeled "Standard English Level, Informal Variety"; "Standard English Level, Formal Variety"; and "Standard English Level, Literary Variety." Pooley's groups contain three cultural levels (illiterate, homely, standard) and three functional varieties of the standard cultural level (informal, formal, literary).

The misapplication to colloquial English of the term *level*, metaphorically appropriate only to cultural gradations, is especially misleading. We often read of English that is "on the colloquial level." For example, Krapp writes: *"Who do you mean?* . . . has passed into current spoken use and may be accepted on the colloquial level."[8] This implies that colloquial English is on a different cultural level from formal English (literary, scientific, etc.), and a too frequent assumption, owing to this and other misuses of the term *colloquial*, is that its cultural level is below that of formal English. This supposition, tacit or explicit, that colloquial style is inferior to formal or literary style, leads inescapably to the absurd conclusion that, whenever scientists or literary artists turn from their formal writing to familiar conversation with their friends, they thereby degrade themselves to a lower social status.

This misuse of *level* encourages the fallacy frequently met with of contrasting colloquial with standard English, logically as fallacious as contrasting white men with tall men. For instance, Mencken writes: " 'I have no doubt *but* that' . . . seems to be very firmly lodged in colloquial American, and even to have respectable standing in the standard speech."[9] This contrast, not always specifically stated, is often implied. For example, Kennedy writes: "Colloquial English is, properly defined, the language of conversation, and especially of familiar conversation. As such it may approximate the standard speech of the better class of English speakers, or it may drop to the level of the illiterate and careless speaker."[10] *May approximate* should be replaced by *may be on the level of*.

Similarly, on page 440: "Some measure words [are] still used colloquially without any ending in the plural . . . ; but most of these are given the *s* ending in standard English usage." Here *standard* is confused with *formal*.

Kennedy (pp. 534, 616) several times contrasts colloquial English with

[8] *A Comprehensive Guide to Good English* (New York, 1927), p. 641.

[9] H. L. Mencken, *The American Language* (4th ed.; New York, 1936), p. 203.

[10] Kennedy, *op. cit.*, p. 26.

"standard literary English." This implies that colloquial English is not standard, while literary English is. If he means to contrast standard colloquial with standard literary, well and good; but I fear that most readers would understand the contrast to be of colloquial with standard.[11]

The term *colloquial* cannot properly designate a substandard cultural level of English. It designates a functional variety—that used chiefly in conversation—and in itself says nothing as to its cultural level, though this discussion, and the dictionary definitions, are chiefly concerned with cultivated colloquial, a functional variety of standard English. When writers of such standing as those I have mentioned slip into expressions that imply lower cultural status of colloquial English, it is not surprising that colloquialisms should not be represented as standard American speech. But the context of the statement indicated that its author was using *colloquialism* in the sense of 'localism.' I could hardly believe how frequent this gross error is, until I heard it from a well-known American broadcaster.[12]

The best dictionaries, at least in their definitions, give no warrant for the various misuses of *colloquial, colloquially, colloquialism, colloquiality*. I urge the reader to study carefully the definitions in the *Oxford English Dictionary* with its many apt examples from standard writers, and in *Webster's New International Dictionary, Second Edition*, with its quotations from George Lyman Kittredge. Kittredge's views on the standing of colloquial English are well known. It is said that somebody once asked him about the meaning of the label "Colloq." in dictionaries. He is reported to have replied, "I myself speak 'colloke' and often write it." I cannot verify the story, but it sounds authentic.

It seems to me inevitable that the frequent grouping of so-called "levels" such as "Literary, Colloquial, Illiterate," and the like, will lead the reader to suppose that just as Illiterate is culturally below Colloquial, so Colloquial is culturally below Literary. While I can scarcely hope that my humble remonstrance will reform all future writing on "levels of English," I believe that writers who confuse the meaning of the term *level* must accept some part of the responsibility for the popular misunder-

---

[11] Greenough and Kittredge in *Words and Their Ways in English Speech* (New York, 1909), Chap. VII, only apparently treat literary English as the sole standard form: "What is the origin of standard or literary English?" (p. 80). They use *standard* in a special sense for their particular purpose, calling it "the common property of all but the absolutely illiterate," "the language which all educated users of English speak and write" (therefore including colloquial). For the usual current meaning, see the definitions of *standard* quoted in *American Pronunciation* (6th and subsequent eds.), pp. 14–15.

[12] Leonard and Moffett also mention the frequency of this blunder (*op. cit.,* p. 351, n. 5).

38   standing of the true status of colloquial English; for I cannot avoid the belief that the popular idea of colloquial English as something to be looked down upon with disfavor is due to the failure of writers on the subject to distinguish between *cultural levels of English* and *functional varieties of standard English.*

A Projection of Sociolinguistics: The Relationship of Speech to Social Status

Haver C. Currie

The following article is the first formal projection of a field
that has become very important in the last decade. Haver C.
Currie has a wide background of not only ancient and modern
languages, but also philosophy, religion, sociology, and
psychology. He wrote recently: ". . . I understood myself to
have created the term *sociolinguistics*, and [thereby] naming
a new field of study that I was projecting." When he wrote
this article, Mr. Currie was a member of the English
faculty at the University of Houston. At this writing he is a
Consultant with the Regional Research Associates of
Austin, Texas. His publications have been primarily
philosophic essays, poetry, book reviews, and accounts
of research.

40   In recent years linguists have shown a lively interest in the social significance of varying features of spoken English. Upon noting published materials reflecting this interest, the writer entered into a study of which this paper is representative. The study was warranted by the existence of a large body of linguistic facts which could be considered from the viewpoint of their social significance.

The present purpose is to suggest, by the citing of selected and salient studies, that social functions and significations of speech factors offer a prolific field for research. It is the intention in this connection to project, partly by means of identification, a field that may well be given the attentions of consciously directed research. This field is here designated *sociolinguistics*. Attention will be called to certain relevant research done or under way. Possibilities for further socio-linguistic research are, in fact, beyond estimation. Certain data gathered by linguists, sociologists, and specialists in speech call for coordination and mutual implementation.

Attention will be directed primarily to the relationship of speech to social status. This is not necessarily to delimit the projected field but to point up a desiderative approach revealed by the fact that in many linguistic studies and in a large array of popular and academic considerations the factor of social status with relation to speech has prominence either by clear implication or direct recognition.

Data that might be taken into account are so extensive and diverse and so widely scattered that a major problem is that of presenting only such materials as are altogether necessary to the present purpose. It will be understood, therefore, that this paper is not intended as definitive but as authentically suggestive.

Various linguists have remarked upon the social functions of language, and now and again sociologists speak of language as the major social medium. For example, the linguist E. H. Sturtevant, in defining language, makes use of a generalization one expects to find upon consulting a sociology textbook: "The final clause of the definition *by which the members of a social group cooperate and interact* designates the chief function of language in society."[1] It is Sturtevant who goes so far as to speak of linguistics as a social science, although one largely neglected by most groups of social scientists.[2]

The linguist Raven I. McDavid, Jr., in writing directly about speech,

From *The Southern Speech Journal,* Vol. 18, No. 1 (September, 1952) 28–37. Reprinted with the permission of the Southern Speech Association and Haver C. Currie.

[1] Edgar H. Sturtevant, *An Introduction to Linguistic Science* (New Haven, 1949), 3.

[2] *Ibid.,* 6, 7.

calls attention to a certain negligence in the consideration of the social significance of speech in our culture:

> The relationship between speech forms and the cultural configurations and prestige values within a civilization has been indicated by linguistic scientists, but so far most of the study of that relationship has been directed toward languages outside the Indo-European family. It is, however, just as proper to utilize the data of linguistics, as derived from a study of dialect of our own language, in analyzing some of the problems within our own culture.[3]

Both Sturtevant and McDavid, while recognizing the studies devoted to the significances of speech directed toward languages outside the Indo-European family, have complained of a marked neglect of the same subject with respect to our own culture. The anthropologist Branislow Malinowski has from his own viewpoint made a somewhat similar complaint:

> The lack of a clear and precise view of linguistic function and the nature of Meaning, has been, I believe, the cause of the relative sterility of much otherwise excellent linguistic theorizing . . . The study of the above-quoted text has demonstrated that an utterance becomes comprehensive (*sic*) when we interpret it by its context of situation. The analysis of the context should give us a glimpse of a group of savages bound by reciprocal ties of interests.[4]

Malinowski's account of "phatic communion" is pertinent to our present subject, for it was his view that among both savages and civilized people "the function of Speech is mere sociabilities" affords "one of the bedrock aspects of man's nature in society."

> A mere phase of politeness, in use among savage tribes as in a European drawing-room, fulfills a function to which the meaning of its words is almost completely irrelevant . . . The stranger who cannot speak the language is to all savage tribesmen a natural enemy . . . The modern English expression, "Nice day today" or the Melanesian phrase, "Whence comest thou?" are needed to get over the strange and unpleasant tension which men feel when facing each other in silence.[5]

At thought of coordinating linguistic and social facts, the usual American student may feel that even the phase of linguistics that has primarily

---

[3] Raven J. McDavid, Jr., "Postvocalic /ɾ/ in South Carolina: A Social Analysis," *American Speech*, XXIII (1949), 194.

[4] C. K. Ogden and I. A. Richards, *The Meaning of Meaning*, 5th ed. (New York, 1938), 310.

[5] *Ibid.*, 313, 314.

42   to do with the English language assumes such formidable proportions
that he is confronting helplessly a mass of facts and theories. Certain
linguists, however, are beginning to conceive it as of importance to cast
their data into a form providing for more general accessibility to salient
facts. This tendency is reflected by the linguist Hans Kurath and his
associates:

> The linguistic facts are presented in simple, nontechnical form so that
> they may be readily understood not only by linguists, but also by
> historians, geographers, sociologists, and others interested in the social
> and cultural history of New England.[6]

Kurath expresses amazement that a country so democratic as the
United States should be so far behind Europe in the study of folk speech
and common speech and that in this country "the speech of the large
middle class has hardly been touched by trained linguists."[7]

It now appears that phoneticians of departments of speech at certain
of our American universities are coming forward to consider the relationship of speech to social status. A copy of *The Quarterly Journal of
Speech* of February, 1952, with its consideration of the speech and status
of Franklin D. Roosevelt, has just come into the hands of the writer. The
article done by Brandenburg and Braden which brings an analysis of
Roosevelt's speech to bear on his status in the United States might well
be cited at length here, and is properly called to attention.

That Kurath and his associates have given some attention to speech
in its relationship to social class cannot be doubted in view of their identification of informants with respect to occupation and attitudes expressed. Raven I. McDavid, Jr., who has been engaged with the *Linguistic
Atlas,* has been explicit with respect to speech and class status, at least
insofar as the South is concerned. Following his studies of the speech
of South Carolina, he took the postvocalic /-r/ as a symbol of social class:

> A social analysis proved necessary for this particular linguistic feature,
> because the data proved too complicated to be explained by merely
> a geographical statement or a statement of settlement history. In this
> particular problem, moreover, the social analysis seems more significant
> than it might seem to others, because the presence or absence of post-
> vocalic /-r/ as constriction becomes an overt prestige symbol only on
> a very high level of sophistication.[8]

---

[6] Hans Kurath, Marcus L. Hansen, Julia Bloch, and Bernard Bloch, *Handbook of the Linguistic
Geography of New England* (Providence, R. I., 1939), ix.

[7] Hans Kurath, *A Word Geography of the Eastern United States* (University of Michigan Press,
1949), 9.

[8] McDavid, 194.

McDavid found that the Tidewater area of South Carolina has a speech characterized by the postvocalic /-r/ without constriction.[9] This speech, characteristic of the rich coastal plains extending inland for seventy miles to the hills of the Piedmont, was transmitted to inland plantation areas by the plantation class.

McDavid's statement that "in every Southern state one may find locally rooted speakers with constriction in at least some of these words"[10] might well have become a widely accepted generalization long ago. In fact, the logic of his position concedes the majority of the political votes to Southerners of speech characterized by the postvocalic /-r/ with constriction in view of his assumption that the strength of such politically successful men as Blease, Talmage, and Bilbo has been derived from this group.[11]

With his thesis that in the states of the Deep South constriction of the postvocalic /-r/ is a "linguistically peripheral" feature of a "culturally peripheral" group, McDavid is pressed toward the highly popularized concept of a two-class Southern society. This is of peculiar interest to socio-linguistics because it affords a superb illustration of the effort to correlate speech type with social status. It is all the more interesting that, with appeal to linguistic science, he proposes a procedure of social control:

> Consequently, a Southern official whose job dealt with interracial problems might screen with a little extra care those native applicants for, say, police jobs, whose speech showed strong constriction. And those interested in changing racial attitudes of the whites might concentrate their efforts on those areas where constriction has survived in greatest strength. Perhaps this suggestion is extreme, but it shows the possibilities. For language is primarily a vehicle of social intercommunication, and linguistic phenomena must always be examined for that correlation with other cultural phenomena . . .[12]

The linguist Hans Kurath, however, has gone much further than McDavid toward discovering a social and linguistic Southern middle class in his reference to "the Scotch-Irish and Palatine Germans from Pennsylvania and overseas."

> This whole area of the Southern upland populated by these stocks was a land of independent farmers, wholly democratic in character. There was no leisure class, and there were few servants and paupers.

[9] *Ibid.*, 196.

[10] *Loc. cit.*

[11] *Ibid.*, 203.

[12] *Loc. cit.*

On the frontier a poor man could become a man of substance within his lifetime if he used his hands and his head.

This leveling of social differences inevitably entailed a leveling of social dialects. In the course of time a new type of cultivated speech based upon the common speech of an active middle class, came into being in the Midland area.[13]

Although the work of the *Linguistic Atlas* is hardly complete for any except the Atlantic states, Kurath finds significant the southwestern movement of the Scotch-Irish and Germans of the South and their "thrusts" across the Appalachians. It is to be predicted that the speech of the middle class of the inland Southern states will be discovered by future researchers to resemble the Southern-Midland type identified by Kurath.

C. C. Fries is quite definite in speaking of "standard English" in the United States in terms of social class. It is a standard English determined "by the *socially acceptable* of most of our communities." There are, Fries says, "separate social and class groups even in American communities" and "these groups differ from one another in many social practices including their language habits."[14] To the language habits in which the major matters of our country are carried on there attaches "a certain social prestige, for the use of them suggests that one has constant relations with those who are responsible for the important affairs of our communities."[15]

To recent linguists of the United States who have specialized in the English language, it has seemed appropriate to say that each regional dialect furnishes its own standard. J. S. Kenyon, for example, who in dealing primarily with phonetics considers American pronunciation under the classifications of Eastern, General American, and Southern takes a position spoken of as broadminded:

Probably no intelligent person actually expects cultivated people of the South, the East, and the West to pronounce alike. Yet such criticism, or politely silent contempt, of the pronunciations of cultivated people in other localities than our own is common. A student of phonetics soon learns not only to refrain from criticizing pronunciations that differ from his own, but to expect them and listen for them with respectful, intelligent interest. . . .[16]

[13] Kurath, 7.

[14] Charles Carpenter Fries, *American English Grammar* (New York, 1940), 9.

[15] *Ibid.,* 13.

[16] J. S. Kenyon, *American Pronunciation* (Ann Arbor, Michigan, 1946), 4, 5.

Despite the theoretical position of linguists under such terms as that of "respectful, intelligent interest" in "pronunciations that differ," the war of regions over language continues with force, even among certain academicians. Professor Kenyon himself, after protestations of tolerance, responds to his critics with some suggestion of exasperation and a fairly extreme statistical claim: "But apparently this does not satisfy such critics. One must not even describe or speak respectfully of the traditional speech of ninety million people."[17]

Maps delimiting the General-American belt presupposed by Kenyon and others appeal to the eye, it is true, by dint of the vast but sparsely settled West, including all the areas of the prairies and the Rockies and the extended deserts of the Southwest. And now Professor Kurath declares that recent data show that the heralded "General American" does not exist.

The compromise proposed by linguists in connection with regional wars over speech is of significance to socio-linguistics because it presupposes claims of social status for regional speech types. The proposed compromise is of such idealistic nature that ostensibly the regional conflicts over language might well be dismissed, but Professor Kenyon himself has observed that his proposal of compromise has seemed to have no salutary effect on his critics.

The search in the United States for prestige on grounds of language occurs not only intra-regionally with appeal to the conception of a superior class, and not only inter-regionally with appeal to the notion of a more acceptable region; it occurs also on the national scale with appeal to the concept of a speech having significant national identification.

The immense popularity of the various editions of H. L. Mencken's book called *The American Language* is a major social phenomenon within itself. All the interest in this book has not occurred because of an interest in language or linguistics *per se,* but because in its various editions it has been so socially satisfying or harrassing to so many people. The linguists themselves have taken it into account, even if furtively.

After the first publication of the book some thirty years ago, Mr. Mencken discovered he had hit a rich vein. He has come a long way since his early days of taunting the British, amusing himself with the American Southerners, and paying his respects to middle-class language with something of a bow to the Vulgate. Upon an increasing avalanche of letters, not only from general readers but also from American, British, German, and Japanese linguists, Mr. Mencken produced edition after edition of his famous work, until, mellowed by time, he has paid his respects to

[17] *Ibid.,* viii.

46 nearly every writer who has gained a marked distinction as a linguist concerned with the English language and its American manifestations.

Mr. Mencken pleases Americans by indicating that the offensive of the three-hundred-year war over language between England and the United States has been taken by the Americans. By now he pleases Americans in general by pointing out that they have a national language of their own with respectable regional variants.

He goes further to point out heartily that many of the English react negatively to the idea of a standard type of British English, variously called "Southern English," "Oxford English," "the language of the great boarding schools," or "Received English."

Without doing harm to the Oxonians, Mr. Mencken has done something toward satisfying a segment of Britons who can never be certain of their speech. At the same time he has been specially satisfactory to middle-class Americans by declaring the existence of an American language while recognizing regional dialects and an appropriate amount of slang. In addition, he has celebrated the linguists; and for that these fairly obscure scholars have to thank him. The American middle class has for thirty years rewarded him by their share in buying every copy of his book that his publishers would print.

Semantics, which promised to shed light on meaning—and meaning is the only legitimate subject of the field—has by now become so involved with psychiatric speculations, neurological theories of mind, and political theories of empirical radicalism as to have become rather widely suspect.

Semantics has had a special appeal to students of psychology who are novices in psychiatry. It has had an appeal to political reformers and revolutionaries who, through the manipulation of language and the spread of skepticism with respect to word meanings, have sought a means of social control. It has had an appeal also to those who seek an easy neurological formula in explanation of mind.

Moreover, the terrific influence of Korsybski has been such as to immesh semantics in a hotch-pot of the esoteric and obscurant. Upon attenuating sanity to neutral structures in correspondence to physical structures, he spoke as if meaning could best be conveyed by mathematico-physical symbols, despite the fact that an attempt to translate an account of social data into mathematico-physical terminology is peculiarly frustrating and futile.

The present projection of socio-linguistics proposes a fresh start toward researches into the social significance of language in all respects. The present projection is with a view to open researches fully subject to the critical examination of intelligent men who are not hampered by any esoteric, obscurant, or surreptitious clique or cult.

This paper has called attention to certain items of research and specula- tion salient to the consideration of the social significance of English as spoken in the United States. It has emphasized the persisting interest in the relationship of oral English and social status. Several works have been cited which have reflected this interest on the scholarly level, particularly with respect to speech and social class, regional dialects and social status, and national speech and social status. Specifically, a field for quite conscious study here called *socio-linguistics* has been envisioned, by warrant of work already done and possibilities hardly estimable. The coordination and mutual implementation of data presented by professional linguists, social scientists, and speech specialists have been called for.

Attention has been called to the fact that only a beginning has been made in research consciously directed to the social significances of the various manifestations of the spoken English that is the living language of this country. One conclusion of the research which this paper represents is that hardly any phase of speech studies in this country will be irrelevant to the projected field of research, and this conclusion belongs to the broader conclusion that no linguistic field in the United States is so open to researches as that of spoken English. It has been definitely the purpose here to provide a stimulus to relevant research.

Sense and Nonsense about American Dialects

Raven I. McDavid

Raven I. McDavid is at present Editor of the *Linguistic Atlas of the Middle and South Atlantic States.* He has been associated with Atlas work since 1941. With Hans Kurath he co-authored *The Pronunciation of English in the Atlantic States* (1961). He has written one of the most widely known scholarly surveys of American English dialects, "The Dialects of American English," which was published as Chapter Nine in *The Structure of American English* by W. Nelson Francis (1958).

In 1963 Professor McDavid published a revision of H. L. Mencken's *The American Language.* From 1966 to 1968 he was President of the American Dialect Society. He has written many articles for such publications as *PMLA, College English, Orbis, The Journal of English Linguistics, Social Forces,* and *PADS.* A collection of his papers, *Essays in General*

Dialectology, edited by Lee Pederson, Roger Shuy, and   49
Gerald Udell, has been published recently by the University
of Alabama Press. Dr. McDavid is Professor of English at
the University of Chicago.

In my boyhood—more years ago than I care to remember we used
to define an expert as "a damned fool a thousand miles from home."
Since I am considerably less than a thousand miles from where I grew up,
and stand but a few minutes from my residence in Hyde Park, it behooves
me to avoid any claim to expertness about the problems faced in practical
situations where the dialect of the schoolchild is sharply divergent from
what is expected of him in the classroom. For many of these situations,
neither I nor any other working dialectologist knows what the local patterns actually are; for some, there has been no attempt, or at best a partial and belated one, to find out the patterns. Nevertheless, the implications of dialectology for the more rational teaching of English in the
schools—and not only in the schools attended by those we currently
euphemize as the culturally disadvantaged—are so tremendous that I am
flattered to have John Fisher ask for my observations. The problems
are not limited to Americans of any race or creed or color, nor indeed
to Americans; they are being faced in England today, as immigrants
from Pakistan and the West Indies compete in the Midlands for the same
kinds of jobs that have drawn Negro Americans to Harlem and the South
Side, and Appalachian whites to the airplane factories of Dayton. In fact,
such problems are faced everywhere in the world as industrialization and
urbanization take place, on every occasion when people, mostly but not
exclusively the young, leave the farm and the village in search of the
better pay and more glamorous life of the cities. In all parts of the world,
educators and politicians are suddenly realizing that language differences
can create major obstacles to the educational, economic, and social advancement of those whose true integration into the framework of society
is necessary if that society is to be healthy; they are realizing that social
dialects—that is, social differences in the way language is used in a given
community—both reflect and perpetuate differences in the social order.
In turn, the practicing linguist is being called on with increasing frequency to devise programs for the needs of specific groups—most often
for the Negroes dwelling in the festering slums of our Northern and
Western cities; and generous government and private subsidies have
drawn into the act many teachers and administrators—most of them,
I trust, well meaning—who not only have made no studies of dialect

From *PMLA*, LXXXII, No. 2 (May, 1966), 7–17. Reprinted with the permission of the
Modern Language Association of America and Raven I. McDavid.

50   differences, but have ignored the studies and archives that are available, even those dealing with their own cities.

Perhaps a data-oriented dialectologist may here be pardoned an excursion into the metaphors of siegecraft, recalled from the time when under the tutelage of Allan Gilbert I learned something of the arts of war and gunnery, if not all their Byronic applications. In confronting our massive ignorance of social dialects, the professional students of the past generation have been a forlorn hope—burrowing into a problem here, clawing their way to a precarious foothold of understanding there, seizing an outwork yonder. Like many forlorn hopes, they have been inadequately supported, sometimes ignored, even decried—not only by their literary colleagues, with the usual patronizing attitude toward anything smacking of affiliation with the social sciences, but also by their fellow linguists who are interested in international programs for teaching English as a second language, in machine translation, in formulaic syntax, or in missionating to convert the National Council of Teachers of English. It is small wonder that some students of dialects have withdrawn from the assault to participate in these better-heeled campaigns; it is a tribute to the simple-minded stubbornness of the survivors that they have not only persisted but advanced. Today their work, their aims, are embarrassingly respectable, as legions spring from the earth in response to the golden trumpet sounding on the banks of the Pedernales. It is inevitable, perhaps even fitting, that the practical work in social dialects should be directed by others than the pioneers in research. But it is alarming that many of those now most vocally concerned with social dialect problems not only know nothing about the systematic work that has been done, about the massive evidence (even if all too little) that is available, but even have a complete misconception about the nature and significance of dialects. At the risk of drawing the fire of the House Un-American Activities Committee, I would agree with my sometime neighbor James H. Sledd that our missionaries should at least know what they are talking about before they set out to missionate.

I have a particular advantage when I talk on this subject: I am one of those who speak English without any perceptible accent. I learned to talk in an upper-middle-class neighborhood of Greenville, South Carolina, among corporation lawyers, bankers, textile magnates, and college presidents, among families with a long tradition of education and general culture. Many of my playmates, like myself, represented the sixth generation of their families in the same county. It never occurred to any of us to tamper with our language; our only intimate acquaintance with nonstandard grammatical forms in writing came from stories in literary dialect or from the quaint and curious exercises that infested our textbooks—though we knew that less-privileged forms of speech than ours were found in our community, and were not above imitating them for rhetorical effect. Not a single English teacher of an excellent faculty— our superintendent had his doctorate, not from Peabody or from Teachers College, Columbia, but from the University of Berlin in 1910—made a gesture of tampering. Nor have I ever heard anything in the exotic dialects of the Northeast or the Middle West that would make me feel less content with a way of speaking that any educated person might want to emulate. And yet, a few years ago, my younger sister, who has remained in the South Carolina upland, told me over the telephone: "Brucker, you've been North so long that you talk just like a Yankee." Even though I doubt if I would fool many real Yankees, I know that something has rubbed off from my travels and teaching to make me talk a little different from the boys I grew up with. Still, whenever I go back and start talking with them again, I find myself slipping into the old ways; it is natural for us to shift our way of talking, according to the people we are talking with. In fact, it is the people we talk with habitually who give us our way of talking. Here, in essence, is the way dialects originate. And until everybody lives in a sterile, homogenized, dehumanized environment, as just a number on the books of an all-powerful state, we can expect differences in environment to be reflected in those differences in speech that we call dialects.

An appreciation of this fact would avoid a lot of nonsense expressed in categorical statements in educational literature. Two amusing if distressing examples are found in *Language Programs for the Disadvantaged: Report of the NCTE Task Force,* a booklet released at the 1965 convention of the NCTE. These statements, the more distressing because so much of the report is magnificently phrased, probably arose from the inevitable wastefulness of haste (the Task Force was in the field only last summer) and from the imbalance of the Task Force itself: there was only one linguist and not a single sociologist or anthropologist or historian in a group heavily loaded with supervisors and (to coin a term, which is probably already embalmed in educationese) curriculologists:

> Most disadvantaged children come from homes in which a non-standard English dialect is spoken. It may be pidgin, Cajun, Midland, or any one of a large number of regional or cultural dialects. Many preschool teachers are concerned about the dialect of their children and take measures to encourage standard pronunciation and usage. (p. 70)
>
> . . . the general feeling is that some work in standard English is necessary for greater social and job mobility by disadvantaged students with a strong regional or racial dialect. (p. 89)

52   Among the bits of nonsense to be found in these two statements we
may notice:

1) A belief that there is some mystical "standard," devoid of all
regional association. Yet the variety that we can find in cultivated American English, as used by identifiable informants with impeccable educational and social credentials, has been repeatedly shown in works based
on the *American Linguistic Atlas,* most recently and in greatest detail in
Kurath's and my *Pronunciation of English in the Atlantic States* (Ann
Arbor: University of Michigan Press, 1961).

2) A belief that there are "racial" dialects, independent of social and
cultural experiences.

3) A snobbishness toward "strong" dialect differences from one's own
way of speaking. Would Bobby Kennedy, politically disadvantaged after
the Atlantic City convention, have run a better race in New York had
he learned to talk Bronx instead of his strong Bostonian?

4) A glib juggling of terms, without understanding, as in the parallelism of "pidgin, Cajun, Midland." *Pidgin* denotes a minimal contact language used for communication between groups whose native languages
are mutually unintelligible and generally have markedly different linguistic structures; typical examples are the Neo-Melanesian of New
Guinea and the Taki-taki of Surinam. However scholars may debate the
existence of an American Negro pidgin in colonial days, speakers of
pidgin constitute a problem in no Continental American classroom,
though it would be encountered in Hawaii and the smaller Pacific islands.
Cajun properly describes the colonial varieties of French spoken in southwestern Louisiana and in the parts of the Maritime Provinces of Canada
from which the Louisiana Acadians were transported; even if by extension we use the term to describe the varieties of English developing in
the French-speaking areas of Louisiana and the Maritimes, the problems
of teaching English in these areas are really those of teaching English
as a second language. *Midland* is a geographical designation for those
dialects stemming from the settlement of Pennsylvania and embracing
a broad spectrum of cultural levels. At one extreme, we may concede,
are the impoverished submarginal farmers and displaced coal miners
of Appalachia; at the other are some of the proudest dynasties of
America—the Biddles of Philadelphia, the Mellons of Pittsburgh, the
Tafts of Cincinnati, and their counterparts in Louisville and in St. Louis,
in Memphis and in Dallas—people it were stupid as well as impractical
to stigmatize in language like that of the Task Force Report. So long as
such glib generalities are used about social dialects, we must conclude
that our educators, however well intentioned, are talking nonsense.

And regrettably, such nonsense is no new phenomenon in American
culture; it has long been with us. Much of it, fortunately, runs off us like

raindrops off a mallard's back. But enough lingers in the schoolroom to do positive harm. My friend Bob Thomas, the anthropologist—a Cherokee Indian and proud of it, though with his blond hair and blue eyes he looks far less like the traditional Cherokee than I do—tells of his traumata when he moved to Detroit from Oklahoma at the age of fourteen. Although Cherokee was his first language, he had picked up a native command of Oklahoma English. Since he had always lived in a good neighborhood, and his family had used standard English at home, he had no problems in grammar; through wide reading and a variety of experiences he had acquired a large and rich vocabulary. But his vowels were Oklahoma vowels; and some benevolent despot in Detroit soon pushed him into a class in "corrective speech." The first day the class met, he looked around the classroom and noticed everybody else doing the same. As eyes met eyes, it became apparent that the class in "corrective speech" contained no cleft palates, no stammerers, no lispers, no foreign accents, not even any speakers of substandard English— for again, the school was in a good neighborhood. The only thing wrong with the boys and girls in the class was that they had not learned English in Michigan, but in Oklahoma, Arkansas, Missouri, Kentucky, Tennessee, West Virginia, Mississippi and Alabama. "We all realized immediately," Bob told me years afterward, "that they were planning to brainwash us out of our natural way of speaking; and it became a point of honor among us to sabotage the program." To this day, Bob flaunts his Oklahoma accent belligerently; if the teachers had let him alone, he might have adapted his pronunciation to that of the Detroit boys he played with, but once he felt that the school considered his home language inferior, nothing could make him change. The first principle of any language program is that, whatever the target, it must respect the language that the students bring with them to the classroom.

Another kind of nonsense was demonstrated by the head of the speech department at the University of Michigan during my first Linguistic Institute. Impelled by the kind of *force majeur* that only a four-star general can exert, I had compromised with my scientific interest in linguistics to the extent of enrolling in a course in "stage and radio diction," only to find myself bewildered, frustrated, and enraged from the outset. Typical of the petty irritations was the panjandrous insistence on the pronunciation /'pradjus/, though all my friends who raised fruits and vegetables for market, many of them gentlemen with impeccable academic credentials, said /'prodjus/. But far more distressing were the pronunciations advocated in the name of elegance. We were advised to reject the Middle Western and Southern /æ/, not only in *calf* and *dance* and *command,* but even in *hat* and *ham* and *sand,* for an imitation of the Boston /a/ in environments where Bostonians would never use it, so that we would

54   say /hat/ and /ham/ and /sand/, pronunciations legitimate in no American dialect except that of the Gullah Negroes of the South Carolina and Georgia coast. A few departmental underlings even went all out for an equally phony British [ɑ], again in the wrong places, yielding [hɑt] and [hɑm] and [sɑnd], and all of them plumped for replacing the Midwestern [ɑ] of *cot* and *lot* with an exaggerated [ɔ]. Of course, Midwesterners ordering [hɔt hɑm ˈsɑndwɪčɪz] are as suspect as counterfeit Confederate $3 bills. It is possible that some compulsive aspirants to social elegance docilely lapped up this pap; but those of us who were seriously concerned with English structure and usage laughed the program out of court and left the course, never to return. A second principle can be deduced from this experience: to imitate a dialect sharply different from one's own is a tricky and difficult assignment. A partial imitation is worse than none, since the change seems an affectation to one's neighbors, and the imperfect acquisition seems ridiculous to those whose speech is being imitated. Any attempts at teaching a standard dialect to those who speak a nonstandard one should be directed toward an attainable goal, toward one of the varieties of cultivated speech which the student might hear, day after day, in his own community.

At this point, perhaps, some of you may be muttering, "But what do these experiences have to do with dialects? I always thought that a dialect was something strange and old-fashioned." Many will share your opinion, especially in such countries as France and Italy, where an academy accepts one variety of the language as standard and casts the rest into outer darkness. In such countries the word *dialect* implies a variety of the language spoken by the rustic, the uneducated, the culturally isolated. To say that someone "speaks a dialect"—as one Italian professor patronizingly described one of the best soldiers working with me on our Italian military dictionary—is to exclude him forever from the company of educated men. For a dialect, to such intellectuals, is a form of the language they had rather be found dead than speaking.

True, there are other attitudes. Germans and Austrians make a distinction between the standard language—literary High German—and the dialects, local and predominantly rural forms of speech. But educated Germans do not always avoid dialect speech forms; in some areas, such as the Austrian Tyrol, an educated person will take particular pains to use some local forms in his speech, so as to identify himself with his home. The attitude may be a bit sentimental, but it does help to maintain one's individual dignity in a homogenizing world.

A more extreme attitude was prevalent in the Romantic Era. If the Augustans of the seventeenth and eighteenth centuries looked upon dialects as corruptions of an originally perfect language, the Romantics often alleged, in Wordsworth's terms, that people in humble and rustic life used "a purer and more emphatic language" than that to be met with in the cities. In this viewpoint, the dialects represent the pure, natural, unchanging language, unencumbered by the baggage of civilization. This attitude has long prevailed in Britain; even today the English Dialect Survey is heavily slanted toward archaic forms and relics and ignores modern innovations.

Nor are Americans wholly free from this attitude that a dialect is something archaic and strange. Time and again, a fieldworker for our *Linguistic Atlas* is told, "We don't speak no dialect around hyur; if you want *rale* dialect you gotta go down into Hellhole Swamp"—or up into Table Rock Cove, or at least across the nearest big river. To many of us, as my student Roger Shuy put it, a dialect is something spoken by little old people in queer out-of-the-way places.

When we become a little more sophisticated—as we must become on a cosmopolitan campus—we realize that cities as well as rural areas may differ in the ways in which their inhabitants talk. Thus we next conclude that a dialect is simply the way everybody talks but us and the people we grew up with; then, by force of circumstance, we realize that we speak a dialect ourselves. But at this point we still feel that a dialect is something regional or local. When we notice that people of our own community speak varieties of English markedly different from our own, we dismiss them as ignorant, or simply as making mistakes. After all, we live in a democratic society and are not supposed to have class markers in our speech. It is a very sophisticated stage that lets us recognize social dialects as well as regional ones—dialects just as natural, arising out of normal everyday contacts.

By this time we have elaborated our definition of a dialect. It is simply a habitual variety of a language, regional or social. It is set off from all other such habitual varieties by a unique combination of language features: words and meanings, grammatical forms, phrase structures, pronunciations, patterns of stress and intonation. No dialect is simply good or bad in itself; its prestige comes from the prestige of those who use it. But every dialect is in itself a legitimate form of the language, a valid instrument of human communication, and something worthy of serious study.

But even as we define what a dialect is, we must say what it is not. It is different from slang, which is determined by vogue and largely distinguished by transient novelties in the vocabulary. Yet it is possible that slang may show regional or social differences, or that some regional and social varieties of a language may be particularly receptive to slang.

A dialect is also different from an argot, a variety of the language used by people who share a common interest, whether in work or in play. Everyone knows many groups of this kind, with their own peculiar ways of speaking and writing: Baptist preachers, biophysicists, stamp collectors, model railroad fans, Chicago critics, narcotic addicts, jazz musicians, safe-crackers. But in the normal course of events a person adopts the language of such subcultures, for whatever part of his life it may function in, because he has adopted a particular way of life; he uses a dialect because he grows up in a situation where it is spoken. Again, some argots may show regional or social variations; the term *mugging*, to choose one example, is largely found on the Atlantic Seaboard; the sport has different designations in the Great Lakes region and on the Pacific Coast.

Nor are dialect differences confined to the older, pre-industrial segments of the vocabulary. Here European and American attitudes differ sharply. The late Eugen Dieth chided the editors of the *Linguistic Atlas of New England* for including such vocabulary items as window shades, the razor strop, and the automobile, such pronunciation items as *library* and *post office* and *hotel,* on the ground that these are not genuine dialect items. Yet if they have regional and social variants, as all of these have in North American English, they warrant inclusion. In my lifetime I have seen the *traffic circle* of the Middle Atlantic States become the *rotary* of Eastern New England; the *service plaza* of the Pennsylvania *Turnpike* become the *oasis* of the Illinois *Tollway;* the *poor boy* of New Orleans—a generous sandwich once confined to the Creole Gomorrah and its gastronautic satellites—appearing as a *grinder* in upstate New York, a *hoagy* in Philadelphia, a *hero* in New York City, a *submarine* in Boston. Nor will dialect terms be used only by the older and less sophisticated: a Middle Western academician transplanted to MIT quickly learns to order *tonic* for his children, not *soda pop*, and to send his clothes to a *cleanser*. And though some would consider dialect a matter of speech and not of writing, one can find regional and local commercial terms on billboards and television as well as in the advertising sections of local newspapers.

Finally, dialect terms are not restricted to sloppy, irresponsible usage— a matter of personality type rather than of specific vocabulary items. And though regional and local terms and usages are likely to appear most frequently in Joos's casual and intimate styles, the example of William Faulkner is sufficient evidence that they may be transmuted into the idiom of the greatest literature.

All of these comments are the fruit of centuries of observation, at first casual and anecdotal, later more serious and systematic. The grim test of the pronunciation *shibboleth*, applied by Jephthah's men to the Ephraimites seeking to ford the Jordan, the comic representations of Spartan and Theban speech by Aristophanes, the aspiration of the Roman cockney Arrius-Harrius, immortalized by Horace, the Northern English forms in the Reeves Tale—these typify early interest. With the Romantic search for the true language in the dialects came the growth of comparative linguistics, and the search for comparative dialect evidence in translations of the Lord's Prayer and the proverb of the prodigal son. The search for comparable evidence led, in the 1870's, to the monumental collections for Georg Wenker's *Deutscher Sprachatlas*, later edited by Ferdinand Wrede and Walther Mitzka—44,251 responses, by German village school-masters, to an official request for local dialect translations of forty-four sentences of Standard German. Designed to elicit fine phonetic data, the collections proved notably refractory for that purpose, but the sheer mass of evidence corrected the unevenness of individual transcriptions. More important, the discovery that questions designed for one purpose may yield a different but interesting kind of evidence—as *Pferd* proved useless for the /p:pf/ consonant alternation in dialects where the horse is *Roß* or *Gaul*—was reflected in greater sophistication in the design and use of later questionnaires. Less happy was the effect on German dialectology, with later investigations, such as Mitzka's *Wortatlas*, sticking to corre-spondence techniques, a short questionnaire, an immense number of com-munities, and an expensive cartographic presentation of the data. But the *Sprachatlas* and *Wortatlas*, and the Dutch investigations modeled upon them, provided us with the evidence on which to determine their own defects.

A valuable innovation was made at the turn of the century in the *Atlas linguistique de la France*, directed by Jules Gilliéron. Correspondence questionnaires gave way to field interviews on the spot, in a smaller num-ber of selected communities (some six hundred in this instance) with a longer questionnaire; a trained investigator interviewed a native of the community in a conversational situation and recorded his responses in a finely graded phonetic alphabet. As with the German atlas, however, the communities chosen were villages; larger places were first investigated in the Atlas of Italy and Southern Switzerland, under the direction of the Swiss scholars Karl Jaberg and Jakob Jud, who also introduced the prac-tice of interviewing more than one informant in the larger communities. With certain refinements, then, the basic principles of traditional dialect study were established by World War I. Some subsequent investigations have followed Wenker, others Gilliéron; some, like the current Czech in-vestigations, have combined both methods, relying primarily on field interviews but using correspondence surveys in the early stages, so that the selection of communities can be made most effectively. Only the British Isles have lagged, perhaps because Joseph Wright's *English Dialect Dictionary*, with its claim to have recorded ALL the dialect words of Eng-lish, has erected a Chinese Wall worthy of Mr. Eliot's scorn. Not till the 1950's did any kind of fieldwork get under way in either England or Scot-land; in both countries it was handicapped by a shortage of funds and fieldworkers, and in England by an antiquarian bias that overemphasized

58   relics, shunned innovations, and neglected opportunities to provide data comparable to that obtained in the American surveys. Yet both Harold Orton in England and Angus McIntosh in Scotland have enriched our knowledge of English.

Perhaps because American linguists have kept in touch with European developments, the *Linguistic Atlas of New England,* launched in 1930, drew on the lessons of the French and Italian atlases. Although the transition from casual collecting to systematic study was not welcomed by all students, nevertheless—even with the Hoover Depression, World War II, the Korean intervention, and the tensions of the Cold War—a respectable amount of progress has been made toward a first survey of American English. *The Linguistic Atlas of New England* was published in 1939–43; scholars are now probing for the changes that a generation has brought. For four other regional surveys, fieldwork has been completed and editing is under way: (1) the Middle and South Atlantic states, New York to central Georgia, with outposts in Ontario and northeastern Florida; (2) the North-Central states: Wisconsin, Michigan, southwestern Ontario, and the Ohio Valley; (3) the Upper Midwest: Minnesota, Iowa, Nebraska, and the Dakotas; (4) the Pacific Southwest: California and Nevada. Elsewhere, fieldwork has been completed in Colorado, Oklahoma, Washington, and eastern Montana; respectable portions have been done in several other states, Newfoundland, Nova Scotia, and British Columbia; with a slightly different method the late E. Bagby Atwood produced his memorable *Regional Vocabulary of Texas.* In all of these surveys the principles of European dialect investigations have been adapted to the peculiarities of the American scene. Settlement history has been studied more carefully before fieldwork, since English-speaking settlement in North America is recent, and its patterns are still changing. At least three levels of usage are investigated—partly because cultivated American speech has regional varieties, just like uneducated speech, and the cultivated speech of the future may be foreshadowed in the speech of the intermediate group; partly because until very recently general education has been a more important linguistic and cultural force in the United States than in most of the countries of Europe. Urban speech as well as rural has been investigated in each survey, and intensive local investigations have been encouraged. The questionnaires have included both relics and innovations. All of these modifications were suggested by Hans Kurath, first Director of the Atlas project, who is currently drawing on his experience in developing a new theory for the interpretation of dialect differences.

Just as warfare is still decided ultimately by infantrymen who can take and hold territory, so dialect study still depends on competent investigators who can elicit and record natural responses in the field. The tape recorder preserves free conversation for later transcription and analysis, and permits the investigator to listen repeatedly to a response about whose phonetic quality he is in doubt; but the investigator must still ask the right questions to elicit pertinent data. He must remember, for instance, that *chicken coop* is both a vocabulary and a pronunciation item—that the pronunciation in the American North and North Midland is /kup/, in the South and South Midland /kʌp/, that *coop* in the North designates the permanent shelter for the whole flock, in the South a crate under which a mother hen can scratch without an opportunity to lead the little ones off and lose them in the brush. The full record for such an item may require three or four questions, which only a human interviewer can provide.

But if the fieldworker remains essential, the objects of his investigation may change. Recent studies have turned increasingly to urban areas, urbanizing areas, and minority groups. To a long list of impressive early investigations one can now add such contributions as Lee Pederson's study of Chicago pronunciation and Gerald Udell's analysis of the changes in Akron speech resulting from the growth of the rubber industry and the consequent heavy migration from West Virginia. Among special groups investigated in detail are the Spanish-American bilinguals in San Antonio by Mrs. Janet Sawyer, the American Norwegians by Einar Haugen, the New York City Greeks by James Macris, the New England Portuguese by Leo Pap, the Chicago Slovaks by Mrs. Goldie Meyerstein, the Gullah Negroes by Lorenzo Turner, and the Memphis Negroes by Miss Juanita Williamson. In all of these studies the emphasis has been on the correlation between linguistic and social forces.

Another significant development has been the investigation of the way language attitudes are revealed by the choice among linguistic variants under different conditions. The most impressive work of this kind has been done by William Labov of Columbia University, in his study of the speech of the Lower East Side of New York. Limiting himself to a small number of items—the vowels of *bad* and *law*, the initial consonants of *think* and *then*, the /-r/ in *barn* and *beard*—phonological details that can be counted on to appear frequently and in a large number of contexts during a short interview, Labov gathers specimens of linguistic behavior under a wide range of conditions. At one end of the spectrum is the reading of such putatively minimal pairs as *bed* and *bad;* at the other is the description of children's games or the recounting an incident when the informant thought he was going to be killed. The difference between pronunciations in the relaxed situation and those when the informant is on what he considers his best linguistic behavior is an index of his social insecurity. Almost as revealing is the work of Rufus Baehr with high-school students in the Negro slums of the Chicago West Side. It is no surprise

60   that in formal situations the students with greater drive to break out of
their ghetto reveal striking shifts of their speech in the direction of the
Chicago middle-class norm. This kind of discovery should give heart to
all who believe that a directed program of second-dialect teaching can
make at least a small dent in our problem of providing a wider range of
economic and educational opportunities for the aspiring young Negro.

Out of all these investigations two patterns emerge: (1) a better understanding of the origin and nature of dialect differences; (2) a set of implications for those who are interested in providing every American child
with a command of the standard language adequate for him to go as far
as his ability and ambition impel him.

No dialect differences can, as yet, be attributed to physiology or to climate. Perhaps anatomists will discover that some minor speech differences arise from differences in the vocal organs; but so far, there is no evidence for any correlation between anatomy and dialect, and the burden
of proof is on those who propose such a correlation. As for climate: It is
unlikely that nasality could have arisen (as often asserted) both from the
dusty climate of Australia and the dampness of the Tennessee Valley.
And though it is a favorite sport among Northerners to attribute the so-
called "Southern drawl" to laziness induced by a hot climate, many
Southerners speak with a more rapid tempo than most Middle Westerners, and the Bengali, in one of the most enervating tropical climates,
speak still more rapidly. For an explanation of dialect differences we are
driven back, inevitably, to social and cultural forces.

The most obvious force is the speech of the original settlers. We should
expect that a part of the United States settled by Ulster Scots would show
differences in vocabulary, pronunciation, even in grammar from those
parts settled by East Anglians. We should expect to find Algonkian loans
most common in those regions where settlers met Algonkian Indians,
French loans most frequent in Louisiana and in the counties adjacent to
French Canada, Spanish loans most widespread in the Southwest, German loans clustering in cities and in the Great Valley of Pennsylvania,
and indubitable Africanisms most striking in the Gullah country.

Speech forms are also spread along routes of migration and communication. The Rhine has carried High German forms northward; the
Rhone has taken Parisian forms to the Mediterranean; in the United
States, the same kind of dissemination has been found in the valleys of
the Mississippi, the Ohio, and the Shenandoah.

If speech forms may spread along an avenue of communication, they
may be restricted by a physical barrier. As Kurath has observed, there is
no sharper linguistic boundary in the English-speaking world than the
Virginia Blue Ridge between the Potomac and the James. The tidal rivers
of the Carolinas, the swamps of the Georgia coastal plain, have contrib-

uted to making the Old South the most varied region, dialectally, in the English settlements of the New World.

The economic pattern of an area may be reflected in distinctive dialect features. *Fatwood,* for resin-rich kindling, is confined to the turpentine belt of the Southern tidewater; *lightwood,* with a similar referent, to the Southern coastal plain and lower Piedmont. *Case weather,* for a kind of cool dampness in which it is safe to cut tobacco, occurs over a wide area, but only where tobacco is a money crop. *To run afoul of,* a maritime phrase in the metaphorical sense of "to meet," seems to be restricted to the New England coast.

Political boundaries, when long established, may become dialect boundaries; in the Rhineland, pronunciation differences coincide strikingly with the boundaries of the petty states of pre-Napoleonic Germany. In the New World, on the other hand, political boundaries have seldom delimited culture areas. Yet *county site,* for the more usual *county seat,* is common in Georgia but unknown in South Carolina, and Ontario Canadians speak of the *reeve* as chief officer of a township, the *warden* as chief officer of a county, and a *serviette* instead of a table napkin—terms unfamiliar in the United States.

Each city of consequence may have its distinctive speech forms. The grass strip between the sidewalk and the curb, undesignated in South Carolina, is a *tree belt* locally in Springfield, Massachusetts (and hence unlabeled in *Webster's Third New International Dictionary*), a *tree lawn* in Cleveland, a *devil strip* in Akron, and a *boulevard* in Minneapolis and St. Paul. And only Chicagoans naturally refer to political influence as *clout,* or to a reliable dispenser of such influence as a *Chinaman.*

Nor are differences in the educational system without their effect. Where separate and unequal education is provided to particular social groups, we can be sure that a high-school diploma or even a college degree will be no indication by itself of proficiency in the standard language. That this problem is not confined to any single racial or cultural group has been shown by institutions such as West Virginia State College, which have undergone the process of reverse integration. This particular school, which once drew an elite Negro student body, is now eighty percent white, with the white students mostly from the disadvantaged mountain areas along the Kanawha. Since the teachers in the mountain schools are not only predominantly local in origin, but often have had little education beyond what the local schools offer, and then, since most of them habitually use many nonstandard forms, it has been difficult for the college to maintain its academic standards in the face of increasing white enrollment, however desirable integration may be.

Most important, perhaps, is the traditional class structure of a community. In a Midwestern small town, it is still possible for one brother to

62   stay home and run a filling station, and another to go off and become a judge—and nobody mind. But in parts of the South there is a social hierarchy of families and occupations, so that it is more respectable for a woman of good family to teach in an impoverished small college than to do professional work for the government at twice the salary. Here, too, an aristocratic ideal of language survives, and the most cultivated still look upon *ain't* as something less reprehensible than incest—but use it only in intimate conversation with those whom they consider their social equals. Here too we find the cultural self-assurance that leads an intelligent lawyer to ask the linguistically naive question: "Why is it that the educated Northerner talks so much like the uneducated Southerner?"

If social differences among the WASP population are reflected in linguistic differences, we should not be surprised if similar differences among later immigrants are reflected in the extent of linguistic borrowing from particular foreign-language groups, or even from the same foreign-language group at different times. Our longest continuous tradition of borrowing, with probably the largest and most varied kinds of words, is that from various kinds of German. Even the bitterness of two world wars cannot prevent us from seeing that of all foreign-language groups the Germans have been most widely distributed, geographically and socially, throughout the United States—as prosperous farmers, vaudeville comedians, skilled craftsmen, merchants, intellectuals. In contrast, the hundreds of thousands of Italian- and Slavic-speaking immigrants of the last two generations have left few marks on the American vocabulary; most of them were of peasant stock, often illiterate, and settled in centers of heavy industry as basic labor.

Even more striking is the change in the incidence of Texas borrowings from Mexican Spanish. In her study of the bilingual situation in San Antonio, Mrs. Sawyer has shown that although early Spanish loans were numerous, quickly assimilated, and widely spread—*canyon, burro, ranch, lariat, broncho, silo* are characteristic examples—there have been few such loans in the last seventy years. The explanation is the drastic change in the relationships between Anglos and Latins. When English-speaking settlers first moved into Texas, they found the hacienda culture already established, and eagerly took over culture and vocabulary from the Latins who constituted the local elite. Anglo and Latin, side by side, died in the Alamo 4 March 1836 and conquered at San Jacinto seven weeks later. But since 1890 the Texan has encountered Mexican Spanish most often in the speech of unskilled laborers, including imported braceros and illegally entered wetbacks; derogatory labels for Latins have increased in Texas English, and loans from Spanish have declined. We borrow few words from those we consider our inferiors.

We can now make a few clear statements about the facts of American
dialects, and their significance:

1) Even though much work remains to be done, we can describe in some detail most of the principal regional varieties of American English and many of the important subvarieties; we can indicate, further, some of the kinds of social differences that are to be found in various dialect areas, and many of the kinds that are to be found in some of the most important cities.

2) We can be sure that in many situations there are tensions between external norms and the expectations of one's associates. These tensions, most probably, are strongest in the lower middle class—a group anxious to forget humbler backgrounds but not sure of their command of the prestige patterns. Since the teaching profession, on all levels, is heavily drawn from the lower middle class, we can expect—as Marjorie Daunt found years ago—that anxiety is the characteristic attitude of the English teacher toward variations in usage. There is a strong urge to make changes, for the sake of making changes and demonstrating one's authority, without stopping to sort out the significance of differences in usage. This attitude is reflected in the two most widely known programs for teaching better English to the disadvantaged: a socially insignificant problem, such as the distinction between *Wales* and *whales*, is given the same value as the use of the marker for the third singular in the present indicative. Future programs should use the resources of the dialect archives, at least as a start, even though more detailed and more recent information may be necessary before one can develop teaching materials. The inevitable prescription in a pedagogical situation can be no better than the underlying description.

3) There is evidence that ambitious students in slum areas intuitively shift their speech patterns in the direction of the prestigious local pattern, in situations where they feel such a shift will be to their advantage. Some actually achieve, on their own, a high degree of functional bidialectalism, switching codes as the situation demands. In any teaching program it would seem intelligent to make use of this human facility.

4) The surest social markers in American English are grammatical forms, and any teaching program should aim, first of all, at developing a habitual productive command of the grammar of standard English—with due allowance for the possibility that the use of this grammar may be confined to formal situations in which the speaker comes in contact with the dominant culture.

5) Relatively few pronunciation features are clear social markers, though in many Northern cities there is a tendency to identify all Southern and South Midland pronunciations as those of uneducated rural

Negroes. How much one should attempt to substitute local pronunciations for those which are standard in regions from which migrants come would probably depend on the extent to which variations in standard English are recognized and accepted in the community: Washington, for instance, may be more tolerant than New York City. In any event, programs to alter pronunciation patterns should concentrate on those pronunciations that are most widely recognized as substandard.

6) Few people can really identify the race of a speaker by pronunciation and voice quality. In experiments in Chicago, middle-class Middle Westerners consistently identified the voice of an educated urban white Southerner as that of an uneducated rural Negro, and many identified as Negro the voice of an educated white Chicagoan. Similar experiments in New York have yielded similar results. And many white Southerners can testify to personal difficulties arising from this confusion in the minds of Northerners. In Ithaca, New York, I could not get to see any apartment advertised as vacant until I paid a personal visit; over the telephone I was always told that the apartments had just been rented; James Marchand, a Middle Tennessean now on the Cornell faculty, must carefully identify himself as "Professor Marchand," if he wants a garageman to come and pick up his car. And the telephone voice of my Mississippi-born chairman, Gwin Kolb, is racially misidentified with alarming regularity.

7) There can be no single standard in programs for the disadvantaged; the target dialect must vary according to the local situation. In Mississippi, the same program can be used for Negroes and whites, because they share most of the same grammatical deviations from the local standard, and share phonological patterns with that standard; in Cleveland, grammatical features in writing are sufficient to distinguish Negro college applicants from white better than ninety percent of the time, and deviations from local standard pronunciation are far more striking and numerous among Negroes than among locally-born disadvantaged whites.

8) To the suggestion that Southern Negroes should not be taught local standard pronunciation, but some external standard—the hypothetical variety some call "network English"—there is a simple answer in the form of a question: "Do you want integration in the South?" The Southern patterns of race relations have suffered too long from too many separate standards for Negro and white; it would be ironical if those speaking most loudly in behalf of the aspirations of the Southern Negro should create new obstacles to those aspirations. The language problems of the uneducated Southern Negro are the language problems, even to fine detail, of the uneducated Southern white in the same community; the South may well solve the language problems in its schools before Detroit does. Once the races are brought into the same classroom, a community will need only one intelligent program based on a solid body of dialect evidence.

9) While we are planning language programs for our disadvantaged, we must educate the dominant culture in the causes and significance of dialect differences; it is particularly urgent that we educate teachers on all levels, from kindergarten through graduate school. The disadvantaged will have enough to do in learning new patterns of language behavior; the dominant culture must meet them part way, with greater understanding, with a realization that dialect differences do not reflect intellectual or moral differences, but only differences in experience. Granted that this re-education of the dominant culture is bound to be difficult, we should not be so cynical as to reject it, on the ground that it cannot take place. In an age when we are turning the heat off under the melting pot and accepting the cultural contributions of Americans with ancestral languages other than English, in an age when we are learning the art of peaceful co-existence with a variety of economic and political and cultural systems, it should not be difficult to extend this acceptance to fellow Americans of different cultural backgrounds and linguistic habits, and especially to recognize that cultured American English may be found in many regional and local varieties. It is a poor cultural tolerance that would accept all cultivated speech except that in other parts of our own country.

With my deep-ingrained horror of patent-medicine salesmen, I would not leave you with the impression that we already have all the answers, or even all the evidence we need to arrive at those answers. We need many more kinds of investigation, and we should like to think that John Fisher, with his unlimited license to stalk money-bearing animals, might help us conduct some of them. We are still to do even the preliminary surveys in such parts of the country as Tennessee and Arkansas; we need many more studies of the actual patterns of social dialects in most American cities. We really have no serious evidence on regional and social differences in such prosodic features as stress and pitch and juncture. The recognition of paralanguage—the non-linguistic modulation of the stream of speech—is so recent that we have no idea as to the kinds of regional and social differences that may be found in tempo and rhythm, in range of pitch and stress, in drawl and clipping, in rasp and nasality and mellifluousness. We have not even begun to study regional and social variations in gesture and other kinds of body movement. But we do have a framework which we can fill in detail, continually building our teaching programs on solid research into the ways in which Americans communicate in various localities, and into the attitudes of specific speakers toward those whose usage differs from their own. In comparison with the immensity of our social problems, our linguistic knowledge is as a little candle in the forest darkness at midnight; let us not hide that candle under a basket, but put it in a lantern and use it to find our way.

part **2**

INHERITED FEATURES

Early American Speech Adoptions from Foreign Tongues

Thomas Pyles

Although the basis of the English language is to be found in the dialects brought to England by the Angles, Saxons, and Jutes in mid-fifth century, this original word stock has been expanded by infusions from dozens of languages beginning with Celtic, Latin, and Scandinavian in the early centuries of the Christian era. It is true that the small stock of words most commonly used in everyday speech is chiefly of Anglo-Saxon origin. But more than half of the words in the language are borrowings or adaptations over the fifteen centuries of its unbroken evolution. The language continued to expand in America as the country developed and immigration continued. Thomas Pyles here describes this process in early American speech.

Professor Pyles has worked for many years in lexicography and historical linguistics. He has acted in editorial and advisory capacities in the preparation of several dictionaries: *Funk and Wagnall College Standard Dictionary, Thorndike-*

70   *Barnhart College Dictionary, World Book Encyclopedia Dictionary,* and *Dictionary of American Regional English.* His publications include *Words and Ways of American English* (1952), *Origins and Development of the English Language* (1966), and *The English Language: A Brief History* (1968). Dr. Pyles is Professor of English and Linguistics at Northwestern University.

Before there was any permanent settlement of English-speaking folk in this land, a number of Indian words had made their way into the language of England by way of Spanish or Portuguese—words from Nahuatl, the tongue of the Aztecs, who were the most highly advanced of the Indians that the Spanish found in Mexico, as well as from various Indian dialects spoken in Central and South America and the West Indies. Some of these words came in time to be current in all the languages of Europe.

The English language in those exuberant days of Elizabeth, of Raleigh, Drake, Hawkins, Bacon, Marlowe, Jonson, and Shakespeare, had been particularly receptive to augmentations of its already rich word stock from foreign sources—the so-called "inkhorn" terms from the classical languages, along with words from French, Spanish, Italian, and Portuguese. Words from the New World must have had all the charm of lush exoticisms in a period when the language was being enriched from so many nearby Continental sources, though they seem for the most part commonplace enough today—words like *potato, tomato, chocolate, cocoa, canoe, cannibal, barbecue, maize,* and *savannah,* which must have been known to the first Englishmen to come to these shores with any intention of staying. One of them, *maize,* was by a strange perversity of linguistic fate to be replaced by *corn* in the English of America. The British use *corn* in the sense "wheat," while retaining the older meaning of "grain," as in the "Corn Laws." Another of them, *cannibal,* a modification of *Caribal,* "Caribbean native," was used in slightly different form by Shakespeare in his play about the "vexed Bermoothes," for *Caliban,* if not simply a metathesized[1] form of *can(n)ibal,* is a variant of *Cariban,* itself a variant of *Caribal. Barbecue,* while appearing first in British English, is nevertheless much more familiar in America, and its use to designate an outdoor social or political meeting at which animals are roasted whole is exclusively American. But these words, while native to the New World, must be distinguished from those which entered the language of English-

[1] Metathesis involves transposition of sounds or letters: hunderd for hundred; tradegy for tragedy; revelant for relevant. [eds.]

men who chose or were forced to transplant themselves permanently in this strange and savage land.

The colonizers of this country were confronted with a land whose topography, meteorological phenomena, trees, plants, birds, and animals were frequently quite different from what they had known in England. Inasmuch as an understanding of the principles of semantics is not congenital, people generally are wont to ask when they see some new object, "What is it?" and expect in answer to be told its name, supposing then that they have learned something really significant about it. This procedure, or something very similar to it, must have been gone through a great many times in the early days of the colonization of America when Indians were friendly enough to be asked and bright enough to divine what was being asked of them. Sometimes, too, these first white Americans made up their own names for what they saw, if there was no one to tell the "true" names or if the "true" names were too difficult for them to pronounce. As we have seen in the preceding chapter, they frequently combined or modified English words, as in *bullfrog* and *jimson weed* (originally *Jamestown weed*); sometimes they made use of sound alone, as in *bobolink*.

The situation with regard to the American Indian languages, with many tribes speaking apparently unrelated languages which are in turn subdivided into dialects, is extremely complex. Fortunately it need not concern us here, for to American English only one stock, the Algonquian, is important. This huge group of tribes, comprising among others the Arapaho, Blackfoot, Cheyenne, Cree, Delaware, Fox, Micmac, Ojibwa (Chippewa), and Penobscot, formerly occupied a larger area than any other North American Indian stock. It was they whom the first English settlers in Virginia and Massachusetts came in contact with.

As early as 1608 Captain John Smith in his *True Relation of... Virginia Since the First Planting of That Collony* recorded *raccoon,* though he did not spell it that way. He wrote it in various ways—for instance, *raugroughcun* and later, in his *General Historie of Virginia, New-England and the Summer Isles* of 1624, *rarowcun*—in his effort to reduce to symbols, which were, incidentally, ill-adapted to that purpose, what he heard or thought he heard from the Indians. It is highly unlikely, as a matter of fact, that a single English word of Indian origin would be immediately intelligible to an Indian today, for words have been clipped, like *squash* (the vegetable), which was originally *askutasquash,* folk-etymologized like *whiskey-John* "blue jay" from *wisketjan,* or in one way or another made to conform to English speechways.

Early Indian loan words naming creatures neglected by Adam are *opossum, moose, skunk, menhaden, terrapin, woodchuck,* and *caribou. Opossum* usually occurs in speech and often in writing in an aphe013tic form

72   as *possum,* as does *raccoon* as *coon. Woodchuck* is a folk-etymologizing
of Cree or Ojibwa *otchek* or *odjik.* Noah Webster was quite proud, by
the way, of deriving *woodchuck* from an Avestan word meaning "pig"
and made frequent reference to this acute etymological discovery in
lectures and prefaces. *Caribou,* as the spelling of its final syllable indicates,
comes to us by way of Canadian French; an Englishman would have
been more likely to write *cariboo.* These words, all of Algonquian origin,
designate creatures indigenous to North America. Ojibwa *chipmunk*
would seem to belong to this group, though it was first recorded considerably later, in Cooper's *Deerslayer* (1841); it was almost certainly in use
much earlier.

A good many native plants, vegetables, trees, and shrubs bear names
of Indian origin: *hickory, pecan, poke(weed), chinquapin, squash, persim-
mon,* and *catalpa,* all but one of which are Algonquian. That one, *catalpa,*
is of Muskhogean origin. A good many Southern place names are of this
linguistic stock, which includes Creek, Chickasaw, and Choctaw, but
catalpa (with its variant *catawba*) and the topographical *bayou* (from
Choctaw *bayuk* "stream," coming to us by way of Louisiana French) are
the only widely known words other than place names taken from the
languages of these Indians, who formerly occupied an area of our country
including most of Georgia, Alabama, and Mississippi and parts of Tennessee, Kentucky, Louisiana, and Florida.

Other early borrowings from the Indians include words denoting foods,
customs, relationships, or artifacts peculiar to the Indians at the time
of borrowing: *hominy, succotash, johnnycake, pone, pemmican, moccasin,
tomahawk, totem, wigwam, toboggan, powwow, mackinaw, caucus* (perhaps), *wampum, sachem, papoose,* and *squaw. Toboggan* and *mackinaw* are
first recorded later than the others in this group, though their earliest use
in English certainly goes back considerably beyond their first recording.
Both entered English by way of Canadian French; the latter word has
a half-French spelling, *Mackinac,* when used as a name for the strait, the
island, and the town in Michigan. The first element of *johnnycake* is probably from *jonakin* or *jonikin,* apparently of Indian origin and meaning a
thin griddle cake made of cornmeal. *Johnnycake* was folk-etymologized
to *journey cake,* which Noah Webster thought the original form; he assumed that it meant cake to eat when one went on a journey. It has also
been suggested that the word is a corruption of *Shawnee cake,* a kind of
cake supposed to have been eaten by the Shawnee Indians—an explanation which Mr. Mencken in *The American Language, Supplement One*
(New York, 1945) considers "much more plausible" than any other.
Jonikin (usually spelled *johnnikin*) is still used for a corn griddle cake in
the eastern part of the Carolinas and on the Eastern Shore of Maryland.

As for *caucus,* somebody suggested a good many years ago that it was
from a somewhat similar Algonquian word meaning "one who advises,"

and more recently efforts have been made to relate it to *cockarouse,* recorded by Captain John Smith in 1624 as *caucorouse* and designating an Indian chief in Virginia, later extended to designate an influential and wealthy white colonist. It is also possible that *caucus* is a variant form of *caulkers.* The learned John Pickering in his *Vocabulary* thought so, basing his belief on a statement in the *History of the Rise and Independence of the United States* (1788) by the Reverend William Gordon, who stated that in Boston "more than fifty years ago Mr. Samuel Adams's father and twenty others, one or two from the north end of town, where all the ship business is carried on, used to meet, make a *caucus,* and lay their plan for introducing certain persons into positions of trust and power." Pickering inferred from this reference to "the north end of town, where all the ship business is carried on" that it was "not improbable that *caucus* might be a corruption of *caulkers,* the word meeting being understood." The *Dictionary of American English* suggests the possibility that *caucus* may be the name of a long-forgotten neighborhood in Boston called West-Corcus; indeed, the quotation given in support of this suggestion (from the Boston *Evening Post* of August 19, 1745), concerns a caucus-like meeting in that neighborhood to "take into serious consideration the conduct of those reverend clergymen who have encouraged the itineration of Mr. George Whitefield," the Calvinistic Methodist evangelist. Another etymology of *caucus* with which Pickering flirted has recently come to light: among some of his old papers there occurs an explanation to the effect that it consisted of the initials of the names of six men— Cooper, Adams, Urann, Coulson, another Urann, and Symmes. Pickering states that he got this story from "B. Russell, who had it from Sam'l Adams and Paul Revere." The etymology has a familiar ring to it; it is precisely the sort on which the dilettante etymologist dotes. Still another theory is that the American word is simply a borrowing of Latin *caucus* "drinking vessel," which may indicate a feature of the evening's entertainment in the early American gatherings.

All the other words in this last group save *johnnycake* have made the Atlantic crossing, and most of them are now about as familiar to the English as they are to us. In fact, all of them except *mackinaw* are listed in Wyld's *Universal Dictionary;* only *succotash* and *johnnycake* are labeled "U.S.A." The usual British pronunciation of *wigwam* rhymes with *big dam,* a pronunciation never heard in this country. *Pemmican,* the Indian name for dried meat pounded into paste, mixed with fat and dried fruits, and then compressed into cakes, has even acquired the figurative meaning in British English of "condensed statement." On the continent of Europe also, most of these words are quite well known as a result of literary transmission, for generations of European children have thrilled to the novels of James Fenimore Cooper, as well as of his European imitators.

Tammany as a political designation is a well-known Americanism of

74   Indian origin. Tammany was a Delaware chief who flourished in the latter part of the seventeenth century and who was jocularly canonized as an American saint in 1771. His name was later used to designate a political club which ultimately grew into the present powerful Democratic organization in New York City. References to *Tammany* as the name of the club, which was founded in1789, occur from 1790 onwards. The organization uses *the Wigwam* as a designation for Tammany Hall, *sachem* for a high official of the society, and *brave* (not of Indian origin, but long used to mean an Indian warrior) for a rank-and-file member.

A good many other words of Indian origin are included in the *Dictionary of American English,* but most of them are not in wide current use: *tuckahoe* "edible part of a fungus found on roots of trees," which is also used to designate a poor white in Virginia and West Virginia, *carcajou* "wolverine," *manito* or *manitou* "a god," *quahog* or *quahaug* "hard clam," *sagamore* "chief," *samp* "corn porridge," *tamarack* "the American larch," *mugwump* "great man," and others considerably less familiar. *Mugwump,* though known much earlier, came into real prominence in the presidential campaign of 1884, when it was applied to those independent Republicans who, affecting an attitude of superiority, refused to support James G. Blaine as their party nominee. Nowadays the word is chiefly notable for the oft-recorded definition by a Congressional wag (would there were more of his kidney!) to the effect that a mugwump was one who always had his *mug* on one side of the fence and his *wump* on the other.

Some early Americanisms were translations or supposed translations of Indian words or phrases, for example, *paleface* (first used by James Fenimore Cooper), *war paint, warpath, firewater, pipe of peace, medicine man, Great Spirit, big chief, to scalp,* and *to bury the hatchet.* Frequently *Indian* was used in conjunction with another word, as in *Indian meal, Indian file, Indian summer,* and *Indian gift,* originally a gift for which one expected something of more value in return, but later a gift which the giver took back. *Indian giver* is first recorded, as far as we know, in Bartlett's *Glossary* of 1848, with the notation that "this term is applied by children to a child who, after having given away a thing, wishes it back again," though *Indian gift* occurs much earlier. The *Dictionary of American English* lists almost a hundred such combinations, though not all are early, for instance, *honest Injun,* which is not recorded until 1875. *Indian summer* is of special interest. By 1830 it had been used in British English (by Thomas De Quincey) in the figurative sense "declining years." That the term is still perfectly familiar in England in this slightly later sense is indicated by John Galsworthy's use of it as the title of a section of the *Forsyte Saga* dealing with the last years of Jolyon Forsyte. Although the English do not have occasion to use the expression in the meteorological sense that Americans have because the phenomenon it names is much less striking in Europe than here, it is nevertheless perfectly well understood in this sense. It has been suggested that Indian summer is so called because its occurrence was predicted by the Indians to the first batch of settlers; but there is no evidence that the term, which is documented only at a comparatively late date, was ever used by the earliest settlers. Other suggestions are that the Indians were responsible for lighting the brush fires common in the late autumn or early winter; that the period constituted a last chance before the final onset of cold weather for the Indians to harass and bedevil the white settlers; and that, because the early settlers thought of the Indians as false and fickle—an idea reflected in the term *Indian giver*—the sham summer weather was called *Indian summer.* The real origin of the term remains as hazy as the weather it designates.

Before passing on to other non-English influences it is interesting to note that British English borrowed *Mohawk,* which it usually spelled *mohock,* early in the eighteenth century to designate, according to the *Oxford English Dictionary,* "one of a class of aristocratic ruffians who infested the streets of London at night," but the term has only a historical interest today. It has never had any currency in American English save among professors of eighteenth-century English literature. The *Apache* of *Apache dance,* a rowdy, sexy dance performed by a pair of dancers attired as a Parisian gangster and his "moll," did not come to us directly from the well-known American aborigines of that name. It came instead by way of French, which in the early nineteenth century borrowed the name of the Indian tribe, Gallicized its pronunciation, and used it to designate a Parisian street bully.

It is perhaps not surprising, considering the ultimate reduction of the American Indians to the status of a conquered people, that the Indian element in American English is no larger than it is. As a matter of fact, if we leave out of consideration place names, of which there are an overwhelming number—more than half of our states bear Indian names, and a large portion of our rivers, lakes, mountains, towns, and cities as well—the Indian influence on our vocabulary must be characterized as slight.

The Indian languages were not, however, the only non-European influence on the English of America in colonial days. More than a year before the Pilgrims landed on Plymouth Rock in search of religious freedom, a group of people were against their will brought here from the west coast of Africa—principally from Senegal, Gambia, Sierra Leone, Liberia, the Gold Coast, Togo, Dahomey, Nigeria and Angola—and forthwith sold into slavery. The traffic in Negro slaves continued until shortly before the Civil War, though slackening somewhat after 1808,

76 when the Slave Trade Act went into effect. A great majority of these Negroes were brought direct from Africa; some, however, had previously lived in the British West Indies, where they had picked up a bare working knowledge of English.

Most of the descendants of these transplanted Africans living in the South now speak conventional American English. Because of lack of social contacts with whites and lack of schooling, relics of older standard speech may occasionally be heard from them, such as the pronunciation *deef* for *deaf* and *obleege* for *oblige*. When a colored charwoman with some embarrassment informed me that her small daughter had suffered an injury in her *grine*, she was not using an un-English, "darky" pronunciation, but merely saying *groin* in a manner which went out of fashion in more sophisticated usage years ago. There is, of course, no connection whatever between race and the ability to articulate given speech sounds, though it is popularly believed that the Southern Negro speaks as he does because of a peculiar conformation of speech organs, aided and abetted by indolence and stupidity. I was once gravely informed by a professor of government that the Negro does not have an *r* sound (my informant was of course referring only to *r* before a consonant sound and in final position) because the "letter *r*" did not exist in African languages—not one of which he had any acquaintance with, incidentally. When I presumed to disagree with his explanation, a corollary of which was that the speech of white Southerners was *r*-less because of the linguistic influence of Negro "mammies," and to point out that an Ohio-bred Negro has no difficulty whatsoever pronouncing *r* in all positions, he was grievously offended with me. The fact is that uneducated Negroes in the South by and large differ little in their speech from the uneducated whites. As for the presence of archaisms, they may also be heard from whites who have lived for a long time in cultural isolation, for instance, the Southern mountain folk.

There are, however, communities of Negro Americans engaged largely in the cultivation of rice, cotton, and indigo along the coastal region of South Carolina and Georgia, both on the Sea Islands and on the mainland, who have lived in cultural and geographical isolation for many generations. Most of them have had little contact with whites; some, indeed, have seldom seen white people. These Negroes, numbering about a quarter of a million, speak a type of English which has been so heavily influenced by the African languages native to their remote ancestors that it is not readily intelligible to people, white or colored, from other parts of the country. Their language, Gullah or Geechee, retains a good many African characteristics in its system of sounds, its syntax, its morphology, its vocabulary, its methods of forming words, and, most striking of all to one hearing it for the first time, its intonation. The word *Gullah* is probably either from *Gola*, the name of a Liberian tribe and its language, or from *Angola*. *Geechee*, also used in the upcountry of South Carolina as a derisive nickname for a low-country white, particularly one living in the Charleston area, is probably derived from the name of another Liberian tribe and language.

It was very unlikely that Africans from the same tribe or language area would find themselves thrown together on a single plantation in sufficient numbers to enable them to maintain their native languages. The chances were all that they would be considerably dispersed upon their arrival at the various Southern ports. Consequently, it became necessary for them to learn English as well as they could. It is not likely that anyone helped them to do so, unless there were prototypes of Mrs. Stowe's Little Eva gliding or floating about the plantations (for Little Eva seldom merely walked) in the seventeenth and eighteenth centuries. The only English many of them ever heard from native speakers was that of the illiterate or semiliterate white indentured servants with whom they worked in the fields or who were set over them as overseers. It was for them not simply a matter of translating word for word their native idioms into English. This cannot be done successfully even with related languages, where it may result in something intelligible if un-English, like *the bread is all*, a Pennsylvania Germanism (though heard in other parts of the country) from German *das Brot ist alles*. It was for these Negroes a matter of acquiring a quite different linguistic psychology, a new attitude toward the phenomena of life as expressed by language. It is not surprising that their accomplishment fell considerably short of perfect. Their English was a sort of jargon or pidgin, which passed into use by their descendants as a native language. This type of so-called creolized language has been preserved largely in the speech of the Gullahs, Negroes who "stayed put" in a region in which they have always been far more numerous than whites and in which they have developed the only distinctive Negro speech in this country.

The principal importance of Gullah, aside from its intrinsic interest as a remarkable linguistic development, is that recent studies of it have been the means of identifying beyond doubt the African source of a number of words in Southern American English, a few of which have passed into other types of American English and one of which, *banjo*, if it is indeed of African origin, is part of the English language wherever it is spoken. Until Lorenzo Dow Turner began his investigations about twenty years ago, Gullah was traditionally regarded as "a quaint linguistic mongrel," to quote from one serious commentator; it was thought to be characterized by "intellectual indolence," "slovenly and careless," a debased form of the "peasant English" of poor whites, a sort of baby talk. One writer even went so far as to attribute its phonological characteristics to the "clumsy tongues," "flat noses," and "thick lips" of the Negroes who speak it.

Professor Turner's studies of Gullah, culminating in his *Africanisms in the Gullah Dialect* (Chicago, 1949), identify thousands of words in Gullah which have or may have African sources. Unlike earlier commentators, who assumed that many words which seemed strange to them were either nonsense words or mispronunciations of English words, Turner, himself of African descent, took the trouble to acquire a good working knowledge of West African languages. His studies and conclusions have made short shrift of some of the theories of previous writers, who assumed, for instance, that a Gullah word for "tooth," which sounded to them something like *bong,* was merely a childish, clumsy-tongued, flat-nosed, thick-lipped mispronunciation of English *bone,* and that the Gullah word *det* or the expression *det rain* "a long, hard rain" was really *death rain,* which involved the further assumption that to the Gullahs a long, hard rain is an omen of death to come—as it were, folklore made to order. The fact that in the Wolof language, spoken in Senegal and Gambia, the word for "tooth" is very like *bong* (it is impossible to indicate the exact pronunciation of the un-English final sound of this word, a palatal nasal, without using phonetic symbols) and that in the same language the word for "long, hard rain" is *det* ought to dispose of the "baby talk" explanation for good and all—though of course it will not, for most people prefer "quaint" explanations of linguistic phenomena to the true ones.

From many Gullah informants, some of them bearing names which are a delight to contemplate—among them Saki Sweetwine, Prince Smith, Samuel Polite, Sanko Singleton, Balaam Walker, Scotia Washington, Shad Hall, and Paris Capers—Dr. Turner collected more than five thousand African words in the Gullah region. About four-fifths of these are now used only as personal names, but most of the remainder are everyday words in the speech of the Gullahs. Some of these words, doubtless the common possession of Negroes in all the slaveholding states, passed into the vocabulary of whites at what must have been a very early date.

How did words from the language of humble slaves get into the speech of their white masters? M. M. Mathews, who devotes the final chapter of his *Some Sources of Southernisms* (University, Ala., 1948) to Africanisms in the word stock of Southern American English, speculates with some reason that such words were transmitted by white children, who would not have resisted the influences of what their elders considered an inferior culture. Dr. Mathews cites his aged aunt's aversion to the "Negro word" *cooter* "turtle" and her regret that her brother, Mathews' father, had sullied the "purity" of his speech by ever using the word.

Actually, the African contribution is rather meager. The remarkable thing is, considering the social and economic relationship of black to white, that there should have been any contribution. Many a white Southerner has imbedded in his vocabulary words whose African origin he probably never suspects. *Banjo* and *cooter* have already been cited. The first word has usually been considered as originating in a Negro mispronunciation of *bandore,* an English word of Spanish transmission denoting a musical instrument whose similarity to the banjo consisted mainly in the fact that it had strings to be plucked. According to Turner, the most probable source is Kimbundu, a language spoken in Angola, in which the word *mbanza* refers to an instrument very similar to the banjo. *Cooter* is very likely from *kuta,* a word appearing in two French West African languages, Bambara and Malinke, in which it has the same meaning as in the language of the Gullahs and in the English of many white Southerners.

Goober "peanut" is a modification of Kimbundu *nguba,* with similar forms occurring in Imbundu (also spoken in Angola) and Kongo (Belgian Congo and Angola). *Pinder,* with the same meaning, is from Kongo *mpinda.* Both these words are freely used on a colloquial level in the South; the first has probably gained a limited national currency.

A number of gustatory and culinary terms of African origin testify to the skill of Negro cooks. Many of these, however, are local terms, like *cush* "corn meal stuffing" and *cala* "sweetened rice"—the latter term confined to the New Orleans area. *Gumbo* is confined to no locality or region, nor is *yam,* which is found also in British English and which is of Portuguese transmission; in Scotland it is used for the common white potato. If the word *yam* was brought to these shores by our early settlers, as it may have been, it is of course not to be regarded as belonging with the group of words under discussion; but there is no reason to insist that, because it occurs also in British English, we could not have got it independently. The same people from whom the Portuguese got the word were right here, and the word might well have entered the American vocabulary, as Dr. Mathews points out, from the language of the slaves. At the least, its use in American English would have been reinforced by their use of it. The word survives as an Africanism in the Gullah dialect (in the form *yambi*) to mean a red sweet potato, which is its usual meaning in Southern American English.

Buckra "white man" is also of African origin, appearing as *mbakara* in Efik and Ibibio, spoken in Southern Nigeria. Loss of the initial nasal sound in the word probably occurred in Negro speech before the word was transmitted to whites and is due to the influence of English on the speech of the Negroes. Simplification of the initial consonant combinations *mb-, mp-, nd-, nt-,* and *ng-,* which do not occur in this position in English, is frequent in the Gullah pronunciation of African words.

80   The great blue heron is frequently called *poor Joe* (or *po' Joe*) in those regions of the South in which the bird is found. There can be no doubt that this is the same word as Vai (Liberia and Sierra Leone) *pojo* "heron." It is likely that *chigger* and its variant *jigger*—the dictionaries give a spelling *chigoe* which suggests a pronunciation seldom if ever heard—are of African transmission as far as their use in American English is concerned, and perhaps of African origin as well. At any rate, *jiga* "flea" is found in a number of African languages spoken in Senegal, Gambia, Togo, Dahomey, and Northern and Southern Nigeria. The word got into British English probably by way of the British West Indies and has been thought to be of Carib origin. It is likely, however, that its use in American English is due independently to Negro transmission, regardless of its ultimate origin.

Pickaninny, which is probably used nowadays by whites more frequently than by Negroes, is of African transmission, but its source is Portuguese *pequenino* "very little." It is not impossible that the last part of the Portuguese word may have been identified by the Negroes with the Mende (Sierra Leone) word *nini* "female breast," *pequenino* being folk-etymologized into *pickaninny* after these Negroes acquired their English. The word is not exclusively American (the same is true of *buckra, jigger,* and others), though it is probably more commonly used here than elsewhere. It is, nevertheless, recorded in British English almost a century and a half earlier than in American English.

Hoodoo and its New Orleans variant *voodoo* are Africanisms. Both forms are in use by the Gullahs. They have, however, become somewhat differentiated in meaning, the latter usually referring to the cult which flourished in the West Indies and was later introduced into this country. *Hoodoo* is applied to a person or object that is thought to bring bad luck, *to hoodoo* consequently meaning "to bring bad luck to someone." Voodoo worship was introduced into Louisiana very early by slaves from the French colonies of Martinique, Guadeloupe, and Santo Domingo, where the cult—probably of African origin, as its name would indicate—raged furiously. It would seem to have grown rather slowly at first, but was a source of worry among the whites by 1782, when the Spanish governor of Louisiana prohibited further importation of Negroes from Martinique because slaves from there were thought to be "too much given to voudouism and make the lives of the citizens unsafe." Later, and partly for the same reason, a similar prohibition was extended to Negroes from Santo Domingo. After the American occupation, however, there were no such restrictions, and with the sudden influx of Negroes into Louisiana by way of New Orleans between 1806 and 1810, voodoo began to exert a strong influence on the Louisiana Negroes. For a long time thereafter —until well after the Civil War, in fact—voodoo "queens" and "doctors" were persons of tremendous power and prestige among the Negroes, and even to some extent among the lower-class whites.

The most famous of the queens, who were the priestesses of the cult and much more influential than the doctors who shared with them their powers of sorcery, was the remarkable Marie Laveau, a free mulatto of striking beauty in her younger years, who was by vocation a hairdresser and by avocation a procuress for white gentlemen. For more than forty years absolute ruler of the cult, she has remained a legend to this day. The visitor to New Orleans, if he is lucky, may still hear old Oscar "Papa" Celestin, a Robert Frost in ebony, sing *Marie Laveau,* an original composition which recounts some of the miracles performed by this celebrated "cunjer-lady."

Transmission into general use of African *zombi,* a word intimately associated with voodooism, is probably rather recent, though it must have been known to whites in certain areas of the South at an early date. Its present familiarity may well be credited to the cycle of "horror" films some years ago. The word originally designated the snake god which was the object of adoration in the voodoo cult. It later came to mean a supernatural force thought to restore corpses to life, and ultimately a corpse brought to life by means of this force. Recently it has been used, with an obvious appropriateness, to designate a mixed drink of (usually) rum and brandy.

Juke, which has come into general use among whites comparatively recently, mainly in the compounds *juke box* and *juke joint,* has been a part of the vocabulary of the Gullahs for a long time in the sense "disorderly," particularly in the combination *juke house.* Turner shows that the word is of African origin. In standard colloquial use its meaning has been considerably toned down, as has been that of *jazz,* which, though of unknown origin, is said to have been long used by Negroes, particularly in the New Orleans region. *Jazz* is very likely of African origin, though no African etymon has been found. These two words are included here because they have probably appeared in the English or creolized English speech of Negroes since pre-Revolutionary days, even though they may have been late in reaching the standard language. Their very nature would of course sufficiently explain the fact that they were not earlier transmitted to whites. *Jazz* as a verb is, as a matter of fact, sometimes used by whites, though only on a rather low social level, in the sexual sense which it seems originally to have had among the Negroes.

It would be pleasant to be able to record that Professor Turner's researches in Gullah have cleared up the origin of *to tote,* long an etymological puzzle, but there are circumstances in respect to it which indicate that final judgment had better be reserved. It is true that no satisfactory English etymon has been found. *Tote* is one of that sizable number of

82 words of which the dictionaries can say only "orig. uncert.," "unknown origin," or something to that effect. Professor Turner found possible African sources in Kongo and Kikongo *tota* "to pick up," with related words in other West African languages meaning "to carry." The fact that *tote* is used in Gullah does not rule out the possibility of an unknown English source, for very many English words are used by the Gullahs. It is likely, however, that if the word is not of African origin, its use has been reinforced, at least in the South and particularly among the Gullahs, by the African words. Though it is usually thought of as a Southernism, *tote* is of fairly frequent occurrence in parts of New England; it has also been found in upstate New York, Northern Michigan, and Northern Minnesota, occurring alone and in the combinations *tote road, tote wagon, tote team,* and *tote sled.* The fact that the word crops up in parts of the country where Negro influence is highly unlikely suggests that there may after all be an English source for the word which has been lost to us. If so, the fact that words of similar sound and meaning occur in West African languages would have to be due to sheer coincidence, like the similarity in American Indian *Potomac* and Greek *potamos* "river."

Contacts with other colonizing peoples have also contributed to the American vocabulary. Relations between the English and the New Amsterdam Dutch were, it is true, never very friendly; nevertheless from the language of these Dutch settlers American English gained *coleslaw, cooky, cruller, boss, dope, hay barrack, spook, stoop* "porch," *poppycock* (from *pappekak* "soft dung"), *patroon* (which the Dutch had in turn taken from Latin *patronus*), *sleigh, scow, to snoop, bowery* "a farm" (but now more famous as the street name), *pit* "fruit stone," *boodle, Santa Claus, waffle,* and probably *Yankee.* In addition American English incorporated a number of geographical terms used in the region of the Hudson: *kill* "creek, stream, river," *dorp* "village," and *clove* "valley," which also appear in place names. Many of these Dutch words were not used by writers until well into the nineteenth century but we may be fairly sure that they occurred in English contexts much earlier; and we may be equally sure that many more Dutch words than are recorded were once in use. *Hay barrack* represents what English-speaking people did to Dutch *hooi-berg.* *Coleslaw* is from Dutch *koolsla* "cabbage salad"; folk etymology frequently converts it to *cold slaw.* *Dope* has acquired a good many slang uses, as in *to dope out, to get the dope on,* and *he's a dope* (i.e., a dolt). It seems to have begun its career in American English meaning simply a drug, later adding the connotation "narcotic." *Boss,* from *baas* "master," was a very useful word, for it allowed the American working man to enjoy the satisfying if purely verbal illusion that he had no master; only slaves had masters in early American democracy. *Father Christmas,* not *Santa Claus,* visits good English children on Christmas Eve. Our name for the jolly saint is from *Sante Klaas,* a Dutch dialect form of *Sant Nikolaas,* that is, "St. Nicholas"; it seems to have taken a long time catching on, and was probably not very common until the nineteenth century. In my childhood *Santa* was always pronounced *Santy* even by the most highly cultured; people nowadays have become much more conscious of spelling and many use a pronunciation which the spelling *Santa* seems to indicate to them.

The source of *Yankee* is uncertain, but the word is most probably from *Jan Kees* (a variant of *Jan Kaas,* which has been in Germany and Flanders a nickname of long standing for a Hollander), used by the English to designate a Dutch pirate, a sense in which it apparently came also to be used in New York as an expression of the contempt in which the English held the Dutch. Because of the final *-s,* the name seems to have been misunderstood to be a plural; the form *Yankee* is thus what is known to linguists as a back formation, like *shay* from *chaise.* It should also be noted that *j* in Dutch has the sound of English *y;* hence the initial sound of the English form of the word. It is a little difficult to understand why the word was transferred from Dutchmen to people of English descent. Perhaps the shift in application was the result of the same type of humor involved in nicknaming the fattest boy in school "Skinny"—the *lucus a non lucendo* principle.

There are, however, many rival theories, for *Yankee* has presented a fascinating problem to etymologists, both professional and lay. One of them, that *Yankee* represents an Indian effort to pronounce the word *English,* is rendered improbable by the fact that the Indians had their own words for the whites; there is no evidence that they ever attempted to use the word *English.* Because Indian etymologies have always been popular, an alternative theory has been proposed, to the effect that *Yankee* was an Indian mispronunciation of *Anglais;* this is just as improbable as the preceding etymology, and for the same reason. Still another "Indian" derivation traces the word to *Yankos,* the name of an apparently mythical Indian tribe; no trace of their existence has ever been discovered. According to Washington Irving's *History of New York . . . by Diedrich Knickerbocker* (1809), the "simple aborigines" called the whites *yanokies,* "a waggish appellation since shortened into the familiar epithet of *Yankees.*" Unfortunately for Irving's reputation as an etymologist, no trace of any such Indian word has ever come to light. A nonexistent "Cherokee" word has also been cited as an etymon. Non-Indian theories attempt to derive *Yankee* from Scots dialect words, from a word in the Lancashire dialect, and from numerous Dutch words.

The meaning of *Yankee* has been anything but static. By the mid-eighteenth century its use in this country to designate a New Englander seems to have been well established. During the Civil War Southerners

84 were employing the term, usually derogatorily, for any Northerner; and it was not long before it acquired what was in the usage of many Southerners the inseparable prefix *dam,* as in *damyankee.*

Since the Revolutionary War the British have used the word to designate any American, with connotations no more derogatory than those of the word *American* itself as it is used by them. It is difficult to imagine any experience more painful to most deep Southerners than to be called *Yankees;* yet there is only sporadic evidence that G.I.'s of Southern origin stationed in England during either World War ever objected very vigorously to the appellation. *Yank* is about as common in British colloquial usage as the unabbreviated form; the clipped form has never been very frequent in American use, though it was the title of a magazine distributed to American soldiers and occurs in a line of the World War I song *Over There* ("The Yanks are coming").

Despite the large number of Germans in this country long before the outbreak of the Revolution, few German words entered the American vocabulary until about the middle of the nineteenth century, when many new immigrants from Germany arrived. The first large groups of Germans came from the Palatinate; they arrived on Delaware Bay in the early years of the eighteenth century, and, finding that the good lands around Philadelphia were already taken by descendants of Penn's colonists, proceeded to settle the back country. Those who subsequently moved on to other parts with the Scotch-Irish soon abandoned their native language. Those who stayed on in Pennsylvania kept pretty much to themselves—on farms and in villages where they continued speaking their dialect of German, which was in time considerably influenced by English but which had no appreciable effect on English outside the areas in which they were settled. *Sauerkraut* appears in British English as early as 1617, though neither the word nor the food it designates ever really caught on in England. It is most likely that it was borrowed independently in this country. Similarly, *noodle* is recorded in England before its first known appearance in America, but was probably reborrowed here.

It is not improbable that other words which entered American English through Pennsylvania German were known outside the immediate German settlement area before the nineteenth century, but most of them are of such a nature that we should not expect to find them recorded as early as the eighteenth century. Some of them, like *ponhaus* "scrapple," are not listed in modern abridged dictionaries, probably because lexicographers do not consider them "standard," despite the fact that they are known and used by many speakers of standard American English at the present day. *Rainworm* "earthworm" is used in settlements of German origin and is probably a translation of *Regenwurm.* It occurs in the Pennsylvania German area and in the German settlements on the Yadkin in

North Carolina, as well as in Nobleboro, Maine, which was settled from the Palatinate. Old English *regenwyrm* is doubtless the ancestor of the term as it occurs elsewhere, for instance, on Buzzards Bay in Massachusetts. *Sawbuck* is now widely disseminated but it originated in German and Dutch settlements from, respectively, *Sägebock* and *zaagbock*. The fact that each end of the rack on which wood is sawed is shaped like the letter X—the Roman symbol for ten—has given rise to the slang use of the term for a ten-dollar bill. *Woodbuck* is also heard over the entire German settlement area, obviously a partial translation of German *Holzbock*. *Hex* "a witch or the spell cast by a witch" and *to hex* "to cast a spell on" are fairly well known all over the country nowadays. *Ponhaus* (also occurring as *ponhoss, ponhorse, ponehoss,* and *pondhorse*) corresponds to standard German *Pfannhase;* it is current from the Pennsylvania German area proper westward to Ohio and is also well known in Northwestern Maryland and Northeastern West Virginia. Other gastronomical and culinary terms of Pennsylvania German origin are *sots* "yeast," *snits* (also *schnitz*) "dried apples; pieces of fruit cut for drying" (also used as a verb "to cut into pieces"), *fat-cakes* "doughnuts" (*fettkuche*), *fossnocks* (*fasnachskuche* "Shrovetide cakes"), *thick-milk* "curdled milk" (*dickemilich*), *smearcase* "cottage cheese" (*schmierkäs*), and possibly, but by no means certainly, *applebutter. Clook* "setting hen," with its less frequent variant *cluck,* is from Pennsylvania German *kluck* (standard German *Klucke*). According to Hans Kurath's *Word Geography of the Eastern United States* (Ann Arbor, 1949), "the derogatory phrase *dumb cluck* obviously contains this word." *Belsnickel* (or *Belschnickel*) was, and still is, the southern Pennsylvanian equivalent of *Santa Claus;* the last part of the name is an affectionate diminutive form of German *Nikolaus.* Another name of long standing for the unhappily commercialized saint who rewards good children at Christmas is *Kriss Kingle* (or *Kriss Kringle*); it is a modification of *Christkindl* "Christ child." *To dunk* "to dip (doughnuts usually) into coffee or milk" is from Pennsylvania German *dunken* "to dip," corresponding to standard German *tunken.* It has not really been widely current for more than about twenty years, although it spread very rapidly once it caught on. There is no usage label for the word in the *American College Dictionary,* so that it is apparently considered standard American English nowadays. *Dunker* (or *Dunkard*) is the popular name of a member of the German Baptist Brethren, a pietistic sect which practices baptism by immersion, that is, by dunking.

From French explorers and colonizers American English acquired, usually by way of the Canadian border, such words as *prairie, bateau, voyageur, chowder, buccaneer, carryall* (vehicle), *levee, calumet,* and perhaps *gopher. Chowder* is a modification of *chaudière* "caldron." Although it is recorded first in England, *buccaneer* should probably be regarded as an Americanism by virtue of its many American historical associations; it is ultimately a Carib word, but comes to English by way of French *boucanier. Carryall* is a folk-etymologizing of *cariole. Gopher* is most likely from *gaufre* "honeycomb," in reference to the animal's burrowing habits. *Prairie* is of frequent occurrence in American English, alone and in a number of compounds such as *prairie dog, prairie wolf* "coyote," and *prairie schooner* "small covered wagon." The word is now perfectly familiar in British English also. *Levee* is a derivative of French *lever* "to raise." Its use to designate an embankment for preventing the overflow of a river is largely confined to the South, as is also its later sense "landing place for vessels." *Calumet,* ultimately a derivative of Latin *calamus* "reed," was the word used by the French explorers for the ceremonial tobacco pipe of the Indians.

A number of Spanish words, such as *mosquito* "little fly," *negro* "black" (an adjective which was soon converted into a noun), *pecadillo* "little sin," *armada* "armed (naval) forces" (originally a past participle), and *alligator* (from *el lagarto* "the lizard"), along with Nahuatl words adopted by the Spanish, such as those cited at the beginning of this chapter, entered the English language as early as the sixteenth century. These words, though some of them are more frequently used in this country than in England, should be distinguished from words taken from Spanish by English-speaking people settled on this continent. Such words are very numerous at a later date but very rare before the nineteenth century. *Calaboose* "jail" is a modification of Spanish *calabozo,* used chiefly in the Southern states; it is recorded first in the latter years of the eighteenth century. *Cockroach* (as *cacarootch*) first appears in the *General Historie* of Captain John Smith, who refers to it in a somewhat ambiguous passage as "a certaine India Bug, called by the Spaniards a *Cacarootch,* the which creeping into Chests they [that is, the "cacarootches"] eat and defile with their ill-sented dung." The word used by Smith is a modification of Spanish *cucaracha* "wood louse," or possibly a variant form of it. It was later folk-etymologized to *cockroach* (just as Latin *asparagus* is converted by some speakers into *sparrow grass*) and subsequently clipped to *roach* in this country, American verbal prudery perhaps playing some part in the elimination of the first element of what deceptively appeared to be a compound of *cock* and *roach. Key* "reef or low island" from Spanish *cayo* was in English use before it was recorded in America, but its use is now mainly confined to this country, particularly to Florida. *Key West* is a modification of *Cayo Hueso* "bone key." The form *cay,* rhyming with *day,* is now more usual in British English than *key. Stevedore,* from Spanish *estívador,* occurs first in the form *stowadore* by association with English *to stow.*

Early Loss of [r] Before Dentals

Archibald A. Hill

Archibald A. Hill, a widely published and eminent linguist, has been Professor of English and Linguistics for many years at the University of Texas, a major center of research in linguistics in the United States. He is the author of the well-known text *Introduction to Linguistic Structures* (1958). He has been Secretary-Treasurer of the Linguistic Society of America since 1952.

Professor Hill here discusses the loss of historical /r/ that occurred about the year 1300, in some but not all British dialects. This loss carries some meaning for students of American English, for it sheds light on forms found in regional varieties of American English. Readers wishing to pursue this subject further are referred to the Appendix following the article in PMLA but not reprinted here. The Appendix is a rich source of information, including the list of forms discussed in the article with notations of the documents in which the forms originally appeared, with place names and authorities cited.

88   It is well known that stressed postvocalic [r] has been lost in many dialects of Modern English. Besides this recent loss, historians of English have recognized that some [r]s in stressed syllables were lost at an earlier date. The causes and conditions assigned to these early losses are the following:

1) An early and general assimilation of consonants in the familiar forms of Germanic personal names.[1] This, of course, does not affect [r] alone, but could result in the loss of any consonant. It is not of importance in the general vocabulary, but is often important in the history of place-names derived from personal names.

2) Borrowing of Norse words in [r]-less form, since an assimilation of [r] to following front consonants took place in Scandinavian dialects at a fairly early date.[2] Related to this would be the possible Scandinavianizing of English words, resulting in an assimilation similar to that in Norse.

3) Borrowing of French words in [r]-less form, since a general loss of postvocalic [r] took place in many Old French dialects. Further, the influence of French scribes on Middle English orthography was considerable, and many *r*-less spellings of English words can be traced to them.[3]

4) Loss of [r] by dissimilation, when a second [r] occurred in the same word. This type of loss could take place in early Middle English or at any time thereafter.[4]

From PMLA 55 (June, 1940), 308–321. Reprinted with the permission of the Modern Language Association of America and Archibald A. Hill.

[1] Cf. Mats Redin, *Studies on Uncompounded Personal Names in Old English*, "Uppsala Universitet Årsskrift" (Uppsala: Berling, 1919), pp. xxxv-xxxvi. Examples of this process are *Æffa<Ælfbeorht, Bugga<Burga, Beonnu<Beorn*. Rudolf Müller, "Untersuchungen über die Namen des nordhumbrischen Liber Vitae," *Palaestra*, IX (1902), 11, 25, quotes some additional Old English examples.

[2] Adolf Noreen, *Altisländische und Altnorwegische Grammatik*, 4th ed. (Halle: Niemeyer, 1923), pp. 185, 197–198. On similar changes in modern Scandinavian dialects, cf. Gösta Langenfelt, *Select Studies in Colloquial English of the Late Middle Ages* (Lund: Ohlsson, 1933), p. 51 *n.*

[3] Dietrich Behrens, "Beiträge zur Geschichte der Französischen Sprache in England. I. Zur Lautlehre der Französischen Lehnwörter im Mittelenglischen," *Französische Studien*, V, pt. 2 (1886), 196. Emil Busch, *Laut- und Formenlehre der anglonormannischen Sprache des XIV. Jahrhunderts*, (Greifswald: Abel, 1887), 45. Louis Emil Menger, *The Anglo-Norman Dialect, a Manual of its Phonology and Morphology* (New York: Columbia University Press, 1904), p. 90. Johan Vising, *Étude sur le dialecte Anglo-Normande du XIIe siècle*, (Uppsala: Edquist, 1882), p. 87. On Middle English *r*-less spellings under French influence, cf. R. E. Zachrisson, "Two instances of French Influence on English Place-Names," *Studier i Modern Språkvetenskap, utgivna av Nyfilologiska Sällskapet i Stockholm*, V (1914), 19.

[4] Zachrisson, *op. cit.*, pp. 19–23; and "A Contribution to the Study of Anglo-Norman Influence on English Place-Names," *Lunds Universitets Årsskrift*, N.F.Afd. I, IV, no. 3 (1909), 136. On dissimilation of [r] in modern English dialects, cf. Fritz Franzmeyer, *Studien über den Konsonantismus und Vokalismus der neuenglischen Dialekte auf Grund der Ellis'schen Listen und des Wright'schen Dialect Dictionary* (Strassburg: Dumont-Schauberg, 1906). Eilert Ekwall, *The*

5) An assimilation of [r] to certain front consonants said to have occurred about 1300, and to have extended to some but not all English
dialects.

6) General loss of postvocalic [r] in certain southeastern dialects at a
date earlier than that usually assigned. This has been established by
Wyld and Matthews,[5] and their [r]-less forms are important since they
are early enough to have shared in Early Modern English sound changes.

It will be the purpose of this paper to study the fifth of the above
changes to distinguish it from the other changes named, determine its
nature and extent, and make clear its relation to the insertion of [r] which
appears occasionally at about the same time as the loss. To define the
change more exactly, it is the total disappearance in EMnE., or earlier,
of [r] in stressed syllables before the consonants which can be loosely
called dentals, namely [d], [t], [n], [l], [θ], [ð], [s], [ʃ], [dʒ] and [tʃ];—every
dental phoneme of the language, except [ʒ], which is not found after [r].

The first task is to set up criteria for distinguishing examples of this
change from those which are or may be caused by one of the other conditions named above. In the examples I have collected, the first change is
ruled out by the exclusion of any familiar name forms among the place-
name examples unless there is clear evidence that they had an [r] in Old
English or later. It is somewhat more difficult to rule out forms in which
Norse or French influence might be suspected. I am unwilling to rule out
all words of Norse or French etymology, since many such words are undoubtedly examples of the English change. However, no words have been
included in the count unless there is evidence that they contained [r] at
the time of borrowing, though for the sake of completeness a number of
doubtful forms, so marked, are given in the appended list. Typical of
such doubtful forms are *foss,* "waterfall," and [skæs] "scarce." The fourth
change is easy to rule out. No examples of words which contained a second [r] are given in the list.

Concise Oxford Dictionary of English Place-Names (Oxford: Clarendon Press, 1936), refers many
[r]-less forms to dissimilation. Important as this process is, it seems to me less so than
Zachrisson and Ekwall believe. It is noticeable that many more examples of dissimilation occur
when the following consonant was one which, as this paper will show, could produce loss by
assimilation, than when it was one which could not produce such a loss. (Eduard Eckhardt,
"Die konsonantische Dissimilation im Englischen," *Anglia,* LXII (1938), 92–93, lists eight examples of dissimilatory loss before dentals, and only one where no dental follows). Apparently
the one tendency aided the other.

[5] Henry Cecil Wyld, *A History of Modern Colloquial English* (New York: Dutton, 1920), 293–
300. William Matthews. "The Vulgar Speech of London in the XV–XVII Centuries," *N & Q,*
CLXXII (1937), 218. Langenfelt, *op. cit.,* pp. 46–52, has other early examples of loss of postvocalic
[r] from the same district. Wyld, though right in his conclusions, did not distinguish between
loss by assimilation and the general loss in postvocalic position, so that many of his examples
belong to the earlier change.

90   A major difficulty exists in distinguishing examples of the early loss
before dentals from the later general postvocalic loss. It is obviously true
that examples from a region where the second loss did not occur must be
due to the first loss. Thus, examples from the western dialects are safe.
But a second criterion exists, or may exist, in the quantity of the resulting vowel. A form which has lost its [r] in the second loss contains regularly a long vowel, or a diphthong, since the manner in which this second
loss operated was gradual vocalization of the [r] and consequent absorption into the preceding vowel. The early change was, as I will show, a
consonant assimilation which did not affect the quantity of the preceding vowel. Thus, forms such as [baɪn] or [baan] for *barn* would normally
be the result of the second loss since they show either a long vowel or
diphthong in place of the short vowel plus [r] of ME. On the other hand,
[bæn] or [bɑn] with short vowels, would normally be the result of the first
loss. This test, however, would not distinguish which loss of [r] had taken
place if the vowel preceding was long in ME. Words with ME long vowels
are therefore omitted from the appended list.

The validity of short quantity as a test for the early [r] loss, although
attested by Luick,[6] and used in this paper, may now be questioned by
some. The work of Wyld and Matthews has shown that in East Anglia
and London [r]'s were lost as a part of the general postvocalic weakening
as early as the fifteenth century, rather than in the seventeenth or eighteenth century, as previously supposed. In late Middle English and early
Modern English many long vowels which stood, or which came to stand
before single final consonants were shortened in sandhi when the next
word began with a consonant. The result was the production of alternate
long and short forms which existed side by side until one was generalized
at the expense of the other. This tendency explains such forms as *red* and
book, with the product of EMnE. short vowels, though the ME. vowels
were long. It is thus possible that in East Anglia a form such as [baɪn]
might have arisen early enough to share in this sandhi shortening, giving
an EMnE. [bɑn] which would become present English [bæn], the same
form as would have resulted from the first loss. Such a development, of
course, would be impossible if the general loss of postvocalic [r] had not
taken place until 1700 or thereafter. Forms such as [bæn], [fʌst], etc., from
East Anglia are clearly enough the result of an [r] loss which took place
early, but are ambiguous as to whether the [r] was lost by assimilation to
the following dental without change of quantity, or by general postvocalic
loss and later shortening.

[6] Karl Luick, *Historische Grammatik der englischen Sprache* (Leipzig: Tauchnitz, 1921), 695–
696. Richard Jordan, *Handbuch der mittelenglischen Grammatik* (Heidelberg: Winter, 1925),
pp. 150–151.

Since some forms might have resulted from either of the above processes indistinguishably, it is probable that my list of examples may err by including some products of the second loss. Though I cannot rule these forms out, I can gauge their frequency by observing the number of [r]-less forms with short vowels which must have been the result of the second loss and nothing else. Only one such word has been found: Modern English [wʌk], [wʊk], or [wɑk] for *work*.[7] The scarcity of such words argues that short vowels after the second loss were rare, and therefore that the appended list of examples of [r]-less forms with short vowels before dentals contains few examples where the development was like that of [wʌk]. Furthermore, as can be seen from the accompanying map,[8] the [wʌk] area not only falls, except for one slight extension, within Ellis' area of loss or vocalization of postvocalic [r], but is closely centered on East Anglia and London. This is just the area in which Wyld and Matthews have said that the second loss took place early. This distribution offers confirmation of their findings, and gives evidence that forms with [r] loss and short vowels before dentals are not ambiguous outside this area.

It is therefore impossible to say that forms such as [bæn] and [bʌd] for *barn* and *bird* are not from the general loss of postvocalic [r] when they come from the counties of Norfolk, Suffolk, Essex, Middlesex, London, Hertford, Cambridge, Huntingdon, Bedford, Buckingham, Rutland, Northampton, Leicester, Nottingham, Southern Derby and Southern Lincoln. But as I have said the danger of ambiguity is slight, and I feel safe in saying that the majority of the short vowel forms from these counties are the result of the loss of [r] before dentals.[9] The fact that in

[7] A possible second form is the pronunciation ['omθɑt] for Ormathwaite in Cumberland, cf. Alexander J. Ellis, *On Early English Pronunciation, Part V, Existing Dialectal as Compared with West Saxon Pronunciation* EETS, extra series LVI; (London: Trübner, 1889), p. 605. But this form may be due to dissimilation, since the etymon is probably the ON personal name *Ormarr*. Cf. W. J. Sedgefield, *Place-names of Cumberland and Westmorland* (Manchester: Manchester University Press, 1915), p. 83.

[8] The statements on which the [r] regions in this map are based are found in Ellis, *op. cit.*, pp. 17, 189, 234, 293–294, 495.

[9] It should be noted that some of the dialect grammars, as for instance, Theodor Albrecht, "Der Sprachgebrauch des Dialektdichters Charles E. Benham zu Colchester in Essex," *Palaestra*, CXI (1916), 81–82, and Harold Orton, *The Phonology of a South Durham Dialect, Descriptive, Historical, and Comparative* (London: Kegan Paul, Trench, Trübner, 1933), 43, explain all [r]-less forms with short vowels as the result of shortening of long vowels resulting from the general post-vocalic loss. Both these grammars, however, list only examples of [r] plus dental as giving rise to such forms. Similarly, Joseph Wright, *A Grammar of the Dialect of Windhill, in the West Riding of Yorkshire*, "English Dialect Society," XXVI (London: Kegan Paul, Trench, Trübner, 1892), states that [r] is uniformly lost before all consonants, and results in a long vowel or diphthong, and then lists two examples of short vowels before dentals, without comment.

MAP 1. THE DISTRIBUTION OF VARIOUS TYPES OF [r]
AND THE AREA IN WHICH WORK SHOWS LOSS OF [r]
AND A SHORT VOWEL. BASED ON ELLIS

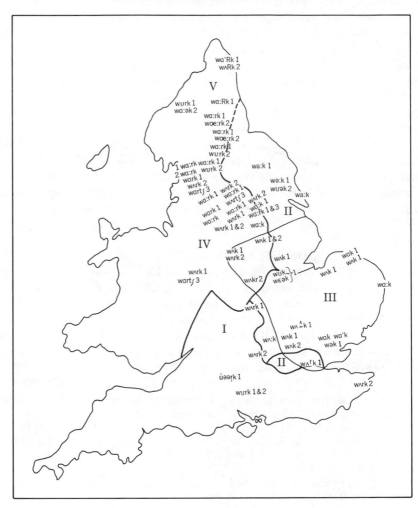

I. Region in which [r] is strongly inverted in all
positions.
II. Area of "loss" of postvocalic [r].
III. Area of "vocalization" of postvocalic [r].
VI. Area in which consonantal [r] is preserved, either
as trill, tap or continuant.
V. Area of uvular [R].

work 1, noun.   *work* 2, verb.   *work* 3, verb, "ache."

this area both changes could have resulted in forms of this type might account in part for the relatively high number of such forms from Norfolk, Suffolk, and Essex, but aside from this fact, I think no further importance need be attached to ambiguity in this region, and forms therefrom are treated in the same manner as forms from elsewhere.

Once the examples are as fully as possible freed from ambiguity, the next step is to take up in greater detail the nature of the change. The loss was earliest noticed before [s] and [ʃ], but though more recent investigators have added loss before such other consonants as [l], [n], [ð], [d], etc., the list of examples supplied with this paper is the first to make a systematic list of all consonants which could bring about [r] loss. The group contains all the consonants made by placing the tip or tip and blade of the tongue against or near the roof of the mouth in the region from the back of the upper front teeth to the alveolar ridge. The consonants not liable to bring about [r] loss are the labials, labiodentals, those made by closure or constriction between the surface of the tongue and the back part of the roof of the mouth, and the various glides. In other words, tongue-tip articulation was necessary to bring about the loss of [r]. It is clear, of course, that the loss was brought about as Pogatscher suggested, by consonant assimilation.[10] It is also clear that the type of [r] assimilated must have been a tongue-tip consonant of some sort, else the assimilation would not have taken place.

More than this cannot be said with safety. The type of [r] assimilated may have been fricative, trilled, or tapped, and may have been darkened by velarization or lip rounding, or been without such darkening. It may also have been made in any position from dental back to postalveolar. It is worth pointing out, however, that there is nothing in my evidence which suggests that [r] at the time of assimilation was not a trill. Examples of [r] loss occur, at any rate, in Modern dialects where the [r] is still strongly trilled.

It is, however, clear that the type of [r] assimilated was not the modern type of slightly inverted vowel, or indeed noninverted vowel which postvocalic [r] has become in the eastern dialects. The process by which the assimilation took place might, however, have proceeded by more than one route. A possible route is by the production of identical double consonants, simplified along with other double consonants late in the ME period. According to this view the development of such a modern form as [læn] would have been [lɑrn]>[lɑnn]>[lɑn]>[læn].

A second possibility is an intermediate stage during which the [r] was phonemically still present, since its retroflexion might have been communicated either to the preceding vowel, the following consonant, or

---

[10] Alois Pogatscher, "Etymologisches und grammatisches," *Anglia*, xxxi (1908), 261–265.

94   both. This would then have been followed by a loss of retroflexion, at which stage all trace of the [r] would be lost. The development of [læn] would then be [lɑrn]>[lɑ̣n]>[lɑn]>[læn].[11] It is, of course, possible that the two processes were more or less combined, giving a series of steps in which the intermediate stage was a double retroflex consonant. Thus the development of [æn] would have been [lɑrn]>[lɑ̣ṇ]>[lɑn]>[læn].

The evidence I have collected is unfortunately inconclusive on these points. There is no positive evidence that double consonants were the immediate result of assimilation, since such double spellings as are found at an early date are very probably indications of the shortness of the preceding vowel. It is, moreover, true that in one particular dialect region, the Northwest, a strongly trilled [r] is lost before dentals, producing an intermediate stage of retroflexion. Thus in Lorton, Cumberland, *hurt* becomes [ʊɪt] or [ʊt], and purse becomes [pʊʃ].[12] There are, however, two things which make me loath to accept the view of Langenfelt that the process represented in Lorton was that which took place everywhere in ME. First, a process resulting directly in the production of a single consonant from [r] plus consonant would be subject to compensatory lengthening. Indeed, a long vowel is the usual result in Lorton. Yet we have seen elsewhere that the result of the assimilation of [r] to tongue-tip sounds was an unlengthened vowel. Second, in the case of [rs] retroflexion would have produced a sound in danger of falling together with [ʃ], as has happened in Lorton in the form [pʊʃ], quoted above. The result elsewhere of the group [rs] is simply [s] as in [pæsl] for *parcel*. Langenfelt has quoted one or two spellings which seem to show a confusion of [rs] and [rʃ] in EMnE., but there is no trace of it at present except in the Northwest. Perhaps the most that can be said is that the present evidence does not disprove the existence of either process.

To pass to the geographical distribution of forms as shown on the second map, it will be seen at once that the distribution is general. The only county not represented is Monmouth, an absence probably to be accounted for by the lack of word-lists from that county. Some other inequalities which appear on the map should likewise be disregarded. At first sight the 123 words from Yorkshire would suggest that that county

[11] This is the view of the process that is taken by Langenfelt, *loc. cit.*, which is the fullest discussion of the steps of the assimilation that I have found. Langenfelt is, however, wrong on two points. First, the occurrence of the assimilation does not prove that all ME. [r]'s were weakly trilled before consonants, since as I have shown above, [r] loss can occur in Modern dialects where [r] is strongly trilled in all positions. Second, the assimilation does not prove that all ME. [r]'s were alveolar rather than true dental, since assimilation took place before [ð] and [θ] which were certainly not alveolars, and there is no proof that ME. [d], [t], [n] were alveolar in all dialects.

[12] Börje Brilioth, *A Grammar of the Dialect of Lorton* (*Cumberland*), Publications of the Philological Society, I (London: Oxford University Press [1913]), 74–76, 197.

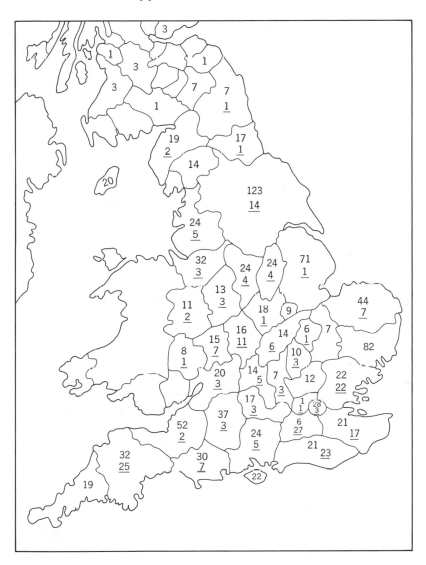

Underlined figures represent the numbers of [r]-less
forms in place-names, figures without underlining
represent [r]-less forms in words.

96   was the center of the change. It should be remembered that Yorkshire is
a large county, and that it has been more thoroughly studied than most
others. The 14 place-name forms from the county are less disproportionate, and suggest, therefore, a truer picture. The large number of words
from Suffolk may be accounted for by the thoroughness of Kökeritz'
grammar of that county, which gives the pronunciation of many words
not recorded elsewhere. In general the distribution of place-name forms
agrees with that of words, but there are some apparent differences. The
four Southeastern counties, Suffolk, Cambridge, Hertford, and Rutland,
show no place-name forms. It has been suggested that this is perhaps the
result of Norse influence, working to protect the [r], but it seems to me
rather the result of the fact that there are no separate studies of the
place-names of these counties.[13] Ekwall's *Concise Dictionary* is the only
source of information about them, and Ekwall is admittedly far from
complete. It should be noted that these counties are between regions
in which there are a high number of [r]-less forms in place-names, and
that the [r]-less forms in words from these counties are likewise high.
The apparent absence of place-name forms from these counties can
therefore, I think, be dismissed as accidental.

This general distribution of [r]-less forms disposes of the possibility
that the loss was stimulated notably by either Norse or French influence.
Wallenberg[14] has remarked that the place-name forms of Kent are remarkably free from Celtic, Norse, or French influence, but nevertheless
the number of [r]-less place-name forms from that county is high, 17 in
all. Conversely, there is no evidence that the influence of either Norse
or French operated to preserve the [r], since there is no diminution of
[r]-less forms in regions especially exposed to the influence of these
languages, such as the eastern coast for Norse, or London for French.
In addition, it seems unlikely that either of these languages could have
exerted an influence to preserve [r], since, as has been pointed out, both
of them suffered somewhat similar [r] losses.

If the first and second maps are compared, it will be seen that [r]-less
forms occur in the regions of all four of Ellis' types of [r]. The change
cannot, therefore, be exclusively related to any one type of [r] pronunciation. We have seen, however, that a uvular [R] would not be subject to
tongue-tip assimilation. Yet [r]-less forms occur in the region of the
uvular [R]. The assimilation must therefore have preceded the development of the uvular type. We have likewise seen that the fully vocalic
[r] of the eastern dialects would not have been subject to assimilation.

---

[13] There exist only the notes on special problems found in Curt Schererz, "Studien zu den
Ortsnamen von Cambridgeshire," *Zeitschrift für Ortsnamenforschung*, III (1927–1928), 13–26,
176–199.

[14] J. K. Wallenberg, *The Place-Names of Kent* (Uppsala: Appelberg, 1934), p. iv.

It is therefore clear that the first loss must have antedated the final stages of the general loss of postvocalic [r]. But, though it must have antedated the final stages of postvocalic loss, it by no means follows that it must have antedated the first stages of weakening of [r] in postvocalic position. A weakly pronounced consonant [r] would be more rather than less subject to assimilation. Thus, though the two types of [r] loss are quite different, the presence of both tendencies would increase the number of early [r]-less forms, but the resultant forms would be due primarily to the first loss and have a short vowel like other forms due to it. Two other explanations of the large number of [r]-less forms in the eastern counties have been suggested, namely, that the eastern counties have been specially well studied, and that the [r]-less forms with short vowels from these counties have been increased by forms due to the second loss with later shortening. Both these factors have undoubtedly contributed to the large number of [r]-less forms in the eastern counties, but it seems to me probable that the speeding up of the first loss, which I have just described, may have been even more important.

I have said above that the distribution of [r]-less forms is general. General distribution could come about by borrowing of the [r]-less forms from the locality where the change took place. However, if the distribution of forms had taken place in this way, there ought to be a center where the change was regularly carried through, and a gradual diminution of the number of forms in the territory adjoining it. No such center of spreading exists, unless it is the counties on the east coast, where we have seen there may be several explanations of the large number of [r]-less forms. No gradual diminution of forms, moreover, in the adjoining territory appears from the evidence I have gathered. The midland counties immediately adjoining have relatively few forms, while the distant southwestern counties have a relatively high number. Further, dialect borrowing would not account for [r]-less forms of purely local words such as the northern [ban], "child," or of place-names. Dialect borrowing would also fail to account for [r]-less forms resulting in specifically local pronunciations, like the Cumberland [puʃ] for *purse,* quoted above. A general sound change is thus the best explanation of the distribution of the [r]-less forms.

It has often been supposed that the change did not take place in London, or at least in the cultured speech of London, since, as is evident to anyone who knows the Standard Language, [r]-less forms are rare in it. According to this view the few [r]-less forms found in the Standard Language are the result of borrowing from dialects where the change took place.[15] It is not possible to prove that upper-class London speech

---

[15] This is the position of Pogatscher, *loc. cit.,* and Luick, *op. cit.,* p. 703, and elsewhere.

98   ever shared in the early [r] loss, but there is good evidence that the change took place in London speech of some sort, since there are a total of 31 London forms, 3 of which are place-names. It would be strange, however, to find upper-class London speech unaffected by a development that took place in all the surrounding dialects, and in England generally. And in view of these facts, I should prefer to say that the sound change at least made itself felt in the Standard Language, whether or not it was ever completely carried out there. The argument that there are few forms without [r] in the Standard Language should not be used, since there are, after all, few forms without [r] in any specific dialect, whether that of London, Somerset, or the Isle of Man, and, as is shown below, this condition is not incompatible with the existence of the sound change everywhere.

As I have just said, the [r]-less forms in any given locality are relatively few. Further, the forms with retained [r] or the product of retained [r], in any given locality, are too numerous to count. Such a state of affairs, if the loss of [r] is to be considered a general sound change, as I maintain, offers the paradox of a sound change with exceptions always more numerous than the examples. There are, too, in the modern dialects examples of excrescent [r]'s without historic justification. It is significant that these excrescent [r]'s appear in words which are exactly similar in phonetic structure to those in which [r]'s are lost. It is further significant that excrescent *r*'s appear in spelling at just about the time when the assimilation of [r] was taking place. Any explanation of these contradictions must take in all three facts: the loss of [r], the retention of [r], and the unhistoric [r]'s. We have seen that the relation of lost [r]'s to retained [r]'s cannot be the result of a change which took place in one dialect, the results of which were sporadically borrowed into the others, since the conditions are everywhere the same. Further, the excrescent *r*'s cannot be explained away as mere inverse spellings, in which the [r] was never pronounced. Such an explanation could be applied perhaps to the earlier excrescent *r* spellings, where we do not of course know how the writer pronounced the word he wrote; but it could not be applied to the forms from the modern dialects which are in phonetic notation and clearly indicate the pronunciation of the [r]. Further the modern dialect forms support the genuineness of the earlier spellings. An explanation such as that of Koeppel,[16] that [r] is unstable ('unfest') between a vowel and a sibilant, will fit all the facts perhaps, but explains nothing, since it does not give us any understandable process by which this unstable [r] could appear and disappear at its own will.

The only explanation which seems to me to fulfill all the necessary conditions is to assume that the tendency toward assimilation of [r]

---

[16] Emil Koeppel, "Zur englischen Wortbildungslehre, Nachträge," *Archiv*, CIV (1900), 279–286.

before the tongue-tip sounds was felt everywhere, but was everywhere checked by a desire to correct the change, and that this correction not only destroyed most of the examples of loss of [r] but went further and thrust in unhistoric [r]'s in words which were structurally like those in which the loss had taken place. Such a process of correction is the well-known phenomenon of regression, so ably studied by Dauzat and others in the history of French. The reasoning back of it can be exemplified in the excrescent [r] in *parsnip,* which must have been caused by a belief that if [pɑrsl] was more elegant than [pæsl], then [pɑrsnɪp] must be more elegant than [pæsnɪp].

It should be pointed out that the process of regression is not synonymous with spelling pronunciation. Spelling pronunciation is one type of regression, but as Dauzat has shown, regressions frequently take place in the speech of people who speak a local dialect without any strong spelling tradition. It is of the nature of sound change that it takes place gradually, and that speakers living in a community at any time will represent different levels of development. At any point in the gradual assimilation of [r] an individual might have consciously restored its full value, or might have elected to imitate the usage of the older or more traditional speakers of the community, a form of regression without the influence of spelling. The sole condition necessary is that the assimilation must have reached a stage where it penetrated the speaker's consciousness, since regression is in the main a conscious change. It should be pointed out, therefore, that regressions could take place at any time after the early stages of the assimilation, and that restored [r] forms so produced would have again been subject to loss, as long as the tendency to assimilation was in operation. It is this tendency to successive regressions and assimilations which in most instances accounts for the variant forms such as [læn] and [lʌn] for *learn,* which are of different periods of origin, but often exist side by side. There need not, therefore, ever have been a period when the loss of [r] was carried through in all words without exception, since regressive forms can always have existed side by side with forms not affected. If the [r]'s before tongue-tip sounds had ever totally disappeared from pronunciation they could have been restored only by imitation of traditional spellings, which would have been surprising in a period of the language when there were comparatively few literate speakers.

As I have said, regression is in the main a conscious change. It should therefore exhibit the inconsistency characteristic of conscious changes—the kind of inconsistency which makes a Middlewesterner correct [bæθ] to [bɑθ], but leave [bæθmæt] unmodified. Just this inconsistency in the relation of regressive forms to nonregressive is shown by the forms in Somerset (where regression is common enough almost to produce the appearance of a sound change) where *marsh* is [mæʃ], but *mash* is [mʊrʃ].

100   Similar inconsistency is found frequently elsewhere, as when *haslet* is found as [hɑrzlɪt] or [ɑrzlɪt] beside *parson* as [pæsn] or *parcel* as [pæsl].

A possible objection, however, has to be met. It may seem surprising that retention or gain of [r] before tongue-tip sounds is explained as regression, when the later loss of all postvocalic [r]'s has not produced any such sweeping series of regressions, even though this latter change took place in a period when literacy exercised a much more important influence on the language. It should be noted that in most if not all dialects affected by the second loss the preceding vowel is long, or accompanied by an off-glide when *r* still appears in the spelling. There is thus a phonemic representative of the [r] still present. Compare in this connection the explicit statement of Ellis[17] that southeastern speakers maintain that they are pronouncing an [r] before consonants, even when there is no trace of trill, tap, fricative, or inversion.

Though the aim of this paper was to study the change as it appears in the modern dialects, rather than to collect a complete list of older forms, there are some observations I should like to make about the date. It is usual to date the change as running from about 1300 to 1500. The later date will be acceptable in most dialects, though there is no positive evidence that the tendency could not have continued considerably longer. The change, however, can hardly have continued to 1500 in East Anglia, where it now seems probable that by that time postvocalic [r] was no longer a consonant, and so would not have been subject to assimilation. On the other hand, I have found some evidence that 1300 is considerably too late for the beginning of the tendency. The earliest forms without *r* that I have found, one occurrence each of *cress* and *gorse*,[18] are in eleventh-century manuscripts. In addition several *r*-less forms are quoted by Ekwall from the Domesday Book, 1086. The Domesday Book forms are quite numerous, but are unfortunately ambiguous, since they may represent either the French scribe's foreign habits of pronunciation, or his failure to hear an [r] still evident to the native, but weakened before the following dental. A more certain form is the place-name *Sholing* (Hampshire) which is found without *r* from the thirteenth century. Thus, Pogatscher's date of 1300 would represent the period at which the tendency had resulted in complete disappearance of [r]'s, or the first stage at which *r*-less forms would be common in spelling, while the rarer spellings above probably represent the earlier stages of the assimilation.

---

[17] Ellis, *op. cit.*, p. 189.

[18] F. Kluge, "Zur Geschichte der Zeichensprache, Angelsächsische Indicia Monasteriialia," *Internationale Zeitschrift für allgemeine Sprachwissenschaft,* ɪɪ (1885), 123, "Cesena tâcen" (the sign of cress, g. pl.). The MS is placed by Kluge in the southeast and dated ca. 1050. Thomas Wright, *Anglo-Saxon and Old English Vocabularies,* 2nd ed. (London: Trübner, 1884), 1 col. 139, "accidenetum, gost." The form is a transcript of an eleventh-century MS of Ælfric.

Some Aspects of Atlantic Seaboard English Considered in Their Connection with British English

Hans Kurath

The tentative views of the sources of American-English dialects offered in 1928 by Hans Kurath in his article "The Origin of the Dialectal Differences in Spoken American English" are supported by the evidence in this paper, written some thirty-seven years later. In the period between these two articles, the *Linguistic Atlas of New England,* of which Professor Kurath was Director, was begun under the sponsorship of the American Council of Learned Societies and was completed; and the greater part of the Middle and South Atlantic states was surveyed. Several studies based on the records of these surveys provided information on the relationships between British English and American English. Notable among them were *A Word Geography of the Eastern United States* (1949) by Professor Kurath, and *The Pronunciation of English in the Atlantic States* by Professors Kurath and Raven

102 I. McDavid. Professor Kurath's most recent book, *A Phonology and Prosody of Modern English* (1964), also includes relationships between American and British English.

The regional dissemination of words, forms, and pronunciations in the Eastern States can often be correlated, with some probability, with specific factors in the history of the population, such as the original settlement, the development of important centers of trade and culture, the influence of formal schooling, and so forth. The "homely" words *whiffletree, sook* (a call to cows), and *lightwood* "kindling" clearly occupy major settlement areas; *quarter till eleven* is confined to areas in which Ulster Scots and Scots settled in large numbers; *I holp* (for *helped*) *myself* falls largely within the Southern settlement area; the New England settlement boundary is strikingly reflected in certain features of pronunciation, some of them sharply recessive. On the other hand, Dutch *cruller* "doughnut" has been disseminated eastward and southwestward from the Hudson Valley; the Virginian *nicker* (for *whinny*) has spread throughout the Appalachians, and far beyond; Southern *corn shucks* (for *husks*) and *you-all* have nearly reached the Pennsylvania line, though the northern Appalachians were settled chiefly by Pennsylvanians; and a rather conspicuous bundle of isophones runs directly South of the Mason-and-Dixon line, including the northern boundaries of [æu] in *down,* of /æ/ in *stairs,* of /o/ in *poor,* of contrastive /o:ɔ/ in *four* vs. *forty.* The flaring of these isophones in Maryland and in northern West Virginia suggests a gradual northward expansion of Southern features, but the elimination of old folk pronunciations in Pennsylvania, through early intensive schooling, has doubtlessly contributed substantially to the present location of these isophones.

The effects of the settlement, of the post-settlement expansion from important centers across old settlement boundaries, and of formal schooling are not the only factors that can be isolated when we undertake to trace the history of specific regional features, but they are the most important ones. As we succeed in dealing with one feature after another, we acquire insight into the dynamics of the major areas and their subdivisions, so that we can try our hand at interpreting more complex situations. In the end, through patient work and some shrewd guessing, we may succeed in reconstructing the history of English usage on the Atlantic Seaboard in realistic terms. The task will not be easy; three centuries are a fairly long time.

From *Communications et Rapports,* Troisième Partie (Louvain 1965), pp. 236–240. Reprinted with the permission of A. J. Van Windekens, Directeur, Centre International de Dialectologie Générale (L'Université Catholique de Louvain) and of Hans Kurath.

Tracing the history of English on this continent over a period of 300 years or so is surely our immediate task, a task for which a systematic survey of present-day usage, however modest in scale, is a necessary prerequisite. Thereafter we may raise questions concerning the British sources of our varieties of English and consider the problem of American innovations of one sort or another.

We may then ask questions like these: What kinds of English were brought to this country from Great Britain during the century and a half of our Colonial Period? Did Standard British English (SBE) continue to exert an influence on American English after the Revolution? How uniform was SBE up to our War for Independence? Did it have marked regional variations? Were some of its features unsettled even in the London area? What are the contributions of English folk speech to American English? Surely, the majority of the American colonists did not talk Standard English and only a minority of them were literate. It would be surprising indeed if no traces of English folk speech had survived in America, especially in folk speech or in common speech.

Such questions must be kept in mind, when we undertake to relate any regional feature of American English to British English. I shall try to suggest a procedure by outlining one general and two specific problems in matters of pronunciation.

But first a few general remarks.

All American English dialects have the same system of consonants, except that the coastal dialects that lack /r/ in postvocalic position have an additional consonant, an unsyllabic /ə/, as in *hear, care, four, poor.*

In the vowel system there are several differences between the regional dialects spoken on the Atlantic seaboard: (1) Dialects that lack postvocalic /r/ have a free low vowel /ɑ~a/, as in *car, garden,* which the «r-dialects» do not have. (2) The New England dialect has a checked midback vowel /ɵ/, as in *stone, coat, whole,* that all other dialects lack. (3) The dialects of Eastern New England and of Western Pennsylvania lack the checked low vowel /ɑ/ of *lot, rod, rock,* which is here merged in the free low-back vowel /ɒ/ of *law, loss,* etc.

The vowel system of those American dialects that lack postvocalic /r/, and therefore have consonantal /ə/ and the free vowel /ɑ, a/, is nearly identical with that of SBE.

Though structural differences between the dialects spoken on the Atlantic Seaboard (and between these dialects and SBE) are few, phonic differences in the vowel units shared by these dialects are quite numerous, and differences in the incidence of the vowel phonemes are of frequent occurrence (e.g. /u, ʋ/ in *room, roof, soot,* /e, ɛ, æ/ in *care,* /ɔ, ɑ/ in *tomorrow*).

These observations lead to the inference that SBE has been the domi-

104   nant influence in shaping the vowel system, or systems, of American English, whatever the sources of the phonic characteristics of the phonemic units of the system may be. If this inference is justified, the question arises how the structural differences between the regional dialects of American English developed. Are they derived from English folk dialects or from successive stages in the vowel system of SBE? Are both factors involved? Are they American innovations?

Let us look first at the unique checked /ə/ phoneme of the New England dialect, which occurs in such words as *stone, road, smoke,* etc.

It is well known that the old long vowels of *tale* and *no* merged with the old diphthongs of *tail* and *know* in SBE, resulting in the loss of two phonemes. All dialects of AE, except that of New England, exhibit the same merger. As in SBE, /e/ and /o/ are upgliding free vowels in America, excepting only the Low Country of South Carolina and coastal Georgia, where they are monophthongal in free position, ingliding in checked position.

When we turn to English folk speech of today (as recorded by Dr. Guy S. Lowman in the early thirties), we find that merging in upgliding [ou, ɔu] appears in a limited area centered on London (the Home Counties), coalescence in ingliding [oə, uə] or a short [ɔ, ʌ, ʋ] in East Anglia and in parts of the Southwest, while the old diphthongs and the long monophthongs remain distinct over large areas.

Is the survival of contrasting vowels in New England to be attributed to English folk speech or to an earlier stage of SBE? Are both factors involved? One hesitates to give a pat answer. However, since all other regional dialects of AE exhibit the merger, one is inclined to assume that it took place rather early in SBE as spoken in the London area. Hence, New England usage in this matter probably derives from English folk speech or from a regional type of SBE reflecting folk usage.

It is interesting to observe that this New Englandism is now sharply recessive. Its erratic incidence from place to place, from person to person, and from word to word gives us welcome insight into the complicated way in which regionalisms are eliminated step by step.

Now let us consider another feature of coastal English. In four geographically separated subareas on the Atlantic Seaboard—Eastern New England, Metropolitan New York, Eastern Virginia, and South Carolina-Georgia—/r/ is lost after vowels. In its place these dialects have an unsyllabic phoneme /ə/ after high and midvowels, as in *here, care, four, poor,* and, by assimilation of this /ə/ to the preceding low vowel, a free low vowel /ɑ, a/, as in *far, garden* (much as Standard British English of today).

Are these features derived exclusively, or even primarily, from SBE?

If so, why are they not current elsewhere in the Eastern States, except as an idiosyncrasy of some urbanites?

Closer inspection of these four areas reveals (1) that relics of postvocalic /r/ survive on the New England coast, in tidewater Virginia, and in the pine barrens of Georgia; (2) that the avoidance of /r/ is on the increase in the margins of these areas, as evidenced by social distribution. These two observations lead to the inference that the so-called "*r*-less" type is spreading as a prestige pronunciation from the old cultural centers within these areas, a process that in all probability has been in progress for generations.

But when did this type become fashionable? Before or after the Revolution? Before attempting an answer to this question, let us look at some other data.

Spellings gathered from town records and diaries by Orbeck, Simpson, and Gibson, such as *libity* for *liberty, patchis* for *purchase,* and *ort* for *ought* leave no doubt but that as early as 1700 some New Englanders did not pronounce an /r/ after vowels. W. Matthews reports similar unconventional spellings from London records of the same period (in positions other than before /s, š/ and dentals). Hence, postvocalic /r/ must have been lost as such in some British dialects in the seventeenth century.

Today English folk speech shows a clear-cut isogloss: /r/ is pronounced as a constricted [ɚ] (as in inland American) south of the Thames and from Buckingham westward but not in the eastern counties north of the Thames. In view of the spellings cited above, this isogloss may well have run the same course two and a half centuries ago. If so, both types must have come to this country as folk pronunciations, and presumably to all of the colonies.

We know little about the time postvocalic /r/ was lost in SBE. H. C. Wyld was of the opinion that the loss of /r/ in this position, originating in Essex and Suffolk, had reached the upper classes of London by 1650. This is probably too early a date. The change was not observed by the orthoepists until more than a century later (John Walker). However, it must have achieved prestige in SBE some time before the American Revolution, otherwise its adoption in the American seaports that had the closest contact with London society would be hard to understand. On the other hand, the retention of postvocalic /r/ in the Quaker seaport of Philadelphia and throughout the inland of the Eastern States points to a rather late date for the loss of this /r/ in Standard British English.

One of the most tantalizing historical problems is that of the low vowels in such words as *half, glass, bath, pasture, aunt, can't,* etc. In New England this feature is most common in the culturally dominant Boston area and again in conservative Maine; in the lower Connecticut valley, it is distinctly a feature of cultivated speech, as also in Metropolitan New York and Philadelphia. In eastern Virginia, it is widely current in the old plantation words *pasture* and *master,* and again in fashionable *aunt,* but exceedingly rare in other words of this group. Elsewhere the low vowel does not occur in the Eastern States, except as a personal affectation. On the other hand, there are relics of /ɑ/ in folk speech, as in *hammer* and *Saturday* both in New England and in Virginia. The present social dissemination of these pronunciations suggest a folk origin, which in certain positions was later supported by SB usage in areas that had close contact with England before the Revolution, and perhaps again after the Napoleonic Wars.

In SBE, the rise of /ɑ/ in *half, bath, aunt* is a complicated story. As late as 1797 John Walker reports /æ/ in *glass, pasture, staff, dance, answer,* etc., but /ɑ/ in *laugh, half, calm, aunt, launch* and (surprisingly enough) in *master, bath, path.* This split of older /æ/ into /æ/ and /ɑ/ is therefore rather late in SBE, but must have been in progress before the Revolt of the American colonies, otherwise New England cultivated usage would be hard to account for. On the other hand, SB usage is ultimately derived from the folk speech of the eastern counties, the only area of England that exhibits this split today. Here the split may have occurred much earlier. At any rate, the fact that New England received a high percentage of its early population from these counties and that New England is the only area in which the low vowel /a/ is fairly widely current in *calf, aunt, glass,* etc., today favors the assumption that this feature was brought to New England by the common people and later supported by SB usage.

In conclusion let us consider one more problem. In *room* and *broom* the checked /ʊ/ of *book* is common in Eastern New England (though recessive), in Eastern Virginia, and in the Low Country of South Carolina. According to Daniel Jones, London English now has checked /ʊ/ as well as free /u/ in these two words. In English folk speech checked /ʊ/ is confined to the eastern counties, being especially common between the Thames and the Wash. The location of London on the /u/ : /ʊ/ line accounts for unsettled usage in SBE of today. The appearance of checked /ʊ/ in three of the four subareas on the Atlantic seaboard that had intimate contacts with London society in Colonial times supports the view that this pronunciation, though partly of folk origin, was supported by SB usage.

On the evidence of the probable history of the features of American pronunciation outlined above one is tempted to make the following generalizations: (1) Structural features of pronunciation shared by all American dialects spoken on the Atlantic Seaboard reflect Standard British usage fully established by the middle of the eighteenth century. (2) Structural features restricted to certain focal areas on the Atlantic coast and most widely used by cultured speakers point to late developments or to unsettled usage in SBE of the eighteenth century. (3) Features of pronunciation now more widely current in rural areas than in the great population centers derive either from British folk speech or from earlier stages of SBE.

Some Dialectal Verb Forms in England

W. Nelson Francis

W. Nelson Francis, Chairman of the Department of
Linguistics at Brown University, is probably best known
for his book *The Structure of American English* (1958), which
has been widely used as a college text. His most recent book,
co-authored with Henry Kucera, Professor of Slavic Languages
and Linguistics at Brown University, is *Computational
Analysis of Present-Day American English* (1968)

Using field records of the *Linguistic Atlas of England,*
Professor Francis discusses here a small group of verb forms
found in American English and British English. His tentative
conclusion is compatible with those of Kurath and Brooks
elsewhere in this collection—that some American English
forms originated in regional varieties of British English.
His call for more extensive research in seventeenth- and
eighteenth-century speech of the American colonies is a
reminder that much work remains to be done in English and
American dialect study.

In the chapter on "Conclusions" in his *Survey of Verb Forms in the Eastern United States*, Bagby Atwood makes some cautious statements about the origin of the verb forms whose distribution he has discussed. He finds that very few forms seem to be of America origin, the great majority being recorded either in Early Modern English or in nineteenth- and twentieth-century British dialects. He abjures any attempt to trace particular forms to specific dialects of seventeenth century England, on the grounds judiciously stated in the following footnote:

> Our knowledge of the present-day distribution of dialect features in England is far from complete, and our knowledge of Early Modern English dialects is extremely limited. To argue from present-day distribution that a certain form must have been brought to an American colony from a certain area of England is risky and neglects the possibility that many forms may have become obsolete in certain areas in the course of two or three hundred years. Such a study should be undertaken only after many cautions and much historical research, and preferably only after a complete survey of England on *Linguistic Atlas* lines.[1]

Now that such a survey of England has been completed,[2] it is possible to begin the process of cautious comparison which Atwood here suggests. On the basis of the field records for the *Linguistic Atlas of England*, which supply data for 300 localities in all areas of the country,[3] we can begin to see some suggestive patterns of distribution. This paper will deal with a few of these.

Before coming to specific cases, however, two general points must be made. In the first place, since the two surveys used different questionnaires and somewhat different methods, the comparability of the results is only partial. Many of the verb forms which show interesting

From *Orbis*, Bulletin International de Documentation Linguistique Vol. X, No. 1 (1961) 1–14. Reprinted with the permission of A. J. Windekens, Directeur, Centre International de Dialectologie Générale, and W. Nelson Francis.

[1] E. Bagby Atwood, *A Survey of Verb Forms in the Eastern United States* (University of Michigan Press, 1953), p. 42, n. 18.

[2 *Survey of English Dialects* (A and B) ed. Orton and Halliday and based on the work of Orton and Dieth is now available. (Leeds: E. J. Arnold, 1962, 1963). Eds.]

[3] For information about the *Linguistic Atlas of England,* see H. Orton, "An English Dialect Survey: Linguistic Atlas of England," *Orbis* IX (1960), and my article "Some Dialect Isoglosses in England," *American Speech,* XXXIV (1959), 243–250, fn. 3 and 6. Some of the data from the field records used in this paper I took directly from the records; the rest were kindly transcribed for me by Messrs. Stanley Ellis and Robin Brown of Leeds University. I am indebted to Professor Harold Orton of Leeds, Director of the *Atlas,* for permission to use this material and for many other courtesies.

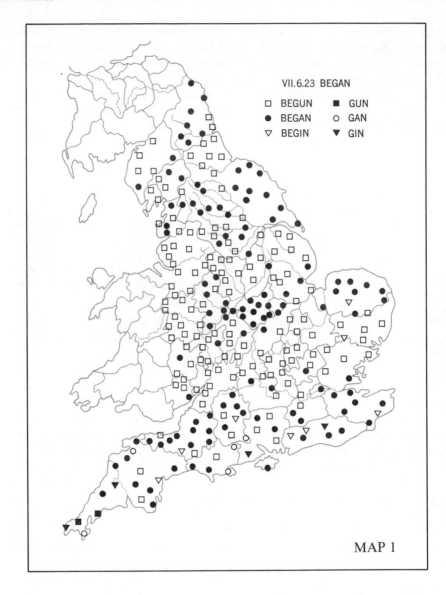

VII.6.23 BEGAN

□ BEGUN   ■ GUN
● BEGAN   ○ GAN
▽ BEGIN   ▼ GIN

MAP 1

regional distribution in the United States were not included in the English survey. Nor were the contexts in which the forms were sought always comparable semantically and grammatically. Secondly, the English survey is confined almost entirely to the kind of informants classed in the American *Atlas* as Type I or IA = older, old-fashioned, poorly educated, and rustic. It is thus not possible with existing material to make for English speech the kind of comparisons of class dialects that the American survey makes possible and that Atwood has taken full advantage of. With the English materials we are confined to studying regional distribution in uneducated speech.

This is well illustrated when we look at the map for the preterit of *begin* (Map 1), which was elicited in the frame "dark clouds gathered and soon it . . . . to rain." Since this item is marked with a dagger in the questionnaire, fieldworkers pressed for this verb, though some informants preferred other verbs, especially *started*. As the map shows, responses are fairly evenly divided between *began* forms and *begun* forms, with only a few widely separated instances of *begin*, which Atwood found to be fairly common in the South Atlantic States.[4] Except perhaps for some localized concentrations of *began*—as in the East Riding of Yorkshire, Leicestershire and Rutland, Norfolk, and Somerset—no meaningful regional pattern is perceptible here. Instead, the intermingling of forms indicates a competition in uneducated rural speech between the Standard English form *began* and the leveled form *begun*. It is to be noted that historically speaking *begun* may represent either a late Middle English leveling on the preterit plural instead of the preterit singular, or a later leveling of the preterit to the past participle, since *begun* is the modern reflex of both the Middle English preterit plural and past participle.

Atwood finds the same kind of mixed usage in Type I speech everywhere in the eastern United States. In the preterit of *come*, however, he finds the class distribution somewhat complicated by regional differences.[5] Thus *came* is standard in Type III (educated) speech everywhere and *come* is standard in Type I speech everywhere except in the vicinity of New York City. But in the middle group—the Type II speakers—he finds the ratio of *come* to *came* varying from 1:2 in New York to 7:1 in North Carolina.

Once again the English map (Map 2) shows a pretty thorough mixing of forms. Greater phonological variety somewhat obscures the morphological distribution, since the reflex of a Middle English long ā may range all the way from Northern [ɪə] to Norfolk [æɪ], and there is a third form, [kɐm], descending from a Middle English (or Danish) form with a short low-back vowel, which appears in the North, especially along the Pennine Ridge and in the Yorkshire Dales. In general, however, it is possible to sort out the forms and observe that *come* forms predominate everywhere except in the Northeast Midland area of Leicestershire, Rutland, and Lincolnshire. The ratio of *come* to *came* is about 5:1, with 16 instances of [kɐm] and 3 of weak forms like *comed*.

---

[4] *Op. cit.,* p. 6.

[5] *Ibid.,* p. 9.

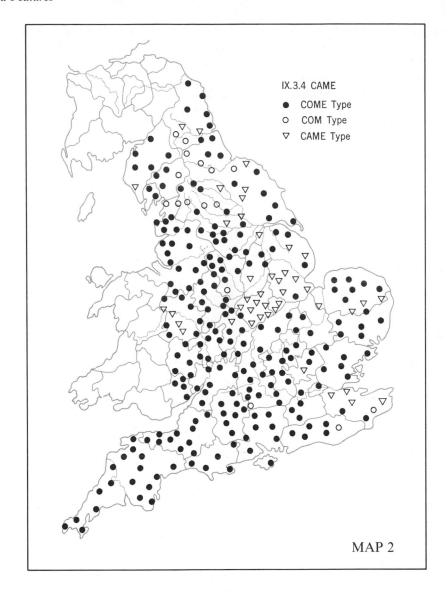

IX.3.4 CAME
● COME Type
○ COM Type
▽ CAME Type

MAP 2

More significant regional distribution on both sides of the water begins to appear when we turn to the past participle of *drink*. Since the American atlas recorded the preterit as well as the past participle, Atwood was able to observe that leveling of preterit and past participle is the prevalent practice among the large number of informants who do not use the standard form.[6] The usual nonstandard forms for the past participle

[6] *Ibid.*, pp. 10f.

are the leveled preterit *drank*, which is common in New England, and the
weak form *drinked*, which prevails in a sizable area of Virginia and North
Carolina. The form *drunken*, which Atwood labels "archaic," is reported
from only 15 informants, 9 of them cultured.

The English distribution of nonstandard forms of the past participle
(Map 3) is more clear-cut. North of the Humber virtually the only form

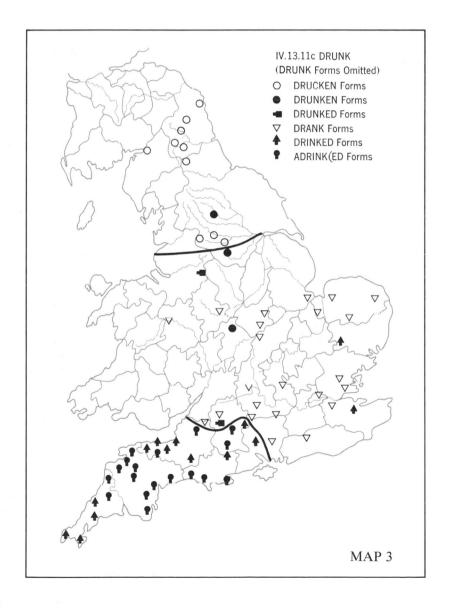

IV.13.11c DRUNK
(DRUNK Forms Omitted)

O DRUCKEN Forms
● DRUNKEN Forms
◄■ DRUNKED Forms
▽ DRANK Forms
♠ DRINKED Forms
♟ ADRINK(ED Forms

MAP 3

114   other than standard *drunk* (commonly pronounced /drunk/) is *drucken*, which either did not go to America at all or has died out there. In the whole Midland area and in the South as far west as the middle of Hampshire, the only nonstandard form (except for one instance of *drinked* from Suffolk and one from Kent) is *drank*, while *drinked* and its variants *adrinked* and *adrink* dominate the Southwest.

A marked difference between the usage of uneducated informants on opposite sides of the water shows up in the past tense of *catch*. Atwood notes that "the standard *caught* /kɔt/ is dominant in all areas among all classes, though limited in Type I."[7] The weak preterit *catched*, usually pronounced /kečt/, he finds to be scattered rather sparsely over the whole area except for eastern Massachusetts, western Vermont, and central New York.

The situation among the Type I informants in England (Map 4) is just about the reverse: that is, weak forms outnumber *caught* forms in a ratio of about 5:1. As the map shows, the *caught* forms occur all over the country, from Northumberland to Cornwall and Kent, with more or less prominent concentrations in the Yorkshire dales, northern Lincolnshire, and Norfolk. This is clearly an instance of greater conservatism in England, for while the two forms have existed together since the thirteenth century, the older *catched* was dominant even in educated speech until the nineteenth century.[8]

Though our concern here is with morphology rather than phonology, I cannot forbear commenting on the regional distribution of the pronunciation /kečt/ with the mid-front vowel. This pronunciation, which McDavid found to be used by more than three fourths of the informants in all areas of the eastern United States except Ohio, central Pennsylvania, central Massachusetts, and the New York City area,[9] is confined in England to two well-marked regions, one corresponding precisely to the West Midland area of Middle English and the other including the Home Counties, Kent, and Sussex, and extending into East Anglia on one side and Hampshire and northern Wiltshire on the other. A narrow corridor through Oxfordshire joins these two /kečt/ areas, which separate Northern [katʃt] from Southwestern [kætʃt]. The difference between these last two is best considered subphonemic (or diaphonic), since [a] is the customary Northern form of the low-front vowel. But [kɛtʃt] definitely represents a phonemic variant, since [ɛ] contrasts with [a] in the northern

---

[7] *Ibid.,* p. 8 and Figure 4.

[8] *OED, s. v.* Catch, v.

[9] Raven I. McDavnd, Jr., "Notes on the Pronunciation of *Catch*." *College English, XIV* (1952–53), 290–1.

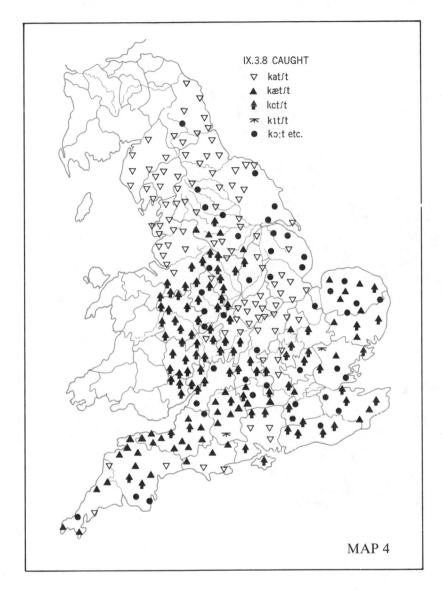

IX.3.8 CAUGHT

▽ katʃt
▲ kætʃt
⬆ kɔtʃt
⊼ kɪtʃt
● kɔːt etc.

MAP 4

part of the West Midland and with [æ] in the southern part and the Home Counties.

A clear-cut pattern of regional distribution appears in the preterit of *grow*. The strong form *grew*, which is also the standard form of cultivated speakers, is almost universal in the North, the Northeast Midland, and East Anglia, while in the West and Central Midland and the South,

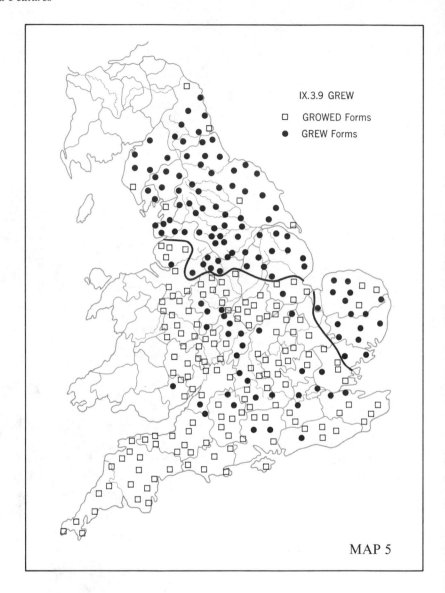

IX.3.9 GREW

□ GROWED Forms

● GREW Forms

MAP 5

growed is heavily preponderant (Map 5). As might be expected, there are scattering *grew* forms, attributable to the influence of Standard English, in the *growed* area; but there are only six instances of *growed* northeast of a line running from the mouth of the Ribble southeast to the Isle of Ely and thence southward to the mouth of the Thames estuary. An almost similar line (Map 6) a bit farther north separates a northern and

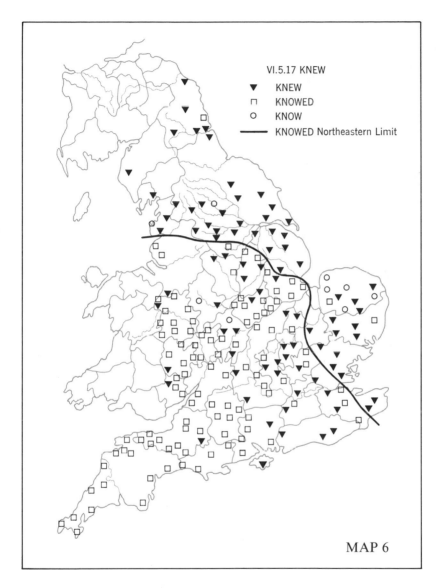

VI.5.17 KNEW

▼ KNEW
⊓ KNOWED
○ KNOW
— KNOWED Northeastern Limit

MAP 6

eastern *knew* area from one where *knowed* preponderates. This pair of isoglosses, which are plotted on Map 7 together with a third which marks the boundary between Northern *he doesn't* and a Midland and Southern *he don't*, are of great interest, because they correspond closely with a major bundle of lexical isoglosses. The dialect boundary thus established historically marks the southwesterly extent of strong Danish influence,

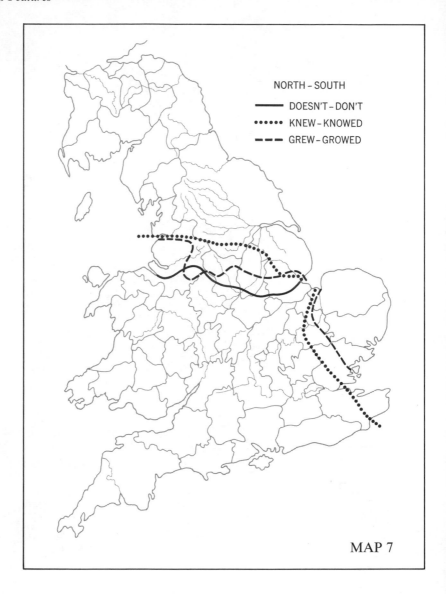

NORTH – SOUTH
―――― DOESN'T – DON'T
•••••• KNEW – KNOWED
― ― ― GREW – GROWED

MAP 7

though it lies some fifty to seventy-five miles northeast of the boundary of the Danelaw.

In America, *growed* is a form having general distribution in Type I speech, though varying in intensity from one region to another. Atwood finds that

> It is used by about three fourths of Type IA informants in northeast New England and by from one fourth to one third of the other non-

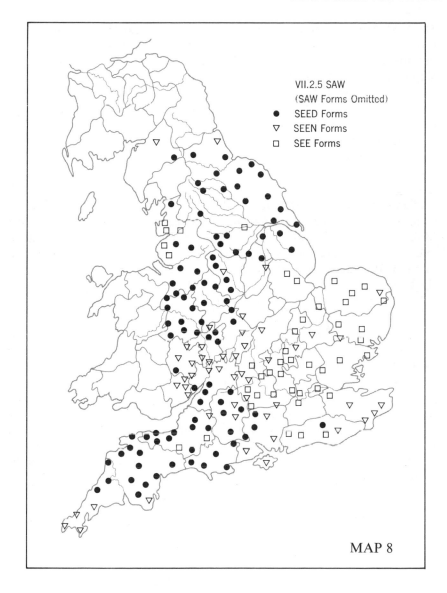

VII.2.5 SAW
(SAW Forms Omitted)
● SEED Forms
▽ SEEN Forms
□ SEE Forms

MAP 8

cultured informants. Elsewhere *growed* occurs in Type I speech with a
frequency varying from about one third (east N.Y and N.J.) to well over
nine tenths (N.C.). In Type II it is rare in N.Y., N.J., and Del.; elsewhere it is used by from one fourth to nearly one half of this group.[10]

One final case, the preterit of *see* (Map 8), shows a clear case of well-
marked regional distribution on both sides of the Atlantic. In the United

[10] Atwood, p. 15.

120   States, as Atwood points out and his map makes clear,[11] the predominant
form throughout New England is *see*, identical with the present. Throughout the Midland area of New Jersey, Pennsylvania, Maryland, West
Virginia, and the Shenandoah Valley of Virginia, the dominant form is
seen, identical with the past participle. Tidewater Virginia again shows
see, while in North Carolina and inland South Carolina, the dominant
form among Type I informants is the weak *seed*.

As Map 8 shows, these three forms are in clear-cut regional distribution
in England. Standard *saw*, not entered on the map, is preferred by the
uneducated rural informants only in the Scottish border counties of
Northumberland, Cumberland, and Westmoreland, and in a northeast
Midland area comprising Leicestershire, Rutland, and southern Lincolnshire. Otherwise, *seed* is almost universal in the North and Northwest
Midlands and in the Southwest, *see* in the East Midlands, East Anglia,
and the Southeast (except Kent), and *seen* in the Southwest Midlands and
in a corridor going through northern Wiltshire and Hampshire south to
the Isle of Wight.

What has been here presented is only a very small series of samples of
varying types of distribution of nonstandard verb forms among the uneducated rural speakers of England. This evidence does not justify us in
advancing very far beyond Atwood's caution about attempting to find
the prototype of a certain form in a specific area of England, though some
examples like *drinked, see* /kečt/, and *growed*, are tempting. They further
point up the need for study of seventeenth and eighteenth century speech
in the colonies. I should be surprised if we did not find that most regions
were dialectal melting-pots, in which individual lexical and morphological
items were in more or less open competition, so that each settlement area
ultimately established its own composite. But we must scrutinize all the
available evidence before we can be sure.

[11] *Ibid.,* p. 20 and Figure 17.

Notes
on the Sounds
and Vocabulary
of Gullah

Lorenzo D. Turner

There are in the United States several relic areas. Among
these are the communities of Negroes living on the Sea Islands
and mainland of coastal South Carolina and Georgia. They
have had limited contact with English speakers in the years
since their forebears came as slaves to work in the rice and
cotton plantations. Thus their speech, known as Gullah
or Geechee, has preserved many of the features of the African
languages of their ancestry. Lorenzo D. Turner, for many
years Professor of English at Roosevelt University, published
in 1949 the most complete study that has been made of the
speech of the Gullahs: *Africanisms in the Gullah Dialect.*
His study of the Gullah dialect was made possible by grants
from the American Council of Learned Societies. In the
following article he discusses some of the features of the
dialect.

THE GULLAH AREA

The dialect known as Gullah or Geechee[1] is spoken by a large number of ex-slaves and their descendants who live in the coastal region of South Carolina and Georgia, both on the Sea Islands and on the mainland nearby. The present writer's fieldwork on this dialect covered the area extending southward along the Atlantic coast from Georgetown, S. C. to the northern boundary of Florida, a territory approximately two hundred and fifty miles in length. The communities in South Carolina that furnished the most distinctive specimens of the dialect were Waccamaw (a peninsula near Georgetown) and James, Johns, Wadmalaw, Edisto, St. Helena, and Hilton Head islands. Those in Georgia were Darien, Harris Neck (a peninsula near Darien), Sapeloe Island, St. Simon Island, and St. Marys. On the mainland of both South Carolina and Georgia, many of the communities in which specimens of the dialect were recorded are situated twenty miles or further from the coast.

METHOD OF COLLECTING MATERIAL

In each community where the dialect was studied, at least three informants were selected. These three persons, two of whom were above sixty years of age, were born in their respective communities[2] and had had a minimum of contact elsewhere. Their parents were also born there. In studying the vocabulary of Gullah, however, the writer consulted a great many additional informants in each of the several communities.

Specimens of the dialect were gathered by means of interviews with informants during which worksheets were used similar to those prepared by the staff of the *Linguistic Atlas of the United States and Canada,* but

From *Publications of the American Dialect Society,* No. 3 (May, 1945), pp. 13–28. Reprinted with the permission of the American Dialect Society and the University of Alabama Press.

[1] There are two theories regarding the origin of the word *Gullah,* pronounced ['gʌlə] and, by many of the ex-slaves, ['gula]. One is that it is derived from *Gola,* a tribe and language of Liberia. The name of this tribe and language is pronounced in different ways by the different neighboring tribes. Among these varying pronunciations are the following: [gola, gula, gura, gɔla, and gɔra]. See F. W. H. Migeod, *The Languages of West Africa* (1913) 2. 345. The other theory is that the word *Gullah* is derived from *Ngola* [ŋgɔla], the name of a tribe in the Hamba Basin of Angola.

The word *Geechee (Geejee)* usually pronounced by the Gullahs ['ɟɪ ic ɟi] (['ɟ ɟɪɟ ɟi]), is very probably derived from the name of another tribe and language of Liberia, among the different pronunciations of which are the following: [gitʃi], [gidʒi], [gitsi], [gisi], etc.

[2] See footnote 5.

made suitable for use among the Gullahs. In addition, phonograph re- **123** cordings were made of many varieties of Gullah material, including auto-biographical sketches of informants, narratives of religious experience, prayers, sermons, religious and secular songs, folk tales, proverbs, superstitions, descriptions of living conditions on the Sea Islands, recollections of slavery, methods of planting and harvesting crops, methods of cooking, systems of counting, etc.

AFRICAN BACKGROUND OF THE GULLAHS

The Gullahs are descendants of slaves brought to South Carolina and Georgia, prior to the Civil War, principally from the West Coast of Africa. Those sections of West Africa supplying the largest numbers were Senegal, Gambia, Sierra Leone, Liberia, the Gold Coast, Togo, Dahomey, Nigeria and Angola. A conservative estimate of the number of Africans brought to South Carolina and Georgia direct from the West Coast of Africa during the one hundred years prior to 1808, when the Slave Trade Act prohibiting further importation of slaves to the United States became operative, would be at least 100,000.[3] Between 1808 and 1860 this traffic, though less active, continued nevertheless.[4] Records revealing the number of these slaves who remained in coastal South Carolina and Georgia and of those who were taken there from other places are not available; but the large number of Africanisms still surviving among the Gullahs would seem to indicate that a large percentage of these "new" slaves (i.e., those who were coming direct from Africa to Charleston and other places nearby until almost the beginning of the Civil War, and who on arriving in the United States presumably had little or no acquaintance with the English language) were occupying the Gullah region, and thus were augmenting the Africanisms of the Gullahs already there and strengthening their African speech habits. Moreover, isolated as the slaves were on the Sea Islands, they found it much easier to retain elements of their native culture than those slaves living in less isolated areas. Africanisms are still numerous in Gullah. They are found in the sounds, vocabulary, syntax, morphology, and intonation of the dialect, and there are many similarities between Gullah and the African languages in the methods used to form words.

[3] See Elizabeth Donnan, *Documents Illustrative of the History of the Slave Trade to America* (1935) 4. 278–587.

[4] See W. E. Burghardt DuBois, *The Suppression of the African Slave Trade to the United States of America* (1896) 108–150. See also Frederic Bancroft, *Slave-Trading in the Old South* (1931) 359–360.

124   THE SOUNDS OF GULLAH

This treatment of Gullah sounds is based on a study of the pronunciation of twenty-one Gullah informants. The following letters and numerals will be used when reference is made to these informants:

Edisto Island, S.C.:
    Diana Brown   E1
    Anne Crosby   E2
    Hester Milligan   E3
Wadmalaw Island, S.C.:
    Saki Sweetwine   W1
    Prince Smith   W2
    Sarah Ross   W3
Johns Island, S. C.:
    Lucy Capers   J1
    Sanko Singleton   J2
    Susan Quall   J3
St. Helena Island, S. C.:
    Samuel Polite   H1
    Anne Scott   H2
    Paris Capers   H3
Sapeloe Island, Ga.:
    Katie Brown   S1
    Shad Hall   S2
    Balaam Walker   S3
St. Simon Island, Ga.:
    Wallace Quarterman[5]   SS1
    David White   SS2
    Belle Murray   SS3
Harris Neck and Brewer's Neck, Ga.:
    James Rogers   HN1
    Bristow McIntosh   HN2
    Scotia Washington   BN1

The following are the sounds of Gullah together with a few of the words in which they were observed:

VOWELS AND DIPHTHONGS

[i]—feel; hair; James, ra*i*sin; give, itch, whicker
[ɪ] ([ɪ])—hill; weave, screech; creek; general, deaf; calabash, January; such, put; tombstone; casket, Jenkins; Mary; Saturday

---

[5] Wallace Quarterman was born in Liberty County, Georgia, and when quite young moved to St. Simon Island, where, until his death recently, he lived more than seventy years.

[e]—day; air, bear; clear, beard; bed, egg
[ɛ]—edge; make, take; brother, shut, touch, etc.
[a] ([aˑ, ã])—at, back; after, half, aunt; barn, marsh; calm, palm, father; can't
[ɒ] ([ɒˑ])—body; borrow; corn, cork; coffee, office; dog, hog; wash; daughter; all; August; bundle, color
[ʌ]—bucket, month; bird, burn
[o]—boat, post; door; oven
[u]—cool, goose, do; Luke, Matthew
[ʊ]—bull, look; coop, hoop, room, etc.
[ɝ] ([ɝ])—about; daughter, Martha
[ɪu]—duty, Tuesday
[ɒɪ] ([ʙɪ])—boy, join, boil; by, die, while; bite, nice, like, right
[ɒU] ([ʙU])—cow, plow; house, about

These sounds require further explanation:

[i]. [i] in Gullah is practically Cardinal No. 1.[6]

[ɪ]. In addition to the principal member of the [ɪ]—phoneme, there is a considerably retracted variety, the central vowel [ɨ], which is heard occasionally when there is an adjacent *k, g, l,* or *r*. A shorter variety of the central vowel [ɪ] occurs in the final open syllable of a word. A still shorter and less retracted variety of [ɨ] occurs in words and phrases of more than two syllables: ['satɨde] "Saturday," [ɸɔ̃ tɨ'mɒrɔ̃] "for tomorrow," etc.

[e]. Gullah [e] is slightly higher than Cardinal No. 2. It is never diphthongized. W1 uses a slightly lower [e] in all positions than any of the other informants.

[ɛ]. [ɛ] is practically Cardinal No. 3. A few of the informants used a more open variety of [ɛ] before nasals—a pronunciation quite common also among Negroes in Charleston, S. C. HN1 used a very open variety of [ɛ] in all positions.

[a]. [a] is practically Cardinal No. 4. It is used regularly in positions where in General American [æ] and long [ɑ] are usually heard. Before and after palatal plosives, E2, J2, W1, and W2 used a variety of [a] that was slightly above cardinal. W1 and J2 used a slightly retracted variety of [a] after [h]. A nasalized variety of the phoneme occurs in the word [cㅏã] *can't.*

[ɒ]. In the pronunciation of Gullah [ɒ], the tongue is held very low and almost fully back. The lips are usually somewhat rounded. In the speech of HN1, HN3, E3, and J2, the lips are quite rounded, and in that of SS1 the sound is fully back and has less lip-rounding after [k] and [t] than elsewhere. In Gullah, [ɒ] is regularly used in positions where in GA [ɑ]

[6] For a description of the cardinal vowels see Daniel Jones, *An Outline of English Phonetics* (1932) 31–36.

126 and [ɔ] occur. In many words it occurs where [ʌ] and [aʊ] or [ɑʊ] would be used in cultivated American speech.

[ʌ]. In the pronunciation of Gullah [ʌ], the tongue is slightly lower than for Cardinal [ɔ] and somewhat more advanced.

[o]. [o] is slightly above cardinal and is never diphthongized. The lips are fully rounded.

[u]. The principal member of the [u]-phoneme in Gullah is practically Cardinal No. 8. An advanced variety occurs after alveolar consonants.

[ʊ]. The position of the tongue in the pronunciation of Gullah [ʊ] is slightly higher than half-closed and is considerably advanced from the position required for [u].

[ə]. The [ə]-phoneme comprises two varieties: (1) a short one with a tongue position somewhat higher than half-open, and (2) a fairly long one with a more retracted tongue position and approximately half-open but more advanced and higher than that required for [ʌ]. The former is indicated by the notation [ə], and the latter by [ɜ]. [ə] is used always in unstressed positions, as in the first syllable of *about*. [ɜ] occurs in final syllables and is used in the newer type of speech to replace [ʌ] by persons who try to distinguish stress.

[ɒɨ]. In the pronunciation of the principal member of the [ɒɨ]-phoneme, the tongue begins at a low and almost fully back position, frequently with lip-rounding, and moves in the direction of [ɨ]. When adjacent to [l] (which in Gullah is clear in all positions), [c], [ɟ], or [ʃ], the first element of the diphthong is usually advanced, sometimes to [a]. The first element is considerably advanced and raised to [ɐ] when the diphthong is followed by a voiceless consonant and frequently also when preceded by fricative *r*.

[ɒʊ]. Before a voiceless consonant, the first element of [ɒʊ] is regularly advanced and raised to [ɐ].

CONSONANTS

[p] ([p'])—pen, stopper, swamp
[b] ([b̥])—baby; tube; coop
[t] ([t'], [t̪], [t̬], [ɾ])—take, Tuesday, cut; month, think; butter; little
[d] ([ɾ])—dog; this, with, teethe; brother, puddle
[c̪] ([c̪ ʰ])—chew, March; fence
[ɟ̪]—Jack, edge; measure; reins; zigzag; rubbish
[k] ([k'], [k̟], [c̪])—cool; case, careful, cat
[kp]—['kpãkpã] "to pound" (from Mende [kpãkpã])
[g] ([g̟], [ɟ̟])—gutter; egg; gable, garden
[gb]—[gbla] "near" (from Mende [gbla])

[m]—March, former, bottom

[mb]—[m'bila] a personal name (from Kongo [mbila] "a call")

[mp]—[m'puku] "rat" (from Kongo [mpuku])

[n]—turn; palm, mushroo*m*

[nd]—[n'dɔmbe] a personal name (from Kongo [ndɔmbe] "blackness")

[nt]—[n'tama] a personal name (from Twi [n₁ta₁ma₃]^{i} "a dress")

[ɲ]—[boɲ] "tooth" (from Wolof [boɲ] "tooth"); new, young, united

[ŋ]—long; round, pound, down; [ŋ'di] a personal name (from Ewe [ŋ₁di₃] "morning"; [ŋ'gaŋga] a personal name (from Kongo [ŋgaŋga] a "doctor")

[l]—sale, long; B*r*ewer, p*r*oud, f*r*itter; M*a*ry, bu*r*eau; wa*r*

[ø]—fall, staff

[β] ([ϑ])—river, very; we, weary; white, while

[ʃ] ([ʃ'])—dish, shine; ashe*s*, rushe*s*, *c*edar, *s*ister, shoe*s*, *s*oda, etc.

[s]—seven; shrimp, shrink

[z] ([ʐ])—rose; examine; mouse

[j]—yonder; ear, hear

[r]—right, bright, tree; Sarah

[h]—hand, hard, heap; ashes, altar

[p]. [p] is generally unaspirated in Gullah. Before long vowels in very emphatic speech, however, it is often followed by slight aspiration. Some informants used the ejective (glottalized) *p* [p'] at the beginning of a

---

[7] Tones are given for words from the following West African languages: Twi, Fante, Ewe, Ibo, Efik, Ibibio, Vai, and Yoruba. The low, mid, and high level tones will be indicated, respectively, by the inferior numerals 1, 2, and 3 placed after the syllables whose tones they represent. Glides from one tone level to another will be indicated as follows:

$3-1$ = a tone falling from high to low
$3-2$ = a tone falling from high to mid
$2-1$ = a tone falling from mid to low
$1-3$ = a tone rising from low to high
$1-2$ = a tone rising from low to mid
$2-3$ = a tone rising from mid to high

The accentuation of Gullah words of more than one syllable is indicated by the mark (') placed before the syllable for the main stress and (,) placed before the syllable for the secondary stress, when it is thought necessary to indicate the secondary stress. Wholly unstressed syllables are not marked. The accentuation and intonation of Gullah words vary somewhat with individual speakers. A word is given the pronunciation used by the particular speaker from whom it was obtained. In the case of many Gullah words the syllables differed not so much in stress as in tone. These differences are indicated by inferior numerals placed after the syllables. Whereas Gullah does not have significant tone in the sense in which the West African tone languages do, it does have a characteristic intonation and rhythm. In the case of words from non-tone African languages the accentuation is given only when there was an opportunity to obtain it from native speakers of the language.

Other diacritics are as follows: ' glottalization; ^{h} aspiration; ~ nasalization; ₒ unvoicing; ⊣ fronting; ⊦ backing; the sign : when placed after vowel or consonant indicates that the sound is relatively long; the sign · indicates intermediate length.

128 stressed syllable. Here the glottal stop was weak and occurred just after the mouth closure was released. These variants of *p* are not distinctive in Gullah.

[b] Some informants used an unvoiced variety of *b* in such words as [bə̥'nanə̄] *banana,* [kʊb̥] *coop,* [cɟ ub̥] *tube,* etc.

[t]. [t] appears regularly in all positions where in G A the voiceless inter-dental fricative [θ] is used. Several varieties of *t* were observed. Between vowels the alveolar tap is the usual sound in Gullah. J2 used the voiced *t* between vowels and between a vowel and *l*; W1 used the postalveolar *t* before front and back vowels; HN1 regularly used the dental *t* in initial position; E3 frequently used the retroflex *t* in medial position, as in [bɨ'ɸoʈɒɨm] "formerly." As in the case of *p*, a weakly glottalized *t* [t'] was sometimes heard at the beginning of a stressed syllable.

[d]. [d] occurs regularly in all positions where in G A the voiced inter-dental fricative [ð] is used. The retroflex flap [ɽ] occurs between vowels and medially before *l* as a substitute for the G A alveolar [d] and [ð]. HN2 used the retroflex *d* in these positions. SS1 and HN1 used the dental *d* in all positions. E2 and E3 used an unvoiced *d* in final position.

[cɟ]. The voiceless palatal plosive usually occurs in those positions where in G A the voiceless palato-alveolar affricate [tʃ] would appear. In emphatic speech [cɟ] is sometimes slightly aspirated.

[ɟ]. The voiced palatal plosive usually occurs in those positions where in G A the voiced palato-alveolar affricate [dʒ] and the voiced palato-alveolar fricative [ʒ] would be used. Occasionally it is heard where [z] or [ʃ] would be found in G A. A voiceless variety of [ɟ] frequently appears in final position.

[k]. Before front vowels (including [a]), a very advanced variety of the [k]-phoneme occurs. Several informants used the voiceless palatal plosive [cɟ] here, making it difficult for the listener to distinguish such a word as *chat* from *cat* or *chase* from *case*. As in the case of [p] and [t], a few informants used a weakly glottalized *k* [k'] as a nondistinctive variant of *k* at the beginning of a stressed syllable.

[g]. Before front vowels (including [a]), a very advanced variety of the [g]-phoneme occurs. Several informants used here the voiced palatal plosive [ɟ]. An unvoiced variety of *g* is frequently heard in final position.

[n]. [n] is replaced by [m] when a bilabial sound precedes, as in ['kɒɸm] *coffin,* ['hɛβm] *heaven,* ['opm] *open.* It is replaced by the palatal nasal [ɲ] when [c] or [ɟ] follows: [ɸɛɲcɟ] *fence,* [reɲɟ] *reins.* [n] regularly replaces G A final [ŋ] in words of more than one syllable.

[ɲ]. [ɲ] is heard in Gullah in many positions where [n] or [j] occurs in G A.

[l]. [l] in Gullah is generally clear not only before vowels but finally and before consonants. Two informants (J2 and W3) occasionally used a dark *l* finally and before a consonant. SS1 used only dental *l*'s, all of which

were very clear. In many words *l* replaces G A *r*. Some informants used *l* and *r* interchangeably, especially between vowels. On Edisto Island, S.C., G A initial *l* was occasionally replaced by *n*: [nʌl] *lull*, etc.

[ø]. The voiceless bilabial fricative in Gullah is used regularly in positions where in G A the voiceless labiodental fricative [f] occurs. W3 and SS1 frequently articulated the sound with slight lip-rounding.

[β]. The voiced bilabial fricative in Gullah generally replaces G A [w], [hw], and [v]. E2, E3, H3, and HN1 used the frictionless continuant [ϑ] in positions where the other informants used [β]: [ϑɨʃ] *wish*, [øɒɨϑ] *five*, etc.

[ʃ]. [ʃ] frequently replaces G A [s] and [z]. In some words [ʃ] was rather weakly glottalized by H3, W3, and SS1: [ʃeβ] *shave*, [ʃɑɨn] *shine*, etc.

[s]. With some informants, [s] was fronted a great deal more than with others. This fronting appeared to be more marked on the Sea Islands of Georgia than on those of South Carolina. In the speech of H2 and H3, [s] was postalveolar. [s] replaces [ʃ] in [sβɪmp] *shrimp* and [sβɪŋk] *shrink*.

[z]. A voiceless variety of the [z]-phoneme is frequently heard in final position. [z] was palatalized by H3 in several words: [øʌz] *furs*, [t'ʌʐde] *Thursday*, etc.

[j]. [j] was inserted by many informants in the following words and phrases: ['mʌSmɪljə̃n] *muskmelon*, (pɒɨ'jazɔ̃) *piazza*, [ɟ ɫjɛm] *give them*, ['mɒɨjont] *my own*. S3 substituted [j] for [r] in ['jabɨt] *rabbit* and a few other words.

[r]. In Gullah, *r* never occurs finally nor before consonants, but only before vowels. With many informants it is used interchangeably with *l*, especially between vowels. HN1 used an alveolar *r* with slight uvular articulation in the word [rʁɐɨt] *right*. Examples of the intrusive *r* appear in ['stʌdɔ̃rɨn] *studying*, [tɔ̃rɔ̃m] *to them*, etc.

[h]. Initial [h] is heard in many words which in G A begin with a vowel sound: ['hambrɐɫə] *umbrella*, ['haɾɨcɫ ok] *artichoke*, ['hɛmptɨ] *empty*, etc.

Nasal + Plosive

The combination of initial nasal plus a plosive consonant is frequently heard in the Gullah speaker's pronunciation of African words containing such combinations. With the exception of [ŋd] each of these combinations observed in Gullah consisted of homorganic nasal plus plosive.

Labio-velar Plosives

[gb] and [kp], each articulated as one sound, are sometimes heard in the Gullah speaker's pronunciation of African words containing these sounds.

130   Other Consonant Combinations

The Gullah speaker usually avoids most consonant clusters familiar to speakers of General American English. He does so either by dropping one of the consonants or by using a vowel to separate them.

Vocabulary

The most distinctive feature of the Gullah vocabulary is to be found in the large number of African words which it contains. These words have come from several of those West African languages spoken by the slaves who were being brought to South Carolina and Georgia direct from Africa until almost the beginning of the Civil War. Among these languages are Wolof (Senegal and Gambia), Bambara and Malinke (French West Africa), Mende (Sierra Leone), Mandinka (Gambia), Fula (West Africa), Vai (Liberia and Sierra Leone), Temne (Sierra Leone), Twi, Fante, and Gã (Gold Coast), Ewe (Togo and Dahomey), Jeji (Dahomey), Hausa (Northern Nigeria), Yoruba, Ibo, Efik, and Ibibio (Southern Nigeria), Kongo, Kimbundu, and Umbundu (Angola), and Tshiluba (Belgian Congo).

The writer has collected between five and six thousand African words in the Gullah region of coastal South Carolina and Georgia. Approximately four-fifths of these are now used only as personal names. Most of the remainder are used daily in conversation. There are also many African words which one hears only in songs and stories. Only a few examples of each of these three groups of African words can be given here.

SOME PERSONAL NAMES

In addition to the English names which the Gullahs give their children, they frequently use an African word or group of words describing some circumstance connected with the child at the time of its birth or later. Very often they use English words for the same purpose. The practice is well known among the various African tribes of whom the Gullahs are descendants. The following Gullah personal names will illustrate the nature of this practice:

1. Time of Birth

[alan'saro] "three-o'clock prayer time" (Mandinka, [alansaro])
[a'me] name used in greeting persons born on Saturday (Ewe, [a₁me₃])

[aŋ'ku] name given a boy born on Wednesday (Ewe, [a₁ŋku₃])
['asigbe] "market day" (Ewe, [a₁si₁gbe₁])
[ba'øata] "high tide" (Mandinka, [ba fata])
['bimbi] "five-thirty in the morning" (Fula, [bimbi])
[øi'tiro] "six o'clock prayer" (Mandinka, [fitiro])
[ɟu'nala] "early" (Mandinka, [dʒunala])
[mpi'aza] the season when the grass is burned—from July to October
 (Kongo, [mpiaza])
[ŋ'di] "morning" (Ewe, [ŋ₁di₃])
[o'ruŋgɟ an] "Night is reproaching him" (Yoruba, [o₂ru₃ŋ₃gã₁:])
['oʃumi] "my month" (Yoruba, [o₂ʃu₁ mi₂])
['pɛgba] the Mende month corresponding to January (Mende,
 [pɛgba])
['pɪndɨ] "night" (Mende, [kpɪndɪ])
[suŋ'gila] "to visit at night" (Kimbundu, [suŋgila])
['zãzɒzɒ] "walking about at night" (Ewe, [zã₃zɔ₁zɔ₁])

2. Physical Condition or Appearance of the Child

[adi'ti] a deaf person (Yoruba, [a₂di₂ti₃])
[a'ɲika] "She is very beautiful" (Vai, [a₁ɲi₁ka₃])
[a'rupɛ] a short person (Yoruba, [a₁ru₃kpɛ₁])
[ban'duka] "to be disfigured" (Kongo, [banduka])
['doɟi] "to speak loudly" (Jeji, [doɟi])
['gɒɨgɒɨ] "sluggishly" (Yoruba, [gɔ₁igɔi₁])
['hudidi] "bleeding" (Jeji, [hũdidi])
[ka'male] "vigorous, active" (Bambara, [kamale])
[la'øija] "to be well" (Jeji, [lafija])
[laku'muna] "to move the tongue" (Kongo, [lakumuna])
[ma'bibi] "faintness, fatigue" (Kongo, [mabibi])
[si'nola] "sleeping" (Mandinka, [sinʊla])
['βande] "filthy" (Ewe, [βa₁nde₁:])
['zaŋga] "to soil, to defecate"—used in reference to babies only
 (Kongo, [zaŋga])

3. Temperament, Character, and Mental Capacity of the Child

['abeʃe] a worthless person (Yoruba, [a₂be₁ʃe₂])
[a'diβe] "to be industrious" (Ewe, [a₁di₁ve₃])
[a'dodo] "to be obstinate, quarrelsome" (Ewe, [a₁do₁do₁])
[a'ɲani] "to beg habitually" (Wolof, [aɲani])
['bede] "to be intelligent" (Yoruba, [gbe₃de₁])
[bet'siβi] a mischievous person (Ewe, [gbe₁tsi₁vi₃])

132
[bum'bulu] a fool (Kongo, [bumbulu])
[go'jito] "haughty, proud" (Jeji, [gojito])
['momo] "to pry into" (Bambara, [momo])
[ji'nisa] "to make dissatisfied" (Kongo, [jinisa])

4. Religion, Magic, and Charms

['bambali] "immortal" (Bambara, [bambali])
[e'salu] the bundle of charms of the witch doctor (Kongo, [esalu])
['øuka] the formalities which have to be observed in approaching a
    great chief or in the worship of God (Kongo, [fuka])
[ɟonɛ'gɬeni] an amulet (Bambara, [ɟonɛgɛni])
['kuɟɬi] "sudden death" (Ewe, [ku$_3$ɟɬi$_{1-3}$])
['puka] a string of beads (Twi, [pu$_3$ka$_3$])
['sambi] a worshipper (Kongo, [nsambi])
['sɛbɛ] an amulet made of leather (Twi, [sɛ$_3$bɛ$_2$])
[βi'luki] a penitent (Kongo, [mviluki])

5. Greetings, Commands, and Exclamations

[a'gali] "Welcome!" (Wolof, [agali!])
[da'jije] "Sleep well" (Twi, [da$_1$ji$_3$je$_2$])
[o'guøɛtimi] "Ogū [the god of war] likes mine" (Yoruba, [o$_1$gu$_3$fɛ
    ti$_2$mi$_2$])
[o'kɒɲe] "Oh, my friend!" (Ewe, [o$_{3-1}$ xɔ̃$_3$ɲe$_1$])
['tiɟu-'iku] " Be ashamed to die" (Yoruba, [ti$_2$ɟu$_3$-i$_2$ku$_3$])
['tiβɒni] "It is thine" (Yoruba, [ti$_2$wɔ$_2$ ni$_2$])

6. Place of Birth

[ala'βaɲo] name of a place in the Ewe country (Ewe, [a$_1$la$_1$va$_1$ ɲo$_1$])
[a'mamøo] a decayed dwelling or habitation (Gã and Twi,
    [a$_1$ma$_1$mfõ$_3$])
[ba'male] a platform (Bambara, [bamale])
['daji] on the ground (Jeji, [daji])
[øɒ'kɒmba] a valley (Kongo, [fɔkɔmba])
['lɑɨnde] a forest (Fula, [lainde])
['mɒŋgɒ] a hill (Kongo, [mɔŋgɔ])
['ɲaba] a swamp (Kongo, [ɲaba])
[ɒbo'daŋ] a cave (Twi, [ɔ$_1$bo$_1$da$_3$ŋ])

['randa] a thicket (Wolof, [randa])

[tɒk'pɒmbu] "under the palm tree" (Mende, [tɔkpɒmbʊ])

[tili'buŋko] a man from Tilibo, a country to the east of the Gambia (Mandinka, [tilibuŋko])

SOME OTHER WORDS USED IN CONVERSATION

['anduɲu] "I was not with you" (Wolof, [anduɲu])

[ban!] "It is done" (Vai, [ban$_1$] "to be finished"; [a$_3$ ban$_1$] "It is finished"; Bambara, [ban] "to be finished"; "the end")

['bidi'bidi] a small bird (Kongo, [bidibidi])

['bɒbɒbɒ] "woodpecker" (Kongo, [mbɔbɔbɔ])

['bɒma] a large snake (Kongo, [mbɔma] the black python)

[boɲ] "tooth" (Wolof, [boɲ])

['bʌkrə̄] [(bʌ$_1$krʌ$_3$)] "white man" (Efik and Ibibio, [m$_1$ba$_1$ka$_2$ra$_2$])

['daøa] "fat" (Vai, [da$_3$fa$_1$])

['dede] "correct" (Yoruba, [de$_3$:de$_3$:])

['dɛt] a hard rain (Wolof, [dɛt])

['dɪndɨ̄] a small child (Vai, [dɪn$_3$ dɪn$_1$])

[də̄] "to, towards" (Ewe [ḍə$_3$])

[də̄] "to be" (Ibo, [de$_1$])

[do] "child" (Mende, [ndo])

[enu'øole] "to be pregnant" (Ewe, [øo$_1$ le$_1$ e$_3$nu$_1$] "She is with child")

[øa] "to take" (Twi and Fante, [fa$_1$])

['øuøu] "dust" (Ewe, [fu$_3$fu$_{1-3}$])

['øuøu] "mush"; flour made into a thin batter and cooked (Mende [fufu] food made of cassava, grated and fermented; Ewe, [fu$_1$fu$_1$] yam or cassava boiled and pounded; Jeji, [fufu] food made from maize, fish, and palm oil; Hausa, [fu:fu:] a food made from cassava)

[ˌøula'øaøa] "woodpecker" (Mende, [fulafafa])

['gʌmbo] "okra" (Tshiluba, [tʃiŋgɔmbɔ]; Umbundu, [otʃiŋgɔmbo])

['guba] "peanut" (Kimbundu, [ŋguba]; Umbundu, [oluŋgupa]; Kongo, [ŋguba])

['gulu] "pig" (Kongo, [ŋgulu])

['ɟamba] "elephant" (Umbundu, [ondʒamba])

['ɟambi] a red sweet potato (Vai, [dʒa$_1$mbi$_3$])

['ɟiboli] a large fly (Vai, [dʒi$_3$bo$_1$li$_1$] any insect or animal that is afraid of water)

['ɟiga] a species of flea (Ewe, [ɟi$_1$ga$_3$] "sand-flea"; Yoruba, [ɟi$_1$ga$_3$]; Wolof, [ɟiga]; Mandinka, [dʒiga]; Hausa, [dʒiga])

['ɟɒgal] "to rise" (Wolof, [ɟɒgal])

134   ['ɟoso] "witchcraft" (Mende, [ndʒoso] fabulous spirits dwelling in the
       woods)
       [ɟuk] ([ɟug]) "disorderly" (Wolof, [ɟug] "to be disorderly"; Bambara,
       [ɟugu] "wicked")
       [kiŋ'kβaβi] "partridge" (Kongo, [kiŋkwavi])
       ['kunu] "boat" (Bambara, [kunu])
       ['kutə̄] "tortoise" (Bambara and Malinke, [kutə])
       [ma'laβu] ([ma'laϑu]) any alcoholic beverage (Kongo, [malavu])
       ['muŋgβa "salt" (Kongo, [muŋgwa])
       [na] "and" (Twi, [na₁]; Ibo, [na₁])
       ['nanse] ([a'nanse]) "spider" (Twi and Fante, [a₁na₁nse₁])
       ['ɲinɨ] (['ɲɪnɨ]) "female breast" (Mende, [ɲini])
       ['poɟo] "heron" (Vai, [po₃dʒo₃])
       ['sɒ ɛ a 'dufe] "Put wood on the fire" (Vai, [sɔ₃₋₁: ɛ₁ a₁ du₁fe₁] "The wood
       has been consumed")
       [so! so!] a call to horses (Vai, [so₂] "horse"; Mende and Jeji, [so] "horse")
       ['sβaŋgɒ] "proud" (Mende, [suaŋgɒ])
       [tot] (['totə̄m]) "to carry" (Kikongo, ['tota] "to pick up"; Kongo, [tɔta]
       "to pick up"; Kimbundu and Umbundu, [tuta] "to carry." Cf. Mende,
       [tomɒ] "one who carries a message")
       ['tutu] "excrement" (Hausa, [tu:tu])
       ['unə̄] "you"; "your" (Ibo, [u₃nu₁])
       ['βaŋga] "witchcraft" (Umbundu, [ɔwaŋga]; Kimbundu, [ɔwaŋga])
       ['βudu] "witchcraft" (Ewe, [vo₁du₃] a tutelary deity or demon; Jeji, [vodu]
       a fetish)
       [βulisã'kpãkpã] "woodpecker" (Mende, [wulisãkpãkpã])

Some Words, Phrases, and Sentences
Heard Only in Songs and Stories

       [a'βɒkɒ]. Mende, [a wɒkɒ], ([a gbɒkɒ]) "in the evening"
       [baka'leŋga]. Mende, [mbakaleŋga] a group of musicians playing their
       instruments
       [øa'lani]. Vai, [fa₁la₃₋₁:n₁] "He died long ago"
       [gbla]. Mende, [gbla] "near"
       [ha]. Mende, [ha] "to die"; "death"
       [hola'tɪtɨtɨ]. Mende, [hoʊ la tɪtɪtɪ] "Hold the door tightly"
       ['hũma]. Mende, [hũma] "to steal"
       ['ɟamba]. Mende, [dʒamba] "to give a present to"
       ['kamba]. Mende, [kamba] a grave; Vai, [ka₃mba₃]
       ['kara'bara]. Vai, [ka₁ra₁gba₃ra₁] "Rise with the beads"
       [kasɨ'tɛ]. Vai, [ka₁sɪ₃tɛ₃₋₂:] "surrounded by rust"

['komɛ]. Mende, [komɛ] "to assemble"

['kpaŋga]. Mende, [kpaŋga] a field burned before clearing; that which remains

[ku'hã]. Mende, [kuhã] "distant"; "from afar"

['mɒnɛ]. Mende, [mɔnɛ] "affliction"; "to suffer"

[na]. Vai, [na₁] "to come"

[nu]. Vai, [nu₃:] "there"

[ŋ'go]. Mende, [ŋgo] "word, voice"

[pi]. Vai, [pi₁:] "grass"

[pon]. Vai, [po₃n] "far away"

['sihã]. Mende, [sihã] "to borrow, to steal"

[tu]. Vai, [tu₁:] "to beat"

[βa]. Mende, [wa] "to come"

['βoŋga]. Mende, [woŋga] "family, relatives"

[ji]. Mende, [ji] "to sleep"

The English Language of the South

Cleanth Brooks

Cleanth Brooks, a distinguished literary critic, is Gray
Professor of Rhetoric at Yale. Among his publications are
The Well Wrought Urn (1947) and *William Faulkner: The
Yoknapatawpha Country* (1963). In this article, Professor Brooks
sweeps away several misconceptions about Southern speech
and advances the thesis that Southern speech is derived not
only from seventeenth century British Standard but also from
the provincial dialects of Dorset, Wiltshire, Devon, and
Somerset. Conservative in language, the South has clung to
older native English forms which are shared by Negroes and
whites alike. Especially interesting is his contention that
Joel Chandler Harris's Uncle Remus uses forms found in the
south and southwest counties of England.

One of the prices of democracy and democratic education is that you
want to speak like everybody else. And one of the ills of isolation—one,
if you like, of the limitations of the provincial—is that you are nervous,

From *A Treasury of Southern Life and Literature* (C. Scribner's Sons, 1937). Reprinted in
several anthologies, including *A Vanderbilt Miscellany* (Vanderbilt University Press, 1944).

or may become so, as to what is done in the great world outside. It follows, therefore, with regard to the South and Southern people, that sometimes they are not sure of themselves, that they abandon too readily their own guns, and are apt to be defenseless before accusations that are mainly limited, if not even ignorant. It is not necessary to speak a language that is archaic and out of tone with our present world. But, on the other hand, we are not obliged to be exactly like the general mass spread over the entire United States; nor must we, on a lower plane, seek that generalization of speech that represents everybody who is not anybody. Within limits, it is a good thing to speak your own way, the way of your own part of the world. It follows, therefore, that it is not a bad idea to look into the background of your inherited speech, with the mingled purposes of justification, defense, and, if need be, compromise. Tone of voice is one thing and so is rhythm. The present article is about the language spoken.

A Southern pronunciation—lumping it all together, despite the fact that in the South there are many different ways of speaking—is usually thought to have emanated from the Negro; on the lips of a Virginia girl, pleasantly quaint, like other relics of the influence of the Negro mammy, but corrupt English after all. This popular belief has from time to time acquired the dignity of publication. Dr. Embree, for example, in his *Brown America* unhesitatingly attributes the Virginia lady's accent to the influence of the Negro. The origins of Southern speech, however, cannot be accounted for under a theory of Negro influence. Moreover, Southern English is not a corrupt form of "standard English." To make this point is to raise a number of questions with regard to the criterion of correct English—questions which divers people with their dogmatic assumptions on the subject never take into account.

In the first place, the speech of the Southern states represents an older form of English than that which is found in Standard British English today. Indeed, it conforms rather closely to the description which A. J. Ellis gave in the last century of the behavior of the speech of a colony. The speech of a colony is conservative. It is in the language of the mother country that innovations are made. For example, few people other than professional students of the language know that the so-called broad *a*, heard in the British pronunciation of words like *path, staff, last,* and *dance,* is a later form than the vowel that is usually met with in these words in America. The broad *a*, most scholars agree, did not become fashionable in England until late in the eighteenth century. The settlement of America by Englishmen began early in the seventeenth. Obviously, the form used by Englishmen today could not have been the pronunciation carried over by the seventeenth-century colonists.

It can be said that a large part of the United States is capable of making criticisms of Southern speech that are merely refined criticism; for the

138   speech of other sections of this country is in its origins also seventeenth-century English. Such criticisms are usually based on a hazy assumption that present Standard British (the speech of the educated classes in London) is "correct," and that the nearer American speech approximates this, the more nearly correct it is. The assumption is not necessarily true, and only ignorance and fear can make us think so. What we can say, however, is that if American English is based originally on seventeenth-century English, the South has clung more tenaciously to these original forms than have other parts of the country. Indeed, many of the pronunciations usually regarded as specifically "Negro" represent nothing more than older native English forms. The pronunciation, for example, of *get* as "git," so widespread in America and certainly not confined to the Negro, was the Standard English form in the eighteenth century; and the pronunciation of *yellow* as "yal-uh" was also the polite eighteenth century pronunciation. Examples could be multiplied. To give only a few: *boil* pronounced as "bile"; *oblige* as "obleege"; *china* as "chainy." The so-called dropping of the *g* in final *-ing* as in "darlin'" for *darling* was perfectly correct in England itself in the eighteenth century, not to mention its practice nowadays by the British upper classes.

        You will hear pronunciations in the South, however, which do not go back to any pronunciation in earlier *standard* English. This does not mean that they originated on our side of the Atlantic. They represent forms from the provincial dialects—pronunciations which occurred in the dialects of certain parts of England but which did not, as such dialectal forms occasionally did, obtain a footing in the standard language. These dialect forms are of great importance because they offer a possible means for determining the regions in England from which came the colonists who set the speech pattern of the South. Joel Chandler Harris has Uncle Remus pronounce *until, unsettle,* etc., as "awn-til," "awn-settle," etc. *Un-* is still pronounced "awn" by dialect speakers in Devon. Uncle Remus pronounces *corner* as "cawnduh," inserting a *d* in it. The living dialects of Somerset and Devon give the same form. When Uncle Remus pronounces *whether,* he leaves out the *th*, but so do the dialects of Wiltshire, Dorset, Somerset, and Devon. Again, the word *seven* is frequently heard in the South as "sebn," but the same form occurs in a number of dialects of England, including those of the southwest. In the southwest of England, "gwine" occurs for *going.* Even the dropping of a final *d* as in *told,* "tole," or in *hand,* "han'," or of a final *t* as in *last,* "las'," is not a corruption. If it is corruption at all, it is one which probably came into this country by passage across the Atlantic. Such forms are the regular developments in many of the living dialects of Great Britain.

        As a matter of fact, a number of words in the South which appear to be new words entirely, represent in their origin merely dialectal forms of standard English: *roil* is a purely literary word, but "rile," which is related to it in the same way as "bile" to *boil,* is common. "Ingun" is a variant of *onion,* still to be found in many of the counties of England and Scotland. The word *frail,* used in the South in the sense of a severe beating (I'm going to *frail* the life out of him) has no relation to *frail* in the sense of "fragile." It is a development of *flail* which has occurred in many of the provincial dialects of Great Britain. The word *rare* as used in the phrase "rarin' to go" is related to the word *rear* in the same way that "quare" is related to *queer.* Both "rare" and "quare" are widely distributed through the dialects of Great Britain. "Peart" is a development of *pert* and must have been brought across the Atlantic by the early settlers, for it still exists in a number of English counties.

In this connection one may point out that the Southern *r* is connected with the south of England as well as with the Southern states of America. In this part of England the consonant *r* was lost very early, before consonants and at the end of words. From the seventeenth century onward this development had penetrated the standard language, and this treatment of *r*, far from being a slurring or a corruption, is the treatment standard in British English today. It is the normal treatment also in some other parts of America—Eastern New England, for example. On the western edges of the Southern states, Midwestern influence has come in, bringing the *r* with it; in the mountain regions of the South also (under Scotch-Irish influence?) the *r* is preserved.

As one instance after another of Southern speech traces itself back to England, either to earlier Standard English or to provincialisms of the south and southwest counties, it rapidly becomes apparent that any theory of Negro influence must be abandoned. The Negro learned his speech from the colonists, who must have come predominantly from the English Southwest. The Negro has then preserved many of these original forms, even after most of the whites have discarded them. This is not to state, of course, that Uncle Remus speaks the dialect of Hardy's peasants. But the fact that his dialect, wherever it deviates from modern British English, differs together along *with* the dialects of the Southwest counties indicates that Southern speech has been colored by the English Southwest.

The only alternative to this theory is to accept what amounts to a staggering coincidence. The magnitude of the coincidence will be made more vivid by consideration of a few more specific cases. Take the Southern variants of *muskmelon,* for instance. *Melon* is often heard as "million" in the South, especially among Negroes; and *muskmelon* is frequently, even among whites, pronounced "mushmelon." The form "mushmillion," which Harris has Uncle Remus use, and which may still be heard among old people in the South in country districts, would accordingly be con-

140   sidered by most people as about as thoroughly "Negro" as a word could be. The form seems obviously to be a corruption. But one holding such a view will be disconcerted to find in the Oxford Dictionary precisely this form occurring in a passage written by one Jerome Horsey in 1591. . . .

The interpretation of the origin of Southern speech given above raises questions with regard to the origin of the speech used in other parts of the country. If the speech of the Southern states shows forms from seventeenth- and eighteenth-century standards and from the provincial dialects of England, why do not such forms appear in the states of the North? The answer, of course, is that they do. In James Russell Lowell's *Biglow Papers,* written in the New England rustic dialect, occur many spellings which indicate such pronunciations. We find even more parallelisms with Southern forms when we consult early New England records, with their occasional spellings which indicate dialectal pronunciations, or else the remarks on pronunciation made by the early grammarians of this section. To take only a few examples collected by the late George Philip Krapp in his *English Language in America,* "skase" for *scarce* must have occurred frequently in the earlier speech of this country, in the North as well as in the South. It probably derives from the southern part of England, where the *r* was lost early before consonants and at the end of words. *Itch* is pronounced "each" by Uncle Remus, but formerly it was so pronounced in parts of the North. "Drap" for *drop* and "crap" for *crop* are still frequently heard in the South, but such forms were once found in New England also; and in the case of both sections, their ultimate origin was probably in the dialects of the Southwest of England.

Most scholars who have worked on the subject believe that the New England coast was predominantly influenced by the south and east counties of England. Pronunciations from the eastern counties, Norfolk, Suffolk, and Essex, are to be found there: for example, the pronunciation of *whole* as something resembling "hull," *stone* resembling "stun," etc. The evidence would seem to indicate, however, in my opinion, considerable influence from the counties of the Southwest as well. The influence of the Southwest, as has been pointed out, seems dominant in the South, though some forms occurring in Virginia seem to point back to the eastern counties, and other influences may be present in other parts of the South. At any rate, the language of both New England and the South —whatever differences existed between them—in the eighteenth century must have differed very considerably from the British English of today. The marked difference between Eastern New England and the South did not exist at this period. These differences came later, and came, not with laziness and corruption in the South, but with innovation in New England through the influence of spelling, the elocution book, and the diligence of the New England schoolma'am. Probably no other part of the English-speaking world in any one period has produced so many spelling books and dictionaries as New England produced in the early nineteenth century.

There is also evidence to indicate that New England has consciously imitated British pronunciation by taking over from it later developments of the qualities of certain vowel sounds, and imposing them in whole classes of words like *corn, morning, short, thorn,* etc., which were distinguished in pronunciation from words like *divorce, store, pork, fort,* etc. The first group had an *aw* vowel, the second a long *o*. Today in British pronunciation, both groups have *aw*, but this development did not take place in England until the nineteenth century. Consequently, the appearance of examples of the present-day British pronunciation in New England (or elsewhere in America) suggests a late imitation of British English.

This difference in attitude toward speech in New England on the one hand and the South on the other is an indication of more fundamental cultural differences. The desire to cultivate "correctness" of speech, the reliance on spelling, the diligence of the New England schoolma'am, may, if you choose to do so, be interpreted as marks of the cultural continuity existing between the New England and the Old. They are susceptible, however, of another account not quite so favorable, perhaps; they may be interpreted as symptoms of a feeling of cultural inferiority —of anxiety, that is, as to status. But it might be more graceful to let a New Englander speak in this matter of New England's dependence on the mother land. Henry Adams, writing of the mid-nineteenth century, says: "The tone of Boston society was colonial. The true Bostonian always knelt in self-abasement before the majesty of English standards; far from concealing it as a weakness, he was proud of it as his strength."

The attitude of the South (again speaking in relative terms) was quite different. The South never had quite the reverence for the written word which prevailed in New England. Like England itself, especially among country families and the aristocracy in general, it was content to rest the criterion of speech on a living oral tradition. Unconsciously at least and by its very lack of extreme self-consciousness, the South ceased to be a colony. Whatever general conclusion one may wish to draw, it would be hard to deny that the attitude toward speech in the South exhibits a culture in a very healthy state. The continuity between class and class and even between race and race was not severed by that artificial and irritating barrier, a *class* pronunciation.

The influence of spelling has, of course, exerted itself on Southern speech, but less than it has on that of most other sections of the country. Otherwise, there has been little or no attempt to keep up with the later developments of British English. Many Southerners, educated persons as well as the uneducated, consistently pronounce *better* as "bedduh," *bottle* as "boddle," etc., thus carrying on regularly in their speech a devel-

142   opment largely to be found in the dialects of the English Southwest. "Taripin" is the almost universal pronunciation of *terrapin,* for few allow themselves to be browbeaten by the spelling. As a matter of fact, *terrapin* is in origin an Algonquin Indian word, and the earliest form seems to have had an *a* rather than an *e.*

The student of language is supposed to be completely objective—to describe conditions rather than to prescribe standards. But perhaps he may be allowed to affect standards, at least in one regard: by giving a true description when a false description is being made the basis for prescriptions. On one fact, scholars are agreed: that the standard of speech for a country is that of the "best" speakers, the educated speakers, of that country. British English is undoubtedly correct for the modern Englishman. It is not correct, by virtue of that reason at least, for the Virginian or Tennessean. Moreover, in trying to find a standard for modern America, the best authorities are agreed that there is no virtue in trying to impose an artificial and synthetic criterion. If the Virginian is not to be forced into imitation of the Oxford don, there is logically no reason for him to be forced into imitation of Boston—or, for that matter, of Chicago or Hollywood.

If the South—or, for that matter, any other sections of the country—under the influence of radio, talking pictures, or other "cultural" forces, cares to abandon its characteristic speech, the pronunciation then adopted by the educated speakers of the region will, of course, then be the standard. But that adoption need not be made under the delusion that something poor is being abandoned for something "better." Certainly the heritage the South possesses is not one to be ashamed of—neither the seventeenth-century standard forms, nor the coloring of Devon, Somerset, and Dorset. The men of the west country were active in the conquest and settlement of America. One of the most prominent of them, Sir Walter Raleigh, was not ashamed of his provincial accent, even at Elizabeth's court. John Aubrey, the gossipy biographer of the seventeenth century, tells us that he heard one of Raleigh's contemporaries say that "notwithstanding his so great mastership in style and his conversation with the learnedest and politest persons, yet he spake broad Devonshire to dying day." It would be odd, indeed, if Raleigh's fellow countrymen, mariners, adventurers, and colonists, not courtiers at all, had not bequeathed forms of their sturdy speech to their descendants in the New World.

part **3**

LITERARY REPRESENTATIONS OF AMERICAN ENGLISH DIALECTS

A Theory of Literary Dialect

Sumner Ives

When "A Theory of Literary Dialect" was published, it
served to correct and update the earlier work of George Philip
Krapp. It has been an essential reference point for all students
working in literary dialects for the past twenty-five years
and remains the single most important source on the subject.
After revising the article slightly for this collection, Professor
Ives wrote to the editors as follows: "I wished to review
it, for it was originally written in late 1950, and much has
happened since then. I made several deletions of material
which no longer seems necessary, but I decided to leave the
time references as they were, with a few exceptions which
are clearly marked. Some readers may wish to visit a time
when E. H. Sturtevant's *Introduction to Linguistic Science*
(1947) could be referred to as a recent work and Zellig
Harris's *Methods in Structural Linguistics* had not yet been

published. Those who think that modern linguistics started in 1957 may be interested in seeing that dialictology was already near its current state." Dr. Ives is Professor of English at Hunter College.

A literary dialect is an author's attempt to represent in writing a speech that is restricted regionally, socially, or both. His representation may consist merely in the use of an occasional spelling change, like FATHUH rather than *father*, or the use of a word like *servigrous*; or he may attempt to approach scientific accuracy by representing all the grammatical, lexical and phonetic peculiarities that he has observed. By framing the definition in this manner, I include for consideration only serious attempts to suggest an actual speech—the real dialect of real people. The sheer misspelling exuberance of Josh Billings' "Essa on the Muel," the hodgepodge of traditional misconceptions found in Al Capp's Dogpatch dialect, and the same author's ingenious inventions in the language of Lower Slobovia are all excluded.

According to the definition of literary dialect given here, it is neither new nor confined to little-known works. Whoever wishes precedent can find it in the stories of Chaucer (*The Reeve's Tale*), the poetry of Spenser (*The Shepherd's Calendar*), and the plays of Shakespeare (*King Lear*). The term is generally associated, however, with such nineteenth-century writers as Joel Chandler Harris, Mark Twain, Mary N. Murphree, Sarah Orne Jewett, Edward Eggleston, and James Russell Lowell. Literary dialect is still popular, and many modern authors, among them Marjorie Kinnan Rawlings, George Sessions Perry, and Roark Bradford, have employed it freely. The aim of these authors has been the literary use of a genuine but restricted version of the English language. Although they have sometimes exploited the possibilities of humor in this speech, serious writers have employed literary dialect as a means of realism. They have tried to give an impression of literal accuracy, to show actual speech as actually used.

When representing a dialect, these authors have been acutely conscious that they were depicting something peculiar, something different from their own conception of the "standard" language. The characters who speak "dialect" are set off, either socially or geographically, from the main body of those who speak the language. Usually the suggested difference carries some connotation of inferiority, but not always. For example, in the Jeeves stories of P. G. Wodehouse, it is the master, Bertie Wooster,

From *Tulane Studies in English II* (1950), pp. 137–182. Reprinted with the permission of Purvis E. Boyette, Editor, *Tulane Studies in English* and Sumner Ives.

who speaks a dialect, and the servant, Jeeves, who speaks the conventional language, although the pedantic flavor of his conversation itself suggests dialect.

The dialect characters are made to speak a language that has unconventional features of pronunciation, grammar, and vocabulary. Pronunciation features are suggested by systematic variations from the conventional orthography, or "phonetic" re-spelling; grammatical forms are used that do not appear in the textbooks—except as awful warnings; and words are employed that are not commonly found in abridged dictionaries —unless followed by an italicized caveat. Nearly all examples of literary dialect are deliberately incomplete; the author is an artist, not a linguist or a sociologist, and his purpose is literary rather than scientific. In working out his compromise between art and linguistics, each author has made his own decision as to how many of the pecularities in his character's speech he can profitably represent; consequently, examples of literary dialect vary considerably in the extent to which they are "dialectal," and no very definite rules can be given regarding what to consider in that category. Regardless of the inclusiveness of the term, however, every variation from the conventional system of writing the language is a linguistic problem, and a valid theory of literary dialect must be based on linguistic evidence, especially that supplied by dialect geography.

The following discussion is an attempt to formulate principles by which the representations of American English dialects in literature may be evaluated. Concomitantly, the limitations and possibilities of such representations become part of the discussion. The greater part of these principles had their conception in a study of the Uncle Remus stories of Joel Chandler Harris which I completed recently as a dissertation under the direction of E. Bagby Atwood; hence, most of the practices of dialect writers will be illustrated from these stories. However, both in connection with that study and later I have examined the writings of many other authors, and those principles which seem to be most general in their application have been most fully developed.

To be sure, other studies of literary dialect have been made. The chief, and still definitive, analysis of literary dialects is that found in the first volume of George Philip Krapp's *The English Language in America*, published in 1925.[1] The importance of Krapp's work in American English is

---

[1] The reliance which is still placed on Krapp's treatment is indicated by the following references. The first is taken from H. L. Mencken's *Supplement II* of *The American Language* (1948), p. 118: "In the first series of 'The Biglow Papers' Lowell lay down [*sic*] seven rules for distinguishing the Yankee dialect, but Krapp has shown that only two of them, both relating to the pronunciation of *a*, had any validity." The second is found in E. H. Sturtevant's *Introduction to Linguistic Science* (1947), p. 32. It is quoted in the final section of this discussion.

148   widely known; however, there has been a quarter-century of active scholarship in the field since the publication of his two volumes. The most important single project has been, I think, *The Linguistic Atlas of the United
States and Canada*.[2] The published maps, the unpublished field records,
and the studies which have been based on these materials have gradually
made more clear the facts of American English and have made possible
more certain generalizations about the regional and social speech variations. It is inevitable that this greater knowledge will make possible the re-
evaluation of many previous notions concerning American English and
conclusions based on these notions.[3]

    Krapp's notions about the nature of dialect and of the standard lan-
guage should be made clear, for his conclusions about the use of dialectal
representation in literature obviously derive from these notions. Moreover, many laymen still, in 1970, hold the same notions that he did. Essentially, he assumed that there was a single national standard for American
speech and a relatively uniform "dialectal" speech, which he called "low
colloquial." His method for dealing with the representation of dialectal
speech in literature was to select small samples and then to compare the
occurrence in them of certain nonstandard forms. When he discovered
that these forms appeared more or less consistently in his samples, he
concluded that the dialect writers did little more than draw on this common "low colloquial."[4]

[2] The general director of this project, Hans Kurath, very kindly made the field records available to me for study during the summer of 1948. At that time the fieldwork for the Atlantic
states had been completed as far south as South Carolina, and between twenty and thirty
additional records were available for that state and Georgia. All statements in this paper regarding the facts of American English usage which are not otherwise credited are based on
these field records or on my own observations.

[3] One should realize that, since 1950, migration, education, and the mass media have altered
the dialectal patterns of the country, especially in urban areas. Also, the *Linguistic Atlas* project
was designed primarily to secure historically valuable evidence while it was still available. This
evidence is still valid for the first half of the twentieth century, and, if judiciously handled, for
a generation or so earlier. But one must be very cautious when using it for current conditions.

[4] Following is a statement of Krapp's position: "Both the terms 'the language' and 'a dialect'
designate merely the peculiar body of linguistic detail which the speakers of a particular group
under observation at a given moment are seen to have in common. The question of approval
or disapproval, that is of standard language or dialect, arises only after the event. . . . It thus
appears that in a true sense the standard speech also is a dialect. . . . Dialects of all kinds are
merely the convenient summaries of observers who bring together certain homogeneities in
the speech habits of a group and thus secure for themselves an impression of unity." (*op. cit.*,
p. 226).

    "When it is said that there are no true dialects in America, the meaning plainly intended is
that the characteristics of American speech are in no region or no social level so obviously
distinguished from those of the customary standard speech that they make of the dialect
speech an easily recognizable kind of language in itself, perhaps intelligible only to those who
are instructed in its peculiarities. . . . Such dialects as have been used for literary purposes in

A different approach would, I think, be more fruitful. In developing the following theory, I have assumed that the authors of literary dialects have been seriously concerned with the validity and justice of their representations; consequently, I have based my analysis on an examination of the actual practices followed by the authors, and I have generalized from the practices rather than from a hypothetical concept of perfection. The two major conditioning factors have been the teachings of linguistic geography and the recognition of limitations in the conventional orthography.

The principles of linguistic geography which apply to the study of literary dialects have not ordinarily come within the scholarly cognizance of students of literature; moreover, these principles themselves are still the subject of lively controversy among the persons actively studying the problems of American dialects. For these reasons a rather elaborate statement of those principles which apply to the literary representation of dialect has been considered a necessary prelude to the main discussion. The abstract theories which are defined in the first section are then recapitulated as they apply to particular problems and the work of particular authors. The result of this organization has been some repetition, but the complexities of the subject are such that I have seen no better way of presenting the material. Following these discussions of separate problems, I have gone into the analysis and evaluation of a particular

America represent on the whole relatively slight departures from the forms of standard speech, and they always imply the standard speech as the background against which the dialect speech is contrasted." (p. 228).

After analyzing passages from several writers who have employed various regional speech types in literature, Krapp concludes: "The main conclusion to be drawn from this analysis of passages from American dialect literature is that all local dialects of this kind are at bottom merely general colloquial or low colloquial American English, with a slight sprinkling of more characteristic words or pronunciations, some of which suggest fairly definite local associations, often in the case of words by connection with some peculiar local occupation or activity. . . . The statement quoted earlier in this chapter, that there are no true dialects in America, is thus seen to be in the main defensible, so far as dialects have been utilized for literary purposes. One may say that there have been only two forms of speech in America, the more or less formal standard and the more or less informal colloquial." (pp. 242–243).

The main difference between Krapp's position and that which has been outlined here is that Krapp assumes a general uniformity within what he calls "low colloquial" which, in the light of more recent research, simply does not exist, and that he implies a "standard speech" which is an oversimplification so great as to lead to misunderstanding of the state of American English, in which the presence of regional standards is too well proved to allow any further doubt. His concept of a dialect fits the traditional notion regarding the linguistic patterns of Western Europe, but even there a study of the various speech atlases shows that such different speech areas as the Ile de France, Provence, and Milan have some features in common that differ from the pronunciation in Florence (standard Italian), and that Milan and Provence have features in common that differ from the pronunciation in the Ile de France (standard French). Moreover, in at least one important characteristic (development of Latin [k] as in *canis*) Florentine pronunciation is not that of "standard" Italian.

150   literary dialect and have formulated a procedure which can be used in the interpretation and criticism of a particular author's work.

Before beginning a discussion of literary dialects—that is, dialects which have existence as an author's impression of regionally or socially restricted varieties of the language—one must necessarily settle on a satisfactory definition of dialect. What, in terms of area linguistics, or dialect geography, is a dialect?

So far as anyone knows, all persons who communicate by means of oral noises, even those who have no written literature, have some recognition of speech conventions, or patterns to which the actual noises conform. These conventions are not always systematically analyzed and recorded in a grammar, but when new words are added to the verbal stock, they are added (with rare exceptions)[5] in terms of the existing conventions, even though no speaker of the language could formulate a satisfactory statement of them. And when a young person or a stranger deviates perceptibly from the accepted usage, the offending utterance is noticed and may be corrected, unless indolence or politeness restrains. It is this communally recognized body of conventions that constitutes a language.

Although the language is a corpus of implicit agreement, there are some differences which exist in the practices of the individual members of the linguistic group. Most such differences are so slight as to be imperceptible in the continuum of speech, or belong to categories that the speakers have been conditioned to overlook—as the phonetically different qualities of /t/ in different contexts; but there are also variations that are common to a certain class or residents of a certain area—such as the phonetically different qualities of "short *o*." Those variations which are systematic in one group are generally noticed by members of other groups.

Moreover, the usages of the language are fluid. Consequent changes in the conventions (such as may be described by a phonetic law) operate more rapidly among some groups than among others, and vary widely in the extent of their operation. Furthermore, people move about and carry their speech with them, and even without such movement the speech of one group affects the speech of adjoining groups. All these factors contribute to the formation of dialects of the language, and all users of a language speak some dialect rather than the "language" itself. So far as known, no language, not even if we include modern Latin, exists in a "pure" or non-dialectal state.

This rather abstract discussion may be made clearer by an extended

---

[5] Charles C. Fries and Kenneth L. Pike. "Coexistent Phonemic Systems," *Language*, 25: 29–50.

comparison. The word *horse*, for example, is an abstraction which has detailed and specific meaning only by reference to a particular horse or horses. In calling any particular animal a horse, we indicate that we see in it certain features common to other horses in our experience, but we do not mean that the specific horse under consideration is exactly like any other specific horse. When we go further and say the animal at hand is a specimen of breed A, we indicate that he has characteristics which in their total combination belong only to that breed. But the discrete characteristics of that breed may all be individually shared with other breeds. For example, horses of breed A may be alike in build to those of breed B, in color to those of breed C, and in adaptibility to training to breed D. Similarly, at any one moment a dialect appears as eclectic rather than homogeneous; its individuality exists in the peculiarity of its combination of features, not in the peculiarity of the discrete features themselves. In fact, there may be no single feature which is found in that dialect and that dialect alone.

The process by which a dialect is localized can be illustrated by two pronunciations which are regionally restricted. These are the pronunciation of *white* as [waɪt] rather than as [hwaɪt][6] and the pronunciation of *garden* with initial [gj] rather than with initial [g]. These pronunciations might be represented in a literary dialect by the spellings W'ITE and GYARDEN, respectively. The pronunciation of *white* with initial [w] rather than with initial [hw] is found as a natural pronunciation along the coast of Georgia and South Carolina to the Peedee River, farther north roughly between Baltimore and New York (and inland), and in some coastal areas of New England.[7] The pronunciation of *garden* with initial [gj][8] occurs fairly often in all the eastern states south of the Potomac River. Thus the use of [w] in *white*, and [gj] in *garden* by the same person would localize him in the coastal region south of the Peedee River; although both fea-

[6] Phonetic symbols are the customary ones of the IPA. However, the symbol [a] in transcriptions of Southern speech represents a vowel sound that is considerably retracted from the position assumed for the vowel sound usually indicated by this symbol. It should also be realized that the transcriptions are "broad" rather than "narrow."

[7] Krapp (*op. cit.,* p. 233) said this feature is "common to all popular English speech." The information which I have given is based on a tracing of the feature in a representative word through about 1,200 *Linguistic Atlas* field records. (Most of the *Linguistic Atlas* informants represented relatively old-fashioned speech in the selected localities. Since they were elderly, their life-spans overlapped the period during which Krapp was active. Krapp's generalization is evidence that he did not have access to any systematically gathered evidence on this point. However, a survey of younger informants made in 1970 would show that this pronunciation is now much more widespread than it was when the *Atlas* records were made.)

[8] The pronunciation of this initial consonant, or consonant cluster, actually varies from that indicated to a palatal, somewhat affricated stop. There is, however, almost always an impression of glide following the initial sound.

152   tures are widespread, they are widespread in otherwise different areas. Hence, a local dialect is not a homogeneous set of speech conventions that differs from other homogeneous sets of conventions in each feature, but it is rather a combination of features which are individually diverse in their distribution but which are found in a particular combination in only one limited area—that area being the region in which their diverse distributions overlap.[9] It follows, of course, that the greater the number of features considered, the more narrowly the area where they overlap can be defined.

Scholarship on American English recognizes certain major dialect areas. These areas may be delineated according to the presence or absence of selected features that seem to be more noticeable or more uniformly found in one area than in others. Or the delineation may be based on the coming together in a relatively narrow transition belt of several distributional margins (isoglosses). This second method, which seems to be sounder and which is gaining favor, is described and employed by Hans Kurath, who, in *A Word Geography of the Eastern United States*, used the distribution of native terms for certain familiar objects as a basis for setting up dialect areas.

A dialect, then, represents the use in one locality of speech traits that may be individually found somewhere else, but nowhere else in exactly the same combination. The delineation of major dialect areas tends to emphasize certain features often to the neglect of others less easily observed. In part, this result comes from the use, in delineation, of features that display a high level of consistency in occurrence and in part from the correlation of dialect boundaries with such factors as settlement history, influence of a cultural center, and socioeconomic levels.

The discussion so far has dealt primarily with speech communities rather than with individuals. It has been assumed that the individuals of each locality, or social class within the locality, will have uniform speech patterns. This assumption, however, is a simplification of the actual facts. It is a truism of linguistics that no two utterances are ever completely the same, and it follows that the speech pattern of every individual is unique. The degree of difference that exists between the speech of individuals in the same class and locality is generally very small, especially if there has

---

[9] In his discussion of John Hay's Pike County dialect, Krapp remarks: "The so-called Southwestern dialect as it has existed in literature has been in reality merely low colloquial speech with an addition of certain details from New England and from Southern speech." Here, and in many places, Krapp shows that he believes only the presence of unique individual features permits a local speech to be called a separate dialect. How it would be possible for the Southwest, in view of the fact that it had been newly settled by persons from other areas, to have developed any wholly unique features Krapp does not say. Any individuality a Southwestern speech could possibly have had at that time could have come only from its peculiar combination of features brought in from more than one other section.

been reasonable stability in their communities. Consequently, there will be some relatively uniform speech habits which are associated with a particular group, although not all members may use all of them all the time.

For example, it can be found that one speaker may frequently pronounce a final [f] rather than [θ] in such words as *mouth, both,* and *teeth*; another person from the same area may use a final [θ] in all these words, but he may pronounce most words ordinarily beginning with [ð], such as *them, those that,* with the initial consonant [d]. If these habits are found in the speech of many other persons in the same region, or same class within the region, two features of the dialect can be stated: initial [ð] becomes [d], and final [θ] becomes [f] when preceded by a vowel.[10] A close study of the speech of many informants in that region will show that not all the informants necessarily have both features in their speech, and that—among those who have them—the distribution of the features in individual words varies from speaker to speaker. The same man may say BOFE but not MOUF, and another may say DIS but not DEM. Moreover, the same person might say DIS in some contexts, or under some circumstances, but not on every occasion. Nevertheless, it is the combination of speech habits characteristic of the group that constitutes the dialect of the group, even though every one of the habits may individually be found in other groups, and even though no one member of the group may employ all of them.

When an author uses a dialect as a literary medium, or represents any of his characters as speaking dialect, it is this typical set of usages—this sort of koiné—that he employs. It is true that his characters are individuals, and that the dialect of the group appears only through the speech of its individual members; but just as the author constructs the characters themselves from his experience with many persons, gathering traits from many individuals, so he develops his dialect from his observations of many persons speaking it. From the total linguistic material available, he selects those features that seem to be typical, to be most representative of the sort of person he is portraying. These features he generalizes so that the literary dialect is likely to be more regular in its variants than the actual speech which it represents. The character is likely to use initial [d] in every word in which an educated character would use initial [ð], in spite of the fact that it is by no means certain that the man in real life would do so.

However, a writer who is a close observer of dialect may detect certain irregularities in the patterns themselves and his representation of the dialect may reflect these irregularities. For example, Joel Chandler Harris

---

[10] The word *becomes* implies nothing regarding the history of the usage nor the intention of the speakers. It is simply a convenient, noncommittal designation of correspondence and is to be so interpreted.

154 has Uncle Remus say CONSATE for *conceit*, but the "correct" vowel is indicated in the historically and phonetically related word *deceit* by the spelling 'SEETFUL (deceitful). As a matter of fact, both words have had both vowels at one time or another in "accepted" English. This practice of Harris is explained by the well-known principle of dialect geography that each word has its own history. Consequently, the failure of an author to spell in the same manner all words which are historically or phonetically related is not to be considered evidence of inaccuracy in his representation of the dialect.

If the character's speech is one which the author regards—even though kindly—as one which is somewhat grotesque, humorous, or socially inferior, the relative frequency of its more obvious peculiarities is likely to be exaggerated, for the author will notice these peculiarities more readily than he will notice usages that may sometimes appear in his own speech. Hence, the literary dialect may justifiably contain more socially disapproved, old-fashioned, or local pronunciations than are present in the speech of any member of the actual group. A similar exaggeration of grammatical features, of local terms, and especially of exotic word formations (like SOLLUMCHOLLY) will probably be found. It follows, then, that the literary dialect is a composite, a compilation of features found in the speech of some members of the dialect group and associated with that group by others. It does not follow that any one member of the dialect group will have exactly the same features in the same words as he is represented to have in the literary dialect. Hence, an author may, without consciously wishing to deceive, exaggerate slightly the frequency of "dialectal" features.

A further type of exaggeration comes from the fact that all dialect writers, so far as I know, sometimes use spellings that mean nothing at all phonetically; they are merely a sort of visual signal to the reader that the dialect speaker is not literate. Such "eye dialect" forms occur with reasonable frequency in the writings of all the authors whose works are being considered here; in none of them, however, do they appear with the annoying, or humorous, frequency that can be noticed in the nineteenth century humorists such as Petroleum V. Nasby and Sut Lovingood. To the extent that an author *relies* on this purely visual dialect, he can be said to be deliberately overstating the ignorance or illiteracy of his characters. Some of it, however, seems to be inevitable even in the most carefully done literary dialect. In fact, some of it actually facilitates the reading. For example, the addition of a final [t] to *once* necessitates the spelling of the first part of the word as WUN-, since ONCET would suggest a two syllable pronunciation; similarly, the EE in P'LEECEMAN, though it indicates the conventional vowel, is justified in order to prevent the unwary reader from pronouncing P'LICE- to rhyme with *slice*.

Opposing this tendency towards exaggeration, however, are counter forces which will prevent the literary dialect from giving a fully complete record of the actual speech. One of the forces is the author's consciousness of his status as an artist and the other is the limiting influence exerted by the inadequacies of the conventional orthography as a representation of phonetic values.

At some point, the author must restrain his desire to be comprehensive and give some thought to the patience and understanding of his readers. If the dialect which is being represented is very different from better known varieties of the language, the author's selection of features to represent it is proportionately restricted. A literary dialect based on the speech of the Gullah Negroes of the South Carolina and Georgia coast is necessarily a less complete representation of the actual speech than a literary dialect based on the speech of southern Indiana or eastern Massachusetts.[11]

This compromise with the ingenuity and endurance of his readers will particularly limit an author in the representation of pronunciations. In English, considerable liberty can be taken with the forms of verbs and pronouns without impairing seriously the clarity of a passage. I SEEN may offend a reader's taste or engender in him a surreptitious feeling of superiority, but it is hardly likely to baffle his understanding. The vocabulary used by a character can likewise contain a great many words that are not in the reader's normal verbal stock without confusing him to the point of irritation. The context, a footnote, or a short glossary can generally provide sufficient understanding of the terms to permit easy reading. However, the selection of appropriate spellings for the pronunciation features of the dialect calls for a great deal of ingenuity on the part of the author and, if the author has used very many "phonetic" spellings, considerable knowledge of variant pronunciations on the part of the reader.

No matter how conscientious an author is, and no matter how complete a representation of his character's speech he may wish to convey, he is limited in his accomplishment by the deficiencies of English spelling as a representation of English pronunciation. Part of his trouble will come from the fact that literary alphabets are not phonetic alphabets. Although each literary alphabet originally had some phonemic base, a one-to-one correlation between sound and letter need not be preserved, and has not been preserved in English. All that is required of a literary alphabet is that it provide a means of visually distinguishing one word

---

[11] For a brief note about Harris's use of Gullah, see my "Dialect Differentiation in the Stories of Joel Chandler Harris," *American Literature*, 17; 88–96 (March, 1955). Ambrose E. Gonzales, in *The Black Border*, has used Gullah as a literary dialect, although in a patronizing manner.

156   from another, but it may preserve enough of its phonological base for reasonably clear designation of sounds at the phonemic level, but this phonemic level is by reference to the regional standards of pronunciation. The spelling *hot* represents a different word than the spelling *hat,* yet the *o* in *hot* will be pronounced differently in Milwaukee, in Boston, and in Atlanta. It is not a visual signal for a certain phonetic value; it is rather a visual signal that, whatever the sound is, it is not the same as that suggested by the *a* in *hat.*

Presumably there was a time when the orthography of English was at least an approximate representation of the sounds in the language. However, a little reflection will show that by this time many spellings have become distressingly obscure. A few vowels can still be represented rather easily and with a reasonable degree of accuracy, such as those of *bit* and *bet,* and the spellings of *i* or *e* plus a single final consonant are interpreted without too much trouble. However, some vowels, such as the low back vowels generally found in *water, wash, bought, moss,* and *law* require considerable ingenuity in representation and care in interpretation, for there seems to be no letter or combination of letters which can be used consistently in all words having these sounds. The problem of spelling is complicated further by the fact that some letters or letter combinations do not consistently represent the same sounds, even in the same dialect. This difficulty is obvious from such a list of words as *lot, lost, fog, roll, stone, hose,* and *lose* in which the letter *o* represents at least three different sounds in some dialects and four in others.

For these reasons it is doubtful that an author can manage any very extensive portrayal of subphonemic, or purely phonetic, variations by means of the literary alphabet. The following pronunciations for the vowel of *can't* can all be found along the Atlantic coast: [æ], [æ:], [æ⁻], [æ¹].[12] Yet these differences in pronunciation can hardly be indicated by "phonetic" re-spelling. It might be argued that [æ:] can be indicated by the spelling DAANCE, but to expect a uniform interpretation of this spelling as [æ:] calls for considerable faith in the discernment of the reader. However, the author can generally indicate a difference in phonemes, or rather a difference in the distribution of a particular phoneme, in the word stock of the dialect. In other words, he can usually indicate when a particular word has a different phoneme in the dialect he is representing from what it has in the dialect which he is regarding as "standard." Since the phoneme already exists in his "standard" speech, there is a spelling tradition associated with it, or a spelling device may usually

---

[12] George L. Trager (*American Speech,* 15: 255–258) has demonstrated that the distinction between [æ] and [æ⁻] is phonemic in some dialects. Since this distinction has been recognized through phonemic analysis and has not been incorporated in the orthography of the language, it is doubtful that a writer of dialect would observe it or be able successfully to represent it.

be improvised to show it. He can improvise a representation by re-spelling the word to resemble other words which have the desired sound in the "standard" dialect. As for the word *can't,* two more pronunciations can be found for it. One is [kɑnt] (with the vowel of *father*); the other is [keɪnt] (with the vowel of *Cain*). Both [ɑ] and [eɪ] are phonemically different from [æ] in all dialects of English, and there are spellings for them in all dialects. The pronunciation of *can't* as [kɑnt] can be shown by the spellings CARNT[13] and CAHNT, and its pronunciation as [keɪnt] can be shown by the spelling CAINT.

It has been possible to consider the theory of literary dialect so far with very little reference to who the author of a particular dialect might be or in what section of the country he might have resided. Further discussion—especially discussion of how pronunciations are represented—must recognize the fact that the author is himself a speaker of dialect. This "standard" language which has been mentioned can only be the variety of the language which the author himself considers to be "standard," not what some dictionary-maker or later critic may wish to judge him by.

There are many pronunciation features found in all varieties of speech which are not considered "dialectal" in the sense of being substandard, even though the persons using the pronunciations may know that other persons in other areas pronounce the same words somewhat differently. The facts that in some regions *mourning* and *morning,* or *hoarse* and *horse,* are homonyms, in others *pin* and *pen* are not distinguished, and in still others *Mary, merry,* and *marry* are all pronounced with the same vowel indicate clearly that there is no generally accepted standard of pronunciation for the entire United States. Rather than a single national standard of pronunciation in this country, we have regional standards, with some usages relatively common to all educated persons, and with some others common to all members of the educated group of each region but differing from usages common to the corresponding groups of other regions.[14]

---

[13] This spelling for *can't* can be found in the Negro dialect of Thomas Nelson Page. An explanation of the use of the letter R in this manner will be made in a later paragraph.

[14] The presence of regional standards rather than a single national standard of speech is really too well known to require belaboring, and any of the recent treatments of American English, such as C. K. Thomas, *Introduction to the Phonetics of American English,* or the Kenyon-Knott *Pronouncing Dictionary,* will provide adequate proof. The latest statement by a recognized scholar is the following quotation from Hans Kurath's *Word Geography of the Eastern United States* (1949), p. 9: "For these reasons the speech of the cultured is less earthbound than that of the folk. It is regional rather than local in character. In grammar and in vocabulary it is apt to strip off even some of the regional features, but in America the pronunciation remains largely regional since there is no national standard of pronunciation."

158   We can not expect a Georgian or Virginian author, believing himself literate and familiar with "good" English, to feel that this pronunciation of *water* as [wɔːtə] is "dialectal," even though he may be aware that people in, say, Oklahoma generally say [wɑtr]. And in representing the speech of persons in his area, he would not make any change in the spelling of this word. Similarly, a writer living in certain parts of the South is no more likely to write both *pen* and *pin* as PIN than a writer living in Pennsylvania would write both *hoarse* and *horse* with the same spelling. It is true, of course, than an author who has traveled, or who has made a study of American dialects, or who has consulted a dictionary with some frequency, will be aware that some of the features of his own speech are considered "dialectal." In a few details, he might make concession to that knowledge, especially if his own pronunciation is not a spelling pronunciation. For example, Joel Chandler Harris writes *catch* as KETCH in representing the speech of Uncle Remus, even though he probably used the pronunciation himself, at least on some occasions. On the other hand, neither Harris nor James Russell Lowell dropped the *r* from such words as *hard* and *part,* although an [r]-like sound in those words was pronounced neither by Uncle Remus nor by the Biglows.

Lacking a uniform standard for spoken English, the author has no choice but to use the accepted criteria of his own region. This is perhaps the most important single axiom in the study of literary dialects.

In summary, then, a dialect is simply the corpus of speech habits associated with a particular group which has some geographic or social unity, but these speech habits are individually diverse in distribution. It is the combination which is unique rather than the discrete features themselves. By a selection of particularly well-defined features, dialect areas can be set up, but that delineation does not guarantee the occurrence of every feature in the speech of all individuals within the line, nor the consistent use of every feature by the same speaker on all occasions. The literary artist must make his own selection of those features which will serve best his purpose of presenting a character who is real but who is likewise a recognizable social type. In this process, he is likely to regularize the speech of his character. Thus, the frequency of occurrence of particular "dialectal" forms may be somewhat different in the literary dialect from the frequency of their occurrence in the speech which is being represented. Moreover, some exaggeration of the more striking peculiarities may result from their very noticeableness, and further exaggeration may result from the fact that authors may employ "eye" or visual dialect. On the other hand, some of the genuinely distinctive characteristics of the represented speech will not be given. Both the author's desire to keep his representation within readable limits and his difficulties in finding suitable spelling devices will inhibit his portrayal of a speech type. Any literary dialect, therefore, will necessarily be a partial and somewhat artificial picture of the actual speech. It is the analyst's task to eliminate the spurious and interpret the genuine.

An author, like everyone else, speaks some variety, or dialect, of a language, not "the language" itself. When he reads, or spells, he associates certain pronunciations with the various vowel and consonant combinations in the conventional orthography. These pronunciations differ in some respects from the phonetic associations made by other persons in other regions. Therefore a proper interpretation of a literary dialect can be made only in terms of the speech of the man writing the dialect. It is, in the main, the pronunciation of his usual speech that he associates with a particular spelling; and when he selects a spelling to represent a phonetic feature of the literary dialect, he selects a spelling that represents that phonetic feature in his own speech.

The preceding section has been a rather abstract dissertation on the theoretical principles that are involved in the writing and interpretation of literary dialects. The pertinence and truth of these principles must be evaluated through an examination of actual specimens of these literary dialects. The essential question is whether the principles are useful in giving pragmatic solutions to the problems of interpretation and whether they explain the practices which are discovered in the dialect stories.

Some notion of the necessity for interpreting spellings in terms of the native speech of the author can be gained from seeing what happens when this principle is not followed. H. L. Mencken, in *Supplement II* of *The American Language* condemns Joel Chandler Harris for the spelling BRER, and he represents what the Negro would say by the spelling BRUH-UH or BRUH.[15] It is clear that Mencken's objection is to the use of ER rather than UH as a representation of the unstressed, indeterminate vowel [ə]. However, in the speech of Harris (probably), and in that of most people in the old plantation areas, unstressed syllables spelled *er*, as in *father, river, consider,* and so on, are pronounced with final [ə] rather than with an [r]-like sound. The ER spelling, therefore, does not suggest a constricted sound to a native of the "*r*-less" areas.[16] Harris actually meant the same pronunciation by his spelling BRER that Mencken meant by his spelling BRUH, namely [brə] or perhaps [brʌ]. This ER spelling was not used for the first time by Harris, and it has been used by many other writers of Negro dialect since his time.

---

[15] p. 265.

[16] See James N. Tidwell, "Mark Twain's Representation of Negro Speech," *American Speech,* 17: 174–176, for Twain's similar use of this spelling.

160   Harris also used the letter R after the letter A to indicate a particular pronunciation of the letter A in stressed position. Some words, such as *master, plaster,* and *after,* which have the vowel [æ] in most varieties of American English, are spelled by Harris with AR (MARSTER, PLARSTER, ARTER) to indicate a much more retracted, and possibly lengthened, vowel, i.e. [a] or [a:]. A study of the speech of educated persons in the Middle Georgia area, where Harris was reared, shows that he probably pronounced such words as *part, hard,* and *cart* with a low back, unrounded vowel, similar to the vowel of *pot, hot,* and *cot,* but longer and followed by a slight central off-glide. Regardless of the phonemic interpretation of this vowel, there is no trace of the constricted [r]-like sound which is found in those words in most regions of the country. The letter R is very likely no more than an indication that the preceding A does not represent [æ] but that instead it represents a more retracted (and possibly lengthened) vowel [a] or [a:]. It would be a prime error to regard such spellings as indicative of the "intrusive *r*" as found in the speech of many Oklahomans in *wash,* or in the speech of many New Englanders in "the idear of it." This practice of using AR to represent a low back vowel has been followed by many writers of Southern dialect, among them Harry Stilwell Edwards and Thomas Nelson Page. Since Page is representing the speech of the Virginia Piedmont Negro, and since this feature—the retracted vowel of *father* in place of the front vowel of *fat*—is found in more words in the Virginia Piedmont than in other sections of the South, he uses the AR spelling more frequently than Harris or Edwards. For example, the spelling LARS' (last) and CARN'T (can't) occur in the Negro stories of Page but not in those of Harris or Edwards.

The use of AR as a spelling device to show that the vowel is not the expected [æ] is a characteristic of the *Biglow Papers* of James Russell Lowell as well as of the Negro stories of Page and Harris.[17] Eastern New England, with some exceptions, is likewise an "r-less" area, and the letter R is therefore available as a spelling device. Hence, the spelling ARTER (after) is probably no more than an indication that the vowel is a more retracted sound than the usual American [æ]. True, this retracted sound is now considered regular in that area before [f], [s], and [θ]; but the "loss" of [f], reflected in the spelling without the letter *f,* would leave such a possible spelling as ATTER without the visual signal which a following *f* would give. It should not be assumed, however, that the spelling *ar* in the *Biglow Papers* represents a sound that is phonetically identical

---

[17] For a more comprehensive discussion of the literary dialect in the *Biglow Papers,* see the University of Michigan dissertation (1958) by James Downer, which was in progress at the time this article was originally written. Professor Downer very kindly gave me access to some of his earlier work.

with the sound it represents in the Uncle Remus stories. The eastern New Englanders pronounce words like *cart* and *hard* with a vowel that is not nearly so retracted as the vowel heard in these words in Piedmont Virginia and Middle Georgia, i.e., [hɑːd] as opposed to [hɑːd] or [hɑːᵊd].

Lowell also used the AR spelling in SLARTER (slaughter) and SARSE (sauce).[18] Here it is likely that he is indicating an unrounded vowel like that of *father* rather than the rounded vowel which the conventional *au* spelling would suggest to most educated New Englanders. This unrounded vowel, or one very similar, which Lowell indicated in the speech of his "dialect" characters, can be heard as the "accepted" pronunciation in many regions west of the Appalachians.[19]

Now it is true that eastern New England does contain an area in which words spelled with post-vocalic *r* are pronounced with an [r]-like sound. This area is the northeast corner of Massachusetts, including the town of Marblehead, the speech of which is suggested by John Greenleaf Whittier in "Skipper Ireson's Ride." It is probable that Whittier, like Lowell, spoke an "*r*-less" dialect; hence he would be likely to use some "phonetic" spelling device to indicate the presence of an [r]-like sound that he would not use himself. In this poem, the words *hard, heart,* and *cart* sometimes appear as HORRD, HORRT, and CORRT. The spelling with RR is certainly an indication to the readers that, actually, the women of this town do pronounce an *r* in these words, contrary to the practice of most other inhabitants of eastern New England. The use of the letter O rather than the letter A suggests, I think, that these same women had a more retracted vowel in these words than Whittier did. It is significant that Lowell, in representing a socially disapproved dialect of his own speech area, did not change the spelling of *hard, heart,* and *cart;* on the

---

[18] A similar interpretation is to be assumed for the spelling HARNSOME (handsome), also found in the *Biglow Papers*. Citations from the *Biglow Papers* used here are taken from the first series, first published in book form in 1848.

[19] A consideration of Krapp's discussion of Lowell's dialect writing will, I think, be illuminating. Krapp said: "He [Lowell] did not omit *r* finally or before consonants, nor did he spell words like *while, when, where* as *w'ile, w'en, w'ere*. He made no attempt in the *Papers* to reduce to spelling the pronunciation of . . . *au* in his sixth [rule, i.e., *slaughter,* etc., has the vowel of *father*], or of broad *a* in handsome . . ." (p. 233).

Krapp quotes six stanzas of "The Courtin'," found in the second series of the *Biglow Papers,* as illustrative of Lowell's dialect writing. It is true that Krapp's objections are valid for this entire poem, and possibly for the greater part of the second series of the papers; however, in the first series of the *Biglow Papers,* examples of the spellings WEN (when), WILE (while), WARE (where), also WITE (white), WUT (what), etc., are very common. The spellings SLARTER and HARNSOME, which also appear in the first series, refute another part of Krapp's statement. Part of the reason why Lowell would be unlikely to omit *r* from such words as *part, pare,* and *more* has already been given, and the matter will be further discussed in later paragraphs.

162   other hand. Whittier, himself from the same speech area as Lowell and the Biglows, doubled the letter R when writing the dialect of Marblehead, which differed from his own speech in being an "*r*-pronouncing" dialect.

Although Joel Chandler Harris did not drop the letter *r* from such words as *part, heart,* and *cart,* when representing the speech of a character whose pronunciation of these words would be similar to that of his own, there are many examples in his Negro dialect of the omission of *r* in his writing of other words. The omission of *r* is generally found in his spelling of words like *poor, your,* and *pour, hoarse, door,* and *more,* which are represented in the speech of Uncle Remus as PO', YO', and PO', HO'SE, DO', and MO'. Now Harris himself, I think, generally pronounced the words listed above with "long *o*" followed by [ə]. His spellings in the Uncle Remus stories seem to indicate that Uncle Remus did not have this post-vocalic schwa, and pronounced them [poʊ], [joʊ], and [poʊ], [hoʊs], [doʊ], and [moʊ]. The apostrophe in these words means only that some letters have been omitted and that the pronunciation is represented by the remaining letters. In a few words, however, like HO'SE and DO', the apostrophe may prevent confusion with other words like *hose* and *do* (verb). Since these pronunciations [poʊ], [joʊ], and [poʊ], [hoʊs], [doʊ], and [moʊ], are all well attested by *Linguistic Atlas* records from Middle Georgia, the omission of the letter R can mean only the omission of the final schwa, which Harris himself would have generally pronounced.

It should be clear by this time that the phonetic interpretation given to the letters and combinations of letters in the conventional orthography varies in different sections of the country, and that an author, seeking spellings to represent pronunciations that differ from his own, will select those which "stand for" the deviant sounds in his *own* speech type, not in that of other varieties of English. Hence, in order to interpret his dialect spelling, it is necessary to know how these spellings would be pronounced in the region to which the author belongs. It is true that a literary dialect is written with the phonetic signals of English orthography in mind; but it is equally true that these signals have reality only in terms of particular dialects or regional standards of English, not in terms of any hypothetical "pure" or "standard" English.

This conditioning factor in the representation of sounds by spellings governs, as we have seen, the spellings which the author chooses, and, as a consequence, the proper interpretation of those spellings. Hence, it is obvious that anyone who attempts the interpretation of literary dialect without first learning something about the speech of the author can hardly expect to arrive at valid conclusions. If, by chance, the dialect of the investigated author happens to be that of the investigator, no difficulty will be apparent. When, however, an investigator from the Midland areas judges an author from any Southern area or from eastern New England, considering his own Midland dialect to be "standard" English, he is almost certain to misread some of the spellings in the literary dialect and to conclude that the author has done an inept job.

The fact that the author is himself a speaker of a regional type of speech will determine to a large extent both what he will attempt to represent and what he will not represent. Many of the regional features of speech which are common to all levels of culture and education will probably not be shown, for the author is not likely to be aware of them as "dialect." Some speech habits, such as the fact that words spelled with *r* following a vowel in the same syllable are pronounced differently in different sections, are well-known and may have been well-known in the nineteenth century. But it still comes as a matter of surprise to many residents of the Midwest that their pronunciation of a word like *dog* could be considered dialectal, and that a New England author, representing their speech in literary dialect, might feel constrained to spell that word DAHG to show that the pronunciation was [dɑg] rather than [dɔg], the pronunciation indicated in the Merriam-Webster dictionaries.

Further illustration of this point is found in the dialect stories of Joel Chandler Harris. In his stories, whether of white or Negro characters, there is no indication of the monophthongal variety of "long *i*." This type of the vowel, generally [a:], is found in at least some words in nearly all varieties of Southern speech; hence, Harris saw no need for such spellings as AH and MAH, for *I* and *my*—which writers from other sections sometimes employ as indications of this feature—for there was no reason why he should consider the monophthongal vowel in these words a "dialectal" type. It follows, then, that an author will fail to represent many features of his character's speech which may be regionally characteristic but which carry no implication of inferiority or "difference" within those regions where they are found. There are some features which are "dialectal" in some regions but "standard" in others. An author from a region where the feature is "dialectal" may represent this type of pronunciation. For example, Lowell considered the vowel of *father* [a] to be "dialectal" in *slaughter* and represented it by the spelling SLARTER; whereas, it is unlikely that an author from some areas west of the Mississippi would see any need to change the conventional spelling of the word.

As a matter of fact, the speech of educated persons is not ordinarily represented in "dialectal" spelling by authors who are portraying their own region. In the stories of Joel Chandler Harris (middle Georgia), Thomas Nelson Page (eastern Virginia), Mary Wilkins Freeman and Sarah Orne Jewett (eastern New England), and Edward Eggleston (southern Indiana), the speech of persons from the educated classes is shown without the "dialectal" indications found in the speech of the

164   less educated.[20] This similarity in the writing of the speech of educated
persons cannot be taken as evidence that all these persons spoke with
the same pronunciations, or that the authors are attempting to create a
false impression of conformity to a national standard. So far as an author
would be conscious of conformity to a standard in pronunciation, he
would assume that a reader would take his conventional spelling to mean
only that the character spoke according to the commonly accepted standards for educated persons of his own region.

An author does not, of course, wish to confuse or deter his readers by
the strange appearance of his written dialogue, but even without this
reason for restraint, he would find the conventional alphabet quite inadequate to represent regional differences in speech. The major regional
differences fall into a small number of categories, but they appear individually in a great number of words. Some, such as loss of R, could be
shown with some consistency, but others would give him more difficulty.
There are two pronunciations each for *tune, duke, nude,* and similar
words, but a person who pronounced the first to rhyme with *moon* would
probably not recognize the conventional spelling as a sign that the vowel
of *mute* was intended and that the author would write TOON when he
wished to show the pronunciation with the vowel of *moon.* Thus, for this
group, and for other groups with two pronunciations, the author would
have to devise two spellings other than the conventional one—e.g., TOON
and TYOON. Even greater difficulty would be encountered in representing the distribution of the low back vowels /ɔ/ and /a/. Some people
pronounce *cot* and *caught* alike. Some of these use the vowel usually
illustrated in dictionaries by *order,* and others use that illustrated by *hot*
or *box.* Also, there are many regional differences in the occurrence of

[20] Regarding the practice by writers in Southern regions, Krapp commented (p. 238): "But
writers who have attempted to depict what may be called reputable Southern persons on the
whole have sedulously avoided the deviations from standard grammar and standard pronunciations common to most forms of familiar American English. That the 'Southern gentleman'
always spoke with strict grammatical propriety and with nice precision in enunciation, one
may doubt. If he seems to have been much more a man of the conventional world than local
characters elsewhere in America, this is probably an illusion cherished by the transcribers of
Southern life, who perhaps have been willing to sacrifice certain elements of realism and truth-
fulness in order not to seem to imperil the dignity of the accredited conservers of the social
tradition of the Southern community." Krapp apparently overlooked the fact that authors
from all regions have likewise "sedulously avoided" representing the speech of what "may be
called reputable persons" living in their own regions in "dialectal" spellings. The writers listed
above all have characters in their stories whose speech is not given regional or social distinction, and the list of such authors could be extended almost indefinitely. The fallacy is, indeed,
so palpable that no point would be served by mentioning it except that Krapp has, in the
statement quoted here, revealed the *suus cuique mos* basis for his use of the term "standard
English" and thus impugns his own qualifications as a judge of literary dialects whose authors
did not share his own speech conventions.

these two vowels in the speech of persons who use both. Furthermore, if an author wished to indicate phonetic differences, such as the qualities of /ɔ/, he would have even greater difficulty, for alphabetic writing systems are not designed to show phonological differences beyond the phonemic level, and the English alphabet is not an exception to this rule.

On the other hand, if an author associates a particular system of sounds (his own) with a particular system of spelling (English orthography), he is able to represent, by systematic variations in the spelling, the phonemic contrasts of a dialect which has the same phonemes as his own speech, even though these phonemes occur in different words. Thus, when Eggleston writes *poor* as POAR, he is indicating that Mrs. Means, in *The Hoosier Schoolmaster,* pronounced the word so that it would rhyme with his own pronunciation of *boar;* and when James Whitcomb Riley writes *water* as WORTER, as he does in "The Old Swimmin'-hole," he is indicating a pronunciation that suggests to him his own pronunciation for *mortar.*

These reasons vindicate the practice which authors follow of not trying to represent regional pronunciation in the speech of persons from the educated classes. They do not represent as "dialect" those features of pronunciation which, though regional in distribution, do not conflict with their notions of "correct" English, and persons from educated classes are presumed to speak "correct" English. First, the authors see little reason to write as dialect what is to them good English; second, the attempt to represent regional variations in dialogue would increase the unconventional spelling to a repellent degree; third, the attempt is not feasible. The author can represent only those phonetic features for which spellings exist or can be improvised. These improvised spellings can be interpreted only by reference to the phonetic associations with the orthographic conventions, and these associations differ from region to region. Hence, the author cannot re-spell his own dialect in terms of his own dialect except by using alternate spellings that are phonetically the same, and to the author and to readers in his own region, this would simply be "eye" or visual dialect.

If, then, an author does not ordinarily try to show regional differences in the speech of educated characters, what is he able to represent with his spellings?

A major effect of a literary dialect is to show that the speech represented is a restricted type, even in its own region. By the very fact that he has represented the speech in unconventional spellings, the author has passed judgment; he has indicated that it is *not,* in his definition of the term, standard English. For one thing, he will represent many features which are relatively common in his own area (possibly in all areas of the country), but which are, for the most part, not socially acceptable any-

166   where. Some of the pronunciation features of this type probably occur
in the author's own speech and in that of other educated persons of the
area, on occasion, although all educated persons "know better" and use
more approved forms when they consider them appropriate. Examples
are pronunciations like final [ə] in words such as *fellow* and *arrow,* and
like [ðɪʃjɪr] for *this year.* Other pronunciations of this type, much lower
in the social scale, are those indicated by the spellings JANDERS (jaundice),
DREEN (drain), and H'IST (hoist), which are very common everywhere
along the eastern seaboard, and probably elsewhere, but which are not
generally found in the speech of well-educated persons. Still other forms,
even farther away from social approval, are L'ARN and SOT, which were
probably far more widespread once than they are now. By a judicious
selection of speech forms, an author can give a good impression of the
level of education represented by his "dialect" character. It goes without
saying, of course, that one who says SOT is also likely to say DREEN and
THISH YEAR.

A literary dialect which is based on a regional "vulgate" should nevertheless contain evidence of regional differences on that level of speech.
The examples of dialect writing which have been used earlier to illustrate
the practices of dialect writers have largely been representations of the
local "vulgate," and the represented features have been geographically
limited in the extent of their occurrence. When Harris writes PO' for *poor,*
or DE for *the,* he is indicating pronunciation features which differentiate
the speech of Uncle Remus from that of Biglow, as represented by Lowell;
and when Lowell writes SLARTER for *slaughter,* he is indicating a pronunciation which Uncle Remus would not have. A more convincing demonstration of how dialectal differences within the "vulgate" can be shown
is provided from a consideration of how the same author has handled
two differing dialects.

Since Harris has written some stories in which the speech of the Negro
and that of the white yeoman class are both represented in "dialect"
spelling, a comparison of his practice in writing the two dialects will be
instructive. Further pertinence can be given to this comparison by selecting "Mingo," the story from which George Philip Krapp took his example
of Harris's representation of rural white speech, as the source of evidence.
The scene of this story is given by Harris as Middle Georgia with a clear
reference to Jones county, which is located about ninety miles southeast
of Atlanta. The conclusion following Krapp's analysis has been quoted
earlier.[21] Later in the same chapter he considers a passage from one of
the Uncle Remus stories. (Uncle Remus lived in Putnam county, which

---

[21] Footnote 4.

adjoins Jones county on the east.) As indications of Negro speech, rather than white speech, in his analysis of the Uncle Remus passage, Krapp finds only the writing of *d* for *th*, which he (incorrectly) supposes to be "merely a very much voiced [ð]," the persistent use of present forms and the use of the preterit *cotch*.[22] Following this analysis of the Uncle Remus material, he concludes:

> That the speech of Uncle Remus as Joel Chandler Harris heard it differed markedly even from Southern low colloquial is possible, but if so, his literary transcription of the dialect of Uncle Remus gives remarkably few clues which will enable one to realize this difference. . . . Negro English as written by such representative authors as Thomas Nelson Page and Joel Chandler Harris is in fact not different from any other dialectal form of American English, that is, it is merely general low colloquial English with a sprinkling of words or phrases which by custom have come to have closer associations with Negro speech.[23]

The misleading implications of this conclusion can be exposed by a somewhat more careful look at "Mingo" than Krapp apparently considered necessary—supplemented, of course, by information which was not available when he made his study. In the story there are two leading characters whose dialogue is represented with "dialectal" spellings. One is Mrs. Bivins, an independent-minded white woman of the class that did not own slaves but that certainly did not consider itself inferior to persons who did. The other is Mingo, an elderly colored man who had once belonged to "de Bushrods of Ferginny," but who had spent most of his life on a Middle Georgia plantation—therefore, a member of the same race and class as Uncle Remus. I have made a representative selection from the speech of the two persons throughout the story, matching their pronunciation of the same words as Harris represents it. Most of the spellings are indeed the same: for example, DRAPS (drops), SHET (shut), CLE'R (clear), GIT (get), CHEER (chair), EF (if), and CAMMER (calmer). These pronunciations all represent the relatively common uneducated, and somewhat archaic, speech of the area.

The comparison of the spellings, however, reveals several systematic differences in the representation of the two dialects. An examination of the following list, in which the spellings in the dialogue of Mrs. Bivins are matched with the spellings in the dialogue of Mingo (which are exactly those which Harris used in writing the dialogue of Uncle Remus), will make obvious some of these differences.

---

[22] *English Language in America,* I, p. 249.

[23] *Ibid.,* pp. 250–251.

168

Mrs. Bivins	Mingo	Mrs. Bivins	Mingo
shorely	sholy	what	w'at
tooby shore	tooby sho'	when	w'en
pore	po'	white	w'ite
'fore	befo'	never seen	never seed
thes (just)	des	taken (pret)	tuck
this	dis	hepped	holp
that	dat	betweenst	'tween
they	dey	betwix'	'twix'
the'r (their)	der	mightent	moutent
with	wid	airter	arter
thar	dar	famerly	fambly
wher'	whar	tell (till)	twel
somewheres	some'ers	ast (pret)	ax'

These differences can be found in a sample of not more than approximately six pages of material from the speech of each character. A full study of the considerable number of stories in which Harris has represented white speech in "dialectal" spellings should bring out many more. Among the features illustrated above are the use of [r] by Mrs. Bivins, the use of [d] for [ð] by Mingo, the use of initial [hw] by Mrs. Bivins and the use of [w] in corresponding words by Mingo, the differences in the verb forms, the apparent use of an [r]-colored unstressed vowel sound in *where* by Mrs. Bivins and the use of [a:] or [a:ə] in the same word by Mingo, the intrusive (excrescent) [st] in *between* by Mrs. Bivins, the aphesis in that word and in *betwixt* by Mingo, the apparent use of a front vowel in *after* by Mrs. Bivins and the use of a back vowel by Mingo (although both have medial [t] rather than [ft]), and the historically different forms of the verb *ask* used by each.

Although I have not made the extensive study of the white speech of Middle Georgia which would be necessary before judging the indication of Mrs. Bivins' speech that Harris has given, I have found confirmation for many of the characteristics which are represented. As a matter of fact, even Mrs. Bivins' use of an [r]-like pronunciation in *pure* and *sure* can be justified by comparison with a field record of the *Linguistic Atlas* made from an elderly, uneducated white informant who lived in a rural community of Baldwin county, which adjoins both Putnam and Jones counties.[24]

There are thus two major categories in which an author can give some individuality to his literary dialect. He can indicate many features which are social in their distribution, and he can indicate a few features which

---

[24] For a more extended discussion comparing Harris's treatment of various social dialects, see the article referred to in footnote 11.

are regional within the social groups which are depicted. He can contrast
the speech of the educated with that of the uneducated, and he can show
some variation in the degree of departure from the regional standard.
Furthermore, he can contrast, to a more limited extent, the uneducated
speech of one area with the uneducated speech of other areas.

There is, however, another type of speech feature which is useful in
reflecting geographical distinctions in language. In the conversation of
everyone, except the most elegant, there are some usages which are not
"correct" in a narrow sense. These usages, some of which belong to the
category referred to in speech manuals as "careless," may be called
"marginal" usages, for they are habits which the speaker may follow in
ordinary conversation, even though he may "know better," and he may
eliminate them on more formal occasions. As already indicated, some of
these usages are hardly regional but others seem to be restricted to certain
areas; hence, the presence of them in a literary dialect may give regional
significance to the dialect. Some of these features, which are commonly
found in the speech of educated persons in the Southeast, are [b] for
orthographic *v* in the morphemes *seven* and *eleven,* especially in *seventy;*
[d] for orthographic *s* in *isn't* and *wasn't;* and *don't* rather than *doesn't* in
the third person singular. Such features as these will ordinarily, and I
think legitimately, be found in the literary dialect. Once an author has
decided to represent the speech of a character in "dialect," he is likely to
give a "dialectal" spelling to all pronunciations he observes that do not
conform to his notions of "proper" English, which in such usages are
likely to be influenced by the conventional spelling. On the other hand, if
he is not representing the speech of a character in "dialect"—that is, if
the character does not, in his opinion, speak "dialect"—he is unlikely to
represent such features as these in his conversation.

The result of this practice will be some exaggeration of the "dialectal"
status of the character's speech as contrasted to the speech of educated
persons; however, the elimination of usages of this type from the representation of the actual speech would be artificial, and would give a false,
even a contradictory, picture of its nature. His inclusion of genuine features, even though these features are not confined to the characters speaking "dialect," is hardly more than an attempt to reproduce as faithfully as
he can the facts of the speech he is portraying. The important point is
that the speech of "dialect" characters is already in contrast to the speech
of educated characters. In his representation of the speech of educated
persons, or persons from educated classes, the author simply follows the
traditional method of representing such speech; and, indeed, no other
course is feasible. However, in the representation of socially restricted, or
disapproved varieties, he gives as many clues to the actual practices as he
is able to within the limitations of the conventional alphabet and the re-

170   strictions imposed by his sense of artistic fitness. This, at any rate, has been the custom.

Some further information regarding the regional speech can sometimes be drawn by inference from a literary dialect. Since the "dialectal" spellings are chosen in terms of the regional standard, the investigator may find some hints of what the author's pronunciations are, or at least, what he considers the proper pronunciations to be. When Lowell represented *when* with the spelling WEN, one can infer that he considered the correct pronunciation to be [hwen]—that is, with [hw]. When, on the other hand, William Gilmore Simms *does not* write present participle with a final -N', but retains the -NG spelling in dialect writing, we can infer that he considered the pronunciation [n] natural for that spelling, for there is too much evidence confirming the final [n] pronunciation for him to have ignored it on any other basis. To be sure, evidence of this nature is very elusive; it should be handled with considerable care and regarded with considerable suspicion.

The contention, therefore, that the authors of literary dialects have written those dialects with regional concepts of standard pronunciation is thus seen to be justified by the evidence of the literary dialects themselves. Moreover, a proper interpretation of the spelling devices which they have employed can be arrived at only from a recognition of this principle. As native speakers of some regional standard speech, authors are not likely to represent the "correct" features of their own dialect; nor have authors represented the speech of persons in the educated class by means of dialect spellings. Even if an author should be so conscious of the regional nature of his own speech as to try to spell by association with some hypothetical "pure" or nonregional language, he would find such a procedure extremely unwise, if not impossible.

There are, however, some things in a literary dialect which can be suggested with a reasonable degree of fidelity. Social gradation between the characters can be fairly well indicated, and some regional differences on the "vulgate" level can ordinarily be incorporated. Furthermore, some usages which are marginal, in that they appear or do not appear in the speech of educated persons according to the occasion, can be justifiably utilized in a literary dialect. The critic, or the student of dialects, therefore cannot expect to find very much direct representation of regionally "correct" or formal English, but he can usually find considerable evidence on social and regional features which are not a part of this regionally "correct" speech pattern.

The central problem, so far, in this discussion of literary dialects has been the means by which pronunciations have been indicated. Phonology, however, is not all of speech, nor is it the whole of the problem of dialect representation in literature. A very large part of the written dialect consists of unconventional morphology, local expressions, and local names for things. The spelling devices for pronunciations have been discussed most fully because their interpretation is the most difficult part of the problem. But the same principles which apply to an understanding of the spelling devices apply also to the evaluation of the other linguistic forms. Full recapitulation of these principles with illustrative materials from verb forms, idioms, and lexical items is hardly necessary, but a quick digression to consider them briefly may be of some value.

E. Bagby Atwood, in . . . a study of the verb forms in the speech of the eastern states,[25] has shown that many nonstandard verb forms are regional in their distribution; hence, these verb forms will serve to indicate regional, as well as social, limitations in the literary dialect. Such forms as the use in one area of *be* and in another of *is* in the first person indicative; the use of *clum, clam,* or *clim* rather than *climbed; driv* rather than *drove; cotch* rather than *caught;* and *holp* rather than *helped* are all relatively restricted to certain sections at the present time. It is likely, of course, that they would have been found to be more widespread at an earlier time, and their value as regional criteria may be less for the older literary dialects than for those more recently written.

The easiest and one of the most effective methods of giving regional flavor to speech is the use of local expressions and names for things. These are particularly effective because they can be used on virtually all levels of speech. In the lowland and piedmont South, a young man, regardless of his class, *carries* a girl home from a party, even though both go on foot. In the same area, most fires are kindled with *lightwood*, and cows are said to *low*. South of the Mason-Dixon line, people buy *light-bread* at the grocers, and (including part of Pennsylvania) eat *roasting ears*. North of a line roughly corresponding to the 40th parallel, people carry things in a *pail* and cook in a *spider*. New England boys ordinarily play in a *brook*, Pennsylvania boys in a *run*, and North Carolina boys in a *branch*. These terms are not all, of course, on the same cultural level, but it is clear from a study of Kurath's *Word Geography,* from which these examples have been taken, that many words in common use have definite geographical associations.

There is, in fact, a great deal to be said for relying predominantly on regional and social peculiarities of grammar, of idiom, and of vocabulary in giving a folksy connotation to the speech of uneducated persons. Some of the most successful of modern authors utilizing literary dialect make little attempt to represent pronunciation, other than the elisions, assimilations, and contractions associated with a very informal style. Damon Runyon, for example, has given almost no clue to the vowels and con-

25 Published in 1953 as *A Survey of Verb Forms in the Eastern United States.*

172   sonants of his Broadway characters, yet he has created a highly indi-
vidualized dialect out of other linguistic materials. Ring Lardner and
Marjorie Kinnan Rawlings have given more hints on the sounds of their
dialects, but they lean far more on local terms, grammar and speech
rhythms than on pronunciation for their effects. It is true that the speech
of Roark Bradford's Mississippi plantation Negroes and his river roust-
abouts is more heavily "dialectal," but Bradford came at the end of a
long history of Negro dialect and much of the manner of indicating it has
become traditional in American literature. As a general rule, however, the
modern practitioners of literary dialect are far less concerned with exact
representation of pronunciation features than were their nineteenth century predecessors.

If the principles which have been described and illustrated in the foregoing discussion are valid, what is the procedure which would lead to
better results? Many of the principles and rules for a better analysis of
literary dialects can, I think, be derived from the preceding remarks.
But they are implied rather than clearly expressed, and a systematic statement of them should be made.

It is obvious, of course, that any examination of a literary dialect
should be guided by the principles of descriptive linguistics and should be
controlled by the findings of linguistic geography. It is apparent, first of
all, that the investigator should have a concept of dialect which fits the
facts of American English as they have been determined by research in
the field. He cannot define a dialect according to criteria which permit the
statement that there are no regional distinctions of speech in this country.
Should he do this, he will be puzzled by spelling devices based on pronunciations that differ from his own; he will find that some pronunciations
which he considers "dialectal" are not indicated; and he will be unable to
find any satisfactory criteria by which literary dialects can be regionally
identified. He is limited at the outset to concluding that only social distinctions have been represented.

The published descriptions of speech habits found in various parts of
the country are many, but they differ greatly in quality and scope. Some
are excellent studies of individual features, such as Guy Lowman's examination of the pronunciation of *house* and words with a similar vowel
in Virginia; some are detailed analyses of limited areas, such as O. F.
Emerson's *The Ithaca Dialect*; and some are mere lists of words with
notes of dubious validity regarding their pronunciation. It is very doubtful
that such material as this can provide sufficient evidence on individual
features for the analysis of literary dialects. Studies of individual features
obviously give only a limited picture of the local speech, and studies of
local speech give only a limited picture of the distribution in other areas

of the speech features found in the locality studied. Above all, the completeness with which individual studies cover all regions and all features is dependent on the interests of many individual scholars and their access to the requisite evidence. Moreover, the problems of correlation and evaluation would be stupendous and their solution time-consuming. Hence, a proper analysis of literary dialects, like a proper understanding of real speech patterns, is practically dependent on such questionnaire studies as the linguistic atlases of France, Italy, and the United States and Canada.

A comprehensive and accurate knowledge of American English, however, will not in itself guarantee valid results. The investigator must use a sufficiently large sample of the literary dialect to insure the consideration of all the pertinent data. No reputable linguist would attempt a phonemic analysis of any language or dialect on a basis of such a sampling as that given in the "Arthur the Rat" story or one side of a phonograph record. Likewise, any student who tries to analyze a literary dialect on a basis of one or two poems, or a short story or two, does not have enough material in his analysis to permit reliable findings, especially if his conclusions are negative.

Up to this time, I think, the evaluations of individual literary dialects have been based on inadequate evidence and have been arrived at by questionable methodology. The inadequacy of the evidence in the work of George Philip Krapp comes, first, from the fact that he used too small a sample of each dialect and, second, from the fact that the regional patterns of American speech and the distributions of individual features were imperfectly understood when he made his analysis. Some question might also be raised concerning his practice of judging the representation of each dialect by an irrelevant standard of pronunciation, and of evaluating the represented features without having accurate information on which to base the evaluations. A comparison of the several evaluations of dialect features in his study will show that some are not justified by present-day knowledge and some are even contradictory. Since he compared each dialect separately with these opinions (which included the presupposition of regional uniformity in American speech) and did not compare the dialects with *each other*, it is not surprising that he failed to detect differences between them.

If the method used by Krapp is inadequate for reliable evaluation, some other procedure is advisable. Not even the most comprehensive knowledge of American English or the use of all the literary dialect which the author has written will insure a proper analysis unless the actual procedures which are followed are themselves wisely chosen.

The first step, I think, in the analysis of any literary dialect is the phonetic interpretation of the spelling devices with which it is written. It

174   should be obvious by this time that this interpretation can be made only in terms of the speech sounds ordinarily associated with those spellings by the author. Hence, a reconstruction of the author's speech, or at least of his speech type, is a necessary prelude to the interpretation of his dialect spellings. If the author is no longer available for direct query, this speech type must be worked out from other evidence. However, with reasonably complete records of the speech of educated persons who live in the author's immediate locality, a pragmatic solution to the problem can generally be arrived at. It cannot be emphasized too strongly that this step must come before any other.

Once this understanding of the author's speech is attained the material of the literary dialect can be interpreted. At this point, it is advisable to assume that every word which is not spelled as it would be found in a dictionary has some kind of significance. These words should be taken out and grouped according to the spelling found in the literary dialect. If the spelling shows the possibility of more than one "dialectal" feature, it must be listed for each possibility and assembled under each potential category. Thus, the spelling 'FO' (before) would be listed both under the aphesis of initial syllables and under the "loss" of *r*. Once these categories have been derived from the dialect spellings themselves, they can be interpreted phonetically, and the nonsignificant spellings may be eliminated. If the spelling KOAM (comb) has been found, it may probably be discarded; but if a spelling like P'LEECEMAN (policeman) has been found, it must be retained under the "loss" of [ə], although it may be removed from its listing under spellings with EE.

When a group of words with like spellings is further examined, it is usually seen that various subcategories can be set up on a basis of how each word would be pronounced by speakers of "standard" English. For example, the list of words with the vowel letter *e*, suggesting [ɛ], may contain several which are conventionally spelled with the letter *u*, denoting [ʌ]; whereas some others listed with the *e* spelling may ordinarily be spelled with the vowel letter *a*, denoting [æ]. Thus, the first category, which contained SHET (shut), BRESH (brush), KETCH (catch), and GEDDER (gather), is now divided into two subcategories with SHET and BRESH in one and KETCH and GEDDER in the other. It is by this method that the distribution of the speech sounds in the lexical stock of the dialect can be seen to differ from their distribution in the "standard" language. From such evidence, the phonetic "laws" of the dialect can be derived. If, for example, the letter D is found consistently written for *th* [ð] in initial position, we can say that initial [ð] "becomes" [d] in the dialect. The statement of these "laws" cannot, however, go beyond the evidence of the spellings themselves. As seen earlier, the finding of CONSATE (conceit) is not evidence that *deceit* ought to be spelled DESATE.

In determining what to consider the "standard" pronunciation, the investigator must rely on his reconstruction of the author's speech. If evidence is lacking or uncertain in this reconstruction, decisions have to follow the lead of the dialect spellings. In other words, whenever an unconventional spelling is found, as KETCH for catch, the first assumption is that the author considered the indicated pronunciation [kɛtʃ] to be "dialectal," even though the reconstruction may suggest that the author may have used it sometimes himself. At any rate, it is a genuine feature of the dialect and is retained in the analysis.

Once all the spellings have been interpeted and the variations of the dialect isolated, they may be examined for authenticity. A reasonably satisfactory verification of the existence of the individual features can be found in: (1) the present occurrence of the feature in the speech of some person whose biography puts him in the same category in the same area; (2) the present occurrence of the feature in the speech of areas which are known to have contributed settlers to the critical area; or (3) the presence of the feature in certain scattered areas which are known to retain consistently once-common features that have passed out of most varieties of the language—the "relic areas," like the Merrimack valley, the North Carolina mountains, and the points of land along the seacoast both in New England and in the Southeast. These categories are arranged in order of validity. Once the individual features have been examined for verification, some estimate of the author's accuracy and skill as a writer of dialect can be made.

The next test will be to determine what degree of individuality the dialect has, whether it is a truly restricted type, and whether the restriction is regional, social, or both. It is at this point that the recognition of a dialect as a unique *combination* of features rather than as a unique *concentration* of features becomes important. There are, of course, some areas which have features that are practically confined to these areas, for example the use of *toot*[26] as the name for a paper bag in southeastern Pennsylvania; but most speech features are rather widespread, and local areas are defined by the overlapping of distribution boundaries (or isoglosses) as described earlier in this discussion. Hence, the distribution of a number of genuine features which the author has represented must be worked out. If it can be shown that the region of overlapping features includes the locale of the story, and if this region of overlapping features is relatively limited, then the literary dialect has regional significance. The more narrowly the region of overlapping can be delimited from the features in the literary dialect, the more regional significance the literary dialect has. It follows, of course, that the dialect does not have regional validity if there

[26] Kurath, *Word Geography,* Fig. 2.

176   is no area where its features overlap. It may then be nothing more than a social dialect with features applicable to its social level anywhere in the country, or it may be nothing more than a mess of spurious and generally meaningless re-spelling like that found in the modern comic page version of Uncle Remus.

This procedure will not, of course, provide any certain means of determining whether the author has presented *all* the characteristics of the dialect—or even all those which could be presented without detriment to the value of the story as literature. The determination of the *extent* to which an author has presented a dialect, as opposed to the *accuracy* of his presentation of *selected* features, is not possible without complete data on the phonology, morphology, syntax, and lexicon of the dialect concerned. Studies which give so complete a coverage of regionally or socially restricted speech communities are extremely rare. The *Linguistic Atlas* does not give this completeness of information about any region, for it is a survey designed to bring out major regional differences and based on significant sampling rather than full coverage.

Should it be found that the procedure which has been outlined here produces nothing linguistically significant, one of several things may be deduced. First, it may be decided that an insufficient sample of the literary dialect was used, or the evidence regarding the speech of the class or region was unreliable. If the raw material and the control material were both adequate, the next possibility is that the author has not included enough significant features, or that he has used features which are not genuine examples of the actual speech. Only after these possibilities are explored can a valid judgment of the author as a writer of literary dialect be made. Of course, if there are so many nonsignificant spellings, or "eye" dialect, that the residue of genuine forms is disappointingly small, he may be criticized on that basis. However, the problem of the linguist is over; further evaluation of the author is a problem of literary criticism and is based on nonlinguistic criteria.

The remaining question regarding literary dialects is whether they have linguistic value. E. H. Sturtevant, in one of the most authoritative recent works on linguistics, gives the opinion:

> In modern novels the use of dialects is a favorite means of securing local color, but such material is far too inaccurate for scientific purposes. . . . As a rule little or no effort is made to tell the reader how he should interpret the dialect spelling employed; if anyone interprets Joel Chandler Harris' *Brer* (*Brer Rabbit,* etc.) as [brə] he must get this from independent knowledge of Negro dialect, not from any hint in Harris' pages. . . . About all we can grant the novelists is the basic observation that there are regional and class variations in speech.[27]

[27] *Op. cit.,* pp. 33–34.

At the end of the first sentence . . . quoted here, Sturtevant has a footnote to Krapp's treatment, which I have already commented on at some length. As for the statement concerning *Brer,* it is possible to say that the form can be properly interpreted from a knowledge of Harris' speech, although it is true that some special information is required. And as for the concluding sentence, more careful studies of individual dialect authors will probably show that their work has greater worth than Sturtevant has granted.

Just how valuable literary dialects are to the student of language is still, I think, an open question, and the value will have to be decided for individual authors rather than for the device as a whole. The dialect stories of Mark Twain would obviously be fitter subjects of study than, say, the remarks of Artemus Ward, and Snuffy Smith is a better representative of "hillbilly" than Abner Yokum. There can be no doubt that the pages of a story are a poor substitute for adequate fieldwork by a competent phonetician; however, if it can be decided that a particular author is, in general, reliable, it is possible that his literary dialect will supply details, especially in vocabulary and structure, that are missing from the phonetician's record. There is possible service also to the historical study of English. Some competent linguists are convinced that many of the conclusions concerning earlier speech, based on spelling analysis, should be re-evaluated. The evidence given in a carefully and competently written literary dialect regarding pronunciations is similar in many respects to the evidence on which some historical conclusions are based. In fact, the problems of interpretation and the complexities brought in by literary and by scribal tradition are remarkably alike in both types of study. Hence, the analysis of those literary dialects for which verifying evidence is available can quite possibly bring out clues to a more certain interpretation of evidence on historical developments.

Eye Dialect as a Literary Device

Paul Hull Bowdre, Jr.

The most recent scholarly analysis of literary dialect is
"A Study of Eye Dialect," a dissertation by Paul Hull
Bowdre, Jr. In the excerpts which follow, Dr. Bowdre reviews
the uses of Eye Dialect from the pre-Civil War humorists
through the "local color" writers to later writers who use
dialect more consciously and realistically. Elsewhere in his
study he points out that readers tend to take the printed page
as a completely accurate record of speech. Even though Eye
Dialect includes phenomena that commonly occur in ordinary
standard speech (assimilation, syncopation of vowels,
reduction of consonant clusters, etc.), readers invariably feel
Eye Dialect is substandard in some way. These findings
underline the need for distinctions among dialect representations to be made in the light of sound linguistic knowledge
rather than preference, guess, or whim both by those teaching
literature in which dialect is included and those working with
persons speaking a dialect other than their own. Dr. Bowdre
is professor of English and Head of the Department at West
Georgia College.

In using nonstandard spellings to portray the speech of a character, the literary artist is faced with the problem of deciding how far he wishes to go in attempting to convey the peculiarities of the speech he has in mind. Despite the fact that regional speech differences are not plentiful in the United States, it is still exceedingly difficult to represent these differences, plus the peculiarities of substandard speech, by means of the conventional alphabetical symbols. Nor is it ordinarily the writer's intention to give an exact representation of all the peculiarities of a character's speech. Rather he is concerned with certain artistic values—he wishes to choose telling details of pronunciation which will give the reader the impression that his character is an actual person. He does not wish to clutter the reader's mind with too many small details, nor does he wish to resort to such complicated or unusual spellings that the reader will have difficulty in deciphering what the character is saying. The reader's attention should be free to appreciate the artistic values rather than be taken up in trying to read the words themselves.

George Philip Krapp has pointed out that "it may be safely put down as a general rule that the more faithful a dialect is to folklore, the more completely it represents the actual speech of a group of people, the less effective it will be from a literary point of view."[1] It is for this reason that the use of Eye Dialect is often justified even though it actually represents nothing more than a standard pronunciation. It is better to use Eye Dialect than to burden the reader with outlandish forms intended to represent all the intricacies of regional speech or substandard speech. Eye Dialect does provide a hint to the reader that the speech of a character in some way differs from normal conventional speech. At the same time, because Eye Dialect consists of quasi-phonetic spellings which represent what are the reader's own pronunciations, it may usually be deciphered by the reader without much difficulty.

It is true that the same nonstandard spelling may on occasion represent different pronunciations to different readers. For example, the spelling *haid* for *head* may appear to one reader to be intended to rhyme with *aid,* in which case it would be a substandard dialect form, perhaps intended to represent a pronunciation heard in some parts of the South, but recognized in all regions as nonstandard. To another reader it may appear that *haid* is intended to rhyme with *said*—in which case it is an Eye Dialect form. . . .

To arrive at the status of various pronunciations indicated by dialect

From "A Study of Eye Dialect," unpublished dissertation (The University of Florida, 1964). Printed with the permission of Paul Hull Bowdre, Jr.

[1] George Philip Krapp, "The Psychology of Dialect Writing," *The Bookman,* 63, (Dec., 1926), p. 523.

180   forms, Kenyon and Knott's *A Pronouncing Dictionary of American English* has been used. This dictionary has as its purpose "to give only pronunciations that are in general cultivated use—to give none that need to be avoided as incorrect or substandard."[2] It records "Cultivated Colloquial English," not the English of "formal public address or public reading." If a nonstandard spelling appears to represent a pronunciation that according to the dictionary is standard throughout the United States, it is considered Eye Dialect. While it is true that there is a theoretical difficulty involved in using a relatively recent (1953) dictionary to determine mid-nineteenth century standard pronunciations (as has been necessary at times in this study), in actuality changes in standard pronunciations have been so slight during the period covered by the study that its use presents no real difficulty.

In discussing the use of Eye Dialect as a literary device by American writers it is obviously not possible to examine all the works of every American writer and to point out each example of its use; nor would there be any value in doing so. Therefore, a number of American authors have been selected who have made use of Eye Dialect, and examples from their works are given in an effort to indicate how they have used it and for what purposes.

The first writer to be considered is the "frontier humorist," George Washington Harris. Harris belongs to that group of writers which includes Seba Smith (Major Jack Downing), Johnson Jones Hooper (Simon Suggs), David Ross Locke (Petroleum V. Nasby), H. W. Shaw (Josh Billings), T. C. Haliburton (Sam Slick), Charles Farrar Browne (Artemus Ward), and others who developed humorous "dialect characters" during the period from 1830 until the end of the Civil War. Harris called his "dialect character" Sut Lovingood. Sut is supposed to be a rough, "ornery" Tennessee mountaineer. His idea of a good time is the playing of crude, sometimes cruel, practical jokes. Harris, apparently to give the reader the pleasure of being continually aware that Sut is a complete ignoramus and buffoon, uses a nonstandard spelling for practically every word Sut says. Sut's speech is a concentration of Substandard Dialect, some Regional Dialect and a great deal of Eye Dialect. Here is a sample of Sut's way of speaking:

> Well, to cum tu the serious part ove this conversashun, that is how the old quilt-mersheen an' coverlidloom cum tu stop operashuns on this yeath. She had narrated hit thru the neighborhood that nex Saterday she'd giv a quiltin—three quilts an' one cumfurt tu tie. "Goblers, fiddils, gals an' whiskey," were the words she sent tu the

---

[2] John Samuel Kenyon and Thomas Albert Knott, *A Pronouncing Dictionary of American English* (Springfield, Mass.: G. C. Merriam Company, 1953), p. xxvii.

menfolk, an' more tetchin ur wakenin words never drap't ofen an 'oman's tongue. She sed tu the gals, "Sweet toddy, huggin, dancin, an' huggers in 'bundance." Them words struck the gals rite in the pit ove the stumick, an' spread a ticklin sensashun bof ways, ontil they scratshed thar heads wif one han' an' Thar heels wif tuther.[3]

Probably the most noticeable aspect of this kind of writing is the heavy concentration of nonstandard spellings. Such writing is not easy to read. There is too much variation from conventional spelling to allow a reader to skim over a passage and get its meaning. There are words which defy the reader's effort to decipher them such as "coverlidloom" and "quilt-mersheen." (These may stand for "coverlet loom" and "quilt-machine" but it requires some study to arrive at even this probable solution.) The many Eye Dialect spellings indicate that the writer is not making a serious effort to convey any regional or class dialect. Rather he is using an easy method of conveying to the reader the impression that Sut Lovingood is funny, an ignorant yokel to be laughed at.

The spellings which are easily recognizable as Eye Dialect include *tu* (to), *cum* (come), *ove* (of), *conversashun* (conversation), *operashuns* (operations), *Saterday* (Saturday), *cumfurt* (comfort), *fiddils* (fiddles), *wer* (were), *sed* (said), *rite* (right), *sensashun* (sensation), and *scratshed* (scratched). There are other spellings (such as *an'* in an unstressed position) that also may be considered Eye Dialect on closer examination. It is not necessary, however, to consider each individual nonstandard spelling in writing of this type to understand what purpose the author has in mind. He is not attempting a scientific delineation of a regional or class dialect, but "is laying it on thick" to give the reader a laugh. It is doubtful whether many readers today would have the patience to wade through such a conglomeration of nonstandard spellings. They no longer seem humorous enough to justify the deciphering effort involved.

Writers like G. W. Harris, Locke, and Browne are representative of a group that made use of quasi-phonetic spellings haphazardly to indicate the lack of education of their comic characters. In some cases—Sut Lovingood, for example—these quasi-phonetic spellings are intended to convey a character's speech and may properly be called Eye Dialect, while in others—such as Petroleum V. Nasby—the spellings are contained in letters and are only evidence that the dialect characters cannot spell. In either case, there is no careful effort to convey either substandard speech or regional speech but only to give a crude, broad, undifferentiated "comical" effect.

[3] George Washington Harris, "Mrs. Yardley's Quilting," in Richmond Croom Beatty *et al.*, *The Literature of the South* (Chicago: Scott, Foresman and Company, 1952), p. 400.

182   In 1871 Edward Eggleston wrote *The Hoosier Schoolmaster,* a book which he later in a preface to the edition of 1892 called "the file leader in the procession of American dialect novels."[4] Certainly it was a forerunner of a number of novels and short stories which dealt with particular locations in the United States. These literary works concentrated on depicting the actual customs, speech, habits, and mannerisms of natives of a certain area; that which gave rise to them is often called the "Local Color" movement in American Literature. Among the leaders of this movement were: Bret Harte, Mark Twain, and Joaquin Miller, who wrote of the West; Joel Chandler Harris, Lafcadio Hearn, and George Washington Cable, who wrote of the South; Sarah Orne Jewett and Mary Wilkins Freeman, who wrote of New England; Edward Eggleston, Joseph Kirkland, and Hamlin Garland, who wrote of the Middle West.

As the aim of the local colorists was to give to the reader the full flavor of the locales they had chosen to depict, often with an accent on what was quaint and picturesque, it was natural that they would seek to provide an impression of the actual sound of the speech of their characters. Consequently, they made some use of genuine Regional Dialect. The motive of the local colorists in writing dialect thus differed from the motive of the pre-Civil War dialect writers such as G. W. Harris, Locke, Browne, and Lowell. While the earlier writers, for the most part, merely wished to make their dialect characters appear ignorant and rustic (and thus funny), the local colorists wished to display the actual regional speech of their characters. Thus, while the earlier writers were content to mix together Eye Dialect, Regional Dialect, and Substandard Dialect at random, the local colorists were confined to the use of Regional Dialect for depicting the standard speech of the locale, or to Substandard Dialect for depicting its nonstandard speech. Any Eye Dialect that crept into the nonstandard spellings of the local colorists would, at least in theory, constitute a mistake on the part of the author. In actual practice, however, there is enough Eye Dialect in the writing of some of them to indicate either that they were often inaccurate in their attempts to analyze the characteristics of the regional speech or substandard speech they wished to portray, or else that they recognized Eye Dialect, perhaps unconsciously, as a useful and legitimate literary device.

A study of the works of Edward Eggleston by W. L. McAtee reveals a number of Eye Dialect forms. In the section called (by Mr. McAtee) "Phonetic or Near-Phonetic Spellings" we find the following forms used by Eggleston: *akordin'* for *according, apposil* for *apostle, fether* for *feather, giv* for *give, ov* for *of, penitenshry* for *penitentiary, rite* for *right,* and *tho'*

---

[4] Edward Eggleston, *The Hoosier Schoolmaster* (New York: Grosset and Dunlap, 1913), p. 6.

for *though*.[5] All of these, save possibly the first, appear to be Eye Dialect; and there are in addition a number of other spellings listed by Mr. McAtee, in other sections of his study, which may be classified as such, either wholly or in part. For example, there are the spellings *liker* for *liquor,* and *wuz* for *was,* both of which are Eye Dialect in their entirety. Some examples of words that are at least partially Eye Dialect are *keerlessness* (carelessness) and *kyard* (card) in which *k* has replaced *c* without indicating any change in the initial sound of the words (in the case of both, the *k* is preferable to *c* also because they might be read with an initial [s]); *nuff* (enough), in which the *nuff* has replaced *nough* with no phonetic significance; and *larf* (laugh), in which *f* has replaced *gh*, also with no change in sound. Eggleston spells *creature* on one occasion as *creetur*—the replacing of *ea* by *ee* is certainly Eye Dialect, but there is no way of knowing with certainty whether he intended the *t* of the last syllable to represent [č], as it does in the standard spelling, or [t], as it does in such nonstandard spellings as *critter*. He spells the Substandard Dialect form meaning *once* as *oncet, onst,* and *wunst*. The last of the three spellings is partially Eye Dialect in its use of the quasi-phonetic spelling *wuns* to represent the usual spelling *once*. The addition of the *t* at the end, of course, makes the word Substandard Dialect rather than Eye Dialect, since the pronunciation indicated is not standard in any section of the United States, or, for that matter, the English-speaking world. Of the three spellings used by Eggleston, however, the *wunst* spelling best represents the sound of the word to the reader, and this is an example where quasi-phonetic spelling is actually necessary to prevent conveying the wrong sound—the other two spellings could easily be taken to represent [ɔnsət] and [ɔnst].

There can be no doubt that Eggleston was making a serious attempt to give a true picture of Hoosier speech. He dedicated *The Hoosier Schoolmaster* to James Russell Lowell "whose cordial encouragement to my studies of American dialect is gratefully remembered." The same book contains numerous footnotes in which the author explains why he is using certain spellings and how they represent some particular characteristic of pronunciation. But it is difficult to understand how Eggleston could have thrown in spellings such as *rite* for *right* or *giv* for *give* without realizing that they do not convey any peculiarity of Hoosier pronunciation but rather simply standard pronunciation. It seems more likely that he willingly used a certain amount of Eye Dialect knowing that the reader would not hold him to strict account for it, or perhaps he was unconscious of it.

---

[5] W. L. McAtee, *Studies in the Vocabularies of Hoosier Authors: Edward Eggleston (1837–1902)* (Chapel Hill, N. C.: Printed by the Compiler, 1961), p. 124.

184   Also belonging to the local color movement was the "Hoosier Poet," James Whitcomb Riley. Riley wrote a very large number of short poems with midwestern settings about farmers, children, local characters, and old-timers. His tone was one of "folksiness." Certainly he was one of the most prolific users of Eye Dialect among American poets. A recent study of five of Riley's dialect-poems[6] revealed no less than thirty-three separate instances of its use with a number of the Eye Dialect spellings having been used on two or more occasions. The spelling *ust to* for *used to* [justə] was in fact used eight times in the five poems under consideration.

It is difficult to point to any specific purposes in Riley's use of Eye Dialect. For the most part it appears that he uses it along with Regional Dialect and Substandard Dialect to indicate that the people the poems are about are "just good old folks like you and me." The dialect of the poems is supposedly Indiana Hoosier dialect. However, Krapp has shown in an examination of one of Riley's dialect-poems, "The Old Man and Jim," that it is "made up of an abundance of ordinary colloquialisms, including much eye dialect, with some archaisms of speech which survive as low colloquialisms."[7]

A short passage from one of Riley's poems should be sufficient to illustrate his inclusion of a number of obvious Eye Dialect spellings among other nonstandard spellings which he uses to produce his "folksy" effect.

> Does the medder-lark *complane,* as he swims high and dry
> Through the waves of the wind and blue of the sky?
> Does the quail set up and *whissel* in a disappointed way,
> Er hang his head in *silunce,* and sorrow all the day?
> Don't the buzzards ooze around up *thare* just like they've
>   allus done?
> Is they anything the matter with the rooster's lungs or voice?
> Ort a *mortul* be complainin' when dumb animals rejoice?[8]

I have italicized the obvious cases of Eye Dialect. It is interesting to note that *complainin'* and *complane* are both found in the same stanza. Of course, the title of the poem, "Discuraged," is itself Eye Dialect.

Leaving the local colorists, we now turn to the use of Eye Dialect by Stephen Crane in his two well-known naturalistic novels, *Maggie, A Girl of the Streets* and *The Red Badge of Courage. Maggie* was Crane's first

---

[6] Dale B. J. Randall, "Dialect in the Verse of 'The Hoosier Poet,'" *American Speech*, XXXV (1960), pp. 36–50.

[7] George Philip Krapp, *The English Language in America*, New York: Frederick Ungar Publishing Co., I (1960), p. 228.

[8] James Whitcomb Riley, *When the Frost Is on the Punkin and Other Poems* (Indianapolis: The Bobbs-Merrill Co., 1911), p. 17.

novel. With reference to it one critic said: "It was, I believe, the first hint of naturalism in American letters. It was not a best-seller; it offers no solution of life: it is an episodic bit of slum fiction . . ."[9]

The dialect used in *Maggie* is intended to represent the nonstandard speech of a slum section of a large city. Pete, the hero of the novel, if it can be said to have one, has this to say on one occasion, "Dere was a mug come in d'place d'odder day wid an idear he was goin' t'own d'place."[10] Most of the dialect is of this type—Eye Dialect is used sparingly, and most of the spellings appear to represent Substandard Dialect. Where Eye Dialect does occur it is largely found in such spellings as *t'own* in the quotation given above, which may be considered an Eye Dialect spelling of *to own* [təon] in which the unstressed *to* [tə] is represented by *t'*. However, even in the representation of prepositions, pronouns, and conjunctions in unstressed positions, Eye Dialect is used very little in this first novel.

The same is not true, however, of *The Red Badge of Courage*. Crane is not concerned here with showing class differences, nor is there any effort to show that his soldiers come from a particular region of the United States and speak the dialect of that region. The dialect spellings Crane uses appear to be, for the most part, an attempt to convey the rough informality of the soldiers in camp and in battle. There is no appreciable difference in the speech of the generals and colonels and that of the privates. In both cases Crane makes heavy use of Eye Dialect to give the impression of informality. The following passage is typical and . . . shows how he goes about creating the effect he desires:

> Th' lieutenant, he ses: 'He's a jimhickey,' an' th' colonel, he ses: 'Ahem! he is indeed a very good man t'have, ahem! He kep' th' flag 'way t' th' front. I saw 'im.'[11]

This quotation is supposed to represent the speech of one of the soldiers, who is telling Henry Fleming of a conversation he has overheard between the lieutenant and the colonel. The most noticeable thing about the nonstandard spellings used is the replacing of various vowels in unstressed positions with apostrophes. *The* in unstressed position [ðə] is spelled *th'* four times, while unstressed *to* [tə] is spelled *t'* twice. Also *and* and *him* are spelled *an'* and *'im,* spellings that reflect a standard pronunciation of these two words in unstressed position—[æn] and [ɪm]. It can be seen

[9] Vincent Starrett, Introduction to *Maggie, A Girl of the Streets, and Other Stories* (New York: The Modern Library, 1933), p. 15.

[10] *Ibid.,* p. 271.

[11] Stephen Crane, *The Red Badge of Courage,* ed. Max J. Herzberg (New York: D. Appleton-Century Co., 1926), p. 207.

186   that Crane relies most heavily on Eye Dialect forms which indicate the effects of lack of stress on the pronunciation of certain words in a sentence. The effect on the reader is an impression of informality, without the definite feeling of ignorance and crudity that the dialect in *Maggie* produces. The soldiers and officers are, after all, not being portrayed as slum characters, but as men in surroundings and under conditions that make more formal language inappropriate.

Not all of Crane's Eye Dialect in *The Red Badge of Courage,* however, is of the type just discussed. A somewhat different type may be noted in the spelling *kep'* for *kept* in the passage quoted. Here lack of stress is not the factor involved. Instead it is the loss of the final [t] due to the initial [ð] of the following word. This is a loss that normally occurs in the standard pronunciation of *kept* when certain consonants follow ([č] being one of them). Also Crane uses a number of common Eye Dialect spellings such as *licker* for *liquor,*[12] *sed* for *said,*[13] and *minnit* for *minute.*[14] The nonstandard spelling *ses* for *says* is used frequently throughout the book wherever speech is depicted. It is obviously Eye Dialect, though the more usual Eye Dialect spelling is *sez.*

Crane allows a number of inconsistencies to creep into his use of Eye Dialect. Henry Fleming uses both *yestirday* and *yesterday* on the same page.[15] And there would appear to be an unnecessary apostrophe or else an unnecessary letter in the spelling *gota 'nough* for *got enough* [gɑtənʌf].

The fact that some errors manage to creep in does not, however, make the dialect of *The Red Badge of Courage* difficult reading. Since the book relies heavily on one particular kind of Eye Dialect—the substitution of alternate spellings in places where the standard spelling doesn't take into account the effect of lack of stress—and uses relatively little Substandard Dialect, the reader soon becomes adjusted to nonstandard spellings and has little trouble deciphering them. They prove to be quite effective in conveying the impression of informality.

---

[12] *Ibid.,* p. 9.

[13] *Ibid.,* p. 48.

[14] *Ibid.,* p. 137.

[15] *Ibid.,* p. 158.

Dialectology Versus Negro Dialect

W. Edward Farrison

In the following article, W. Edward Farrison defines the term
dialect as it should be used and understood by educated people.
He then discusses the "myth of Negro dialect" in the light
of modern scholarship in dialectology and with reference to
representations of "Negro dialect" in the works of American
authors, both Negro and white. He pinpoints a number of
misconceptions which have persisted among educated people
and even among educators. Dr. Farrison is Professor of
English at North Carolina Central University at Durham.

Generally familiar, I believe, is the story of the diffusion of languages
which resulted from the building of the Tower of Babel. It is indeed a
miraculous story but no more fanciful than many other pronouncements
about language have been—especially about dialect. For a long time the
popular notion has persisted that dialect is a more or less primitive, corrupted, or amusingly interesting group of speech habits which are quite

From *CLA Journal,* Vol. XIII, No. 1 (September, 1969) 21–26. Reprinted with the permission
of the College Language Association and W. Edward Farrison.

188   inferior to what is assumed to be standard speech, and which, therefore, stand condemned by it. So generally has the term *dialect* been used to mean this, that even for many otherwise well-educated people it seems to have no other meaning. Some thirty years ago, for example, when I began a study of the speech of illiterate Negroes of Guilford County, North Carolina, many persons told me that they did not know that there was anything "so unusual" about the Negro speech of the area, or that they thought that I could find much better samples of "Negro dialect" along the southern coast of South Carolina than anywhere else. After I finished the study, a Columbia University professor of English read it and remarked that he found nothing unusual in the dialect described in it. Apparently, to the persons just referred to, the study of dialect meant only the study of the unusual or the bizarre.

In the scientific study of language, the application of the term *dialect* to a group of speech habits does not necessarily mean that these habits are either corrupted, undeveloped, strikingly peculiar, or inferior in comparison with some other group of closely related speech habits. The term is used to refer to any group of speech habits which possess a considerably higher degree of homogeneity than is possessed by the larger body of speech habits to which they belong. It is presupposed, of course, that the smaller group is peculiar to a more or less clearly distinguishable class within the larger class to which the language as a whole belongs, for otherwise it would not remain homogeneous very long.[1]

It is in this sense that philologists speak of the ancient Greek and Roman dialects, the medieval dialects of French, English, and other languages, and the present-day dialects of the several modern languages. As philologists have also known for a long time, the differentiation of dialects resulted first from geographical isolation and second from the division of society into classes. In this fact are found the bases for distinguishing, although not mutually exclusively, regional and class dialects, the latter being what some linguists now call social dialects.

The dialects of Attica and Thrace, for instance, differed originally as regional dialects; but as Athens, the capital of Attica, emerged as the cultural capital of Greece, its prestige distinguished the Attic dialect as a class, or social, dialect somewhat superior to the dialects of the other Greek city-states. Likewise, when Paris and London became political and cultural capitals, their dialects became socially superior class dialects. On the contrary, in the United States no one city or region has ever

---

[1] Among Indo-European philologists, the term *dialect* is sometimes used to refer to what are more generally known as the branches of the Indo-European family of languages. See Henrik Birnbaum and Jaan Puhvel (editors), *Ancient Indo-European Dialects* (Berkeley and Los Angeles, 1966), Preface and *passim*.

achieved cultural preeminence, nor has any one regional dialect become preeminent as a class dialect—except in the opinions of the linguistically uninformed.

One of the earliest attempts by an American author to write what has become known as Negro dialect was made by Hugh Henry Brackenridge in his *Modern Chivalry,* Part 1, Volume II, which was first published in Philadelphia in 1792. In Book V, Chapter I of that volume, Brackenridge recorded an oration by an illiterate Negro slave named Cuff. One cannot tell from Brackenridge's transcriptions what he heard or thought he heard any Negro say. One can only deduce from the context that his c-a-s-h means *catch,* f-a-t means *what,* g-r-a-t-e means *great,* and i-b-e-d-y means *every.*

As the nineteenth century advanced, the writing of so-called Negro dialect became a vogue. As early as the 1850's William Wells Brown, a pioneering American Negro man of letters, contributed to this vogue. In several chapters in his *Clotel; Or, The President's Daughter,* which was published in London in 1853, and in his *The Escape,* a drama which was published in Boston in 1858, he tried, without remarkable success, to represent the speech of illiterate Negro slaves by means of mutilated spellings, ridiculous blends, malapropisms, and substandard grammar. Neither historians of American literature nor historians of American English refer to Brown's writing in dialect—if they refer to him at all. They generally refer not altogether accurately to Irwin Russell of Mississippi as a pioneer in this kind of writing, although he seems to have published nothing of this kind until the 1870's. By that time white writers of Negro dialect were rapidly multiplying, probably no more because they found in antebellum and postbellum Negro life suitable subjects for literature than because they found a ready market for this kind of writing, notably in *Scribner's Monthly.* Russell, Joel Chandler Harris, and Thomas Nelson Page early became most prominent in this group. Among others who figured in it for a while were Sidney Lanier and his brother Clifford.

When Paul Laurence Dunbar began writing late in the 1880's, he fell in with the vogue, and within ten years he wrote some of the best dialect poetry he ever wrote. Meanwhile, in *Harper's Weekly* for June 27, 1896, there appeared William Dean Howells's well-intentioned but none the less patronizing review of *Majors and Minors,* Dunbar's second book. Howells dismayed Dunbar by praising the minors—the dialect poems in the book—at the expense of the majors—the poems in standard English —in it. Howells's review not only heralded but also branded Dunbar as a dialect poet, which was indeed something less than he wanted to be considered. In a letter he wrote from London to a friend on March 15, 1897, he said, "I see now very clearly that Mr. Howells has done me

190   irrevocable harm in the dictum he laid down regarding my dialect verse."[2]
Four years later he explained to James Weldon Johnson that "You know,
of course, that I didn't start as a dialect poet. I simply came to the conclusion that I could write it as well, if not better, than anybody else I
knew of, and that by doing so I should gain a hearing. I gained the hearing, and now they don't want me to write anything but dialect."[3] In a
poem entitled "The Poet," in *Lyrics of Love and Laughter,* published in
1903, he complained that the world had turned from his poetry in standard English "to praise / A jingle in a broken tongue."

At the turn of the nineteenth and twentieth centuries, somewhat under
the influence of Dunbar, Johnson wrote an appreciable amount of dialect
poetry, some of which he eventually collected under the heading "Jingles
and Croons" in his *Fifty Years and Other Poems,* which was published
in 1917. But having found dialect too narrow a medium of expression,
he experimented successfully with the representation of the speech of
illiterate and semiliterate Negroes without using Negro dialect. One of
his first successful experiments was "The Creation," which was published
in *The Freeman* in 1918, and which he made the first sermon in *God's
Trombones* when he published that volume in 1927. In the meantime, in
the Preface to his *The Book of American Negro Poetry*, first published in
1922, he briefly explained his views concerning Negro dialect. In his opinion that was a medium suitable for the expression of only two moods,
namely, humor and pathos—the two moods which traditionally but
erroneously had been assumed to be peculiarly characteristic of Negroes.
He argued quite correctly that there were phases of Negro life, like those
of the lives of other people, which could not be treated in Negro dialect
"either adequately or artistically."

Johnson did a great deal to close the school of dialect poetry, but he
did not succeed, alas, in eradicating many misconceptions concerning
dialect which often prevail where one would not expect to find them.
Illustrative of these are the popular notions to which I referred at the
beginning of this discussion. Basic among these misconceptions is the
notion that there is such an entity as Negro dialect; that is, a group of
speech habits which are the result of Negroness rather than the product
of regional and class influences, which in fact they are. It was this notion
which led Richard Wright to assume that a voice he heard over a telephone one day in 1942 was, says one of his biographers, "that of a Negro
or a Southern male";[4] and it still leads many into snap judgments that

---

[2] Quoted by William Stanley Braithwaite in *The New Negro: An Interpretation,* edited by
Alain Locke (New York, 1925), p. 38.

[3] James Weldon Johnson, *Along This Way* (New York, 1933), p. 160.

[4] Constance Webb, *Richard Wright: A Biography* (New York, 1968), p. 230.

somebody talks or does not talk "like a Negro." As dialectologists know, there is no such entity as Negro dialect nor a racial dialect of any other kind. If there were, one might well expect to find a Jewish German dialect in Germany, a Jewish French dialect in France, a Jewish Spanish dialect in Spain, a Jewish British dialect in Great Britain, and a Jewish American dialect as well as a Negro dialect in America, for Jews have been in all of these countries for centuries—certainly long enough for linguistic adaptations to occur.

Incidentally, a seemingly trivial but indeed troublesome question comes to mind. If Negro dialect is a function of Negroness, how much of a Negro need one be for it to be endemic to him? Is it fully characteristic of only full-blooded Negroes, fifty percent characteristic of mulattoes, twenty-five percent characteristic of quadroons, and so on? Or should Negroness be considered an immeasurable sociological quality, which is basically a matter of class, and which, therefore, leads back to the consideration of the speech habits in question as the product of regional and class influences, without regard to the imponderable called race?

Other misconceptions concerning so-called Negro dialect pertain especially to vocabulary, grammar, and pronunciation. The differences between the vocabulary and the grammar of this dialect and those of general American English have long been much more imaginary than real. Ever so many of the words and locutions and most of the substandard grammar which have been said to be characteristic of Negro dialect have been current at one time or another in almost every section of the United States, including areas in which the number of Negroes has always been incomparably small. This fact is supported by the numerous word lists which have been published in *Dialect Notes* since 1900 and by many articles which have appeared in *American Speech* since its beginning in 1925.

The worst and most notable feature of this dialect is its representation —rather, misrepresentation—of pronunciations by various misspellings. Many of these are only mutilated English. They are only what has been called eye-dialect, something which has been made to look different but which signifies nothing unusual. When, for example, one writes *We'n'sday* as Joel Chandler Harris did, or *Cun'l* as Thomas Nelson Page did, or d-u-z or i-z or s-e-z, he indicates nothing different from the respective pronunciations *Wednesday, colonel, does, is,* and *says* have in the several varieties of standard American English. And still worse, many of the misspellings tell the reader nothing in particular about pronunciation. When, for instance, Irwin Russell wrote *Mahrs John*, Page wrote "he kyahn git no perter," Harris wrote *Whoa,* and James Weldon Johnson wrote *prah*, just what pronunciations, one wonders, did they mean to in-

192   dicate respectively for *master, can't,* what one says to stop a horse, and the word *prayer?*

As phoneticians have long known, the dialectal peculiarities of the several languages can be accurately represented, not by the twenty-six letters of the ordinary alphabet, but only by the phonetic alphabet. Of course, writers cannot write in this alphabet for ordinary purposes, but they need not write either mutilated English or phonetic script to convincingly approximate regional or class dialects. They can do so by means of vocabulary, grammar, homely figures of speech, context, etc. This is what Johnson did in *God's Trombones* and what Langston Hughes did more extensively in his books about Jesse B. Simple. The preacher in Johnson's "The Prodigal Son" intoned, "Young man—/Young man—/ Your arm's too short to box with God"; and on one occasion Simple said, "My wife is the most opera-listening woman I know."[5] In these remarks these characters revealed themselves more effectively than pages of mutilated English would have done. Moreover they argued well by example in behalf of dialectology, the scientific study of dialects, versus the myth of Negro dialect.

[5] James Weldon Johnson, *God's Trombones: Seven Negro Sermons in Verse* (New York, 1927), p. 21. Langston Hughes, *Simple's Uncle Sam* (New York, 1965), p. 40.

Poe's Use
of Negro Dialect
in "The Gold-Bug"

Eric Stockton

Although Negro characters appear in several Poe stories, Jupiter is Poe's only speaking Negro. In this article, Eric Stockton, Professor of English at the University of Tennessee, offers a thorough analysis of Jupiter's "Negro dialect," an example of literary dialect as used by antebellum writers. He believes the main purpose of the dialect is to "show low social status, not regional *mise en scene*." Several literary conventions, noted by Professor Stockton, had a bearing on the development of Jupiter as a character and on the representation of his dialect; some of these served to maintain the social distance required in antebellum society. Of particular interest to students of literary dialect are stereotypic elements underlying these early conventions and the effect of the conventions on both the language and the behavior of characters they govern.

194   Poe's use of Negro dialect has received severe condemnation.[1] The judgment of the great Poe scholar Killis Campbell will serve as representative: ". . . such examples of the Negro dialect as Poe attempts are stiff and unconvincing."[2] Ten years later Professor Campbell saw no reason to change this opinion in his "Poe's Treatment of the Negro and of the Negro Dialect"[3]; for seven pages he admirably characterizes Poe's sentimentally pro-Southern and passionately pro-slavery outlook, but devotes only a brief page of complaints to the dialect. It is the conclusion of this paper that Poe's use of Negro dialect in "The Gold-Bug" demonstrates reasonable competence and possesses some interest for the study of language and literature.

The Negro appears or is mentioned by Poe in six other tales and sketches—"How to Write a Blackwood Article," "A Predicament," "The Man Who Was Used Up," "The Oblong Box," "The Journal of Julius Rodman," and "The Elk"—as well as Poe's one novel, *The Narrative of A. Gordon Pym;* but he plays a speaking role only in "The Gold-Bug." Hence the data for analyzing the dialect are not as full as desirable. But in "The Gold-Bug," the old body-servant Jupiter makes some 46 utterances consisting of 1031 words, which is as much dialect as many a full-length novel affords, and enough of a corpus to allow some observations. Moreover, in this story, for which Poe exerted considerable effort to achieve verisimilitude,[4] he does not indulge in such dialectal farcicality as that of "The Devil in the Belfry," for example. (That story takes place in the old Dutch borough of Vondervotteimittiss, the proposed etymology of the place name being "Donder und Blitzen.")[5]

Poe carefully revised "The Gold-Bug," rightly thinking the story one of his best. Despite his attempt for accuracy, however, he is guilty of a basic linguistic inconsistency: Jupiter is a manumitted slave who has followed his master Legrand, "of an ancient Huguenot family," from New Orleans to Sullivan's Island off the Charleston coast. To localize the atmosphere

From *Studies in Language and Linguistics in Honor of Charles C. Fries,* ed. Albert H. Marckwardt, (Ann Arbor: The English Language Institute, The University of Michigan, 1964) pp. 249–270. Reprinted with the permission of the English Language Institute and Eric Stockton.

[1] *Poe's Short Stories*, ed. Killis Campbell (New York: Harcourt, Brace, 1927) p. xx.

[2] *The University of Texas Bulletin*, No. 3626, Studies in English, No. 16 (July 1936) pp. 106–114.

[3] It is a pleasure to thank Professors Albert H. Marckwardt and James Downer for their encouragement and helpful criticism of this paper.

[4] See Arthur Hobson Quinn, *Edgar Allan Poe: A Critical Biography* (New York: Appleton-Century, 1941) pp. 129–132 and 393: *The Gold-Bug* ed. Thomas Ollive Mabbott, with a Foreword by Hervey Allen (New York: Rimington and Hooper, 1928) pp. xx–xxiv.

[5] There is much of this verbal frivolity in Poe, but perhaps his use of the French and Cockney dialects will pass inspection. Van Wyck Brooks rightly commends Poe's Irish (*The World of Washington Irving* [New York: Dutton 1944], p. 280) as "no less good natured than clever." But any purported *German* dialect with a "Mynheer Herman" speaking it simply will not do.

of the tale, Poe gives the Louisianian Jupiter's speech something of the
flavor of the Southeastern coastal region, in part by using some Gullahisms.[6] Thus if one kind of regional accuracy is lost, another kind is partly
gained. The main purpose of the dialect, however, is to show low social
status, not regional *mise en scène*. Surely it was not Poe's intention to
imply that because of long residence in South Carolina, Jupiter had
picked up some speech traits of Negroes there and superimposed them
on his former dialect. There is no such accurate linguistic geography in
"The Gold-Bug," just as there is very little in the brief observations of the
several critics who have reprimanded Poe for failure to reproduce a
Charleston dialect, or some hypothetically unvarying national Negro
speech.

It should be noted here that at the time Poe wrote the story—1843—
there was very possibly a literary convention of having Negro body-serv-
ants speak a *quasi*-Gullah, regardless of the fictional locale. This theory
is considered below. Following another literary convention, Poe does not
have the two Southern gentlemen in "The Gold-Bug" speaking Southern
dialect. Nor is there any reason that he should, for most authors do not
represent dialectally what is standard speech to them.[7] Poe's own speech
was Southern. He spent his formative years in and around Richmond and
always thought of himself as a Virginia aristocrat.[8] He does not show
Jupiter's speech as *r*-less, because there was no difference in this regard
between Jupiter's pronunciation and his own—or that of the whites in the
story. Consequently, there was no need to call attention to the fact that
Jupiter would pronounce *here* and *hear* as [hɪə] or *paper* as /pepə/, these
pronunciations being "standard" for Poe.

These brief remarks about postvocalic *r* call attention to two important
qualifications of the term "Negro dialect" as used in this paper: First, the
term should not be understood to mean that any particular linguistic

---

[6] A nonlinguistic inconsistency that has escaped many annotators is that on Sullivan's Island,
where much of "The Gold-Bug"'s action takes place in and under a huge tulip tree, "No trees
of any magnitude are to be seen" (p. 95). All quotations from the text of "The Gold-Bug" are
taken from *The Complete Works of Edgar Allan Poe,* ed. James A. Harrison (New York: Crowell,
1902), V, 95–142. A convenient edition in which the text of Jupiter's speeches is almost exactly
the same as in Harrison's edition is *The Selected Poetry and Prose of Edgar Allan Poe,* ed. T. O.
Mabbott, Modern Library (New York: Random House, 1951), pp. 249–279. A few contractions
are spelled differently in this edition.

[7] Sumner Ives, "A Theory of Literary Dialect," *Tulane Studies in English.* II (1950), 151 ff.,
esp. 159.

[8] Killis Campbell, *The Mind of Poe and Other Studies* (Cambridge, Mass.: Harvard University
Press, 1933), pp. 113, *n.* 2, and 115. It may be added here that Poe was not reluctant to criticize
the South; see pp. 122 and 125.

For five years, beginning in 1815 when he was six, Poe lived with his foster-parents in England. This period very likely contributed to his retaining an *r*-less speech. His Southern speech
is also of some significance for his poetry. For example, Poe rhymes "kissed her," "vista," and
"sister" in "Ulalume," 11. 72, 75, 78. These were pure rhymes for him, not "Cockneyisms."

196 feature to which it applies is completely confined to Negroes in contradistinction to whites. Conceivably, any linguistic usage associated with Negroes in the minds of white speakers is also employed by some whites, no matter how few. Second, the term "Negro dialect" does not mean that all Negroes, especially Southern Negroes, had at the time of the story or now have any particular linguistic feature, whether phonological, morphological, syntactic, or lexical. These two qualifications do not render the term "Negro dialect" meaningless, but emphasize that it represents a quantitative judgment, in regard both to the dialect as a whole and to the details the sum of which composes the dialect.

To return to Poe's own Southern speech briefly, it is impossible to gather much about it from "The Gold-Bug," but it does make clear Poe's joke in the very first sentence that Jupiter speaks (p. 98). His master Legrand begins to comment on the bug's *antennæ* when Jupiter interrupts, "Dey aint *no* tin in him, Massa Will. . . ." Professor Campbell objects that Poe "reads somehow the word 'tin' out of 'antennae.' Such stupidity is meant perhaps as humor, but the reader finds little humor in it."[9] Not if the reader is a Northerner who has ever felt the amused if momentary bafflement of being asked, say, by a Tennessee or Oklahoma girl whether he can "lind" her a "pin." Many regions of the United States, including Poe's own Richmond and the South Carolina of the story, lack a contrast between the phonemes /ɛ/ and /ɪ/ before nasals. Hence, it is quite plausible for Jupiter, suffering from both entymological and etymological confusion, to analogize the second syllable of the Latin word with "tin." (Jupiter's customary aphesis of initial unstressed syllables is dealt with below.) The syllable would sound very much like "tin" to Poe, too, despite his awareness of the "correct" difference.

Professor Campbell rightly objects to Poe's spelling of *rap* for "wrap," *nose* for "knows," *dare* for "there," and *syphon* for "ciph'n'" ("ciphering"). Such needless misspelling is "eye-dialect." It serves the unfair purpose either of implying that a pronunciation is substandard when it is actually a variety of standard, or of claiming that an unlettered person would adopt the homonymous or otherwise incorrect spellings given him, were he to write the words in question. The proportion of eye-dialect is one criterion of an author's skill or lack of it in handling literary dialect. Poor writers, including those of many so-called comic strips, often overdo such misspellings. Even the best writers, however, seldom avoid them entirely, so some instances of eye-dialect are not sufficient in themselves to condemn Poe. Furthermore, some eye-dialect spellings assist an author in establishing spelling-phoneme correlations. His other uses of it are: *bin* for "been" (twice), *cum* (twice), *enuff* and *nuff*, *feered* and *feerd* for

---

[9] "Poe's Treatment of the Negro and of the Negro Dialect," p. 113.

"feared" ("afraid"), *fru* for "frough" ("through"), *gose* for "ghos'," *pisset* for " 'pistle," *sep* for " 'cep' " ("except") and *trubble*, as well as two spellings analyzed below, *fuss* for "fus,' " ("first") and *soldiers* for "shoulders." At the very most, only eighteen words in Jupiter's speech appear as eye-dialect, and in a frequency amounting to some twenty-four times or roughly two percent of the total. Some of these spellings, moreover, are not amiss. (These figures ignore the doubling of *r* in *berry* and of *b* in *debbil*, *ebber*, and *hebby*, spellings which insure the vowel /ɛ/ in these words; "never" occurs both as *nebber* and *neber*.)

While eye-dialect is orthographical overstatement of affectation, regionalism or illiteracy, good literary dialect, on the other hand, is of necessity a kind of understatement. It is of course too much to expect that the English alphabet can indicate with precision certain phonetic features of Jupiter's speech. Poe cannot indicate whether a [d] is dental or alveolar in contrast with whichever is "normal" in his conception of his own standard, or even whether he was aware of such a possible difference. Similarly, the printed page does not show the phonetic nature of Jupiter's *b* as substituted for *v* in *neber*. The spelling is merely a clue that Jupiter's *v* does not have the "standard" pronunciation but one that sounds something like *b*, the actual phonetic value of which is probably the voiced bilabial spirant [β]. It had become the reasonable and conventional compromise by Poe's time to indicate this Negro pronunciation by *b*. The spelling *berry* for "very" is not crudity; indeed, it is hard to find the word spelled any other way in early Negro dialect.

Poe's Negro dialect does not show phonetic values for their own sake. As is true of so many linguistic phenomena, the basic method of literary dialect is contrast. Since there is no significant contrast in Legrand's pronunciation of "long-i" as in *life* with Jupiter's, there is no need to adopt the hypothetical spelling "lahf" for either character. But when Legrand orders Jupiter to *take this beetle,* and the Negro objects *what for mus tote de bug?,* there is far-reaching phonetic, syntactical, and lexical contrast. This contrastive method serves the basic purpose of literary dialect, which is also contrast,[10] in this story a social rather than a regional one, despite

[10] Such contrast can operate in a number of ways. There can be regional contrast within the upper class, as in Peter de Vries' story "Split-Level" (*The New Yorker*, June 9, 1956): " 'Have you seen Tom?' he asked. 'Tom who?' 'Tom magazine' " (p. 106). There can be social contrast within a group even when most nonmembers preconceive that those within the group will have the same dialect. For an example involving Negroes, see Bucklin Moon's penetrating novel *Without Magnolias* (New York: Doubleday, 1948), in which the respectable Negroes North and South speak almost indistinguishably from the whites, while colored riffraff uses Negro dialect. For an example involving upper-class Southern whites see George W. Cable, *Gideon's Band: A Tale of the Mississippi* (New York: Scribners, 1914), pp. 470–472; here a passel of Dixie belles sets itself apart from its compeers, turning on the charm by means of a wonderfully exaggerated Southern speech.

198   some regional qualities in Jupiter's speech. Yet the dialect in the story has more than once been attacked solely for lack of regionalism.

Since there have been so many hasty and subjective condemnations of Poe's use of Negro dialect, the rest of this paper is largely devoted to a thorough-going analysis of Jupiter's speech. This detailed critique should determine the acceptability or inacceptability of that speech by making possible a quantitative judgment, perhaps the only kind possible upon a literary dialect, but one which Poe has not received. Some interpretive generalizations then follow. Poe's inconsistencies are noted in passing. It should be understood that the analysis does not make silent reference to the speech of the two white men in the story. The first three sections of the analysis attempt to establish the phonemic contrasts between Poe's own dialect (or at times simply standard English) and Jupiter's Negro dialect. The cumulative effect of the literary dialect results in a plausible mixture of Negro, Southeastern Coastal, and widespread substandard forms, all of which show social contrast with the presumed speech of Poe.

PHONOLOGY OF STRESSED VOWELS[11]

/i/ receives its conventional spellings in such words as *be, feel,* and *speak*. It substitutes for /ɛ/ in *eend* and for /ɪ/ in *leetle* (also spelled *little*), old-fashioned pronunciations not yet extinct in the Southeastern Coastal area (hereafter referred to as SEC). Joel Chandler Harris' Uncle Remus pronounced the two words in this fashion. The latter Negro spoke a Middle Georgia dialect. It is of some literary and linguistic interest, however, at times to compare Poe's representations with those of Harris, an acknowledged master of literary dialect, especially since Uncle Remus and Jupiter are not too far removed from each other in time, geography, and social status.

/ɪ/ receives its conventional spellings in such words as *bit, queerest,* and *sick*, and serves several dialectal uses. /ɪ/ occurs for /i/ in *nigger* (regarding this and *Negro* as the same word in this dialect) and for /ɛ/ in *git*, pronunciations common in many regions of the country. It also occurs for /ɛ/ in *gin* "again," a frequent colloquialism. The pronunciation *tin* has been treated above. /ɪ/ (or /ɨ/) occurs for /ʌ/ in *sich*, heard in several regional dialects, and in *jis*, a very common colloquialism. (Poe also writes *just*.)

[ɪə] receives its conventional spellings in *here* and *near*. (Allowing for the alternation of [kwɪərɪst] with [kwɪrɪst], *queerest* could also be placed here.)

---

[11] My debt in the phonological portion of this paper is heavy to Professor Sumner Ives' excellent study, "The Phonology of the Uncle Remus Stories," *PADS*, No. 22 (Nov. 1954).

It substitutes for Poe's own "standard" /ɜ/ in *heered,* and is a possible pronunciation for Jupiter, although [hjɜd] or [hjɪɜd] is now more likely for a Negro in the SEC area. The form *feerd* (also *feered, feared*) "afraid" is a well-known conservatism in substandard English. [ɪɚ] also occurs for [ɛɚ] (or [æɚ]) in *keer* "care" and *skeerd,* fairly common usages in the SEC area today.

/e/ receives its conventional spellings in such words as *break, day, spade,* and *weigh.* It occurs unconventionally only in *dey* (twice), as shown in the illiterate usage *Dey aint bin noffin,* in which "they" is falsely analogized to the expletive "there."

/a/ receives its conventional spellings in *not, rotten, solid,* etc. It replaces "standard" /ɜ/ in *-marcy, sarcumstance,* and *sartain.* This pronunciation is a common dialectal conservatism retained as standard in a few words, such as *sergeant.* /a/ substitutes for /æ/ in *cotch,* an analogical form of "catch" used as a preterite.[12] (Cf. Uncle Remus' "fetch/fotch".) /a/ also substitutes for /æ/ in the common Negro pronunciation /masə/. /mæsə/ is unlikely for *massa;* many dialect writers insure the pronunciation /a/ by an "ar" spelling such as "marster" or "marse" for this word. (Cf. the Cockney spelling "'arf" for *half.*) Poe himself uses the same "ar" spelling for this very purpose in *arter* "after."

The "ar" spelling indicates [aɚ] (prevocalic [aɚr]) to replace "standard" [ɛɚ] (or [æɚ] in *dar, nowhar,* and *whar,* though the use of *dare* upsets the pattern by seemingly indicating a "standard" phoneme. The same spelling also indicates a "standard" [aɚ] (prevocalically [aɚr]) in *far.* Again Poe upsets the pattern by writing *fur* [fɜ]. Here as elsewhere, however, Jupiter uses his own pronunciation first, and then shifts to a "standard" one just after hearing it used by one of the two white men.

/ɔ/ receives its conventional spellings in *all, off, pon* "upon," *cause* "because," *claws,* etc. The sound occurs in this dialect's *on-pleasant,* the only instance of the prefix *un-* in Jupiter's speech. This prefix (which receives either primary or secondary stress) and the word *hungry* have the vowel /ɔ/ in the speech of Negroes in several parts of the South, and are often spelled "aw" as in Uncle Remus' "hawngry." Poe's observation, as often, is correct. In his *Africanisms in the Gullah Dialect,* Dr. Lorenzo Turner says that the sound of [ɒ] for [ʌ] is a Gullah feature.[13]

/o/ receives its conventional spellings in *so, fore* "before," *four, own, gose* "ghost," etc. It does not seem to be used as a dialectal substitution.

---

[12] In his *A Survey of Verb Forms in the Eastern United States* (Ann Arbor: University of Michigan Press, 1953), E. Bagby Atwood records the preterite of "catch" with the pronunciation [katš] for some Negroes and old whites in the South Atlantic states; s.v. "Catch," p. 8. See also p. 266 and n. 36 below.

[13] (Chicago: University of Chicago Press, 1949), p. 18.

200   Poe did not indicate the pronunciations [po], [polɪ], and [jo] (or [poə̯],
[poə̯lɪ], and [joə̯] for *poor, poorly,* and *your.* These pronunciations were
(and are) commoner in the SEC than those with /u/ or /ʊ/ with in-glide
/ə̯/, although both the latter occurred.

The converse is true of *sure.* Uncle Remus and many other Negroes
said "sho'" but /ʃʊə̯/ is commoner in the SEC area today, and Jupiter
could have said it. /ʊ/ also receives its conventional spellings in *curous*
/kjʊrəs/, *good,* and *put.* It substitutes for /ɪ/ or /ɨ/ in *putty* "pretty," often
spelled "pooty" by dialect writers. But the spelling *putty* is allowable, by
analogy with *put.*

/u/ receives its conventional spellings in such words as *fool, shoe,* and
you, and an eye-dialect spelling in *fru* "through." The word *goole,* which
occurs consistently nine times (including the compound *goole-bug*), is not
a grotesque pun on "ghoul" primarily, but an interesting survival of the
conservative pronunciation of "gold" as /guld/. This pronunciation is
historically correct and was used as late as the nineteenth century,
"though by that time it was doubtless old-fashioned" (H. C. Wyld, *A
History of Modern Colloquial English,* 3rd ed. [New York: Dutton, 1937],
p. 239). The "double-o" spelling is hence not eye-dialect, nor is it in *troof,
noovers,* and *boosed,* wherein it also insures the vowel /u/. The pronunciation of these latter two words undoubtedly indicates a retracted form of
the diphthong [ɪu], and therefore meant a substandard usage to Poe.
Southerners still widely regard this diphthong as "standard" in such
words as *news* and *Tuesday.*[14] The spellings are not completely fair to
Jupiter, however, for /ɪu/ after /r/, in such a word as *truth,* is very rare in
the United States; /ɪu/ in *maneuvers* is unhistorical and possibly an affectation when it occurs; and /u/ in *abused* is not fully plausible: /ɪu/ after
labials is still retained in nearly everyone's speech, as in *beauty, few,* and
mule, although some writers use "bootiful" as a Negroism.

/ʌ/ receives its conventional spellings in many words. A few are *mus*
"must," *noffin* and *notin* "nothing," *skull,* and *trouble* (also spelled
trubble.) The spelling *fuss,* while conventional for "fuss," is also dialectal
for /fɜs/ "first" in Jupiter's speech. /fɜs/ is a well attested form for "first,"
but to avoid eye-dialect this latter word might well have been *fus'.* But
Poe is very fond of using eye-dialect for this sound: *cum, enuff,* and other
examples have already been cited. He might well have indicated colloquial pronunciations for *what* and *was,* for Jupiter probably said /hwʌt/
or /wʌt/ and /wʌz/, like Uncle Remus. Poe indicates the sound correctly
for dialectal purposes in *rudder* "rather," where /ʌ/ substitutes for /æ/.

/ɜ/ (prevocalically /ɜr/) receives its conventional spelling in *worf*

---

[14] By the same token Somerset Maugham has Mildred Rogers in *Of Human Bondage* use the
"vulgar" pronunciation "stoodent," a spelling which puzzles Midwestern collegians, who
seldom hear the word pronounced any other way.

"worth," and occurs dialectally in *fur* "far," although Poe also writes "far." /fɜ/ (rather than /fʌ/) is an attested SEC pronunciation for "standard" /faɚ/. Similarly, *fudder* [fɜdə] occurs for "further" or conceivably "farther."

/ɑu/ receives its conventional spelling in *bout* "about," *out*, and *widout*. It occurs as a dialectal form only in *mought*, a substandard conservatism still heard in various regions of the South and elsewhere.

/ɑɪ/ receives its conventional spellings in *buying, I, mind,* and *sky*. It appears as a dialect form only in the common Negro usage *gwine*, which Jupiter undoubtedly would pronounce as [gwɑɚn].

/ɛ/, /ɔɪ/, and /æ/ do not occur dialectally in Jupiter's speech, which is an indication of the limitation of the corpus.

UNSTRESSED VOWELS

There are not many changes of spelling to indicate dialectal or colloquial pronunciations of unstressed vowels in Jupiter's speech. He undoubtedly used the /ə/ and /ɪ/ (or /ɨ/) of general English, and they are not substituted for each other in the dialect, each receiving its etymological spellings in all occurrences of unstressed syllables, except in *syphon* "ciphering" and *massa*. Examples of /ə/ in open syllables are *de* (once spelled *the*) for *the* (probably /də/ even prevocalically), and *massa*. /ə/ occurs epenthetically (or as an "*a*-prefix") in *I keep a tellin* and *he keep a syphon* "ciphering," a usage Uncle Remus shares, and which is a conservatism going back to an old indefinite article before a verbal noun. /ə/ in closed syllables occurs in *ob* and *of, blessed* and *departed, little* and *trouble,* and *rotten*. Uncle Remus is more phonetic with "blessid," and it is quite likely that both Poe and Jupiter said this, too. Hence there would be no need to re-spell.

As noted above, Jupiter's speech is *r*-less, so final -*er* regularly indicates /ə/, as in *answer, matter,* and *nigger,* etc. The spelling *fer* "for" is /fə/, and is thus differentiated from *fur* /fɜ/ meaning "far." Uncle Remus makes this same distinction between *fer* and *fur;* unfortunately, Poe upsets the pattern by also writing both *far* and *for*. Three spellings show /ə/ in words having "standard" /ɪɚ/ or /jə/: *curous* /kjʊrəs/, *figgurs* /fɪgəz/, and *ventur* /vɛntə/. This lack of palatalization in final unstressed syllables, perhaps a conservatism, occurs in a variety of dialects, including Uncle Remus'. It is possible that /ə/ is substituted for /jə/ in *soldiers* "shoulders" in the same fashion.

/ɪ/ (or /ɨ/) receives its etymological spellings in all positions. As a final open syllable it is consistently "y" as in *berry* "very," *ebery* "every," *mighty, putty* "pretty," etc. In closed syllables it is once "ai" in *sartain;*

202   otherwise "i" as in *buying, debbil, funnin, looking, notin* "nothing," *solid,*
and *tellin.* Its sole non-etymological spelling is the eye-dialect *syphon*
"ciphering," a spelling which also involves substitution by folk etymology.
But it does not receive dialectal spelling, as it does in Uncle Remus'
"Atlanty," "baskit," "blessid," and "eddycation."

The spelling *hollo* indicates /'halo/, another standard pronunciation
of an unstressed vowel.

CONSONANTS

Poe's changes of consonantal spellings to convey dialectal
effect demonstrate acceptable if not complete consistency, and reasonable fidelity to actual colloquial and Negro speech practices. Given certain phonetic contexts, it is usually not difficult to interpret the "standard"
value of most consonants in the corpus. Attention will therefore be given
here only to the departures from conventional spelling. It may be pointed
out here that Poe does not use the apostrophe to indicate dialectal omissions of letters from conventional spellings, so he is behind some of his
contemporaries in the employment of this handy orthographical device.
He reserves the apostrophe for its conventional uses in contractions and
with genitives, with the exceptions that Jupiter always says *aint* (or *taint*)
and uses *'t was—twas* and *'t is—tis* indiscriminately.

/b/ for /v/ and /d/ for /ð/ make up the most familiar consonantal
substitutions to show Negro dialect in nineteenth-century American fiction. In Jupiter's speech /b/ occurs regularly for initial /v/ in *berry,* for
medial /v/ in *debbil* and *debbil's, ebery,* and *sabage,* and for final /v/ in
fibe, gib, and *hab.* (Poe might well have doubled the medial consonant
in all these words, to insure retention of the original stressed vowel.)
Jupiter says *ob* twelve times and *of* three times, which is undoubtedly an
oversight on Poe's part rather than an indication of his awareness that
this word receives more than one pronunciation in many varieties of
English. Phonetic contexts do not demonstrate any distribution: Poe
writes *ob de* and *of de.* Except for the /v/ in *blieve,* the only other inconsistency is *noovers* "maneuvers." Perhaps "noobers" would have been
too remote from standard spelling to enable a confident guess at the
word, although *syphon* for "ciphering" is just as obscure.

/d/ is found regularly for /ð/ in all positions. It is seen initially in
dan "than," *dar* and *dare* "there," *dat, de* (once *the*), *dem, den* "then,"
dey "they," and *dis.* The same substitution is consistent for medial /ð/,
as in *fudder* "farther," *todder* "the other," and *widout.* In final position
/d/ occurs for /ð/ in *wid.* These last two words show what are still predominantly Negro pronunciations in the SEC region. Final /d/ is "lost"

after /l/ and /r/ in *goole* and *Lor-* and retained somewhat unexpectedly in the final consonant cluster /nd/ of *eend, hand,* and *mind,* where Uncle Remus "loses" it. These last three spellings may indicate that there was no contrast between the author's speech and the dialect.

/t/ is a common Negro dialect substitution for /θ/ in all positions, but Poe's regular practice is to use it only initially, as in *ting, tink,* and *tree* "three." It does occur medially in *notin* "nothing," but standard /θ/ also becomes /f/ medially in *noffin* "nothing" and initially in *fru* "through"; false regression causes Jupiter's plausible divided usage in this regard. For the final /θ/ and /ð/ in most varieties of English, he uses /f/, in *mouff, syfe* "scythe," and *worf.* Of these, *mouff* is well attested in the SEC area for Negroes, and by analogy the labiodental for the voiced interdental of "scythe" is also plausible.

Historical /t/ is "lost" in *massa,* a very common Negro pronunciation, and *pissel* "epistle," an eye-dialect spelling for a word which has syncopated the /t/ sound in Modern English. Capable of a thousand outrageous puns, Poe may have intended one here on "pizzle." Final /t/ after voiceless consonants is regularly omitted: *fuss* "first," *gose* "ghost," *jis* (Poe also writes *just*), *lef* (both where /t/ is inflectional and morphemic), *mos* "almost," *sep* "except," and *sis* "insist." Final /t/ is retained after voiced sounds, as in *bit, don't, wouldn't,* etc. A nice bit of transcription is *mus go,* without the /t/, versus *must ha got,* with prevocalic /t/ retained.

The spelling *ventur* indicates the pronunciation /t/ rather than /tʃ/, possibly a substitution but more likely an extreme conservatism. It is common in words such as *pasture* in more than one variety of Southern speech, including that of the SEC.

Poe should have observed more consistent handling of "-ing" forms. He indicates the alveolar nasal /n/ in *noffin* and *notin* "nothing," *funnin, gittin, syphon* "ciphering," and *tellin,* but the velar nasal /ŋ/ in *beating, buying,* and *looking.* Although divided usage is common among even educated speakers of American English, such division on Jupiter's part was probably mere oversight on Poe's part. He might better have retained the conservative pronunciation, the alveolar /n/, for Jupiter throughout.

/j/ and postvocalic /r/ have been treated above under unstressed vowels, although it does remain to point out that even intervocalic /r/ is "lost" in the pronunciation *syphon* for "ciphering." Another syncopation is that of /f/ in *arter.*

The respellings *sarcumstance* and *sartain,* with historical *c* replaced, are obviously to preserve /s/ in these words.

Jupiter's substitution by folk etymology of *soldiers* for "shoulders" has been attacked as an absurdity, since the Negro of course would know the meanings of both words. It is necessary to consider, however, whether

204   in addition to being eye-dialect the substitution might be plausible phonetically. The unstressed syllable in each word could readily have the same sound, namely /əz/. The difficulty concerns the initial consonant. Poe had spent considerable time in Gullah-speaking areas and "The practice of substituting [ʃ] for the English [s] is fairly common among the Gullah: e.g., / ʃʌm/ "see them," / ʃoda/ "soda," / ʃup/ "soup," etc.[15] It is not therefore utterly inconceivable that Jupiter said /ʃoldəz/ for both "shoulders" and "soldiers," though it must be admitted that this puts an unfair burden upon the reader. Uncle Remus substitutes an occasional /ʃ/ for /s/ but only postvocalically as in "slishe," so this is probably not the same feature.

    There is a similarly tentative explanation for Jupiter's misunderstanding of *claws* for *cause*. If only Jupiter had used "kase" /kez/, a common Negro pronunciation of "because," then it would be easy to think that a very ready analogy to /kɔz/ in his speech would be *claws*, with the intrusion of only one consonant. But alas, a moment later he says *cause* for "because" (with aphesis of the initial unstressed syllable). Poe had undoubtedly heard the pronunciation /kez/ and it may have been in the back of his mind to have Jupiter say this a moment later. If so, he forgot to give further plausibility to the *cause-claws* pun by having the pronunciation /kɔz/ unfamiliar to Jupiter. This effect defective comes by *cause*. Poe was primarily interested in the white narrator's deliberate but good-humored mystification of the old servant by the question, "And what cause have you, Jupiter, for such a supposition?"

STRESS MODIFICATION

    Such features as sentence intonation being impossible, or nearly impossible, to describe on the basis of orthography, the last feature of pronunciation to be considered here will deal with segments no longer than individual words. It is true that Poe's liberal use of italics, dashes, and exclamation points indicates anything but a monotone for Jupiter's intonation, but a more exact description of it cannot be given. (The speech of the two white men, by the way, likewise reveals Poe's fondness for these punctuational tricks.) As is true of Uncle Remus' dialect, the most apparent stress modification consists of reduction of stress.[16] There is syncope within three words: *blieve, syphon* "ciphering," and *spose* "suppose." There is reduction of four words lightly stressed in conversation: "have" becomes /ə/ in *he must ha got;* "of" or conceivably "have" be-

[15] Turner, *Africanisms in the Gullah Dialect,* pp. 245–246.

[16] Ives, "The Phonology of the Uncle Remus Stories," pp. 56–58.

comes /ə/ in *Lor-gol-a-marcy;* "it" is reduced to only its consonant in the frequent words *taint, tis,* and *twas;* and "them" becomes *em* /əm/, a common conservatism of the very old *h* pronoun *hem.*

By far the most frequent kind of reduction in stress is Poe's very consistent aphesis of initial unstressed syllables. Every polysyllable that Jupiter utters receives primary or secondary stress on its first syllable, a usage not confined to Negroes but very common in literary dialect purportedly theirs. Jupiter's aphetic forms are: *boosed* "abused," *bout* "about," *cause* "because," *feered* "afraid," *find* (falsely substituted for the white narrator's "confined"), *fore* "before," *gin* "again," *mos* "almost," *noovers* "maneuvers," *nuff* "enough," *pissel* "epistle," *plain* "complain," *pon* "upon," *sep* "except," *shamed* "ashamed," *sis* "insist," *tin* (falsely substituted for "antennae"), and *way* "away."

MORPHOLOGY AND SYNTAX

The morphology of Jupiter's speech has probably been more of a target for critics than his pronunciation. The condemnation of Ambrose Gonzales, who rendered the Gullah dialect excellently for literary purposes in his *The Black Border,* is typical: ". . . Poe, in 'the Goldbug' [sic], put into the mouth of a Charleston Negro such vocables as might have been used by a black sailor on an English ship a hundred years ago, or on the minstrel stage, but were never current on the South Carolina coast."[17] Yet many of Jupiter's linguistic features can be found in Gonzales' own rendition of the Gullah dialect—which is no more that of a "Charleston Negro" than Jupiter's is. (As might be expected, many Gullah features do not appear in Poe, since he was not writing literary Gullah *per se.*) It is valid to show a Negro with a mixture of Gullah and non-Gullah speech, as Poe does. Some Gullah features gradually spread westward among Negroes and some coastal whites,[18] and a number of lexical items entered general English, especially in the South.[19]

Other writers use a mixture similar to Poe's. The theory has long been suggested that there was a literary convention of representing a *quasi-*Gullah speech for fictional Negro servants, on the basis of certain writings

---

[17] *The Black Border: Gullah Stories of the Carolina Coast* (Columbia, S. C.: The State Company, 1922), pp. 12–13.

[18] Raven I. McDavid, Jr., and Virginia Glenn McDavid, "The Relationship of the Speech of the American Negroes to the Speech of the Whites," *American Speech,* XXVI (Feb. 1951), 13–16.

[19] H. L. Mencken, *The American Language, Supplement II* (New York: Knopf, 1948), p. 267. See also McDavid and McDavid, *loc. cit.*

206   of Poe, William Gilmore Simms, James Fenimore Cooper, and others.[20] This theory has been questioned by Professor Tremaine McDowell: ". . . it is evident . . . that Caesar's speech possesses none of the unique peculiarities of Gullah dialect, and that the eccentricities of Scipio's speech are merely linguistic achievements of his own."[21] Caesar is a Negro servant in Cooper's *The Spy,* and disregarding the eccentricity, of which Jupiter is not guilty, that Caesar "spoke excellent English in one breath and excellent Negro dialect in the next" (p. 294), his speech shows Gullahisms similar to Jupiter's. Scipio is a Negro servant in Mrs. Tabitha Tenney's *Female Quixotism; Exhibited in the Romantic Opinions and Extravagant Adventures of Dorcasina Sheldon* (2nd ed. 1808). I have not seen the latter novel, but most peculiarities of the quotations given and features described by Professor McDowell (pp. 292–293) could be shown to exist in Gullah—and "The Gold-Bug." Similarly, on page after page, the Gullah Hector in Simms' *The Yemassee*[22] sounds very much like Jupiter.[23] A literary convention of pseudo-Gullah is still a possibility, and may have been based on something close to the facts as derived from at least some non-Gullah Negroes. To conclude this morphological-syntactical preface, many a strange barbarism found in Negro dialect can likewise be found in Gullah (as recorded in Gonzales and Turner), so it behooves the critic not to reject any usage as unthinkable or attributable solely to an author's erratic imagination.

To turn to Jupiter's morphology in detail, he inflects seven nouns to show pluralization, e.g., *claws, crows, eyes,* etc. Three nouns are uninflected in the plural, as in Gullah: *limb, spade,* and *wing.* The corpus affords only two nonperiphrastic genitives, but it is significant that one of them, *de bug mouff,* is uninflected as in Gullah. Poe's noun-inflection is thus inconsistent but does achieve something of a Gullah flavor.

The same statement can be made concerning Jupiter's pronominal inflections (wherein Gullah itself is not fully consistent). First person singular follows standard English, with nominative *I,* genitive *my,* and accusative *me.* (Gullah uses these forms plus "me" for "I" but Jupiter's *Me feered de bug!* is hardly an example of this.) His second person forms, whether singular or plural, are also like standard English, with nominative *you,* genitive *your,* and accusative *you,* as well as the reflexive *yourself.*

---

[20] C. Alphonso Smith, "Dialect Writers," in *The Cambridge History of American Literature,* 1-vol. ed. (New York: Macmillan, 1946) Book III, pp. 351–352. George Philip Krapp, *The English Language in America,* 2 vols. (New York: Century, 1925), I, 254.

[21] "Notes on Negro Dialect in the American Novel to 1821," *American Speech,* V (April 1930), 295.

[22] Ed. Alexander Cowie (New York: American Book Co., 1937).

[23] Their resemblance is close in other ways, too. See C. Alphonso Smith, *loc. cit.*

(In all three cases Gullah uses /unə/, a form avoided by most writers of pseudo-Gullah; true Gullah also uses "you" in the nominative and accusative, e.g., Turner, p. 268.) The corpus affords no first person plurals, and is sparse with third person plurals. *Dey* occurs twice, but only as an analogous form to the expletive "there," as in *Dey aint no tin in him.* (Poe also uses *dar* for this form.) *Him* is twice used as a nominative where it conceivably replaces "they": *Him syfe, massa, and spade. . . . Him de syfe and de spade what Massa Will sis pon my buying. . . .*[24] But more likely the "standard" is, "It is a scythe, master, and spades. . . . It is the scythe and spades that Master Will insisted upon my buying. . . ." (Nominative *him* for "it" is a Gullahism.) Third person plural accusative *em* makes its sole appearance in this same sentence. (The form "them" in *dem goolebugs* is a substandard conservatism for the old definite article *þæm.*)

Elsewhere Jupiter uses *him* unambiguously as third person singular. His third person singular pronouns are interesting, despite the fact that contexts do not admit of any feminine forms. With the exception of the expletives *tis, taint,* etc., in all but two instances—*piece ob it* and *It's all cum ob de bug*—he substitutes masculine forms for neuter, as does Gullah. Jupiter's masculine forms for third person singular subject are *he* and *him* in about equal proportions.[25] (Both forms are common in Gullah [Turner, p. 227].) Thus we find in Poe *him berry sick* and *he talk about it,* etc. The same two forms both serve for the genitive, as in Gullah:[26] Jupiter says *him head, him noovers,* and *him wing,* but *he head, he life,* and *in he sleep.* Poe is to blame neither for the inconsistency nor for the barbarism of the forms.

The common relative pronoun is *what,* as in *ebery ting what cum near him,* a substandard usage not regionally confined.

Most verb forms (exclusive of negatives and other forms with function words) consist of the simple verb, uninflected for person and tense, as in Gullah. Representative first person singular present indicative forms are *hear, keep, know, mean, tell,* etc. Along with these are the Negro usages *chops, is* (Poe also writes *I'm*), *nose* "knows," and the present progressive forms *I'm gwine* and *Ise gittin.* The forms with function words

[24] p. 104. The narrator notices "a scythe and three spades."

[25] This is disregarding the expletives in *taint, tis,* and *twas.*

The "Savannah Darkey" in *Uncle Remus: His Songs and Sayings* (New York: Appleton, 1884) has the same divided usage: "Him po' country fer true . . . he no like Sawanny" (p. 194).

[26] Turner lists no genitive *he* in his paradigm of pronouns, p. 227, but he records some instances, e.g. "he wife" (p. 267). Joel Chandler Harris' old Gullah, Daddy Jack, uses the form, e.g. *Nights with Uncle Remus* (London: Routledge, n.d.), pp. 130, 138, 329. For other examples see *The Yemassee,* ed. cit., pp. 44 and 166; *The Black Border,* p. 25.

The same usage can be heard in a lyric sung by Harry Belafonte on "Calypso," RCA Victor Record No. LPM-1248: "White girl she ain't know she father." Cf. also William Faulkner, *The Sound and the Fury,* Modern Library (New York: Random House, 1946), p. 59: "in he eye."

208   are *don't blieve, is got, mought ventur, mus do, mus go, mus look,* and *mus tote.* The only second person forms are *you mus git* and (you) *needn't hollo.*

The third person singular present indicative forms of "to be" are *aint* (also *taint*) and the standard *is.* All other simple verbs except *keeps* and *fastens* are uninflected: *climb, keep, know, make, pinch, plain* "complain," *say* and *talk* (taking *talk* to be a present on p. 103). Since the stereotype for Negro dialect during the last hundred years has been "I goes, you goes, he goes, we goes, they goes," and since a consistent zero inflection is a Gullah feature widely found in American fiction during the first half of the last century, Poe's usage lends further support to the theory of a conventional literary Gullah of sorts for Negro characters.

The past tense in Gullah has the same uninflected form as the simple present, but this is also true of verbs of high frequency, in substandard English, such as *come* and *give.* Therefore, the use of the present form for the preterite is not a peculiarly Gullah feature. For the first person singular preterite indicative Jupiter has the Gullah zero-inflectional forms *bring, cotch, feel, got* (a preterite present), *rap* "wrapped," and *stuff.* His Negroisms are *done pass, I'm feared, Ise gittin, is got* (both as a preterite present and a true preterite), and *Ise heerd.* The forms with function words are *did see* (emphatic) *didn't like,* and *hadn't.* Standard *had* also occurs. The only second person form is an occurrence of the substandard *you was.*

For the third person singular past tense are the uninflected forms *bite, cotch, cum, gib, kick, look, make, see,* and *sis* "insisted." The only simple verb with standard inflection is *had.* Forms with function words are *aint bin, aint find, aint got, could get, did come* (emphatic), *It's all cum,* and *must ha got,* as well as the Negroisms *done gobble, done departed,* and *is got.* Probably a Gullahism is the preterite passive *he bit by de goole-bug* (Turner, p. 209); and most certainly a Gullahism is the interesting verb form in *somebody bin lef him head.* The same feature is very common in Harris' Daddy Jack's Gullah, e.g.: "Me bin yeddy one tale" ("I have heard a tale") and " 'E bin mek fine nuss" ("He made a fine nurse").[27]

As for other passive forms, with the exception of *all dat done* ("all that is done" or "has been done"), Jupiter shares with the Gullah (Turner, p. 209) an avoidance of them. Thus he twists the narrator's "Is he confined to bed?" to *he aint find nowhar.* This could mean, "He isn't to be found anywhere," but more likely the context indicates, "He hasn't found [what he has been looking for] anywhere."

To complete the analysis of function words with verbs, Jupiter once uses *to* with the infinitive, *to speak de troof, massa.* But his usual signal

---

[27] "How the Bear Nursed the Little Alligator," *Nights with Uncle Remus,* ed. cit., p. 329.

for this mood is *for to* or simply *for* (also *fer*). *For to* is a widespread sub-standard conservatism used with infinitives of purpose, and has been shortened to *for* in the speech of many coastal South Carolinians, both white and black.[28] Jupiter uses *for to* as purposive, e.g., *a big stick ready cut for to gib him d - - d good beating;* but he also uses both *for to* and *for* as nonpurposive: *go fer trubble dat bug; Mos feerd for to ventur;* and *How much fudder is got for go?,* among other instances.

Jupiter's use of the multiple negative is a conservatism which needs no comment here as a mark of social status. One example, *noffin at all aint de matter,* is reminiscent of such Gullah usages as "Nobody ain't worry" and "That ain't not do now."[29] Or, perhaps such negatives are Negroisms: Uncle Remus says, "Nobody ain't ans'er." When they appear, other function words with verbs usually follow standard usage, as can be seen from the examples cited above for tenses or from the sole instance of a future, *de limb won't break.* But one feature of Jupiter's speech, which he shares with Gullah (Turner, pp. 217–218), is frequent syntactical "omission" of words, including that of function words with verbs. Thus there is only the simple verb in *Jup climb any tree, How I know?,* and *What I keer?* There are many uses of the noun-adjective sentence pattern, as in Gullah:[30] *him berry sick, him rotten,* etc.; or perhaps it is better to say that the contrast for Poe consists in the fact that the copula is often "omitted" as in *him syfe* "it is a scythe" and *What de matter?,* likewise as in Gullah. In negative statements the copula is at times "omitted" but more often is expressed by *aint,* a token of substandard usage to Poe, if not to all Southerners.[31]

Pronouns are "omitted" where the first person singular would be expected in standard English, as in *Which way mus go?* and *What mus do wid it?* Other "omissions" are similar to those in the colloquial speech of many areas: (I) *Hab for to keep,* (I) *mought venture,* and (you) *needn't hollo at poor nigger,* though it is impossible to guarantee precisely these parenthetical insertions as "understood."

The last example cited also illustrates the frequent "omission" of the article, probably the indefinite as in *I stuff piece ob it and gib him d - - d good beating.* Jupiter "omits" the definite article, too, as in *he gib me slip fore de sun up.* In this last quotation, *up* functions as a verbal adjective

[28] McDavid and McDavid, "The Relationship of the Speech of the Negroes to the Speech of the Whites," p. 15.

[29] Turner, p. 263, where there are several other examples.

[30] Turner, pp. 217–218. Cf. the well-known Negro utterance in Conrad's *Heart of Darkness:* "Mistah Kurtz—he dead."

[31] McDavid and McDavid, p. 15, n. 48.

210 in a noun-adjective sentence pattern, not as a verb, as it does in Uncle Remus' "he up en say."[32] (For *de* to be the common Gullah verb of incomplete predication "de" [də], the reading would have to be "sun de up.")[33]

On is undoubtedly pleonastic for Poe in *I keep a tellin on you,* where the meaning is "inform," not "inform against." (The occurrence of *a* is discussed above, p. 201.) Uncle Remus is guilty of the same false analogy.[34] "Of" is pleonastic for Poe in *what fastens ob it* and "omitted" in *Me feered de bug!*

As would be expected of an uneducated speaker, Jupiter's utterances usually consist of coordinate clauses.[35] He strings them together somewhat abruptly, which Poe emphasizes by connecting them with dashes, though he does this for the whites on occasion, too. Representative examples for Jupiter are his last utterance on p. 101 and his first on p. 102. Similar to Gullah (Turner, pp. 220–221) are his repetitions of words and phrases, as in *Yes, I nose dat—nose all bout dat,* or *And dis all cum ob de goole-bug! de putty goole-bug! de poor little goole-bug . . .!* One of these repetitions smacks wonderfully of camp meeting oratory, with its crescendo of solemnity: *Him dead as de door-nail—done up for sartain—done departed dis here life.* This of a tree limb!

VOCABULARY

As do his phonology and morphology, Jupiter's lexicon possesses the conservatism so characteristic of national substandard English. There is the old function word *mought* with verbs, archaic indefinite articles (see above, p. 201), and the trace of the old definite article *pæt* in *Todder* "the other." In *Ise sich a fool dat I hadn't de heart* the word *fool* retains its obsolete meaning of a term of endearment or pity (see *NED,* s.v. Fool, *sb.* and *a.,* A.I.1.c.). In *to keep mighty tight eye,* the word *tight* has the figurative meaning of "alert" or "capable," now obsolete except dialectally (*NED,* s.v. Tight, *a.,* 3.). The Negro's use of the word *style* may also be obsolete (*NED,* s.v. Style, *sb.* III. 19; but see also No. 25.)

---

[32] *Uncle Remus: His Songs and Sayings,* p. 36. He is fond of this expression, sometimes as "he ups an' sez, sezee" (p. 215). The usage of *up* as a verb is of course still a widespread colloquialism.

[33] Turner, pp. 209–210.

[34] *Songs and Sayings,* p. 39.

[35] Charles Carpenter Fries, *American English Grammar* (New York and London: Appleton-Century-Crofts, 1940), pp. 206 ff. Turner makes the same point for Gullah, attributing its habitual parataxis to the syntactical influence of African languages (p. 209).

Funnin, an occasionally used colloquialism of the nineteenth century   **211**
(*NED,* s.v. Fun, *vb.,* 2.), still exists in some rustic parts of the South as
a synonym for "joking." (Flannery O'Connor, a Georgian, uses it in her
television play, "The Life You Save.")

Poe's very accurate ear enabled him to reproduce not only conservatisms but also usages which were and are both racially and regionally
correct. Professor E. Bagby Atwood has stated that among the forms
which are almost "characteristically Negro" in the South Atlantic States
to this day are *cotch, gwine, mought,* and *what make.*[36] To this list *tote*
may well be added.

Jupiter shows the same fondness as Uncle Remus and many other
Negroes for polysyllables whether rightly understood or not. He proudly
uses *sarcumstance* (correctly) and substitutes the fancy and impressive
noovers for "doings" or "carrying-on." (This comic formula is still a main-
stay of blackface commercial entertainment.) At the same time his vocabulary can show the essential poverty of substandard: he overworks the
word *get,* employing it eight times (see Fries, *American English Grammar,*
p. 288).

The old Negro's oaths and outcries are common ones for Negroes of
his day. Jupiter says *my golly* (and an expanded version, *Lor-gol-a-
marcy!*), and Mencken notes of "by golly" that "down to the Civil War
it was the characteristic oath of the Negro slaves—at all events in the
literature of the time."[37] *Blessed* occurs in the Uncle Remus stories (there
spelled "blessid"), in which Daddy Jack, like Jupiter, utters the cry of
surprise *hoo!* Among both whites and blacks this is still widely heard in
the South, often as [hu'wu] or [hu'wi], with a sharp rise in intonation on
the second syllable.

It is a bit of a surprise, at least in fiction, to have Jupiter swear *d--d*
(once it is *d--n*) so often in the presence of his white superiors. The
profanity does assist in portraying him as an individual, although his
name does not do so. His Olympian appellation is not burlesque but
convention. Antebellum Southerners often assigned the names of Roman
gods and heroes to their male slaves—and dogs.[38]

---

[36] *Verb Forms in the Eastern United States,* p. 41. (Page 34 points out that an *a*-prefix with
present participles is also characteristic of the untutored in this region.)

[37] *The American Language,* 4th ed. (New York: Knopf, 1937), p. 316.

[38] "Neptune" is the name of a big dog in Poe's "The Journal of Julius Rodman." On slave
names, see Mencken, ed. cit., p. 523; Hennig Cohen, "Slave Names in Colonial South Carolina," *American Speech,* XXVII (May 1952), 102–107; George Walton Williams, "Slave Names
in Ante-Bellum South Carolina," *American Speech,* XXXIII (Dec. 1958), 294–295. Ironically,
assigning Negro slaves the names of mythological divinities proves to be symbolic of the black
race's spiritual mastery (as in Faulkner), despite the onomastic cruelty intended.

JUPITER AS A LITERARY CHARACTER

Jupiter's dialect is basic in establishing or damaging him as a literary character, but narrative exposition, action, and commentary, which are closely tied in with his speech in the story, help to round out a full picture of him. Jupiter has been the subject of harsh criticism, even in his nonspeaking role. For example, "The character . . . is unconvincing, being far too simple and naive, and full of the most surprising contradictions. He is able to look out for his master, and yet cannot tell his right hand from his left. Although a devoted menial, well knowing his place, he actually prepares a club with which to discipline the wayward Legrand."[39] Why shouldn't the old Negro be inconsistent? This is truth. Furthermore, nothing could be more inconsistent than Legrand's treatment of his faithful slave, and equivalent contradictions in race relations are still very much alive.[40] It is nothing new for a Negro not to know exactly where he stands, or to pretend ignorance and lack of comprehension. Nor is it anything new for a Negro (or white) to indulge in what are genuine contradictions by any standards.[41]

Jupiter does confuse right and left, but understandably: At the end of a long climb while carrying the gold-bug and enduring the threats and curses of his master, out on a dead limb he suddenly faces a skull. The skull's left eye is exactly opposite his right eye, it can be said, provided the skull is face outward *and* its jaw points toward the tree trunk. But Legrand fails to establish the second of these two conditions. Jupiter himself (somewhat indignantly?) expostulates that he certainly does know which hand is his left. As for his threatening to beat his master, the Poe scholar T. O. Mabbott says, ". . . I am assured by descendants of old families that in a case of incipient madness, this probably would have been considered admirable, like hitting a drowning person."[42] Poe avoids making Jupiter a caricature in part by having him talk back to his master, at times a bit sharply. But he possesses the deeply ingrained caution of the Southern Negro and knows when to stop and to obey.

As does Hector in Simms' *The Yemassee,* he refuses his freedom. He follows his master from New Orleans to South Carolina because of undeviating loyalty—a stereotyped devotion dear to ante-bellum South[43]

---

[39] John Herbert Nelson, *The Negro Character in American Fiction,* Bulletin of the University of Kansas Humanistic Studies, IV, No. 1 (Lawrence, 1926), p. 40.

[40] See Gunnar Myrdal, *An American Dilemma,* 2 vols. (New York: Harper, 1944), *passim.*

[41] See for example Will Alexander Percy, *Lanterns on the Levee* (New York: Knopf, 1941), esp. the vivid ch. 23, "A Note on Race Relations," pp. 298–309.

[42] *The Selected Poetry and Prose of Edgar Allan Poe,* p. 423 (Notes).

[43] See Tremaine McDowell. "The Negro in the Southern Novel Prior to 1850," *JEGP, XXV* (Oct. 1926), 455–473.

which chose to misjudge the three hundred slave revolts before the Civil War. He responds with an alacrity still seen in many Southern Negroes at the promise of unexpected hard cash. He is gingerly reluctant in the face of what seems danger to him and quick to make up ridiculous evasions of it. Yet he has the ultimate capacity for any toil and hardship. Thus Jupiter's character is in no small measure conventional, but not banally so.

His greatest charm lies in his comicality, which is of course inseparable from his speech. He reacts to the bantering so favored by Southern gentlemen toward Negroes (and amongst themselves) by doing his best to keep up with them, immediately seizing upon any analogy that will enable him to sustain the conversation. To show the typicality of such keeping up of appearances, here is a fairly recent real-life instance. A friend of mine teased his old colored mammy by remarking that the weather was very inclement that day. She replied, "That's right, ain't no lemon in it." Such an anecdote is not given to belabor the obvious, but from regret that few critics seem to have laughed at the right things in "The Gold-Bug."[44]

Despite his other traits, Jupiter must stand or fall because of his dialect. He does not commit the worst fault of Negro dialect, speaking like a colonel on the piazza in one paragraph and a fieldhand chopping cotton in the next.[45] Analysis reveals his linguistic inconsistencies as minor; they even lend some verisimilitude, absolute consistency being a blemish in any literary dialect.[46] He speaks a *quasi*-Gullah, a literary convention which rests on two bases, Negro speech of the Southeastern Coast with some not-unexpected Gullah features, and "the common body of folk-speech which underlies American dialects in all sections of the country,"[47] a speech marked by conservatisms of several kinds. Jupiter talks something like Uncle Remus' Charleston and Savannah acquaintances;[48] if he does not speak exactly like any other literary character, that is in some measure a tribute to his individuality and to Poe's accuracy of observation.

This analysis has attempted to show that Jupiter's phonology, morphology, syntax, and vocabulary form an excellent contrast with Poe's

---

[44] For good examples of similar anecdotes see Mamie J. Meredith, "Negro Patois and its Humor," *American Speech*, VI (June 1931), 317–321.

[45] More than one Negro in fiction written before the Civil War occasionally does this, including the most famous of all, Uncle Tom. See n. 47 below.

[46] Ives, "A Theory of Literary Dialect," pp. 145–146.

[47] Tremaine McDowell, "The Use of Negro Dialect by Harriet Beecher Stowe," *American Speech*, VI (June 1931), 322.

[48] *Uncle Remus: His Songs and Sayings*, pp. 193–195, 204–205.

214   conception of his own "standard" Southern speech. The primary contrast emerges as social; Jupiter's speech is as much substandard as it is Southern Negro. The author, however, took race and the story's locale into consideration successfully. Save for two or three humorous folk etymologies, Poe invented no linguistic features for him; they are all duplicable elsewhere, and the overall dialect is enjoyable. While Poe loved, as he said, to "exaggerate the witty into the burlesque," he usually restrained himself with his one vocal Negro, and the result is not just another pleasant old darkey shuffling around. Jupiter is a less stereotyped character than the decadent, hypersensitive hero and moribund, tubercular beauty who hover through tale after tale by Poe, speaking in the manner of Rasselas, Prince of Abyssinia, if not always with Johnsonian wisdom. It is a pity that Poe did not oftener endow them with Jupiter's linguistic vitality.

Geographical Delimitation of the Dialect Areas in The Adventures of Huckleberry Finn

Curt M. Rulon

Curt M. Rulon here takes issue with Mark Twain's claim that in *The Adventures of Huckleberry Finn* he used several dialects, one carefully distinguished from another. Twain lists these dialects in a puzzling way as "Missouri Negro," "Backwoods South-Western," "Pike County," and "four modified varieties of the last." Does Twain here indicate a minimum of three, a maximum of seven, or something in between? Professor Rulon shows the relationship between the geography and the dialects of the novel. He is a member of the Department of English, North Texas State University.

Mark Twain has given the reader of *Huckleberry Finn* numerous clues concerning its specific geographical setting. This information is of interest

From *The Mark Twain Journal.* Vol. XIV, No. 1 (Winter 1967) 9–12. Reprinted with the permission of *The Mark Twain Journal* and Curt M. Rulon.

216   to the general reader, the literary scholar, and the dialectologist, or linguistic geographer, as he is sometimes called. Generally, the locale is the Central Mississippi River Valley in the 1840's. One can learn this much by a glance at the title page. Moreover, Robert F. Stowell[1] and Leo Marx[2] have independently constructed maps of the geography of the novel which contain inaccuracies: Both scholars have incorrectly placed the Grangerford Plantation and the Phelps Farm. Otherwise, their maps are quite useful and accurate.

My interest in the geography of the novel stems from the fact that I have elsewhere[3] attempted to analyze the dialects Twain alleges to have differentiated so meticulously and which number variously between a minimum of three and a maximum of seven: Missouri Negro; South-Western; Ordinary Pike-County; and four modified varieties of Pike-County.

Stowell and Marx have correctly suggested that the Grangerford Plantation was located somewhere below Cairo, Illinois, where the Ohio River joins the Mississippi. However, Stowell places it in southwestern Kentucky, and Marx indicates that it is in southeastern Missouri, whereas it would seem that Twain conceived of it as being in northern Arkansas, i.e., if one can rely on his synoptic note to chapter seventeen in the table of contents of the first American edition text[4] which reads: The Farm in Arkansaw.

One learns in chapter sixteen that Huck and Jim have inadvertently gone by Cairo, Illinois in the fog:

> When it was daylight, here was the clear Ohio water in shore, sure enough, and outside was the old regular Muddy! So it was all up with Cairo. (p. 129)

Shortly after this, Huck and Jim become separated when a steamboat threatens to ram them. They dive in the water from opposite sides of the raft to escape injury. Huck comes up for air and relates the following account:

> I sung out for Jim about a dozen times, but I didn't get any answer; so I grabbed a plank that touched me while I was "treading water,"

[1] Stowell, Robert F. 1966. Map entitled: Huck Finn on the Mississippi. MTJ. Front cover page and comments on back page.

[2] Marx, Leo. 1967, p. xli. Map entitled: The Mississippi Valley circa 1835–1845 as found in The Adventures of Huckleberry Finn. Indianapolis. The Bobbs-Merrill Company.

[3] The dialects in Huckleberry Finn. 1967. Unpublished doctoral dissertation. The University of Iowa.

[4] Hill, Hamlin and Walter Blair. 1962. The Art of Huckleberry Finn. San Francisco, Chandler. All following page numbers refer to this volume which contains a facsimile of the first American edition text of Huckleberry Finn.

> and struck out for shore, shoving it ahead of me. But I made out to see
> that the drift of the current was towards the left-hand shore, which
> meant that I was in a crossing; so I changed off and went that way.
> (p. 131)

Stowell perhaps is assuming that Huck was heading downstream after
he came up for air, and thus the "left-hand shore" would be the eastern
rather than the western shore, i.e., southern Kentucky or northern Tennessee rather than southern Missouri as Marx would have it, or northern
Arkansas.

Of course, it is not crucially important to an analysis of dialects in the
novel whether or not the Grangerford Plantation is in one of these locations or the other. What is important for the linguistic geographer is that
the general location is in the proximity of the Mississippi River below
Cairo, Illinois, which point is the heel of an overturned boot configuration delimiting known contemporary dialect areas: Midland and Southern, respectively.

Stowell inaccurately places the Phelps Farm north of Memphis, Tennessee, which is too far north. Marx, on the other hand, in placing it in
northern Louisiana, fixes the location of it too far south. Huck testifies
that the locus of the Wilks episode, which takes place *after* the Grangerford episode and *before* the Phelps episode, is south of Memphis and
north of New Orleans:

> So the next day after the funeral, along about noontime, the girls' joy
> got the first jolt; a couple of nigger traders come along, and the king
> sold them the niggers reasonable, for three-day drafts as they called it,
> and away they went, the two sons up the river to Memphis, and their
> mother down the river to Orleans. (p. 234)

The Boggs-Sherburn episode, found in the novel between the Grangerford and Wilks episodes, apparently takes place in Arkansas; for, just
prior to the Boggs-Sherburn incident, Huck relates that:

> One morning, when we was pretty well down the state of Arkansaw,
> we come in sight of a little one-horse town in a big bend. . . . (p. 180)

Marx conjectures that this "one-horse town" (Bricksville) is really the
town of Napoleon, located in the southern half of Arkansas.

The Wilks episode may have taken place in either Arkansas or Mississippi—but probably in the latter since Huck informs the reader that
he and the king encounter Tim Collins (the lad who gives them information about the death of Peter Wilks) after they have left the duke to his
own devices on the other side of the river:

> . . . the duke said he reckoned he'd lay off and work his brains an hour
> or two and see if he couldn't put up something on the Arkansaw village;

and the king he allowed he would drop over to t'other village (presumably on the Mississippi side of the river) without any plan. . . . (p. 204)

There is one reference in the novel and one in Twain's autobiographical writings which can help one fix the location of the Phelps episode. Twain recalls that:

My uncle, John A. Quarles, was a farmer, and his place was in the country four miles from Florida (Twain's birthplace, not far from Hannibal) . . . I have never consciously used him or his wife in a book, but his farm has come very handy to me in literature once or twice. In *Huck Finn* and in *Tom Sawyer, Detective* I moved it down to Arkansas. It was all of six hundred miles. . . . (p. 392)

Further, Aunt Polly exclaims in the novel that she had to "trapse all the way down the river, eleven hundred miles, and find out what that creetur's up to . . ." (p. 362) Presumably she is speaking of round trip mileage. Thus the Phelps Farm is probably located well south of Memphis rather than above Memphis as Stowell would have it but still in southern Arkansas rather than in northern Louisiana as Marx maintains. Further, one learns from Huck (p. 267) that the name of the town near which the Phelps live is Pikesville, and that it is situated far enough south so that Spanish moss can grow:

We was down south in the warm weather, now, and a mighty long ways from home. We begun to come to trees with Spanish moss on them . . . (p. 266)

The locus of the St. Petersburg episode was Hannibal, Missouri, alias St. Petersburg; for Mrs. Loftus exclaims to Huck:

Goshen, child? This ain't Goshen. This is St. Petersburg. (p. 89)

Finally, the *Walter Scott* episode (involving Huck, Jim, Jake Packard, Jim Turner, Bill, and The Watchman) takes place near St. Louis:

The fifth night below St. Louis we had a big storm after midnight. . . . When the lightning glared out we could see a big straight river ahead. . . . "Hel-*lo*, Jim, looky, yonder!" It was a steamboat that had killed herself on a rock. (p. 96)

Two dialect areas are included in the geography of the novel that Twain has given us: Midland and Southern. In recent years, linguistic geographers have uncovered an impressive list of dialect features peculiar to these speech areas—features which include matters of pronunciation, vocabulary, and grammar. Many of these features have been included in the dialogue and narrative of the novel. By and large the characters in the novel maintain a Midland/Southern dichotomy which fairly well

matches the geographical delimitation Twain placed upon the novel as
a whole. . . .

Some general conclusions concerning the extent and accuracy of dialect differentiation in the novel are as follows: There are basically only two dialects represented, namely, a mixture of Caucasian (South) Midland and Southern speech on the one hand, and a mixture of Negro (South) Midland and Southern speech on the other hand.

Both regional and social dialect features are included in the speech of the characters in the novel. The term *Pike-County dialect* probably refers to a socially restricted, rustic, and historically conservative mode of speech, whereas the term *South-Western dialect* probably refers to the regional loss of postvocalic /r/, the palatalized stops /ky/ and /gy/ in such words as *k'yer* and *g'yirl* (care and girl), and the occurrence of /a/ in such words as *thar* and *whar* paralleling *there* and *where*.

The phonological features found in the Negro dialect are mainly Southern features, and they are historically quite conservative. The phonological features of the Caucasian dialect are mainly (South) Midland.

One of the greatest differences between the Negro and Caucasian dialects is in the area of verb morphology, especially in the formation of preterite verb forms.

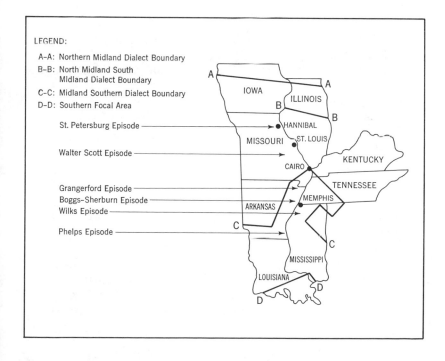

220   Uniform features of the dialects include a generalized present tense morpheme, the lack of a *was/were* distinction, a prefixally inflected present participle, the occurrence of *ain't, hain't, warn't, dasn't,* double and multiple negation, and socially restricted preterite and participial forms of verbs.

In addition to the major widespread features listed above, there are such interesting sporadic minor features as:

1. Lack of the ordinal number morpheme *-th: Louis Fourteen, Louis Fifteen, Looy the Sixteen, Looy the Seventeen.*
2. Generalized comparative and superlative morphemes:
 faithfuller, more pleasanter, bitterer, blessedest, carelessest, foolishest, treacherousest, etc.
3. Phonetic reduction of *on:*
 a-fire, a-purpose, a-horseback. Compare also, *anear, afront, anigh.*
4. Unorthodox verb formation:
 So Jim and me set to *majestying* him . . . But it warn't no time to be *sentimentering* . . . And kind of *lazy along,* and by-and-by *lazy off* to sleep . . .
5. Unorthodox adjective formation:
 rose-leafy, smothery, startlish.
6. Generalized *-s* inflection:
 innerds, upards, som'ers, northards, forrards, whiles, on accounts of, etc.
7. Stressed negative prefix *on-:*
 oncomfortable, oncommon, oneasy, onless, onreasonable.
8. Uninflected intensifiers:
 Considable, considerble, tolable, tolerble, pow'ful, powful occur pervasively without -ly.
9. Puns and malapropisms:
 Bulrushers for *bulrushes, captivated* for *held captive, diseased* for *deceased, putrified* for *petrified, remainders* for *remains, dolphins* for *Dauphin, yellocute* for *elocute.*
10. Analogizing of inflectional *-n:*
 his'n, ourn, yourn, your'n, their'n displacing *his, ours, yours, theirs.* Note also, *his own self, her own self, deyselves, hisself.*
11. *Those* is pervasively *them* in the novel, whereas them (pronoun) is usually *'em.*
12. Unorthodox subordination:
 You don't know about me, *without* you have read a book. . . . (Huck)
 I ain' gwyne to len' no mo' money *'dout* I see the security. (Jim)
 . . . *they bein'* partickler friends o' the diseased. . . . (The King)
 Seein' how I'm dressed, I reckon I better arrive down from St. Louis or Cincinnati. . . . (The King)

This list could be extended almost indefinitely, but for the present we must limit ourselves to these few but significant generalizations. The dialects in the novel, two in number, are authentic and genuine to a certain degree, i.e., there are many dialect features which correspond to well-known contemporary and historical, regional and social restricted features of conservative American and British speech, but there is no evidence which this investigator uncovered in the areas of phonology, morphology, or syntax which might lead him to believe that Twain was serious when he spoke of four modified varieties of Pike County speech.

Dialect Differentiation in the Stories of Joel Chandler Harris

Sumner Ives

Sumner Ives, whose landmark paper, "A Theory of Literary Dialect," also appears in this collection, did extensive analysis of the literary dialects of Joel Chandler Harris. His basic work on Harris, "The Phonology of the Uncle Remus Stories" (*Publications of the American Dialect Society,* 1954), led him to conclude that Harris's nonstandard spellings "reveal a consistent phonology" that could be achieved only through keen observation of the folk speech of the inhabitants of Middle Georgia. Since all the characters in the Harris stories lived in the same region, Harris's dialects are designed to reveal social rather than regional differences. It is of interest to note that the most distinctive dialect Harris uses is the Gullah-based speech of Daddy Jack.

Despite the widespread use of literary dialect by American authors,
this device for realism has been studied very little. True, George Philip
Krapp included an extensive discussion of dialect writing in his *English
Language in America,* published in 1925; but aside from this, very little
original work has been done. And twenty years later E. H. Sturtevant
and H. L. Mencken were simply repeating his conclusions: that all of
our literary dialects are essentially alike, that authors did not succeed
in differentiating them, and "that there are no true dialects in America
. . . so far as dialects have been utilized for literary purposes. One may
say that there have been only two forms of speech in America, the more
or less formal standard and the more or less informal colloquial."[1]

I have already argued at some length that these conclusions have been
unjust to many authors, especially such men as James Russell Lowell,
Mark Twain, and Joel Chandler Harris.[2] This discussion is an extension
of the arguments advanced then and a fuller demonstration of just how
one of them, Harris, was able to use various white and Negro dialects
in his stories and to show systematic differences between them. But first
some review is necessary, for the recognition of differences between literary representations of dialects depends on agreement as to how dialects
themselves are different.

We may apply the term *dialect* to the speech of any group, limited
socially or geographically, which has certain language habits in common,
enough so that there is an appearance of homogeneity within the group
and an appearance of difference between this group and other groups.
These distinguishing language habits, however, have individually their
own separate and distinct distributions. The isoglosses, or lines bounding
their distribution, extend horizontally across the country and vertically
through the social structure of every region. Consequently, the social
status of many nonstandard items is often different in different sections.
For example, both *it don't* and *you was* are found nearly everywhere in
popular speech. But all educated people know that both are condemned
by guides to correct usage. However, a great many Southerners, knowing
this textbook rule, use *it don't* in ordinary conversation, although the
same people would not say *you was.* Thus the social implications of *it don't*
in the dialogue of a story would differ according to the native region
of the speaker. But *you was* in the dialogue of any character would at
least separate him from the company of the educated or their more successful imitators. Another form, *it do,* is practically limited to the rural

From *American Literature* 17:88–96 (March 1955) Reprinted with the permission of Duke
University Press and Sumner Ives.

[1] I, 243.

[2] "A Theory of Literary Dialect," *Tulane Studies in English,* II, 137–182 (1950).

224   South and even there it implies a less educated or more rustic speech than does *you was*.[3] It is through the careful management of such items as these, with their different social and regional associations, that Harris was able to distinguish his dialects from each other and from other popular speech.

When all the characters of a story are residents of the same locality, use of dialect, or nonstandard speech forms, serves chiefly to identify the characters as members of different social groups. These social distinctions are indicated by two devices. One is the density or frequency of the nonstandard forms; the other is the choice of nonstandard forms. In general, the greater the density, the greater the rusticity or the lower the class. Thus, in Harris's stories, the speech of a "poor white" farmer has in it not only the nonstandard forms found in the speech of a middle-class tradesman but many others as well.

But just as the choice of certain dialectal forms can show a difference in social status, so can the selection of other forms give some indication as to the generation to which the character belongs. An elderly plantation owner may use archaisms which would not appear in the speech of a younger person, regardless of his social status.

Harris could indicate such differences in dialect in his stories of Middle Georgia because many distinct speech patterns actually existed there. Middle Georgia was a relatively isolated town and country section. Settlers had come in well after the American Revolution from both the lowland South and the mountain South.[4] These differences in origin must have been reflected in the local speechways, for they can still be discovered in field records of the Linguistic Atlas.[5] And differences in family origin correlated to some extent with occupation and economic standing. Thus there were distinct social classes in town and in country, and town and country differed from each other. Both had their "poor whites" and their local aristocrats, with gradations between. And there were also the Negroes.[6] Thus the local speech mores were more complex than those of other areas with less diversity in settlement and culture. Harris must

---

[3] E. Bagby Atwood, *A Survey of Verb Forms in the Eastern United States* (Ann Arbor. 1953), pp. 27, 28, 41.

[4] J. E. Callaway, *The Early Settlement of Georgia* (Athens, Ga., 1948).

[5] For a general description of the Linguistic Atlas and its methodology, see Hans Kurath, and others, *Handbook of the Linguistic Geography of New England* (Providence, 1939). All forms which have been cited from the Harris stories have been verified by examination of unpublished Atlas records.

[6] The Negroes in Middle Georgia had been born in this country, with rare exceptions. Negro slaves were brought in from the lowland plantations at the time of settlement, and the plantation culture was fully established within a generation of the time when the land was first thrown open for occupancy.

have had a keen ear and exact memory, for he used the distinguishing marks of the several dialects in his characterizations. Whether this use was based on deliberate and systematic analysis, I would not say.

Much of this social dialect is also regional. It is well known that all forms of popular speech are derived from earlier popular and cultured speech through the operation of the same linguistic processes as those which give standard speech. At the same time, each change of each word in each region and in each class is a unique event, and these changes are not necessarily consistent with each other. For example, in some dialects of eastern New England, the form *be* is generalized throughout the present indicative, regardless of the subject. On the other hand, the form *is* has been similarly generalized in parts of the rural South.[7] Thus, when Uncle Remus says *I is,* he is using both social and regional dialect. Such internal causes of dialect difference have been reinforced by education and other enemies of the local folkways. These have not been nationally uniform in their effect. Consequently, "relic areas" appear with distinctive traits, although these same traits might not have been regionally definitive a few generations earlier.

The grammar and vocabulary of local speech can be shown rather fully and with little difficulty, for the conventional alphabet will spell its forms, and the meanings are relatively clear. But the representation of pronunciations is another matter. The function of orthography is to identify the phonemes, or distinctive vowels and consonants, of a language. For it to show regional differences in the pronunciation of these vowels and consonants would be redundant. Although English spelling is defective and awkward, even in its representation of the distinctive sounds, an author is generally able to show which of the traditionally recognized vowels and consonants are used in particular words. Nevertheless, he very seldom shows purely regional pronunciations in the speech of educated people, even when he could do so, unless there is some immediate reason for showing that the character is not native to the locale of the story. He varies from the standard spelling only to show pronunciations which differ from standard speech in the region of the story. At the same time, pronunciations correlating with social class are nearly always circumscribed geographically, just as nearly all social differences in grammar are geographically limited.

In summary, then, an author employs dialect writing to identify a character as a member of some social group to which neither author nor reader is presumed to belong. By exploiting the diverse occurrence and density of nonstandard forms, he is able to distinguish between social groups with some sureness. In dialect writing, structural, lexical, and

[7] Atwood, *op. cit.,* p. 27.

226   rhetorical items can be shown rather fully, and generally are; for they clearly contrast with equivalent forms in the literary standard. However, this literary standard is not uniformly pronounced, and variations in the standard pronunciation are not ordinarily shown, even to the extent they could be. Only when pronunciations are socially indicative does an author represent them. Nevertheless, these socially distinct pronunciations, like socially distinct grammatical items, generally have regional as well as social limits to their occurrence.

The best known of all the dialects which Harris used is the Negro dialect of the Uncle Remus stories. I have shown elsewhere some details of how this dialect differed from rustic white speech, as Harris represented it, and shall give here only a few generalizations.[8] There are, it is true, many items which appear in both his Negro and his rustic white speech, but there are others which appear only in his representation of Negro speech. Among them are the use of *d* for *th* when it indicates a voiced sound, as in *the, that, them,* and *whether;* the use of final *f* for voiceless *th* in words like *mouth* and *tooth;* the omission of *r* in words like *before* and *sure;* and the omission of *h* in words like *what* and *why.* Also, the Uncle Remus speech shows far more assimilation, more loss of initial unstressed syllables, more leveling of preterit and past participle forms, and a greater density of archaic forms. Uncle Remus himself has a peculiarly ornate use of words, with such exotic formations as *sollumcholly, sustonished,* and *rekermember.* He has a rich imagery, with such expressions as *leg-bail* for escape by flight and *you'er thumpin' de wrong watermillion* for barking up the wrong tree. Furthermore, his speech is larded with such proverbs as *'oman tongue ain't got no Sunday* and such comparisons as *ez ca'm ez a dead pig in de sunshine.*[9]

Actually the field records of the *Linguistic Atlas,* aside from a very few Gullah records, show hardly any usages in Negro speech which cannot also be found in rustic white speech. And there are many similarities in usage as Harris wrote the dialects. However, the peculiarity of his Negro speech, in addition to the features already listed, consists in the greater density of nonstandard forms, and in the fact that the nonstandard items include, in greater number, features which are associated with Southern plantation speech rather than with Southern mountain speech. Since the same features can actually be found in the speech of both Negro and rustic white, Harris could more justly be accused of exaggerating the actual difference than of failing to indicate it. One additional point should, however, be mentioned. Some of the Atlas field records of rustic

[8] *Op. cit.,* pp. 165–167.

[9] For many similar expressions, see the list compiled by Stella Brewer Brookes, *Joel Chandler Harris—Folklorist* (Athens, Ga., 1950), pp. 97–110.

white speech show much closer agreement with the Uncle Remus dialect than do others. These other records show features which are neither in the records of cultured informants of the region nor in the records of Negro speech. Instead, they show characteristics of South Midland[10] or Southern mountain speech, and in this respect, their usage agrees substantially with that of the "poor white" as Harris wrote it. Although most of the animal fables are told by Uncle Remus, a few of those in *Nights with Uncle Remus* are told by Daddy Jack, who represents the Gullah Negroes of the coast. The dialect is quite different, in fact so different that any one complete line of text is enough to tell them apart.

According to Lorenzo Turner,[11] Gullah speech has the same vowel in words like *pat* as in words like *pot,* and it has no postvocalic *r.* Thus *pat, pot,* and *part* would all have the same vowel. This characteristic is suggested by Harris in Daddy Jack's speech. For example, he spells *laugh* and other words normally pronounced with "short *a*" with *ah,* sometimes with *ar.* At the same time, he omits the letter *r* from those words which, like *smart* and *part,* have *ar* in their normal spelling, or he spells them too with *ah.* This spelling practice shows that Harris heard the same vowel in all these words.[12] In writing the dialect of Uncle Remus, Harris indicated no dialectal pronunciation for these words.

Another of the peculiarities in the representation of Daddy Jack's speech is the use of a spelling for "short *e*" as in *met* for words which have "long *a*" in the speech of most Southerners, including Uncle Remus. Examples are *shekky* for *shake, yent* for *ain't, bre'k* for *break,* and *sem* for *same.* According to Turner,[13] *met* and *make* have different vowels, but the vowel of *make,* which is a diphthong in Southern standard speech, is a short monophthong in Gullah. There was no way by which Harris could show the actual facts with the conventional alphabet. But of course he may have thought that the two monophthongs were actually the same vowel.

Three consonant features will do for illustration, although there are many others. All these are corroborated by Turner's study and differ from the usage of Uncle Remus. One is the use of *t* for voiceless *th* in all positions. For example: *troo* for *through, nuttin'* for *nothing,* and *mout'* for *mouth.* Second is the use of *f* for final *v,* as in *drife* for *drive* and *lif* for *live.* The third is the spelling of *young* as *noung.* This word occurs in one of

---

[10] For the limits of this speech region, see Hans Kurath, *A Word Geography of the Eastern United States* (Ann Arbor, 1949), p. 36.

[11] *Africanisms in the Gullah Dialect* (Chicago, 1949), pp. 16, 17.

[12] This vowel was probably intermediate between the vowels of *pat* and *pot,* something like that in French *la.*

[13] *Op. cit.,* p. 16.

228   Turner's illustrative texts with an initial palatal nasal,[14] a sound for which there is no precedent in native English.

Differences in grammar and rhetoric are quite obvious, but I shall illustrate them only by giving a portion of a conversation between Daddy Jack and Uncle Remus. Regarding one of the young plantation women, Daddy Jack said, "Da' gal do holler un lahf un stomp 'e fut dey-dey, un dun I shum done gone pidjin-toe. Oona bin know da' 'Tildy gal?"[15]

Uncle Remus replied, "I bin a-knowin' dat gal now gwine on since she 'uz knee-high ter one or dese yer puddle ducks; en I bin noticin' lately dat she mightly likely nigger."[16]

In giving examples to show how Harris differentiated between his white dialects, I shall draw from *Sister Jane*, a novel telling, in the person of William Wornum, the activities of Wornum's sister, Jane, and her associates. In it, some characters use consistently the standard colloquial of literature, deviating only in so far as is consistent with occupation and personality. For example, the dialogue of the narrator, a mild and bookish man, is rather formal and old-fashioned.

On the other hand, the dialogue of Sister Jane herself has in it many nonstandard forms and local expressions which do not appear in the speech of her brother or in that of Colonel Bullard and members of his family. For example, she says *he don't, fetch* for *carry, chany* for *china*, uses *ain't* with subjects in all persons, and has such expressions as *it would look a heap better*. Next is a group of Jane's friends, middle-class townswomen, of whom Mrs. Beshears is representative. She uses all the nonstandard forms which are found in the speech of Sister Jane and many more. Examples of these additional usages are *done took; don't never up and tell me; I ups and says, says I; teetotal;* and pronunciations of the *ee* sound in *guardian, oblige, scare,* and *care; cuss* for *curse;* and *purty* for *pretty*. Such spellings as *bekase* for *because* and *natur'* for *nature* occasionally appear, but the standard spelling for many of these is more common. Next, there is the speech of Jincy Matthews, son of a well-to-do plantation family, but popularly regarded as a half-wit and vagabond. Some forms he uses, in addition to those of the persons already mentioned, are *ast,* preterit of *ask; I seen, I taken,* and *I know'd; jine* and *spile* for *join* and *spoil; allers* for *always; tech* for *touch, drapped* for *dropped,* and *hoss* for *horse*.

There are two further dialects which have all these features and many more. One is that of two elderly gentlemen, Grandsir Roach and Uncle Jimmy Cosby, about whom it is said: "They owned land and negroes,

---

[14] *Ibid.*, p. 263. This sound is similar to that of *gn* in French *agneau*.

[15] Translated, this means: "That girl shouts and laughs and stamps her foot right here, and then I see her walk pigeon-toed. Do you know that Tildy girl?"

[16] *Mighty likely* here means *well-favored* and *desirable*.

horses and carriages; but back of their prosperity were the experience of the pioneer and the spirit of true democracy." The other is that of Mandy Satterlee, a young girl from a "poor white" settlement who is befriended by Sister Jane, and her brother, Bud Satterlee, of whom Sister Jane said, "He was born trifling and he's stayed so." Both dialects have a heavier concentration of nonstandard forms than is found in other white dialects of the story. That of the older people includes *holp* for *helped, mought* for *might*, and in general a greater density of other archaic items such as *ax* for *ask* and *desarve* for *deserve*. Additional forms which appear in their dialogue but not in that of the younger Satterlees are *nother* for *neither, oneasy* for *uneasy; hyearn* for *heard, her'n* for *hers, gwine* for *going*, and *cotch* for *caught*. Both they and the Satterlees have such features in their dialogue as *hain't; hisse'f; out'n* for *out of; e'en about* for *just about; a-nigh* for *near;* and the following phonetic spellings: *ef* for *if; hender* for *hinder; yan* for *yon; quare* for *queer; whar* for *where; arter* for *after; shore* for *sure;* and *creetur* for *creature*. These examples, of course, are only a few of the nonstandard usages found in each dialect.

The mere listing of specific items which occur in one literary dialect but not in others does not, of course, exhaust the distinctions between them. There are differences in syntax and idiom which are not revealed by this type of analysis; moreover an author puts more of such spellings as *sez* for *says*, which indicate no more than the normal pronunciation, into his writing of nonstandard dialogue.

From one point of view, this is an exaggeration of the dialect, an insinuation that it is further removed from the standard than it is. However, such exaggeration is probably defensible, for it adds to the illusion that actual conversation has been reproduced. Once the literary standard has been left behind, the author tends to suggest the actual rhythm and flow of speech as closely as he can. In doing this he is apt to indicate by spelling changes what probably occurs also in the speech of those whose conversation is not represented as dialect. Thus the dialects in literary transcription may actually appear more different from the regional standard than in truth they were.

But if this is a fault it is, so far as Harris is concerned, a happy one, for his writing of conversation in literary dialect seems truer and more natural than his writing of it in the literary standard. In fact, the more one examines the speech of Harris's folk characters, the more one admires the skill with which he worked. He has, in truth, done more than write a more or less informal colloquial, as Krapp put it. A shy man himself, he must have listened keenly and sympathetically, for he caught the various patterns of folk speech in great detail. And whatever his narrative ability, he handled the dialogue of his folk characters with skilful discrimination.

Dialects in Eugene O'Neill's Plays

Ruth M. Blackburn

No less important in the development of literary dialects
than poets and writers of fiction were American playwrights.
Early dramatists, less hampered by literary conventions
than novelists were, used dialect long before the local-color
movement of the nineteenth century. Because O'Neill is a
modern exemplar of this long tradition, and because he
used many dialects in his plays, his work is a rich source
through which to study both the range and authenticity of
his dialects. Here, Ruth Blackburn reviews O'Neill's treatment
of dialects and provides a close look at the dialects of his
New England plays. Dr. Blackburn is a member of the faculty
of the State University of New York at Albany.

American writers of literary dialects usually specialize in one non-standard dialect and use it extensively. A writer who can handle several literary dialects well, as did Samuel Clemens, is an exception. But what of Eugene O'Neill, who employed about twenty dialects in his plays? Are his literary dialects authentic or are they pseudodialects? Did he know the "real" dialects well? Do the dialects enhance his plays or detract from their quality? Earlier critical commentary on his plays showed no agreement on the effectiveness or genuineness of his dialects. This paper gives a summary view of O'Neill's treatment of dialects to serve as a backdrop for a closer view of his representation of a particular dialect. There is no attempt here to deal with all the dialects he employed.

O'Neill peopled his plays with a large assortment of characters, endowing each with speech that would suggest his circumstance in life and individualize him. Of the forty-eight plays that O'Neill completed, over thirty of them contain some variety of nonstandard speech. In some plays several dialects are blended in a medley; in others they provide a kind of modern Greek chorus.

About half of the dialects are major ones, those which are used in several plays and are spoken by characters whose lines bulk large in number and length. These speech types vary from play to play, and often there is a range within a dialect in a given play, the range conditioned by generation, social gradations, time setting of the play, location, sex, occupation, education, and temperament. The types that include a range are Irish-American; Negro; Swedish-American; rural Eastern New England; lower-class urban types—underworld, New York City, traveling salesmen, "Broadway lingo," which is a kind of Damon Runyon, sporting type of slang of the early twentieth century. And Cockney turns up frequently.

The minor ones, used very little, are mostly of the mixed-national variety: Austrian-American, Italian-American, Russian-American, French-American, and a Scots accent. There is also a Pidgin English which, according to region, would be of two varieties—West Indian and Melanesian, but O'Neill showed little if any difference between them. There is a suggestion of deviation from English speech in the lines of a character in an early play, *Thirst*, but there seems to be no way of identifying it as a dialect.

Middle-class American speakers are immediately recognized by the reader because the author made no attempt to differentiate their speech

From "Representation of New England Rustic Dialects in the Plays of Eugene O'Neill," (unpublished dissertation, New York University, 1967). Printed with the permission of Ruth M. Blackburn.

232   from his own. The spelling of their lines is conventional, and the grammatical structure used is that of an educated speaker. But the type of
dialect assigned the less literate characters is delineated generally by the
use of unconventional spellings. These re-spellings are clues to the
phonemes in the dialect that differ from those of the author's own speech.
This is a practice that has been commonly employed by writers of dialectal literature, at least for the English language, to convey the level of class
and education of the speaker, as well as the regional speech group to
which he belongs. The reader understands this. He understands, further,
that the social, educational level of the character is conveyed inversely in
proportion to the density of re-spellings in his lines.

To insure ease in reading, an author does not avail himself of the full
range of these possibilities; he re-spells just enough to give the reader a
sense of what he wants to convey about a character's social level or the
region he comes from. Occasionally a playwright, when treating a nonstandard dialect well known to the readers, represents it fully for a few
lines and then, with a direction to the reader that representation of the
phonetic peculiarities will be thereafter omitted, ends the unconventional
spellings and relies on grammatical and lexical cues to remind the reader
of the character's dialect. The actor, of course, is expected to carry on
with the full dialect. This was the practice of George Bernard Shaw and
J. M. Barrie with Cockney speech in *Pygmalion* and *A Kiss for Cinderella*,
a dialect well known to Londoners.

But this was not O'Neill's method. He chose his method of representing
a dialect in a play at the outset of writing it and carried through with that
method meticulously to the end. His system of representing a certain dialect might change somewhat from play to play, but within a play his
method of treatment was consistently maintained.

The way in which he re-spelled is a system in itself, a simple system
which he adhered to rather consistently. A few re-spelled words from
some dialects will suffice to show his method. The value of some vowels,
particularly the low ones, may not be clear to every reader because of the
dialect situation in the United States. The phonemic symbols used here
are largely those employed in *The Pronunciation of English in the Atlantic
States*.[1] The symbols listed in column I represent approximations of the
vowels in the playwright's own speech. Column II shows the pronunciation of the re-spelled words in the rustic New England speech in *Desire
under the Elms* (1924); words in column III, Cockney, and column IV,
Irish, are from *The Long Voyage Home*. (1917).

[1] Hans Kurath and Raven I. McDavid, Jr., *The Pronunciation of English in the Atlantic States*,
(Ann Arbor, 1957), pp. 6–7.

Samples of Re-spelled Stressed Vowels

I O'Neill's Stressed Vowels	II Rustic E.N.E..	III Cockney	IV Irish
/i/ asl*ee*p			asl*a*pe /e/
l*ea*ve			l*a*ve /e/
/I/ h*e*re[2]	h*a*r /æ₂~a/[3]		
/e/ t*a*ke		t*i*ke /aI/	
s*a*me		s*ai*me /aI/	
/ɛ/ ag*ai*n	ag*i*n		
rem*e*mber			rem*i*mbcr /I/
y*e*llow	y*a*ller[4] /æ/		
/æ/ s*a*t	s*o*t /ɒ/[5]		
/a~a/ h*a*lf		'*ar*f[6] /a/	
/ɜ/ *ea*rn	'*ar*n /a/		
f*i*rst	f*u*st /ʌ/		
/ʌ/ s*u*ch	s*e*ch /ɛ/		
/u/ y*ou*	y*ew* /u/ "eye dialect"		
/ʊ/ y*our*[2]	y*ewr* /ʊ₂/[3] "eye dialect"		
/o/ h*o*me	h*u*m /θ/[7]		
d*o*n't		d*ow*n't /au/	
/ɒ~ɔ/ P*a*	P*aw*[8]		
h*o*rse	h*o*ss[8]		
G*o*d		G*aw*d /ɔ/	
*o*ff		*or*f /ɔ/	
/aI/ f*i*ve			f*oi*ve /ɔI/
/au/ ab*ou*t		ab*a*ht /a/	
m*ou*th		m*ar*f[9] /a/ (lengthened)	
/ɔI/ j*oi*n	j*i*ne /aI/		

[2] Normally, O'Neill does not re-spell /I/ and /ʊ/. Approximations with *r* would be /I₂/ and /ʊ₂/.

[3] /₂/ = nonsyllabic /ə/, which substitutes for /r/ after /æ/ and /ʊ/ when final.

[4] See below for unstressed *er*.

[5] /ɒ/ is pronounced somewhere between /a/ and /ɔ/. It occurs in dialects in which *cot* and *caught* are homonyms.

[6] *ar* suggests that the playwright intended the low back vowel /ɑ/ rather than /a/, Eastern New England vowel. See below for *r*.

[7] /θ/ is 'New England short *o*'. It is a mid vowel close to /o/ but lower and more fronted.

[8] *Paw* and *hoss* re-spellings are commonly used to suggest a rustic dialect and, therefore, are not clear indicators of the sounds the playwright intended to represent. /ɒ/ is possible.

[9] See below for *f* and *r*.

Phoneme	Corresponding Grapheme	Spelling Pattern	Example
/I/	*i*	__C(C) (C=consonant) ((C)=optional C)	ag*i*n
/e/	*a*	__C(C)ę (ę=silent *e*)	aslape
	ai[10]		a*i*sy
/ε/	*e*	__C(C)	s*e*ch
/æ/	*a*	__C(C)	y*a*ller
/æ᷈/	*ar*	(in final position)	h*ar*
/a/	*ar*		'*ar*n
/ʌ/	*u*	__C(C)	f*u*st
/u/	*ew*		y*ew*
/ʊ᷈/	*ewr*	(in final position)	y*ewr*
/θ/	*u*	__C(C)	h*u*m
/ɑ/	*ar*		m*ar*f
	ah		aba*h*t
/ɒ/	*o*	__C	s*o*t
/ɔ/	*aw*		G*aw*d
	or		*or*f
/aI/	*i*	__C(C)ę	t*i*ke, j*i*ne
	ai	(alternate re-spelling)	sa*i*me
/aʊ/	*ow*	__(C)	d*ow*n't
/ɔI/	*oi*		f*oi*ve

Unstressed *er* is used frequently to represent /ə/, the unstressed neutral vowel in "sofa." Examples: *yaller, fergive, yer,* as well as *ye,* for unstressed "*you*." Unstressed /I/ correlates with *i* in *minit* "minute." In Irish, *av* "of" is commonly used to indicate that the vowel is lowered.

Re-spelled consonants pose only a few problems for the reader. In Cockney *marf* "mouth" is confusing because of *f*, which replaces *th*, and *r*, which represents a lengthening of /a/ and is not otherwise articulated. Representing stressed /a⁓ɑ/ by *ar* and unstressed /ə/ by *er*, as above, is a practice of writers who do not pronounce postvocalic /r/. In Irish, words like *thricks* "tricks," *sthripped* "stripped," and *dhry* "dry," show aspiration of *t* and *d*; and *girrls* "girls" and *harrd worrk* "hard work" show that /r/ is to be pronounced.

O'Neill's re-spelling system relies heavily on the use of apostrophes. In fact, *Desire Under the Elms* seems peppered with them, making reading of the text rather difficult. However, close inspection reveals that every apostrophe is very carefully placed to do one of the following: to reduce the

---

[10] When silent *e* is not available as in *aisy* "easy" (Irish), phoneme /e/ correlates with grapheme *ai*.

number of syllables, as *'spect* "expect," *s'pose* "suppose"; to show omission of a consonant, *on'y* "only"; to show substitution of a final /n/ for /ŋ/ in an unstressed syllable, as *speakin'* "speaking"; to show difference in vowel value, as *'arn* "earn"; to make a distinction between homonyms, as *p'int* "point" in contrast with *pint* (unit of measurement); and to represent a very short /ə/ in phrases, often where two consonants are not permitted to cluster, as in *t'bed* "to bed," in *t'get* "to get," and even in *t'* at the end of a sentence: "Cuss all ye've a mind t'." The overall effect of the extensive use of apostrophes is to give the speech relaxed articulation and a distinctive rhythm.

O'Neill made very little use of "eye dialect," re-spellings that are simply alternate spellings for the usual pronunciations of words, as in *sez* and *wuz*. This device was used commonly in the nineteenth century in humorous dialectal writings. "Eye dialect" would not have served O'Neill's serious purpose. Furthermore, he was writing primarily for the stage production where its effect would, of course, be lost.

He relied chiefly on phonological and grammatical deviations from educated speech. With the exception of early twentieth-century underworld and sporting slang, which he used abundantly in some of his plays, he made little use of words or expressions to remind the reader of a regional dialect. A word or two, like *bloke* "fellow" and *bleedin'* "bloody" (intensive expressions in Cockney), sufficed. In most of his plays he relied on words and expressions that are either colloquial, slang, or low-colloquial clichés, almost all commonly used in the United States. In plays where old-fashioned rustic speech was called for, as in *Desire Under the Elms*, he made extensive use of a few little function words in types of expression that are survivals. Examples show that their connotations would be quite understandable to an American audience:

"There's more to it *nor* yew know, makes him tell."
"I got a lot in me folks don't know *on*."
"It's wa'm [warm] down *t'* the barn."
". . . . twenty-dollar pieces—thirty *on* 'em."

The few metaphors that he used seem appropriate for the New England countryside, as for example:

"hard 'n' bitter's a hickory tree!"
"It's just t'spite us—the damned old mule."
"Wait'll we see this cow [woman] the Old Man's hitched t'."

Because the function words and metaphors give the speech a rustic and often old-fashioned flavor without hindering communication, I feel O'Neill might have used them more extensively.

The play lacks the local vocabulary that larded the verses in James Russell Lowell's *Biglow Papers*, written in the same dialect. But *Biglow Papers* had to be glossed for the reader. This would be very inappropriate

236   for O'Neill's plays, which were written for a twentieth-century audience. The need for easy communication across the footlights rules out archaic vocabulary in a play.

There was no attempt made by the author to differentiate middle-class American speech according to regions. In the case of two educated Englishmen, O'Neill made no attempt, on the phonological level, to give them British speech. Their speech was made distinct, in a few instances, by sentence structure but more often by some characteristic expressions.

Irish brogue occurs more often in his plays that do other dialects. It ranges the widest, from speech that is full of re-spellings and has some Irish expressions, like those of Matt Burke in *Anna Christie* and of Paddy in *The Hairy Ape:*

BURKE: "Is it losing the small wits ye iver had, ye are?"

". . . aisy for a rale man with guts to him, the like of me."

PADDY: "Ho-ho divil mend you? Is it to belong to that you're wishing?"

"Me back is broke. I'm bate out—bate."

to the Irish "brogue" and "lilt" that one is apprised of in the directions of the playwright for *Long Day's Journey into Night,* but which is not easily detected in the written lines. If the reader knows the Irish dialect, he can supply the brogue in the speech of the Irish maid and, as mentioned in the stage directions, the touch of "Irish lilt" in the mother's voice "when she is merry." The reader who does not know it can do without it very well in that play.

When O'Neill knew a dialect well, as he did Irish-American, he would use it to convey the subtleties usually available only to a native speaker: humor, sarcasm, irony, lack of respect, ridicule, complete humiliation, feelings he conveyed to the reader largely by the switching and lapsing of the speaker from an acquired dialect to a native one, or vice versa. *A Touch of the Poet* and *Moon for the Misbegotten* reveal the shadings of emotion that O'Neill was linguistically capable of expressing in writing. Indeed, his virtuosity suggests a near-to-native command of that dialect. In both plays there are bidialectal characters.

In *A Touch of the Poet* Con Melody, the Irish-immigrant tavern owner, has acquired careful educated speech to match the aristocratic airs of the gentleman he imagines himself to be. On rare occasions, when he is off-guard and in a convivial mood, the brogue slips back into his voice. But in the end of the play, when he suffers deep humiliation and shock that shatters his pretensions completely, he lapses into thick brogue:

MELODY: "But he's dead now, and his last bit av lyin' pride is murthered and stinkin'."

"So let you be aisy, darlint. He'll nivir again hurt you with his sneers, and his pretendin' he's a gentleman, blatherin' about pride and honor,

and his boastin' av duels in the days that's gone, and his showin' off
before the Yankees, and thim laughin' at him, prancing around drunk
on his beautiful thoroughbred mare—
>   (He gulps as if he were choking back a sob.)
For she's dead, too, poor baste."

This slipping back into the mother dialect in time of great emotion is a
psychological aspect of bilingualism that O'Neill seemed to understand.
Con's daughter Sara, second-generation American, switches dialects to
suit her mood, but her normal speech is standard American with occasional grammatical slips. When Sara is talking to her mother, who speaks
with a broad brogue, she uses a few Irish expressions. The daughter's
switching to the mother's dialect is not quite so skillfully handled here
as it is, say, in Sean O'Casey's *Juno and the Paycock* when Mary is talking
to her mother, Mrs. Boyle; but O'Neill's linguistic insights seem right.
When Sara is talking to her father, she normally uses educated speech,
but when she wishes to show contempt for his pretentions, she switches
to an exaggerated brogue that never fails to irritate him.

In *Moon for the Misbegotten* there is a ribald and raucous scene in
which the Irish ne'er-do-well tenant farmer, Phil Hogan, and his gargan-
tuan daughter, Josie, drive off an aristocratic neighbor who has come to
complain about Hogan's pigs. They succeed in ridiculing him beyond
endurance by their switching into a stronger brogue delivered more
rapidly than usual.

Being himself the son of an immigrant father, O'Neill had opportunity
to become aware of the linguistic difference between parents and children
in a bidialectal family. Just as he showed Sara's educated English as different from her father's, so O'Neill also distinguished second-generation
Negroes in New York from their parents, though not so skillfully. In
All God's Chillun Got Wings, Jim Harris, as a small boy, speaks his
mother's Southern dialect; but later, when both he and his sister Hattie
are educated adults, their speech is middle-class American without a trace
of Southern accent, even when talking to their mother. In "The Dreamy
Kid" there is a grandmother speaking with a Southern accent. Her grand-
son, who was brought to New York from the South as a baby, has become
a gangster. His speech still has Southern features, but his vocabulary
includes underworld slang.

MAMMY: "Does yo' know—I gives you dat name w'an yo's des a baby—
lyin' in my arms."

DREAMY: (to Irene) "Leggo o'me! Why you come here follerin' me? Ain't
yo' got 'nuff sense in yo' fool head ter know de bulls is liable to shadow
you when dey knows you's my gal? Is you pinin' ter git me kotched
an' sent to de chair? . . . Can dat bull or I'll fix you."

The density of Southern features in his speech would be more credible

238   if their home were in Harlem instead of Carmine Street in Greenwich Village. The other Negro characters who appear in O'Neill's plays without their parents, have idiolects which seem to be more credible. Joe Mott, also of the underworld and an habitué of Harry Hope's saloon in *The Iceman Cometh,* differs very little from other characters in respect to speech, having only four distinguishing features as shown in: "I's going to," "No, suh, never no more," and "I got idea." Joe, it is clear, has been raised in a lower-class neighborhood of New York. But Brutus Jones in *The Emperor Jones,* a pullman porter, seems to be first-generation Negro removed from the South. Though O'Neill was aware of the sub-dialects within Negro speech and treated them quite well, he did not make use of switching and lapsing as he did in Irish brogue.

With careful combing it is possible to find inconsistencies in O'Neill's treatment of the dialects he employed. As I have mentioned above, however he planned at the outset to treat a certain dialect, he usually maintained the treatment consistently. But by its very nature, language is not consistent. Changes are always at work in a dialect of a community of speakers and also in the idiolect of an individual member of that group. So, while a language is always systematic, there are some features in a dialect that are stable and other features that vary between competing forms. Therefore, consistency itself cannot be said unreservedly to be a criterion by which to judge a representation of a dialect. Rather we must ask, is the writer being consistent in the right places and inconsistent in the right places? We should qualify it further and say "the important right places." What reader or audience could object to a character's saying "It's a matter between him and me," and a few minutes later saying, "There was never any trouble between he and I." But for a writer to let a lower-class character say "he don't" in one breath and "he doesn't" in the next is less likely. What is important is that the native speaker of the dialect must feel that the choice is right, given a certain situation. Let us consider O'Neill's consistency or lack of consistency in his treatment of Cockney. Basically, a Cockney speaker does not pronounce initial /h/ in a word, but frequently initial /h/ occurs in his speech. And where will he be apt to put it? Very likely on a stressed word beginning with a vowel, and his uncertainty will lead him often to place it mistakenly on a stressed word where there is no initial /h/; Example: "Six 'ard boiled heggs." O'Neill's re-spelling system, in each of the plays with a Cockney speaker, apparently was to drop initial *h* in a consistent fashion and to put it on a very few emphatic words where /h/ was not permitted in standard speech. It calls for a chuckle when he does so—words reserved for moments when dignity is at stake: for example, in *The Long Voyage Home,* "You don't get drunk an' hinsult poor gels. . . ." (Freda); "H'abusin' me like a dawg. . . ." (Meg). This is a fairly accurate rendering of the linguistic phenomenon of a Cockney speaker consciously using a dialect he is uncertain about. There are a few exceptions, as when O'Neill did not drop the initial *h*, probably unintended; but, on the whole, we can say that he was consistent and inconsistent in the right places in respect to this particular feature.

O'Neill used variations from character to character within a dialect community, depending on occupation, age, sex, and temperament. These subdialects within a regional dialect are observable in the plays with New England characters. Female characters in roles calling for sympathy of the audience have standard speech; the speech of less likeable ones contains rustic features. In two plays the wife's speech is quite different from that of her husband. In *Beyond the Horizon,* the wife, Kate Mayo, employs educated speech, and the farmer-husband James, the rustic old-fashioned Eastern New England dialect, but in the stage directions O'Neill explains that the wife was a former schoolteacher. That makes the situation more plausible to the reader, but the playgoer is left to wonder—if he notices it at all. Also, in the same play, Mrs. Atkins, an irritable, talkative, illiterate widow, has a rustic dialect, though not as old-fashioned as that of her neighbor, James Mayo, and it is sprinkled here and there with Calvinistic phrases. The Mayo sons, Robert and Andrew, have slightly different dialects. Robert, who has had a year in college, speaks standard English; the speech of Andrew, who did not go to college, is slightly rustic, with a few grammatical features like "ain't" and ". . . the way us two feel about the farm."

The difference between the dialect of James Mayo and that of his seafaring brother-in-law, Captain Dick Scott, is conditioned by occupation:

SCOTT: "You fellows look as if you was settin' up for a corpse. God A'mighty, there ain't anyone dead, be there?

MAYO: Don't play the dunce, Dick! You know as well as we there ain't no great cause to be feelin' chipper.

SCOTT: You shouldn't be taking it so hard. 's far as I kin see, this vige'll make a man of him. I'll see to it he learns how to navigate, 'n study for a mate's c'tificate right off—and it'll give him a trade for the rest of his life, if he wants to travel."

As young men they may have had the same rural old-fashioned dialect; but in time the farmer's become less old-fashioned, and the New England seafarer took on more of the speech features that generations of captains, most of whose more isolated lives were spent at sea, had passed on to those who followed them.

So, in *Beyond the Horizon* these seven characters, closely related by blood and marriage, are speaking five different subdialects within the Eastern New England dialect. Each of the dialects is influenced largely by level of education or by occupation or by generation. The social level is the same.

240   It should be clear from these summary impressions of O'Neill's treatment of some dialects that his Eastern New England rustic dialect was only a small part of his total dialectal writing, but it was an important part. It was used throughout one long play, *Desire under the Elms,* and in parts of others. Moreover *Desire under the Elms* was one of the plays generally considered important enough to stand as a major work of O'Neill, one of the few on which his reputation would probably rest in the future. His treatment of the dialect in that play had been adversely criticized.

The unfavorable criticism is understandable—but unfair to O'Neill. Unless the reader knows how to interpret the re-spellings, he may read it with distortion and thus assess O'Neill's representations adversely. It was Sumner Ives' theory of literary dialects that offered the key to interpretation: Persons whose speech is regionally different from that of a writer of a literary dialect will misinterpret the writer's unconventional spellings, thus distorting the sounds the author intended.[11]

Examining the dialect in *Desire* through the filter of O'Neill's dialect, which is phonologically different from my own, I was able to compare items of this dialect with items covered in the *Linguistic Atlas of New England* and with items of the same dialect in James Russell Lowell's *Biglow Papers,* which James W. Downer had found to be authentic.[12] O'Neill's representation is substantially accurate phonologically and grammatically. Regrettably, it is too meticulously rendered; five years later, in *Mourning Becomes Electra,* the dialect is used again, but this time more artistically. The distinctive features of the dialect are there, but density of re-spellings and apostrophes has been toned down. The dialect is suggested, and reading of the text is made easy.

SETH BECKWITH, gardener: "No, ye don't! I'm onto your game! He's aimin' t git so full of Injun courage he wouldn't mind if a ghost sot on his lap! Purty slick you be, Abner! Swill my licker so's you kin skin me out o' my bet!"

This line, taken from the drinking scene, shows re-spelling at the fullest, but the following line is more representative:

"Oh, hers and a hull passel of others. The grave-yard's full of Mannons and they all spent their nights to hum here. You needn't worry but you'll have plenty 'o company, Abner!"

O'Neill knew this dialect well when he employed it thirteen years earlier in the short play "Ile," but his rendering of it in a total of six plays improved gradually over the years. Although O'Neill knew this dialect well

---

[11] Sumner Ives, "A Theory of Literary Dialect," *Tulane Studies in English,* II (1950), pp. 146–53.

[12] James W. Downer, "Features of New England Rustic Pronunciation in James R. Lowell's *Biglow Papers,*" (unpublished dissertation, University of Michigan, 1958).

and could represent several variations of it, he was never as versatile in using it as he was when he wrote Irish brogue.

Explaining the methods O'Neill used in treating dialects raises the question of the effectiveness of his techniques. A brief comment on the use of dialects on the American stage at the time O'Neill began to write plays suggests the answer. It also reveals a handicap he faced in using nonstandard dialects in serious plays.

It had been the practice in the nineteenth and early twentieth centuries to use dialect to inject humor into a play. From the rustic Yankee's first entrance on the American stage in 1787 in *The Contrast,* the humor of his dialect had been exploited. Large immigrations from Europe in the nineteenth century added varieties of "broken English" to the repertoire of humorous dialects on the American stage. Occasionally a modified version of these national dialects was used in serious plays of intrigue; but, in general, the moment a character spoke nonstandard English the audience's reaction was amusement. Actually this was not peculiar to the American stage. It is well known that the Elizabethan stage used "broken" English for the same effect.

The tradition that nonstandard dialects were used on the American stage for levity was one of the many conventions that O'Neill broke. The biographies and critical reviews of his plays have not, to my knowledge, indicated that an audience ever laughed derisively at the nonstandard dialects in his plays. In *Welded,* the audience tittered over the banal talk of the middle-class characters, we are told by Ludwig Lewisohn; but the lower-class characters and rustic folk in O'Neill's plays have always commanded the serious attention of an audience.[13] Though there may be other reasons why "broken" English has ceased to be the "rib tickler" it once was on the American stage, O'Neill did much to establish a serious tradition of using dialect for characterizing and individualizing people in plays. His intention was always serious, and the dialects helped him to achieve his intention. Perhaps the authenticity of his dialects helped to break an old stage tradition.

To depict life as he knew it was the motivating principle that guided O'Neill's writing career for forty-five years. When he chose to re-create in his plays the assorted people he knew at sea, on the waterfront, and in the saloons of New York and New London, he undertook the tremendous task of giving each the type of speech that belonged to him and distinguished him from others. That O'Neill did this with great care and attention to details was the burden that plagued him many times in the career that he decreed for himself.

[13] Oscar Cargill, N. Bryllian Fagin, and William J. Fisher, eds., *O'Neill and his Plays: Four Decades of Criticism,* (New York, 1961), p. 164.

part 4

ASPECTS
OF REGIONAL
AND SOCIAL
DIALECTS

What Do You Call It?

Hans Kurath

Until the late 1940's there were thought to be three major
speech areas in the United States: Eastern (New England);
Southern; and General American, spoken everywhere except
in the East and South. In 1949 Professor Kurath published
his *A Word Geography of the Eastern United States,* one of the
most important and influential of the studies of the dialects
of the United States. In this book he summarized the
vocabulary evidence of the *Linguistic Atlas* materials and
showed that the earlier designations did not fit the evidence.
There are, as Professor Kurath indicated, three areas:
Northern, Midland, and Southern, each of which has subareas.
His evidence showed that there is a definite speech area,
Midland, separating the Northern and Southern areas; this
had not been known before his study. Subsequent studies have
confirmed his findings. In "What Do You Call It?" Professor
Kurath deals with a number of vocabulary items, showing
how terms differ from region to region, and how they reflect
cultural and settlement patterns.

246   Do you call it a *pail* or a *bucket?* Do you draw water from a *faucet* or from a *spicket?* Do you pull down the *blinds,* the *shades,* or the *curtains* when it gets dark? Do you *wheel* the baby, or do you *ride* it or *roll* it? In a *baby carriage,* a *buggy,* a *coach,* or a *cab?*

Do children rock on a *seesaw,* a *teeter board,* a *teeter-totter,* a *dandle,* a *tilting board,* a *ridy-horse,* a *hicky-horse,* or on a *tippity-bounce?* Do boys *skip school, hook school, bag school, lay out of school,* or do they *play hookey* or *truant* to go fishing? Do they bait the hook with an *earthworm, angleworm, angle dog, fishworm, redworm,* or with a *night crawler* or *night walker?*

Where is a *dragonfly* called a *snake doctor,* a *snake feeder,* a *darning needle,* a *mosquito hawk?* Where is the *skunk* a *polecat,* the *chipmunk* a *ground squirrel* or a *grinnie,* the *screech owl* a *scrooch owl* or a *shivering owl,* and the *sycamore* a *buttonwood* or a *buttonball?*

On the farm, is it a *haystack,* a *rick,* or a *barrack;* a *haycock,* a *shock,* a *doodle,* or a *tumble?* Are cows kept in a *cowpen,* a *cuppin,* a *brake,* a *pound,* a *milk gap,* or a *pightle?*

Do horses *whinny,* or do they *whicker* or *nicker?* Do cows *moo, low, loo,* or *hum?* Is the bull called *the critter, the toro, the brute, the beast, the masculine,* or simply *the bull?*

Where is a *doughnut* known as a *cruller,* a *fried cake,* a *fatcake,* a *cookie;* a *corn griddlecake* as a *corncake,* a *johnnikin,* a *johnnycake,* a *hobby;* a *wheatcake* as a *battercake,* a *flannel cake,* a *fritter,* a *pancake,* a *hotcake?* Do you fry your eggs in a *spider,* in a *skillet,* or in a *frying pan?*

Is an illegitimate child known as a *woods colt,* an *old-field colt,* a *come-by-chance,* or as a *Sunday baby* in your part of the country? Where is a mock serenade a *chivaree,* and where is it called a *horning,* a *belling,* a *skimerton,* or a *calathump?*

Such questions can be answered for the Eastern States now that the survey of this, the oldest, part of our country has been completed for the forthcoming *Linguistic Atlas of the United States,* a research project sponsored by the American Council of Learned Societies. Partial answers can also be given for the Middle West, since the survey of the Great Lakes Basin, the Ohio Valley, and the Upper Mississippi Valley, which is going forward under the joint sponsorship of the University of Michigan and the Universities of Wisconsin and Minnesota, has made such excellent progress.

We can now say, for instance, that *pail, whiffletree, teeterboard* (seesaw), *darning needle* (dragon fly) and *angleworm* (earthworm), and the cow

From *The Michigan Alumnus Quarterly Review* 55 (Summer, 1949) 293–299. Reprinted with the permission of *The Michigan Alumnus Quarterly Review* (now *The Michigan Quarterly Review*) and Hans Kurath.

call *boss!* are current only in New England and in the New England settlement area, which extends from the Hudson River to the Upper Mississippi Valley and beyond; that *blinds* for the roller shades, *skillet* for the cast-iron frying pan, *smearcase* for cottage cheese, *quarter till ten* for quarter to ten, and the cow call *sook!* are found only in Pennsylvania and the Pennsylvania settlement area, which includes the Ohio Valley, the Valley of Virginia, and the Appalachians; and that *lightwood* for kindling, *turn of wood* for an armful of wood, *snapbeans* for string beans, and the cow calls *co-wench!* and *co-ee!* occur only in the old plantation country of the South and the cotton belt of the Gulf States.

The surveys show, furthermore, that some expressions are restricted to certain parts of the New England settlement area (the North), to parts of the Pennsylvania settlement area (the Midland), or to parts of the Southern settlement area (the South).

Drag for the stone boat, *double runner* for the bobsled, *pigsty* for the pigpen, *lean-to* for the shedlike addition to a barn, *whicker* for whinny, *bonny-clapper* or *bonny-clabber* for curdled sour milk, *tonic* for soda pop, *rock maple* for the sugar maple, and *buttonwood* for the sycamore are heard only in Eastern New England (sometimes including the Upper Connecticut Valley). Rhode Island alone has *johnnycake* for a corn griddlecake, *dandle* for the seesaw, *eace worm* for the earthworm; while *tempest* for a storm and *cade* for a pet lamb are found from Narragansett Bay to Cape Cod.

In the Dutch settlement area on the Hudson and in East Jersey one hears *hay barrack* for a square haystack with corner posts and sliding roof, *pot cheese* for cottage cheese, *skimerton* or *skimilton* for the mock serenade, *suppawn* for corn mush, *sapbush* for the maple grove, and *teeter-totter* for the seesaw. Some of the old Hudson Valley expressions have spread into Upstate New York and into western New England, especially *coal scuttle, sugarbush* for the maple grove, *cruller* for the sweetened un-raised doughnut, and *stoop* for a small porch at the front or back door.

Parts of the Midland have equally distinctive local expressions. *Coal oil* for kerosene, *flannelcakes* for griddlecakes, *pavement* for the sidewalk, and *baby coach* for the baby carriage are characteristic of southeastern Pennsylvania (the Philadelphia trade area). A Philadelphia schoolboy has *hotcakes* (griddlecakes) for breakfast, and he *bags school* when he takes a day off.

In Western Pennsylvania (the Pittsburgh area) and in the Appalachians a paper bag is a *poke,* string beans are *green beans,* sugar maples are *sugar trees,* and kerosene is called *lamp oil* (around Pittsburgh also *carbon oil*).

Fatcake for the doughnut, *thick milk* for curdled milk, *ponhaws* for scrapple, *sawbuck* for the sawhorse, *saddle horse* for the near-horse, all patterned on Pennsylvania Dutch expressions or borrowed from this

248   German dialect, are current in large parts of Pennsylvania and in the mountain valleys to the south.

     The Appalachians, too, have their unique regional expressions, but they are not as numerous as is generally believed. Here a cowpen is a *milk gap* or *milking gap,* a sugar maple grove is a *sugar orchard,* a man's vest is a *jacket,* and the mantle piece of a fireplace is called the *fireboard.* In the main, however, the Blue Ridge and the Appalachians agree either with Pennsylvania or with the Southern Piedmont in word usage.

     In the old plantation country of the South, especially in the Tidewater area, regional and local expressions abound. The Eastern Shore of Maryland, the Western Shore and the Virginia Tidewater, the Piedmont of Virginia, Albermarle Sound, the valleys of the Cape Fear and the Peedee, and the Low Country of South Carolina each has its characteristic expressions.

     The Piedmont of Virginia is perhaps the most distinctive subarea of the South (unless it be the Low Country of South Carolina). In this part of Virginia the corncrib is a *cornhouse,* the cow barn a *cow house,* the cowpen a *cuppin,* the near-horse a *line horse* or *wheel horse;* horses *nicker* and cows *low* or *lower;* a man's vest is still a *wesket,* and a burlap bag is a *croker sack; school breaks* or *breaks up* in the *evening* (afternoon); the freestone peach is a *soft peach,* the clingstone a *plum peach;* the dragonfly is a *snake doctor,* an illegitimate child an *old-field colt* (not a *woods colt,* as in the Carolinas).

     Some of these Virginia Piedmont expressions have been carried westward into the Blue Ridge and the Appalachians, as *nicker* and *snake doctor.*

     Strictly local expressions are current in various parts of the largely rural Southern coast, which is deeply indented in so many places and mostly sparsely settled. On the Eastern Shore of Maryland one hears *cornstack* for the corncrib, *caps* for the cornhusks (which elsewhere in the South are called *shucks*), *cocky-horse* for the seesaw, and *'mongst-ye* by the side of the general Southern *you-all.* On the coast of North Carolina cows *hum,* and you listen to the call of the *shivering owl* (screech owl) while your head rests on the bolster that runs *slam across* the bed. On Chesapeake Bay and on the Carolina Coast every major point of land has such local expressions, probably as a heritage of Colonial times.

     Regional and local expressions are most common in the vocabulary of the intimate everyday life of the home and the farm—not only among the simple folk and the middle class but also among the cultured. Food, clothing, shelter, health, the day's work, play, mating, social gatherings, the land, the farm buildings, implements, the farm stock and crops, the weather, the fauna and the flora—these are the intimate concern of the common folk in the countryside, and for these things expressions are handed down in the family and the neighborhood that schooling and reading and a familiarity with regional or national usage do not blot out.

Until recently scholars have not paid much attention to regional usage, although even the most casual observations make it clear that Detroiters don't talk like New Yorkers or Bostonians, nor like Philadelphians, and certainly not like people in Richmond, Nashville, or New Orleans. And if the speech differences are so great between rather well-schooled city people, how about the country folk? Could anyone who has been in different parts of our country mistake, sight unseen, a Maine fisherman or farmer for one from the Eastern Shore of Maryland, the Gulf Coast, or the Great Lakes? If four farmers from these four areas met, they could doubtless talk shop or swap stories; but again and again utterances would have to be repeated or paraphrased for the benefit of one or the other of them.

Regional differences in the vocabulary and in the pronunciation of American English being what they are, why have scholars devoted so little time and effort to recording them? Why have no significant efforts been made to account for them?

Several reasons suggest themselves.

1) During the nineteenth and the first quarter of the twentieth century linguistic research was focused on the earlier periods of English and on the history of Standard British English.

2) American English was viewed as a deviation—if not as an aberration—from Standard British English, and therefore hardly worthy of serious and painstaking investigation.

3) The dictionaries of Noah Webster and of Worcester and the great Standard Dictionary edited by W. D. Whitney, all of them the work of New England scholars during the period of New England's predominance in literature and scholarship, gave the illusion that American usage was more uniform than it is, simply because many Southern and Midland terms failed to be included for lack of information. The prestige of the dictionaries in school and college was such that all unrecorded terms were apt to be looked down on as "dialect," and to be shunned.

4) Scholarly interest in regional culture and in the everyday life of the folk is of very recent date in this country. F. C. Turner gave the decisive impulse to the study of the region or section as an integral part of the nation, including in his purview not only physiographical, economic, and political factors but also the traditional attitudes and folkways of the settlers.

With the recognition of the fact that our national culture is essentially a configuration of regional cultures, the study of the culture of the several regions and their component parts assumes a new importance and a dignity that it has lacked in the past. We must know the parts before we

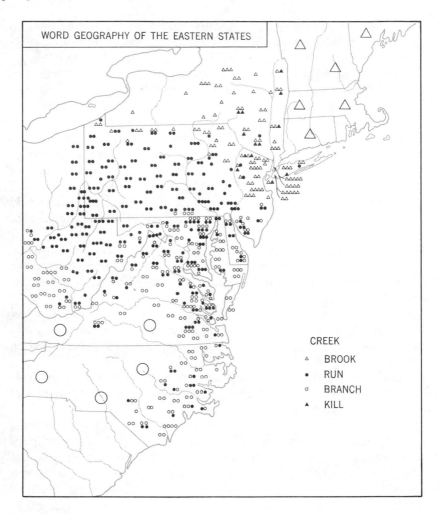

WORD GEOGRAPHY OF THE EASTERN STATES

CREEK
△ BROOK
• RUN
ᵟ BRANCH
▲ KILL

can understand the whole, and in turn we must strive for a view of the whole before we can hope to see the parts in proper perspective.

Applying this point of view to the study of our language, which is an integral part of our culture and in which all phases of our national and regional life of the present as well as the past are somehow reflected, we come to realize that the student of American English must investigate not only those features of grammar, vocabulary, and pronunciation that

[1] These maps are reproduced from Hans Kurath, *A Word Geography of the Eastern United States,* (Figs. 93 and 124) with permission of the University of Michigan Press. Copyright 1949 by the University of Michigan.

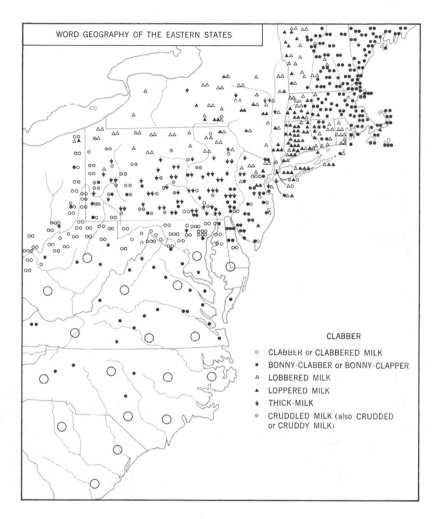

WORD GEOGRAPHY OF THE EASTERN STATES

CLABBER

○ CLABBER or CLABBERED MILK
● BONNY-CLABBER or BONNY-CLAPPER
△ LOBBERED MILK
▲ LOPPERED MILK
↓ THICK-MILK
◉ CRUDDLED MILK (also CRUDDED or CRUDDY MILK)

are common to educated Americans in all parts of the country, but also those in which the cultured Bostonian's speech differs from that of the cultured New Yorker, the Chicagoan, the Virginian, the Texan. Not only that; the speech of the common man and of the simple country folk in all parts of the country must also be brought within the range of observation and research on the part of trained linguists. We must know the usage of the simple folk if we want to get a historical perspective of the speech of the large middle class, and we must know the speechways of this middle class of farmers, tradesmen, and businessmen before we can hope to trace the development of the various regional types of cultivated

252   American English. In a society like ours, where all social groups freely intercommunicate, where no hard and fast lines are drawn between social classes, where a man of humble background can rise to a position of influence within his lifetime, the give-and-take in speechways between social groups and the social revaluation or devaluation in usage is so many-sided and so rapid that all forms of speech must be known to us before we can deal satisfactorily with the speech of any one of the social or regional groups.

The plans laid for the *Linguistic Atlas of the United States* two decades ago called for a systematic sampling of usage on all social levels. Trained observers have visited the homes of nearly fifteen hundred persons from all walks of life and have questioned each one of them from ten to twenty hours to determine their habitual usage on about a thousand carefully selected points. Almost every county in the Eastern States, from Maine to Georgia and as far west as Eastern Ohio, is now on record, so that the geographic spread and the social dissemination of many words, phrases, grammatical forms, and pronunciations can be readily plotted for this part of our country, which includes all of Colonial America and now holds nearly two-fifths of the population of the Union.

When one maps the individual words as recorded for the *Atlas,* one finds that perhaps no two of them occupy precisely the same area; but one also discovers quite soon that certain types of geographic distribution recur. Boundaries drawn for the various words showing similar distributions will coalesce in some sectors and diverge or flare out in others; but they will either form irregular concentric circles or more or less parallel straight lines. Thus we find that numerous word boundaries (isoglosses) encircle the Piedmont of Virginia and the Lower Hudson Valley, and that strands of parallel isoglosses run in a westerly direction through Northern Pennsylvania and in a northerly direction through the central part of New England. These bundles or strands of isoglosses mark dialect boundaries; and—given an adequate sample of usage—the number of isoglosses contained in such a bundle is an index to the relative importance of the boundary so identified.

On the basis of the isoglosses for more than four hundred regional or local words recorded for the *Linguistic Atlas* we find that there are two clearly marked dialect boundaries of outstanding importance in the Eastern United States. One runs in a westerly direction through the northern counties of Pennsylvania, separating the North from the Midland; the other follows the crest of the Blue Ridge in Virginia, from the Potomac to the James, separating the South from the Midland.

Some of the isoglosses running through northern Pennsylvania may be mentioned here:

North	Midland
pail	bucket
whiffletree	s(w)ingletree
johnnycake	cornbread
angleworm	fish(ing)worm
button ball	sycamore
boss!	sook!
lobbered (loppered) milk	thick-milk, clabber

Some of the dividing lines that follow the Blue Ridge are:

South	Midland
shades, curtains	blinds
gutters	spouts, spouting
snake doctor	snake feeder
quarter to ten	quarter till ten
co-wench! co-ee!	sook!
clabber cheese	smearcase
snap beans	green beans

Other boundaries of importance run as follows:

1) In a northerly direction from the mouth of the Connecticut to the Green Mountains, separating Eastern New England (the Bay Colony) from Western New England (the New Haven and Connecticut River settlements);

2) From the fork of the Susquehanna in Pennsylvania to Sandy Hook in New Jersey, separating the New England and Hudson Valley settlements from the Pennsylvania settlements;

3) From Dover in Delaware by way of Baltimore to Harper's Ferry on the Potomac, separating the Pennsylvania settlements from the Maryland and Virginia settlements;

4) From the lower James through the central Piedmont of North Carolina to Roanoke in the Blue Ridge, separating the Virginia settlements from the Carolina settlements;

5) Along the northern watershed of the Kanawha in West Virginia, separating the predominantly Pennsylvanian settlements of Northern West Virginia from Southern West Virginia.

As has been already indicated, all of these speech boundaries reflect settlement boundaries. Some of them are sharply defined; others have rather the character of transition belts, partly because of the early mingling of settlers, partly because of later spreading of speech forms across old settlement boundaries (as from the Philadelphia area onto the Eastern Shore of Maryland, from the Virginia Piedmont into the Valley of Virginia, and from Metropolitan New York in the direction of Philadelphia).

By establishing the correlation between the speech areas of today with

254   settlement areas and with the shifting boundaries of trade areas and the radiation of influence from cultural centers, the linguist opens up a new approach to the problems of tracing the history of our English during the three centuries that have elapsed since the first English colonies were planted on the Atlantic Seaboard. Our work has just begun. It will take years to complete the collection of the facts and to interpret the findings with reference to the history of the population before we will have a realistic account of the character and the history of our varieties of English. Not until then can we undertake the much more difficult task of separating American innovations from traditional British usage.

Some Eastern Virginia Pronunciation Features

E. Bagby Atwood

The speech of Eastern Virginia, although essentially Southern, has a number of distinctive features that set it apart from the surrounding area. Using *Atlas* materials, Professor Atwood charts selected speech features that are common to the area.

E. Bagby Atwood was Professor of English at the University of Texas. For a number of years he was engaged in making a survey of the vocabulary of Texas, and in 1962 he published *The Regional Vocabulary of Texas.* His study, *A Survey of Verb Forms in the Eastern United States* (1958) is one of the most important of the studies based on the *Linguistic Atlas* materials.

For many generations the "Tuckahoes," or inhabitants of the plantation areas of Eastern Virginia, have maintained a culture which distin-

From *University of Virginia Studies* IV (1951) 111–124. Reprinted with the permission of E. D. Hirsch Jr., Chairman of the Department of English, University of Virginia, and Mrs. E. Bagby Atwood.

256   guishes them from their neighbors on all sides. That this group developed a distinctive set of speech habits—a "dialect"—of their own has frequently been observed and commented on. Since the publication, in 1925, of E. F. Shewmake's "Laws of Pronunciation in Eastern Virginia," a considerable number of scholars have contributed their observations of phonological or lexical features thought to be peculiar to the area.[1]

In spite of the extensiveness of the previous observations, there has been considerable disagreement as to the limits of the Eastern Virginia speech type, and even, in some quarters, as to whether it exists as a separate type—that is, apart from coastal, or "plantation," Southern speech in general. The confusion arises chiefly from the facts that (1) many of the features adduced for Eastern Virginia are known to exist in other portions of the South and probably elsewhere; and (2) other features appear to be confined to only a portion of the area and thus do not characterize the region as whole, though they also may be shared with speech areas in other portions of the United States.

In order to obtain a clear picture of the Eastern Virginia area—or indeed of any other speech area—it is necessary to proceed from a systematically gathered body of data rather than from random observation. The field records of the *Linguistic Atlas of the United States and Canada* provide by far the best body of linguistic material as yet collected, and they will serve as the basis for the present study. These records consist of phonetic transcriptions of the usage of native informants chosen from well-spaced communities throughout the Eastern United States. The survey of the Eastern states has now been completed, although only the New England materials have been edited and published.[2] Something like

---

[1] Shewmake's study appeared in *Modern Language Notes,* XL (1925), 489–492. He has since published his doctoral dissertation, *English Pronunciation in Virginia* (Davidson, N. C., 1927) and a study entitled "Distinctive Virginia Pronunciation," *American Speech,* XVIII (1943), 33–38. Among other studies of Virginia pronunciation should be mentioned Argus Tresidder, "Notes on Virginia Speech," *American Speech,* XVI (1941), 112–120, and "The Sounds of Virginia Speech," *American Speech,* XVIII (1943), 261–272; W. Cabell Greet, "A Phonographic Expedition to Williamsburg, Virginia," *American Speech,* VI (1931), 161–172; Guy S. Lowman, "The Treatment of [au] in Virginia," *Proceedings of the Second International Congress of Phonetic Sciences* (Cambridge, 1936), pp. 122–125; A. K. Davis and A. A. Hill, "Dialect Notes on Records of Folk Songs from Virginia," *American Speech,* VIII (1933), pp. 52–56. Some features of Virginia speech are also treated in J. S. Kenyon, *American Pronunciation,* 10th ed. (Ann Arbor, 1950), especially pp. 210–213. Failure to cite these and other works in detail does not imply disparagement of any of them. They were, with the exception of Lowman's study, based on a different type of data from that used here, and none of them duplicate the geographical analysis here attempted.

[2] Hans Kurath and Bernard Bloch, *Linguistic Atlas of New England,* 3 vols. in 6 parts (1939–43). For a full explanation of *Atlas* methodology, see H. Kurath and others, *Handbook of the Linguistic Geography of New England* (1939).

550 records are available for the South Atlantic States, of which about 150 were made in Virginia.[3] The informants, it should be noted, fall into three groups: I, aged and poorly educated; II, middle-aged or younger, with average education; and III, highly educated, or cultured. Thus we may determine not only the geographical distribution of a speech form but also the social and educational levels on which it is current. The *Atlas* records have already been utilized by Phyllis J. Nixon, Elizabeth J. Dearden, and Hans Kurath in the analysis of Virginia vocabulary features, while Guy S. Lowman has likewise drawn data from the *Atlas* for a thorough study of a single pronunciation feature: the treatment of the diphthong in such words as *house*.[4] Many other features, of course, remain to be charted; only after a considerable number of individual distributions have been collected may we speak with any confidence of the "limits" or "boundaries" of a dialect, or of the subareas into which it may be divided. The present study is meant as a contribution of data, not as a conclusive demonstration.

In order to interpret the distribution of speech forms in Eastern Virginia, it is necessary to keep in mind the historical facts that might have a bearing on the development and spread of linguistic peculiarities.[5] The early Virginia settlements, it will be recalled, clung to the Tidewater, or Coastal Plain, for something like a century, because of the necessity of water transportation. In the eighteenth century, tobacco culture moved into the Piedmont, with various results. The shortage of laborers led to the introduction of African slavery on a large scale, and a degree of prosperity was achieved that far exceeded that of the more modest planters of the Tidewater. In the early years of Piedmont settlement, probably the trading centers along the Fall Line facilitated communication to such an extent that no sharp cleavage existed between Piedmont and Tidewater. However, after the development of overland transportation, the Tidewater area (particularly the easternmost points of land) and the Eastern Shore were to a considerable extent isolated. The tobacco culture

---

[3] All of the Virginia fieldwork was done by the late Guy S. Lowman. The records, which are now filed at the *Atlas* headquarters at the University of Michigan, were made available to me through the courtesy of Professor Kurath.

[4] Phyllis J. Nixon, *A Glossary of Virginia Words* (Publications of the American Dialect Society, No. 5 [1946]); Elizabeth J. Dearden, "A Word Geography of the South Atlantic States" (Brown University dissertation, 1941); Hans Kurath, *A Word Geography of the Eastern United States* (1949). Lowman's study is cited in the first footnote.

[5] It is hardly necessary in this study to document the facts of Virginia history, though they are of course subject to some controversy. I have been particularly indebted for background material to the works of R. A. Billington, U. B. Phillips, T. J. Wertenbaker, Rupert B. Vance, R. B. Bean, and F. L. Paxson. C. O. Paullin and J. K. Wright, *Atlas of the Historical Geography of the United States* (New York and Washington, 1932), has been immensely valuable.

258   of the Piedmont extended itself across the Potomac into the "Western Shore" of Maryland (lying to the South of Baltimore), and into two or three of the northernmost counties of North Carolina; yet it did not to any great extent advance beyond the Blue Ridge. The difficulties of transportation in the Valley were considerable; moreover, this area had begun to fill with a stream of migrants from Pennsylvania—chiefly "Scotch-Irish" and Germans—who were not only settling the choicer areas but also using the valleys as routes of travel to the Piedmont of North Carolina and ultimately to more westerly areas. Thus the Blue Ridge formed a fairly sharp and permanent boundary between two cultures and two types of population—between "Tuckahoe" on the east and "Cohee" on the west.

To be sure, a good many Eastern Virginians themselves migrated to other areas. Throughout the eighteenth century the yeoman farmers, finding themselves unable to compete with the large slaveholders, removed themselves in various directions—to northern and western North Carolina; across the Blue Ridge to the Valley settlements[6] and often southwestward to the Wilderness Trail; or over the divide to the New River leading into southern West Virginia. At the beginning of the nineteenth century, as a result of rapid and unchecked soil exhaustion, rich and poor alike were moving to new lands[7]—the former frequently to Middle Georgia and ultimately to other cotton lands of the Gulf States.

These migrations might be expected to have a bearing on the distribution of speech features in Eastern Virginia and the adjoining areas. Yet the spread of linguistic forms is by no means dependent entirely on direct migration. An area of prosperity and prestige—as the Piedmont of Virginia undoubtedly became—may serve as a center for the spread of linguistic behavior, and from it some features may advance even to rather remote areas. Still, speech forms travel not as the birds of the air but along the established lines of human communication; a study of individual linguistic distributions may therefore reveal to us something of the earlier pathways of social intercourse.[8]

The most frequently cited pronunciation features of Eastern Virginia will not be the primary concern of the present study. Among these features are (1) the use of a centralized first element in the [au] diphthong

---

[6] Thomas P. Abernethy estimates that as many as one-third of the early Valley settlers were Virginians. See "The First Transmontane Advance," *Humanistic Studies in Honor of John Calvin Metcalf* (1941), pp. 120–138.

[7] "Between 1790 and 1800 thirteen counties in Maryland and twenty-six in Virginia lost population, so rapid was the migration." R. A. Billington, *Westward Expansion* (1949), p. 247.

[8] See Kurath, *Word Geography*, pp. 41–43.

before voiceless consonants, as in *house* [həus]; (2) the similar treatment of the [ai] diphthong in such words as *white* [hwəit]; (3) the incidence of a palatal glide after the initial stops in such words as *garden* [gjɑədən]; (4) the appearance of the "broad *a*" [ɑ] in *pasture* and a few other words. Of these, the first has been thoroughly discussed by Lowman, on the basis of *Linguistic Atlas* data; it, as well as others, will certainly form a part of Kurath's phonology of American English, which is now in preparation. It will suffice here to point out (as J. S. Kenyon has already done[9]) that the first two features, though admirable criteria for Eastern Virginia, are shared with the Low Country of South Carolina as well as with much of Canada. The third ([gj-] in *garden*), though somewhat more frequent in Virginia than elsewhere, is actually current among the more ancient speakers throughout the South Atlantic states. The [ɑ] in *pasture* needs further investigation, since it apparently does not extend to many analogous words, as *glass, half,* etc.

The features which have been charted for the present study[10] represent for the most part matters of phonemic *choice* rather than phonemic *system*—that is, they do not raise the question of whether a phonemic distinction is possible, but merely of which one of two phonemes is chosen in a particular word. Some of these choices are no doubt systematic, in that they would apply to other words of similar phonological structure and similar history; others appear to be unsystematic, in that no law of any kind seems to govern them.

The first chart shows the pronunciation of *afraid* to rhyme with *said,* [ə'frɛd]. The incidence of this form marks what might be regarded as the approximate normal limits of the Eastern Virginia dialect. The feature is well established in both Piedmont and Tidewater. It occurs on the Western Shore of Maryland and in the Norfolk area; only on the Eastern Shore is it of rare occurrence. The two occurrences west of the Blue Ridge (Roanoke and Washington counties) are both in the speech of educated informants, and may represent recent adoptions of the form as a prestige feature. The pronunciation [ə'frɛd], it should be noted, is perfectly standard within its area, being used by all categories of informants. The same chart shows the distribution of the archaic form *afeard,*

---

[9] *American Pronunciation,* 10th ed. (1950), pp. 210 ff.

[10] None of the features here discussed have hitherto been plotted on the basis of *Linguistic Atlas* data; some of them, of course, have previously been observed and mentioned, either as "Southern" or as Virginia features. For example, J. S. Kenyon and T. A. Knott, *Pronouncing Dictionary of American English* (1944), label [laŋ] for *long* and [ə'frɛd] for *afraid* as Southern; Shewmake and Tresidder (see Footnote 1) regard [ə'frɛd] as Eastern Virginian; Greet and Shewmake mention [jæs] for *yes;* Shewmake observes that *home* is sometimes pronounced with [ʊ]. So far as I know, the peculiarities of *guardian* and *vegetables* that are discussed in this study have not previously been recorded.

260 which occurs in various conservative areas more or less surrounding
Eastern Virginia.

The next feature which is charted is the medial [-dʒ-] in *guardian*
—[gɑrdʒən] or [gɑrdʒənt] (to avoid confusion, the "Virginia" [gj-]
is not entered on the map). Although this pronunciation occurs at
a few points around Narragansett Bay, it is otherwise characteristic only
of Eastern Virginia—elsewhere in the East the almost universal popular
pronunciation is [ˌgɑr'din]. The ['gɑrdʒən] type covers most of Eastern
Virginia, though it does not reach to the vicinity of Alexandria or to the
Western Shore of Maryland. It is almost exclusively an uneducated pronunciation. An examination of this item provides some rather striking
examples of blended forms, which are characteristic of transition belts
between two geographically distributed speech forms. At various points
on the fringes of the ['gɑrdʒən] area (particularly in North Carolina), this
form is blended with the more usual American [ˌgɑr'din] to produce
[ˌgɑr'dʒin]. How this in turn is transmuted into [ˌgar'dʒin] defies conjec-
ture. In any case, we can observe a clear influence (though some would
regard it as a highly perverse one) operating to the southward from the
Virginia Piedmont.

Whether the medial [-dʒ-] would show a similar distribution in other

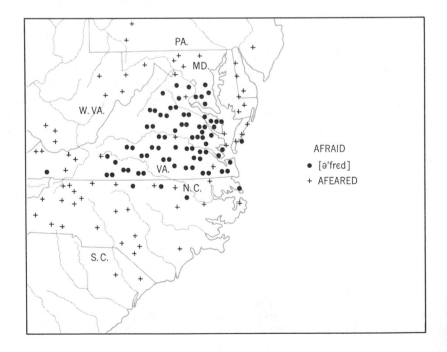

words where "standard" usage has [-diə-] (as *tedious, Indian,* etc.) is highly
problematical, since the *Atlas* provides no data on the matter.

The next feature to which attention is drawn is the occurrence of [æ] (the vowel of *hat*) in *yes.*[11] This trait, it can be observed, is concentrated in the central Piedmont, though its occurrence at several points around Chesapeake and Delaware bays, as well as on the North Carolina coast, would indicate that it is an older coastal feature. It was no doubt carried from the Tidewater to the Piedmont and there acquired some currency and prestige. Since [jæs] is often thought to be a Negro speech feature, it may be surprising that not one of the *Atlas* Negroes from Virginia uses this pronunciation. Within the area of its greatest currency, [jæs] is fully as common among the younger speakers as among the more elderly.

The next feature that is charted is the pronunciation of *home* with the vowel of *foot*—[hʊm]. This is concentrated in the middle Tidewater and the middle Piedmont areas; it does not extend to the Eastern

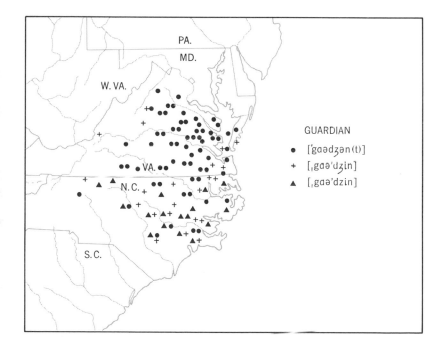

[11] I am indebted to Dr. Sumner Ives for having plotted this feature, which he studied in the preparation of his doctoral dissertation, "The Negro Dialect of the Uncle Remus Stories" (University of Texas, 1950). I am indebted to Miss Narcissa White for assistance in drafting all of the maps.

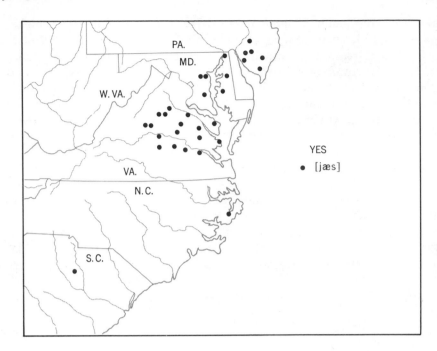

YES
• [jæs]

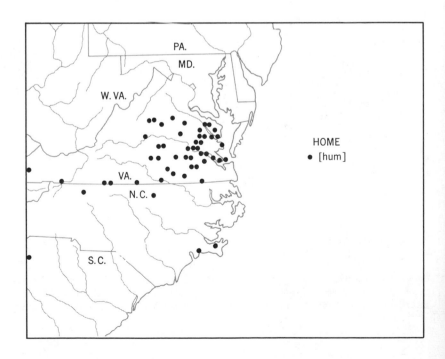

HOME
• [hum]

Shore, or the Norfolk area, or the Western Shore of Maryland, or even the northern portion of the Piedmont. What is particularly interesting is the westward string of occurrences pointing toward the southwestern corner of Virginia. A good many Southern forms show a similar thrust, or bulge, in this area south of the Roanoke River, though few so sharply as this. The old Richmond Road, opened before the Revolution, ran approximately in this direction; it joined the Valley Road at Ft. Chiswell and led on to the Cumberland Gap. This overland route undoubtedly served as an important avenue of travel for Eastern Virginians who sought homes in the Western wilderness.[12]

A somewhat different distribution may be observed in the case of the word *vegetables*. The characteristic Eastern Virginia feature is the occurrence of a secondary accent on the penultimate syllable—so that the word makes a reasonably good rhyme with *bubbles*. This feature is very common in most of the Tidewater and Piedmont, though it is missing from the Eastern Shore and the Norfolk area. It extends no further to the southwest than Campbell County; thus, it falls somewhat short of reaching the Blue Ridge in the Southern Piedmont. However, the feature again occurs with considerable frequency in the South Carolina Low

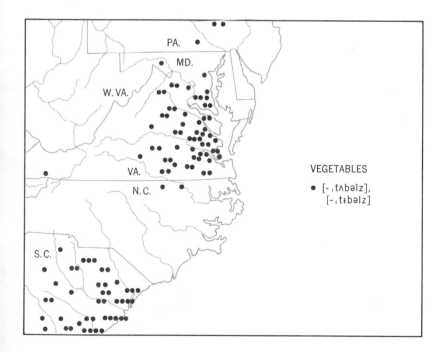

[12] See R. A. Billington, *op. cit.*, pp. 248–249.

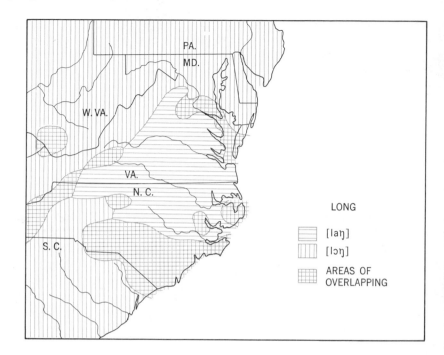

LONG

[laŋ]

[lɔŋ]

AREAS OF
OVERLAPPING

Country and the adjoining portions of Georgia. If it is a "Southern" feature, it is discontinuous; in any case it marks off the Eastern Virginia type so far as immediately contiguous areas are concerned.[13] Although the *Atlas* offers no further evidence on the point, it seems probable that the feature is systematic—that is, that it would occur in other words containing the element *-able* [-əbəl].

An interesting instance of the spreading of a speech feature from the Eastern Virginia area can be observed in the case of the word *long*. Throughout nearly all of Eastern Virginia this word is pronounced with [ɑ], the vowel of *father*, rather than [ɔ] (as in *taught*). The Eastern Shore of Virginia, the Western Shore of Maryland, and a small area to the southwest of Alexandria show a mixture of usage; otherwise the Tuckahoe area uses [ɑ] very solidly. The same pronunciation prevails in approximately the northern half of eastern North Carolina; and to the southward

[13] Possibly because of the preponderance of "Midland," or Pennsylvania-derived, settlers in North Carolina, the "Southern" speech forms in Virginia sometimes coincide with those in South Carolina without being shared by the intervening areas, particularly the territory between the Roanoke and Peedee rivers. Cases in point are the diphthongs in *house* and *white,* as well as such vocabulary features as *croker sack* (as against the upland Southern and North Carolina *tow sack*). See Kurath, *Word Geography,* pp. 41, 57; Figure 71.

as far as the valley of the Peedee the [ɑ] occurs alongside [ɔ]. Similar areas of mixed usage may be observed in westernmost North Carolina and in a small southern sector of West Virginia. Now, the southwestward thrust of this feature may well be due to the direct migration of Virginians into the uplands; the [ɑ] is clearly receding in these areas in favor of the more usual American [ɔ]. However, in Eastern North Carolina we must be dealing with linguistic irradiation independent of migration. In thirteen communities where older and younger informants differ in usage, the younger offers the pronunciation [lɑŋ]; in only three such communities does the younger speaker give [lɔŋ]. This indicates rather clearly that eastern North Carolina is now in the process of adopting the Virginia pronunciation [lɑŋ] as a prestige feature.

The [ɑ] in *long* is almost certainly a systematic phonological development. The similar word *strong* was recorded from most *Atlas* informants (some used *stout*, etc., instead); it shows [ɑ] in almost precisely the same geographical areas as does *long*. Although other such words (as *song*, *wrong*) are not available for comparison, it seems pretty clear that "short *ŏ*" before [ŋ] appears regularly as [ɑ] in the territory in question.

The last item on which comment will be made is really a morphological rather than a phonological feature: that is the use of [klom] (rather than the usual Southern [klɪm] or [klʌm]) as the preterite of *climb*.[14] The center of currency of this form is clearly the Piedmont; although [klom] is common along the Fall Line, it has not penetrated into the lower Tidewater or into Maryland. Yet the occurrences of this form seem to reflect the early exodus of Tuckahoes in rather typical directions—directly westward along the Virginia–North Carolina line; into western North Carolina; probably up the Roanoke to the Valley; almost certainly down the New River into southern West Virginia; and far southward into the plantation area of Middle Georgia. Only the most elderly informants offer [klom] except in Eastern Virginia—here it is used by a considerable number of younger speakers as well. This would indicate that it is not without prestige, though it is of course confined to uneducated speech.

The conclusions which we may draw are not so concise as we might wish. On the basis of previous studies (particularly those of Kurath) as well as the evidence adduced here, it seems quite justifiable to speak of an Eastern Virginia dialect, in the sense of an area set off from its neighbors by a considerable body of speech forms. To delimit the precise extent of the area is not easy; in fact, it is hardly possible until all the phonological, morphological, and lexical evidence has been assembled. What we find in general is that the Piedmont, which was the chief focal area,

[14] In my *Survey of Verb Forms in the Eastern States* (which is now awaiting publication) this verb, as well as numerous others, is discussed in detail.

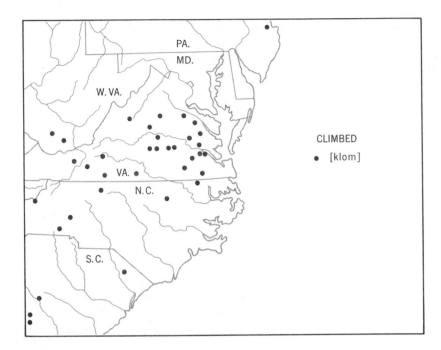

CLIMBED

● [klom]

shows a considerable uniformity in its usages. These usages may or may not be shared with surrounding areas. Usually they are found in the upper Tidewater, and not infrequently on the Western Shore of Maryland. The easternmost points of land very often lack the characteristic Piedmont usages; that is particularly true of the area east and south of Norfolk. Finally, the Eastern Shore even more frequently fails to share the linguistic peculiarities of the remainder of Eastern Virginia.[15] Some of these marginal areas probably share more features with other dialects than with that of the Virginia Piedmont.

The southern and southwestern limits of our dialect area have been somewhat obscured by the spreading of Piedmont forms in these directions—the [ɑ] in *long* is a case in point. Such spreading has in some cases gone even further; as has been shown in a previous study,[16] the [z] following the first vowel in *Mrs.* is clearly of Eastern Virginia origin, and has

[15] Kurath, *Word Geography*, groups the Eastern Shore and the Norfolk area with northeastern North Carolina. His term for the dialect of the remainder of Eastern Virginia is "Virginia Piedmont," which is a satisfactory label, provided we understand that the area normally includes a good many points to the east of the Fall Line.

[16] E. B. Atwood, "The Pronunciation of *Mrs.*," *American Speech*, XXV (1950), 10–18.

spread into the whole of the South Atlantic area. The existence of such expanding features certainly does not invalidate the idea of a single and unified speech area; on the contrary, it is in the nature of a speech center to irradiate forms in various directions, some forms extending, of course, much further than others. Thus the Eastern Virginia dialect, while remaining distinctive and recognizable, has at the same time contributed no little to the flavor of South Atlantic English.[17]

---

[17] Much of the material presented in this study was included in a paper read before the summer meeting of the Linguistic Society of America in Ann Arbor, Michigan, July 29, 1950.

North Carolina Accents

Lucia C. Morgan

North Carolina is a part of two major speech areas, Southern and Midland. The speech of eastern North Carolina is Southern while the speech of western North Carolina is South Midland, a sub-area of Midland. In turn, both Southern and South Midland in North Carolina have several distinguishable sub-areas. Professor Morgan deals with selected pronunciation and vocabulary items found in three of the sub-areas of North Carolina.

Lucia Morgan was co-author with C. M. Wise of *A Progressive Phonetic Workbook*. She is Associate Professor of Speech at the University of North Carolina at Chapel Hill. She has been observing, recording, and analyzing North Carolina accents for many years. Through her able description in the following article flows deep affection for the accents of the Tarheel State.

NORTH CAROLINA'S COASTLINE AND ITS EFFECT   269
UPON COLONIZATION

The North Carolina Coastline from the Virginia border to Cape Fear is the most inaccessible of all the states along the Atlantic Seaboard. The Outer Banks, which are shaped like a menacing bent bow, form an arc of islands whose hidden reefs and shifting sands defy even the most experienced mariner. This strip of coastline is called the most dangerous between Canada and Florida, yet it was the site of the first colony in America.[1] Sir Walter Raleigh's 1585 effort to establish a settlement on Roanoke Island failed and almost 100 years elapsed before a permanent colony was established on the Albemarle Sound. The absence of harbors and safe passage over the reefs had retarded colonization seriously.

The Albemarle Colony did manage to survive despite its political problems with its governors and boundary disputes with Virginia. Efforts were made to attract settlers from England but the population was composed chiefly of an overflow from Virginia, Pennsylvania, and South Carolina. The pioneers who came to North Carolina had little in common with their aristocratic plantation owners to the North and to the South, so once they were inside the boundary of North Carolina there was little communication with the outside world.

FIRST TOWN INCORPORATED

The political picture improved at the end of the seventeenth century. In 1705 (or 1706, by the new style calendar)[2] the town of Bath on the Pamlico River was incorporated. By 1714 a colonial legislature had been created and laws were enacted to encourage future settlers. One of the laws enacted was the *pilotage law*, which provided for the establishment of experienced seamen on Ocracoke and Roanoke to "constantly and diligently make it their business to search & find out the most convenient channels," to keep them properly marked, and to pilot vessels safely over the sandbars.[3] This assistance to incoming ships led to an increase in immigrants and trade.

From *Southern Speech Journal* 34 (Spring 1969) 223–229. Some background material added. Reprinted with the permission of the Southern Speech Association and Lucia C. Morgan.

[1] Hugh T. Lefler and Albert Ray Newsome, *North Carolina, The History of a Southern State* (Chapel Hill: University of North Carolina Press, 1944) pp. 17–18.

[2] Lefler and Newsome, p. 50.

[3] *Ibid.,* p. 62.

270   By 1720 the arrival of the Scots and German Palatines (along with a few Swiss and English) strengthened the coastal settlements; and new towns were laid out at New Bern on the Neuse River and Wilmington on the Cape Fear River. But as significant as these advancements were, they did not keep pace with those of other Atlantic Seaboard states.

Without seaports, adequate river transportation, or railroads, eastern North Carolina could not develop and expand. It is interesting to note that with the exception of the Cape Fear, the other major rivers of eastern North Carolina—the Chowan, the Neuse and the Pamlico—were not navigable for more than 100 or 150 miles inland and that no rivers from the central Piedmont area enter the Atlantic via North Carolina, but drain through South Carolina. Thus communication between the northeastern counties and the rest of the state was virtually impossible.

NORTH CAROLINA EMERGES IN TWENTIETH CENTURY

Until the twentieth century when the Piedmont suddenly erupted with industry to make North Carolina the most industrialized state in the South, North Carolina was known as the Rip Van Winkle State of the Union.[4]

While the state lay sleeping quietly, the speech patterns of the early settlers were handed down from generation to generation, so that we can still hear remnants of Elizabethan speech and pronunciations similar to those heard among the English and Irish seamen. Some pronunciations resemble those of the Southern and Midland counties of England. One occasionally hears a sprinkling of words with an Ulster flavor. The North Carolina Department of Conservation and Development actually publishes a small dictionary designed to acquaint the tourists with the "foreign language" they will hear. The pamphlet, known as *The Queen's English*,[5] lists colorful phrases and pronunciations still heard in remote parts of North Carolina. They are the pronunciations and phrases common to the language of Sir Walter Raleigh, Marlowe, Dryden and even Shakespeare.

[4] Charles B. Hitchcock, Editor, *These United States*, (Pleasantville, New York: The Reader's Digest Association, 1968) p. 50.

[5] *The Queen's English* (Raleigh, North Carolina, The Department of Conservation and Development, 1968).

PURPOSE OF STUDY

It is not the purpose of this study to analyze the present day speech of North Carolina in its entirety, but rather to point out the areas in which remnants of colonial speech are found and to mention some of the particular words and pronunciations common in North Carolina which may or may not be known in other areas of the South. Most of the informants were students at the University of North Carolina at Chapel Hill. They were natives of the state and their parents had been lifelong residents of the particular area in which they were living. Additional observations and recordings were made of adults and children who also qualified as lifelong residents. These observations concentrated on three particular areas: (1) the mountains, (2) the northeast counties bordering on the Outer Banks and (3) the Outer Banks Islands themselves.[6] Occasional references to the speech of the industrialized Piedmont are used for comparisons.

Variations among the Sounds [i] [ɪ] [eɪ] [ɛ]

The substitution of the vowel [ɪ] for [ɛ] as in *pin* for *pen* is still as strong in North Carolina as it is in other Southern states, but surprisingly enough it does not occur with marked frequency on the Outer Banks Islands.

Closely related to the lack of distinction between [ɪ] and [ɛ] is the tendency to pronounce all three vowels in *sit*, *set* and *sat* with the [ɛ]. When the pronunciation was first heard in speaking situations, it was judged to be an error in grammar, but when students read all three with [ɛ] the lack of vowel distinction became evident. Only rarely did the inappropriate word appear in written material.

The pronunciation of *git* for *get* is very common. This vowel substitution is widespread throughout the United States and is not necessarily peculiar to North Carolina.

The vowel in the second syllable of *experiment* is seldom pronounced with [ɛ], but is usually [ɪ]. *Chevrolet* is pronounced with an [ɪ] in the first syllable.

On the islands and the areas adjacent to the coast where fishing is a major activity, the vowel [ɪ] shifts to [i] so that we hear *feesh* for *fish, deesh*

---

6 Lucia C. Morgan, "The Speech of Ocracoke, North Carolina: Some Observations," *Southern Speech Journal,* XXV (Summer, 1960), p. 314

272   for *dish*, and *weesh* for *wish*. Throughout the state the shift from [ɪ] to [i] is clearly heard in *thing, hill, inch* and *zinnia*.

In the words *dear, fear, ear, year,* and *beer* the [ɪ] predominates, particularly when the final *r* is [ə]. However, a shift to [ʌ] was recorded on numerous occasions in the words *year, gear,* and *steering*. One man wanted to *oil the gears on his steering wheel*. He said [ɔl ðə gjʌz oʊn ðə stʌrɪn hwil]. *Last year* became [læs jʌ].

In the eastern area and especially on the Outer Banks and the counties bordering Albemarle and Pamlico sounds the [ɪ] is so centralized in *sister, river,* and *filling* (as in *filling station*) that one needs to listen carefully to get the words. In many instances the vowel shifts to the back [ʊ].

The vowel [ɛ] and the diphthong [eɪ] are both used in *egg* and *leg,* but the [eɪ] in *head* was rarely heard among the informants used in these observations. However, the use of [ɛ] in words normally pronounced [eɪ] was marked in the coastal area and in the Piedmont. With many informants there was no distinction between *tale* and *tell, sale* and *sell, Yale* and *yell*. All were pronounced with [ɛ]. One student told me she was going to wear her grandmother's *wedding vell*.

The Vowel [æ]

In general, no significant changes were observed in the production of the vowel [æ] as in *calf, glass* and *dance* except for a few interesting words on the Outer Banks and some isolated words in the mountains and the Piedmont. The prolongation of the vowel to [æə], [æɪ] and even to [æˈjə] was heard throughout the state. Assimilation nasality was common when the vowel was followed by a nasal consonant, and harshness from a tense [æ], rather than a relaxed one, was particularly noted in the Piedmont.

On the Outer Banks a shift toward [ɛ] was clearly observed in *fatback* [fɛt bɛк], *Hatteras* [hɛtrəs], *calico* (a variety of shell) [кɛlɪкɛʊ], *captain* [кɛpm̩], and *salad* (greens) [sɛlɪt]. In this same area a shift to [aɪ] was heard in *lacking* [laɪкɪn].

In the mountains and in several of the Piedmont counties, Alamance in particular, [æ] shifted to [a-a] in *bear, bare,* and *hair*. He *was barefooted* was heard as [hɪ wʌz ba(a)rfʊtɪd]. *Can I get my hair combed* was [кɪn a gɪt ma ha(a)r коʊmd]. In both of these sentences the *r* quality of the vowel was a dominant feature.

Both [ænt] and [ɑnt] were heard for *aunt,* with the latter more frequent in the eastern areas than in the western portion of the state. The pronunciation [ɑnt] is prominent among the older Negro population in Chapel Hill. Negro teachers from all areas of the state who attended

ummer school classes at the University in Chapel Hill had a preference
or [ɑnt]. Several indicated that they felt that the pronunciation was more
ultured.

The [æ] was expected in *calm* in the folk speech of the mountains and
he Outer Banks; but it was heard only three times, once in a rural store
car Asheville and twice from fishermen on Ocracoke. All three usages
eferred to either the sea or the wind. Students who frequent the islands
uring the summer and those who live in the mountains report that the
æ] is still used, but there seems to be a tendency to eliminate it when
ourists or city dwellers come around. The pronunciation [ĸæm] is a rem-
ant of the Colonial pronunciation which enjoyed extensive currency in
North Carolina.

The Diphthong [aɪ]

The residents of the Outer Banks are called the *Hoy Toiders*
because of their characteristic pronunciation of the diphthong [aɪ].
Words such as *high tide* and *night* are pronounced with a sound re-
embling the diphthong [ɔɪ] as in *boy*. This variant was expected; and it
s definitely present, not only among the islanders, but it is heard inland
or several hundred miles. The frequency of the variant is not as great
nland as it is on the coast, but it has been heard in both Chapel Hill and
n Chatham County, south of Chapel Hill.

While the acoustic value of the sound resembles the diphthong [ɔɪ],
areful observation reveals that it is produced without the customary lip
ounding of [ɔɪ]. The sound seems to be made entirely in the oral cavity
vith no assistance from the lips. Hours of imitative practice were re-
uired to determine exactly what the speakers were doing. When several
eamen were observed speaking with their pipes clenched between the
eeth and the lips immobile, a pencil was used to simulate the pipes. The
ongue was retracted and lowered. The resulting sound was similar to that
f the Outer Bankers.

Wise[7] lists two other variants of [aɪ] which are pertinent to this study.
The [aɪ] becomes [ʌɪ] or [ɜɪ] in Irish dialects. He points out that [ɔɪ] char-
cterizes individuals and communities rather than the Irish dialect as a
vhole. He further states that the [ʌɪ] for [aɪ] is more widely used in Ireland
han the [ɔɪ]. These variants are known to exist among the Irish settlers of
Eastern Ontario in Canada and they have been recorded in the area east
f the Blue Ridge Mountains in both North Carolina and Virginia. Both
vere heard in Ocracoke. The phrase *my wife* was heard as [mɪ wʌɪf] and
nɪ wɜɪf]. It seems safe, therefore, to assume that these pronunciations,

Claude M. Wise, *Applied Phonetics* (Englewood Cliffs, N.J.: Prentice Hall, 1957) p. 277.

274   including the [ɔɪ], could well have been brought to North Carolina by the Irish who came to the area around 1720.

The diphthong [aɪ] is reduced to [a] or [ɑ] in the mountains and spor adically throughout the state. One elderly mountain resident described the fall leaves in this way:

"*Hits a beauteous sight. Hits like a bright light was turned on from*
[hɪts ə bjutɪəs sat hɪts lak ə brat lat wəz tɝnd oʊn frəm *heaven.*"
hɛvən]

When the full diphthong [aɪ] is followed by nasal consonants, assimila tion nasality is more common than when they follow just the vowels [a] o [ɑ]. The tendency toward assimilation nasality is more characteristic o the Piedmont and coastal areas than in the mountains. In fact, it now ap pears that there are pockets of extreme nasality in parts of the industrial ized Piedmont. Detailed studies in this area should reveal interesting data

The Diphthong [aʊ]

One of the most rewarding aspects of the observations o North Carolina speech was concerned with the changes in the diphthong [aʊ] as in *cow, house, around, mountain, out* and *our*. Not only were the expected variants heard, but a new and hitherto unrecorded one ap peared.[8] The sound was a clear and distinct substitution of the diphthong [aɪ] for [aʊ]. It was heard first in the expression *down town* which came out as [daɪn taɪn]. When it was first recorded in a speech class, the sub stitution was considered to be a deviation peculiar to that one student, bu ten years of careful observations and recording have amassed overwhelm ing evidence in favor of the sound in varying degrees from the Oute Banks as far inland as Orange, Alamance, Chatham and Lee counties, a distance of about 200 miles.

The expected variants of [æʊ], [ɛʊ], and [ʌʊ], as listed by Kurath and McDavid,[9] were readily observable. When the [æʊ] was used, the sound was frequently characterized by harshness and nasality, even when no nasal consonant was present to encourage assimilation nasality. When the sound was followed by an *r*, as in *our*, the glossal muscles became more restricted and the sides of the tongue were raised in contact with the upper molars. Both [æˆʊr] and [aɪr] were heard for *our*. When the

---

[8] A summary of the findings of the *Linguistic Atlas of the Eastern United States* failed to revea any mention of the variant under discussion. A conversation with C. M. Wise in June 196 disclosed that he was unaware of the presence of this variant of /aʊ/.

[9] Hans Kurath and Raven I. McDavid, Jr., *The Pronunciation of English in the Atlantic State* (Ann Arbor: The University of Michigan Press, 1961) maps 28 and 29.

word was pronounced as [aʊə] or prolonged to [aʊwə], the diphthong [aʊ] tended to return to its position as [aʊ] or [ɑʊ].

The [aʊ-aɪ] variant was heard in numerous words. *Brown* was *brine*, *round* was *rind*, *house* was *hice* and even *heist*. A filling station attendant directed a customer to turn *roit* at the *cryin' station*. He meant *right* at the *Crown station*.

In several isolated communities the words *flower*, *flour*, *shower*, *our*, and *hour* had an additional sound treatment. *Flower* and *flour* were both [flaɪvə], *rain shower* was a [raɪn ʃaɪvə] and *our* and *hour* were both [aɪvə].

Influences of Colonial Speech on [aʊ]

Two influences of the speech of the Colonial period seem to be in effect here. The substitution of [ɑɪ] for [aʊ] has been heard in the speech of British visitors from the South and Midland counties of England. The sound was heard for the word *brown* in a broadcast over the British Broadcasting System during a discussion of Irish handwoven fabrics. A merchant from Ulster indicated that the most popular color in hard woven woolens was *brine*. Exchange students and teachers from these areas of the British Isles attest to the presence of the [aɪ] for [aʊ] among many of the speakers on the common speech level.

The other influence of Colonial speech concerns the *v* for *w* in *flower* and *shower*. This, of course, is common among persons of German descent. The communities in which the addition of the [v] for the orthographic *w* was heard both had German settlers in the 1720's.

One additional comment may be of interest here. The Elizabethan pronunciation for the word *fought* is still to be heard among the older residents as [faʊt]. It is more common in isolated rural areas where folk speech is to be found.

The Sounds [ɔ] and [ɔɪ] in Certain Words

When an individual is interested in attempting to guess the place of birth or the place of residence of a person, he usually has a series of words he uses to "cue him in." Such well-known words as *merry, marry,* and *Mary, water, fog, Florida,* and *aunt* may be used. If North Carolina is suspected as the place of residence, either by birth or by adoption, an attempt should be made to elicit the three words *on, gone,* and *oil*. These are not the only needed clues, but they will help.

In the words *on* and *gone* three separate phonemes are heard. The [ɔn-ɑn] pronunciations are both known, but the most popular one in common speech is [oʊn] as in *own*. No distinction is made between *on* and

276 *own.* The same situation exists with *gone.* Both [gɔn-gɑn] are heard, but [goʊn] appears more often, even among those individuals who think they have cultivated speech.

The other characteristic word is *oil* and the related words *soil, toil,* and *boil.* In the word *oil* there is an overwhelming tendency to say either [ɔl] or [ɔəl].

In a random sampling of 136 white North Carolina male students at the University of North Carolina at Chapel Hill, Whitehurst[10] found that 75.7% said [ɔəl] or [ɔl], 21.4% said [ɔɪəl] and only 2.9% used the [ɔɪl] diphthong. The students surveyed represented every part of the state, both urban and rural.

On the Outer Banks the diphthong in *oil, boil,* and *oyster* was often produced with [ɔɪ] or [oə]. The word *oil* was noted particularly as [oəl].[11] A related shift of sounds on Ocracoke was heard in *frog, called, ball* and *along.* The vowel [ɔ], which is more common than [ɑ] in these words, shifted to the diphthong [oʊ] or [oə].

The Treatment of the Central Vowels [ɜ ɝ ə ɚ]

The free mid-central vowel [ɜ] in *thirty,* which has been characteristic of much of the early speech of the Atlantic states, is seldom heard on the North Carolina mainland. The current vowel sound is more constricted with the sides of the tongue raised against the upper molars. The degree of constriction and the tension of glossal and related muscles determines the amount of so-called "*r* quality" given to the sound. A detailed study of this vowel is now under way and the data to date show a general tendency for less constriction and a slight rounding of the lips in the eastern portion of the state, with the greater constriction occurring in the Piedmont and mountains.

When these words (which are known as "vowel *r* words" when teachers are working with students who are not familiar with phonetic symbols) appear in an unaccented position in the ends of words such as *mother, better, mister,* and *speaker,* the [ə] is used more often than is the [ɚ]. One teacher was drilling her class with vigor and determination to get them to produce a very constricted vowel in *bird* and *turn.* She went into facial contortions to emphasize her point. When she was asked why she was trying to eradicate any vestige of the [ɜ] which is used by English speaking people the world over, she replied that she thought it sounded [bɛtə].

---

[10] Lee Whitehurst, *A Study of the Pronunciation of Oil in North Carolina.* Unpublished paper. University of North Carolina at Chapel Hill, 1968.

[11] Lucia C. Morgan, "The Speech of Ocracoke, North Carolina."

On the islands of the Outer Banks the [ɜ] was heard. At times it shifted to the lower central vowel [ʌ]. The word *girl* was both [gɜl] and [gʌrəl].

Consonant Deviations

In North Carolina, as in many southern states, consonants continue to be neglected through omission or substitution. Ease of pronunciation and imitation of parents, teachers, and friends are the major factors influencing this neglect. While all teachers of speech should be interested in the improvement of consonant production, this study is concerned with those particular consonants which may be peculiar to North Carolina or which may be related to the speech of the early settlers.

Postvocalic Final r

The omission of *r* after the vowels [ɑ] and [ɔ] as in *farm* and *form* is heard, but the change to the constriction of the tongue, in recognition of the orthographic *r*, is marked. The influence of the British treatment of this sound has continued to some extent in the eastern counties and to a strong degree on the outer islands. The British influence is more strongly preserved among the Negro teachers enrolled in summer school classes than it is among the white teachers. The recognition of the *r* is stronger in the industrialized Piedmont and in the mountains.

The use of [ə] following other vowels as in *here, dear, sure,* and *door* is holding longer than was first suspected. When students are asked to pronounce a list of words, they make a conscious effort to pronounce the orthographic *r*, but a few moments later when free speech is heard, the [ə] is used. One student was pronouncing a list containing the word *floor*, which she pronounced in isolation as [floʊr]. Just then her papers fell from her desk and she said, "Just a minute. My paper fell on the floor." [dʒʌst ə mɪnɪt ma peɪpə fɛl oʊn ðə floʊə]. The student had denied the presence of the [ə] in her speech so the class enjoyed her return to normalcy.

The Treatment of [θ] and [ð]

For several years the teachers of speech therapy in the eastern counties had been reporting an unusual number of sound substitutions for the voiced and voiceless *th*. It is not unusual for first- and second-grade children to use *t* or *d, f,* or *v* for these two sounds, but when the substitution continued on into the upper grades, into high school, the university, and among the adults of the area, it was time to take a look at the histor-

278   ical background of the speakers. When the voiceless *th* appeared in a final position such as *with, bath, both, birthday, tooth,* and even the name of the state, *North Carolina,* an *f* was used so that the words became *wif, baf, bof, birfday, toof* and *Nof Carolina.* The state is [nɔf kəlanə] to a great many people who live here.

While this substitution is preserved through imitation, its original cause was not in defective articulation, but in the Cockney and Irish speech of the seamen who were established on Ocracoke and Roanoke islands. Since *th* is typically English, the German and Swiss settlers did not have the sound in the language they brought with them to the new land. The substitution may be traced to the speech of these ancestors as well as to the Cockney and Irish.

Words and Expressions

Hit. The pronunciation *hit,* the historical form from which *it* evolved, is still heard in folk speech. *Hit* appeared in writing in North Carolina as late as 1853.[12]

Holp. The word *holp* (sometimes spelled *hope*) for *helped* is also historical. It, like *hit,* is still heard in folk speech. Eliason records the spelling *hope* in 1830, 1837 and in 1857.[13]

Salet. These are cooked greens, usually turnips. The word, pronounced [sælɪt] and [sɛlɪt] is no doubt a corruption of the word *salad.*

Creasies or *Creesies.* These are a wild type of greens which resemble watercress. They are boiled and seasoned in much the same way turnip greens are prepared. The pronunciation [krisɪz] is probably a folk etymology originating from *watercress.*

Poke. This word has two meanings. First, there is *poke salet.* The tender young leaves of the pokeberry weed are prepared like turnip greens and creasies. The second meaning is a bag or sack. This word originated with the Scots who settled in North Carolina. Their word for *sack* or *bag* is *poke.* It also means a beggar's wallet. It sometimes referred to a baglike pocket women wore under their aprons or skirts.

Roke. This unusual word used for the past tense of *rake* has been recorded several times in folk speech. No mention of the word has been seen in any publication except for a related one in the *Random House Dictionary of the English Language.*[14] *Roke* is a term used in metallurgy

---

[12] Norman E. Eliason, *Tar Heel Talk* (Chapel Hill: The University of North Carolina Press, 1956) p. 229.

[13] Norman E. Eliason, p. 312.

[14] Jesse Stern, *The Random House Dictionary of the English Language,* (New York: Random House 1967) p. 1241.

and it refers to a seam or scratch which has been filled with slag. It lists
roke as dialectal meaning "to scratch." No clearer relationship can be
established with the North Carolina folk word *roke* meaning *to rake up*
or *scratch up*.

Right much. This expression is used in common speech as well as folk
speech. On Ocracoke the pronunciation is [rɔ⁺ᵉɪt mɛtʃ].

Gracious plenty. Thank you, this is a gracious plenty. This is well established among the older residents. It has been heard in the University
environment only once.

Wont. This is not *won't*, but is a word meaning *wasn't*. *It wont any
trouble to help you.* The word enjoys extensive currency in both folk and
common speech. It may be an unusual usage of the archaic word *wont*
which meant one was *accustomed to* doing something.

Fault. The verb of the present day is usually *to find fault with him.* The
word is used in North Carolina without the words *find* or *with. Don't fault
her for wanting to see her family.*

Bunk. The word *bunk* is supposed to have originated in North Carolina.
A legislator from Buncombe County was always presenting bizarre ideas
to the General Assembly. His bills were called pure Buncombe. Later, the
word was shortened to its present form *bunk*.

SUMMARY

North Carolina dialects and folk speech are rapidly dying out
as the twenty-first century approaches and automation replaces the folk
ways. But until it docs . . .
The speech of Nof Ca'lina, hits a beauteous sound.

The Speech of Ocracoke, North Carolina

Robert Howren

The Outer Banks region of North Carolina, of which Ocracoke is a part, is one of several relic areas in the Atlantic states. Such areas, because of their isolation, have kept many pronunciations and forms that have been lost in other varieties of speech. The Outer Banks were not included in the *Linguistic Atlas* surveys of the Eastern states; and outside the region itself, its speech is little known. "The phonological and lexical characteristics of the area are of considerable relevance for the historical development of American dialects," Robert Howren stated in a letter to the editors. He is Professor of Linguistics and English at the University of Iowa.

The Outer Banks of North Carolina, a rope of sandbanks flung out from the coast in an irregular, 200-mile arc extending from the Virginia border southeast to Cape Hatteras, which lies some twenty-five miles

From *American Speech* 37: 161–175 (October 1962). Reprinted with the permission of Columbia University Press and Robert Howren.

from the nearest point on the mainland, and looping from Hatteras back southwest toward the mainland, have changed in recent generations from the isolated habitat of a hardy fisherfolk to the popular destination of tourists in search of the quaint and picturesque. The relative isolation of the Banks has produced a dialect sufficiently distinct from the speech of the coastal South that every North Carolinian has heard—and many believe—that the Bankers speak "Elizabethan English" (a dialect related, no doubt, to the form of English popularly supposed to be spoken in the more isolated coves in the mountains at the opposite end of the state). However, the motorcar and the ferryboat—a combination inevitably fatal to quaintness and picturesqueness—have brought perceptible changes to the Outer Banks. A good many linguistic archaisms and localisms perhaps have long since passed from usage, and inevitably further leveling will eventually result from close and continuous contact with the speech of the mainland. One observer noted as early as 1910 "greater changes in the speech of the people [of Hatteras] since the coming of the daily mail in motor boats just ten years ago, than . . . in the preceding thirty years, and the songs of the mothers and the grandmothers are well nigh forgotten by the daughters."[1]

The aim of this article is to describe in some detail the speech of Ocracoke, one of the oldest of the fifteen or twenty villages scattered up and down the Outer Banks and the latest to succumb to the influences, both good and bad, of tourism. Ocracoke is the sole village (population about 600) on Ocracoke Island, which lies in a northeast-to-southwest position between Hatteras and Portsmouth islands, separated from them by Hatteras Inlet on the northeast and Ocracoke Inlet on the southwest. The small fishing village of Ocracoke is located at the southern end of the island, clustered around Silver Lake, a circular harbor opening into Pamlico Sound. The village originated in 1715, when the North Carolina Assembly passed a bill providing for settling and maintaining pilots at Ocracoke Inlet, which had become an important but dangerous point of entry for shipping. By the end of the Colonial period a sizable community, then called Pilot Town, had grown up around Cockle Creek[2] (that is, Silver Lake; the natives still refer frequently to the harbor by its earlier name).

For more than a century the Ocracokers had relatively little contact with the mainland. The first regular communication was established sometime after the turn of the century, with the inauguration of mail-

---

[1] Collier Cobb. "Early English Survivals on Hatteras Island," *North Carolina Booklet*, XIV (1914), 99.

[2] See David Stick, *The Outer Banks of North Carolina, 1584–1958* (Chapel Hill, 1958), pp. 298–304.

282   boat service. From that time until 1957, when a paved road was constructed from Hatteras Inlet to Ocracoke village, thirteen miles away at
the southern end of the island, the village was most easily reached by
means of the mail boat, which made one four-hour trip each morning
from the mainland town of Atlantic up Core and Pamlico sounds to
Ocracoke, returning to Atlantic in the afternoon. The completion of the
road in 1957 made it possible to drive all the way down the Banks from
Kitty Hawk, at the mouth of Albemarle Sound, to Ocracoke, crossing
Oregon and Hatteras inlets on free, state-operated car ferries. Early in
1960 a private company inaugurated car-and-passenger ferry service between Atlantic and Ocracoke, thus closing the final gap of inconvenience
between Ocracoke and the mainland and pointing up the desirability of
an early systematic study of the speech of the Bankers.

Because of its long isolation, the Outer Banks dialect should prove
valuable in what it may eventually reveal about the development of American English. Since the Banks were not included in the *Linguistic Atlas*
fieldwork, and since there have been no systematic studies of the dialect,
this study may perhaps partially fill in this considerable blank space in
our knowledge of the speech of the coastal South.[3] It is hoped that the
following presentation of the vowel phonology and some of the regionally
distinctive lexical features of Ocracoke speech may provide a starting
point for a thorough treatment of the Outer Banks dialect.

The system of stressed vowels in Ocracoke speech differs structurally
only in minor details from the systems of the other dialects of the Atlantic
states, just as these systems differ only slightly from each other. In the
following display of the Ocracoke stressed vowel phonemes, I have adjusted my phonemicization to correspond with that used by Kurath and
McDavid in their study of American pronunciation[4] and have listed the
vowels in such a way that the place of the Ocracoke system in the
typology suggested by Kurath and McDavid may be readily seen. In
Table 1, the checked vowels /ɪ,ɛ,ʊ,ɒ/ are paired with the free vowels
which are phonetically most similar to them. The low-front checked
vowel /æ/, the mid-central vowel /ʌ/, and the low-central free vowel /ɑ/
are the only ones not so paired.

A comparison of Table 1 with those of Kurath and McDavid[5] indicates
that the dialect spoken in Ocracoke shares with all the major Eastern
dialects the nuclei /ɪ/ in *crib,* /i/ in *three,* /ɛ/ in *ten,* /e/ in *eight,* /æ/ in

---

[3] The fieldwork and the distribution of lexical questionnaires were aided by grants from the
Southern Fellowships Fund and from the Wake Forest College Research and Publication
Fund.

[4] Hans Kurath and Raven I. McDavid, Jr., *The Pronunciation of English in the Atlantic States*
(Ann Arbor, Mich., 1961), pp. 3–6. This work will subsequently be cited as *PEAS.*

[5] *Ibid.,* pp. 6–7.

Table 1

crib : three/ɪ: i/		/U: u/ wood : tooth	
ten : eight /ɛ: e/	/ʌ/ sun/thirty	/o/	road
bag /æ/	/ɑ/ car	/ɒ: ɔ/ crop : law	
down /au/		/ʊi/	buoy
		/ɔi/	boil
		/ɒi/	five

bag, /au/ in *down*,[6] /ʌ/ in *sun*,[7] /U/ in *wood*, and /u/ in *tooth*. It also shares the free nucleus /o/ in *road* with all dialects save that of eastern New England (especially in the speech of older informants), which often, but not consistently, has the checked vowel /ŏ/ in this and a few other words.

In the low-back region, however, where most of the differences in vowel incidence are found, Ocracoke speech aligns itself as follows:

Table 2

/ɒ/ in *crop*	Ocracoke with eastern New England, western Pennsylvania, and Middle Western and Western derivatives from western Pennsylvania; also Standard British (all others have /ɑ/)
/ɔ/ in *law*	Ocracoke with all (including Standard British) except eastern New England, western Pennsylvania, and Middle Western and Western derivatives from western Pennsylvania, which have /ɒ/
/ɑ/ in *car*	Ocracoke with upstate New York, eastern Pennsylvania, South Midland (New York City, upper and lower South, and Standard British have /ɑᶧ/;[8] western Pennsylvania and its derivative dialects have /ɒ/; and eastern New England has /a/)
/ɒi/ in *five*	The phonetic charts in *PEAS* show no diphthong with an open low-back rounded onset in the word *five*. The nearest approximation of such a diphthong in this word occurs in the chart for an informant in Georgetown, S.C., who uses the diphthong [ɑᶧⁱɪᶧ] in *five*.[9]
/ɔi/ in *boil*	Ocracoke with all except eastern New England and western Pennsylvania and its derivative dialects, which have /ɒi/

[6] /au/ is listed here with the front vowels because its onset is most generally, in all positions, markedly fronted.

[7] The nucleus of *sun* is consistently paired with a back vowel in the *PEAS* charts. I have placed it in the central column because of its noticeably fronted articulation in Ocracoke speech. Moreover, I find no contrasts in Ocracoke speech to justify a phonemic separation of the stressed nucleus of *thirty* and the vowel of *sun*. These words are usually pronounced [θʌ� ɪn] and [sɜ˞ⁱn], with the more retracted vowel occurring before /r/.

[8] However, the degree of retraction of this vowel is considerably greater in New York City and New Orleans speech, for example, than it is in Standard British.

[9] *PEAS*, p. 91.

284   No particular pattern of affinity of Ocracoke speech with the major dialects is evident in the system of vowel phonemes, except that the Ocracoke system aligns itself less frequently with that of the coastal South than with the systems typical of the other major dialects. The frequent lack of affinity with the Southern dialect becomes even more apparent when we turn to the phonetic particulars of the Ocracoke stressed vowels, as presented in Table 3:

Table 3

Phoneme	Principal Allophones	Distribution	Incidence
		1. CHECKED VOWELS	
/ɪ/	[ɪ]	Generally, except as follows	*inlet, any, penny, jingle, dip, here* [hjɪ⁺ə] (sometimes has /ɛ/), *career*
	[ɪ⁺ə⁺∼ɪə⁺]	Before final or preconsonantal /l/; under terminal contour before apico-alveolars, labials	*it, is, went, dip, bit, keelson, hill*
/ɛ/	[ɛ]	Generally, except as follows	*ever, edge* (sometimes has /e/), *kept, yet, wreck, Methodist, catch, Mary*[10]
	[ɛ⫫ə∼ɛə]	Before final or preconsonantal /l/; before /ð/; under terminal contour before apico-alveolars, labials	*ebb, bell, weather, net, bed, kept*
/æ/	[æ]	Generally, except as follows	*after, half, square, married, dance, aunt, can't, Wahab* ['we⁺ˌhæb] (a surname), *bad, bat, back, shallow*
	[æə]	Before final or preconsonantal /l/; under terminal contour before apico-alveolars, labials	*half* [hæəf], *bass, bad, gal, dance, can't, aunt, have*
	[æɪ]	Before /g,ŋ,ʃ/	*keg, smashed, tanker, ashes*

[10] *PEAS* shows considerable currency of /ɛ/ in *Mary* around Albemarle Sound and in the eastern peninsular area of Carteret County, which juts out between the Outer Banks and the mouth of the Neuse (Map 50). Otherwise, eastern North Carolina usage conforms to the Southern pattern, with some diaphone of /e/ generally current in this name. I have observed that in many respects the speech of the easternmost part of the Carteret peninsula (on the coast of which the town of Atlantic is located) seems quite similar to Ocracoke speech.

Table 3 (Continued)

/ʌ/	[ɜ⁺]	Generally, except as follows	*up, tubs, husband, lucky, jug, nothing* ['nɜ⁺θɪŋk], *Fulcher* (a surname), *rum, judge*
	[ʌ⁺]	Before /r/	*earth, girl, hurricane, far*
	[ɜɪ]	Before /ʃ/	*Russian, hush*
/ʊ/	[ʊ⁺]	Generally, except as follows	*one* [wʊ⁺n~wɜ⁺n], *woman, full, wood, took, put, could*
	[ʊɪ]	Before /ʃ/	*bush, push*
/ɒ/	[ɒ]	Generally, except as follows	*otter, hog, log, water, box, forwards, Florida*
	[ɒɪ]	Before /ʃ/	*wash, Washington, the Swash* (a section of Ocracoke Island)

2. FREE VOWELS AND DIPHTHONGS

Phoneme	Principal Allophones	Distribution	Incidence
/i/	[ïi~ɪi~i⁺]	Alternate rather freely; [ɪi] most frequent; [i⁺] generally before dorso-velars	*either, east, inch, really, creek, fish, big, sea, lee*
	[i⁺ə]	Before final or pre-consonantal /l/; under terminal contour, occasionally, before final /z, n/	*eel, reel, knees, mean*[11]
/e/	[ɜɪ~ɛɪ~e⁺]	Alternate rather freely; [ɜɪ] most common	*age, April, days, Hazel, weigh, sailor*
	[e⁺ə]	Before final or preconsonantal /l/	*nail, sail*
/u/	[ʊ⁺u⁺~u⁺]	Alternate rather freely; [ʊ⁺u⁺] more frequent and occurs before /r/ almost invariably	*school, New Bern* ['nʊ⁺u⁺ bən][12] *room, cured, bluefish, crew*

[11] A similar diphthongal allophone of /i/ before voiced apico-alveolars is characteristic of the speech of the Charleston, S.C., area (see *PEAS*, Map 16, showing the pronunciation of *grease*).

[12] The first syllable of the name of this city is consistently pronounced without the palatal semivowel /y/, but *new, due,* and so on, are generally /nyu, dyu/.

Table 3 (Continued)

/o/	[œᵻʊ⁺~o⁺ʊ~o⁺]	Alternate rather freely; [œᵻʊ⁺] most frequent; frequently [o⁺ʊ] before /r/	*over, old, Ocracoke* ['œᵻʊ⁺krɪ͵kœᵻʊ⁺k], *boat, 'course* [ko⁺ʊs], *four, Portsmouth, know*
/ɔ/	[oᵀ]	Generally, except as follows	*all, on, dog, lost, caught, war, horse, morning, forty, storm, along, draw*
	[oᵀə]	Under terminal contour before apico-alveolars, final or preconsonantal /l/	*all, across, Claude, ball, called*
/ɑ/	[ɑ]	(Single major allophone)	*honest, fire, calm, barkentine, copper, pond, pa*
/au/	[a⁺ʊ̈~aʊ~ɐʊ⁺]	Alternate freely, except that (1) [a⁺ʊ̈] occurs most frequently, and is the sole variant before /n/; (2) [ɐʊ⁺], in its relatively infrequent occurrence, is found only before voiceless consonants; and (3) only [aʊ] is found before /r/	*out, trout, south, sound, flounder, house, now, hour, sour, ourselves*
/ʊi/	[ʊ⁺ɪ]	(Single major allophone)	*ruin, buoy*
/ɔi/	[oᵀɪ]	(Single major allophone)	*oyster, boys, boil, boiler, Roy*
/ɒi/	[ɒɪ~ɑɪ~aɪ]	[ɒɪ] is regular; [ɑɪ, aɪ] occur infrequently in all positions[13]	*eyes, island* ['ɒɪᵀlənt], *pirate, tide, tight, mile, pilot, high*

Several details of Table 3 are worthy of further emphasis. The two most immediately evident phonological features of Ocracoke speech are: (1) the general and regular retention of postvocalic /r/, in contrast with the very mixed patterns of eastern North Carolina;[14] (2) the quality of the diphthong in *tight, tide, tie,* and so on. Unlike the coastal Southern dialect, Ocracoke speech generally has /r/ in all positions. Moreover, this sound

---

[13] The diphthong /ɒi/ does not normally occur before a final or preconsonantal /r/, but is replaced in these positions by the phoneme /ɑ/, as in /ɑrn/ *iron,* /fɑr/ *fire.*

[14] See *PEAS*, Map 156.

is notable for its sharp constriction in all positions except finally in unstressed syllables. Also, unlike various types of Southern speech, Ocracoke
speech has essentially the same diphthong before the voiced consonant
and finally in *tide* and *tie* that it has in *tight* and other words ending in a
voiceless consonant. The diphthong is further distinguished by its low-
back, very slightly rounded onset: [ˈɒɪˉlənt] *island,* [tɒɪ⁺t] *tight,* [tɒˈɪˉd]
tide, [mɒɪˉɫ] *mile,* [tɒɪˉ⁻] *tie.* Though the diphthong /ɒɪ/ does not occur,
in my records, before final or preconsonantal /r/, being replaced in this
position by the simplex /ɑ/, it does occur before intervocalic /r/, as in
pirate [ˈpɒɪˉrət].

A clear distinction between the diphthongs of *tie* and *toy* is maintained
by the rather close mid-back rounded onset of the latter, as in *oysters*
[ˈoˉɪstəz], *noise* [noˉɪz], *boil* [boˉɪ̈ɫ],[15] and *toy* [toˉɪˉ]. Similarly, the vowel
of *all, along, draw, hawk,* and so on, is a noticeably closer vowel than one
is accustomed to hear in mainland North Carolina speech. Moreover, it
is normally a lengthened monophthong in Ocracoke speech, without the
usual Southern and South Midland back-rounded offglide, except under
a terminal contour before an apico-alveolar consonant, where a central-
gliding diphthong occurs: thus, under terminal contour, *all* [oˉːɫ], *hawk*
[hoˉˑk], *dog* [doˉːg], *draw* [drɔˉː]; but *Claude* [kloˉˑəd], *bought* [boˉˑət],
across [əˈkroˉˑəs]. Around Albemarle Sound and the mouth of the Neuse
River, the *PEAS* map for the word *dog*[16] shows a considerable sprinkling
of [ɔˑ~ɔˑə] in this word. The Ocracoke records show no central-gliding
diphthongs before dorso-velars, but perhaps the monophthongal variant
in these two areas reflects a vowel related to the close monophthong in
Ocracoke speech.

A third distinctive characteristic of Ocracoke pronunciation—and one
which, it would seem from an examination of *PEAS*, is unique—is the
centralization of the onsets of the diphthongal allophones of /i/ and /e/
in all positions except after the dorso-velars /k, g/ and the fronto-palatal
fricative /ʃ/. The words *east, ceased, beach, creek, three, age, same, great,*
and *way* are normally heard as [ïist, sïist, biitʃ, krïik, θrïˑɨ, ɜˑïdʒ, sɜˈïm, grɜɨt,
wɜˈïˉ).

A fourth prominent phonetic feature is the distinctive quality and distribution of the diphthong occurring in words such as *house, sound,*
and so on. This diphthong may be described as beginning at a somewhat
retracted low-front position and terminating at an open, slightly rounded,
high-central position; thus, the words *out, house, flounder, sound,* and *now*

[15] The *PEAS* charts show a somewhat similar diphthong in the word *boil* in the field records
from Atlanta; Charleston and Georgetown, S.C.; Georgetown, D.C.; Cassville and Philadelphia, Pa.; Providence, R.I.; New London, Conn.; and Billerica, Mass.

[16] Map 24.

288 are normally pronounced [a⁺ʊt, ha⁺ʊs, fla⁺ʊndɚ, sa⁺ʊn, na⁺ʊ]. Occasionally, however, one hears a second allophone of /au/, a diphthong [ɐʊ] with a central onset and a back-rounded glide, before voiceless consonants. One can detect some similarity between the distribution of the variants of /au/ before voiceless consonants in Ocracoke speech and the speech of certain areas of the Southern coast. A diphthong transcribed with an advanced rounded offglide in the *Atlas* records—evidently similar to the [a⁺ʊ] of Ocracoke—occurs in alternation with [ɐʊ, əʊ, ʌʊ] before voiceless consonants in the Charleston area, in most of Virginia, and on Chesapeake Bay.[17] It would seem, however, that nowhere except on the Outer Banks does such a diphthong occur before voiced consonants or finally.

It should be noted here that in Ocracoke speech [a⁺ʊ] does not have an unlimited distribution. A variant [aʊ] is regularly heard before /r, l/, and a similar diphthong alternates occasionally with [a⁺ʊ] elsewhere, particularly in final position.

The mid-central vowel also exhibits some peculiarities worthy of mention. The first of these is the extreme fronting of the vowel in all positions except before /l/ and /r/, but particularly before the apico-alveolars. Phonetically, this vowel is so closely similar to [ɛ] that the two are easily confused at first hearing. During my first visit to Ocracoke, I overheard a housewife complaining to the clerk in the community store that the last cornmeal she had bought from him was 'mesty.' It was only much later, after having heard the same vowel in *husband, must, run,* and *other,* that I realized that the woman's cornmeal had not been infected with some exotic blight, but was simply *musty* (not fresh). This fronted variant of /ʌ/ contrasts with [ɛ] in such pairs as *says* [sɛz]: *husband* ['hɜ˧zbən], and *rest* [rɛst]: *rust* [rɜ˧st].

Before /r/, however, we find a different positional variant of the mid-central vowel. Here the vowel is open central, but more noticeable than its position of articulation is the relative absence of 'r-coloring'—the vowel and the /r/ remain quite distinct from each other. Typical incidences are in the words *earth, furrow, Burrus* (a surname), *burned,* and *far,* which are regularly pronounced [ʌ˧ɹθ, 'fʌ˧ɹə, 'bʌ˧ɹəs, bʌ˧ɹnd, fʌ˧ɹ]. A similar variant of /ʌ/ in the word *furrow* is not infrequent in northeastern North Carolina, eastern Virginia, New York City, the Hudson Valley, and New England,[18] but would seem to be rare in monosyllables.

In the word *one,* the mid-central vowel is occasionally replaced by /ʊ/ —a relic usage evidently related to the pronunciation of *home* as /hʊm/ recorded frequently in a wide area of eastern Virginia and in scattered

[17] See *PEAS*, Map 29.

[18] See *PEAS*, Map 55.

stances in eastern North Carolina.[19] A related usage in Ocracoke eech is the pronunciation of *woman* with the stressed nucleus /ʊ/ ther than with the more generally current /ŏ/ or /o/. The pronunciation wʊmən/ seems to be more widely current than /wʊn/ *one* in Ocracoke eech.

The diphthong heard in *Ocracoke, boat, show,* and *froze* regularly has onset approaching a mid-front rounded position: [ˈœ˫ʊ˧krɪˈkœ˫ʊ˧k, e˫ʊ˧t, ʃœ˫ʊ˧, frœ˫ʊ˧z]. This particular diphthong, one of the most dis- ıctive characteristics of Ocracoke speech, is similar to one which has nsiderable currency in the Albemarle Sound area of North Carolina, ong the upper Ohio River, and in the Philadelphia area.[20] A back- iding allophone [o˧ʊ], with a more retracted onset, frequently occurs fore /r/, as in *Portsmouth* [ˈpo˧ʊɹtsməθ], *four* [fo˧ʊɹ], *ashore* [əˈʃo˧ʊɹ].

The vocabulary of Ocracoke speech reveals upon examination some teresting patterns of affinity with the regional dialects of the Eastern ates.[21] Evidently, there are also a number of localisms, which, however, ust await systematic collection before anything significant can be said them. I have not yet made any attempt to collect such expressions stematically, and the lexical observations which constitute the remain- r of the present article are confined largely to the generally established gional expressions included in Kurath's *Word Geography*.[22]

In some respects, the regional words used by the Ocracokers are the gional words of the North Carolina coast, especially the relic area which s around Albemarle Sound—the northeastern section of the state. Of ore interest, however, are the numerous points of usage which dis- ıguish Ocracoke speech from that of the mainland. We may perhaps proach the lexical features of Ocracoke speech most systemically by amining them under four headings: (1) words predominant both on cracoke and on the mainland, with no significant difference in usage tween the two areas; (2) words predominant in both Ocracoke and ainland North Carolina speech but current in Ocracoke usage beside

See *PEAS*, Map 123.

PEAS, Map 21.

Unlike the phonological data, which were collected in personal interviews with selected ormants and by random notes on conversations overheard and engaged in during visits Ocracoke, the lexical material was collected mainly by means of questionnaires mailed to y-three native residents of Ocracoke, twenty-five of whom responded by marking the ques- nnaires more or less completely. The questionnaires consisted of 115 items for which variant pressions occur. The informant was asked to circle in each group the expression or expres- ns which he employed, and to write in any expression which he employed but which was t included in the group given. Each informant also gave relevant personal information.

Hans Kurath, *A Word Geography of the Eastern United States* (Ann Arbor, Mich., 1955). subsequent statements about regional distribution of terms are based on this work.

290   non-North Carolina words; (3) words predominant in Ocracoke speec but infrequent or apparently nonexistent in coastal North Carolir speech; and (4) coastal North Carolina words which are lacking or in frequent in Ocracoke usage.

A few items will illustrate the first group—words current in both area alike. Two nautical expressions current throughout the East Coast are of the United States, *the wind is breezing* or *breezing up,* and *squall,* a the regular expressions among Ocracokers for "the wind is rising" an "heavy rainstorm." The words *gutters* and *kerosene* flourish as region terms among the Ocracoke informants and on the mainland. The fenc made of upright slats, known as a *paling fence* or *palings* throughout tl Southern area, is called by those names, especially the former, by Ocra cokers, though a few use *picket fence,* which appears as a modern ter in, among other areas, northeastern North Carolina. The word *whicke* (for the sound made by a horse) and its variant *whinker,* both firmly estat lished folkwords in the Carolinas, and the coastal expression *mosqui hawk* (for "dragonfly") are regularly current also on Ocracoke.

The second group of words, those shared by Ocracoke and the mai land but current in Ocracoke usage beside expressions not found i eastern North Carolina, are relatively few. One such expression is tl Southern *quarter to eleven,* which predominates in Ocracoke speech b side the fairly frequent Northern *quarter of* and the Midland *quarter ti Quarter till* was offered by four, and *quarter of* by three, informant *Quarter to* is the sole usage recorded in the *Atlas* records for the Nor Carolina coast from the Virginia line to the Neuse River, with the excep tion of a single instance of *quarter of* on Albemarle Sound. Perhaj *quarter to* and *quarter of* are the oldest expressions on the Banks, an *quarter till* may have spread to the Outer Banks from southeastern Nort Carolina, where the Midland form has come by way of the Cape Fear Peedee "corridor."

Another instance of a Midland term which crops up in the Ocracok materials along with a more frequent Southern word is *skillet* (besic *spider*). There are three occurrences of *skillet* in the Ocracoke record none at all is recorded for coastal North Carolina.

A similar situation may be observed in the occurrence of the term *co hod* beside the more frequent *coal scuttle* and *coal bucket,* and of *cor husks* beside *corn shucks.* Both *coal hod* and *husks* are Northern expre sions on the mainland. The word *husks* is not recorded in a single instanc in central or eastern North Carolina in the *Atlas* records, but it appear in the Ocracoke questionnaires seven out of seventeen times. The *Atlc* records show two occurrences of *coal hod* in northeastern North Carolin and the term appears twice in the Ocracoke materials, both times offere by older informants. Possibly *coal hod* is a recessive form on the Banks, but *husks* seems as current among younger as among older Ocracokers.

The group of words which represents the greatest difference between the usage of Ocracoke and that of mainland North Carolina is a sizable one; these are the expressions which predominate on Ocracoke but occur infrequently or not at all in the rest of North Carolina. Possibly the most striking example of this group is the Northern term *stone wall*, in the sense of the fence or low wall constructed of flat stones piled one on another without the use of mortar. This term was offered by thirteen out of seventeen informants; the other four gave *stone fence,* the usual North Midland expression. Few instances of any name for this particular type of fence are recorded on the Carolina coast, but Piedmont and western North Carolina, as well as all of Virginia from the Tidewater west, show the Southern and South Midland *rock wall* and *rock fence,* especially the latter. A single instance of *stone wall* recorded on Albemarle Sound suggests the possibility, at least, that there flourishes on Ocracoke a usage that used to be more frequent in northeastern North Carolina than it is today. Ocracokers employ the simple term *rock* for the throwing-size piece of stone, but the word *stone* has an equally vigorous currency.

A situation similar to that of *stone wall* or *fence* vs. *rock wall* or *fence* is seen in the relative frequency of the expressions *an armful (of wood)*, a Northern and North Midland usage which does not occur in North Carolina except sporadically in the west; and *a turn (of wood)*, which is the regular expression throughout the Southern area and the only one in eastern North Carolina. Ocracokers seem to prefer *armful;* only five out of eighteen offered the Southern expression.

Another Northern term principally found in eastern New England and regularly current on Ocracoke is the form *comforter* as the name of the thick, cotton-padded bedcover. This term, which was offered by all but four of the Ocracoke informants, has no currency at all in the Midland or Southern areas, with the exception of four isolated occurrences across Pamlico Sound from Ocracoke. In all of North Carolina the regular form of the word is *comfort.*

Finally, we may look briefly at a group of words which, though characteristic of the mainland adjacent to Ocracoke, are evidently employed infrequently or not at all by Ocracokers. The typically Southern Coast expressions *lightwood* (or /láitəd/) for "kindling wood," and *curtain* for "roller shade," seem surprisingly infrequent on Ocracoke: they occur five and three times, respectively, in the Ocracoke records. The Southern and South Midland *dog irons,* which is the regular expression along the coastal plain of North Carolina as far south as the Cape Fear River, was not offered by any of the Ocracoke informants, nor were the related forms

292   *dogs* and *firedogs,* which are current in the rest of North Carolina. In the total absence of *dog irons, dogs,* and *firedogs* in Ocracoke usage, we may consider *andirons,* which together with one instance of *handirons* takes their place, a true folkword in Ocracoke usage.

Two peculiarly North Carolina expressions should be mentioned in connection with the group of North Carolina words without wide currency in Ocracoke speech: *shivering owl* (and its variant *shiveling owl*), of which there are no occurrences in the Ocracoke records; and *tow sack,* which was offered by five out of twenty-one informants. The term *screech owl,* which in eastern North Carolina has less currency than the regional term, was used by all the informants; and *burlap bag* was generally preferred over the North Carolina expression.

I shall conclude this rather general discussion of noteworthy lexical features of Ocracoke speech by mentioning a handful of expressions gleaned from casual conversation with Ocracokers, and included here simply as interesting points of usage which seem to have a more or less limited geographical distribution. One of these, a usage with a nautical flavor, is the word *abreast* meaning "across from," employed regularly as a simple preposition, as in "He lives up here abreast the post office" and "She went aground abreast the island."[23] Another term connected with the sea and used quite regularly is *fatback,* pronounced /fǽd bæ̀k/, the popular name for the menhaden, a fish plentiful in Pamlico Sound. A grove of trees is generally called a *hammock* /hǽmək/, and two hills on the island which support some vegetation are called "First Hammock Hill" and "Second Hammock Hill," in order of their distance from the village. A single cow is frequently referred to as a *cattlebeast.* An item of syntax which is particularly interesting in view of its currency also in New England speech and of its similarity in that respect to other Northern terms like *coal hod, stone wall,* and *comforter* which are current on Ocracoke, is the use of the preposition *to* in a locative sense, as in "She was borned up to Buxton" and "the new hospital over to Sealevel." Finally, there is a holly-like shrub which grows wild on the Outer Banks, as well as in some other parts of the South, and which is known by the Ocracokers as *yaupon* /yópɒ̀n/. What is interesting about this word is not the name itself but the Ocracoke pronunciation of it, for unless the lexicographers have erred, the pronunciation elsewhere is /yɔ́pən/. It is tempting to speculate that both the first vowel and the slightly stressed second syllable of the Ocracoke pronunciation represent a more authentic rendering of the original Catawba Indian word, *yopún.*

---

[23] The word *island* here means, as it frequently does in Ocracoke, the village itself, i.e., the inhabited part of Ocracoke Island. Thus, "She went aground at about the latitude of the village [but on the ocean side of Ocracoke Island]."

Much more study of the speech of the Outer Banks must be done before firm patterns emerge; this article is admittedly preliminary and incomplete. However, we may be justified in making a few tentative generalizations about Ocracoke speech on the basis of the foregoing details of vowel phonology and vocabulary.

It is immediately evident, for instance, that the speech of Ocracoke in several respects differs markedly from the Southern dialect, particularly in: (1) the retention of postvocalic /r/; (2) the general occurrence of the stressed nucleus /ɛ/ in both *merry* and *Mary;* and (3) the considerable currency of such non-Southern expressions as *quarter of, quarter till, skillet, cornhusks, coal hod, stone wall,* and so on. Moreover, there are certain features of phonology which seem to set Ocracoke speech apart from all the major dialects—for instance, the diphthong /ɒi/, the pronunciation of the mid-central vowel plus /r/ in monosyllables as [ʌɨɹ], and the extreme fronting of the onset of the diphthongal allophone of /o/ (which more closely resembles Standard British usage than that of any type of American English). But these differences should not be permitted to obscure the numerous similarities between Ocracoke speech and that of the upper South, particularly of eastern North Carolina (and more particularly of the Albemarle Sound area) and eastern Virginia.

Perhaps the most fitting generalization with which to conclude is that the speech of the Outer Banks is obviously a fertile field for investigation, and one too-long neglected. It should be cultivated at once, for the Banks are becoming year by year less isolated and more susceptible to outside linguistic influence.

Florida Pronunciation

Charles K. Thomas

As might be expected from the settlement patterns of the
state, the speech of Florida is different from that of the
surrounding Southern states. Professor Thomas discusses a
number of the features of the speech of Florida and compares
the usage of Floridians with that of other areas. Professor
Thomas was at the time of his death Professor of English at
the University of Florida.

Florida represents a curious amalgamation of American dialects. It is
the purpose of this writer to study Florida pronunciation and its history.

From the *Southern Speech Journal,* Vol. 33, No. 3 (Spring, 1968) 223–229. Reprinted with
the permission of the Southern Speech Association, and Mrs. Charles K. Thomas.

The late Charles K. Thomas (Ph.D., Cornell University, 1930) was Professor of Speech at the
University of Florida when Prof. Philip H. Constans was department chairman. A graduate
student—Voncile Marshall Smith, who, incidentally, is a native-born Floridian—presented her
master's thesis (see footnote 1) to the Graduate Council of the University of Florida in April,
1964. Professor Constans served as chairman of her supervisory committee along with Professor
Hal G. Lewis and Professor L. L. Zimmerman. The raw data on which Mrs. Smith based her
work were the author's phonetic tabulations of the records of Florida pronunciation in his
collection. "In a substantial degree," wrote Dr. Thomas, "she has been my co-author."

The native pronunciation of English in the state of Florida varies widely from an urban style to one that is generally labeled "Florida cracker." These forms shift from the urbanized variations of Miami and Fort Lauderdale, which have virtually no Southern elements, to some of the northern and western interior counties such as Liberty, Gadsden, and Columbia, where Southern style predominates. It is a paradoxical truism that the speech of Jacksonville, in the north, sounds much more Southern than Miami, which is five hundred miles farther south. Within the last generation the tremendous growth of Florida's population has upset the balance of styles until there is now more variation in pronunciation than in Pennsylvania, which has a much longer history of changing population and variations in pronunciation.

MIGRATION BROUGHT VARIATION

The principal reason for this variation is to be found in the population history of the various sections of the state. In brief, the earliest settlers represented an overflow from the coastal South; later migrations came from the southern Appalachians; in the boom period of the twentieth century the Miami area filled up with people from New York and New Jersey, and the St. Petersburg area drew many inhabitants from the northern Midwest. Currently Miami is experiencing a large infusion of Cuban refugees.

When people migrate, they carry with them the language patterns of the region from which they come. The extent to which these characteristics become established in the new area depends on the number of immigrants from any one region, the number of people already living in the area, and whether or not other groups from different sections join them in large numbers. An analysis of the pronunciation of any given region should therefore take into consideration the historic backgrounds of the people of that region and the subsequent effect these backgrounds have on the spoken language patterns. In this connection a survey of the population changes that have occurred in Florida is most illuminating.

Florida's first settlers came from adjacent southern states to the most northern and western sections of the state. This was a rural farming region settled by Scotch-Irish immigrants who had been farmers, chiefly in Georgia. Some came from Alabama, and a few from other southern states.

When Florida was admitted to the Union, in 1845, the state's population totaled about 70,000. The census of 1850 records a population of 87,445, of whom only 25 percent were native-born white Floridians. About 29 percent were born in other states, and 3 percent were of foreign

296   birth. No record was made of the birthplaces of Negroes, who made up nearly half the population at that time.

By 1860 the percentage of native-born white people had dropped to 20 percent. Of those born outside Florida, Georgia contributed nearly 50 percent, South Carolina 20 percent, and Alabama and North Carolina a little more than 10 percent each. In this early period only a few settlers had come from outside the South. One thousand had come from New York, fewer than five hundred from Massachusetts, and only a few from the Northeastern and North Central states. Only five had come from the West—four from California and one from Idaho Territory. West Florida's population in 1864 was six times greater than that of the peninsula area.

In 1900 a line could have been drawn diagonally across a map of the state, running from a point in the northeast, near what is now Cape Kennedy, in mid-Brevard County, down to Lee County, west of Lake Okeechobee, to separate the northern populated portion of the state from the relatively unsettled southern part. As railroad tracks were laid down as far as Tampa and extended along the east coast to Palm Beach and later to Miami, the first real flow of population began to be noticeable in those areas, beginning in the 1890's and increasing steadily after 1900.

Before 1920, while most of the towns shared in the general growth in population, the state remained predominantly rural, farms and villages accounting for nearly two thirds of its inhabitants. In sharp contrast, most of the increase in population since 1920 has been in the cities. By 1950 nearly two thirds of the people living in the state were city-dwellers—a complete reversal within a short span of time. In 1920 more than a third of the state's people were non-white; by 1950 this proportion had decreased to barely 20 percent.

The total population in 1950 numbered nearly 2,800,000. The eight leading states of origin, in order, were Florida, Georgia, Alabama, New York, Pennsylvania, Ohio, South Carolina, and Illinois. Only ten years later this number had increased to about 5,000,000.[1]

DETAILS OF VARIATION

This study is based on data compiled from 1938 to 1963. Tape recordings were made of the speech of 1,117 white students enrolled in four Florida universities: the University of Florida, Florida State University, the University of Miami, and Stetson University. All these young men and women were native-born, each a lifelong resident of the partic-

---

[1] See the unpublished thesis (Florida, 1963) by Voncile Marshall Smith, "An Analysis of the Pronunciation of Life-long Florida County Residents Who Have Enrolled in Florida Colleges, 1938–1963," pp. 2–12.

ular county from which he or she had been accredited. Their ages ranged from the late teens to the early twenties. So, in general, the recordings were made of speakers of similar age and educational background. These students represented all the sixty-seven Florida counties. Their numerical distribution was roughly in proportion to the populations of the counties they represented in relationship to the total population of the state. Analysis of the speech sounds recorded from their oral reading of a written page of key words woven into a simple narrative yielded the following findings concerning speech patterns current in particular localities in Florida.[2]

To the visitor from the North or West the most noticeable feature of Florida pronunciation is the variation in the treatment of *r*, whether consonantal or vocalic, in words like *car, card, hear, heard,* and *better.* West of Jacksonville, *r* usually is not heard except in the neighborhood of Tallahassee. South of Jacksonville, *r* returns strongly in Daytona Beach and Brevard County, drops out again in Indian River, St. Lucie, and Martin counties, and then returns in Palm Beach, Broward, and Dade counties. Southwest of Jacksonville, *r* drops out all the way to the Gulf Coast, then stays out through Alachua and Marion counties and the small counties south and west of them till it comes back into such words at St. Petersburg, in Pinellas County, and Bradenton, in Manatee County. From Tampa, in Hillsborough County, across the northern Everglades to the Atlantic, *r* is gone once more.

Thus, the total picture with respect to *r* can be summarized as dependent on the background of the original settlers. Where northerners predominate, except for settlers from New York city, *r* remains predominant; where Southerners predominate, *r* drops out. The history of the state in the twentieth century is such as to make the pattern an irregular patchwork.

Somewhat more characteristic Southern forms occur in the unstressed syllables of such words as *city, chimney, coffee, foggy,* and *heavy.* Regardless of the nature of the stressed vowels in these words, the unstressed vowels in the north and west are qualitatively the same as the vowel in *beet* and may be recorded as *ee*: thus *citee, chimnee, foggee, heavee.* In Florida and for some distance to the north the unstressed vowel is much more likely to be qualitatively the same as that of *bit* and may be recorded as *ih*: thus, *citih, chimnih, foggih, heavih.* The unstressed *ee* occurs in less than 5 percent of the usages on the unstressed vowel in Okaloosa, Walton, Holmes, Washington, Bay, Gulf, Gadsden, and Glades counties, and less than half the time in the populous Northern-influenced sections of south Florida and the East Coast. This feature, though not conspicuous in the

[2] Smith, p. 12.

298   individual occurrence, nevertheless gives a distinctively Southern flavor
to Florida speech as a whole.

In *Mary, various,* and *area,* usage is mixed; though in the north and
west, Mary is normally pronounced *merry,* perhaps with a vowel that is
slightly longer in duration but identical in quality. In Florida and elsewhere in the South it is predominantly *mayrih. Vayrious* also predominates, but *ayrea* occurs only in west Florida and points westward along
the Gulf Coast.

Similarly, in words like *hero* and *zero* the Florida pronunciation has *ee*
in the first syllable in contrast with the north and most parts of the west,
which have *ih.* Thus, in Florida *heero* is in contrast with *hihro* in most
places outside the South.

A characteristic variation, particularly hard to describe without the
help of a phonetic alphabet, is the treatment of long *a* along the Gulf
Coast of west Florida. *Gate* and *get* are pronounced *gayt* and *geht* in most
parts of the country, though the respelling of *get* is perhaps exaggerated.
In west Florida, however, the pronunciation of *gate* combines the first
part of *get* with the second part of *gate:* thus, *geh-yt*—a subtle difference
that may be hard to analyze.

The so-called broad *a* of New England is completely foreign to Florida;
thus, *hahf, dahnce,* and *clahss* are not heard. Instead, the normal form is
diphthongized to something like *ha-eeff, da-eence,* and *cla-ees,* and *can't*
becomes virtually *caint.* This usage is uniform throughout the Deep South
but variable in Florida except for the Miami and St. Petersburg areas,
where the sounds are like those of northern and western America.

In *joy, enjoyed,* and *boiled* there is a great deal of variation in the *oi*
diphthong. *Joy* may sound either like *jaw* or *jo-ey* so that it is sometimes
difficult to tell the girl's name *Joy* from the boy's name *Joey.* When the
author was first living in Alachua County, he was puzzled by small-boy
peddlers who seemed to be selling *bald* peanuts, whatever they were. It
took him a while to interpret the hawkers' cries as *"boiled* peanuts," a
Southern delicacy with which he was unfamiliar. The regional variation
of these versions of the *oi* diphthong are mixed throughout the state, the
occurrence of the standard *oi* being largely limited to those areas which
have a history of northern infiltration in population.

In the country as a whole such words as *forest, horrid, corridor, Florida,
Oregon,* and *torrents* have two main types of pronunciation. The short *o*
followed by the *r* sound and another vowel in the same word is predominantly pronounced *ah* in the East and South, *aw* in the North and West.
The seam between the two types runs down through central Vermont,
cuts across western Massachusetts and a bit of western Connecticut, and
southeastern Pennsylvania, crosses the Maryland line at the panhandle,
and keeps all of West Virginia except a small part of the southernmost

area of the state in *aw* territory. From Kentucky to Texas the line slopes west and south. The South from Virginia to Georgia is clearly in the *ah* territory.

Not so, Florida. Except for a few counties along the Georgia border, most of Florida calls the state *Flawrida*. The same is true of *fawrest, hawrrid, Awigon,* and other words in the class. The only cities of any size to use *Flahrida* predominantly are Jacksonville, Gainesville, and Tallahassee. Even in the Miami area, where the New York City background should have produced *Flahrida,* the pronunciation is *Flawrida.*

Similarly, before velar consonants there is considerable variation between *ah* and *aw: donkey, honk,* and *logs* are predominantly *dawnkey, hawnk,* and *lawgs; fog, frogs, hogs,* and *mahogany* are predominantly *fahg, frahgz, hahgz,* and *mahahgony.* This variation characterizes the country as a whole, because mappings of words in this class—e.g., *donkey, fog, foggy, frog, hog, mahogany, clogged,* and *gong*—show variations in predominant vowels everywhere.

Before *l, ah* predominates throughout the state, as in *doll, follow, golf, involve,* and *solve:* thus, *dahl, fahllow, gahlf, invahlve,* and *sahlve.* This variation is characteristic of most of the country except for western Pennsylvania and the areas derived from it, where *aw* is often predominant.

VARIATIONS IN CONSONANTS

Aside from *r,* there are not many variations in the pronunciation of consonants. One is between *s* and *z* in *greasy* and the verb *grease.* In Florida, as in the rest of the South as far north as central New Jersey and southern Pennsylvania, *greasy* is predominantly *greazih;* elsewhere, except for scattered areas in the Pacific Northwest, it is *greassee.* In the South the words rhyme with *easy;* elsewhere, with *fleecy.* Similarly with the verb *grease:* In Florida and throughout the South, up to New Jersey and Pennsylvania, you have your car *greazed:* elsewhere, you have it *greast*—a pronunciation that rhymes with *east.*

The other consonantal variation characteristic of Florida and the rest of the South is the survival of *yoo* instead of the more recent *oo* in words like *due, new, tune, student,* and even *suit.* This survival, universal in *union, unit, use, huge,* and similar long-*u* words, has been largely eliminated in most parts of the country except in the stressed position at the beginning of a word or syllable, as in *used* and *unused,* after *h* as in *huge,* after *k* as in *cube,* after *g* as in *argue,* after *m* as in *mute,* after *p* as in *pew,* and after *b* as in *beauty.* Thus, instead of *dyoo,* the rest of the country pronounces *due* and *dew* as *doo, tube* as *toob, lucid* as *loosid,* and *suit* as *soot.* But Florida and the rest of the South largely retain the old consonantal *y.*

300   Many parts of the country often insert an unhistorical *y* in words like *column, coupon, escalator, metabolism,* and *percolator.* Since Florida makes more use of this consonantal *y* than most other areas, it is not surprising frequently to hear *colyum, kyoupon, eskayalator, metabyolism,* and *perkyolater.* As elsewhere in the country, these pronunciations spring from ignorance of the history of the words, combined with a false quest for elegance.[3]

[3] Smith, pp. 32–63.

From Cockney
to Conch

Frank K. La Ban

The speech of the Conchs of the Florida Keys has a number of
features that are notably different from the speech of South
Florida. Like the people of Ocracoke, North Carolina,
the Conchs have been isolated from others in the region.
Professor La Ban describes some of the features of the
speech of the Conchs and seeks the sources of these in British
speech, Southern speech, and General American, a term
he uses, as Claude M. Wise does, to mean generally the
speech of the North Midland area. Dr. La Ban teaches
speech and phonetics at the University of Arizona. This
paper is based on his unpublished doctoral dissertation
"A Phonological Study of the Speech of the Conchs, Early
Inhabitants of the Florida Keys, at Three Age Levels"
(Louisiana State University, 1965).

If you were to hear people say locker ['lɑkə] instead of closet, kitchen
safe ['kɪˈtʃɪnˌseɪf] instead of pantry, grits box ['grɪtsˌbɑˈks] instead of

This unpublished paper is based on the author's dissertation "A Phonological Study of the
Speech of the Conchs, Early Inhabitants of the Florida Keys, at Three Age Levels" (Louisiana
State University, 1965). It is printed here with the permission of Frank K. La Ban.

302 stove, first oldest (fɜɪst 'ɜuldɪs] instead of oldest, natural sponge ['nætʃrəl ˌspɔ⌐ntʃ] instead of dishcloth, and bumbershoot ['bʌmbə,ʃut] instead of umbrella, and if the people you heard pronounced these terms as transcribed above, where would these people be most likely to live? Maine? Massachusetts? England? No, none of these. The answer is southern Florida or, more correctly, the Florida Keys.

Why such remnants of pronunciation and lexical items can be found in the speech of some people living in the Florida Keys today can best be explained by noting the background of these people and their ancestors.

In 1649, a company, the Eleutherian Adventurers, was formed by a group of Cockney Englishmen in London with the expressed purpose of seeking political and religious freedom.[1] Shortly thereafter, they traveled to Bermuda. Later, around 1770, this group migrated to the island of Cigatos in the Bahamas, which they renamed Eleutheria.[2] These Bahamans and their descendants settled in the Florida Keys in the early 1800's. Fishermen by trade, these English settlers were soon given the name "Conch" because of their reliance on the conch, a gastropod, for food, and the use of the giant conch shell as a trumpet used for communication from key to key and from ship to shore.

In 1819 the Conchs began settling on the Keys, and by 1860 had built homes on the upper Keys as well as on Key West. Instead of mingling with people already settled in Key West, the Conchs built homes on both sides of the island; and, being bound by close family ties, they remained apart from other settlers.[3] The Conchs made a living doing three things: fishing, gathering sponges, and wrecking, and all three involved the sea.

After hearing the speech of a few of these individuals, I felt that changes taking place in the speech of the Conchs could be determined by studying the recorded speech of informants representing three age groups: young adults aged 17, middle-aged adults between 40 and 55, and adults 65 years old or older.[4] As far as possible, selection of informants was limited to those individuals willing to be interviewed and who had not resided, traveled, or been educated outside the Keys area. My investi-

[1] Work Projects Administration, Federal Writers' Project. *A Guide to Key West* (New York: Hastings House, 1941), pp. 29–30.

[2] *Ibid.*

[3] Marie Louise Cappick, *The Key West Story* (unpublished manuscript, 1946), p. 70.

[4] The number of informants representing each group is as follows: age 17 (2), age 40–55 (3), age 65 or older (2). The seven informants in this study were used to represent the speech of less than thirty-four thousand people. This was a more favorable people-to-informant ratio than that used in the Kurath and McDavid study of the Atlantic States. See Hans Kurath and Raven I. McDavid, Jr., *The Pronunciation of English in the Atlantic States* (Ann Arbor, Michigan: The University of Michigan Press, 1961), p. 11.

gation tried to determine the phonological characteristics of the speech of the Conchs with attention to (1) the characteristics of British speech present, (2) the characteristics of standard and substandard Southern speech present, (3) the characteristics of standard and substandard General American speech present, and (4) trends indicated by differences in speech at three age levels. The reason for assuming British speech characteristics would be present in the speech of these informants has already been established. The possible presence of Southern American speech characteristics was considered because of the location of the Keys in the Southern speech region. And finally, it was felt that characteristics of General American speech might be present in the speech of the Conchs through the possible influence of tourists to the Keys from General American dialect areas, and perhaps even the influence of radio and television.

After informants had been selected, interviews were arranged. These interviews were based on the workbooks for the *Linguistic Atlas of the U.S.A. and Canada* as edited by Hans Kurath for the South Atlantic section.[5] All interviews were tape-recorded. During the interview, questions were asked in such a way that the interviewer never pronounced the response sought from the informant.

Upon completion of the fieldwork, the responses on the tapes were transcribed into symbols of the International Phonetic Alphabet. The transcriptions were then analyzed in comparison to descriptions of standard southern British speech, and standard and substandard Southern and General American dialects as found in Claude Merton Wise's *Applied Phonetics*.[6] This analysis led to the following conclusions: (1) The speech of the Conchs in the Florida Keys is actually a mixture of British, Southern American, and General American dialects. (2) The speech of the oldest informants is primarily a mixture of British and Southern American dialects. (3) The speech of the informants in the middle-age group contains elements of British, Southern American, and General American dialects. (4) The speech of the youngest informants is composed of characteristics of Southern and General American speech, and although an occasional feature of British dialect can be found in the speech of the youngest informants, these are so rare they must be considered negligible.

The number of features of each dialect presented here are only a few of those found in the speech of the informants interviewed.

---

[5] I further edited the workbooks before they were used in the Keys area. Items relating to snow, sleet, heavy farming, and the like were not considered pertinent to this area and so were deleted. Also, since this study was mainly concerned with phonology, many grammatical items were omitted.

[6] Claude Merton Wise, *Applied Phonetics* (Englewood Cliffs, New Jersey: Prentice-Hall, Inc., 1957), pp. 182–220, 239–244.

One of the characteristics of British dialect present in the speech of the Conchs is the tendency to use the sound [ɪ] in unstressed suffixes spelled *-ace, -ain, -ate, -ed, -en, -es, -ess, -et, -ice, -id, -in, -ip, -is, -ist, -it, -ite,* and *-uce.*[7] For example, the suffix *ace* in the word *palace* would be pronounced [ɪs] as in ['pælɪs]; the suffix *ess* in the word *actress* would be pronounced [ɪs] as in ['æktrɪs]. This was the most prevalent characteristic of British speech (and in this case of Southern speech as well) recorded in the speech of the informants. So strong was the tendency to use [ɪ] by all seven informants in these unstressed suffixes that only three out of fifty such words produced exceptions.

Another characteristic of British speech indicated by Wise is the use of [ɪ] in medial syllables spelled with *e, i,* or *y.*[8] In the following fifteen words of the above category, the number of informants indicated in parentheses in the right-hand column used [ɪ] in the medial syllable.

1.5[9]	*seventy*	(7—*all*)
9.3	*furniture*	(7)
40.2	*anywhere*	(7)
56.7	*honeydew*	(2)
62.5	*boysenberry*	(1)
65.1	*pregnancy*	(1)
73.5	*carpenter*	(1)
74.6	*negligent*	(1)
82.7	*celebration*	(1)
86.7	*Florida*	(7)
86.8	*California*	(7)
90.6	*terribly*	(1)

In "short o" words, such as *not, bottle, what,* etc., a low-back vowel, [ɒ], is commonly heard in British speech.[10] This sound was used often in words of this category by the oldest informant, *not* (57.5) and *October* (1.8) being examples. The other informant in the oldest age group used this sound occasionally, as did two informants in the middle-age group.

Another important feature of British dialect found fairly consistently in the speech of the oldest informant was the use of the diphthong [ɜʊ] in

---

[7] *Ibid.,* p. 240. (The term *suffix* is used here in the sense that it is used by Wise in *Applied Phonetics.* For example, Wise considers the final syllables *-ad* in the word *salad* and *-en* in the word *kitchen* as suffixes. This pattern is followed throughout this study.)

[8] *Ibid.*

[9] The number 1.5 indicates that the word *seventy* is the fifth item in section one of the workbooks used in this study. Other such numbers indicate similar information.

[10] Wise, *op. cit.,* p. 241.

syllables where only the diphthong [oʊ] would be used in most American English.[11] Forty-one words in the workbooks called for the [oʊ] sound in the stressed position, for which the oldest informant offered responses to thirty-four. In his responses he used [ɜʊ] twenty times, [ɜº] once, [oʏ] three times, and [oʊ] seven times, clearly indicating a preference for [ɜʊ]. The other informant representing the oldest age group used [ɜʊ] in the stressed position on just two occasions: *posts* [-ɜᵗʊ-] (16.6), and *crowbar* [-ɜʊ-] (22.2).

According to Wise medial [t] is aspirate in British speech.[12] Of the eight words in the workbooks in which [t] appeared medially, an aspirate [t] was used by all informants in pronunciation of the following: *prettier* (26.6) and *cottage* (47.4). Other words in which a medial [t] was used by the informants are: *pretty* (26.5), *water* (48.7), *sitting* (49.5), *lettuce* (56.2), *excited* (75.4), and *better* (76.2).

STANDARD SOUTHERN SPEECH

A characteristic of Southern American speech is the use of [ɑ] for the orthographic combination *ar* in words such as *car, park,* and *cigar*.[13] The oldest informant used [ɑ] in such words, while the other informant in the 65 or older age group and two informants in the 40–55 age group used either [ɑ] or [ɑə] in *car* (23.5) and *park* (24.1).

In Southern speech, [l] is usually clear before front stressed vowels.[14] In words where *l* preceded front vowels such as [i] in *cleans* (10.3), [ɪ] in *lit* (44.2), [ɛ] in *eleven* (1.3), [æ] in *glass* (48.7), and front rising diphthongs such as [aɪ] in *library* (84.1) the informants recorded in this study always used a clear [l].

In contrast to the use of clear [l] as stated above, Southern American

[11] *Ibid.*

[12] *Ibid.*, p. 242. In his discussion of medial aspirate [t], Wise includes such words as *city, ditty, pity, jetty, nettled, little, battle, kitten, cotten, rotting, witty, Saturday,* and *flutter.* All these words follow a pattern in which the /t/ phoneme considered to be medial is preceded immediately by a syllable of primary stress and followed immediately by a syllable of weak or no stress. This writer did not consider words such as *little* and *battle* in his discussion of medial aspirate [t] when they were pronounced [lɪtl̩] and [bætl̩]. In such pronunciations, the tip of the tongue remains in contact with the alveolar ridge long enough to cause the stopped air to be released bilaterally to produce the following [l] and thus prevents the [t] from being aspirate. In words like *kitten* and *cotton,* when pronounced [kɪtn] and [kɑtn], medial [t] is not aspirate because the stopped air is not exploded over the tip of the tongue but released nasally for the production of [n] which follows.

[13] *Ibid.*, p. 207. (This is also a characteristic of British speech.)

[14] *Ibid.*, p. 209.

306   speech is characterized by the use of dark [l], [ɫ], before back vowels as in *load*, finally as in *fill*, and in intermediate positions after stressed back vowels, as in *pulley*.[15] Four informants were consistent in their use of [ɫ] in a list of eleven such words as described above.

MIXED DIALECT FEATURES

In standard southern British "[ɑ] is used in 'broad a' words ... which are in most cases spelled with *a* plus [f] ([v] in some plurals), [s], [θ] ([ð] in some plurals), and *n* plus a consonant."[16] In Southern American[17] and General American[18] *a* = [æ] in "all 'broad a' words." Two of the informants in the 40–55 age group used [ɑ] in words of this category (*rather* (90.5) and *glass* in conversation). It is interesting to note that the informant who pronounced *glass* as [glɑs] in isolation pronounced the same term as [glæs] in the expression *a glass of water* (48.7). The rest of the informants used [æ] in "broad a" words without exception.

In standard southern British and Southern American dialects, words containing the spelling *ear, er, ir, or, our, ur,* and *yr* in their stressed syllables are usually pronounced [ɜ].[19] In General American speech, words in this category are pronounced [ɝ].[20] The two informants in the 65 or older group used [ɜ] or [ɜ¹] in such words consistently. Two of the three informants in the middle-age group, 40–55, used [ɜ] and [ɝ] on an almost equal basis. The youngest informant indicated the strongest General American influence as represented by this feature. In nineteen words containing the vowel sound in *bird*, he used [ɝ] eighteen times and [ɜr] once.

In Southern American English "*r* is silent finally and preconsonantally after [ɑ], [ɜ], and [ə], as in *car* [kɑ], *harm* [hɑm], *turn* [tɜn], *buttered* ['bʌtəd]."[21] The workbooks indicate that in many instances where *r* is silent after [ɜ], as in *thirteen* (1.4), *first* (1.6), and *heard* (71.8), [ɪ⁺] often occurred as an offglide from [ɜ] thus producing ['θɜ¹tin], [fɜ¹st], and [hɜ¹d]. The workbooks also show that the youngest informant used [r] after [ɑ] in *park* (24.1), *garden* (50.7), *cigars* (57.3), and *starts* (83.4). Since Wise in-

15 *Ibid.*

16 *Ibid.*, p. 240.

17 *Ibid.*, p. 205.

18 *Ibid.*, p. 183.

19 *Ibid.*, pp. 241, 207.

20 *Ibid.*, p. 185.

21 *Ibid.*, p. 209.

dicates that *r* is always pronounced in General American speech,[22] we may conclude that such an influence is present in the speech of the youngest informant.

DEVIATIONS FROM STANDARD SOUTHERN AND GENERAL AMERICAN

Many deviations from standard Southern and General American speech were recorded for all seven informants. One of the deviations recorded in the workbooks is the reduction of a diphthong to a pure vowel. The tendency was most noticeable in the diphthong [aɪ] being reduced to [a].[23] The oldest informant never reduced the [aɪ] diphthong to a pure vowel, but one of the younger informants did so most of the time.

Another of the deviations from standard Southern and General American dialects revealed in the interviews was that of unvoicing. Numerous instances occurred in the speech of each informant whereby a consonant, usually voiced in that particular linguistic environment, was unvoiced. In fourteen words in which unvoicing occurred, it appeared in the final position in ten and in a medial position in four. Some examples of the utterances recorded follow.

4.7	*ages*	['eɪdʒɪs]
4.7	*visit*	['vɪsɪt]
8.7	*coals*	[koʊls]
9.6	*closet*	['klɑsɪt]
11.3	*shutters*	['ʃɑdɪs]
16.3	*pointed*	['pɔɪntɪt]
100.4	*recognize*	['rɛkəɡˌnaɪs]

The word *shutters* produced a combination that could be labeled voicing-unvoicing. Two informants pronounced this word as ['ʃɑdɪs] thus voicing [t] to [d] and unvoicing [z] to [s].

Among other deviations of standard speech recorded in the interviews is the simplification of consonant clusters.[24] Examples of such simplifications noted in the workbooks are the loss of [v] from the cluster [lv] as

---

[22] *Ibid.,* p. 187.

[23] Such a tendency is described by Wise as monophthongization. He says this reduction of [aɪ] to [a] occurs often in Southern American speech. See Wise, *Applied Phonetics,* p. 215.

[24] This simplification is merely the loss of one or more elements of the cluster. Many reasons exist for the simplification of such clusters, such as ease of articulation, and the assimilation of one consonant to that of another. See Wise, *Applied Phonetics,* p. 162.

308 in *twelve* (1.3) producing [twɛl] instead of [twɛlv]; the loss of [f] in the cluster [fθ] as in *fifth* (1.6) producing [fɪθ] and the loss of [θ] in the cluster [fθ] producing [fɪf].

A review of the material gathered in the workbooks will show that there are additional characteristics of British, Southern American, and General American dialects present in the speech of the informants interviewed other than those characteristics mentioned here. A review of the data will also show that the trend is away from the British dialect features contained in the speech of the older informants and toward the characteristics of Southern and General American English as contained in the speech of the younger informants.

It is possible that intermixing of social groups in the Keys, the cessation of British dialect speaking immigrants, and the influence of radio and television have helped to bring about changes in the speech of the Conchs.

That a change has taken place in the dialect of the Conchs from predominantly British speech to predominantly Southern and General American speech within three generations is evident. Such changes within the sound pattern of a language (dialect) are to be expected. As John T. Waterman observed:

> Sound-changes are historical events that take place quite without intention on the part of the generations of speakers involved. Each generation uses the same general sound pattern and no one perceives that certain classes of sounds are "drifting" away from a previous norm.[25]

---

[25] John T. Waterman, *Perspectives in Linguistics* (Chicago: The University of Chicago Press, 1963), p. 65.

A Southeast Texas Dialect Study

Arthur Norman

Studies of the speech of Texas have shown that there is an east Texas variety and a western variety. The eastern variety has many features of Southern speech of the plantation area, the western more of the South Midland or "hill Southern" type.

In the following article Professor Norman of the University of Texas discusses the speech of a part of the eastern Texas area. He treats at some length the vocabulary of the area, comparing the forms he found with those of the Eastern Seaboard area discussed by Professor Kurath in his *Word Geography*. Professor Norman also makes a few comments on the pronunciation and selected verb forms of the speech of the area.

310 THE AREA OF INVESTIGATION

This study represents a detailed investigation of the speech of Jefferson County, Texas, with attention to the speech of Chambers, Hardin, and Orange counties.[1] These four counties are located in the southeasternmost tip of the state.

Jefferson, the largest of the four counties in this study, had in 1950 a population of 195,083 persons, 147,633 of whom were native-born whites and 44,122 blacks. There were 3,225 foreign-born whites in the county, and 103 persons of other races. Jefferson is the most urban of the counties in this investigation, being only 1.5% farm rural, 8.1% non-farm rural, and 90.4% urban.

Chambers County had in 1950 a population of 7,871 persons, 6,291 of whom were native-born whites and 1,526 of whom were colored. Twenty-six were foreign-born whites and 28 of other races. Chambers County is entirely non-urban, being 14.1% farm rural and 85.9% non-farm rural.

Hardin County in 1950 had a population of 19,535, of whom 16,361 were native-born whites and 3,079 colored. Eighty-nine were foreign-born whites and six belonged to other races. Hardin is 16.3% urban, 64.0% non-farm rural, and 19.7% rural in composition.

From *Orbis*, Bulletin International de Documentation Linguistique, Vol. V (1956), 61–79. Reprinted with the permission of A. J. Windekens, Directeur, Centre International de Dialectologie Générale, and Arthur A. Z. Norman.

[1] This paper attempts to summarize the most important findings of my doctoral thesis, which was supervised by Professor E. Bagby Atwood, University of Texas, in 1955.

Previous investigations of Texas dialect have been limited to pronunciation or vocabulary studies, usually at the county level. These investigations include Oma Stanley's "The Speech of East Texas," a study of the phonology of Smith County with attention to a number of neighboring counties, which was serialized in *American Speech*, XI (1936), 1–36, 145–166, 232–255, and 327–355; Carmelita Klipple, "The Speech of Spicewood, Texas," *American Speech*, XX (1945), 187–191; Zelma Boyd Hardy, "A Vocabulary Study of Kerr County, Texas," (M. A. thesis, University of Texas, 1950); and Randoph A. Haynes, Jr., "A Vocabulary Study of Travis County, Texas;" (M. A. thesis, University of Texas, 1954). E. Bagby Atwood's "A Preliminary Report on Texas Word Geography," *Orbis*, II (1953), 61–66, contains an important presentation of the Spanish, French, and Southwestern influences in the state.

In 1962, less than a year before his untimely death, Professor Atwood's last book, *The Regional Vocabulary of Texas*, was copyrighted and later released for publication by the University of Texas Press in Austin. In Chapter IV, "Geographical Aspects of Usage," Atwood shows that a major dialect boundary exists, "one that tends to set off southern Louisiana from the remainder of the territory that has been surveyed." Many of the isoglosses, in fact, "pass just to the eastward of Jefferson and Hardin Counties, setting these off from Orange County and the Louisiana parishes of Calcasieu, Acadia, and St. Martin, as well as from all the other points lying closer to New Orleans." Still, the "presence of a good many of the Louisiana terms in southeastern Texas" leads Professor Atwood "to consider this corner of Texas as being a transition zone" (pp. 97–98).

In 1950, the population of Orange County was 40,567, of which 35,797
persons were native-born whites and 4,387 were colored. There were 335
foreign-born whites and 48 of other races. For the most part, Orange is an
urban county. Its population is 5.0% farm rural, 36.5% non-farm rural,
and 58.5% urban.[2]

Chambers County contains the oldest settlement in the area, dating
from 1821, when the Spanish placed a fortress at Anahuac and invited
American colonists.[3] Three years later, in 1824, the first settlement in
Jefferson County was made on the Neches River by Noah Tevis and was
called Tevis Bluff. By 1835, for no convincing reason, the Tevis settlement became known as Beaumont, the city which is now the county seat
of Jefferson. Here at Spindletop, in 1901, the American oil industry was
revolutionized by the appearance of the Lucus Gusher, which spouted oil
two hundred feet into the air and could not be controlled for nine days.[4]

In order to learn how this area was settled, I have constructed nativity
tables based on microfilm copies of the census returns for Jefferson
County in 1850 (at which time Hardin and Orange counties were largely
a part of Jefferson County, and Chambers County was a part of both
Liberty and Jefferson counties).[5] My figures show that, as early as 1850,
35.7%—more than a third—of the 1567 inhabitants were Texas-born (and
presumably born in the Southeast Texas area). The main source of migration was from Louisiana, which contributed 33.6% of the settlers. The
other important sources of migration were from Mississippi (5.8%),
Georgia (3.4%), Alabama (2.0%), and Tennessee (2.1%). Migration from
New York, Ohio, and Pennsylvania—all outside the speech area known
as Southern—was 4.2%. The only large foreign-born element was German
(1.7%).

If we assume that the chief influence on a child's speech habits is the
mother, it is possible to suggest even more precisely which states exerted
greatest influence on the dialect of these earliest settlers. By re-examining
the 1850 Census returns and tabulating all informants according to the
birthplace of the mother, we discover that 49.4%, or almost half, of the
1567 inhabitants were born in Louisiana or had mothers from Louisiana.
Some 9.6% were born in Mississippi or their mothers were born in Mississippi. Some 5.9% were born in Georgia or were of Georgia matriarchy.
Some 3.8% were of Tennessee extraction; 3.5% were of South Carolina

[2] *Texas Almanac, 1954–55,* (Dallas, 1953), pp. 100–102; 529; 559–560; 570; and 593.

[3] *Handbook of Texas,* ed. Walter Prescott Webb (Austin, 1952), I, 327.

[4] Federal Writers Project, *Beaumont* (Houston [no publisher or date]), pp. 36; 39–40; 97–104.

[5] Manuscript returns of the United States Seventh Census, 1850, Schedule No. 1, Free Inhabitants, for all counties of Texas. The originals are in the National Archives, Washington 25,
D. C. Microfilm copies are in the Library of the University of Texas in Austin.

312   matriarchy; and 3.4% were second generation Texans of Texas-born mothers.

The nativity tables printed for the Tenth Census provide us with information concerning the settlement of the area in 1880.[6] We find that by 1880, the entire area was two-thirds populated by native-born Texans. We also note that Louisiana contributes considerably less to the population than in 1850, but is still the greatest source of settlers in all counties except Hardin. Migration from Louisiana has evidently slackened, and the Louisiana-born settlers are being diluted in the increasingly Texas-born population. The next largest contributions are from Alabama, Mississippi, and Georgia.

	Chambers	*Hardin*	*Jefferson*	*Orange*
Total Population	2101	1858	3353	2789
% Alabama	3.7	8.8	3.0	3.0
% Foreign-born	4.1	0.1	4.1	5.3
% Georgia	0.9	6.2	3.9	1.7
% Louisiana	7.3	6.2	10.9	16.3
% Mississippi	1.8	8.6	2.6	2.5
% Texas-born	77.2	65.2	67.5	66.2

WORKSHEETS AND INFORMANTS

The worksheets used for this study are based on Hans Kurath's "short" worksheets of 1939, revised for the North Central states in 1949 by A. L. Davis and Raven I. McDavid, Jr. In May, 1951, E. Bagby Atwood re-edited these worksheets for the Southwest, adding a number of expressions illustrative of the Spanish, French, and ranching influences of the area.

The worksheets' format differed somewhat in construction from the format hitherto in use in the United States. Instead of writing down an informant's response on a tablet of blank paper, "books" were used on which the questions were actually mimeographed at suitably spaced intervals. The technique proved successful in the field and helpful in the process of editing.

Among the additions to the worksheets made by Professor Atwood are the following items (items printed within virgules were included chiefly for pronunciation):

---

[6] *Statistics of the Population of the United States at the Tenth Census* (Washington, 1883), pp. 528–530. The reports of the Ninth Census and the Tenth are the only ones that give nativity tables for counties.

Acadian French
Acequia (main irrigation ditch)
Arroyo (dry creek bed)
/Bar/
Brioche (small cake)
Buck (to try to throw the rider)
Burro (small donkey)
Canyon
/Car/
Chaparral (place where mesquite grows thick)
Chaps (leather leggins for riding)
Chigger
Cinch (band that holds the saddle on)
Corral (place where horses or cows are enclosed on a ranch)
Cush (a kind of mush)
Dogie (a motherless calf)
Feedbag (bag attached to horse's head to feed him)
Gate (place to let cars or trains through a fence)
Gumbo (soup made with okra)
Hackamore (rope halter to control a wild horse)
Haunches
/Hem/
Horned toad (small, flat lizard with horns on head and back)
Hunker down (to squat)
Junk room
Lagniappe (bonus or gift given with purchase or when bill is paid)
/Lamp cord/
Lasso (rope with a loop)
/M and N/
Maverick (an unbranded calf)
Mesa (high, flat land)
Mexican
Mexican brown beans
Mustang
Name for a band or herd of saddle horses
Name for workers on a ranch
Niggershooter (boy's weapon made of forked stick with rubber strips)
Olla (large jar to hold drinking water)
Paint (mottled Indian pony)
/Partner/
/Pecan/
Pillow slip
/Playing card/
Prairie (flat grassy country)

314   Praline (sugar candy made with pecans)
         Racket store (store where all kinds of cheap things are sold)
         Rawhide rope
         /Safety pin/
         Shinnery (land where scrubby oak grows)
         Sidewalk
         /Strength/
         Tacky (slovenly)
         Tank (artificial pool to water livestock)
         /Tar/
         Texan of Mexican ancestry
         /Tin can/
         Town square
         Wasteland

The informants were chosen to represent as broad a distribution as possible with regard to social, educational, and age levels. Three age groups were set up: Group A, of people 60 and over; Group B, of informants 40 to 59 years old; and Group C, representing a younger generation 39 years and less. Group C is something of an innovation in American dialect studies, since heretofore this younger generation has been ignored in favor of the speech of the older generations. Three educational levels are considered: Type I, informants with as little formal schooling as possible; Type II, informants with a fair education (approximately high school level); and Type III, informants with two years of college or more.

Twelve informants were interviewed, including four of Group A, five of Group B, and three of Group C. Four informants, moreover, are of Type I, four of Type II, and four of Type III. Two of the informants are Negroes; one is Acadian French. One is a farmer by profession, but eight of the others have farmed or have a rural background. Nine of the informants are from Jefferson County and one each is from Chambers, Hardin, and Orange counties.

The informants, who will be identified by Arabic numerals, may be classified according to age and educational levels and by sex:

Informant 1.	Type IA.	Male
Informant 2.	Type IA.	Female
Informant 3.	Type IA.	Male (Acadian French.)
Informant 4.	Type IIIA.	Female
Informant 5.	Type IB.	Female (Negro.)
Informant 6.	Type IIIB.	Male (Negro.)
Informant 7.	Type IIIB.	Female
Informant 8.	Type IIB.	Female

Informant 9.   Type IIB.   Female
Informant 10. Type IIC.   Female
Informant 11. Type IIIC. Male
Informant 12. Type IIC.   Male

VOCABULARY: INCIDENCE
OF EASTERN DIALECT WORDS

Since the publication of *A Word Geography of the Eastern United States,* it has become possible to compare the vocabulary of an inland area with the vocabulary features of the principal dialect areas of the Eastern Seaboard.[7] These Eastern dialect areas have been succinctly defined by Raven I. McDavid, Jr.:

> . . . the term *North* designates New England, the Hudson Valley and their derivative settlements; *North Midland,* Pennsylvania and Northern West Virginia; *South Midland,* the Shenandoah Valley and the Southern Appalachians; *Southern,* the plantation settlements from Chesapeake Bay to Northern Florida, plus their immediate derivatives.[8]

In order to estimate the influence of Eastern dialect vocabulary on the four Texas counties of this investigation, we must examine Kurath's key words for the North, the Midland, and the South with the South Midland, listing the number of times each word was elicited from the Southeast Texas informants:

North

Key Word	Occurrences
Pail (a bucket)	8.00
Whiffletree *or*	1.00
Whippletree (a singletree)	0.00
Boss! (a call to cows)	0.00
Johnnycake (cornbread)	0.33
Darning Needle (a dragonfly)	0.00
Angleworm (an earthworm)	2.00
Stone Wall (a wall made with rocks)	0.00
Nigh-horse (horse on the left)	0.00
Total	11.33
Frequency	11.8%

[7] Hans Kurath, *A Word Geography of the Eastern United States* (Ann Arbor, 1949). Comparisons of this type have been done a number of times; for example, by Mrs. Hardy in her study of Kerr County and by Randolph Haynes in his investigation of Travis County.

[8] Raven I. McDavid, Jr., "The Position of the Charleston Dialect," *Publication of the American Dialect Society,* No. 23 (1955), p. 41.

316 *Midland*

Key Word	Occurrences
Blinds (roller shades)	3.00
Skillet (frying pan)	12.00
Spouting *or*	0.00
Spouts (eaves troughs)	0.00
[Little] Piece (a short distance)	3.33
To Hull (to shell beans)	0.00
[Arm] Load (an armful)	7.00
Snake Feeder (a dragonfly)	0.00
Sook! *or*	1.00
Sookie! (a call to calves)	0.00
Bawl (cry of a calf being weaned)	4.33
I Want Off	5.00
Quarter Till Eleven	2.00
Total	37.66
Frequency	28.5%

South and South Midland

Key Word	Occurrences
Light Bread (wheat bread in loaves)	7.66
Clabber (curdled milk)	8.00
Snack (food taken between meals)	10.33
Middlins (salt pork)	2.00
Ash Cake (a type of corn cake)	0.00
[Hay] Shock (a small heap of hay)	5.33
[Corn] Shuck (corn husk)	11.00
You-all (you)	12.00
Waiter (best man)	0.00
Pallet (a makeshift bed)	12.00
Gutters (eaves troughs)	10.66
[Barn] Lot (barnyard)	3.00
Rock Fence (a wall made with rocks)	3.00
Total	85.00
Frequency	54.5%[9]

[9] See Kurath, pp. 12, 28–29, and 38. From Kurath's list of typical words, the expressions *roll the baby* (wheel the baby) and *salad* (garden greens) were not asked for in these interviews and are therefore omitted from consideration.

The percentages for the three speech areas are derived from:

$$\frac{\text{(Number of responses from Texas informants)} \times 100}{\text{(Number of key words given by Kurath)} \times \text{(12 informants)}}.$$

Suggested responses (responses recorded when, in the opinion of the fieldworker, the informant accepted the suggested word enthusiastically, used it in an illustrative sentence, or amplified the word's definition) are here valued at one-third the weight of a spontaneous response.

A number of the various expressions listed by Kurath as characteristic of the subareas of the North, Midland, and South may also be pointed out as very common in the Southeast Texas area. *Coal oil* (kerosene, for example, which is found in eastern Pennsylvania and the Chesapeake Bay area, is used by ten of the Texas informants. *Baby buggy* (baby carriage), a term common throughout western Pennsylvania and northern West Virginia, is given by eight of the Texas informants. Of the expressions listed by Kurath as typical of the Southern Coast, *curtains* (roller shades) is used by five of the Southeast Texas informants, *mosquito hawk* (a dragonfly) by twelve, and *earthworm* (a worm) by five of the informants.

Kurath also provides lists of words quite common throughout the North and the Midland; the Midland and the South; and the North and the South.[10] Of these expressions, the following were used by half or more of the Southeast Texas informants:

North and Midland

Key Word	Occurrences
Moo (noise made by a cow)	7.33
Wishbone (clavicle of a chicken)	9.00
Sheaf (of grain)	6.00
Bacon (smoked bacon)	7.00
Cling [-stone Peach] (a type of peach)	8.66
Freestone [Peach] (a type of peach)	9.00
Stringbeans (a type of beans)	6.00

Midland and South

Key Word	Occurrences
Singletree (on a one-horse rig)	7.00
Seesaw (children's game)	11.00
Comfort (a quilted blanket)	8.00
Polecat (a skunk)	9.33

North and South

Key Word	Occurrences
Quarter to Eleven (ten forty-five)	6.00
Gutters (eaves troughs)	10.66

It will be noted that the frequency with which dialect terms from the North were used was 11.8, 28.5 for the Midland, and 54.5% for the South and South Midland. These frequencies stand in a proportion of 1 to 2.2

[10] Kurath, pp. 28–29, 38, and 48–49.

318   to 4.9. In other words—if we may run the risk of oversimplification—in the dialect vocabulary of Southeast Texas, Southern words are used twice as much as Midland expressions, which in turn are used twice as much as Northern terms.

VOCABULARY: OLD VERSUS NEW

The Southeast Texas counties illustrate quite well the changing usages of all living vocabulary. Though these changes follow no logical pattern, it is demonstrable that formally schooled informants do not keep their folk words to the extent that elderly and/or rural informants do.[11] The words chosen to demonstrate this changing Texas vocabulary deal chiefly with foods, artifacts, and customs.

The expressions used for an ear of corn cooked on the cob show an interesting variation between older and younger informants. The distinctly modern term is *corn on the cob*, reported by informants 7, 9, 11, and 12. *Sugar corn* is used by only one informant, number 5. The term *sweet corn* (informants 2, 6, 8, 9, and 12s)[12] and *roasting ears* (informants 1, 3, 4, 7, and 12s) are characteristic of the elderly and middle-aged informants, *sweet corn* appearing more among the middle-aged and *roasting ears* more among the elderly; neither expression is in active use among the youngest informants.

The word *cracklins*—fried pieces of pork rind from which the fat has been cooked out—is known to informants 1, 2, 3, 4, 5, 6, 7, 9, 10, and 12s, leading us to think that perhaps the increasing urbanization may account for the younger generation's relative unfamiliarity with the term. This view is supported by the informants' acquaintance with *chittlins* (informants 1, 2, 4, 6, 7, 9s, and 12s) and *chittlings* (informants 3, 5, and 8)—the fried small intestine of swine—which is a term almost unknown to the youngest informants.

The usual term for the cheese made from milk curds is *cottage cheese* (informants 1, 2, 3, 4, 7, 8, 9s, 10, 11, and 12s), which one informant (number 1) characterizes as a modernism. The older folk-name for this homemade curd cheese is *cream cheese* (informants 2, 4, 5, 6s, 7, 8, 9, and 12s), which informant 7 labels old-fashioned. Another informant (number 3) reports having heard the term *clean cheese*, obviously a folk variant of *cream cheese*. From a comparison of these two expressions, the first current among all three generations of informants, the second used only

---

[11] Kurath, p. 8.

[12] The letter *s* appended to an informant's code number is used to designate a suggested response in contrast to the spontaneous responses of other informants.

by the elderly and middle-aged groups, we may infer that *cottage cheese* has been encouraged in recent years by the commercial use of the name, while the term *cream cheese* has been displaced by *Philadelphia Cream Cheese*, a sweet cheese spread altogether different from curd cheese.

An interesting distinction showing the preference of the more modern speakers for grammatically "correct" usage is illustrated by *hog head cheese* (informants 1*s*, 3, 5, and 6) versus *hog's head cheese* (informants 4, 7, 8, 9, 10, and 11). This latter expression for the food made from the head-meat of swine is employed by the middle-aged and youngest informants plus informant 4, all of whom evidently regard it as a more educated form than *hog head cheese* (possibly under the influence of the word *hogshead*). If we remember that informant 4, a well-educated lady, often tends to give very modern expressions, while the colored informants 5 and 6 are considerably more conservative, we see a clear-cut dichotomy in the use by the older informants of *hog head cheese* and by the younger informants of *hog's head cheese*.

A striking example of a word that has been made old-fashioned by the advent of the automobile is *singletree* (known to informants 1, 2, 3, 4, 5, 6, and 8). The fact that a term for the swivel to which the traces of a horse are connected is unknown to the informants under fifty can be used rather exactly to date the automobile. On the other hand, words for the more prominent and less intricate parts of a wagon—the *tongue*, for example— are still known to all informants.

Gallery is a word which has gone out of fashion even to the two groups of informants who report it. It is used by informants 1, 2, 3, 4, 5, 6, 7, 8, and 9 (the elderly and middle-aged groups) and is characterized as old-fashioned by all these informants except 1, 3, and 7. *Porch*, the standard term, is used by informants 2, 3, 4, 5, 6, 7, 8, 9, 10, and 11; informant 1 also mentions the word, calling it an expression heard from others.

For the portable device to protect against rain, *umbrella* is the universal word among the Southeast Texas informants. Its cousin, *parasol* (in the sense of a *sunshade*), is reported by informants 3, 4, 5, 6, 8, and 9; called old-fashioned by informant 2; and noted as heard from others by informant 10. We note in *parasol*, therefore, a type of apparel that has gone into disuse, taking the word with it.

Dishrag and *dishcloth* offer us a contrast between old and new based on fashion and gracious living. *Dishrag*, a name for the cloth with which dishes are soaped and washed, is used by informants 1, 2, 4, 5, 7*s*, 8, 9, 10, and 12. *Dishcloth* is given by informants 7, 9, 10, and 11 (three of whom are women). *Dishcloth* is a young word (as contrasted with words which, though known to the older folk, attain their real currency among the younger), just beginning to make inroads in the *dishrag* province. If we consider how inappropriate the *rag* element of *dishrag* must seem to

320　urban, well-educated Southern ladies (and gentlemen), *dishcloth* appears to be a well-considered substitute and one destined to replace *dishrag* eventually.

For a group of trees growing in an open meadow or prairie, the elderly and middle-aged informants use the word *island*. *Island* was elicited from informants 1, 2, 4, 6, 8, 11*s*, and 12*s*. It is known to the modern informants chiefly as a place-name element. *Pine Island Bayou*, for example, was mentioned by informants 4, 6, 8, 9, and 12 as the name of one of the local streams.

Terms of address to one's father show a marked distinction between the use of *papa* by the elderly and middle-aged informants (including 1, 2, 3, 4, 6, 7, 8, 12, and 5, who terms it old-fashioned), and *dad* or *daddy* (words known to informants in all age levels, but almost the exclusive term of the younger informants). *Dad* is given by informants 5 and 12. *Daddy* is used by informants 1, 8, 10, and 11.

The word *niggershooter,* a child's weapon for shooting birds, is reported by informants 1, 2, 3, 4, 6, 7, 8, 9, 12, and called an old-fashioned expression by informants 10 and 11. The variant *slingshot* is used by informants 1, 2, 4, 5, 7, 8, 9*s*, 12, and by 10 and 11 (who term it a modernism). Informant 6 uses *sling,* and the word *beanshooter* was given by informants 3 and 9. It may be noted that the mention of *niggershooter* by informant 6, who is colored, indicates a certain currency among Negro speakers. Likewise, informant 9, who states that she would never use the word *nigger,* does use the compound *niggershooter,* along with its variant *beanshooter.*

The burlesque serenade accorded newly-wedded couples is called a *shivaree* by informants 1, 2, 3, 4, 7, and 8, and (by a process of folk etymology) a *chivalry* by informant 9. Inasmuch as the younger informants do not recognize the custom, the demise of the *shivaree* would seem to have occurred in the first decade or so of this century.

The custom of *lagniappe*—any small gratuity given, for instance, with a purchase or with the payment of a bill—is limited to the elderly and middle-aged groups. The word is reported by informants 1*s*, 2, 3, 4, 5*s*, 6, 7, 8, 9, and 10*s* (who calls it a word heard from others). No synonym for *lagniappe* exists among the younger informants; it is a bit of the old South, displaced forever by the more businesslike practices of the chain stores and urban civilization.

Another expression which is vanishing from Southeast Texas is the greeting, *Christmas Gift*! Originally, the expression was a Christmas-day game in which children tried to be first in surprising one another with the greeting, the loser being obliged to present a gift to the winner. As a greeting, it is used by informants 1, 2, 5, 7, and 8, and upon suggestion by

informants 4 and 6 (who terms the expression old-fashioned). The more   321
prevalent greeting, *Merry Christmas*, is used by all informants.

VOCABULARY: FRENCH, SPANISH, AND OTHER SOUTHWESTERN INFLUENCES

Since the Old Spanish Trail cuts through the four Southeast
Texas counties that make up this study, we might expect to find in the
area Spanish words brought from the West as well as French words imported from Louisiana. In addition we should look for ordinary English
and American expressions which take on new meanings under the influence of a ranching, farming, or rice-growing culture.

Of the group of Louisiana French expressions which E. Bagby Atwood
suggested might be found in East Texas,[13] *bayou, cush,* and *lagniappe* are
the only ones having any real currency in Southeast Texas, although
many others, such as *banquette* (a sidewalk), *armoire* (a wardrobe), *batteau*
(a boat), *boudin* (a sausage), and *piroque* (a boat), are to be found.

Bayou was used by informants 1, 2, 3, 4, 5*s*, 6, 7, 8, 9*s*, 10, 11*s*, and 12 as
a name for a small stream. The word is an Acadian French derivative of
the Choctaw Indian *bayuk*.[14] *Cush* or *cush cush* is the Texas version of the
Acadian *couche-couche,* a fried preparation ˙of cornmeal dough and
sugar.[15] *Cush* was reported by informants 5 and 6 as a name for *mush* and
by informants 2*s*, 4, 5, 6, 8, and 11*s* as the name for a preparation made of
seasoned cornmeal dough fried with onions. *Cush cush* was used spontaneously only by informant 3, who is Acadian French, but upon suggestion by informants 1 and 9. *Lagniappe*, a combination of the French
definite article *la* with Spanish *ñapa* (ultimately from Kechuan), is used
by most of the elderly and middle-aged informants, as discussed above.[16]

In addition to these expressions, two other words borrowed from the
Acadian dialect are current among most informants. These are *gumbo*, a
word obtained by the Acadian French from an African term for the okra

---

[13] E. Bagby Atwood, "A Preliminary Report on Texas Word Geography," *Orbis,* II (1953), 64.

[14] William A. Read, *Louisiana French,* Volume V of *Louisiana State University Studies* (1931),
p. 82.

[15] Read, p. 122. Raven I. McDavid, Jr., in "Africanisms in the Eastern United States," an
unpublished paper read to the Modern Language Association in 1952, points out that *cush* is
also used in the areas of Chesapeake Bay, Albemarle Sound, the Neuse River, and the South
Carolina low country. He does not find enough evidence to support the recent suggestion that
cush is an Africanism.

[16] Read, p. 442.

322 plant,[17] and *Cajun*, an aphetic form of *Acadian* which is in use among the Acadian French themselves. *Gumbo* is reported by informants 1, 2, 3*s*, 4, 7, 8, 9, 10, 11, and 12. *Cajun* was elicited from all informants except 3, who used it upon suggestion.

Of the various terms mentioned by Atwood as typically Southwestern,[18] only *norther, lariat,* and *corral* are in common use. *Norther* was given spontaneously by all informants except 2 and 3, both of whom used the word upon suggestion. *Lariat* was reported by informants 1, 2, 3, 4, 6, 8, 10, 11, and 12. *Corral* is a popular word, used by informants 2*s*, 4, 7, 8, 9, 10, 11, and 12*s*.

Two other expressions of local currency are *canal* and *bellyband. Canal* is the usual word for a drainage ditch, reported by informants 1, 2, 3, 4, 5*s*, 6, 8, 9*s*, 10, 11, and 12. Because Southeast Texas does a vast amount of rice farming, it is natural that the irrigation canals should become associated with drainage ditches. *Bellyband*, a saddle girth, is used by informants 2, 3, 6, 7, 8, 9, and 12*s*.

PRONUNCIATION

A study of pronunciation must take into account three possible types of differences: (1) variations in the system of phonemes (such as the /ɜɪ/ phoneme of New York City speech); (2) subphonemic differences in the pronunciation of the same phoneme (for example, the mutually nondistinctive voiceless stops in *paper* [pᶜeɨpɚ]); (3) systematic and individual differences in the occurrence of phonemes (such as the use of /z/ or /s/ in *greasy*). With regard to (l), no differences in the phonemic system are posited for Southeast Texas. In order to survey (2), brief summaries will be made of the subphonemic differences of the vowels. Only two of the consonants, /l/ and /r/, show variations important enough for consideration in this abstract.

/i/ as in *grease*: regularly a high front vowel with either an up-gliding element or lengthening. Its usual forms are [iiˆ,i·] and also [ɨi,i·ˆ,ɪˆi] in that order of frequency.

The phoneme /i/ is distinguished from /ɪ/ before tautosyllabic /r/ only in the word *ear* (by informants 1, 2, 4, 6, 7, 8, 9, and 11).

/ɪ/ as in *dish*: a mid-high front vowel whose usual forms are [ɪ',ɪ]. Before nasals, /ɪ/ is no longer distinct from /ɛ/ and appears phoneti-

[17] Read, p. 122.

[18] Atwood, pp. 65–66.

cally as [ɪˈ,ɪ] with the variants [ɪ²,ɛˢ], which show lowering.[19] The variant [ɛˢ] is used chiefly by the oldest informants, 1 through 5, and possibly indicates the increased variation that may occur when two phonemes (/ɪ/ and /ɛ/) cease to be distinctive in a certain position (here, before nasals). The younger informants apparently tend to use a retracted /ɪ/ which is phonetically close to [ɛ³] both for /ɪ/ and for /ɛ/ before nasals, as in *chimney, Cincinnati,* and *clingstone*; and in *hem, hen,* and *strength.*

/e/ as in *way*: regularly a high-mid front vowel with a high central glide. Its usual forms are [ei, eˇɨ].

Before intersyllabic /r/, /e/ is irregularly distinguished from /ɛ/ by seven of the twelve informants in the words *dairy* and *Mary.* In *dairy,* /e/ is used by informants 4, 8, 9, and 10; in *Mary,* by informants 3, 4, 5, and 9.

Before tautosyllabic /r/, /e/ is distinguished from /ɛ/ in the word *chair* by informants 5, 7, 9, and 10, who use /e/.

/ɛ/ as in *seven*: a mid-front vowel with the usual form [ɛ].

Before nasals /ɛ/ is not often distinguished from /ɪ/. Before /m/ as in *hem,* [ɪˈ] and [ɛˢ,ɪ] are used by informants 1, 2, 5, 6, 7, 8, 9, 10, 11, and 12. Before /ŋ/ as in *strength,* [ɪ², ɪˈ] are used by informants 1, 4, 5, 8, 9, 10, 11, and 12; [ɛ²] by informants 2 and 7; and [ɛ,ɛˈ] only by informants 3 and 6.

Before /n/ as in *end,* [ɪ², ɪˈ] are used by informants 1, 2, 5, 6, 7, 8, 9, 10, and 11, while informants 3, 4, and 12 use /ɛ/. Pronunciations such as [ɪ²] (which may be phonemicized here as /ɪ/), as in the words *cents, fence, hen, men, pen, ten, M,* and *N,* are most common among the Groups B and C informants, who use it 4½ times more often than the Group A informants.

/æ/ as in *bath*: a higher low-front vowel with the usual phonetic forms [æ,æˆ].

Before the fricatives /f/ and /s/ and less frequently before /š/, nasal clusters, and velar stops, /æ/ sometimes develops a mid-high central glide with the usual phonetic form [æɨ], as in the words *answer, ashes, aunt, bag, basket, calf, chance, class, dance, glass, hamper,* and *lamp.* This diphthongization is to be found most often among the Groups A and B informants, although it is recessive even in their speech.

/ɑ/ as in *father*: a low central vowel whose usual form is [ɑ] with the principal variants [ɑˈ, ɑˈ, ɑˈ].

Before tautosyllabic /r/, /ɑ/ and /ɔ/ are no longer distinct (as in *card: cord*), and /ɑ/ shows a number of phonetic variants ranging from

---

[19] Diacritics showing nasalization are here omitted.

324   [ɑ', ɑ, ɑ·] through [ᴅ, ᴅˆ, ɔ], as in *armful, bar, barbed wire, barn, car, card, cartridge, garbage, garden, harmonica, hearth, Martha,* and *tar.* For the twelve informants, the overall ratio of [ɑ] to [ɔ] before /r/ in this group of words is two to one. The well-educated informants 4, 6, and 7 rarely use [ɔ] at all in these words. Informants 1, 2, and 3 (Group A) prefer [ɑ] to [ɔ] in a ratio of five to one, while informants 5, 8, and 9 (Group B) use it in a ratio of three to one. With informants 10, 11, and 12 (Group C), the ratio is reversed, and these informants are found to use [ɔ] to [ɑ] with a frequency of two to one.

/ʌ/ as in *judge:* a retracted and stressed low-mid central vowel whose usual phonetic quality is [ʌ]. The form [ʌ̹] with lip-rounding occurs as a free variant, but is used most frequently in the word *onion.*

Before intersyllabic /r/, /ʌ/ combines to produce [ʌr] and also [ʌ-r, ɜ-r] as in *furrow* and *worry.* The variant [ɜ-r] is limited to informants 4 and 7 (Type III).

Before /rC/, /ʌ/ usually becomes [ʌr] with the variants [ɜ ͥ, ərͥ, ɜ, ɵ], as in *first, girl,* and *worm.* The latter variants are limited to the Negro informants 5 and 6 (with whom they are quite frequent) and to informant 1 (who uses them occasionally).

/ə/ as in *sofa:* a weakly stressed mid-central vowel whose phonetic quality is [ə] or [ə²].

/u/ as in *tooth:* a high back vowel with lip-rounding which appears either as a diphthong with an advanced first element or as an advanced and lengthened monophthong [uʻu, u·ʻ].

/ʊ/ as in *foot:* a mid-high back vowel with moderate lip-rounding, the usual phonetic forms of which are [ʊ, ʊʻ].

/o/ as in *boat:* a high-mid back vowel with lip-rounding, which appears fronted with a high central rounded glide [oʻʉ].

Before tautosyllabic /r/, all informants distinguish /o/ from /ɔ/ (as in *hoarse: horse*); /o/ takes the phonetic form [o].

/ɔ/ as in *caught:* a mid back vowel with lip-rounding which, as a monophthong, is usually [ɔ, ɔˆ]. The phoneme diphthongizes in all positions except before /r/ to [ᴅˆɔ, ᴅᴅˆ]—that is, the vowel becomes higher and more rounded during its utterance. The diphthong is used in a ratio of one to one with the monophthong of this phoneme in the words *all, brought, caught, costs, cough, daughter, dog, fought, law, loft, moth, saw, trough,* and *water.* The diphthong appears twice as frequently among the younger six informants than among the older six.

/aɪ/ as in *five:* a diphthong composed of a low front element and a mid front glide, somewhat retracted. It usually appears as [aᵋ] with the variants [aᵻ, a·ᵋ, a·]. In all positions, [aᵋ] is used four times as much as the fuller diphthong [aᵻ]. Before /r/, as in *barbed wire* and *andirons,* the monophthongal [a] is usual.

/aʊ/ as in *drouth:* a diphthong composed of a low or higher-low front element and a high central glide with lip-rounding. Its usual forms are [æʉ] and [aʉ]. The variant [æʉ] is used in a ratio of one to one with [aʉ] for all informants. The well-educated informants (4, 6, 7, and 11) use [æʉ] in a ratio of one to three with [aʉ]. The Type IA informants (1, 2, 3) use [æʉ] in the proportion three to five with regard to [aʉ]. The younger informants of Types IB, IIB, and IIC (5, 8, 9, 10, and 12) use [æʉ] considerably more than anyone else, in a ratio of five to one with regard to [aʉ].

/ɔɪ/ as in *boy:* a diphthong composed of a mid back vowel with lip-rounding followed, usually after a slight "pause," or drop in breath pressure, by a mid-high central glide. Its usual phonetic form is [ɔ-ɪ].

/l/ as in *Billy:* intervocalically before mid-high or high front and central vowels, a "bright *l*" [l̩] or a non-velarized [l] regularly appears, as in the words *Dallas, Illinois, jelly, Nelly,* and *pallet.*
Before /j/, as in stallion, /l/ usually appears as the palatalized [l̩].

/r/ as in *father:* postvocalically, /r/ is usually a retroflex or "constricted" vowel [ɚ]. Informants 1, 3, 4, 5, 6, and 7, however, substitute /ə/ freely. Informants 4, 5, and 6, in whose speech this feature is more noted than in the other informants, nevertheless use the constricted vowel twice as frequently as the vowel without *r*-coloring. Of those who use only the constricted vowel, informants 2, 10, and 12 occasionally give pronunciations with only weak retroflexion.
In the words *oyster, wash, washing,* and *Washington,* an intrusive /r/ is used by all informants except 4, 7, 8, and 12 about three times out of every eight occurrences. The /r/ always appears in the form of a mildly retroflex vowel.

PRONUNCIATION: SYSTEMATIC DIFFERENCES IN THE PATTERNING AND OCCURRENCE OF PHONEMES

Before /w/, /h/ is regularly pronounced by all informants, as in the words *wheat* and *whip.* Before /j/, /h/ is frequently pronounced by all informants, as in *humor* and *Houston.*
After the alveolar consonants /t, d, n/, /u/ is frequently preceded by /j/ in one of two forms. In the word *Tuesday,* for example, informants

2, 3, 4, 5, 6, 7, 8, 9, 10, and 12 use either a palatalized /t/ plus a diphthong: [ʧɪʉ], or a palatalized /t/ with /j/ glide and vowel: [ʧjʉ]. In the word *tube,* palatalization is restricted to informants 3, 4, 6, and 7, while in *student* it is limited to informants 4 and 7. Informant 1 uses /t/ and a diphthong without palatalization: [tɪʉ] in *Tuesday* and *tube;* in *student* he employs [tu].

After /d/ in *due,* palatalization before /u/ occurs in the responses of informants 1, 2, 3, 5, 6, and 7. In *dues,* however, palatalization is limited to informants 3, 4, 5, and 6. The unpalatalized consonant plus diphthong, [dɪʉ], is given by informants 9 and 12 in *due* and by informants 1 and 2 in *dues.* The use of [du] is apparently typical of the younger Group C informants.

After /n/, as in new and New Year, palatalization before /u/ occurs in the responses of informants 1, 2, 3, 4, 6, 7, 8, 10, and 12. Informants 9 and also 12 (in other responses) use the diphthong [nɪʉ] without preceding palatalization, and informants 4 and 11 (and also 8 and 10 in other responses) use a monophthong without palatalization: [nu].

In final unstressed syllables, as in *evening, laughing, lightning, nothing, singing, something,* and *thinking,* /n/ alternates with /ŋ/. This substitution is random, appearing about once in every three occurrences of these words in the speech of all informants except 4, 8, and 11.

Before /g/, Middle English "short *o*" is regularly pronounced /ɔ/, except in the speech of several of the well-educated female informants. In *fog* and *foggy,* for example, /ɑ/ is employed by informants 4, 7, 8, and 10. Informants 7 and 8 use /ɑ/ in *log.* In *hog,* /ɑ/ is used by informants 4 and 8, and in *frog* by informants 4 and 7.

In words with intersyllabic /r/, as in *borrow, Florida, orange,* and *tomorrow,* the Middle English "short *o*" category (into which *orange* and *Florida* have fallen) regularly becomes /ɔ/ in the speech of all but some of the well-educated female informants. *Borrow* is pronounced with /ɑ/ by informants 4, 6, and 7. In *Florida,* informants 4, 7, and 8 use /ɑ/. In *orange,* /ɑ/ is given by informant 4, and in *tomorrow* by informant 6.

In words in which Middle English /ɑ/ follows /w/, as in *swamp, wash, washing, Washington,* and *wasp,* /ɔ/ appears twice in every three occurrences. With the exception of the word *swamp,* in which informants 10 and 12 use /ɑ/, the use of the /ɑ/ phoneme in these words is restricted to informants of Groups A and B. Informants 4, 6, and 7, moreover, who are of Type III, account for half of all occurrences of /ɑ/.

Before alveolar consonants in weakly stressed syllables, both "short *e*" and "short *i*" regularly become [ɪ], as in *basket* and *dishes.*

When final in weakly stressed syllables, as in *borrow* and *yellow,* /o/ is replaced by /ə/ once in every two occurrences.

VERB FORMS AND SYNTACTICAL PECULIARITIES   327

Urbanization (and with it, better education) makes itself most apparent in the "correctness" of grammar in use throughout the area of investigation, where it is difficult to elicit a double negative, the word *ain't,* or a nonstandard verb form even from the least educated of the informants. But as Atwood has pointed out, this is to be expected in an urban area,[20] and does not mean that nonstandard verb forms are not in use. Notwithstanding this apparent purity of Southeast Texas grammar, a number of idiosyncracies may be pointed out.

Dive. For the preterite of *dive, dove* and *dived* are used about equally. Such a mixture is typical of a "belt" along the upper Ohio in north-central and eastern Pennsylvania.

Drink. Among the Texas informants, *drank* is the regular preterite of *drink.* Usage is divided between *drunk* (informants 3, 4, 6, 7, 8, 9, and 10) and *drank* (informants 1, 2, 5, 10, 11, and 12) for the past participle. It will be noted that *drank* is favored by all three of the Group C informants (10, 11, and 12). This usage may be compared with Atwood's findings for the East, which show that the standard *drink-drank-drunk* forms are not usual, being rejected by half of the "cultured" New England informants and two-thirds of the well-educated informants in the Middle Atlantic States, but finding acceptance among the well-educated informants of the South Atlantic States.

Lie. *Lie* and *lay,* as present tense forms, show an interesting division in usage between the older and younger informants. *Lay,* used by informants 1, 2, 3, 4, 5, and 8, is the distinctly older usage; *lie,* given by informants 6, 7, 9, 10, 11, and 12, is the schoolroom expression of all the younger informants with the exception of 8. This contrast in usage is lost in the preterite, where *lay* is used by informants 1, 3, 4, 8, 9, and 10, and *laid* by informants 5, 6, 11, and 12. Throughout the East, *lie* predominates in the present tense and, except for a few small areas and in cultivated speech, *laid* predominates in the preterite.

Sweat. *Sweated* is used as the preterite of *sweat* by all informants except 2, 3, and 4, who employ the uninflected form *sweat.* *Sweat* is characteristic of the North, although used equally with *sweated* in some parts of the South, including Virginia and South Carolina.[21]

Cain't. A pronunciation of *can't* rhyming with *ain't, cain't* probably represents a diphthongization of *can't* to [kæɪnt] with subsequent raising

---

[20] E. Bagby Atwood, *A Survey of Verb Forms in the Eastern United States* (Ann Arbor, 1953), p. 37.

[21] Atwood, *Verb Forms,* pp. 9, 11, 18, and 22.

328   to [eɪ]. It is limited in use to informants 1, 2, 4, 5, and 8 (Types I and II informants except for 4).

Sick at the Stomach. Informants 1, 2, 4, 5, 6, 7, 8, 9, 10, 11, and 12s use the Midland and Southern construction *sick at the stomach.* Informants 8, 9, and 10 report the expression *sick to the stomach,* but informant 8 terms it old-fashioned and informant 10 characterizes it as heard from others. This construction is typical of the New England settlement. Informant 3 and informant 4 (who reports it as heard from others) mention *sick in the stomach,* an expression found in southeastern Pennsylvania and in the South from southern Maryland as far as the Neuse in North Carolina.[22]

It is not likely that any of the speech features of the four Southeast Texas counties are unique when compared with the rest of East Texas. Since it is the combination of typical speech patterns which gives individuality to an area, the probability is that no other four counties in Texas will produce the same configuration of vocabulary, pronunciation, and verb usages which have been shown to characterize this area.

[22] Kurath, p. 78.

The Speech
of Spicewood, Texas

Carmelita Klipple

Spicewood, Texas, in the western section of Texas, has
many of the features of the South Midland or the
"hill Southern" dialect. The following article discusses a
number of pronunciation features of the speech of Spicewood
as they appear both in individual words and in connected
speech.

Spicewood, a very small town about forty miles northwest of Austin,
was settled more than a hundred years ago by people who fought in the
Texas Revolution. It has been isolated from any considerable communication with rather nearby towns until comparatively recent times. Even
now one must go by way of unimproved mountain roads in order to get
there from any direction. From Austin one must in addition be ferried
across the Pedernales River.

The speech of Spicewood is what is often termed the "hill-southern"
type, having most of the traits of ordinary Texas speech, but being peculiarly characterized by an extremely retroflex *r*, the preservation of nu-

From *American Speech*: Vol. XX, No. 3, 187–191 (October 1945). Reprinted with the permission of Columbia University Press.

330 merous archaisms, and the total lack of any main features of plantation-southern speech.

My material is based on the speech, both as sampled by phonograph recordings by a number of informants of various ages and as observed in the natural conversation of Spicewood citizens. In this paper I enumerate the features in which Spicewood speech differs from General American (GA), giving special attention to deviations from East Texas speech, as set forth by Mr. Oma Stanley.[1]

VOWELS

[e]: Mr. Stanley records (æ^I) for *ant,* with [e^I] as a variant. My records also show a pronunciation of *ant* as [e^Int].

[ɛ]: Both GA [ɪŋ] and GA [æŋ] appear in Spicewood speech as [ɛ^Iŋ]: *I drank water out of the spring* (a drɛ^Iŋk wɔt̢ɚ æət̢ə ðə sprɛ^Iŋ]. For GA [ɪ] one hears [ɛ] in *literature* [lɛt̢ɚtjʊɚ] and *picnic* [pɛknɛk].

[u]: The phonetic quality of this phoneme in Southern American speech is in general [ü^u]. For Spicewood speakers it is of a central variety which moves backwards: *food* [fü^ud], *school* [skü^ul], *boot* [bu^ut]. No monophthongal variety occurs unless it is rapidly spoken or without stress: *I have two cows* [a hæv tu kæəz].

[o] occurs for [ʊ] in *woman* [wo⁻mən], for [ɑ] in *want to* [wo⁻ntə]. The word *on,* which in GA speech is pronounced [ɑn], in Texas and especially in Spicewood speech is usually [ɔn], but under full stress it frequently occurs as [o^Un]. For instance, as in *come ón* [kʌm 'o^Un] and *he fell right on it* [hi fɛl ra^It o^Un ɪt]. Even when it is unstressed it may appear as [o^Un] or [on]: *The bird is on the wing* [ðɪ bɚd ɪz on ðə wɛɪŋ].

[ʌ]: Besides *put, took,* and *soot,* which are pointed out by Stanley as having [ʌ] for GA [ʊ], I also find *good* [gʌ⁺d], *could* [kʌ⁺d], *would* [wʌ⁺d], and *cook* [kʌ⁺k]. *Want,* which Stanley found to be pronounced as [wɔnt] or [wɑnt],I find most frequently as a centralized reduced form [wʌnt], possibly because it is often used as an auxiliary pro-word: *I don't want to go* [a dõ wʌ̃nt̢ə go^U]. I do not hear *stood* [stʌd] nor *shook* [ʃʌk] as in East Texas, but [stʊd], [ʃʊk].

[ə] appears with the *r*-coloring in words ending in [o] such as *fellow* [fɛlɚ], *window* [wɪndɚ], *hollow* [hɑlɚ], *potato* [tetɚ], etc., as was noted by Stanley, and in numerous proper names ending in *a: Emma* [ɪmɚ], *Lelia* [lilɚ], *Stella* [stɛlɚ], *Ina* [a^Inɚ], etc.

[aɪ] appears as [a^I], [a:], or [a] in Texas speech. *I* and *my* are commonly

---

[1] Oma Stanley, *The Speech of East Texas* (*American Speech: Reprints and Monographs,* ɪɪ), New York, Columbia University Press, 1937.

heard with [a], as most students of speech agree. I do not find *nice, bind,* *kind, mind, bite* with the monophthong, as in East Texas, but as a diphthong with the second element extremely light. On the other hand, I hear *science* [sa:ᵊns], *try* [tra:] *try to do it* [tra: t̬ə du ɪt]. I also hear *child* [tʃa:ᵊl], *while* [ʍa:ᵊl], and *style* [sta:ᵊl].

[au] shows raising and fronting of the first element and centralization of the second. The first element is lengthened and the second extremely light. Phonetically it is [æ:ᵊ]. It appears in such words as *proud* [præ:ᵊd], *mouth* [mæ:ᵊθ], *how* [hæ:ᵊ], *about* [əbæ:ᵊt], *scouts* [skæ:ᵊts], *out* [æ:ᵊt], etc. I found it nowhere pronounced [æu], as Mr. Stanley has it recorded.[2] I can imagine it appearing as such only in the speech of meticulously careful Texas speakers.

[ɔɪ] appears with the first element of a rather unrounded quality and with its second element slightly pronounced. Words containing this phoneme are as follows: *destroy* [dɪstrɔˈɪ], *noise* [nɔˈɪz], *boy* [bɔˈɪ], *join* [dʒɔˈɪn], *oil* [ɔˈɪl], etc.

CONSONANTS

1. *Loss.* Initial *d* is lost in unstressed and intervocalic position in the nasalized form of the expression *I don't know* [ã õnt nõᵁ]. Initial *g* is lost under the same circumstances in *I'm going to* [ãmə̃nɔ̃]. Initial [w] is unvoiced and seems lost in an idling *well* at the beginning of a sentence. This occurs especially where there is no hesitation, but very weak stress: *Well, not altogether* [ɛl nɑt ɔltəgɛ⁺ðɚ]. *Well, I thought you liked it* [ɛl a θɔtʃu laɪkᵗ ɪt]. Loss of *t* occurs in the syncopated combination *Let us* *see* [ɛs:ii]. Loss of medial [j] occurs in *royal: They wouldn't be getting drunk* *and having a royal time* [ðe wᵁdn bi gɪtn drʌnk ɛn hævɪn ə rɔəl taɪm].

2. *Addition.* [j] appears between [h] and a high front vowel in *here* [hʲɪɚ] and after [n] in *near* [nʲɪɚ] . [h] often appears at the beginning of certain words when emphasized. Besides *hit* and *hain't* for *it* and *ain't*, I find *hyonder* for *yonder: it just* [hɪt dɪs], *ain't* [heɪnt], and *down yonder* [dæən hjɑndɚ]. Intrusive [p] appears in *something* [sʌmpθɪn]. Additions appear in rebuilt grammatical forms. Although Spicewood people say [kraɪs] for *Christ* [kraɪst], when they come to forming the possessive, they *know* [kraɪsɪz] is wrong, so they say [kraɪstɪz]. They frequently use the past participle for the preterite of a strong verb and vice versa. However, when they use *taken* in the preterite they often go on to pattern it after weak verbs and say *takened* [tekənd].

---

[2] Here the difference between Mr. Stanley's findings and mine is probably one of symbol rather than sound.

332   3. *Elisions.* Elisions in words and word phrases in Spicewood speech are numerous. I find the following: *wasn't no* [wɑno], *going to* [gonə], *go to the* [goθə], *there would* [ðɛɚd], *it is awful* [tsɔfəl], *I'm going to* [ãmə̃nə̃]. Elision of syllables occurs in the following words: *Carolina* [kɛlaɪnɚ], *president* ['prɛzˌdɪnt], *material* [mətɪrəl], *particularly* [pətɪkəlɪ], *furniture* [fɝntʃɚ], *probably* [prɑblɪ].

4. *Metathesis.* In Spicewood *handerchief* is usually [hæɪntʃəkəf], showing metathesis of [k] and [tʃ]. One informant, with regard to my given name, said to me, "My little girl can say *Carmelita* [kɑləmiṭə] just as good as I can." Here we see the interchange of [l] and [m]. The word *tarviate*, with a reduction and re-expressing of the vowel *i,* goes from [tɔɚvɪeːt] through [tɔɚveːt] to [tɔɚɪveɪt]. *Pedernales* [pɛðɛrnɑlɛs] (the name of a river, meaning 'flint rocks'), with strong articulation of [r] and the unvoicing of [d] goes through [pɛḍɛrnɑlɛs] and [pɛtərnælɪs] to [pɝtɪ'nælɪs]. Metathesis of [r], often mentioned in connection with such pronunciations as *children* [tʃɪldɚn], *perspire* [prɛspaɪɚ], etc., is really just the reducing and re-expressing of [ɚ], [ər] as [rə] or the restating of a syllabic [r], [ər] as [rə], [rɛ].

5. *Miscellaneous.* For *Mrs.* neither GA [mɪsɪz] nor formal Southern [mɪzɪz] is heard. It is pronounced Southern [mɪz] or more frequently [mɪzrɪz]. The latter form is also used elsewhere in Texas among the less literate classes. Whether the appearance of [r] in [mɪzrɪz] comes from the old pronunciation [mɪstrɪs] in which the [s]'s have become voiced after the [t] has been lost, I can not say. It may be that through some trick of the imagination they think they are really pronouncing the written form 'm-r-s.'

The loss of medial *t* in *started* is a real elision, but it is in a strange position. The word is pronounced [stɔɚɪd]: *Some fellow started that up, you see* [sʌm fɛlɚ stɔɚɪd ðæṭ ʌp jə sɪi]. I believe this pronunciation is frequently used among the more careless speakers of Texas—as for instance, in *you started it* [u stɔɚdɪt].

It just has been discussed under 'Addition.' Here I am interested particularly in the pronunciation of *just.* In this combination the first phoneme, [dʒ], is unpalatalized: [hɪt dɪs]. In the same manner, one sometimes hears [juzlɪ] for *usually* instead of GA [juʒjuəlɪ]. Here with the reduction and elision of the second syllable containing the [u] sound, the [ʒ] becomes unpalatalized because the factors conditioning palatalization have disappeared.

The [s] in *terrace* [tɛrɪs] is palatalized to [ʃ], [tɛrɪʃ]. For *crystal* [krɪstəl] one hears [krɪstʃəl], and for *Corpus Christi* [kɔɚpəs krɪstɪ] one hears [kɔɚpəs krɪstʃə], possibly because of the influence of *Christian* [krɪstʃən].

6. [r]. Preconsonantal and final *r* is considerably retroflex. It is more strongly articulated than the West Texas or plantation-southern pre-

consonantal and final *r*. For example, in the sentence *I hear Martin* [a hɪɚ mɔɚtən], both *r*'s would be strongly articulated. This *r* is seldom weakened and rarely omitted.

There is heard as [ðɛ] or [ðe] so often in syncopated combinations like *there was* [ðɛəz] and *there is* [ðe:z] that apparently *they* has come to be used for *there* [ðæɚ], even when not in such combinations. For instance, *Are there a pencil on the table?* [ɔɚ ðe: ə pɪns]̣ on ðə teb]̣].

An intrusive *r* often occurs in preconsonantal position after back vowels in such words as *hush* [hɝʃ], *ought* [ɔɚt], etc. In the same position *r* appears in *wash* [wɔɚʃ], as was noted by Mr. Stanley.

I do not notice any great difference between linking-*r* and final *r*. For example, in *their* and *their ice* the *r*'s are of practically the same quality.

7. [l]. In contrast to East Texas speech, [l] before [j] is extremely dark, as in *Lillian* [lɪłjən]. [l] may be lost before [d] in *told: I told her the other day* [a tod ɚ ðɪ ʌðɚ deɪ].

8. *Odds and Ends.* When a certain speaker wished to say that the country was 'sparsely settled' or that there were only a few families 'scattered out' in the country, he said the country was 'scatterly settled' [skætəlɪ sɛtəld].

For *unless* [ənlɛs], 'lessen' [lɛsən] often appears.

TRANSCRIPTION

As a sample of Spicewood speech, I present parts of a transcription of a recording of *Horace,* a test piece written by Miss Katherine Wheatley of the University of Texas for the study of Texas speech. The speaker is a fifteen-year-old girl, who was born and raised in Spicewood and who was attending the Spicewood High School. She speaks in a slow tempo, even in ordinary conversation, which increases the otherwise normal lengthening and diphthongization of vowels.

. . . hɛlo wɔltɚ| ʃi seᵊd| hæə ɔɚ jüᵘ‖ hɛlo| sɛd wɔltɚ| aɪ dɪdnt noʊ ju wɝ ɪn sküᵘl| a θɔt ju wɝ in foɚt wɝθ‖ . . . bəfoɚ ʃi kʊd æɪnsɚ| wɔltɚ rɪmɛmbɚd hɔ⁺rɪs hæd ɪntɚdjust hɪᵊm‖ ðe wɪnt ɪntʊ ðə drʌg stoɚ æn hæd sʌmθɪn tə dreɪŋk æ⁺t ðɪ sodɪ fæᵊntn‖ lɪłjən hæd ɔɚndʒ dʒüᵘs æn hɔ⁺rɪs hæd ə tʃuklɪt mɔltɪt mɪᵊlk‖ ðɪn ðe wɪnt draɪvɪn ɪn wɔltɚz foɚd| ðæt wəz bɪfoɚ hi gat hɪz njüᵘ ʃɪvɚleɪ‖ . . . lᴵłjən wəz ɔfᵊlɪ mæᵊd‖ ʃi dɪdnt kæɚ ʍat ʃi sɛd‖ ʃi færlɪ ʃæətɪd| hɪɚ a æm ɪn ðə mɪțəl əv noʍɚ wɪð ə nɔɚðɚ kʌmɪn ʌp æn ə fɔg raɪzɪn‖ av mɪs mə treɪn tüᵘ‖ . . . hi hæd ðɪ kɔɚ toᵁd tʊ e gəradʒ tə hæv ðɪ bæțərɪ rɪtʃɔɚdʒd‖ hi æst ðɪm tʊ grɪiz ðə kɔɚ tüᵘ‖ . . . vədʒɪnjəz pærənts lɪvd ɪn mɪmfɪs tɪnəsii‖ . . . hi θɔt hi hæd nɛvɚ hæd ə tʃæᴵns‖ hi wɔnțɪd tə

334 teɪk ə kɔɚəspandəns koɚs| bəţɪ kʊtnt əfoɚd ðə fii‖ ɪt kɔst fɔrtɪ foɚ dalɚz‖
. . . ðe hæd ə bɪg blæk læn fɔɚm| bət ðɪs jiɚ ðə krɑp wəz pʊɚ‖ ðe hæd bɪn
ə bæd dræət| æ̃ən pɔɚt əv ðɪ taɪm ðæɚ waznt iven ɪnʌf wɔtɚ fɔɚ ðə stɑk‖
ðɪ pɑnz æn bɑgz hæd draːd əp‖ hɔˉɚs kʊtnt kɛtʃ ĩnĩ moɚ frɔgz‖ hi laɪkt
frɔg leɪgz‖ hɪz fɑðɚ hæd sɛd jɛstɚdeɪ ðæt ðe maɪt bi lʌkɪ ɪf ðe dɪdnt stɔɚv‖
hɔˉɚs θɔt hiəd rɛðɚ stɔɚv ðɪn iit ĩnĩ mo poɚk sɔsɪdʒɪz ən hæəm‖ hi waz
taəd ə vɛʒtəbəls tüᵘ‖ ðe hæd kɔlɪflæɚz| ən kæbɪdʒ ən tɚnəps| ən spɪnɪʃ ɪn
ðɪ gɔɚdn‖ hɔˉɚs dɪdnt laɪk spɪnɪʃ‖ ðe hæd ʌnjɘnz| ən rædɪʃɪz ən lɛtɪs tüᵘ‖
hɔˉrɪs dɪdnt laɪk ʌnjɘnz iðɚ| n̩ hi nɛvɚ| eɪt ɪnɪ kaɪnd əv sælɪd‖ sʌmtaɪmz
ðe hæd kɔɚnbrɛd ən sælɪd fɔɚ dɪzɚt‖ hɔˉɚsɪz fɑðɚ kɔld sɚəp məlæsɪz‖
ɛvɚ wʌns ɪn ə ʍaəl hi ʃʌt ə skwɚl ɔɚ ə dɔg| bət juzlɪ hi hætə iit sɔsədʒ ɚ
hæəm æn sæəs‖ sʌmtaɪmz ðe hæd eɪgz| bət nɑt ɔftən‖ ðe hæd lɔst ə gʊd
mɪnɪ tʃɪkɪnz‖ hɔəks ətæktɪd ðɪəm| æn pɑsəmz gɑt ɪntʊ ðɪ tʃɪkɪn kʊp| tə
seɪ nʌθn əv ðɪ hʌŋgrɪ nɪgɚz wɪθ ðɛɚ hæŋkrɪn fə tʃɪkɪn stju‖ sʌm əv ðə
kæəz wɚ draɪ| ən ðe dɪdnt hæəv mʌtʃ mɪək‖

Some Social Aspects of the Speech of Blue-Grass Kentucky

Lawrence M. Davis

The current interest in the speech of black persons is attested to by the increasing number of articles dealing with their speech which are appearing in learned journals. Many of the articles label the speech of white persons "white English" and that of black persons "black English." In this article, Professor Davis, using the records of the *Linguistic Atlas,* begins an investigation of the validity of these terms. He deals with a number of features of the language used in the Bluegrass area. The time for the research on which this paper is based was provided by a Faculty Research Fellowship, granted by Illinois Institute of Technology, 1969–70. Professor Davis is a member of the Center of American English at Illinois Institute of Technology.

336   Discussions of the social dialects of American English have proliferated of late, and at least two equally fashionable points of view regarding the speech of Negro Americans seem to be emerging. Though both see Black English as different from White English, one maintains that the former is in fact a different language because of an African creole substratum;[1] the other says that "the language [of Negro children in Florida] is, of course, in no way impoverished or pidginized."[2] Adherents of both these viewpoints loudly (and in the best journals) proclaim their certitude, but neither group has published data in support of their major premise—the one they share—that, indeed, there is any worthwhile distinction between White speech and Black speech in the first place. The evidence for so-called "Negro features," when it does not come from literary sources (a highly unlikely place to find accurate phonetic information), is simply anecdotal.

Since the *Linguistic Atlas* records do provide data from both Negro and White informants of comparable social, economic, and educational levels, this seems a good place to begin to study this question. And the Blue-Grass area of Kentucky provides a place where there was historically little contact between the races, at least compared to areas farther south.

Clearly, this admittedly preliminary study will not provide any conclusive statement about the relationships between Black and White speech.[3] What it may provide, however, is a basis for further research, and a plea that those truly interested in the dialects of American English avoid facile generalizations having no basis in fact.

The eleven Kentucky informants were divided as follows: seven were Type I, uncultivated,[4] including one Negro informant; two were Type III, cultivated; three were in between, Type II. For the most part, the lin-

From *Orbis,* Bulletin International de Documentation Linguistique, Vol. 19, No. 2 (1970), 337–341. Reprinted with the permisson of A. J. Windekens, Director, Centre International de Dialectologie Générale, and Lawrence M. Davis.

[1] See especially Beryl Loftman Bailey, "Toward a New Perspective in Negro English Dialectology," *AS,* XL (1965), 171–177; J. L. Dillard, "Negro Children's Dialect in the Inner City," *The Florida FL Reporter* (Fall, 1967); William A. Stewart, "Continuity and Change in American Negro Dialects," *The Florida FL Reporter* (Spring, 1968); "Nonstandard Speech Patterns," *Baltimore Bulletin of Education,* Nos. 2–4 (1966–1967), 52–65.

[2] Susan Houston, "A Sociolinguistic Consideration of the Black English of Children in Northern Florida," *Language,* XLV (1969), 606.

[3] The idea of the uniformity of White and Black speech is not new. See especially McDavid, Raven I., Jr. and McDavid, Virginia, "The Relationship of the Speech of American Negroes to the Speech of Whites," *AS,* XXVI (1951), 3–17.

[4] For a detailed description of these three informant types see Hans Kurath, *Handbook of the Linguistic Geography of New England* (Providence, R.I.: Brown University Press, 1939), p. 41.

guistic forms which will be classed as "uncultivated" here are to be found in the speech of both Type I and Type II informants, and in the speech of Whites and Negroes alike.

Table I

The informants came from three counties in the Bluegrass—168 (Fayette County), 169 (Bath County), and 178 (Menifee County). Their ages, education, and professions are as follows.

Informant Number and type	Age	Education	Occupation
168.N.1	67–77	Fifth grade	Stonemason, farmer
168.1	83	none	Farmer
168.11	71	Four years	Farmer, sharecropper
168.2	50	High school	Housewife
168.3	67	Two years at Bryn Mawr; graduate University of Kentucky	Housewife
168.31	23	Graduate Brown University	Housewife, teacher
169.1	68	Grade school	Farmer
169.11	75+	Common school	Blacksmith, farmer
169.12	62	none	Farmer, blacksmith
169.2	78	High school	Housewife
178.1	88	Eighth grade (three months a year)	Farmer
178.2	81	Three months	Farmer, sheriff, magistrate

One further point deserves mention here. Unfortunately, these results are not very neat; that is, there are no clear emergent patterns. This will come as no surprise to anyone who has actually worked with large masses of linguistic data, since, unfortunately, informants seldom talk the way linguists would like them to. For almost every form which seems to suggest a pattern, there is another which obviates against it.

Verb forms provide an excellent example. Only the uncultivated informants, Negro and White, use the forms *we was* and *I'z a-gowna*, but the Negro informant also used *I'm going*. Furthermore, both cultivated and uncultivated informants omit the copula in *we gonna, they gonna*, and so on. And *we a-gowna* is also common to all types of informants.

The following past tense forms are all common to only Type I and II informants: *I taked, I seen, I ketched, I done*. *Have rode* is common only to Type I informants, but *drownded* is common to all types. Other markers of uncultivated speech, as far as the morphology is concerned, are *oxens, hisn*, and *hern*.

338   The best, or at least the most conclusive, social markers in central Kentucky can be found in the phonology, and the clearest-cut phonological marker is a [θ>f] shift in final position. The forms *toof, teef, harf,* and *mauf,* though they occur only seldom, do occur in the speech of only Type I informants, both Negro and White. Similarly, only the cultivated informants use the pronunciation [draṵt]; all the others say [draṵθ]. The [nd] cluster in the cultivated pronunciation [bʌndl̩] generally becomes [bʌnəl] in uncultivated speech, though one of the cultivated informants used both terms.

      Furthermore, for the cultivated pronunciations [kəmfət] and [tū͞ınti] or [tuɛnti], a few uncultivated informants used [kə̃fət] and [tū͞ıdi]; in other words, they had no postvocalic nasal, only a nasalized vowel.[5] In both cases, incidentally, the Negro informant used the form, without the /n/. The uncultivated informants also pronounce the word for the substance that causes bread to rise as [ii̯s] or [ii̯st], while the cultivated informants say [ji̯i̯st]. Likewise, while the cultivated informants say [to̰dz], the uncultivated say [two̰dz] or [təwo̰dz]. [roṵstɪn] in cultivated speech becomes [roṵsn̩] in uncultivated, and, conversely, [twai̯stəz bɪg] is common only to uncultivated speech, though not all the uncultivated informants use this pronunciation.

      These examples are hardly conclusive. They seem to be more morpheme or word specific than evidence of any pattern, yet they are the most clear-cut markers in the records. Others, which "common sense" dictates must be markers, are not so. For example, only uncultivated speakers say [θu] or [θoṵd] for the preterite of *throw,* leading one to expect this omission of prevocalic /r/ to be a feature of uncultivated speech.

      But then one finds that all types of informants omit the /r/ in [ei̯pən] (*apron*), [ei̯pəl] (*April*), and [jɪəgoᵘ] (*year ago*). We all know that the so-called r-less pronunciation of barn ([baə̰n]) is not a negative social marker in the South, but these nonsignificant absenses of /r/ in heterosyllabic positions is rather interesting, though the pronunciation [lai̯bɛrii̯] (*library*) is common only in uncultivated speech.

      Likewise, only uncultivated speakers pronounce the fourth day of the week as [wɪnzdɨ], leading to the notion that [ɛ>ɪ] before nasals. The fact is that though this may be true for the pronunciation of the fourth day of the week, it is not true for the dialect in general. In fact, [ɪ] and [ɛ] seem to vary freely before /n/, so that speakers of all types will say both [hɛn] and [hɪn]. What does seem likely, however, is that uncultivated speakers are more likely to use [ɪ] intead of [ɛ]; those with only [ɪ] were all Type I. Furthermore, one cultivated informant consistently used a sound in-

---

[5] See James McMillan, "Vowel Nasality as a Sandhi-Form of the Morphemes *-nt, -ing* in Southern American," *AS,* XIV (1939), 120–123.

between the two, indicated by the field worker with shift signs; the other cultivated informant used both, with a predominance of [ɛ].

Even more confusing is the fact that [sɛə̯f] (*self*) occurs only in the speech of uncultivated informants, but [tʉɛə̯v] (*twelve*) occurs in the speech of cultivated and uncultivated alike. Similarly, we have all read that so-called nonstandard speech is characterized by the reduction of final consonant clusters; but cultivated speakers in Kentucky say [lɔf] and [lɔft] (*loft*), [læn] and [lænd] (*land*), [kol] and [kold] (*cold*), [paʉn] and [paʉnd] (*pound*); uncultivated speakers do likewise. And here not even a statistically relevant conclusion is possible, as was the case with [ɛ] and [ɪ] before /n/.

Cultivated speakers in Kentucky say [tʃɪmliḭ] (*chimney*), [hʉps] (*hoops*), and [hʉfs] (*hoofs*). And, horror of horrors, they say [ɪlɛbm̩] (*eleven*), with a [b] rather than a [v], and [θɜḭtiḭn] (*thirteen*), [pəḭs] (*purse*), and [wɜḭmz] (*worms*). Only the Negro said [θɜḭzdɨ] (*Thursday*), however.

The data revealed a total of only five or six *words* which the Negro informant pronounced differently from the Whites of his social and educational background, and in no case did the Negro informant have an inventory of sounds different from that of the Whites. The Negro informant did say [θɜḭzdɨ] differently from the Whites, but the Whites used [əḭ] in words like [pəḭs], [nəḭs], and so on. But one thing is clear; though the other informants use this pronunciation, and though the Negro informant also says such things as [θɜɚrtiḭ] on occasion, the incidence of [əḭ] is more frequent in the speech of the Negro. The same kind of conclusion as for the [ɛ~ɪ] alternation.

There simply were no systematic differences between the speech of the Negro and that of the Whites.[6] There may, however, be some significance in the fact that some forms are used more regularly by one race or the other. No other conclusion is permitted by the data investigated. Perhaps, in fact, the very terms Negro and White used to describe language might be worthless. A man, White or Black, in Atlanta does not talk like a man in Lexington, and perhaps race is less important than is the Midland dialect boundary. Such certainly seems to be the case in the Bluegrass, and some transdialect boundary studies should certainly be undertaken. All the informants in this study can more easily be characterized as South Midland than as either Black or White. . . .

This, however, is no time to make any firm conclusions about the relationships between White and Black speech in the Bluegrass. Because

---

[6] In fact, there is no real evidence that people can tell Whites from Blacks by linguistic cues alone. Roger Shuy, *et al., Field Techniques in an Urban Language Study* (Washington: Center for Applied Linguistics, 1968) showed that 80% of the Detroit informants could distinguish Whites from Blacks after listening to taped conversations, but Shuy did not include samples of the speech of the some 300,000 in-migrants to Detroit in his samples.

340   the *Linguistic Atlas* interviewed only one Negro there, any further research must be based on additional fieldwork. But the *Atlas* does provide a beginning, and much more work is needed before any scholar can
afford to be satisfied. We need controlled research, utilizing comparable
data from informants of both races, and all the appeals to the "common
sense" which tells us that "there ought to be a difference" cannot substitute for that needed research.

Grammatical Differences in the North Central States

Raven I. McDavid, Jr. and
Virginia G. McDavid

One of the first regions to be investigated outside the area of
primary settlement, the Atlantic Seaboard area, was the
North Central states. The *Linguistic Atlas of the North
Central States*, under the direction of Professor Albert
Marckwardt, was begun in 1938. In this article, Raven and
Virginia McDavid summarize and interpret the grammatical
data found in the records of the North Central States.
  Professor Raven I. McDavid, Jr., several of whose
articles are included in this collection, is one of the best-
known American linguists. Virginia G. McDavid
(Mrs. Raven I. McDavid, Jr.), also a linguist, is Professor
of English at Chicago State College and editor of the
Illinois Schools Journal.

  Descriptive linguistics, in its broadest aspects, tells us not only what
forms occur and in what combinations, but also in what parts of the

From *American Speech* 35:5–19 (February 1960). Reprinted with the permission of Columbia
University Press and the authors.

342   linguistic community and in the speech or writing of what social groups
particular variants may be found.[1] By examining these regional and
social differences within the generally uniform structure of a language,
dialectologists are able to correlate linguistic data with patterns of settlement history, regional growth, and social structure; furthermore, they are
able to provide a solid basis of fact for the value judgments necessary in
such applications of linguistics as lexicography and the teaching of
English.[2]

   These regional and social differences have been summarized, for the
older settlement area along the Atlantic Seaboard, in Hans Kurath's
Word Geography of the Eastern United States, in E. Bagby Atwood's
Survey of Verb Forms in the Eastern United States, and in Kurath and
Raven I. McDavid, Jr.'s *Pronunciation of English in the Atlantic States*.[3]
This article summarizes the grammatical evidence in the field records for
the *Linguistic Atlas of the North Central States*.[4] Besides the general interest of dialectologists in accurately delineating regional and social
patterns of usage, there are several reasons why an examination of grammatical evidence from the North Central area should be of interest to the
student of American English:

---

[1] Preliminary versions of this study have been presented at the Linguistic Forum, Ann Arbor
(July, 1955), and at the Madison, Wis., meeting of the Present-Day English group of the MLA
(September, 1957). The evidence on verb forms, as gathered to September, 1955, is found in
Virginia McDavid, "Verb Forms of the North-Central States and Upper Midwest" (disserta-
tion [microfilm], University of Minnesota, 1956).

   Permission to utilize the North Central field records has been given by A. H. Marckwardt,
of the University of Michigan, Director of the Linguistic Atlas of the North Central States,
with whom the authors have worked closely for more than a decade.

[2] Like all studies of the social distribution of grammatical forms, this one owes much to the
precept and example of Charles C. Fries, especially to his *American English Grammar* (New
York, 1940).

[3] The *Word Geography* (Ann Arbor, Mich., 1949) went to press before fieldwork was complete
in South Carolina, Georgia, and upstate New York. For these areas see R. I. McDavid, Jr.,
"The Folk Vocabulary of New York State," *New York Folklore Quarterly*, VII (1951), 173–91,
and "The Position of the Charleston Dialect," *Publications of the American Dialect Society*, No.
23 (1955), pp. 35–53. Atwood's *Survey* was published at Ann Arbor in 1953.

[4] Duplicate archives of the North Central field records are housed at the University of Michigan and the University of Chicago. Checklist studies, which have been used in subsequent
regional surveys to supplement the field records, were first employed in the North Central
region in Alva Lee Davis, "A Word Atlas of the Great Lakes Region" (dissertation [micro-
film], University of Michigan, 1949), which covered Michigan, Ohio, Indiana, and Illinois.
Subsequently, Kentucky was surveyed by checklists in Christine Duncan Forrester, "A Word
Geography of Kentucky" (M.A. thesis, University of Kentucky, 1952). Checklist archives have
been gathered for Ohio, Indiana, and Illinois; as yet, all of these checklist collections are incomplete. Because literate Americans are self-conscious about grammatical propriety, checklists have not been used to sample grammatical differences.

1) Since the North Central states are an area of secondary settlement, it is desirable to see whether regional dialect differences, established for the Atlantic Seaboard, persist inland, in the heartland of the traditionally uniform "General American."

2) More specifically, conceding that the well-recognized relic areas of the Atlantic states preserve characteristic local grammatical forms, it is desirable to know whether secondary settlement areas also show regional differences in grammar, contrary to Mencken's theory of a uniform American vulgate.

3) Since the teaching of standards of grammatical usage is one of the most important tasks of our schools—and is the touchstone by which teachers of English, at all levels, are most commonly judged—it is imperative to know what are the grammatical practices which actually differentiate cultivated from uncultivated usage, so that the teacher— whether dealing with native speakers of English or with those who come from other language-communities—may work on those practices which are most likely to stigmatize a student in the judgment of his peers or of his future employers.[5]

Fieldwork for the *Linguistic Atlas of the North Central States*, under the direction of Albert H. Marckwardt, of Michigan, began in the summer of 1938, with a preliminary survey of Michigan and Indiana; further preliminary investigations the following summer, in Ohio and Illinois, indicated enough clear regional differences to warrant a full-fledged linguistic atlas of the region, but only Wisconsin was fully covered before the United States became involved in the Second World War. Fieldwork was resumed in 1948, and by now is essentially complete except for a few areas in Indiana and the adjacent section of Kentucky. These last areas should be completed in 1960, so that editorial work—already in its preliminary stages—may proceed to publication. In their present form the North Central archives comprise approximately 450 field records.

The principles on which American linguistic geography is based have been discussed many times.[6] The following summary indicates the modifications required by the practical situation in the North Central states, where the director has had relatively little money for the Atlas as an or-

---

[5] A comparison of handbook judgments and Atlas data on selected grammatical items is found in Jean Malmstrom, "A Study of the Validity of Textbook Statements about Certain Controversial Grammatical Items in the Light of Evidence from the Linguistic Atlas" (dissertation [microfilm], University of Minnesota, 1958).

No social scientist will be surprised to discover inconsistencies between the unguarded usage of informants and their reactions to direct questioning. Such discrepancies are a part of the record of usage, and should be recorded wherever possible.

[6] See, for example, R. I. McDavid, Jr., "The Dialects of American English," ch. 9 in W. Nelson Francis, *The Structure of American English* (New York, 1958), pp. 488–494.

344　ganized project, and where the fieldwork in each state has been conducted
according to the conditions which local institutions have attached to
their financial support:[7]

1) A network of communities, representative of the economic and
demographic history of the region: 25 to 40 communities, providing adequate coverage for a survey of an area of secondary settlement.

2) Informants native to their communities, representing at least two
different groups in each community by age, education, and sometimes
by ethnic origin. As in the Atlantic states, cultured informants are interviewed in most of the important cultural centers.

3) A questionnaire composed of items from the daily experience of
most informants and designed to reveal regional and social differences
in vocabulary, pronunciation, and grammar. Since the dialectologist is
interested not only in describing the present dialect situation but in establishing the historical affiliations of the present-day dialects, the selection of items—as well as of communities—is slightly weighted in the
direction of rural and small-town life.

4) Field investigators, normally with intensive training under more experienced workers in: (*a*) the handling of informants; (*b*) the purposes of
the questionnaire; (*c*) the phonetic alphabet devised for the *Linguistic
Atlas of the United States and Canada*. More than four-fifths of the North
Central interviews were conducted by fieldworkers trained by the original
Atlas staff in common practices of eliciting and transcribing, so that their
records provide comparable data even on the phonetic level. In a few
areas, however, the fieldworkers did not have adequate training in the
use of the questionnaire or in transcription in the *Atlas* alphabet; as a
result, their records not only differ markedly in the phonetic transcriptions but often skimp the grammatical and lexical data. Fortunately, the
boundaries of these areas never coincide with probable dialect boundaries
and always overlap the areas covered by more experienced investigators.

5) Impressionistic transcription on the spot in a finely graded phonetic
alphabet.[8]

[7] The principal support has been provided by the University of Michigan, through a series of
grants from the Rackham Fund. Other institutions assisting the project have been Augustana
College, the University of Illinois, Indiana University, the University of Kentucky, Michigan
State University, the Ohio State Archaeological and Historical Society, Ohio State University,
Western Reserve University, and the University of Wisconsin.

[8] In some areas, to compensate for the inexperience of the fieldworkers (and, theoretically, to
save time in the field), interviews have been recorded on tape and transcribed later, by the
interviewer or someone else. However, since the tape cannot record what the interviewer has
not elicited, and since a transcriber incompletely familiar with the questionnaire will hardly
recognize a form out of context, it is not surprising that the interviews on tape sometimes provide disappointingly little grammatical evidence, especially (and where the tapes should be
most productive) alternative forms recorded from free conversation.

Differences among fieldworkers, in experience and in practices in the field, naturally com-

In the field records for the North Central Atlas is evidence on the regional and social variants for some 125 items of grammar. Some of these were offered by informants as lexical variants (as *bought bread, boughten bread, brought on bread* for *baker's bread, store bread,* etc.) and hence would not be recorded from every informant. Some forms—such as the preterits of *come, run,* and *take* —might be recorded in several contexts; the same context, on the other hand, might provide data on several forms—as he *became sick, took sick,* or *was taken sick.* The inventory of grammatical items covered by the questionnaire is as follows:

1. *Verbs*[9]

a) Principal parts (preterits only, unless otherwise indicated): *become, begin, bite* (p. ppl.), *blow, boil* (p. ppl.), *bring* (pret.; p. ppl.), *buy* (attributive p. ppl.), *catch* (inf.; pret.), *climb* (pret.; p. ppl.), *come, dive, do, draw up, dream, drink* (pret.; p. ppl.), *drive* (pret.; p. ppl.), *drown* (p. ppl.), *eat* (pret.; p. ppl.), *fetch, fight, fit, freeze, give, give out* (p. ppl.), *grow* (pret.; p. ppl.), *hear* (p. ppl.), *heat* (p. ppl.), *kneel, learn, lie* (inf.; pret.), *lie out, ride* (p. ppl.), *rise* (pret.; attributive p. ppl.), *run, scare* (p. ppl.), *see, shrink, sit* (inf.; pret.), *spoil* (p. ppl.), *sweat, swim, take* (pret.; ppl.), *teach, tear* (p. ppl.), *throw, wake* (up), *wear* (out) (p. ppl.), *write* (p. ppl.)

b) Personal forms of the present indicative: *I be* (etc.), *I'm going, am I going, he does, he doesn't, he looks like* (etc.), *she rinses, it costs*

c) Number and concord: *we were* (etc.), *here are, oats are*

d) Negative forms: *am not, are not, is not; have not, has not; was not; do not; will not; ought not; didn't use to;* multiple negatives

e) Infinitive and present participle: *to tell, singing and a-laughing, going*

f) Phrases: *all gone, get rid of, might could, I shall be, we shall be, I've been thinking, I've done worked, I want to get off.*

2. *Noun plurals: bushel,*[10] *fist, hoof, house, ox, post, pound, shaft, trough, eavestrough, yoke* (*span, pair, team*).

---

plicate the task of interpreting the data. The problem in the North Central states is roughly analogous to that in New England, where nine investigators gathered the data, but Guy S. Lowman, Jr., contributed nearly two-fifths of the total, and Lowman's territory was contiguous to that of every other fieldworker.

[9] The classification of verb forms follows that in Atwood's *Survey of Verb Forms in the Eastern United States.* Statements of the provenience of verb forms along the Atlantic Seaboard are based on Atwood.

[10] For a detailed study of the plurals of *bushel, pound, yoke,* etc., see R. I. McDavid, Jr., and Virginia McDavid, "Plurals of Nouns of Measure," in *Studies for C. C. Fries,* ed. A. H. Marckwardt (University of Michigan Press).

Uninflected plurals of measure are more common than the usual educated layman suspects; a sign on U. S. 23 reads "Ann Arbor 2 mile"; one on the University of Chicago campus, "No load permitted over 5 ton."

346   3. *Pronouns*
    a) Personal pronouns: *it, it wasn't me* (etc.), *you* (nom. pl.; gen. pl.), *ours, yours, his, hers, theirs*
    b) Interrogative pronouns: *who* (nom. pl.; gen. pl.), *what* (nom. pl.; gen. pl.)
    c) Relative pronouns: *who, whose*
    d) Demonstratives: attributive plural.
    4. *Adjective formation: poisonous.*

    5. *Article* (*sandhi-alternation*): *an apple* (etc.).

    6. *Adverbs and adverbial phrases: a little way, a long way, anywhere, at all, look here! rather cold* (etc.), *this way.*

    7. *Prepositional syntax: run across him, not at home, all at once, sick at his stomach, behind the door, named for his father, wait for you, died of diphtheria, fell off the horse, half-past seven, quarter of eleven.*

    8. *Subordinating conjunctions: as far as, as if, because, unless.*

For interpreting the regional and social distribution of these forms and their variants, one needs a brief sketch of settlement and social history, pending a detailed presentation in the published North Central Atlas. The basic patterns of settlement represent extensions westward of the major dialect regions of the Atlantic seaboard states—Northern, Midland, and Southern[11]—with the Northern and South Midland regions providing the bulk of early settlement. Wisconsin, Michigan, southern Ontario, and the nothernmost counties of Illinois, Indiana, and Ohio were all settled primarily by New Englanders and by upstate New Yorkers of New England descent. New Englanders and New Yorkers also established enclaves further south in such communities as Worthington (now a suburb of Columbus) and Marietta, at the confluence of the Mus-

---

[11] This classification, first established in Kurath's *Word Geography,* was originally based on vocabulary evidence but has since proved valid for grammatical and phonological evidence as well. For the Atlantic Seaboard, the North includes New England, the Hudson Valley, and their derivative settlements; the Midland, Pennsylvania, and its derivative settlements; the South, the areas of older plantation culture from Delaware Bay to the Florida line. Within the Midland, the North Midland includes Pennsylvania and northern West Virginia; the South Midland, southern West Virginia, the Shenandoah Valley, and the upper Piedmont and mountains of the Carolinas and Georgia. Because of the cultural dominance of the plantation areas in the former slaveholding states, the South Midland is highly receptive to Southern speech forms.

For a preliminary examination of the North Central vocabulary, see A. H. Marckwardt, "Principal and Subsidiary Dialect Areas in the North-Central States," *Publications of the American Dialect Society.* No. 27 (1957), pp. 3–15.

For the foreign-language groups, the most extensive study is Einar Haugen, *The Norwegian Language in America: a Study in Bilingual Behavior* (Philadelphia, 1953), 2 vols.

kingum and the Ohio. In southern Ontario there were also many United Empire Loyalists who were refugees from the Middle Atlantic states; later came direct migrations from the British Isles. South Midlanders from the western counties of Virginia and North Carolina pushed across the Cumberland Gap and other passes into Kentucky, and from Kentucky infiltrated the bottom lands of southern Illinois, most of Indiana, and southern Ohio. Groups of Kentuckians settled farther north, along the Mississippi and its tributaries, notably in the lead region where Illinois, Wisconsin, and Iowa join. The opening of the National Road provided an overland route for Pennsylvania settlement of the central parts of Ohio, Indiana, and Illinois—a wedge progressively narrowing as it approached the Mississippi—while other Pennsylvanians, chiefly from the Pittsburgh area, descended the Ohio Valley. These last migrations both introduced North Midland forms into the North Central states and reinforced the general Midland contributions of the South Midland settlements.

The large-scale immigration from Northern Europe after 1840 brought fairly compact colonies into both urban and rural areas of the North Central region, but fewest into Kentucky. Although these groups occasionally introduced loan translations of their native idioms, in the long run they probably accelerated the spread of Standard English grammatical forms, since—placing a high value on education—they appear to have often gone directly from their native language to Standard English, without learning the folk speech.

Direct migration from the Southern region proper—the plantation settlements of the coastal plain and lower Piedmont of Virginia, the Carolinas, and Georgia—was comparatively small. It seems to have been strongest in the westernmost counties of Kentucky, particularly the Jackson Purchase west of the Tennessee River, less strong in the Blue Grass area around Lexington and Louisville. However, thanks to the political and economic history of Kentucky, and the ties of cultured Kentuckians with the older plantation areas, the prestige of Southern institutions and Southern speech forms has always been high in the Blue Grass State, and not ignored farther north. With slavery forbidden north of the Ohio by the Northwest Ordinance of 1787, and economically unprofitable in the foothills and mountains that cover most of Kentucky, there were few Negroes among the early settlers, except in the Purchase and Blue Grass regions.

Alongside the pattern of settlement, and often disturbing the dialect areas that settlement had created, the North-Central region has witnessed the dramatic operation of the three forces that have characterized American society from its beginnings—industrialization, urbanization, and the spread of education. From the development of heavy industry near the end of the nineteenth century there has been a steadily accelerating migra-

348   tion from the farms and small towns to the cities and expanded metropolitan areas. The population of these expanded urban areas has been
further augmented by new mass migrations, first of immigrants from
Southern and Eastern Europe, later by Southern Negroes and poor whites.
Each of these later groups has frequently established socially isolated
colonies within urban areas, with the tacit or open cooperative blessing
of industry, political machines, and churches, so that speech peculiarities
of the group may tenaciously persist.[12] In compensation, popular education, inaugurated by the Northwest Ordinance, has been strongly supported north of the Ohio from the earliest settlements, so that there has
been attrition of folk grammatical forms—as well as of words and pronunciations—under the impact of the standard language. The influence
of popular education has so far been less significant in Kentucky, where
industrialization came late, communications have been generally poor
until recently, and the lack of funds and the proliferation of county
governments have hindered the development of a strong state-wide school
system.

Against this background we may now examine the regionally distinctive grammatical features in the North Central states. It should be remembered that in an area of secondary settlement the dialect regions—
Northern, South Midland, etc.—are not so distinctly marked as they are
along the Atlantic seaboard. Furthermore, the occurrence of a particular
form in a particular area does not mean that everybody in that area uses
that form on all occasions.

Among the grammatical features characteristic of Northern speech
(Map 1), *troths* "troughs" (with /-θs/ or /-ðz/), *died from,* and *to* as a
preposition of location—in such contexts as *sick to the stomach,* (he isn't)
to home, and *all to once*—are well established throughout the area of
Northern settlement. Less well established are *scairt* "scared" and *het*
"heated."[13] Except in Ontario, /wʌnt/ "won't" predominates in the
inland North, as it does in New England and upstate New York; in
Ontario, however, /wʌnt/ is infrequent, but the Hudson Valley /wunt/,
/wʊnt/ very common. Apparently expansive Northern forms are *dove*
/dov/ as the preterit of *dive* and *hadn't ought* "ought not"; *hadn't ought*
is found as far south as the St. Louis and Cincinnati areas. On the other
hand, *it wan't me, gwine,* and *be* as a finite verb—old-fashioned in New
England—are very uncommon and seem to be rapidly disappearing.[14]

---

[12] See R. I. McDavid, Jr., "Dialect Differences and Inter-Group Tensions," *Studies in Linguistics,* IX (1951), 27–33.

[13] Both *scairt* and *het* occur occasionally in Kentucky.

[14] *It wan't me* and *gwine* are also fairly common in the coastal South; they are found occasionally in Kentucky.

On Beaver Island (an Irish fishing colony in northern Lake Michigan)   349
and in scattered communities of northern Wisconsin is found the negative form *usen't to,* not uncommon in British English but rare in the
Atlantic states.

Of characteristic Midland forms, *seen* as a preterit has spread widely
throughout the North Central states, except in cultivated speech. Occurring everywhere, without appreciable concentration in any single area,
it is one of the few speech forms of the region that one may safely label
as "General American." *Clum* "climbed" is also an expansive form,
except in cultivated speech, but has spread less than *seen. I want off* and
quarter till occur throughout the areas of Midland settlement, though—
perhaps because of Southern influence—*quarter till* appears infrequently
in the Blue Grass and not at all in the Illinois communities near St. Louis.

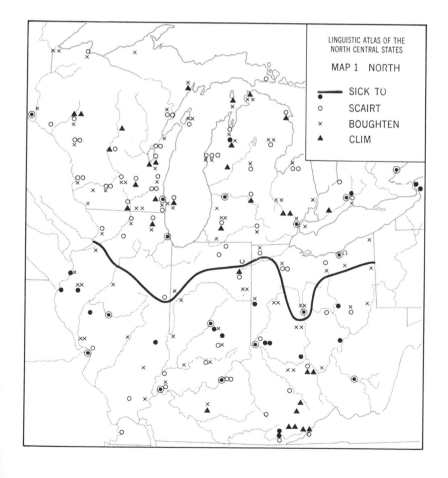

350   *Wait on* "wait for," common in the Midland areas of the Atlantic states, is relatively infrequent in Illinois, and *all the further* "as far as" seems to be receding throughout the area, but particularly in Illinois. *You-uns* "you" (pl.) is rare and old-fashioned; such Pennsylvania Germanisms as *the oranges are all* "all gone" and *got awake* "woke up" are extremely rare (Map 2).

A few South Midland forms are fairly well established in the areas of South Midland settlement, though never to the exclusion of competing forms: *dog-bit* "bitten by a dog," *used to didn't* "didn't use to," *give out* "tired," and *sick in the stomach.* Less well established are *drinkt* "drank, drunk" and *the sun raised* "rose." Receding are *shrinkt* "shrank," *I sot down* "sat," *swim* "swam," and the /-n/ forms of the absolute genitive: *ourn, yourn, hisn, hern, theirn. Drimpt* "dreamed" is well established in

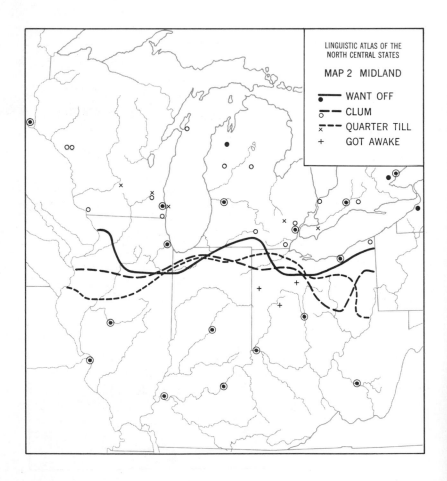

LINGUISTIC ATLAS OF THE
NORTH CENTRAL STATES

MAP 2 MIDLAND

━━━━ WANT OFF
┅┅ CLUM
┉┉ QUARTER TILL
+   GOT AWAKE

eastern Kentucky. Less common, and usually confined to eastern Kentucky, are *fit* "fought," *them there boys,* and *e'er a, ne'er a* in such constructions as *he said ne'er a word about it* (Map 3).

Although previous studies of the vocabulary of the North Central states have not disclosed any characteristic Southern lexical items,[15] several Southern grammatical forms do occur. The most widely distributed of these items is *waked up,* which is most common in eastern Kentucky (sporadic occurrences to *waked up* in the Northern settlement area are probably explained by its appearance in New England and in the Genesee Valley of New York). Southern forms which are old-fashioned

[15] Neither Davis nor Forrester found any characteristic Southern vocabulary items with wide distribution.

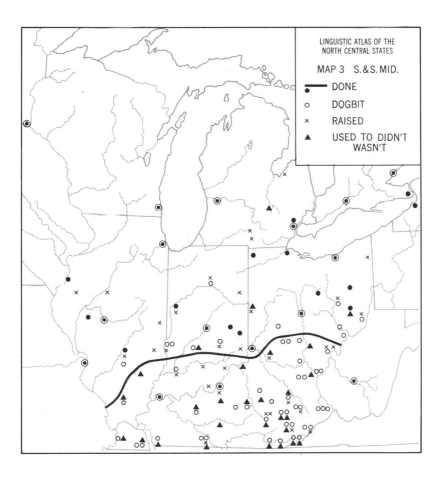

352   in the Atlantic seaboard are rare in the North Central states: *he do, the sun riz, I driv a nail,* and *he div in* are definitely recessive, and largely confined to eastern Kentucky (Map 4). Of dialect areas within the South, eastern Virginia is represented by *I ran up on him* "met," which is fairly common in Kentucky. However, *clome* "climbed," another characteristic Virginia item, rarely appears, and only in northern Wisconsin and northern Michigan, where Virginia influence is improbable.[16]

As with vocabulary and pronunciation, some grammatical items are typical of two of the major Eastern regions, or of parts of them. *Forty*

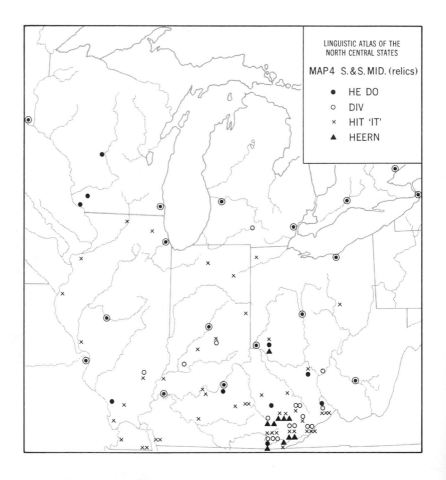

LINGUISTIC ATLAS OF THE
NORTH CENTRAL STATES

MAP 4 S. & S. MID. (relics)

● HE DO
○ DIV
× HIT 'IT'
▲ HEERN

[16] For *clome* as an eastern Virginia form, see E. Bagby Atwood, "Some Eastern Virginia Pronunciation Features," *English Studies for James Southall Wilson,* University of Virginia Studies IV (1951), 111–124.

bushel, found throughout the Northern and Midland regions of the Atlantic seaboard, is common everywhere in the North Central states. The Northern and North Midland *boughten bread* "baker's bread" is moderately common north of the Ohio River; south of the river it appears only in Maysville, Kentucky, where features of North Midland vocabulary and pronunciation are also found (Map 1). The inland North (Vermont and New York State) and western Pennsylvania share *I ran onto him* "met," likewise common north of the Ohio. The Midland and South share *two pound,* one of the most characteristic non-Northern items in the North Central states;[17] in Illinois and Wisconsin it follows the Mississippi (and presumably the migrations of Kentucky rivermen) from the lead region north to the neighborhood of Minneapolis. Outside the area of Northern settlement, the Midland and Southern *oughtn't* is well established, though yielding ground to the Northern *hadn't ought.*

As along the Atlantic Seaboard, there are a few items characteristic of the North and South but not of the Midland: *quarter to eleven, clim* "climbed," and the uninflected preterits *begin* and *see;* the high incidence of *see* in Kentucky and adjacent communities is probably due to its predominance in eastern Virginia. The Northern, Southern, and South Midland parts of our section—but not the North Midland settlements[18]—share *ketcht* (rarely *katcht*) "caught," *off'n* "off," the mistakenly labeled "Common Americanism" *half after seven,* and *oxen* as a singular, with a new analogical plural *oxens.*[19] The singular *oxen* and the plural *oxens* seem to be more recessive in Wisconsin and Michigan than in Kentucky and the Ohio Valley; better education, better communications, and the earlier disuse of oxen in agriculture are obvious explanations.

As we have mentioned, the Southern and South Midland areas of the Atlantic Seaboard have many items of vocabulary, grammar, and pronunciation in common, and Southern forms often infiltrate the South Midland—a situation to be expected since not till the twentieth century did the South Midland develop cultural centers important enough to resist the pressure of such plantation focal areas as the Virginia Piedmont and the South Carolina Low Country. A large number of grammatical items shared by South and South Midland are common in the North Central states: *you-all* (dominant south of the Ohio, but sporadic and

---

[17] See A. H. Marckwardt, "Folk Speech in Indiana and Adjacent States," *Indiana History Bulletin,* XVII (1940), 120–40.

[18] Kurath and McDavid have found that many old-fashioned pronunciations—e.g., –drin–"drain"—are found in New York State, West Virginia, and Maryland, but are practically lacking in Pennsylvania.

[19] See R. I. McDavid, Jr., and Virginia McDavid, "*House* and *Ox:* Analogy and Anomaly in the formation of Noun Plurals," to appear in an early issue of *General Linguistics.*

354 considered somewhat quaint further north), *a apple, taken* and *tuck* "took," *tuck* "taken," *sweated* (also occasionally in the North), *bought bread* "baker's bread," *look-a-here, this-a-way, drawed up* "shrank," *seed* "saw" (in old-fashioned speech), the perfective *done* (as *I've done worked all I'm going to*), and apparently a greater tendency toward omission of the relative pronoun in such constructions as *he's the man owns the orchard* and *he's a boy his father's rich.* Less common, and practically restricted to eastern Kentucky, are *might could* and such recessive forms as *brought on bread* "baker's bread," *mout* "might," and the /-əz/ inflection in *it costes, fistes,* and *postes.*

Cutting across the patterns of regional distribution is the social distribution of these forms. This too follows in general the distribution found along the Eastern Seaboard. That is, forms characteristic of the oldest and least-educated group in New York or Virginia continue to be found in the speech of that group; they do not suddenly appear in the speech of college graduates in Wisconsin or Illinois. However, as one goes West, the forms characteristic of the oldest and least-educated group become much less frequent—a testimony to the attrition of the rarer forms by dialect mixture, as well as to the efficiency of public education in eradicating characteristics of nonstandard speech. Throughout the North Central states it is the less sophisticated speakers who use such forms as *blowed, growed, throwed, come* "came," *run* "ran," *eat* "ate, eaten,"[20] *drownded, them boys,* he came over *for to tell me, he was a-singin', he did it a-purpose,* and *I won't go without he goes.* Though *hain't* and *ain't* often occur side by side as negatives of both *have* and *be, hain't* is clearly the more old-fashioned, nearly always restricted to the most old-fashioned informants. Less clearly nonstandard, but certainly not predominant in cultivated speech, are *we was* and *he don't care.*[21] And as Avis and Allen have pointed out,[22] *I have drank* is predominant in educated usage except

[20] In most parts of the United States, *eat* is far more common as a folk preterit than *et,* which (perhaps because it is Standard British) actually has some status in cultivated speech, notably in the Charleston area. Oddly enough, the handbooks often condemn *et* but never seem to mention *eat.*

[21] Of course, the cultured informants who use these forms in familiar conversation—like the cultured Charlestonians who say *ain't* freely among themselves—would never use them in writing or in formal speeches.

There is no systematic study of regional grammatical differences in written American English. In the *American English Grammar* Fries indicated that he had collected material toward such a study, but he has never published it. The conventions of edited English would make such a study, from printed materials, difficult but not impossible.

[22] Walter S. Avis, "The Past Participle *Drank:* Standard American English?" *American Speech,* XXVIII (1953), 106–111; Harold B. Allen, "On Accepting Participial *Drank," College English,* XVIII (1956–1957), 283–285. Is it possible that the preference for *drunk* in Kentucky arises from the local prestige of the distilling industry, licit and illicit?

in Kentucky; perhaps in Wisconsin and Michigan (where this predominance is clearest) there has been a confusion of meaning between the participle of *drink* and the adjective *drunk* "intoxicated."

Despite the disapproval of handbooks and other self-constituted authorities, certain other forms occur everywhere, in the speech of all social groups: *I been thinking* (with omission of *have*), *singin'* with the final alveolar nasal /-n/ rather than the velar nasal /-ŋ/, *like* as a subordinating conjunction in such contexts as *it seems like he'll win,* and *it wasn't me.*[23]

For a final group of forms, the status is indeterminate; that is, on the basis of our evidence we cannot classify the variants regionally or socially or predict the direction of change. Among these are *ran across* and *ran into* "met," *named for* and *named after, died of* and *died with, oats is thrashed* and *oats are thrashed, dreamed* and *dreamt, fitted* and *fit, learned* and *learnt, kneeled* and *knelt,* and the complex of *lie* and *lay,* with the infinitives *lie* and *lay* and the preterits *lay, laid,* and *lied.* Perhaps usage in this complex has been confused by association with *lie* "prevaricate."[24]

On the basis of our evidence, then, we reach the following conclusions:

1. As in vocabulary and pronunciation, regional differences in grammar are less sharp in the North Central states than along the Atlantic Seaboard. This is what one would expect in an area of secondary and relatively recent settlement, favored with a tradition of public education and leavened by large settlements of prosperous Germans and Scandinavians who might tend to approach English through books and the classroom rather than through the regional folk speech.

2. Nevertheless, many regional differences in grammar can be observed, on every level of usage.

3. As one would expect from the history of settlement, the regionally distinctive grammatical forms in the North Central states normally reflect the usage of the Northern (especially Inland Northern) and the South Midland regions of the Atlantic Seaboard. Features from eastern New England are very rare; features from the North Midland are highly recessive except when they also occur in the North or in the South Midland; features from the South appear only when they have infiltrated the South Midland areas of the Atlantic Seaboard or have been adopted in Kentucky—originally a political subdivision and still to some extent a cultural dependency of Virginia—but are more common than previous studies would have suggested.

---

[23] These forms, of course, are characteristic of informal conversation and would rarely appear in formal writing.

[24] An educated Kentuckian commented indignantly: "I know that some people tell us to say *lie down* and not *lay down;* but I also know some folks who can lie standing up."

356   4. Arteries of communication, especially the Mississippi and its tributaries, have facilitated the southward spread of Northern forms and the northward spread of forms from the South Midland.

5. The more spectacular relic forms are rare. Those that occur are most common in eastern Kentucky, still largely rural, with industry, communications, and education lagging behind those in the states north of the Ohio.

6. Finally, the social differences that actually occur in the speech of the North Central region are not accurately reflected in the judgments of usage heretofore made by those who prepare teaching materials.

These general conclusions are likely to stand up, though some particular statements may be modified as the last records come in, intensive local studies are conducted, and the entire body of our evidence is compared with the data from the Atlantic Seaboard. After all, as practitioners of the science of language, we must remember that all conclusions are tentative, the best we can reach with the evidence at hand, and subject to revision when we have more evidence.

Dialect Distribution and Settlement Patterns in the Great Lakes Region

Alva L. Davis

In this article Professor Davis shows the correlation between
speech features of the Great Lakes area and the settlement
patterns of the region. This is the same area with which
Professors Raven I. McDavid, Jr. and Virginia McDavid dealt
in the preceding article. For his study, Alva Davis uses a
number of vocabulary items included in the *Linguistic Atlas
of the North Central States*. He is Professor of English
Linguistics and Director of the Center for American English
at the Illinois Institute of Technology.

The study of dialect distribution in the Eastern United States and in
the secondary settlement areas of the Great Lakes Region has now
reached a point where it is possible to show some interesting correlations

From *The Ohio State Archeological and Historical Quarterly*, 60: 48–56 (1951). Reprinted with
the permission of the Ohio Historical Society and Alva L. Davis.

358   between the linguistic features and the settlement patterns of these regions. It is simple, perhaps even obvious, to say that when large, homogeneous groups of people migrate to new territories, they take with them the speech patterns of their old communities and that these speech patterns will be gradually modified as various cultural influences are brought to bear on them. However, the validity of any correlation depends on a solid foundation of extensive and painstaking research, rather than on generalities; and for this particular problem, such research materials are provided by the collections of the *Linguistic Atlas of the United States and Canada.*[1]

The *Linguistic Atlas,* which proposes to be a comprehensive survey of American English, was begun in 1931 under the directorship of Professor Hans Kurath, then at Brown University. In that year the first of the regional atlases, *The Linguistic Atlas of New England,* got under way. Upon completion of the records for New England, fieldwork was extended to the Middle Atlantic and South Atlantic states, and these records were finally completed during the spring of 1949. *The Linguistic Atlas of New England*[2] has been published, and the Middle Atlantic and South Atlantic materials are on file at the University of Michigan, where they are to be edited and prepared for publication.

The technique employed by the *Linguistic Atlas* is modeled on the personal-interview methods developed by European linguists. After a careful analysis of the geography and history of the region to be surveyed, the director of the project plots the communities for investigation. These communities are spaced so as to furnish a balanced sampling of speech forms in the area, the number of the communities varying with the complexity of the region. A trained phonetician then visits each community and interviews native speakers, asking several hundred standardized questions designed to bring out regional and social differences in dialect. Each interview requires about eight hours and is conducted in such a way that the informant uses his normal pronunciation, grammar, and vocabulary. According to the plan of the *Linguistic Atlas,* two speakers are chosen from each community, one a representative of the oldest gener-

---

[1] This paper is limited to a discussion of Michigan, Ohio, Indiana, and Illinois. For an account of the Wisconsin data, see Frederic G. Cassidy, "Some New England Words in Wisconsin," *Language,* XVII (1941), 324–339. The name "Great Lakes Region" has been applied to this area.

Other articles based on *Atlas* fieldwork in the region are Albert H. Marckwardt, "Folk Speech in Indiana and Adjacent States," *Indiana Historical Bulletin,* XVII (1940), 120–140; "Middle English *o* in the American English of the Great Lakes Area," *Papers of the Michigan Academy of Sciences, Arts, and Letters,* XXVI (1941), 56–71; "Middle English *WA* in the Speech of the Great Lakes Region," *American Speech,* XVII (1942), 226–254.

[2] Hans Kurath, ed. (6 vols., Providence, 1939–1943).

ation with relatively little education, and another of the middle age group (ordinarily from fifty to sixty years old) with considerably more formal education and wider social contacts. Occasionally college-educated informants are interviewed to represent the cultured speech of the area. In the Eastern states—from Maine to Florida—over 1,600 field interviews have been completed. The geographical spacing of the communities permits the plotting of the informants' responses on maps so that regional dissemination of speech forms can be related to topographical, historical, and cultural influences. By using informants from different age groups and from varying social backgrounds much useful data can be obtained about innovation, obsolescence, and prestige values of speech forms.

Since 1937 *The Linguistic Atlas of the North Central States,* under the supervision of Professor Albert H. Marckwardt of the University of Michigan, has been making steady progress.[3] Work in this region was begun with an exploratory survey of Ohio, Indiana, Illinois, Wisconsin, and Michigan, limited to ten field records in each state. This initial survey was completed in 1940 and the project was then expanded to cover from fifty to seventy records per state. The additional fieldwork has already been done in Wisconsin and Michigan and is currently being carried on in Illinois and Ohio.

The historical background for dialect distribution in the Great Lakes Region is well known. The settlement patterns for Ohio, Indiana, Illinois, and Michigan are easily traced, partly because the region is new, comparatively speaking, and partly because a wealth of information on the subject is available.[4] Three main streams of migration entered the area. The southernmost and earliest of these used the Ohio River system and peopled the lands within easy reach of the river and its tributaries. This group of settlers was for the most part from the Middle Atlantic states and the hill regions of the old slave states. In the north the important avenue of approach was the Great Lakes. Although some New Englanders, following Moses Cleaveland's party of 1796, had settled in the Connecticut Western Reserve, the opening of the Erie Canal in 1825 started the great land rush into that area, made up principally of Yankees

---

[3] This atlas includes the five states named above (footnote 1) plus Kentucky. The research in this area has been made possible by grants from the Rackham Foundation of the University of Michigan, from the University of Illinois, University of Wisconsin, Western Reserve University, Ohio State University, and the Ohio State Archaeological and Historical Society.

[4] Information concerning settlement is available in such works as Frederic L. Paxson, *History of the American Frontier 1763–1893* (Boston, 1924); Lois K. Mathews, *The Expansion of New England* (Boston, 1909); Beverley W. Bond, Jr., *The Foundations of Ohio* (*History of the State of Ohio,* edited by Carl Wittke, I, Columbus, 1942); Solon J. Buck, *Illinois in 1818* (Springfield, 1917). Tables I and VII, *U. S. Census, 1870: Population,* are of great value for determining the geographical extent of these settlements.

360   from New York State. This migration, which reached its peak in the 1840's and 1850's, completed the settlement of the Ohio counties bordering Lake Erie and filled up most of Michigan and northern Illinois. The third general migration was the overland movement, especially along the National Road. The Conestoga wagon carried Pennsylvanians into Ohio and westward, and Buckeyes and Hoosiers themselves joined in this search for cheap land.

Within the Great Lakes Region are two important small areas distinctive in the composition of their population: in southeastern Ohio, the Marietta colony, founded in 1788 by the Ohio Company, from Massachusetts, and in northwestern Illinois, the Lead Region settled in the 1820's by miners from all parts of the country.[5]

Even though much fieldwork is still to be done in the Great Lakes Region, the present data is adequate for a preliminary comparison to the Eastern findings. The handiest material for such a comparison is the folk vocabulary, the everyday words of life around the house and farm.

On the basis of the vocabulary variants of the Eastern *Atlas* records, Professor Kurath has discovered three main dialect areas,[6] differing considerably from the traditional threefold Eastern, Southern, and General American classification.[7] The Eastern records show a Northern area including New England, New York, the northern half of New Jersey and approximately the northern quarter of Pennsylvania; a Midland area including the rest of Pennsylvania and New Jersey, parts of Delaware and Maryland, and the mountainous South, beginning at the Blue Ridge; and a Southern area consisting of the coastal South from Delaware to Florida.

None of these areas is completely uniform, but divided into several subareas. The North is composed of Eastern New England (roughly from the Connecticut River), Western New England and Upstate New York, the Hudson Valley, and metropolitan New York. The Midland may be divided conveniently into two large subareas: North Midland for most of Pennsylvania and northern West Virginia, and South Midland for the speech of the mountain area to the south. The South (identified most easily by loss of postvocalic *r*) contains many subareas, many of them centering around such cities as Richmond, Charleston, and Savannah.

The general patterns which folk terms make in the Great Lakes Region

[5] The Lead Region also includes southwestern Wisconsin. See Cassidy, *loc. cit.*, 326. Foreign population settlements, such as that at Holland, Michigan, may be of importance but our present data shows little permanent influence on American English in this area.

[6] *A Word Geography of the Eastern United States* (Ann Arbor, 1949). This work gives a detailed explanation of the Eastern areas, with helpful maps.

[7] George Philip Krapp, *The English Language in America* (2 vols., New York, 1925), I, 35–42.

are shown on the accompanying map.[8] The "Yankee" settlement is consistent in using Northern words, and the area to the south of it is almost
without exception Midland. Between the two major areas, some smaller
transition areas of mixed usage occur.[9] The Lead Region of northwestern

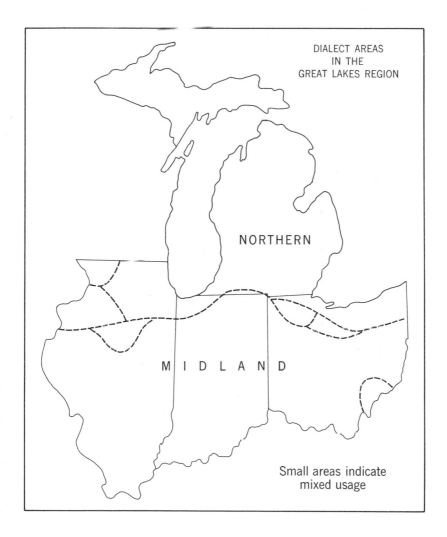

DIALECT AREAS
IN THE
GREAT LAKES REGION

NORTHERN

M I D L A N D

Small areas indicate
mixed usage

[8] The atlas records have been augmented by a correspondence questionnaire given to 233 informants in these four states. See Alva L. Davis, "A Word Atlas of the Great Lakes Region"
(unpublished doctoral dissertation, University of Michigan, 1948). It should be noted that
most of the information thus far obtained is from the older age group.

[9] Raven I. McDavid, Jr. and Alva L. Davis, "Northwestern Ohio: a Transition Area," *Language,* XXVI (1950), 264–273, is a preliminary study of one of these areas.

362   Illinois reflects its different settlement history by the retention of many
Midland forms, and the Marietta region retains many Yankeeisms.[10]
The following words, arranged according to their Eastern distributions,
may be used to demonstrate the folk vocabulary differences in the Great
Lakes Region:

NORTHERN WORDS

A. General North:

pail; swill, "food for hogs"; *comforter,* "tied quilt"; *johnnycake; whiffletree; boss!,* "call to cows"; *angleworm; (devil's) darning needle,* "dragonfly"; *sick to his stomach*

B. Hudson Valley:

stoop, "small porch"; *sugar bush,* "sugar maple grove"; *coal scuttle*

C. The North except the Hudson Valley:

spider, "cast-iron frying pan"; *dutch cheese,* "cottage cheese"; *fills,*
"shafts of a buggy"; *nan(nie)!* and *co-day!,* "calls to sheep"; *curtains,*
"roller shades"; *scaffold,* "improvised platform for hay"; *rowen,* "second
crop of hay"

D. Western New England and Upstate New York:

fried-cakes, "baking powder doughnuts"; *loppered milk,* "thick, sour
milk"; *hard maple,* "sugar maple tree"

This group of words, as a whole, is limited to northern Ohio, Michigan,
and northern Illinois, with rare instances in the Midland area. Those
words restricted to subareas of the East—as in B, C, D—do not make any
definite geographical patterns within the Great Lakes northern area,
though further research may show that some new subareas are to be set
up.[11] Most conspicuous is the fact that many of these words are becoming
old-fashioned, being supplanted by words of wider regional and national
usage, or being forgotten with changes in customs. *Johnnycake* is a childhood memory for many speakers, *dutch cheese* and *fried-cakes* are now

[10] Among the Yankee terms in the Marietta area are *pail, swill, dutch cheese, boss!,* and *angleworm.* In the Lead Region are found *roasting ears, sook!,* and *fishworm.*

[11] *Sewing needle,* "dragonfly," for example, is current in the Upper Peninsula of Michigan and
in the Duluth area of Minnesota.

cottage cheese and *doughnuts* most commonly, the *whiffletree* (sometimes *whippletree*) and the *fills* (or *thills*) are of little use in a tractor and automobile age, the old *spider* is likely to be an aluminum frying pan, and the more fashionable term *window shades* is taking the place of *curtains*. Rarest on this list are *scaffold, rowen,* and *loppered milk* (sometimes *lobbered milk*): the general terms are *loft* or *mow*—the improvised platform is now a permanent structure in the modern barn—*second cutting,* and *sour milk.*

MIDLAND WORDS

A. General Midland:

quarter till (eleven); blinds, "roller shades"; *skillet; dip,* "sweet sauce for pudding"; *sook!,* "call to cows"; *sheepy!; fish(ing) worm; snake feeder,* "dragonfly"; *poison vine,* "poison ivy"; *belling,* "noisy celebration after a wedding"

B. North Midland:

spouting, "guttering at edges of roof"; *smearcase,* "cottage cheese"; *hay doodles,* "small piles of hay in the field"; *sugar camp,* "sugar maple grove"; *baby buggy*

C. South Midland:

fireboard, "mantlepiece"; *clabbered milk,* "thick, sour milk"; *trestle,* "implement to hold planks for sawing"

D. South Midland and South:

evening, "afternoon"; *light-bread,* "white bread"; *clabbered cheese,* "cottage cheese"; *hay shocks,* "small piles of hay in the field"; *nicker,* "noise made by horse at feeding time"

E. Midland and South:

dog irons, "andirons"; *bucket; slop,* "food for hogs"; *comfort,* "tied quilt"; *pully bone,* "wishbone"; *corn pone,* "corn bread"; *cherry seed; butter beans,* "lima beans"; *roasting ears,* "corn-on-the-cob"; *singletree; polecat; granny woman,* "midwife"; *Christmas gift!,* "familiar greeting at Christmas time"

NOTE—No terms limited to the South are common in this region.

364   The General Midland words are in common use in the Ohio Valley, though *poison vine* is obsolescent, and *blinds* may be. *Belling* is now common only in Ohio and scatteringly in northern Indiana and southern Michigan; it has been replaced in most of the area by *shivaree*, the most common term in the Middle West.[12]

The North Midland contains many expressions which are common only in Ohio; some of them have spread into Indiana (especially the northern part of the state), and occasionally they are found in Illinois. *Spouting* is restricted to Ohio; *hay doodle* is old-fashioned in Ohio and Indiana and very rare in Illinois; *sugar camp* is most common in Ohio and Indiana; and *smearcase* is common in Ohio, Indiana, and most of Illinois (*clabbered cheese* is fairly common in southern Illinois and Indiana). These North Midland words as a group form an irregular wedge-like pattern: generally current in Ohio, occasional in Indiana, and rare in Illinois. The Upper Ohio Valley may be the home of *baby buggy*, which is now the most usual of the words for the perambulator in all of the Great Lakes Region. It is, of course, a trade term, and therefore little affected by settlement patterns. The *Dictionary of American English* gives 1852 as the first date for *baby wagon*, the earliest of the terms.

The South Midland has few terms of its own; in vocabulary it seems to be a transition zone between the North Midland and the South. Words typical of the region are those listed, along with *sugar orchard; ridy horse,* "seesaw"; *pack*, "carry"; and *favor*, "resemble." None of these words is especially common in this region, but they are most frequent in the southern portion.

Words common to large parts of the South and the South Midland are well represented in the Great Lakes Midland, and for this reason these terms have been included with the Midland group. They seem to be slightly less common in Ohio than in Indiana and Illinois, further differentiating these subareas. *Light-bread*, for example, is only fairly common in Ohio, but is the prevailing term of southern Indiana and southern Illinois. *Nicker* has probably spread from the Virginia Piedmont; it is common in the entire Great Lakes Midland, even spreading into southern Michigan.

The words shared by the Midland and the South are also well distributed in the Great Lakes Midland, but many are becoming old-fashioned. *Dog irons* become the modern "andirons," *corn pone*, like Northern *johnnycake*, has yielded to "store-bought bread," the general term *skunk* occurs alongside *polecat*, and few communities have a *granny woman* to deliver the babies. *Christmas gift!*, usually a children's greeting, is rather

---

[12] See McDavid and Davis, " 'Shivarre': an Example of Cultural Diffusion," *American Speech,* XXIV (1949), 249–255.

rare in the region, but information is not sufficient to tell whether it was ever more widely used here.

The evidence of regional differentiation shows, in this comparison, surprisingly little disturbance of the "expected" dialect patterns, in spite of the steady leveling influences of national advertising, ease in transportation with its resultant mobility of population, intermarriage, and changes in modes of living. These influences have tended to blur some regional differences, but the vocabulary of everyday usage is so extremely conservative that there is far from complete uniformity. As yet there is no indication that trade and culture centers have developed distinctive dialect areas as has happened in the case of Boston and some Southern cities.[13] The dialect information makes, instead, a faithful reconstruction of the settlement patterns. The significance of this historical comparison, even in its present incompleteness, is that speech habits are brought into the realm of historical fact—the usage of the word *spider*, for example, becomes as real as the use of the Cape Cod lighter or the hip-roofed barn.

---

[13] *Tonic*, "soda-pop," is one of the terms current in the Boston trade area. The prestige of Boston pronunciation is well known.

The Primary Dialect Areas of the Upper Midwest

Harold B. Allen

With the completion of the fieldwork for the *Linguistic Atlas of the Upper Midwest*, of which Professor Allen is director, it was possible to make statements concerning the extension of Atlantic Coast varieties of English into the Upper Midwest. It is an area in which Northern and Midland features mingle. In this article Harold Allen discusses a number of lexical, phonological, and morphological features of the speech of the region and their incidence. He is Professor of English and Linguistics at the University of Minnesota.

In 1949 Hans Kurath, drawing on the materials of the three Atlantic Coast atlases for his *Word Geography of the Eastern United States,* made obsolete the traditional tripartite division of American English into East-

From Studies in Language and Linguistics in Honor of Charles C. Fries, ed., Albert Marckwardt. (Ann Arbor: English Language Institute, University of Michigan, 1964) pp. 303–314. Published under the title "Aspects of the Linguistic Geography of the Upper Midwest." Reprinted here under its original title with the permission of the English Language Institute and Harold B. Allen.

ern, Southern, and General American. Four years later his overwhelming lexical evidence for the existence of what is now called the Midland dialect between the Northern and the Southern areas was supplemented by E. Bagby Atwood's *Verb Forms of the Eastern United States* with its showing that many nonstandard forms are distributed according to the dialect divisions outlined in Kurath's study.

By implication both works raised the question: How far do the principal Atlantic Coast dialect boundaries extend west of the Appalachians? For the immediately contiguous area in the northern part of the country a tentative answer appeared some time ago in a preliminary review of the data collected under the direction of Albert H. Marckwardt for the *Linguistic Atlas of the North Central States*. These unpublished data would suggest that the principal dialect areas in the North Central states are reflexes of the Midland–Northern areas along the Atlantic Coast. The major bundle of Midland–Northern isoglosses stretches west to the Mississippi so that roughly the northern third of Ohio, the northern fourth of Indiana, and the northern third of Illinois lie north of the bundle; that is, in a territory settled largely by people who had moved westward from the Northern speech areas of northern Pennsylvania, New York State, and western New England. South of the bundle lies derivative Midland and South Midland speech territory.

The recent completion of fieldwork for the *Linguistic Atlas of the Upper Midwest* now makes possible for the first time a definitive demonstration of Midland–Northern relationship in the region immediately west of the North Central states. It is the function of this paper to delineate that relationship rather than to establish a correlation between dialect patterns and population history, but a brief covering statement may provide a framework for the language information.

Settlement in the five states designated as the Upper Midwest—Minnesota, Iowa, North and South Dakota, and Nebraska[1]—began with the first inrush of English-speaking families shortly before the Civil War. Into northern Iowa and southeastern Minnesota came settlers from western New England and New York State and from their secondary settlements in Ohio, Michigan, and northern Illinois, and even Wisconsin. Into central and southern Iowa—but with a large overflow into Minnesota—came settlers from the mid-Atlantic area, principally Pennsylvania, and from the derivative settlements in Ohio, Indiana, and Illinois. And also into southern Iowa came a third group, smaller but distinctive, with its source in the earlier movement westward through the Cumberland Gap into Kentucky and thence into southern Indiana and southern Illinois. Gradually, though with waves roughly corresponding to economic cycles,

---

[1] These states have an area of 365,297 square miles and, in the 1950 census, a population of 7,931,298.

368   population spread after the Civil War into western and northern Minnesota, the Dakotas, and Nebraska, reaching some parts of the extreme western sections as late as 1910.[2] This later spreading was caused by an influx of newcomers having the same three origins, by a second westward move on the part of families who already had settled in Minnesota or Iowa, and to a very large measure by the massive advent of thousands of immigrants directly from non-English-speaking countries in Western and, later, Eastern Europe. For all these except the last, the following delineation of the principal Upper Midwest dialect divisions will permit reasonable inferences about the population distribution even though fully detailed treatment of the settlement history must await the future publication of the Upper Midwest Atlas. That in this area such inferences can be drawn safely without regard for any influence of the non-English-speaking immigrants has already been ascertained.[3]

Evidence for the dialect divisions described here is almost entirely that provided in the field records of 206 informants interviewed by fieldworkers between 1947 and 1956. Of this number, 102 are classed as Type I (older and uneducated or old-fashioned), 88 as Type II (middle-aged with high-school education), and 16 as Type III (younger with college education). Except for about twenty-five additions, the questionnaire used is essentially that of the short worksheets of the New England Atlas and of the worksheets of the North Central Atlas. The additions were of some general items thought to be productive, such as *slick* and *boulevard*, and of other items intended to probe lexical differences in the vocabulary of the cattle country west of the Missouri River. Besides the general body of data there is available a supplementary resource in the marking of 136 lexical items on checklists returned by 1064 mail informants in the five states. For these particular 136 items, therefore, there actually is evidence from 1270 informants. Although it is statistically unsound to add the returns from the two groups together in light of the lower validity of the mailed responses, the latter often turn out to have a strong confirming value.

Even though full analysis of the data is only now under way, the preliminary analysis of replies to more than 125 items in the full questionnaire offers clear evidence for the establishment of the primary isogloss patterns shown on the accompanying map. Replies to some two dozen others indicate a gradual dialect variation corresponding to these

---

[2] The region adjacent to the extreme western boundary between the Dakotas had no significant permanent settlement, for example, until the Milwaukee railroad extended its line west to the Pacific Coast in the late 1900's. Previously, of course, a sparse handful of cattle ranchers had occupied the region for three or four decades.

[3] Support for this statement was offered by the writer in a paper, "The Validity of the Use of Informants with Non-English-Speaking Parentage," read before the Linguistic Society of America in Chicago, December 29, 1955.

primary divisions, one so gradual that it can more effectively be shown by percentage comparisons. By "primary" is meant "reflecting Midland–Northern differentiation as carried west by population movement." Secondary patterns, those reflecting ecological, commercial, or other influences peculiar to the Upper Midwest, will be treated in another article for publication elsewhere.

Of the primary patterns revealing Midland–Northern differentiation the major isogloss bundle is shown on the map by the 1–1 line, with certain deviations represented by the a-1 line. (All references to the symbols on the map will read from right to left in conformity with population movement.)

The 1–1 boundary represents generally the northern limit of the following lexical items: *scum* (of ice), *firedogs, bucket* (of metal), *slop* (-*pail* or -*bucket*), *coal oil, nicker, piece* (a distance), *piece* (a lunch), (*died*) *with, slick* (of a pavement), and *taw* and *taw-line*. Of these items *firedogs, bucket, slop-, coal oil, nicker, piece* (distance), and *piece* (lunch) are shown in the

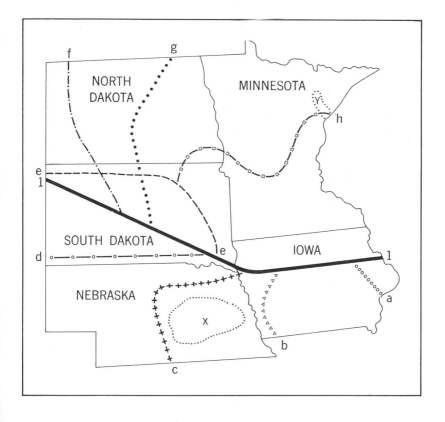

370   *Word Geography* (*WG*) as typical Midland or South Midland forms. Inferentially, the other items may be considered as having at least a typical Midland distribution pattern in the Upper Midwest, although *slick* cannot be checked with materials of the other atlases since it is one of the added items.

Phonological matters occurring largely in this Midland area are /mɪniz/ *minnows*, /ɛ/ in *since*, and /k/ in *spigot*.

The a-1 boundary, which presumably indicates the presence of a strong Northern population element in the Iowa triangle set off by Davenport, Cedar Rapids, and Dubuque, is the northern limit for Midland *draw* "shallow valley," *light bread, snake-feeder,* and *belly-buster,* as well as for the nonstandard morphological item *clum,* the preterit of *climb.* Of these *light bread, snake-feeder,* and *belly-buster* are attested as Midland in the *WG;* and *clum* is similarly classified by Atwood.

The 1–1 boundary is also the southern limit in the Upper Midwest for the common *slough* /slu/ "swamp," *griddle cake,* and the infrequent *quite (cold),* and for the phonological items /ɑn/ *on* stressed, /ɛ/ in *scarce,* /ɔ/ in *caught,* /hj/ in *humor,* and /ɑ/ in *nothing.* Of these, *griddle cake* is dominantly Northern in the *WG,* and /ɑ/ for *o* is revealed as Northern (though not eastern New England) in the *Linguistic Atlas of New England* and in an unpublished summary by Atwood.

The a-1 boundary appears as the southern limit of Northern lexical features such as *devil's) darning-needle* "dragonfly"[4] and *belly-flop,* but of no phonological items. Both of these are of frequent occurrence despite competition with a considerable number of other Northern regionalisms.

Study of the lesser areas within the principal Midland zone reveals at least three isogloss bundles which may represent successive waves of Northern and Midland population, although the first bundle may well indicate also the extension of South Midland features into this area.

The Midland lesser area included within a-1-b or 1-b, southern Iowa, is marked by the occurrence of *spouting* "eavestrough," *branch* "stream," *dogbit, pullybone* "wishbone," *sook!* "call to cows," *corn) pone, sick in* and *sick on* (*one's stomach*), *drying cloth, -towel,* or *-rag* "dishtowel," *french harp* "harmonica," and *rack* "sawbuck," among the lexical evidence, and by fronted beginning of the /au/ diphthong as in [kæʊ] *cow* and by the /e/ in *Mary,* among the phonological evidence. South Midland origins are likely for the infrequent *dogbit* and *pullybone;* the others presumably are Midland.

---

[4] Open and closed parens ( ) denote an explanatory item, such as *curtains* (on rollers). Use of) or (indicates that a whole phrase—such as *devil's) darning needle* or *cling (peach*—was used by the informant, but that Allen wants to draw attention to a certain portion—*darning needle* and *cling.* [Ed. note]

The second Midland lesser area includes southern Iowa and the eastern half of Nebraska below the isogloss line 1-c. Like the first lesser area, it is marked by the appearance of exclusively Midland forms, although the boundary marks also the southern extension of two Northern pronunciation features. Lexical inclusions are *weather-boarding, barn) lot, plumb across, fice(t* "small dog," /pui/ and /hoi/ as calls to pigs, *chickie!, clabber cheese* and *smearcase, barn owl, polecat,* and *baby cab.* Phonological matters include /rɛntʃ/ for *rinse,* /kæg/ *keg, tushes* for *tusks,* /ʌ/ in *rather,* and /ʊ/ in *Cooper.* At the same time the 1-c bundle includes one isophone and one isomorph limiting two expanding Northern forms, /æ/ in *married* and *dove* as the preterit of *dive. Dove,* incidentally, is significantly dominant with all types of speakers despite repeated pedagogical injunctions against it.

The third Midland lesser area, 1-d, includes the southern two-thirds of Iowa and all of Nebraska. Its main lexical features are *till* (in time expressions), *blinds, dust up (a room, comfort* "bedcovering," *pallet, paving* "rural concrete highway," *dip* "sauce for pudding," *hull* (of a walnut), *butter beans, snake-feeder,* and *sick at (one's stomach. Sick at,* which competes with two other Midland regionalisms, interestingly enough is often listed in textbooks as standard in contrast to the dominant Northern form *sick to.* A conspicuous nonstandard phonological characteristic in this area is the excrescent /-t/ on *trough* and *eavestrough.*

At the same time the 1-d bundle serves to set off a fourth area between 1-d and 1-1, southwestern South Dakota, in which is found the maximum extension of a few Northern forms, *parlor match, haycock,* and *tarvy* or *tarvia* for a macadamized road. Of these only *parlor match* was reported as used in Iowa. The *tarvy* item may require further study, as its incidence could be related to variables not related to population distribution.

Although detailed investigation of the Type distribution of each of the terms in these three lesser areas would be needed before accurate classification of each as expanding or receding, a reasonable inference would seem to be that, in general, Midland forms limited to these areas are receding, or at least checked, and that Northern forms found here are expanding.

The converse, then, may with equal reason be inferred with respect to the Midland and Northern forms whose distribution is marked by the isogloss bundles setting off the lesser areas north of the main dialect boundary, 1-1. There appear to be four such lesser isogloss bundles, 1-e, 1-f, 1-g, and 1-h, designating the limits of expanding Midland or checked or receding Northern forms.

Isogloss bundle 1-e, for example, clearly represents the northern limits of the Midland *armload* and *seed* (as in both *cherry-seed* and *peach-seed*), which are found in nearly all of South Dakota. They compete with

372   Northern *armful* and *stone*. On the other hand, it appears to represent also the limit of the rather infrequent Northern expression *pothole*. This last term was not recorded in Minnesota or Iowa during fieldwork, but checklist returns show a spotty frequency in Minnesota in addition to the recorded uses in North Dakota.

Similarly, the boundary l-f is chiefly comprised of isoglosses showing the northern expansion of Midland terms. Here in northwestern South Dakota and western North Dakota the Midland *hayshock* and *haydoodle* have successfully competed with the receding Northern *haycock*. Midland *mouth harp* likewise is found here as far north as the Canadian border; so are Midland *bottoms* or *bottomland, roasting-ears,* and the locution *want off/in.* Only one apparently Northern word has so far been found to be limited by l-f, *boulevard.* This term was not included in any eastern atlas study, so that no comparative data are available except some isolated occurrences reported in private correspondence from northern and central Ohio. However, in the sense "strip of grass between sidewalk and street," this term patterns exactly like a typical Northern word, and strong confirmation of this patterning is found in the responses on the checklists.

Although the line l-e, g, setting off the eastern Dakotas, does indicate the full northern expansion of several Midland terms, it largely denotes the limited western extension of Northern forms which probably are receding or checked. Midland forms which have spread widely, if sparsely, as far as Canada are: *evening* "time before supper," *cling peach, took sick, come back* and *come back again,* and *the baby) crawls.* Northern words rarely found beyond this boundary are *the wind) is calming (down* (mostly in Minnesota), *curtains* (on rollers), *red up* and *rid up, whipple-* or *whiffletree, cluck (hen* "brooding hen," *fried cakes* "doughnuts," and *skip school.* Even in the North Central states the Midland *singletree* was unaccountably well on its way to supplant *whippletree* before the advent of the tractor. The Northern term now appears obsolescent. In addition, several Northern pronunciation items are seldom recorded beyond this boundary: /ɑ/ in *fog* and *foggy,* /gul/ *goal,* /draut/ "drouth," /sut/ *soot,* and /bdrəl/ *barrel.* The last three of these apparently are old-fashioned, used almost exclusively by Type I speakers. The receding and infrequent Northern /klɪm/, nonstandard preterit of *climb,* also occurs only within this lesser area. /ɑ/ in *fog,* it is curious, is obviously receding, while the /ɑ/ in stressed *on,* contrariwise, is expanding with vigor.

Boundary l-e, h, enclosing principally northern Iowa and southern Minnesota with a small margin of South Dakota, chiefly sets off the extreme extension of receding Northern forms. Among them appear to be *spider* "frying pan," *fills* or *thills, brook* "fishing stream" (only in Minnesota), *feeding time,* /ho/ "call to a horse," /kəde/ "call to sheep," *lob-*

bered milk, and *sugarbush.* Also apparently receding Northern forms are
the pronunciations with /θs/ or /ðz/ in *troughs* and *eavestroughs* and /e/
in *dairy,* and the morphological feature *see* as the preterit of *see.* At least
two Midland forms are found throughout the Upper Midwest except in
this limited area, possibly because of reinforcement by population influx
through Duluth. One is *rock,* as in *He threw a rock at the dog;* the other
is *bawl,* to describe the noise made by a cow.

The regional patterns which have been outlined above are slightly
complicated by the presence of at least one enclave and perhaps another.
The area marked X on the map contains a number of Northern forms
not reported generally in southern Iowa or elsewhere in Nebraska. Its
existence probably is to be correlated with the migration of a number
of New York and Ohio families into the eastern Platte River valley after
the Civil War. Within or marginal to this enclave, for example, both
parents of two informants came from New York and the mother of another was born there. One informant reported both parents born in Ohio;
another reported his mother's birthplace in that state. Besides, one informant's father came from Illinois and both parents of another came
from Wisconsin. All other informants are of foreign-born parentage.
Among the hence presumably Northern forms which appear in the Platte
River valley are *parlor match, haycock,* /hoʊ/, /kəde/, *fried cake, boulevard,*
and *quite (cold,* in addition to the pronunciations /ɑ/ in *fog* and *foggy,*
/ɔ/ in *caught,* and /hj/ in *humor.*

The putative second enclave is designated by Y on the map. It includes
Duluth, Minnesota, and communities along the Mesabi iron range. Considerable investigation is called for by the appearance in this area of a
number of Midland forms. Although no one informant has consistent
Midland speech (not one of them has a Midland background), the frequency with which Midland items occur points to a possible Midland
influence because of the contacts between Duluth, a major port, and the
Lake Erie ports of Sandusky, Cleveland, and Erie, which are not far from
the Midland territory of southern Ohio and Pennsylvania. Lexical items
with usual Midland distribution which turn up in this enclave are *cling*
(peach, blinds, lot, bucket (of metal), *spigot* "faucet," *bag* (of cloth), *arm-*
load, coalbucket, bawl, chickie!, dip "sauce," *hull* (of walnut), *butter bean,*
come back again, died with, and *took sick.* Phonological forms recorded
here include /e/ in *chair* and *Mary,* /ʊ/ in *spoons* and *Cooper,* /ɔ/ in *on,*
and /wo/ "call to horse."

But the description of the Midland–Northern differentiation in the
Upper Midwest is by no means complete in terms of isogloss boundaries.
As the existence of the various "lesser areas" reveals, a number of Northern terms have been recorded in various parts of that principal Midland-
speaking territory which is set off by the main isogloss bundle 1-1; and,

374   correspondingly, a number of Midland terms have been recorded north of that bundle. Clearly the Midland–Northern distinction becomes less sharp as the dialect boundary is followed westward. The distinction is clearest in Iowa; it has so far broken down in South Dakota that that state might well be designated a transition area. Actually the degree of the breakdown is much greater than the map would suggest, for the diffusion of many a dialect feature is so gradual that an isogloss cannot be drawn for it. Rather, recourse must be made to percentage of frequency.

For nearly all forms already cited, the distribution patterns are so clear that isoglosses may be drawn with some certainty. For example, a quick glance at a map bearing symbols marking the occurrence of *comfort, comforter,* and *comfortable* is adequate for one to be able to draw the isogloss of *comfort,* which is clearly limited to the Midland l–d area. To establish its distribution pattern there is no need to resort to a study of the percentages. The statistics merely confirm the obvious. How percentages are related to such a clear pattern may be seen in the figures for *comfort:*

0	2
0	
25	35

This table, in which the figures are arranged so as to correspond spatially with the relative positions of the Upper Midwest states, is to be read like this: Two per cent of the Minnesota field informants replying to this particular question use the lexical variant *comfort,* thirty-five percent of those in Iowa, none in either of the two Dakotas, and twenty-five percent of those in Nebraska.

Such a table should now be compared with the following, which shows the percentage of frequency of occurrence of *poison* in the locution "Some berries are poison" (in which it contrasts with *poisonous*):

31	29.5
50	
54	39

Reference to a map bearing symbols for the occurrences of *poison* would indicate no possibility of drawing an isogloss. Even the slight differences in percentage at first appear to be insignificant, easily due to the variables that operate when informants are interviewed by different fieldworkers. But when a corresponding differential appears with item after item, and when each variation correlates consistently with the Midland–Northern contrast, then the gradation must be recognized as significant and not accidental. Examination of numerous tabulations now makes clear that, regularly, some attested Midland forms not susceptible of delimitation by isoglosses occur with greatest frequency in Iowa and Nebraska, less in South Dakota, still less in Minnesota, and, usually, least in North Dakota. Conversely, some attested Northern forms appear regularly with highest percentages in Minnesota and North Dakota, less in Iowa and South Dakota, and least in Nebraska. Since the percentages have been calculated on the artificial basis of the political boundaries, actually the figures are more significant than at first sight, for the Midland percentage for Iowa would be still higher if the informants in the Northern-speech territory of the two upper tiers of counties had been counted in Minnesota rather than in Iowa. The reverse, of course, would hold true for a Northern form, which would have a lower frequency in Iowa if the northern third had been counted in with Minnesota.

Now even though the spread in the percentages for *poison* is not great —between 29.5 and 54—the spread clearly indicates a higher rate of occurrence in Midland territory. Similar spread appears in the percentages ascertained for these words:

the sun) came up		*skillet*		*paper) sack*	
11.5	10.5	27	49.5	70	55
27		65		85	
40.5	22	81	90	81	73

Of these, *skillet* is shown in the *WG* to be the dominant Midland term, with only a scattered handful of instances reported along Long Island Sound. It would seem to be expanding with some vigor in the Upper Midwest, and the checklist replies confirm this expansion. The figures for *sack* may be questioned, but they conversely match those for *paper bag*, which appears to have a slight Northern dominance.

With the phonological items recourse to percentage analysis is particularly productive, for matters of pronunciation seem much less likely than vocabulary items to be characterized by fairly distinct regional patterns. Yet regional variation on a graduated scale appears when the statistics are examined for such as these:

/sʌt/ *soot*		/-waɪn/ in *genuine*	
19	25	56	66
24		59	
30	31	62	73

/-ə/ final in *wheelbarrow*		/ɑ/ in *wheelbarrow*	
19	22	10	22
27		8	
30	50	22	39

/ʊ/ in *root*		/θ/ in *with milk*	
38	23	36	34
25		42	
40	46	41	52

/æ/ in *razor-strap*	
46	37
48	
47	49

A Midland emphasis appears also in the distribution of a few morphological items which do not have sharp isoglottic patterning. With each of these items the variation is heard from only Type I and Type II informants:

bushel (pl. after numeral)		*who-all?*		*begun* (pret.)		*drownded*	
36	40	51	57	0	6	19	19
52		57		0		43	
50	72	78	66	11	19.4	14	35

At least two lexical items exhibit Northern weighting in their distribution:

paper) bag		*warmed up*	
73	74	62.5	62.5
56		61.5	
40	58	38	28

Phonological responses revealing Northern emphasis are:

/bɑb/ *wire*		/ɑ/ in *harrow*		/ɪn/ in ppls. and gerunds	
23	16	16	33	59	82
19		7		47	
11	10	6	12	48	46

Two morphological items may have Northern weighting also, the non-standard inflected genitive *anywheres* (contrasting with *anywhere* and *anyplace*) and the preterit *fitted*:

anywheres		*fitted*	
23	19	28.5	22
16		17	
13	11.7	8	14

Although certainly most of the Upper Midwest worksheet items classed in the eastern atlases as either Midland or Northern reveal, to some extent at least, the same correlation, there are a few for which the evidence is puzzling and will require some special investigation if not supplementary collecting. *Clean across,* for instance, is reported in the *WG* as a "regional phrase" current along the South Atlantic coast; but in the Upper Midwest it turns up twice only in Midland Iowa and Nebraska, four times in South Dakota, and five times in North Dakota. *Mosquito hawk* "dragonfly" is reported in the *WG* only along the South Atlantic coast from southern New Jersey to South Carolina (although Raven I. McDavid, Jr., has additionally recorded a few scattered occurrences in upper New York); in the Upper Midwest this variant shows distinct Northern distribution with its seven occurrences in Minnesota and four in North Dakota but none in either Iowa or Nebraska. *Buttry,* according to Kurath, "is unknown in the Hudson Valley and in the entire Midland and South." Yet as a relic term it appears not only in Minnesota but also in the Midland speech area of Iowa and Nebraska. *Lead-horse,* according to the *WG,* is limited to Midland and South Midland areas; as a relic in the Upper Midwest it has fairly even distribution in the five states. *Fishworm* was recorded frequently in both New England and New York as well as in South Midland territory; in the Upper Midwest it is exclusively Midland. Both the field records and the checklists show that *angleworm* is the overwhelmingly dominant form in the Northern speech regions of the Upper Midwest. *Firebug* is reported in the *WG* as a Pennsylvania vocabulary variant for *firefly,* with only a solitary instance in New York. But in the Upper Midwest the percentage distribution surely is not Midland:

15.4	9.5
16	
2.7	1

Furthermore, the checklist responses number 45 in Minnesota and North Dakota with only ten in Iowa and nine in Nebraska. *Raised* in "The sun raised at six o'clock" Atwood calls Middle Atlantic, but in the Upper Midwest it occurs as a rare nonstandard form seven times north of the 1-1 boundary and only four times in Midland territory south of it.

In summary:

1) The primary Midland–Northern dialect contrast of the Atlantic Coast states is maintained in the Upper Midwest.

2) The distinction is particularly clear in the eastern half of the Upper Midwest, that is, between the lower two-thirds of Iowa and the upper third of Iowa.

3) The distinction is less clear in the western half, that is, west of the

378 Missouri River, where splitting of the major isogloss bundle reveals several lesser dialect areas delimiting expanding or receding forms.

  4) In general, Northern speech forms seem to be yielding to Midland.

   a. The principal isoglosses bend northward, even to the point of indicating a complete blocking of some Northern terms.

   b. Most of the expanding forms are Midland; most of the receding forms are Northern.

   c. Diffusion appears to be more intensive for Midland forms in Northern territory, especially in Minnesota, than for Northern forms in Midland territory, especially southern Iowa.

  5) One Northern enclave occurs in Midland territory; a probable Midland enclave occurs in Northern territory.

The Pronunciation of English in the Pacific Northwest

Carroll E. Reed

The Pacific Northwest was settled primarily by people from the Northern and Midland areas. The speech of the area has, as might be expected, many of the features of the speech of these areas. In this article, Professor Reed describes the pronunciation of vowels and consonants of the Pacific Northwest area and comments on the incidence of selected phonemes in a number of words. Carroll Reed is Professor of Germanic Language and Literature at the University of Massachusetts. Among his publications is *Dialects of American English* (1967), a useful introduction to this subject.

As has been pointed out on several occasions,[1] varieties of American English spoken in the Pacific Northwest are largely derived from Eastern

From *Language,* Vol. 37, No. 4 (1961), 559–564. Reprinted with the permission of the Linguistic Society of America and Carroll E. Reed.

[1] Carroll E. Reed, "The Pronunciation of English in the State of Washington," *American Speech* 1.186–9 (1952); id., "Word Geography of the Pacific Northwest," *Orbis* 6.86–93 (1957); David W. Reed, "Eastern Dialect Words in California," *Publication of the American Dialect Society* 21.3–15 (1954).

380   sources. A good deal of information is already available on the geographical distribution of vocabulary throughout the United States, so
that dialectologists now have a fairly clear idea of lexical continuity in
the vast areas of Western settlement. For this reason it has become
standard procedure to identify dialectal types within these areas in ac-
cordance with the criteria presented by Hans Kurath in his *Word Geography of the Eastern United States* (Ann Arbor, 1949). A monumental
work by Kurath and McDavid on the pronunciation of English in the
Atlantic States has now been published,[2] and new comparisons of dialect
distribution East and West are therefore in order.

In the matter of pronunciation it is possible to examine not only the
incidence of certain phonetic types among the items furnished by the
Atlas questionnaire,[3] but also the basic aspects of phonemic structure in
various idiolects. In this way, a kind of typology can be developed synop-
tically for extended areas of transition. For the purpose of describing
and epitomizing "regional dialects" on a given speech level, therefore,
Kurath and McDavid have devised a large number of "synopses" showing
vocalic incidence among cultivated speakers in the Atlantic States. Individual deviations around such norms have then been dealt with chiefly
from the standpoint of their function as representatives of a phonemic
structure.

The amazing complexity of variations thus revealed is especially striking when the relatively clear-cut distribution of lexical items in the *Word
Geography* is recalled. If pronunciation remains so variegated in older,
longer established colonial areas, what are the linguistic results of their
proliferation in areas of eventual resettlement? The files of the *Linguistic
Atlas of the Pacific Northwest,* incomplete though they are, give an answer to this question.

In general, it seems reasonable to expect that the proportions of regional representation already observed in connection with vocabulary
will also hold good for pronunciation. Synoptic examination of phonemic
patterns, moreover, represents a new approach to the study of dialect
variation. It is at least the first step toward the establishment of a structural dialectology, in the light of which, it may be hoped, some of the
fundamental facts about language change will eventually be brought to
light.

The following treatment of Northwest pronunciation will be concerned
with the reflection of Eastern variants in Washington, Idaho, and adjacent

[2] Hans Kurath and Raven I. McDavid, Jr., *The Prnunciation of English in the Atlantic States*
(Ann Arbor, 1961).

[3] *Work Sheets of the Linguistic Atlas of the Pacific Coast,* selected and adapted by David W.
Reed and David DeCamp (1952) from *A Compilation of the Work Sheets of the Linguistic Atlas
of the United States and Canada,* by Raven I. and Virginia McDavid (Hans Kurath, ed.), (1951).

sections of Oregon and Montana. Foremost among the things to be investigated here are the elements of phonemic structure and the distribution of phonetic data in selected sets of examples.

Vowels

Most native speakers in the Pacific Northwest have the following vocalic nuclei or slight variations of the same:

[i] *three, grease*
[ɪ] *six, crib, ear, beard*
[e] *eight, April*
[ɛ] *ten, egg, head, Mary, stairs, care,* *(married)*
[ɚ] *thirty, sermon, furrow*
[æ] *bag, glass, half, aunt, (married)*
[a] *father, crop, palm, barn, garden,* *borrow*
[aᴵ] *five, twice, wire*

[u] *two, tooth*
[ʊ] *wood, pull, (poor)*
[o] *ago, coat, road, home, know*

[ʌ] *sun, brush*
[ɔ] *forty, morning, corn, horse, (poor)*
[aᵁ] *down, out, flower*

[ɔᴵ] *joint, boil, oil*

A partial list of vowel phonemes can be given as follows: /i ɪ e ɛ æ a ə o ʊ u ai oi au/.[4] There seems to be no reason why [ɚ] cannot be analyzed as /ər/, and, so far, at least, why [ɔ] in *forty* cannot be classed as a variety of /o/ before /r/. In the examples given, furthermore, it should be noted that distribution occasionally varies: /ɛ/ ~ /e/ in *egg* and *Mary*, /ɛ/ ~ /æ/ in *married*, /æ/ ~ /a/ in *half, glass, aunt*, and /u/ ~ /o/ in *poor*.

A low-back rounded vowel is widely represented in *chocolate, moth, coffee, office, frost, sausage, costs, daughter, caught, law, saw, haunted, long, strong, log, fog, dog, launch, haunches, walnut, wash, always, warmed, on, watch, water, swallow,* and *wasps*. With some speakers this may be regarded as an allophone of /a/. Wherever an opposition such as *cot* ≠ *caught*, [a] ≠ [ɒ], is maintained, another vowel phoneme must be posited.

In the speech of some people, the words *forty, horse,* and *morning* contain a low-back rounded vowel which is distinguished from the higher back vowel in *four, pour, hoarse,* and *mourning*. The latter can, in such instances, be regarded as an allophone of /o/, and the vowel of *forty* etc. can be assigned to /ɔ/; the [ɒ] of *caught, log* etc. and the [ɔ] of *forty, horse* etc. can be defined as positional variants of /ɔ/. The maximum list of vowel phonemes thus analyzable is /i ɪ e ɛ æ a ɔ ə o ʊ u ai oi au/. For speakers who have neither of the oppositions /o/ ≠ /ɔ/ and /a/ ≠ /ɔ/,

---

[4] Without wishing to criticize either the "binary" or the "unitary" analysis of vocalic segments, I am adopting the unitary system here, because it facilitates comparison of dialect data.

382 a phoneme /ɔ/ is, of course, not pertinent. Further mention of such cases will be made below.

A few speakers also have the vowel [ɵ] in *home, coat,* and *road.* While it is theoretically possible to recognize a phoneme /ɵ/ in this case, it seems more reasonable to regard this [ɵ] as a free variant of /o/. Because of the weak opposition of [a] and [ɒ] in such pairs as *cot ≠ caught,* the same argument might be suggested for /ɔ/; here, however, the more widespread use and function of /ɔ/ would seem to militate in its favor, particularly with respect to its occurrence before /r/.

Consonants

The inventory of consonants used in the Northwest is almost identical with that given by Kurath and McDavid for the Atlantic States: /p t č k b d ǰ g f θ s š v ð z ž m n l r ŋ w j h/. There is no lack of preconsonantal or postvocalic [r] in this area, and the "linking [r]" is nonexistent. Other matters pertaining to consonant distribution will be dealt with below.

Dialect Variation

The incidence of alternate phonemes or allophones in Northwest English may be considered in three ways, with reference to (1) relative frequency, (2) geographical occurrence, and (3) social correlation. The following outline of linguistic data is divided first according to the relative frequency of the items examined, after which comments are added on geographical or social factors wherever the facts permit.

The first form predominates; the second is infrequent to rare:

[æ] in *glass, half, aunt, can't*	[a] used by a small number of cultured speakers.
[o] in *coat, road, home*	[ɵ] used by a few older people around Port Townsend.
[ɔ¹] in *oil, boil, joint*	[ɑ¹] used by an older speaker in the Port Townsend area.
[ʊ] in *pull*	[ʉ] sporadic in the Port Townsend area, also in southeastern Washington.
[ʊ] in *butcher*	[u] used by an older speaker in the Port Townsend area.
[u] in *blew, suit, two, tube, Tuesday, new, chew, due*	[iu] commonly a prestige form, occurring most often on the east side of Puget Sound.
[i] in *Negro*	[ɪ] infrequent
[ɪ] in *ear, beard*	[i] used by a few older speakers.
[ɪ] in *crib*	[ɪə] occurs in eastern Washington, Oregon, and Idaho.

[ɪ] in *bristles* — [ɨ] rare.

[ɛ] in *again* — [ɪ] occasionally around Puget Sound.

[ɛ] in *chair* — [ɛ¹] sporadically in eastern Washington.

[ɛ] ~ [æ] in *wheelbarrow* — [ɑ] rare.

[ɛ¹] [ɛ] in *egg, keg* — [e¹] [e] infrequent.

[ɛ] [ɛ³] in *deaf* — [i] used by a few older speakers.

[ɛ] in *Mary* — [ɐ] used by some older speakers.

[ɛ] in *married* — [æ] used by some older speakers.

[ɑɚ] in *hearth* — [ɚ] used by some speakers in the Puget Sound area.

[a] in *garden, barn, borrow, to-morrow* — [ɒ] generally infrequent, concentrated in the Puget Sound area.

[a] in *on, calm, haunches, water, watch, swallow, wasps, warmed* — [ɒ] generally infrequent, concentrated in the Puget Sound area.

[ɒ] in *chocolate, moth, coffee, office, frost, costs, sausage, law, saw, daughter, caught, long, strong, fog, dog, log, haunted, launch, walnut, always, wash* — [a] used in all of these to some extent, especially in eastern Washington, Oregon, and Idaho.

[ɔ] in *oranges* — [a] ~ [ɒ] rare.

[ʌ] in *bulk, bulge* — [ʊ] rare.

[ʌ] in *brush* — [ʌ¹] ~ [ɛ] occasionally in southeastern Washington and in Idaho.

[ʌ] in *gums* — [u] used occasionally in the Port Townsend area.

[ʊ] in *put* — [ʌ] rare.

[ʊ] in *soot* — [u] used by cultivated speakers.

[ʊ] in *hoofs,* especially on the west side of Puget Sound. — [u] infrequent, concentrated in eastern Washington.

[u] in *coop* — [ʊ] rare.

[ɑᵁ] in *mountain, house, drought* — [a°] used by some speakers in southeastern Washington, Oregon, and Idaho.

Stressed vowels are generally the same in the pairs *hoarse–horse, mourning–morning, four–forty;* they are opposed in the speech of some speakers in southeastern Washington and adjacent sections of Oregon and Idaho, occasionally also in the Port Townsend area.

[o] in *yolk* — [ol] and [ɛl] rare, the latter restricted to a few older speakers.

[ɚ] in *stirrups* — [ɪɚ] and [ɛɚ] rare.

[i] in the final syllable of *Missouri* — [ə] used by some speakers in southeastern Washington and a few in the Puget Sound area.

[hj] in *humor* — [j] rare.

384   [hw] in *whinny, whip, wheel-*   [w] infrequent.
        barrow
    [w] in *wheat, wharf*   [hw] infrequent.
    [a/ɒ] in *wash*   [aʳ/ɒʳ] used only around Puget Sound.
    [ð] in *without*   [θ] infrequent.
    [s] in *greasy*   [z] rare.
    [f] in *trough*   [θ] used by a few older people.

Items of nearly evenly divided usage follow; the more frequent form is given first.

[ɛ] in *catch*	[æ]	[ʊᶦ] in *push*	[ʊ]
[ɛ] in *wheelbarrow*	[æ]	[ʊ] in *roof*	[u]
[ɛ] in *parents*	[æ]	[ʊ] in *roots*	[u]
[æᶦ] in *bag*	[æ]	[ʊ] in *hoops*	[u] in cultivated speech.

[t] in *drought*, used by cultivated speakers.   [θ]

Relation of Eastern to Northwestern Dialect Variants

A quantitative examination of like variants in the Atlantic States and the Pacific Northwest shows the following general correlations.

(a) Items of widespread occurrence in the Atlantic States are also common in the Pacific Northwest, e.g. [æ] in *half*, [u] in *due*, [a] in *tomorrow*, [u] in *roof*, [ʊ] in *soot*, [ɪ] in *crib*, [ʌ] in *brush*, [ɛ] in *egg*, *deaf*, and *again*, [aɚ] in *hearth*.

(b) Northern and North Midland forms are strongly represented in the Pacific Northwest, e.g. [ɪ] in *creek*, [ɛ] in *chair*, [ɛ] in *Mary* and *married*, [ʌ] in *bulk* and *brush*, [ɔ] in *oranges*, [o] in *Negro*, [ʊ] in *roots* and *hoops*, [aᵁ] in *house* and *drought*.

(c) Midland forms are in a minority generally, but they are more prominent in eastern Washington, Oregon, and Idaho, e.g. [ɪᵊ] in *crib*, [ʌᶦ] ~ [ɛ] in *brush*, [θ] in *without*, [i] in *creek*, [ʊ] in *pull*, [ʊ] in *bulk* and *bulge*, [aᵒ] in *house* and *drought*. Such forms are especially prevalent when they are matched in some Northern areas, e.g. [a] in *water*, [u] in *roots*, and [ʊᶦ] in *push*.

(d) Northern forms are particularly frequent in the Puget Sound area, notably on the west side of the Sound; Midland forms are concentrated in and around Seattle.

(e) The old New England settlement area at the northwest entrance to Puget Sound (here called "the Port Townsend area") preserves a number of New England relic forms, e.g. [ɵ] in *home, coat,* and *road,* [a] occasionally in *glass, aunt,* and *can't,* [e] in *Mary,* initial [j] in *humor,* [a] in *sausage, haunted,* and *long,* [aᶦ] in *oil,* [u] in *butcher* and *gums.*

Some of the forms in this area are found in both New England and the

South Atlantic States, but settlement history would indicate that they are probably to be connected only with the former, e.g. [ʊ¹] in *push*, [ʊ] in *pull*, [e¹] ~ [e] in *egg* and *keg*, and [ɒ] in *fog*. A few speakers around Port Townsend, as well as some others in southeastern Washington, also distinguish opposing vowels in the pairs *hoarse-horse, mourning-morning*, and *four-forty*. It seems highly probable that the two areas inherit this peculiarity from two different eastern sources, that is, from the North and from the South Midland respectively.

(f) Minor folk forms of the Atlantic States also occur sporadically in the Northwest, e.g. [ɪ] in *again*, and [i] in *deaf*.

(g) Prestige forms, occassionally adopted by educated speakers, include [iu] in *Tuesday* and *suit*, [a] in *aunt* and *can't*, [u] in *soot*, and [hw] in *wheat*.

Comparative Structures

There seems to be no significant difference in the vocalic structure of cultured and uncultured speakers in the Pacific Northwest. The basic set of phonemic oppositions here involved equals generally those designated by Kurath and McDavid as belonging to Type 1, which is peculiar to speakers in upstate New York, eastern Pennsylvania, and the South Midland.[5] A total of fourteen vowel phonemes is thus to be posited: /i ɪ e ɛ æ a ɔ ə o ʊ u ai oi au/. A considerable proportion of speakers, however, have only thirteen vowel phonemes, lacking a separate /ɔ/. This system corresponds to Type IV, characteristic of speakers in western Pennsylvania. A notable difference, however, can be observed on the subphonemic level: in the Northwest, /a/ is a low-central unround vowel with slight retraction before /l/ and in some other positions, whereas the Pennsylvania phoneme seems to be more frequently low back rounded. Northwest speakers using this system are predominantly younger and better educated, living chiefly in eastern Washington and Idaho, where Midland characteristics are relatively more common.

From the arrangements of examples in Kurath and McDavid's synopses, it may be noted that the incidence of vocalic phonemes varies appreciably, even among cultured speakers, in the Atlantic States. Similar checking of individual speakers in the Northwest also reveals great variability, but within a more limited range of difference; that is to say, the impositions of dialect provenience very largely restrict the range of possible deviation, while the treatment of any extensive set of examples is characterized by a number of unique combinations.

[5] Op. cit. 6–7.

386   It is, of course, difficult to estimate the extent to which given dialect variants, phonemic or allophonic, have been influenced in their distribution by successive irregular mixtures of settlers coming to the Northwest. In addition to the substantial influx of people from the upper Middle West and from New England, various other groups of immigrants must be taken into account. Contributions of Scottish and Irish speakers to Northwest English (the Irish particularly in Idaho) are difficult to assess, and the effect of Scandinavian and German speakers throughout the Pacific Northwest can hardly be measured at the present time.

Conclusions based on lexical analysis tend to be confirmed by the observations subsequently made in regard to pronunciation. The residual effects of Northern and North Midland speech forms are readily demonstrable in the Pacific Northwest, and a proportionate distribution of dialect variants is clearly in evidence. Especially notable in this regard are the elements of phonemic structure.

part **5**

SELECTED SOUNDS AND FORMS

The New England Short o̲: A Recessive Phoneme

Walter S. Avis

There are very few differences in the phonemic systems
of the major dialects of American English. One of these
occurs in New England speech. The phoneme known as
"New England short *o*" probably occurs in all parts of
New England, but it is now recessive. Professor Avis
discusses this phoneme, its incidence, and its realization.
Professor of English at the Royal Military College of Canada,
Dr. Avis has been editor-in-chief of *A Dictionary of
Canadianisms* and co-editor of *A Dictionary of Canadian
English*.

   This study is intended to illuminate the highly recessive nature of the
"New England Short *o*." The varying stability of the feature from word
to word and from region to region and the extent of divided and unsettled usage from community to community and speaker to speaker pro-

From *Language*, Vol. 37, Pt. 4 (1961), 544–559. Reprinted with the permission of the Linguistic Society of America and Walter S. Avis.

390   vide an unusual glimpse of a linguistic phenomenon long recognized but never adequately documented.[1]

The data used in this investigation are those of the *Linguistic Atlas of the United States and Canada,* housed at the University of Michigan; much of the relevant material has been published in the *Linguistic Atlas of New England,*[2] where the phonetic detail for most of the words referred to below may be found. It should be added that much of what follows is taken from my doctoral dissertation, which was written under the direction of Hans Kurath and which dealt primarily with the status of nonupgliding mid-back diaphones throughout the Eastern United States.[3]

One of the major areas of concentration for nonupgliding phonic types in words like *road* and *coat* is New England, where a highly complex situation exists, for here such diaphones occur only in a limited number of phonetic environments, and in a relatively small number of words, virtually none of which show these types exclusively. In view of this complexity, it is impracticable to present the results of the analysis for the area as a whole; the greater part of the discussion will therefore be based on the *Atlas* records for the Northeastern region, specifically those of Guy S. Lowman, recorded in eastern Vermont, New Hampshire, northeastern Massachusetts, Maine, and southwestern New Brunswick, Canada.[4]

This limitation, in addition to rendering the data manageable, has several advantages. (1) The area includes a large sample of evidence, some 137 informants in 85 communities; (2) it also includes most of the informants who use ingliding diaphones with a significant degree of regularity; (3) the data are uniform, having been recorded by one fieldworker, one of the most competent of those operating in New England;[5] (4) the problem of fieldworker differences in notation can be by-passed, a problem that is more troublesome at the phonetic than at the phonemic

[1] See Charles H. Grandgent. "From Franklin to Lowell: A Century of New England Pronunciation." *PMLA* 14.207–39 (1899).

[2] Edited by Hans Kurath, Bernard Bloch, and others; 6 vols. (Providence, 1939).

[3] Walter S. Avis, The mid-back vowels in the English of the eastern United States: A detailed investigation of regional and social differences in phonic characteristics and in phonemic organization (University of Michigan, 1955: unpublished doctoral dissertation, available in microfilm).

[4] The area referred to is substantially that shown as Area 1 among the speech areas of the Atlantic States in Hans Kurath and Raven I. McDavid, Jr., *The Pronunciation of English in the Atlantic States,* Map 2 (Ann Arbor, 1961). See the line of demarcation drawn on Figure 1 below.

[5] See Hans Kurath, Bernard Bloch, Marcus L. Hansen, and Julia Bloch, *Handbook of the Linguistic Geography of New England* 52–3 (Providence, 1939; second printing 1954).

level;[6] (5) the findings for this area provide a reliable index for the incidence of similar diaphones throughout New England, although as one moves westward from the Northeastern region and away from the East generally, the feature becomes progressively less common and less stable.

In Northeastern New England, then, a set of upgliding diphthongs is regularly found in words like *ago* and *know*, whereas in words like *road* and *smokestack* similar upglides are found together with a set of very different ingliding or monophthongal types, which do not have the same incidence from word to word and which do not necessarily occur in all words of similar phonetic environment. Thus, the ingliding diphthong occurs widely in *road* but not at all in *rode* and seldom in *Rhode Island;* the related monophthong occurs widely in *smokestack*, less widely in *yoke*, and very rarely in *woke*. Such evidence strongly implies the existence of two phonemes.

The phonetic norm for the stressed vowel in *ago* is a diphthong, beginning in a somewhat lowered mid-back position and ending with a prominent upglide, [oˇu]. It should be noted that neither ingliding diphthongs nor monophthongs occur in *ago* or any other word in which the phones occur word-finally.

A similar set of upgliding diphthongs occurs in *road*, and alongside these occurs a set of ingliding diphthongs and monophthongs. The phonetic norm for the latter set is a diphthong, beginning in a fronted and lowered mid-back position and ending with a prominent inglide, [ɵə]. The monophthongal types differ from the diphthongs only in the absence of the inglide. They occur rarely in *road*, more often in *back road, side road,* and similar compounds. The diphthongal types occur predominantly in *toad, stone, coat,* and *boat*, whereas the monophthongal types occur most often in *toadstool, stone wall, stone walk, smokestack, folks, most,* and *whole*. It should be noted that all such diaphones occur only in checked position.[7]

A study of the diaphones [ɵə] and [ɵ] in *road, coat,* and *whole* reveals clear contrast with the diaphones in *good, caught,* and *hull*, indicating that [ɵə/ɵ] do not belong to the phonetically similar and adjacent phonemes /ʊ/, /ɔ/, and /ʌ/. Furthermore, for most speakers the diaphones [ɵə/ɵ] are in contrast with [oʊ] diaphones in such identical or analogous environments as *road/rode, coat/shoat, most/coast, home/loam,* and *whole/knoll*. In these pairs the first member usually has [ɵə/ɵ]; the second member never has these phones.[8] It follows from the foregoing evidence that

[6] See Avis 106 ff.

[7] For a full description of the diaphones recorded, see Avis 81 ff. For a succinct discussion of free and checked vowels, see Kurath and McDavid 3–5.

[8] See Avis 92 (Table 14) for a detailed listing of such contrasts.

392   [ɵə/ɵ] and [ou] belong to different phonemes, which will henceforth be referred to as /ɵ/ and /o/ respectively.[9]

The phoneme /ɵ/ has two dominant positional allophones, an ingliding diphthong and a monophthong, though the alternation is not necessarily clear-cut for every speaker. Probably because of varying prosodic conditions, both types occur to some extent in nearly all the words. Nevertheless, the tendencies are abundantly clear when the total number of responses are taken into consideration: ingliding diphthongs of the type [ɵə] predominate in monosyllabic words before the front stops /t/ and /d/ and before /n/; monophthongs of the type [ɵ] predominate before the back stop /k/, before the fricatives /s/ and /z/, and before /m/.[10] The predominance of one allophone or the other appears to vary according to the position of the morpheme containing the phone: if the morpheme is final, as in *wishbone, freestone, clingstone, grindstone, whetstone,* the usual allophone is that commonest in the simplex (e.g. *stone*), in all instances here listed an ingliding diphthong, though it should be observed that the proportion of monophthongs has in all cases increased; if the morpheme is not in utterance-final position the monophthong appears to predominate, as in *smokestack* (100%), *railroad station, Rhode Island, toadstool,* and *stone wall.* In the few instances where [ɵə] or [ɵ] occur in polysyllabic words, the monophthong also predominates, as in *soldiering, poultry, bonny clabber, harmonica,* and *suppose.* Two other allophones merit mention: a half-long vowel in *home* and, much less commonly, a markedly short vowel in compound words having the relevant morpheme as the first component, e.g. *smokestack, toadstool, stone wall,* and *Rhode Island.*

To make clear the incidence of the phoneme /ɵ/ in the *Atlas* materials for the Northeastern region the following inventory is presented. It will be convenient to gather the words concerned, all of which have been fully charted for the entire New England area, into four groups: (1) those words of reasonably wide dissemination which often have /ɵ/, and a number of others which have a relatively low incidence of /ɵ/ but figure prominently in the discussion; (2) those words for which /ɵ/ was recorded but which for one reason or another are sparsely represented in the data (sporadically recorded compounds containing simplexes listed in Group 1 are shown in parenthesis after the relevant word in that group); (3) those words of reasonably wide dissemination in which /ɵ/ occurs rarely in the data; and (4) those words in which /ɵ/ does not occur at all in the Lowman materials.

---

[9] The unitary interpretation of syllabics adopted here has most recently been defended in Kurath and McDavid 3–5. See also Avis 7–8.

[10] See Avis 94 (Table 15) for a statement of the proportional occurrences of these allophones in 32 words, including compounds.

GROUP 1. These words form the basis for the greater part of the discussion concerning the status of /ɵ/: *boat* (*stone-, motor-*), *coat* (*over-*), *smokestack* (*smoked meat*), *folks* (*home-, kin-*), *most, 'most* "almost," *toad* (*hop-, tree-,* etc.), *toadstool, road* (*dirt-, side-,* etc.), *railroad station, Rhode Island, home, stone* "pit" (*cherry-, peach-*), *stone* "rock" (*-boat, -road*), *stonewall, grindstone, whetstone* (*soup-*), *wishbone* (*pully-, lucky-*), *holt* "hold," *soldiering* "loafing," *whole, yoke.*

GROUP 2. The number of occurrences with /ɵ/ in total occurrences follows each entry: *goat* 1/1, *open* 4/11, *broken* 1/1,[11] *cloak* 4/5, *kofe* 5/15 (a call to cows), *loads* 26/32, *pogey* 18/78 "menhaden," *scupogue* 1/1 "menhaden," *toast* 1/4, *close to* 36/46 (all instances of *close* /kloz/ have //o), *suppose* 39/48, *none* 5/5, *colt* 1/1, *hold* 3/17, *poultry* 25/25, *swollen* /swoln/ 21/75, *yolk* 72/105 (/jolk/; /jok/ without /l/ always has the upglide), *bonny clabber* 54/132, *harmonica* 25/113.[12]

GROUP 3. The number of occurrences with /ɵ/ in total occurrences follows each entry: *oats* 5/132, *cove* 2/102, *posts* 1/134, *post office* 3/133, *don't* 1/137, *doughnut* 4/137, *sofa* 3/138, *tuberculosis* 1/115.

GROUP 4. Words for which the data are scant are marked with an asterisk: *shoat, *toted, write, yolk* /jok/, *pokey* "haunted," *loafing, coast, *ghosts, *wardrobe, rode, blowed, growed, *throwed, dove, drove, grove, stone, close* /kloz/, *clothes, froze, rose, those, *toes, *loam, grown, coal, *hole, *goal, pole, *rolls, *stole, swollen* /swolən/, *cold, old, shoulder, *crocus bag, grocery, hotel, motor car, *motorboat, over, *robust, social, *soda, ago, blow, blowing, beau, *below, depot, *doe, *ewe* /jo/, *glowworm, go, know, low* "moo," *low shoes, lowland, mowing, *no, *show, *throw up, *crowbar.*

It is obvious from the foregoing inventory that the phoneme /ɵ/ occurs in a limited number of words and in an even more limited number of environments, substantially those outlined in the statement concerning positional allophones. It is also obvious from Groups 3 and 4 that /ɵ/ does not occur in word-final position (that is, as a "free vowel") and occurs rarely in polysyllabic words where it precedes a morpheme boundary (*doughnut*) or in so-called open syllables (*sofa*). Even in checked position /ɵ/ occurs in a relatively small number of words, and its incidence varies strikingly from word to word. With respect to the words in Group 1, those for which there is a meaningful amount of evidence, no speaker uses /ɵ/ exclusively, and (in the Northeastern region) very few use /o/ exclusively. In some of the words, the former phoneme predominates throughout the

---

[11] Informant 160.2 in Billerica "uses [ɵ] at home in such words as *coat, broken,* but avoids it in public speaking" (fieldworker's comment).

[12] It appears that /gɵnə/ in the context *am I going to* . . . occurs surprisingly seldom among a wide variety of pronunciations.

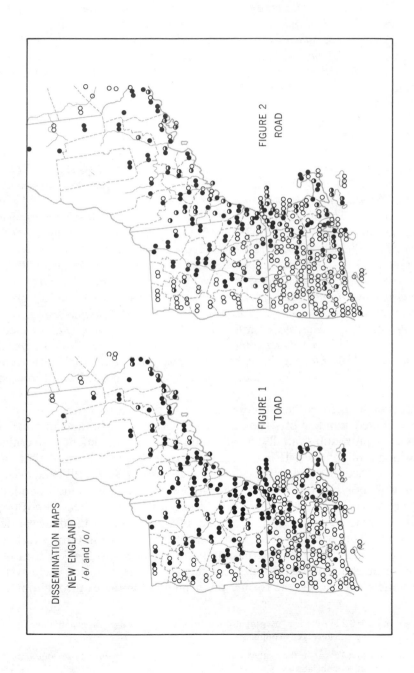

DISSEMINATION MAPS
NEW ENGLAND
/θ/ and /o/

FIGURE 1
TOAD

FIGURE 2
ROAD

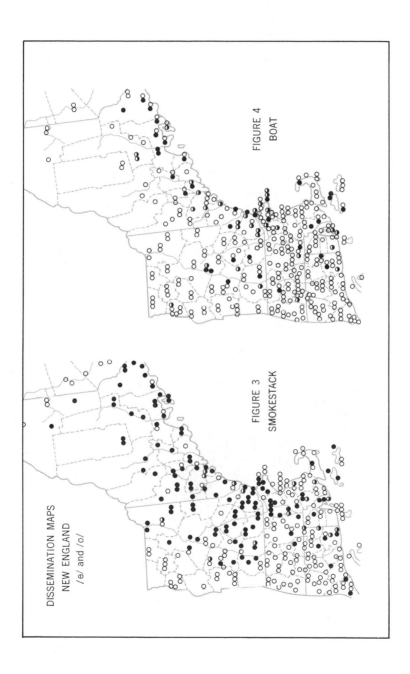

DISSEMINATION MAPS
NEW ENGLAND
/ɵ/ and /o/

FIGURE 3
SMOKESTACK

FIGURE 4
BOAT

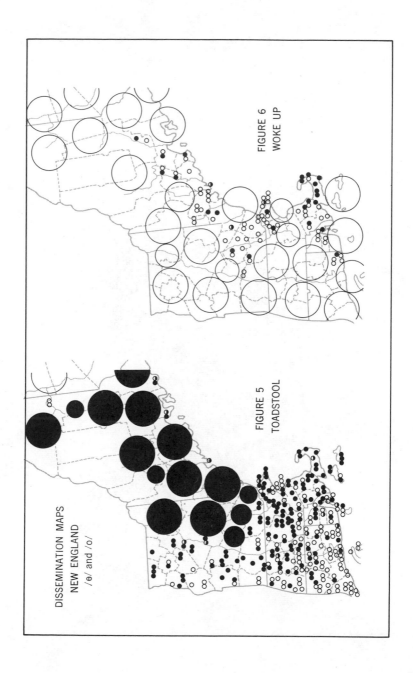

DISSEMINATION MAPS
NEW ENGLAND
/ɵ/ and /o/

FIGURE 5
TOADSTOOL

FIGURE 6
WOKE UP

region, in others the latter. In short, unsettled usage is everywhere the rule from word to word and often from utterance to utterance of the same word. Almost everywhere, moreover, the informants in whose speech the /ə/ phoneme is most stable are members of the older and/or the less-educated social group, especially those in rural or relatively isolated communities.

The evidence for the Northeastern region clearly indicates that /ə/ is to a considerable extent recessive and for this reason has a highly complex regional and social dissemination. This conclusion is reinforced when the evidence for the entire New England area is taken into consideration. Figures 1–6 show the over-all distribution pattern for the words *toad* (Figure 1), *road* (2), *smokestack* (3), *boat* (4), *toadstool* (5), and *woke up* (6).[13] On the maps, a solid circle represents a pronunciation with /ə/, an open circle a pronunciation with /o/, and a half-solid circle pronunciations with both /ə/ and /o/ by the same speaker. The first four maps, showing words in which /ə/ is relatively unstable in the Northeastern region, chart the usage of every informant; the last two, showing words in which either /ə/ or/o/ is relatively stable, chart separately only the instances of unsettled or divided usage, but represent the remaining instances by large circles which indicate uniform use of one phoneme or the other.

As appears from the maps, the incidence of /ə/ varies from word to word, often quite markedly even in Northeastern New England. Thus /ə/ is much more commonly heard in *road* than in *boat*, in *smokestack* than in *woke up*, and so on. This variation can be grasped more readily by comparing the proportional-response figures in Table 1, which shows for the Northeastern region the proportion of informants using /ə/, either alone or beside /o/, in each word, as opposed to the proportion using /o/, either alone or beside /ə/. By comparing the entries opposite each word, one can see both the degree of stability of /ə/ in that word and the tendency to recessiveness from word to word. In the table, the first column shows the relative incidence of /ə/, the second shows the proportion of speakers using only that phoneme; comparison of these two figures indicates the extent of unsettled usage in the word. Columns 3 and 4 give corresponding figures for /o/. Column 5 shows the proportion of all informants who used the word in question, with /ə/ or /o/ or both. All figures in the table are percentages.

Table 1 shows, for example, that in *toad* /ə/ was used by 90% of the informants, whereas in *road* it was used by 81%. Moreover, in *toad* /ə/

---

[13] The following maps in Kurath and McDavid illustrate other words discussed in this article: 20 *ago;* 30 *coat, whole,* and *stone (wall);* 121 *ewe* /jo/; 123 *home;* 124 *loam;* 125 *won't;* 126–8 *yolk.*

398   was used to the exclusion of /o/ by 69% of the informants, whereas in *road* the proportion using /ə/ exclusively was only 57%. The first comparison indicates that /ə/ is more common in *toad* and the second that the phoneme is also more stable. In both of these words, however, the "short *o*" is more common than in *Rhode Island* and less common and less stable than in *railroad*, in which 12% and 94% respectively of the informants responded with /ə/. Further comparisons using other words on the table which have roughly similar phonetic environments will reveal similar disparities, a fact which suggests that the phonetic environments, limited in range though they are, are not the only factor which determines the presence or absence of /ə/ in a given word.

The comparative figures on Table 1 suggest that prosodic factors also exert an influence on the incidence and stability of /ə/. It will be noticed that when the simplexes containing the phoneme appear as parts of compound words, the stability of /ə/ is regularly greater in the latter; cf. *stone wall, whetstone, grindstone, freestone, toadstool, railroad,* and *Rhode Island,* to which may be added *stoneboat, hoptoad,* and *post office.* The higher stability of /ə/ in such compounds is so regular that it seems reasonable to predict that in *smoke* and *bone,* simplexes not recorded for the *Atlas,* /ə/ would be both less common and less stable than in *smokestack* and *wishbone,* both of which appear on Table 1 (p. 399).

Sentence stress and speed of utterance, not clearly identifiable from *Atlas* evidence, appear also to have some connection with the stability of the /ə/ phoneme. The high stability of the phoneme in *whole,* taken in the frame *the whole of it,* seems to be a case in point; certainly the presence of /ə/ before final /l/ is most unusual, for *whole* regularly fails to rime with *pole, knoll,* and *hole,* although evidence for the last is scant. Probably the fairly frequent occurrence of /ə/ in *'most anywhere, I suppose so,* and *am I gonna go?* can be attributed to similar obscure influences.

But neither phonetic environment nor prosodic influences account for all of the variations in the stability of /ə/. Certain factors associated with what may be called "social context" seem to have an important bearing on the presence or absence of /ə/. Thus a word current largely in popular or dialectal speech is more likely to retain /ə/ than a word learned in school. Again, a word which occurs in a relatively limited social environment, for example on the farm, in the family circle, or as a variant peculiar to a certain limited speech area, will more probably have /ə/ than a word in wide general use. Finally, /ə/ will be retained longer in words with a relatively low frequency of use than in others which have a high frequency and which, consequently, are more affected by the movies and radio, to say nothing of outside influences of other kinds.

The significance of such factors as these is implied in Table 1, where the words with /ə/ are ranked according to the stability of the phoneme.

WORD	/ə/	/ə/ ONLY	/o/	/o/ ONLY	Proportion of informants
holt	97	97	3	3	62
whole	95	89	11	5	89
railroad station	94	94	6	6	60
yolk	93	93	7	7	51
toadstool	93	90	10	7	94
whetstone	93	90	10	7	96
toad	90	69	31	10	97
folks	90	86	14	10	78
grindstone	89	88	12	11	95.5
stone wall	89	86	14	11	98.5
freestone	85	83	17	15	58
stone "pit"	85	68	32	15	96
home	84	80	20	16	95
'most midnight	83	79	21	17	70
road	81	57	43	19	99.5
wishbone	79	72	28	21	94.5
smokestack	75	69	31	25	75.5
coat	74	36	64	26	99
most cheeses	71	61	39	29	88
yoke	62	57	43	38	87
soldiering	53	53	47	47	57
boat	31	15	85	69	81
swollen /swəln/	23	23	77	77	54.5
Rhode Island	12	12	88	88	88
woke up	9	8	92	91	85

At the top of the list is *take* (*a*) *holt* (i.e. *hold*), in which 97% of the informants responding used /ə/, all of them exclusively. The high degree of stability for /ə/ in this word is undoubtedly due to the social context in which the expression occurs, for the expression itself is colloquial and the pronunciation /həlt/ for *hold* popular or dialectal. Column 5 reveals that only 62% of the informants offered this response, a low yield due in part to the currency of competing variants, but more importantly to the fact that the pronunciation /həlt/ is relatively uncommon among younger, better-educated informants, especially those in urban areas. It is significant that twenty informants, mostly of this class, offered the expression with the pronunciation /hold/, which like *old* and *cold* has /o/ almost exclusively; /həld/ occurred only three times in the area.

The fact that /ə/ has a higher incidence and greater stability in *whetstone* than in the simplex *stone* is probably due in part to prosodic factors

400 but also to the different social contexts in which the words are used. The former is strictly a farm word, that is, a word used in a relatively limited environment, whereas the latter has a much wider range and also a much greater frequency of use. Several of the words on the list fall into the same rustic category, as *toadstool, stone wall,* and *grindstone.* Moreover, the disparity between the incidence and stability of /ə/ in these words and in such words as *road* and *coat* seems attributable in part to similar influences.

It is illuminating in this regard to compare *toad* and *road* (Table 1), both simplexes in which the phoneme precedes the same final consonant. In *toad,* a word of relatively limited milieu and correspondingly low frequency of use, the incidence and stability of /ə/ are quite high; in *road,* which has a much broader milieu and a much higher frequency of use, the incidence and stability of /ə/ are both appreciably lower. Note, however, that certain less widely used terms—*side road, dirt road, tote road*— occur with /ə/ in the *road* component in the speech of many informants who use /o/ in *road.* Similarly, speakers who use /o/ in *stone* and/or *boat* often use /ə/ in less frequent compounds containing these words, as *stone wall, stoneboat, steamboat, boatlanding.* A speaker may use /o/ invariably in *coat,* but retain /ə/ in the word when it occurs in a particular context, as *coat of paint.*

The position of the preterit *woke* at the bottom of Table 1 is striking. Occurring in the context *woke up* (Figure 6), under prosodic conditions making for stability of /ə/, the word has a far lower incidence of that phoneme than *yoke,* which occurs as a simplex and which, moreover, is a book word for many people, the referent having fallen into disuse. Certain facts in the evidence may explain this apparent anomaly.

Throughout the Northeastern region the preterit *woke up* competes with the variant *waked,* for which there were seventy-five responses.[14] Of these, twenty-eight were suggested by the fieldworker, and many of the informants designated the form as "older," "old-fashioned," or "rare"; on the other hand, several who offered *woke up* designated it "modern." *Waked* must have been formerly of much wider dissemination than at present.[15] It is not unlikely that *waked* was displaced relatively late, perhaps through the schools, by *woke up* /wok/. The evidence also shows that of /ə/ and /o/, the latter is the usual, almost invariable, phoneme in verb forms, as *rode, froze, drove,* and *dove,* a fact which again suggests school influence.

The word *boat* (Figure 4) is another striking example, ranked near the bottom of Table 1. /ə/ is common in this word only among the older,

[14] See E. Bagby Atwood, *A Survey of Verb Forms in the Eastern United States,* Fig. 20 (Ann Arbor, 1953).

[15] Atwood, 25.

COMMUNITY	N.B. 431		Me 422		N.B. 426-7		MAINE 412		406		386		360		352		NEW HAMPSHIRE 302		310		324		328		340		348		MASS 194		200		156		VERMONT 257-8		294	
TYPE	2A	2B	1A	2A	1A	1A	2A	2B	2A	2B	2A	3A	1A	2A	1B	2B	2A	2B	1A	2A	1A	1A	1A	3A	1A	2A	1A	2A	2A	2A	1A	2A	1A	2A	2A	2A	2A	2B

Legend: ● /θ/ ◐ /θ/ ~ /o/ ○ /o/

Communities (left to right): WOODSTOCK-BRIGHTON, FORT FAIRFIELD, ST. STEPHEN-ST. CROIX, CALAIS, GOULDSBORO, WALDBORO-NOBLEBORO, PORTLAND, YORK, SEABROOK, BELMONT-LOUDON, ANTRIM, KEENE-MARLOW, HAVERHILL, CONWAY, NEWBURY, ROCKPORT, CONCORD, NEWFANE-ROCKINGHAM, RYEGATE

WORD																																						
WHETSTONE	○	○	○	●	●	●	●	●	●	●	●	○	●	●	●	●	●	●	●	●	●	◐	●	●	●	●	○	●	●	●	●	●	○	●	●	●	●	●
TOADSTOOL	○	○	○	○	●	●	●	●	●	●	●	●	●	●	●	●	●	●	●	●	●	●	●	○	●	●	●	●	●	◐	●	●	○	●	●	●	●	◐
WHOLE	○	○	○	●	●	●	●	●	●	−	●	○	●	●	●	●	●	●	●	●	●	●	●	●	●	●	○	●	●	●	−	−	●	●	●	●	◐	◐
HOME	○	○	○	◐	●	●	○	○	●	●	●	●	●	●	●	●	●	●	●	●	●	◐	●	●	◐	●	●	○	◐	●	●	●	●	−	●	●	●	○
STONEWALL	○	○	○	−	●	●	●	●	−	●	●	◐	○	●	●	●	●	●	●	●	◐	●	◐	●	◐	●	●	●	◐	●	●	●	●	●	●	●	●	○
FOLKS	−	−	○	○	●	●	◐	●	●	●	−	●	●	●	●	●	●	●	●	●	●	●	●	−	●	●	●	○	●	●	○	○	●	●	●	●	●	○
SMOKESTACK	○	○	○	○	●	●	●	●	●	○	−	−	○	◐	○	◐	●	●	●	●	◐	◐	●	○	●	●	●	−	●	●	○	○	●	●	●	●	−	○
WISHBONE	○	○	○	●	●	●	●	●	◐	◐	◐	−	○	●	●	●	●	●	●	●	◐	◐	○	○	◐	●	●	●	●	●	○	○	●	●	○	●	●	○
STONE	○	○	○	◐	●	●	●	●	◐	◐	●	−	○	●	◐	●	●	●	●	●	●	◐	●	●	●	●	●	◐	◐	●	●	●	●	●	●	●	●	○
TOAD	○	○	○	●	●	●	◐	◐	◐	◐	●	◐	○	◐	◐	○	●	●	●	●	◐	◐	○	○	●	●	●	●	◐	●	◐	◐	●	●	●	●	◐	◐
YOKE	○	○	○	◐	●	●	●	●	●	−	○	○	○	●	●	○	◐	●	◐	○	◐	◐	○	●	●	●	●	◐	●	●	◐	◐	●	●	○	●	○	○
ROAD	○	○	○	●	●	●	◐	◐	◐	◐	●	◐	○	◐	◐	○	●	●	●	◐	◐	◐	◐	○	○	●	●	◐	●	◐	◐	◐	◐	●	●	●	○	○
COAT	○	○	○	◐	●	●	◐	◐	◐	◐	●	●	◐	◐	●	●	◐	◐	●	●	●	−	○	○	●	●	◐	◐	◐	◐	○	◐	◐	◐	◐	●	◐	○
BOAT	−	○	○	○	○	−	○	○	●	○	−	○	○	○	○	●	●	●	◐	○	○	○	◐	−	○	◐	○	○	○	●	●	◐	●	−	○	○	○	○
RHODE ISLAND	○	○	○	○	−	○	○	○	○	○	●	○	○	○	●	●	●	○	○	○	○	◐	○	○	●	●	○	○	◐	●	○	○	○	○	○	○	○	○
WOKE UP	○	○	○	○	○	○	○	○	○	○	−	○	○	○	○	○	○	−	○	○	●	○	○	○	○	○	○	○	○	○	○	−	○	○	○	○	−	○
OATS	○	○	○	○	○	○	○	○	○	○	○	○	○	○	○	○	○	○	○	○	○	○	○	−	○	○	○	○	○	○	○	○	○	○	○	○	○	○
SHOAT	○	○	○	○	○	○	○	○	○	○	○	○	○	○	○	−	○	○	○	○	○	○	○	○	○	○	○	○	○	○	○	○	○	−	○	○	○	○
RODE	−	−	−	○	○	−	○	−	○	○	○	○	○	○	○	○	○	−	○	○	○	○	○	○	○	○	○	○	○	−	○	−	○	○	○	○	○	○
SOFA	○	○	○	○	○	○	○	○	○	○	○	○	○	○	○	○	○	○	○	○	○	○	○	○	○	○	○	○	○	○	○	○	○	○	○	○	○	○
AGO	○	○	○	○	○	−	○	○	○	○	○	○	○	○	○	○	○	○	○	○	○	○	○	○	−	○	○	○	○	○	○	○	○	○	○	○	○	○

relatively uneducated informants along the northeast coast, the very region where the word is apt to have a relatively high frequency of use. Inland, where boats are not so intimately a part of everyday life, /θ/ has almost entirely been replaced by the innovating /o/.

In the Northeastern region the /θ/ phoneme occurs to some extent in every community; there are, in fact, only three informants who do not use it at least once (180.2 Marblehead, 2A; 190.4 Haverhill, 2B; and 422.1 Fort Fairfield, 1A).[16] Regional dissemination in this area can be described as general, variations in the incidence of /θ/ being for the most part dependent on the word and on the age or social status of the informant. Nevertheless, there are several communities in which /θ/ appears to have a lower incidence than others in the same general locality. These atypical communities are of two kinds: some have a settlement history distinct

---

[16] Informants for the *Linguistic Atlas* are identified by a decimal number, in which the part before the decimal point denotes the community and the part after it the individual informant. They are characterized as follows: Type 1, persons with little or no formal education, little reading, and restricted social contacts; Type 2, persons with better education (usually through high school), wider reading, and more varied contacts; Type 3, persons of cultivated background with superior education (usually through college), wide reading, and extensive contacts; Type A, old, or regarded by the fieldworker as relatively old-fashioned; Type B, young, or regarded as relatively modern. Thus the designation 1A refers to an old man with little or no formal schooling, 3B to a relatively young man with considerable education, and so on. See Kurath, *Handbook* 41–2.

402 from that of neighboring communities; some today are urban rather than rural centers.

Differences in settlement history are clearly responsible for the almost exclusive use of /o/ in 422 Fort Fairfield (Figure 7, p. 401), which lies on the Canadian border in northeastern Maine.[17] Like most of adjacent New Brunswick, where /o/ is generally current in the words under discussion, Fort Fairfield was settled by Loyalists who left the neighborhood of New Jersey and New York at the time of the Revolutionary War. Moreover, the town is both culturally and economically oriented toward New Brunswick rather than toward the more distant economic and cultural centers of New England. It is of interest that the people in Fort Fairfield prefer, according to the fieldworker, to call themselves Americans rather than Yankees.

Another Maine–New Brunswick border town, 424 Fort Kent, similarly reflects Canadian usage, though not as strongly as Fort Fairfield. This community has a mixed settlement history; it was first settled by Acadian French, who were later joined by English-speakers from Kennebec County and New Brunswick. The fieldworker reports that there are few English-speaking families in the community, adding that the informant, though of Yankee stock on both sides of the family, is bilingual, and that certain French traits are evident in his speech. No doubt as part of his Yankee heritage, this informant (Type 2B) retains the New England "short *o*" in several words in which it has high stability farther south.

In 384 Waldoboro-Nobleboro, Me. (Figure 7), a settlement largely German and Scotch-Irish in background, there appears to be another enclave with infrequent /ə/. The Type-3A informant uses the phoneme in only three words, *toadstool, home,* and *stone wall* (alongside /o/ in the last). The 2A informant, for whom the record is only partial, uses /ə/ much more commonly, often beside /o/ and often with an intermediate pronunciation. It might appear that the low incidence of /ə/ in the case of the educated speaker simply reflects a difference in social usage; yet in this part of Maine it is most unusual for educated speakers to have /ə/ so rarely. To this group also belong several Scotch-Irish communities: 318 Derry-Londonderry, 320 Bedford-Amherst, 322 Francistown, and 324 Antrim (Figure 7) in the Lower Merrimack Valley, and 294 Ryegate (Figure 7), on the Vermont side of the Upper Connecticut. In these communities /ə/ is common, especially among the older less-educated speakers; but /o/ is common also, more so than in nearby communities of New England–English background. The communities with unstable /ə/ are among those that use postvocalic /r/, a fact not surprising in

[17] See Kurath, *Handbook,* ch. 3, for an outline of New England settlement history; references to settlement history in this part of the discussion are based on that outline and on the detailed accounts of communities and informants in ch. 4.

	1	2	3	4	5	6	Total
coat	16	24	1	3	0	3	47
road	9	15	10	6	0	3	43
stone	12	19	5	3	1	0	40
yoke	16	1	3	0	10	5	35
toad	8	19	2	3	1	0	33
boat	12	6	8	1	3	1	31
Total	73	84	29	16	15	12	229

view of the settlement history: both /o/ and postvocalic /r/ are characteristic of the speech both of the New Brunswick settlements and of Scotch-Irish settlements in the Eastern United States generally.

Especially interesting is 180 Marblehead, Mass., a relatively isolated, self-contained fishing community on the north shore of Boston Bay. Although originally planted from Salem, Marblehead seems to have taken an independent road in linguistic matters. On the one hand, perhaps because of its independence and isolation, it is one of the relic areas of the region, as in the retention of postvocalic /r/;[18] on the other, perhaps because of its long association with the shipping industry, an activity which brought Marbleheaders in touch with many outsiders, it has been receptive to innovations, as in the adoption of the /o/ phoneme. It is possible, of course, that /ɵ/ was never common in Marblehead; but the facts of original settlement and the sporadic presence of the /o/ in the speech of the 1A informant argues against this theory. Proximity to Boston, where /ɵ/ has largely disappeared, may help to account for the prevalence of /o/ in Marblehead.

A number of informants represent the several urban communities in the region: 190 Haverhill, 328 Keene-Marlow (Figure 7), 356 Biddeford, and 360 Portland (Figure 7). The responses of these informants make it clear that /ɵ/ has a relatively low incidence and stability as compared with the status of the phoneme in rural communities in the vicinity. Among the younger, better-educated social group the "short o" is common only in words where it is of especially high incidence throughout the area; among the older, less-educated speakers /ɵ/ is more frequently met with (even in Boston, where /ɵ/ is highly recessive). Nevertheless, it is markedly unstable in most words at all social and age levels.

On the maps (Figures 1–6), circles farthest to the right in any one row represent the younger and/or better educated informants. Even a cursory examination of these maps will show that in most of the communities

---

[18] Kurath, *Handbook* 34 (Chart 16).

Table 3

	wVt.	wConn.	wMass.	seConn.	Narragansett Bay	MV and Nantucket	Cape Cod	Plymouth Region	Boston Bay	cMass.	neMass.	Coastal Me. & NH	Inland Me. & NH	Upper Conn. Valley	swNH
whole	x	x	x	x	x	–	x	x	x	x	x	x	x	x,	x
stone wall	/	o	/	x	x	x	x	x	o	/	x	x	x	x	x
toadstool	/	o	/	/	/	x	x	x	/	x	x	x	x	x	x
grindstone	/	o	/	/	/	x	x	/	o	/	x	x	x	x	x
stone	o	–	o	/	o	x	x	o	o	/	x	x	x	x	/
coat	o	o	–	o	/	/	/	/	–	o	x	x	x	x	o
road	–	–	–	/	/	/	/	/	o	o	x	x	x	x	o
home	–	o	–	/	/	x	o	o	o	–	x	x	x	/	/
wishbone	–	–	–	/	/	x	o	o	o	o	x	x	x	x	/
folks	–	–	–	–	–	–	–	/	–	/	x	x	x	x	x
yolk	–	o	–	–	o	–	/	/	–	–	/	x	x	/	/
poultry	o	o	–	–	–	–	/	/	o	–	/	x	x	/	–
yoke	–	–	–	o	–	–	o	–	–	/	/	x	/	–	
most	–	–	–	–	–	o	–	–	–	–	x	x	x	/	/
(al)most	–	–	–	o	–	–	–	–	–	–	/	x	x	/	/
boat	–	–	–	o	o	/	–	–	–	–	/	/	o	o	o
woke	–	–	–	–	–	–	x	/	–	–	o	o	–	–	–
Rhode Island	o	–	o	o	–	–	–	–	–	o	/	o	–	o	–
post office	–	–	–	–	o	–	–	–	–	o	–	–	–	–	–
oats	–	–	–	–	–	–	–	–	–	–	–	–	o	–	–

with divided usage the recessive /ɵ/ is used by the older and/or less educated, the innovating /o/ by the younger and/or better educated. Exceptions to this rule generally involve educated New Englanders of the Old School, among whom the "short *o*" has prestige value as a symbol identifying them with New England. But even these speakers frequently use /o/, often in free variation with /ɵ/.

All the evidence reinforces a generalization already indicated: If usage in a given community is divided for a particular word, the recessive phoneme /ɵ/ usually occurs, alone or beside /o/, in the speech of the older and the less educated; and the innovating phoneme /o/ usually occurs, alone or beside /ɵ/, in the speech of the younger and better educated.[19] Table 2 shows the incidence of /o/ and /ɵ/ in the speech of older and younger informants in the same communities. Italic numbers at the heads of the columns represent six types of distribution, as follows: *1* older has

[19] See Avis 133–8 (Tables 20–3) for the data on the dissemination of /ɵ/ and /o/ by informant types in the Northeastern region.

/ɵ/, younger /o/; *2* older /ɵ/, younger /o, ɵ/; *3* older /ɵ, o/, younger /o/; *4* older /o/, younger /o, ɵ/; *5* older /o, ɵ/, younger /ɵ/; *6* older /o/, younger /ɵ/. Older informants who use /ɵ/ total 201, younger informants who use /o/ total 202; older informants who do not use /ɵ/ total 28, younger informants who do not use /o/ total 27.

The generalization about the recessive nature of /ɵ/, though based on a detailed study of Northeastern New England only, holds good for New England as a whole. Any word in which /ɵ/ is widely disseminated and stable in the Northeast, as shown in Table 1, will have /ɵ/ fairly often elsewhere as well; any word in which /ɵ/ is rare and unstable in the Northeast will have /ɵ/ rarely or not at all elsewhere. In short, /ɵ/ is receding throughout New England, lingering longest among the older and the less educated, especially in rural areas. Table 3 shows the approximate frequency of /ɵ/ throughout New England.[20] In this table the symbol x indicates that /ɵ/ is common; a slant line / that it is fairly common; a circle o that it is not common; and a dash – that it is rare or lacking.

Diaphones of /ɵ/ occur, though sparsely, in Upstate New York and in the adjacent counties of Pennsylvania, that is, in the New England settlement area north and west of the Hudson-Mohawk Valley.[21] The phoneme in this region is decidedly recessive, as in Western Vermont (Table 3), with which it combines to form a subarea of the Northern speech area.[22] Finally, it occurs as a relic feature on the Canadian side of the border, in the St. Lawrence Valley, an area whose settlement history links it with Western New England and Upstate New York.[23]

[20] For a detailed treatment of the evidence for New England outside the Northeastern region, see Avis 142–66.

[21] The maps referred to in fn. 13 above illustrate the dissemination of /ɵ/ in this settlement area. See also Avis, Figures 54–61 and Tables 33–5.

[22] Area 4, Map 2 in Kurath and McDavid.

[23] It must be remembered that the *Atlas* records here under examination were made almost thirty years ago; many of the informants are now dead. In view of the recessive character of /ɵ/ in the 1930's, it seems improbable that the feature is still common now. If someone were to record comparable data for /ɵ/ and /o/ today, the extent of drift in New England would almost certainly be even more remarkable than is shown by this study.

The Low Central and Low-Back Vowels in the English of the Eastern United States

Thomas H. Wetmore

The pronunciation of the vowels in such words as *cot, caught,* and *crop* varies in the United States. Professor Wetmore discusses the vowels of these words and other low-central and low-back vowels in eight of the dialect areas of the east: western Vermont, metropolitan New York, southeastern Pennsylvania, western North Carolina, eastern Virginia, eastern South Carolina, coastal Maine, southeastern New Hampshire, and western Pennsylvania. The data for this study were the records of the usage of 1450 informants interviewed for the *Linguistic Atlas* (1939–1948) in seven hundred communities in the eastern states from the Canadian border to the coast of Florida and as far west as eastern Ohio and West Virginia. The pronunciation of all speakers was recorded phonically, i.e. without any attempt to identify the phonemic appurtenance of the sounds. Reprinted here are a section of the introduction to the study and all of Chapter IX, "Western Pennsylvania." Western Pennsylvania is unique in that it has one less low vowel phoneme than do other dialects of the eastern United States. Professor Wetmore is Chairman of the English Department at Wright Junior College, Dayton, Ohio.

The purpose of this study is to analyze and describe the low-central and low-back vowel phonemes, their phonic characteristics, and their incidence in selected areas of the eastern United States.

The derivatives of the following historical types are involved:

(1) ME /ŏ/, as in *crop, pot, shock, fog, office, hospital*
(2) ME /ɑu/, as in *law, saw, strawberries*
(3) Early MnE /ɑu/, from ME /ɑ/ before /l/, as in *all, salt, talk*
(4) ME /ou/, as in *brought, fought, daughter*
(5) ME /ɑ/ before tautosyllabic /r/, as in *car, barn*
(6) ME /ɑ/ after /w/, as in *swamp, watch, water, wharf.*

Two other historical types are included for areas in which their derivatives have fallen together with any of those already listed:

(1) ME /ou/ before tautosyllabic /r/, as in *four*
(2) ME /ū/ before tautosyllabic /r/, as in *mourning.*

There are three principal questions to be answered for all of the areas selected for this study:

(1) Which of the regional dialects have unrounded low-central or low-back /ɑ/ in *cot* and fully rounded low-back /ɔ/ in *caught*, and which have a slightly rounded low-back /ɒ/ in both *cot* and *caught?*
(2) What is the phonic range of the phonemes?
(3) What is the incidence of each phoneme in regional dialects which have both /ɑ/ and /ɔ/?

. . .

The system of phonetic notation used in this study is that employed in the *Linguistic Atlas* records, a slightly modified version of the International Phonetic Alphabet. The following are the most frequently used symbols:

ɑ, denoting an unrounded low-central vowel
ɑ, denoting an unrounded low-back vowel
ɒ, denoting a weakly rounded low-back vowel
ɔ, denoting a fully rounded higher-low-back vowel.

For phonemic analysis, it is assumed that such diphthongs as [ɔˇɔ], [ɔə],

From *Publications of the American Dialect Society*, No. 32 (November, 1959). Reprinted with the permission of the American Dialect Society, the University of Alabama Press and Thomas H. Wetmore.

408 and [aᵊ] are phonically complex speech sounds functioning as unit phonemes.

This assumption facilitates the presentation of regional differences found in the eastern United States. The symbols /ɑ/ and /ɔ/ are used to represent the phonemes found in *crop* and *loss*, respectively, in most areas; the symbol /ɒ/ is used for the low-back phoneme in areas in which such words as *crop* and *loss* have the same syllabic. Either the symbol /a/ or the symbol /ɑ˞/ is used for the free phoneme in *car* and *barn* in areas in which it is in contrast with the checked /ɑ/ of *crop* or the /ɒ/ of *crop* and *loss*: in eastern New England the symbol /a/ is used since in this area the most frequent phones are low-front; in New York City, in eastern Virginia, and in eastern South Carolina the symbol /ɑ˞/ is used, since in these areas the most frequent phones are low-back unrounded ones. Whenever the free phoneme in *car* is discussed without reference to a particular area, it is symbolized as /a ~ ɑ˞/, i.e., /a/ alternating with /ɑ˞/.

The following terms used in this study warrant definition:

phone: a speech sound as observed and recorded, treated without reference to its phonemic appurtenance.

phoneme: a speech sound treated as a unit of signaling in a given dialect.

allophone: a positional or prosodic variant of a phoneme.

diaphone: a regional or social variant of a phoneme, or of one of its allophones.

divided usage: divergence in the incidence of vowels in one and the same community.

unsettled usage: variation in the speech of one and the same informant.

dissemination: regional and social spread of a linguistic feature.

incidence: distribution of the phonemes in the vocabulary.

free vowel: a vowel that can occur in word-final position, as the /ɑ˞/ of *car* /kɑ˞/ in New York City or the /ɔ/ of *law* /lɔ/ in most areas in this study.

checked vowel: a vowel which does not occur in word-final position, i.e., one that is always followed by a consonant, as the /ɑ/ of *lot* /lɑt/, *shock* /ʃɑk/, and *crop* /krɑp/ in most areas investigated in this study.

• • •

In dealing with the eight areas, the following procedure has been adopted.

1) Two words are chosen, one of the type of *crop*, which is expected to have the /ɑ/ phoneme in most of the eastern states, the other of the type of *loss*, which is expected to have the /ɔ/ phoneme in most of the eastern

states. The pronunciation of the informants is mapped by phonic types. Then two or three other words for each phoneme are mapped to make sure that the two words taken as examples are typical.

2) The phonic ranges of the presumed phonemes are compared to see whether the phones are distinct or whether they overlap.

3) A graph is made showing for monosyllables in all possible phonetic environments the distribution of the vowel phones and their relative frequency. The graph not only provides further evidence for phonemic analysis, but also indicates any striking allophonic differences within the phonemes.

4) Whenever possible, evidence from minimally contrastive pairs is used to supplement the graph in determining whether the area has the same or different phonemes in *crop* and *loss*. In areas in which minimally contrastive pairs are not recorded, words like *pot* and *brought* are used, since they end in the same stop and have initial consonants which in English do not usually affect the phonemic status of the following vowel.

5) If there is no overlapping of phones and if the minimal pairs are in contrast throughout the area, the existence of both /ɑ/ and /ɔ/ is regarded as established for the area. Conversely, if there is substantial overlapping of phones, and if there are no contrastive minimal pairs, it is concluded that the words under consideration have the same phoneme, which is then designated as /ɒ/, since a slightly rounded low-back phone is the one of most frequent occurrence in such areas.

6) If there is an overlap of the phones in an area which appears to have two phonemes, /ɑ/ and /ɔ/ usage of all individual speakers is investigated to find out whether they have an overlap of phones in the two types of words. In most cases it is found that the individual speakers in such areas do not have an overlap. In such instances, it is concluded that the entire area has both /ɑ/ and /ɔ/. If some informants have such an overlap, this fact is pointed out and an attempt made to explain the phenomenon. Usually such speakers are on the periphery of the area, in which case the neighboring dialect has to be investigated as a possible influence.

7) In areas which have the free vowel /a ~ ɑ/, the same procedure is used to establish the existence of free /a ~ ɑ/, as in *car, barn,* contrasting with the checked /ɑ/ of *crop.*

8) After a decision is reached with regard to the existence in any given area of a single phoneme /ɒ/, of the two phonemes /ɑ/ and /ɔ/, or of the three phonemes /ɑ/, /ɔ/, and /a ~ ɑ/, attention is directed to the positional allophones, the social diaphones, and the subregional diaphones.

9) Finally, for areas having /ɑ/ and /ɔ/, or /ɑ/, /ɔ/, and /a ~ ɑ/ a description is given of the incidence of the phonemes in the vocabulary, arranged by historical types. . . .

WESTERN PENNSYLVANIA

Description of the Area

Except for the northern counties adjoining New York, Pennsylvania west of the crest of the Alleghenies is a subarea of the North Midland.[1] The city of Pittsburgh, at the confluence of the Allegheny and the Monongahela, is the center of this densely populated area, which includes the Upper Ohio Valley and the valleys of its tributaries, the Allegheny, the Beaver, and the Monongahela.[2]

The segment of this area chosen for the present study includes the Ohio Valley proper and the valleys of the Allegheny and the Beaver to the north of it. The following are the counties included: Allegheny, Westmoreland, Indiana, Armstrong, Butler, Beaver, Lawrence, Mercer, Venango, Clarion, Jefferson, and Clearfield. On the map in Figure 1 are shown the location and classification of the informants in these counties.

This area has the free vowel /ɒ/ in *lot*, in *brought, law, loss, corn,* and in *car, barn, garden.*

The /ɒ/ Phoneme

In both the words *crop* and *salt* the range of the phones is from [ɑ], low-back unround, to [ɔˇ], lowered low-back rounded; and the most frequent phones are [ɒ, ɒˆ], slightly rounded low-back, often raised.

When the phones in *crop* and *salt* are charted beneath a phonic spectrum, as in Figure 2, it is apparent that there is complete overlapping of phones. Moreover, identical phones occur in such pairs as *caught* and *cottage, pot* and *brought, John* and *gone, oxen* and *talking,* which have contrastive phones in most other areas. This is conclusive evidence that the two groups of words have the same vowel phoneme, which we shall represent by /ɒ/.

In order to determine whether the phoneme /ɒ/ has more or less marked allophones, the range and frequency of the phones in representative monosyllables are tabulated in Figure 3. Range is indicated by the span of the horizontal line beneath the phonetic spectrum. For phones of primary frequency, the number of occurrences is enclosed in a boldly outlined circle. For phones of secondary frequency, the circle is thinly outlined. Phones of less frequent occurrence are not enclosed; those of rare occurrence are omitted.

[1] Kurath, *Word Geography,* Fig. 3, represented as Fig. 1 of this study.

[2] Charles O. Paullin (John K. Wright, ed.), *Atlas of the Historical Geography of the United States* (New York and Washington: Carnegie Institution of Washington and The American Geographical Society of New York, 1932) Plate 76.

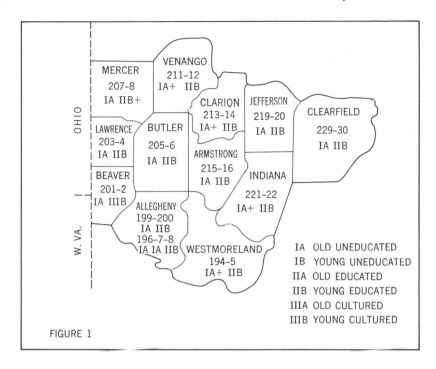

IA   OLD UNEDUCATED
IB   YOUNG UNEDUCATED
IIA OLD EDUCATED
IIB YOUNG EDUCATED
IIIA OLD CULTURED
IIIB YOUNG CULTURED

FIGURE 1

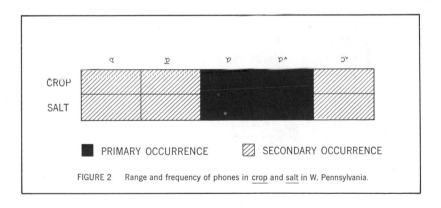

FIGURE 2   Range and frequency of phones in <u>crop</u> and <u>salt</u> in W. Pennsylvania.

Figure 3 shows that the phoneme /ɒ/ in western Pennsylvania has a very wide phonic range, from a retracted low-front [aʾ] to a lowered fully rounded low-back [ɔˇ]. The most frequent phones range from a short slightly rounded low-back monophthong [ɒ] to a lengthened raised slightly rounded low-back ingliding diphthong [ɒˑˆə].

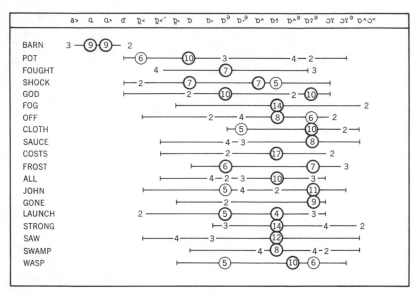

Range of /ɒ/ in W. Pennsylvania and frequency of phones in monosyllables.

Before voiceless stops, as in *crop, pot,* and *shock,* the most frequent phone is a short slightly rounded low-back monophthong [ɒ]. A short raised [ɒˆ] also occurs often.

Before voiced stops the phones are usually longer and occasionally ingliding. Before /b/ in *cobweb* and *bobsled* [ɒ, ɒˆ, ɒˑˆ, ɒˑˆᵊ] occur. Before /g/ as in *fog,* the usual phone is [ɒˑˆ], a raised and lengthened slightly rounded low-back monophthong.

Before voiceless fricatives and before sonorants, as in *cough, cloth, loss, on, strong,* and *all,* two phones occur frequently: [ɒˑˆ], a raised and lengthened slightly rounded low-back monophthong, and [ɒˑˆᵊ], a raised and lengthened slightly rounded low-back ingliding diphthong.

After /w/, as in *swamp* and *water,* [ɒˑˆ] is the usual phone. In *wasps* ingliding diphthongs usually occur: [ɒˆᵊ] most often, but also [ɒᵊ] and [ɒˑˆᵊ].[3]

In final position, as in *law, pshaw,* and *saw,* [ɒˆᵊ] is the usual phone.

Before consonant clusters /ɒ/ is often shorter and lower than before the corresponding single sonorants and fricatives. Whereas *on* and *all* have lengthened raised phones, *launch* and *salt* occur frequently with shorter and/or lower low-back phones: [ɒ, ɒˑ, ɒᵊ].

In polysyllabic words /ɒ/ usually has fewer inglides, less rounding, and less length than in monosyllables with the same phonetic environment.

[3] *Wash*, pronounced /wɔrʃ/ in this area, usually has the same vowel phoneme as *horse* and *wharf.*

Several exceptional pronunciations should be pointed out. In both *God* and *fought* ingliding diphthongs [ɒᵊ, ɒˑˈᵊ] usually occur. Although *dog* usually is pronounced with [ɒˑˈᵊ], as are other monosyllables ending in /g/, six informants have a lengthened lowered fully rounded low-back monophthong [ɔˑˇ]. In the few occurrences of *Mom,* [ɒᵊ] is the usual phone.

The most striking allophone of /ɒ/ is low-central unround [ɑ, ɑ'], which occurs only before tautosyllabic /r/, in such words as *barn* and *garden.* Unless one is willing to posit a phoneme /ɑ/ limited to occurrence before tautosyllabic /r/, the low-central phones in *barn* and *garden* must be assigned to the phoneme /ɒ/. Thus western Pennsylvania has the unique distinction of possessing one fewer vowel phonemes in the range of the low vowels than do other American dialects spoken in the eastern United States.

In eastern New England, where such words as *lot, crop, shock,* and *law, loss, brought* also have the same phoneme, the vowel in such words as *barn* is not a member of this phoneme. Rather, *barn, car, garden* have a vowel that also occurs in *calf, glass, bath. Calf, glass, bath* have /a/, which contrasts with /ɒ/ in *cough, loss, moth.* Therefore, eastern New England has two low vowels, /a/ and /ɒ/. This means that eastern New England has the same number of phonemes in the range of the low vowels as do all American dialects in the eastern states except that of western Pennsylvania.

In western Pennsylvania the vowel phones occurring in *crop, loss* differ markedly from the phones of /o/ in such words as *boat* and *over.* Although *tore, hoarse, horse, war,* etc., have lowered mid vowels [ɔ, ɔˆ], whereas *boat, over,* etc., have upgliding mid vowels (oˇu, ou], these phones must be taken as members of the phoneme /o/, unless one is willing to posit a separate mid-back vowel phoneme that occurs only before /r/. This /o/ before /r/, as in *horse, hoarse,* contrasts in this position with /ɒ/ of *barn* and with the /ʊ/ of *poor,* the only two other back vowel phonemes occurring before /r/ in the dialect of western Pennsylvania.

The vowel of *barn* is in contrast with that of *corn, horse, hoarse, four, forty, war,* etc., all of which have in this position an [ɔˆ]-like allophone of the phoneme /o/, as in *road.* The phones of /ɒ/ and /o/ before tautosyllabic /r/ are shown in Table 1.

The phonic range of the phoneme /ɒ/ of western Pennsylvania is very great, since the contrast between /ɑ/ and /ɔ/ existing in most other dialects is lacking, so that /ɒ/ occupies the entire phonic spectrum between /æ/ and /o/.

The influence of Pittsburgh speech upon the surrounding area can be seen through an analysis of the diaphones in *barn, crop,* and *off.* In all three words the two chief diaphones are found throughout the area, but

414   the one which seems to be expanding is the one used by the middle-class Pittsburgh informants.

In *barn* the principal diaphones are [ɑ] and [ɑ']. The old uneducated Pittsburgh informant has the retracted diaphone in *barn;* the two educated informants have the more fronted variety. The retracted diaphone is the most frequent one in the surrounding area. It is of long standing and is found equally often in the speech of the older and the younger informants, both educated and uneducated. The more fronted [ɑ], on the other hand, occurs usually in the speech of the younger and/or more educated.

Table 1

PHONES OF /ɒ/ AND /o/ BEFORE TAUTOSYLLABIC /r/
IN WESTERN PENNSYLVANIA

	a'	ɑ	ɑ'	ɑ	ɒˆ	ɔˇ	ɔ	ɔˆ	o
barn	3	9	9	2					
tore							9	16	1
hoarse					1		5	19	1
(saw)horse						1	13	8	
war						1	12	13	
wharf							13	13	

The principal diaphones in *crop* are [ɒ] and [ɒˆ]. In Pittsburgh the younger middle-class informant has [ɒ], and both the middle-class and uneducated younger informants have [ɒˆ]. Three-fifths of the younger middle-class informants in the surrounding area have [ɒ].

In *off* the two principal diaphones are [ɒ·ˆ] and ɒ·ˆə]. Both the older and the younger educated Pittsburgh informants have a monophthongal pronunciation in *off*. In the surrounding area pronunciation of *off* with an ingliding diphthong is heard with equal frequency in the speech of all classes of informants. Monophthongal [ɒ·ˆ], on the other hand, occurs, for the most part, only in the speech of the middle class.

Both /ɒ/ and /o/ occur before intersyllabic /r/. The incidence varies greatly from word to word.

The highest incidence of /ɒ/ occurs in *tomorrow* ($\frac{14}{26}$). /ɒ/ in *tomorrow* is preferred by the younger and/or more educated informants in Pittsburgh and in the rest of Allegheny County and in Beaver County. The phoneme /o/ is more expansive in the northern half of the area. /ɒ/ occurs less frequently in *borrow* ($\frac{8}{26}$). In *oranges* only the old uneducated informant in Clarion County has /ɒ/.

In the speech of this area, /ɒ/, pronounced as [ɑ, ɑ'], occurs not only before tautosyllabic /r/, but also before intersyllabic /r/. In *married,* eight of the twenty-six informants have /ɒ/. Of the eight, five are uneducated.

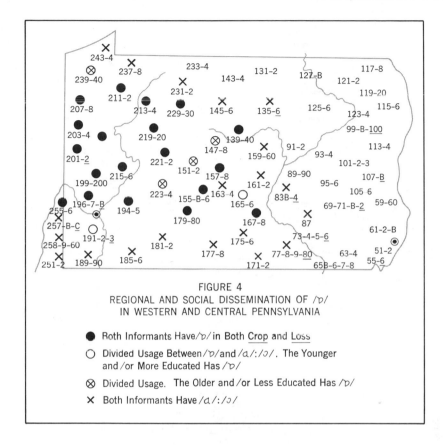

FIGURE 4
REGIONAL AND SOCIAL DISSEMINATION OF /ɒ/
IN WESTERN AND CENTRAL PENNSYLVANIA

● Both Informants Have /ɒ/ in Both <u>Crop</u> and <u>Loss</u>

○ Divided Usage Between /ɒ/ and /ɑ/:/ɔ/. The Younger
and /or More Educated Has /ɒ/

⊗ Divided Usage. The Older and /or Less Educated Has /ɒ/

✕ Both Informants Have /ɑ/:/ɔ/

This old-fashioned pronunciation is not heard in the speech of the Pittsburgh informants.

In *wheelbarrow*, /ɒ/ occurs much more frequently ($\frac{16}{26}$). It does not occur in Pittsburgh speech, but is found elsewhere among all classes of informants.

Figures 4 and 5 show that the lack of the phonemic distinction, /ɑ/ versus /ɔ/, extends eastward into central Pennsylvania. Nine counties east of the area analyzed have at least one informant who pronounces *crop* and *loss* with the same vowel phoneme: Clinton, Center, Blair, Mifflin, Cambria, Bedford, Huntingdon, Perry, and Cumberland. In five of these counties (Clinton, Mifflin, Bedford, Huntingdon, and Cumberland) both informants lack the contrast; in one (Perry) the younger middle-class informant lacks the contrast; and in three (Center, Blair, and Cambria) the older, less educated informant lacks the contrast.

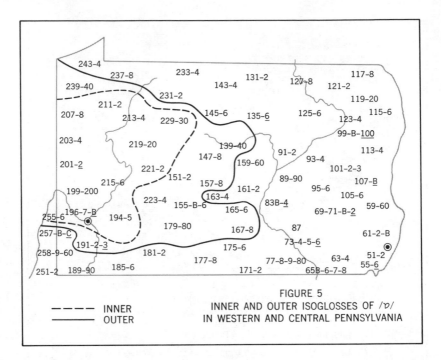

FIGURE 5

INNER AND OUTER ISOGLOSSES OF /ɒ/
IN WESTERN AND CENTRAL PENNSYLVANIA

– – – – INNER
——— OUTER

In northeastern Pennsylvania in Crawford County, at the seam of the New England settlement area, the Pittsburgh pattern is losing ground. Only the older uneducated informant lacks the contrast.

To the south and west of the Ohio and the Monongahela there is evidence that the Pittsburgh pattern is being accepted. In Washington County the younger and more educated informants lack the contrast. In Hancock County in West Virginia both informants lack the contrast.

Mourning
and Morning

Hans Kurath

The pronunciation of the pairs *mourning:morning* and
hoarse:horse is not the same in all parts of the United States.
In some areas the words in each pair sound alike, while
in others they have different vowels. In this article Professor
Kurath discusses the pronunciation of these words and
related words in some parts of the Atlantic slope.

In a paper published in 1923,[1] William A. Read discussed the character of the vowel in words like *four, hoarse, glory* in American English.
Relying on his expert knowledge of Southern speech and on information
secured by correspondence from competent observers in the northern
United States, he reached the conclusion that most Americans have the
[o] vowel in words of this type and that they differentiate more or less
sharply between such words as *hoarse: horse, mourning: morning,* etc.
These observations are borne out in the main by the findings of the
Linguistic Atlas of the U. S. A. in New England and the South Atlantic

From *Studies for William A. Read,* 1940. Reprinted with the permission of Louisiana State
University Press and Hans Kurath.

[1] "Some Phases of American Pronunciation," *JEGP,* XXII, 220–29.

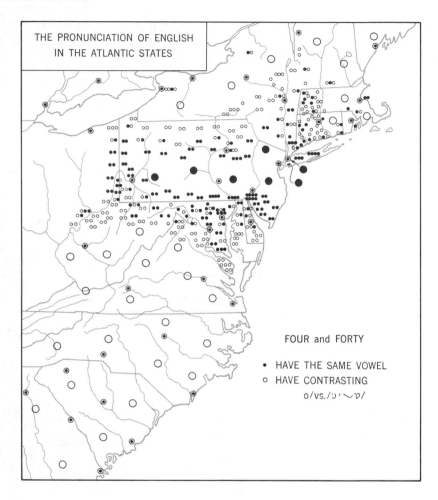

THE PRONUNCIATION OF ENGLISH
IN THE ATLANTIC STATES

FOUR and FORTY

• HAVE THE SAME VOWEL
○ HAVE CONTRASTING
o/vs./ɔ·∽ɒ/

states, the two sections of the eastern United States that have been investigated to date.[2]

The accompanying sketch map presents a somewhat simplified general view of current usage in those parts of the Atlantic slope that have been investigated. Three rather well-defined sections emerge: (1) New England and (2) the states south of the Potomac (the South Atlantic states), where *mourning: morning* and *hoarse: horse* have different vowels;

This map is taken from *The Pronunciation of English in the Atlantic States* by Professors Hans Kurath and Raven I. McDavid (1961). It includes material on areas investigated after 1940. Reprinted with the permission of the University of Michigan Press.

[2] The first of the three volumes of the *Linguistic Atlas of New England* and a *Handbook of the Linguistic Geography of New England* came off the press in July, 1939.

and (3) Maryland and southern New Jersey (and perhaps Pennsylvania) where these word pairs have identical vowels.

West of Chesapeake Bay the southern boundary of the undifferentiated area is formed by the Potomac, the historic boundary between Maryland and Virginia; however, a short distance below Washington, D.C., the boundary swerves east, cutting off the southern point of Maryland, including the counties of Charles, St. Marys, and Calvert. In this part of Maryland the "Virginia type" predominates. East of Chesapeake Bay the dividing line between the two types runs much farther north. It follows the northern boundary of Kent County, Maryland, and Kent County, Delaware, so that nearly all of the Eastern Shore of Maryland and more than two-thirds of Delaware have the differentiating "Virginia type."

How far north the undifferentiated type extends remains to be determined. Upstate New York presumably agrees with New England in having distinct vowels in *mourning* and *morning;* perhaps also northeastern Pennsylvania with its large New England settlements on the upper Susquehanna and northern New Jersey. Since the valley of Virginia differentiates words of this type, one expects to find this differentiation also among the parent stock, the Scotch-Irish of Pennsylvania. According to rather casual observations made by Guy S. Lowman, Jr., the two types are not differentiated in the Philadelphia area. We shall soon know.[3]

The present division of the Atlantic slope into three sections—New England, the South Atlantic states, and an intervening area of undetermined extent—doubtless existed in colonial times, whatever the explanation may be. Since *mourning* and *morning, hoarse* and *horse* are more or less sharply contrasted in the folk speech of all of southern England and the Midland, except for the immediate surroundings of London and parts of Essex and Suffolk,[4] the origin of the New England type and the "Virginia type" is clear. On the other hand, the sources of the undifferentiated "Maryland type" will have to be investigated. Is it historically connected with the London type described by Daniel Jones or has it a broader basis? Were Baltimore and Philadelphia the two centers from which it spread?

West of the Appalachians one expects to find this differentiated type (1) in the belt of New England settlements from central New York westward to the Mississippi and beyond and (2) in the southern area of settlement from the Gulf of Mexico to the valley of the Ohio River, including southern Ohio, Indiana, and Illinois. The undifferentiated "Maryland type" will probably be found along the Old National Road in central Ohio, Indiana, and Illinois. If the Philadelphia area (southeastern Penn-

---

[3] Lowman started a systematic survey of Pennsylvania in the summer of 1939, aided by a grant of the American Philosophical Society.

[4] This statement is based on Lowman's survey (1937–38) of these parts of England.

420   sylvania) should prove to have the undifferentiated type, this type would correspondingly be more frequent in the derivative areas to the west.[5]

The sharpest contrasts between the vowels of *mourning: morning* and *hoarse: horse* are found in eastern New England and on Chesapeake Bay (Tidewater Virginia and the Eastern Shore). (See map, p. 418.)

In eastern New England, *mourning* and *hoarse* almost invariably have the well-rounded mid-back vowel [o], the same phoneme as words of the type of *road, post, oats.*[6] *Morning* and *horse,* on the other hand, have a slightly rounded low-back vowel [ɒ], sometimes raised toward [ɔ]. The same vowel phoneme appears in this part of New England also in words of the types of *off, frost,* of *saw, salt,* and of *rod, crop.*

The two sets therefore contrast sharply as [hoəs:hɒəs] and [moənɪŋ: mɒənɪŋ].

In the older type of eastern New England speech, the [o] phoneme in *road, post, oats,* etc., is fronted and more or less lowered and the tongue glides toward central position; in the modern type it begins fully back, close or open, and the tongue glides up. The vowel in *mourning, four, boar,* etc., differs phonically from both these variants but is certainly a member of the same phoneme. It begins like the modern vowel in *road* [roʊd] but there is no upglide.[7]

In Western New England the contrast between the vowels of *mourning* and *morning* is less sharp. *Mourning* is usually sounded [mornɪn], the vowel being somewhat lower than in *road, post,* but clearly a member of the same phoneme; *morning* is pronounced [mɔrnɪn] and has the vowel phoneme of *off, frost, saw, salt.*

Among over four hundred informants in New England, about ten do not seem to differentiate between *hoarse* and *horse* and about twenty appear to pronounce *mourning* and *morning* alike. Most of these instances are scattered through southern New England, from western Connecticut and Massachusetts to the Boston area. Only a meticulous study of these cases will reveal whether this usage is old or new in New England.[8]

On Chesapeake Bay, exclusive of Maryland west of the Bay, *mourning*

[5] Of seven informants interviewed in central and northern Ohio, three pronounce *mourning* and *morning* alike. But these figures are hardly representative.

[6] References to the maps of the *Linguistic Atlas of New England* are given in the table in p. 421.

[7] The pronunciation of *hoarse* as [hoʊs], common in parts of Maine and New Hampshire, may represent OE *hās* (cf. German *heiser*), since *mourning, four, boar* do not have this diphthongal vowel. But it may also be an isolated relic of a pronunciation corresponding to the Southern variant described below.

[8] Kenyon's statement, *American Pronunciation* (6th ed., 1935), p. 225, that "many speakers in eastern New England and New York City and vicinity" pronounce *four, tore, door,* etc., "with the [ɔ] sound of the word *all*" is erroneous as far as eastern New England is concerned, where [foə, toə, doə] usually contrast sharply with *for, fall, tall, law,* [fɒə, fɒl, tɒl, lɒ].

KEY WORDS	43 ROAD 128 OATS	54 FOUR · 501 HOARSE 532 MOURNING	94 STORM · 77 MORNING 196 HORSE	48 OFF · 98 FROST 208 TROUGH	162 SAWHORSE · 291 SALT 376 DAUGHTER	45 ROD · 124 CROP 131 POT	48 FAR · 101 BARN 121 GARDEN
EASTERN NEW ENGLAND	ou	o^T (o^w)	ɒ (ɔ)	ɒ (ɔ)	ɒ (ɔ)	ɒ (ɔ)	a (ɑ)
WESTERN NEW ENGLAND	ou, o	o^T	c	c	ɔ (ɒ)	ɑ	ɑ
WESTERN MARYLAND AND SOUTHERN NEW JERSEY	ou, o	$ɔ^L, o^T$	$ɔ^L, o^T$	c	c	ɑ	ɑ
SOUTH ATLANTIC STATES	ou, o	ou, o	ɔ (ɒ)	ɔ (ɒ)	ɔ (ɒ)	ɑ	ɑ, ɒ

422 and *morning* contrast sharply as [mo·nɪn, moʊnin] and [mɒnɪn]. The former has the same vowel as *road, post* (and presumably also *moaning*), the latter the vowel of *off, frost,* and of *saw, salt.* It is of interest to note that in this area (the Tidewater of Virginia and the Eastern Shore) many persons have the same slightly rounded low-back vowel [ɒ] in *morning, storm, corn* and in *far, barn, garden*—but not in the cities of Richmond and Norfolk.

In all the rest of the Atlantic slope south of the Potomac the contrast between *mourning* and *morning* is less striking, since *morning, horse* (as well as *off, frost* and *saw, salt*) have the well-rounded raised low-back vowel [ɔ], often with an upglide toward [o]. The type of *mourning* [moʊnɪn] is found in Maryland and in the Tidewater and Piedmont of Virginia and North Carolina, but is entirely lacking in the Charleston area where the vowel in *mourning, hoarse, four* as well as in *road, post, oats* either has an off-glide to [ə] or is a close mid-back monophthong.

By and large, the vowel in *mourning, hoarse, four, boar,* etc., is apt to be lowered more in areas where postvocalic *r* is pronounced (western New England and the Blue Ridge), than in areas where the historical *r* appears in this position as [ə] or is lost (eastern New England and the greater part of the Tidewater and the Piedmont in the South Atlantic states). But the presence or absence of the *r* is not connected in any manner with the preservation of distinct vowel phonemes in *mourning : morning,* etc. It need hardly be pointed out that Standard Southern British English has given up this distinction, whereas in America those areas that sound the *r* only before vowels have preserved (or developed?) sharply contrasting vowels.

In Maryland west of Chesapeake Bay, where *mourning* and *morning, hoarse* and *horse* are homophonous, the character of the vowel varies greatly, apparently without any regional pattern. Sometimes it is a lowered [o], more commonly a raised and well-rounded [ɔ], occasionally simply [ɔ]. In the greater part of this area the vowel is followed by [r], south of Baltimore by [ə] or by a "zero variant" of the [r] phoneme.[9]

The question whether in the "Maryland type" the vowel of *mourning, hoarse, four* and the identical vowel of *morning, horse, storm* is a member of the [o] phoneme of *road, post,* etc., or a variant of the [ɔ] phoneme in words like *saw, salt, off,* etc., is not a simple one. Perhaps the phonemic affiliation of the vowel of *mourning, morning* is not the same for all speakers in this area. Only a thorough analysis of a large body of material will enable us to make a decision. Certain it is, however, that words of this

---

[9] Kenyon's analysis (*American Pronunciation,* 224) of words like *four* into consonant plus "centering diphthong" is unacceptable. *Four* has three phonemes in all types of American English: consonant plus vowel plus consonant (sonorant).

type do not have a vowel phoneme distinct from both the [o] phoneme and the [ɔ] phoneme, since the variant occurring in these words has a distribution complementary to either of them.

In the phonemic analysis of any dialect the attempt must be made to assign all phonetic variants (phones) to phonemes. In other words, since all languages must have a system or pattern of signals for ready intelligibility, this pattern must be established by the linguist. He must *act as if* the pattern or system were clearly defined in every respect and assign the multiplicity of variants to functional entities, the phonemes. However, the system is often not perfect. Dialect mixture, ever present, may upset the system in one respect or another and produce confusion, at least temporarily; and again, accentuation or partial assimilation may produce a variant phonically intermediate between two phonemes and thus leave the phonemic appurtenance in doubt. For example, in western New England *swallow, borrow* often have a sound (phone) in the first syllable that lies halfway between the [ɔ] vowel of *wall* and the [a] vowel of *lot:* to which of the two phonemes does it belong? Some Marylanders may be in this position with regard to the vowel of *mourning* and *morning*.

Grease and Greasy:
A Study
of Geographical
Variation

E. Bagby Atwood

This article is a classic study of geographical variation.
It has been widely known that *grease* and *greasy* are
pronounced differently in the Northern and Southern areas
of the United States. Until the publication of Professor
Atwood's article, however, the exact geographical distribution
of the pronunciations could not be stated. The study is
based on the materials of the *Linguistic Atlas*.

The fact that the verb *to grease* and the adjective *greasy* are pronounced by some Americans with [s] and by others with [z] has long been
well known even to amateur observers of speech.[1] It has also been pretty

From *University of Texas Studies in English* (1950). Reprinted with the permission of the
University of Texas Press and Mrs. E. Bagby Atwood.

[1] Webster's *New International Dictionary* states that [z] in *grease* is found "esp. Brit. and Southern U. S."; [z] in *greasy* is "perhaps more general in England and the southern U. S. than in the
North and East." Kenyon and Knott, *Pronouncing Dictionary* (Springfield, Mass., 1944), give
[s] and [z] for the country as a whole, only [z] for the South. *The Century, Funk and Wagnalls*

well accepted that the incidence of [s] or [z] in the words in question is primarily dependent on the geographical location of the speaker rather than on his social or educational level—that [s] is, in general, "Northern," [z] "Southern."

As early as 1896, George Hempl published a study[2] of these two words, based on a rather widely circulated written questionnaire. His returns enabled him to divide the country into four major areas, according to the percentages of [s] in *to grease* and *greasy* respectively. The "North"[3]—extending from New England to the Dakotas—showed 88 and 82 percent of [s] pronunciations; the "Midland," comprising a fairly narrow strip extending from New York City to St. Louis,[4] 42 and 34 percent; the "South,"[5] 12 and 12 percent; and the "West"—an ever-widening area extending westward from St. Louis—56 and 47 percent. The material which Hempl was able to collect was admittedly "insufficient";[6] moreover, he had no means of selecting strictly representative informants;[7] and the answers may not always have been correct, since, it seems to me, an understanding of the questions would have required a certain degree of linguistic sophistication.[8] Still, in spite of these handicaps, Hempl's study

New Standard, and the *American College Dictionary* merely give [s] or [z] for both words. Kenyon and Knott state that "['grizɪ] and [tə grɪz] are phonetically normal; ['grisɪ] and [tə gris] imitate the noun *grease* [gris]." Certainly many verbs since Middle English times have been distinguished from the corresponding nouns by voicing the final fricative; cf. *house: to house, proof: to prove, wreath: to wreathe, abuse: to abuse*—and (with vowel change) *bath: to bathe, breath: to breathe, grass: to graze,* etc. This paper will not be concerned with the origin or history of the feature.

The pronunciation of the vowels is of no significance in our study. For convenience I am using the symbol [i] for both the stressed and the unstressed vowels in *greasy*.

[2] *"Grease* and *Greasy," Dialect Notes,* I (1896), 438–44.

[3] In addition to New England, this area includes New Brunswick, Quebec, Ontario, New York, Michigan, Wisconsin, North Dakota, South Dakota, Minnesota, and the northern portions of Pennsylvania, Ohio, Indiana, Illinois, and Iowa.

[4] This includes New York City, New Jersey, Delaware, the District of Columbia, southern Pennsylvania, southern Ohio, northern West Virginia, middle Indiana, middle Illinois, and St. Louis, Missouri.

[5] This includes everything to the south of the Midland, as far west as Texas.

[6] *Op. cit.,* p. 438.

[7] For example, he urged his colleagues, especially "teachers of English in colleges, normal schools, and young ladies' seminaries to use the questions as an exercise in English." (*Ibid.,* p. 444.)

[8] Question 45 reads: "In which (if any) of the following does *s* have the sound of *z: 'the grease,' 'to grease,' 'greasy'?*" (Hempl, "American Speech Maps," *Dialect Notes,* I [1896], 317.) Judging from my experience in teaching phonetic transcription to college seniors and graduate students, a considerable proportion of a class would simply not know whether [s] or [z] was used in such words; certainly many students unhesitatingly write [s] in words like *rose* and *has* simply because the *letter s* is used in standard spelling.

426   has not been greatly improved upon by later writers. Most authorities content themselves by stating that [z] in *to grease* and *greasy* is predominantly Southern, and that either [s] or [z] may occur elsewhere.[9] Few investigators have gathered material that would enable them to draw clearer lines between [s] and [z] than Hempl was able to do.[10]

The field records that have been gathered for the *Linguistic Atlas of the United States and Canada*[11] provide us with an excellent basis for delimiting the geographical and social spread of speech forms in the Eastern United States. A number of features of the *Atlas* methodology[12] are conducive to an accurate picture of native and normal speech. The informants, though relatively few,[13] were carefully chosen, each being both native to and representative of his community. The answers to questions were elicited, so far as possible, in a conversational atmosphere, and thus the occurrence of ungenuine forms was minimized. Finally, the forms were recorded by trained phoneticians, who would be very unlikely to make such errors as to write [s] when the informant actually uttered [z].

A few words should be said regarding the cartographical representation of linguistic atlas data. In such works as the *Atlas Linguistique de la France,*[14] in which each community, or "point" on the map, is represented

[9] See footnote 1. It is sometimes pointed out that the same speaker may use both ['grisi] and ['grizi] with a distinction in meaning. This point will be discussed below.

[10] A. H. Marckwardt was able to draw a fairly clear line through Ohio, Indiana, and Illinois, though on the basis of relatively little data. See "Folk Speech in Indiana and Adjacent States," *Indiana History Bulletin*, XVII (1940), 120–40. Henry L. Smith has long been using the word *greasy* as a test word in his demonstrations of regional variation and to determine the origins of speakers, though he has not published his material. I presume that Dr. Smith's observations are the source of Mario Pei's statement: " 'greazy' . . . would place the speaker south of Philadelphia, while 'greassy' would place him north of Trenton." (*The Story of Language* [Philadelphia and New York, 1949], p. 51.) C. K. Thomas considers the word *greasy* in his survey of the regional speech types, but comes to the strange conclusion that "the choice between [s] and [z] in words like *discern, desolate, absorb, absurd,* and *greasy* seems to be more personal than regional." (*An Introduction to the Phonetics of American English* [New York, 1947], p. 154). G. P. Krapp is likewise at fault when he states that, in *greasy,* "popular usage and, in general, standard speech have only the form with [z]." (*The Pronunciation of Standard English in America* [New York, 1919], p. 119.)

[11] The New England materials have been published as the *Linguistic Atlas of New England,* ed. Hans Kurath and Bernard Bloch, 3 vols., Providence, R. I., 1939–43. Field records for most of the Middle Atlantic and South Atlantic states were gathered by the late Guy S. Lowman; recently (summer, 1949) Dr. Raven I. McDavid, Jr., completed the work for the eastern seaboard. The records, in an unedited but usable state, are filed at the University of Michigan, where they were made available to me through the courtesy of Professor Kurath.

[12] See *Handbook of the Linguistic Geography of New England,* ed. H. Kurath and others (Providence, R. I., 1939), for a complete account of the *Atlas* methodology.

[13] Something like 1600 informants have been interviewed, representing communities from New Brunswick to northern Florida, approximately as far west as Lake Erie.

[14] Ed. J. Gilliéron and E. Edmont, 7 vols., Paris, 1902–10.

by a single speaker, it is usually possible to draw lines, or *isoglosses,* separating those communities where a form occurs from those where it does not occur. Often these isoglosses set off a large block of "points," forming a solid area—as, for example, the southern French territory marked by initial [k] in the word *chandelle.*[15] A more complex presentation is sometimes required, as in the case of the northern French occurrences of [k] in this same word: After setting off our solid area we find outside it a number of scattered communities where the feature in question occurs; these must be indicated by additional lines encircling the "points" where the form is found.[16] In still other cases, the communities where a given speech form occurs (for example, *conin* for "rabbit") are so scattered that it is impossible to connect them; in such cases our isoglosses must consist merely of scattered circles here and there on the map.[17] When this situation obtains we would probably do better to assign a symbol (say, a cross, or a dot, or a triangle) to the scattered form in question, lest the labyrinth of lines become too much for the reader to cope with.

Now, in presenting data from the American *Atlas,* we are faced with all these complications, plus others arising from the fact that more than one informant was chosen to represent each community. That is, at nearly every "point" the American fieldworkers recorded the usage of one elderly, poorly educated informant and one younger, more modern informant. In certain key communities a third type was included—a well educated, or "cultured," speaker who presumably represented the cultivated usage of the area. Thus, at the same point on the map we often find such variants as *sot down* (preterite), representing rustic usage, *set* or *sit down,* representing more modern popular usage, and *sat down,* representing cultivated usage.[18] It is obviously impossible to draw isoglosses separating *sot* from *set* or *sat;* it is even impractical to set off the *sot* areas, since the form occurs in about every other community through considerable areas. In other cases, of course, it is quite easy to mark off an area where a certain form is current. *Holp* (for *helped*), for example, occupies a very clear-cut area south of the Potomac.[19] Yet a line marking off this area would by no means constitute a dividing line between *holp* and *helped,* since most of

---

[15] See Karl Jaberg, "Sprachgeographie," *Siebenunddreissigstes Jahresheft des Vereins Schweiz. Gymnasiallehrer* (Aarau, 1908), pp. 16–42; also Plate III.

[16] *Ibid.,* Plate III.

[17] *Ibid.,* Plate X.

[18] In addition, the same informant often uses more than one form; all of these are of course entered at that point on the map. On at least one occasion McDavid picked up from the same informant, as the preterite of *see, I seen, I seed, I see,* and *I saw.*

[19] This verb, as well as the others mentioned, is treated in my *Survey of Verb Forms in the Eastern United States,* 1953.

428 the younger informants within the *holp* area use the standard form *helped.* My point is that an isogloss based on American *Atlas* materials *should in all cases be regarded as an outer limit, not as a dividing line between two speech forms.*

The examples hitherto adduced have, of course, illustrated the incidence of "nonstandard" as against "standard" speech forms. What of those instances of two forms which are equally "standard," each within its area? Kurath's map of *pail* and *bucket* provides an example.[20] Here too we must follow the same principle: We must first draw the outer limit of one form, then of the other. The two lines will lap over each other at some points, enclosing certain communities of mixed usage.[21] Thus, *a dividing line is a double isogloss,* each line being the outer limit of one of the two speech forms in question. The areas of overlapping between the two lines may be wide or narrow, depending on many social, geographical, and historical considerations.

Let us return to *grease* and *greasy.* The variations between [s] and [z] in these words furnishes an almost ideal example of geographical (as against social) distribution. Consider first the verb *grease.* It is unnecessary to describe in detail the incidence of [s] and [z], since the accompanying map tells its own story. The northern line of the [z]-form, it may be observed, takes in the southwestern corner of Connecticut (west of the Housatonic); from there it passes westward just to the north of New Jersey; then it dips sharply southward to Philadelphia, to the west of which it again rises gradually northward to the northwestern corner of Pennsylvania. The transition area (where both [s] and [z] are used) is relatively narrow to the west of Philadelphia; to the northeast, however, it widens considerably so as to include most of northern New Jersey, as well as New York City and eastern Long Island.

Outside our pair of isoglosses there is a surprisingly small number of "stray" forms. All together, there are only six occurrences of [z] in the [s] area and only six of [s] in the [z] area.[22] (It will be observed, of course, that there is a second area, or island, of [s] along the Ohio River extending northeastward from the vicinity of Marietta, Ohio). There is no sign whatever of social variation within the solid [s] and [z] areas; cultivated usage

[20] *A Word Geography of the Eastern United States* (Ann Arbor, Mich., 1949), Figure 66.

[21] Even after drawing the lines we would find a good many scattered, or "stray," occurrences of *pail* within the *bucket* area and vice versa. Kurath's lines, which are all outer limits, do not attempt to indicate the presence of stray forms or small patches which occur outside the main area; however, since he also publishes maps on which each occurence of each word is recorded by a symbol, the reader can easily check and interpret his isoglosses.

[22] This amounts to less than one percent of the informants. Most of the informants who show exceptional usage also give the "normal" form; that is, they use both [s] and [z] forms.

is in strict agreement with popular usage.[23] Within the areas of overlapping there is naturally some variation between older and more modern informants—yet the general trend is not at all clear. In the communities of divided usage to the west of Philadelphia the more modern informant uses [s] in six out of eight instances; in such communities to the northeast of Philadelphia the modern preference is for [s] in six instances, for [z] in six others. As for cultured informants within the areas of overlapping, ten use

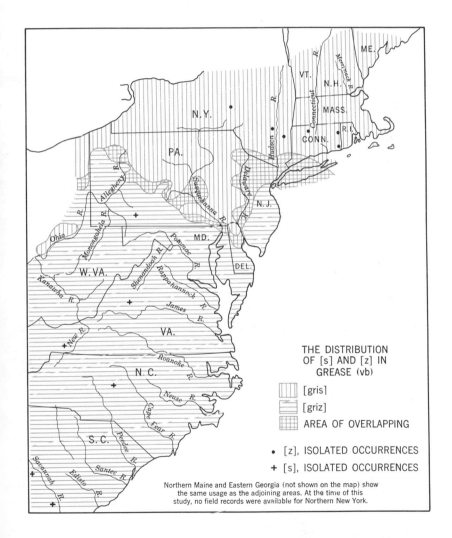

THE DISTRIBUTION
OF [s] AND [z] IN
GREASE (vb)

[gris]

[griz]

AREA OF OVERLAPPING

• [z], ISOLATED OCCURRENCES

+ [s], ISOLATED OCCURRENCES

Northern Maine and Eastern Georgia (not shown on the map) show the same usage as the adjoining areas. At the time of this study, no field records were available for Northern New York.

[23] Although the preterite form of the verb was not called for in the work sheets, Lowman picked up some five instances of *grez* [grɛz] in the [z] area; and a number of other informants reported having heard this form.

430   [griz], five use [gris], and one offers both [s] and [z] forms. One might state, very tentatively, that cultivated usage has tended to favor [griz], particularly in New York City and northern New Jersey.

For the adjective *greasy,* the pronunciations [grisi] and [grizi] show almost precisely the same isoglosses as those for [gris] and [griz]. The northern limit of [z] pushes further northward at three points in Pennsylvania;[24] correspondingly, the southern limit of [s] retreats northward at one point in Ohio, three in Pennsylvania, and two in northern New Jersey.[25] Within the [s] area, there are ten stray forms with [z], scattered through New England and the Hudson Valley; six of these occur in the cultured type of informant. Within the [z] area, we again find six stray occurrences of [s]; and precisely the same island of [s] occurs along the Ohio River. In short, a few more eastern informants use [z] in *greasy* than in *grease,* though the difference is not great. Within the areas of overlapping we find almost exactly the same social distribution as in the case of *grease.* Cultured informants prefer [grizi] by eleven to four; this fact, together with the six "stray" northern uses of [z] in the cultured type, inclines us to believe that [z] in *greasy* has penetrated into northeastern cultivated speech a little more palpably than in the case of *grease*—though still to a very slight extent.

After describing the incidence of the speech forms in question, we are still faced with a number of questions, to which our data can provide only partial answers.

What becomes of our isoglosses in the areas west of Pennsylvania? The materials being gathered for the Great Lakes atlas (under the direction of Professor A. H. Marckwardt) will undoubtedly provide an answer. I have not been able to examine the latest of these materials; but judging from preliminary information, as well as from a map already published by Professor Marckwardt,[26] the northern limit of [z] in *greasy* passes through central Ohio, then swings northward so as to take in almost the whole of Indiana, then bends southward through central Illinois in the direction of St. Louis. Whether the areas of transition are wide or narrow we can probably not determine with accuracy, since, in general, only one social type (the elderly, or rustic) is included in the Great Lakes survey.

Why should the isoglosses run where they do? The answer, in part, is relatively simple. Of the two sets of variants, the [s] forms were evidently generalized in the New England colonies, the [z] forms in the Middle and South Atlantic colonies. The westward migrations and settlements of the New Englanders covered New York State, northern Pennsylvania, Mich-

[24] Lehigh, Columbia, and Lancaster counties.

[25] Columbia, Armstrong, Blair, Cumberland, Hunterdon, and Morris counties.

[26] "Folk Speech of Indiana and Adjacent States," *op. cit.,* p. 128.

igan, Wisconsin, and the northern portions of Ohio, Indiana, and Illinois.[27] Many speech features mark off this Northern area from the "Midland"—the area occupied primarily by Pennsylvanians.[28] Most of the northern lines, to be sure, pass further to the north in Pennsylvania than do those of the [s] in *grease* and *greasy*. Yet the penetration of northern forms to the area of Philadelphia is occasionally to be observed in other instances; for example, the line of Northern *clapboards* (as against Midland and Southern *weatherboards*) dips sharply southward so as to take in Philadelphia and northern Delaware. Another explanation for the prevalence of [gris] and ['grisi] in east central Pennsylvania might be the fact that much of the area was occupied in the early 18th century by Palatine Germans, whose native dialect had no [z] phoneme at all[29] and who may, for this reason, have favored [s] in any English words where variation between [s] and [z] occurred.

What is the British practice with regard to the pronunciation of *grease* and *greasy?* No complete survey has been made; but there seems no doubt that London usage, as well as "Received Standard" usage throughout southern England, is mixed.[30] The questionnaires which Hempl circulated in England (for his study cited above) showed that in London only 25 and 33 percent of the informants used [s] in *grease* and *greasy;* but that in England exclusive of London the percentages of [s] were 84 and 74.[31] We have no ground, even yet, for rejecting these figures; but it should be pointed out that folk speech in England, just as in the United States, shows its isoglosses. A survey of the linguistic atlas type conducted by Guy S. Lowman in 1934[32] shows that the [z] in *grease* (I have no information on *greasy*) occupies East Anglia and a small adjoining area; that [s] is universal in the remainder of southern England (we are speaking strictly of the rustic type of speaker). Since the line passes through (or very near)

[27] Kurath, *Word Geography,* pp. 1–7; see also Lois K. M. Rosenberry, *The Expansion of New England,* Boston and New York, 1909. Even the island of [s] forms around Marietta, Ohio, is to be explained on the basis of early settlement; this area was first settled by New Englanders as early as the 1780's. See Rosenberry, pp. 175ff.

[28] Examples of Northern words (from Kurath) are *whiffletree, pail, darning needle* ("dragonfly"), and *co, boss!* (cow call). Verb forms which I have found to have similar distributions are *hadn't ought* ("oughtn't"), *how be you?, clim* ("climbed"), and *see* as a preterite of *to see.* Note that Kurath's definition of "Midland" does not coincide with that of Hempl; the area, according to the former, extends much farther to the southwestward of Pennsylvania than Hempl indicated. (See *Word Geography,* pp. 27–37.)

[29] See Carroll E. Reed, *The Pennsylvania German Dialect Spoken in the Counties of Lehigh and Berks: Phonology and Morphology* (Seattle, Wash., 1949), pp. 20 and 29.

[30] See Daniel Jones, *An English Pronouncing Dictionary,* 9th ed., London, 1948.

[31] Hempl, *op. cit.,* pp. 442–43.

[32] Lowman's British field records are filed in an unedited state at the University of Michigan.

432   London, it is easy to see why the metropolitan area should show a mixture of usage.

Is there any evidence of a differentiation in meaning between ['grisi] and ['grizi]? The *Atlas* provides no answer to this question, since, in the interest of obtaining comparable data, the words were always called for in the same context ("grease the car, axle, etc." and "my hands are greasy"). In general, such differentiations in meaning are characteristic of areas of mixed usage, not of those where one pronunciation or another is definitely established. The distinction usually given in dictionaries is that ['grisi] may mean literally 'covered with grease,' while ['grizi] may be used with less literal, and sometimes unpleasant, connotations.[33] What we can say with confidence is that speakers to the south of our isoglosses do not follow this practice: ['grizi] is universal with the literal meaning 'covered with grease'; whether or not more speakers in the area of overlapping, and to the north of it, would have used ['grizi] had the context been different, we are unable to determine.

How should we evaluate the *Atlas* data as a picture of reality? What is most important to realize is that the *Atlas* makes no attempt whatever to record the usage of non-native speakers, or even of those natives who have resided for long periods outside their home communities. Such speakers are rather uncommon in some communities, fairly numerous in others; in a few of the latter, the *Atlas* may even reflect the usage of a minority of old-timers. In view of this, we might be inclined to wonder whether the percentage method might not give a truer picture of prevalent usage than the isogloss method. The proportion of non-native speech forms in a community would, of course, roughly correspond to the proportion of non-native residents; such data would certainly be valuable, though to collect it on a large enough scale (say, 100 or so informants from each county) would be so difficult as to be practically impossible. Few investigators are qualified to make extensive phonetic observations, and those few must take their informants from such captive groups as college classes, whose usage may or may not be spontaneous or representative. Another feature of the *Atlas* that must be considered is the prepon-

---

[33] Daniel Jones, *English Pronouncing Dictionary:* "Some speakers use the forms . . . with a difference of meaning, ['gri:si] having reference merely to the presence of grease and ['gri:zi] having reference to the slipperiness caused by grease." *Webster's NID* states: ". . . many people in all sections use ['grisi] in some connotations and ['grizi] in others, the first esp. in the literal sense, covered with grease." Cf. Kenyon and Knott: "Some distinguish ['grisi] 'covered with grease' from ['grizi] 'slimy' " (*op. cit.*). G. P. Krapp states: "A distinction is sometimes made in the meaning of ['gri:si] and ['gri:zi], the later being regarded as a word of unpleasant connotation" (*op. cit.,* p. 119). *Webster's* implies that this distinction is fairly general throughout the country —a very dubious proposition. T. Larsen and F. C. Walker simply prescribe [s] for the meaning 'sticky' and [z] for the meaning 'slippery'—as though this feature were standard and universal (See *Pronunciation* [Oxford Press, 1931], p. 92.)

derance of rather old informants. Since the interviews were conducted several years ago, many of the forms shown to be current among the aged may now be rare or even obsolete; moreover, the *Atlas* records would not reflect the most recent trends, fads, and innovations—some of which are rapid, others extremely slow. It seems unlikely to me that the lines on *grease* and *greasy* have shifted radically in the last few years, yet I have no doubt that usage may have changed in certain individual communities.[34] All things considered, the *Linguistic Atlas* offers the most reliable body of data as yet assembled, or likely to be assembled in the near future, on American speech; isoglosses based on it reflect the usage of a highly important segment of our population, and they are, moreover, of the highest value in a study of our cultural and settlement history.

[34] Dr. Smith expresses the opinion that the younger generation in New York City has gone over almost entirely to the [s] in *greasy*.

A Note on
It Is/There Is

Juanita V. Williamson

A great deal of information about current English usage can
be found in the short articles printed in such publications
as Webster's *Word Study* (now *Word Watching*) and
American Speech. College English for more than twenty
years (until 1962) published brief articles on usage in its
"Current English Usage" section which was sponsored by
the Committee on Usage. The following brief article
deals with one usage found in current English, primarily
in the South.

In several recent publications whose declared purpose is to describe the
speech of ghetto school children and/or to help them learn to speak Standard English, there are a number of statements which can hardly be considered sound. One such statement, found in *Non-Standard Dialect,*[1] asserts that in the ghetto dweller's speech *it* is substituted for *there* in
sentences such as this: "It was one in the hall this mornin'."

From *Word Study* (October, 1969). Copyright 1969 by G. & C. Merriam Co., publishers of
the Merriam-Webster dictionaries. Reprinted by permission.

[1] Published by the Board of Education of the City of New York and the National Council of
Teachers of English, 1968, p. 10.

It is not substituted for *there* in sentences like this. An examination of 435
the entry under *it* in either *Webster's Second* or *Webster's Third,* however
cursory, reveals that the use of *it* is at least several hundred years old.
Webster's Second states that "*it* was formerly often used where *there* is
now used," and quotes a line from Shakespeare: "It is a peerless kins-
man." *Webster's Third,* in addition to showing that the usage is an old
one, gives some information on its present status. It is labeled *dial.,* a term
used to indicate that the pattern of usage is "too complex for summary,"
usually because it may be found in several varieties of English.

The *Oxford English Dictionary* states that the usage may be found as
early as 1300, in *Cursor Mundi.* It also appeared in other early works, including *Sir Gawain and the Green Knight* and Holinshed's *Chronicles.*

C. C. Fries in *American English Grammar*[2] states that this usage is an
"older use of *it* equivalent to the function word *there.*"

E. Bagby Atwood's *A Survey of Verb Forms in the Eastern United States*[3]
shows that the usage occurs "with some frequency" in West Virginia and
the Chesapeake Bay area. The item investigated for the *Atlas* was the
occurrence of *are/is* in the frame "There (are) many people who think so."
About half of the communities in West Virginia and the Chesapeake Bay
area used "It's many people." Atwood states that *it* "is about as common
in Type II as in Type I speech." He found three cultured informants using
it.[4]

Now what about the current use of this structure in the late 1960's? My
material on the language of Southern white speakers indicates that this
usage is found in the speech of Kentuckians, Tennesseans, Mississippians,
and Texans. The following examples were recorded during the 1968–69
school year either on tapes or in phonetic notation as the speakers talked:

> It's three boys in the band.
> > —*Administrator in a Kentucky university*
>
> So it won't be no confusion.
> > —*Clerk in Memphis cleaning establishment*
>
> It's another store out there.
> > —*Woman on a Memphis bus*
>
> It's two older than I am.
> > —*Former Mississippi resident, poorly educated*
>
> It's about fifty words in it.
> > —*Book company representative, native of Texas*

[2] Appleton-Century-Crofts, Inc., 1940, pp. 244–245.

[3] University of Michigan Press, 1953, pp. 29–30.

[4] *Atlas* informants are classed as type I, those with poor education; type II, those with better
education; and type III, those with superior education. The latter are usually classed as
"cultured."

436   As these examples indicate, the structure is found in the speech of both the high and the low classes in the Southern area. It is probable, however, that *it* occurs more frequently in the speech of the less educated, as Atwood's study indicates. This is usually the pattern in language change: a usage often continues in the speech of the less educated longer than it does in the speech of the educated. It is to be expected that it would be found in the speech of the ghetto dweller since the South is the area from which he or his parents came.

The history of this usage is honorable and long. Even though it may be no longer used by a great many standard speakers, any discussion of its place in present-day standard English should be put on a sound basis so that those who read it may at least view the usage in proper perspective.

Speech Variations in a Piedmont Community

Lewis Levine and Harry J. Crockett, Jr.

This study is concerned with the pronunciation of post-vocalic *r* and the social structure of a North Carolina community usually characterized as *r*-less. Professors Levine and Crockett indicate that the *r*-less prestige pronunciation is now being replaced by an *r* pronunciation, a trend noted earlier by McDavid.

This paper presents some results of a study of speech variation and social structure in a North Carolina Piedmont community. Only one linguistic variable is considered here: the pronunciation of postvocalic *r*.

This article was originally published in *Sociological Inquiry,* Vol. 36, No. 2 (Spring, 1966) 204–226. Reprinted with the permission of the *Journal* of Alpha Kappa Delta.

This research has been supported by the National Science Foundation under grants G 24969 and GS 779. The National Science Foundation Program for Summer Undergraduate Research Participation has also supported the following persons as summer assistants during the study: in 1962, Edgar B. Warren and Clarence Dillard; in 1963, Jane Arndt, Gwathney Tyler, and Elaine Weinreib; and in 1964, David Britt and Judith Housermann.

438   The major results to be discussed are the following. The rates at which *r* was pronounced are not normally distributed about a single central value, but tend to be bimodal. Moreover, such bimodality—suggesting the possibility of two *r*-pronunciation norms—is most pronounced among the higher-status residents of the community. That there are two *r*-norms is further reflected by the tendency for younger and newer residents to pronounce *r* and for older ones and those with long tenure in the community to refrain from making the sound. As attention becomes more focused on pronunciation the general tendency is to increase, rather than decrease, the use of the *r*-sound.

Word pronunciations were elicited in two ways: in sentences and in a word list: both methods show these results. Moreover, differences in pronunciation between the two eliciting situations are related to these social and demographic factors; however, overriding differences between the situations also appear.

Just as people differ in their *r*-pronunciation habits, so also do words vary in the extent to which they elicit *r*-pronunciations in postvocalic position. When words are ranked in this respect, we find linguistic factors which affect *r*-pronunciation; these factors are independent of the eliciting situation.

Finally, a study of transcriber reliability shows that perception of *r* in postvocalic position, in at least one sense of the term "perception," is influenced by the speech habits of transcribers as well as syllable structure.

THE STUDY

Although within any community people differ in linguistic behavior—in pronunciation, in grammatical usages, and in choices of common words and idioms—little is known about the ranges of such variations, about their interplay, or about the social and psychological factors which underly them. Perhaps even less is known about intrapersonal variations—"speech lability." Our aim therefore was exploratory, and our study design called for the inspection of many different linguistic and non-linguistic variables.

The Community. The community studied was selected for several reasons. First, it seemed likely to present a particularly interesting linguistic situation. Located just west of the easternmost boundary of the North Carolina Piedmont region, the community is at or near the confluence of several dialect areas.[1] We wondered whether inhabitants spoke some

---

[1] The community is very near the point at which Kurath and McDavid's areas 15 (the Virginia

"transitional" dialect or dialects or, instead, one or more of the nearby dialects in relatively unmixed form.

Second, the community is reasonably small,[2] stable, and old. The legal boundaries of the town, an approximate square enclosing some 400 acres, have remained constant since 1754. The ancestors of all people in our sample were resident in the United States at least for the last 100 years. The town is far from being isolated; it is a county seat, has some agricultural market facilities, and is near major tobacco markets. It has some textile mills, is within 15 miles of a branch of the State university, and is near the State capitol and several Piedmont cities. It attracts some migrants from the region; also, since roads in this area are good, it provides labor for other nearby communities. However, it participates in regional rather than national patterns of mobility; of our sample of 275 people, only twelve were born outside the Carolinas, Tennessee, Kentucky, Virginia, and Maryland.

The legal boundaries of the town do not enclose the whole of the functional community, i.e., the set of people who look upon themselves, and are regarded by others, as community residents. Town officials, merchants, and other long-term residents consider the functional community to include the populous areas adjoining the legal town.[3] This view excludes those relatively sparsely settled tracts nearby where farming is the typical mode of livelihood. We accepted these judgments; and so, even though we may have excluded the odd household whose members consider themselves community residents, the town, as we studied it, is not an agricultural one. The functionally defined community covers an area of between 1,600 and 2,000 acres.

The Sample. The sample was restricted to white residents of the community. Each of the 1,121 dwelling units normally occupied by white residents was located; a random sample of 400 units was selected from

Piedmont), 16 (northeastern North Carolina), and 17 (Cape Fear and Peedee Valleys) come together. This point is in turn reasonably close to the boundary which has been postulated between the Midland and the South. Several "speech models" are thus available to the inhabitants. See Hans Kurath and Raven I. McDavid, Jr., *The Pronunciation of English in the Atlantic States*, Ann Arbor: University of Michigan Press, 1961.

[2] The community has a population of about 5,000—small enough so that most community members are aware of the functional social groupings that segment the community, and practically all are members of at least one such group.

[3] Extensive westward expansion of the legal town occurred early in this century as textile mills were established; this area is heavily populated today by textile workers and other blue-collar families. More middle-class residences have appeared to the east and south of the town proper, while blue-collar residents predominate directly north of the town. All the residents in these areas view themselves as belonging to the community studied.

440   among these.[4] The individual to be interviewed in each selected household was determined by using Kish's method,[5] which provides for adequate representation in terms of such demographic factors as age and sex. Interviewing began on August 7, 1963. Nearly 80 percent of the total number of interviews obtained (216 out of 275) were completed by the end of August; interviewing continued through December 21, 1963.

We attempted to evaluate the sample we obtained in three ways: (1) We compared respondents interviewed early (during August) to those interviewed later with respect to social and demographic characteristics. (2) We compared respondents to nonrespondents (refusals, not-at-homes, those rejected for senility or speech defects). (3) We compared respondents to the larger population from which they were drawn.

1) The earlier group of respondents contained more females, old people, and persons with white-collar occupations than did the group interviewed later; in fact, the total sample approximated the larger population better than did the August sample alone.

2) One hundred and twenty-five of the 400 selected household units did not yield valid interviews.[6] The nonrespondents appeared to differ from the respondents only in having a very slightly higher incidence of males and, contrary to other surveys, in having status somewhat skewed towards the high end of the continuum.[7]

[4] A number of considerations led to our decision to draw a sample of 400. First, we suspected that attrition in interviews obtained would be greater than one usually meets in sample surveys. We expected that the unusual nature of the respondents' task of speaking into a microphone for from 30 to 45 minutes would noticeably raise the refusal rate. Furthermore, most members of the white community displayed some antipathy towards the Civil Rights demonstrations going on at the time in the nearby university community. Thus, we expected our study to be linked to the Negro protest movement by some prospective sample members. The location of this old, stable, and small community within 15 miles of the university community also resulted in its being studied with some regularity, so that we anticipated some refusals from persons who were simply tired of being interviewed. Given these factors, and our estimate that we could hope to handle no more than 300 cases adequately, a sample of 400 seemed indicated.

[5] Leslie Kish, "A Procedure for Objective Respondent Selection within the Household," *Journal of the American Statistical Association,* 44 (September, 1949), pp. 380–387. Briefly, the procedure required that the interviewer list all adult members of the household (persons 21 years of age or older) by sex and age. One of six respondent selection charts, pre-assigned randomly among the 400 sample units, was then used by the interviewer to determine the household member to be interviewed.

[6] Of these 125 units, three were vacant throughout the entire interviewing period; in nine cases respondents could not be found at home during any of a minimum of five call-backs; in eleven cases respondents could not perform the linguistic task because of deafness or some other physical ailment, speech defects, or illiteracy. In 102 cases respondents refused to be interviewed, and maintained their refusals through contacts by at least two different staff members.

[7] Comparing the nonrespondents to respondents revealed the following: 48 percent of nonrespondents were male, compared to 45 percent of respondents. The nonrespondents were

3) Over-all, the sample obtained also compared favorably with avail- able census data and could be considered a fairly accurate representation of the white population of the functional community, with males slightly underrepresented, and with persons aged 45–54 probably slightly over-represented.[8]

Linguistic Materials. Preliminary work in this region indicated that the

evenly distributed among the residence areas into which we divided the community; had these people responded, observed proportionate distributions over residence areas would have changed by less than two percent in the most extreme case. We identified entries in county tax assessment records for 208 of the 275 respondents, and for 72 of the 125 nonrespondent house-holds. These data suggest that respondents, as a group, were more representative than the non-respondent group of the status range pictured by tax valuations. Nonrespondents were skewed towards the high-status categories, in contrast to the situation typical of sample surveys. Twenty-five percent of nonrespondents had tax valuations of $10,000 or more, compared to 20 percent of respondents; 58 percent of nonrespondents had tax valuations of $5,000 or more, compared to 48 percent of respondents. Eleven percent of nonrespondents had tax valuations of less than $1,000, compared to 12 percent of the respondents.

We are indebted to Mr. Sam W. Gattis, County Tax-Assessor, for access to the tax lists. The data are for 1961 property valuations (not assessed taxes), the latest records available to us at the time. Personal property (such as items of furniture, cars, etc.) as well as real property is included here.

[8] Data were obtained from the *United States Census of Population: 1960. North Carolina, General Population Characteristics, Final Report PC (1)–35B,* Washington, D. C.: U. S. Government Printing Office, 1961. Comparing respondents to the population containing them could only be done by an approximation. Tabulations were available for the town as legally defined; this area corresponded exactly to one of the residence areas sampled in the study. These esti-mates are nonetheless crude for a number of reasons. First, the functional community sampled here is larger than the town as legally defined and smaller than the township of which it is a part, but census figures are available only for these latter two civil divisions. Second, census data for persons aged 21–24 are included in the category "15 to 24 years," making comparisons for the youngest members of our sample (persons aged 21–24) impossible. Finally, our sample was obtained some three years after the census materials were gathered.

Assessment of the sample age and sex distributions, for persons aged 25 and older, by means of the binominal test of nonrandomness, with census proportions taken as universe propor-tions, yielded no probability values near or below the .05 level, both in the case of the total sample and for males and females considered separately.

For sample members residing outside the legally defined town we compared sample distribu-tions to census distributions for the township *minus* the town figures. The accuracy of census figures in depicting the population characteristics of the functional community is probably less here than in the preceding analysis; for not only are Negroes included in the present figures, but also the farm population of the township.

The test for nonrandomness yielded probability values near or below .05 for persons aged 45–54 and 65-and-over in the total sample, and for both the male and female groups aged 45–54. Last, when total sample figures for people aged 25-and-older were compared with cen-sus figures for the entire township, the proportions test for nonrandomness yielded probability values near or below .05 only for those aged 45–54 in the total sample, and among females. The reader must remember that the township and functional community boundaries do not coincide.

442 speech of people who evince maximal vowel differentiation in stressed syllables can be described in terms of 15 stressed vowels.[9] We wished to measure variations in pronunciation and distribution of these vowels. We therefore compiled a list of common words and names which represented each of these vowels in stressed syllables in as many linguistic environments as possible.[10] The words in this list were pretested, in communities near the one reported upon here, to get a rough idea of differences, among the linguistic traits, in the amount of interpersonal variation elicited, and, to discover differences among the words representing each trait. The tests showed, first, that the various linguistic traits did not produce coincident distributions of people, and second, that for each trait, words varied widely in their power to elicit interpersonal variation, particularly variation which cross-cut social class boundaries. A second list of words and names was prepared from the first, in which those word-types were over-represented which elicited much variation and in which, for each word-type, both words showing much social-class linked variability and words showing little social-class linked variability were represented. This second list also included repetitions of many words, to provide a measure of speech lability. These words were used as stimuli in two ways.

First, each word was embedded in a sentence. Each sentence contained from one to four of the words chosen, with no rhymes permitted in any sentence. Further, each sentence contained a blank, to be filled in by the respondents. This device was used to distract respondents from their pronunciation; the blanks were also the vehicles for the collection of data on grammar (e.g., preterit-participle choice, adjective-adverb choice) and on idioms and choices of words (e.g., *sick to-, at-,* or *in my stomach; pail* or *bucket,* etc.). The sentences, themselves pretested, were listed in an order which distributed word-types throughout the test instrument.

Second, many of the words appearing in the sentences were presented in the form of a word-list. Respondents were given the set of sentences and the word-list, and, after some rehearsal with dummy sentences, read first the sentences and then the word-list into tape recorders. After this linguistic task, repondents were interviewed for nonlinguistic information.

---

[9] We use the term *vowel* to avoid any discussion of problems of phonemicization. The vowels are those in a New Yorker's pronunciations of *meet, mitt, mate, merry, Mary, marry, mutt, mob, booth, book, bowl, bawl, down, die,* and *toil.*

[10] As linguistic environments we considered mainly: consonant following the vowel, syllable structure, and syllable position. The list also contained words representing other would-be diagnostic features, e.g., palatalization, labialization, and preaspiration of certain consonants, the pronunciation of the final nasals of present participles, the pronunciation of postvocalic *r;* and, also, various shibboleths employed in the literature, e.g., *mourning, morning, pen,* etc.

Eighty percent of all interviews, linguistic and nonlinguistic parts, were completed in one and one half hours or less.

Interviewers were five male students, trained partly through the program of pretesting. Analyses not mentioned here suggested that dialectal differences among the interviewers had little effect on the respondents' pronunciations.

Transcribing, Coding, and Scoring. Coding the nonlinguistic materials was routine for the most part,[11] since the length of the linguistic portion of the interview precluded the use of open-end questions calling for sophisticated coding procedures. Linguistic data were processed in two steps. A booklet of linguistic check-off sheets had been prepared for use in pretest transcription. Each of the words to be studied was listed under each sentence, and codes representing pronunciations were listed under each word. These codes consisted of columns of phonetic symbols. For example, vowels were assigned as many as three columns, each consisting of symbols appropriate to a vowel segment of the word studied, e.g., *nucleus, offglide.* Appropriate columns were included for the consonants under study as well as (where appropriate) for stress patterns, for voicing of the initial sound of the next word, etc. The columns and the rows of each column were numbered; in the second stage of coding, these numbers were transferred to transfer sheets which served as instructions to operators of IBM keypunch equipment. Although this meant that the major transcription task was selecting those symbols from among a number of alternatives which best represented the observed pronunciations of consonants, vowel segments, etc., the transcribers were also permitted to write in phonetic transcriptions where necessary. Analysis of write-ins resulted in the addition of new symbols for certain word-types to the original code; a residual "other" category was also employed. The transcribing was done by three linguistics graduate students, whose training included both advanced course work in phonology under Levine and additional work specifically addressed to the project. These students also participated in the design of the linguistic test instruments and in the transcriptions of the pretest data. Further details will be given below, under *Reliability.*

Postvocalic r. Here we shall deal with only one speech trait—the presence or absence of an *r*-sound which represents an etymological (or spelled) *r,* placed in phonologically final and preconsonantal positions (e.g., in *bare* and *bark,* but not in *barrel*). This trait is one regarded as diagnostic in dialect geography and has also received some attention from

---

[11] Nonlinguistic materials did not present problems of judgment with the one exception of occupation. Hence, Crockett coded the latter variable.

444   a social point of view.[12] Pronouncing these final and preconsonantal *r*'s with little oral constriction or with none at all is characteristic of Eastern New England, New York City, and of the South Atlantic States except for their Appalachian regions. The tendency in these regions is toward only a weak *r* sound or none at all; for example, *guard* sounds like *god.*

The extreme western portions of the Carolinas and Virginia, and much of the North Carolina Piedmont lie within the Midland dialect area, characterized by fully constricted *r*'s.[13] Now the term "characterized by," although perhaps appropriate to linguistic geography, carries no precise quantitative implications; indeed McDavid, Labov, and others have noted *r*-pronunciations in supposedly *r*-less areas and, at least in the case of the South Carolina Piedmont, McDavid has also noted the reverse.[14]

In order to quantify any tendency to make the *r* sound, we constructed a variable called "R" by assigning a score equal to 100 times the ratio of the number of observations for which an *r*-sound was heard to the total number of observations for which the sound might have been heard. R could be computed for a person, a group of people, an area, a word, or a set of words. Distributions of the values of this variable over words and over people, constitute the subject of this paper.

RELIABILITY

Analyses of inter-transcriber agreement and intra-transcriber consistency have not yet been completed. However, work so far done allows us to have confidence in the data we present here. Two reliability tests were included in the research design: One attempted to shed light on systematic changes in transcribers' habits during the many months required for data transcription; the other attempted to provide a relatively simple synchronic measure of reliability at the end of the transcription period. We report here upon the latter.

A reliability sample of 28 respondents, stratified by age, sex, and education, was selected from among the whole set of 275 respondents; and from among the roughly 600 words considered in the sentences, a linguis-

---

[12] See, in particular, Kurath and McDavid, *op. cit.;* Raven I. McDavid, Jr., "Postvocalic *-r* in South Carolina: A Social Analysis," *American Speech,* 23 (October–December, 1948), pp. 194–203; and William Labov, "Phonological Correlates of Social Stratification," *American Anthropologist,* 66 (December, 1964), in John J. Gumperz and Dell Hymes, editors, *The Ethnology of Communication,* Part 2, pp. 164–176. For a discussion of methodological problems in sociolinguistics see also Glenna R. Pickford, "American Linguistic Geography: A Sociological Approach," *Word,* 12 (1957), pp. 211–233.

[13] Kurath and McDavid, *op. cit.*

[14] McDavid, *op. cit.;* Labov, *op. cit.*

tically stratified sample of 70 words was selected. We had intended that, at the end of the data transcription period, each transcriber would redo each of the 28 interviews twice, transcribing only the selected words. This plan did not materialize, however; one of our transcribers left the project early in the data transcription period and a second left during the middle of the reliability test. Nevertheless, since the relative amounts of material processed by our transcribers was grossly uneven—B, the man who left first, transcribed six percent of the interviews; G, the man who left during the reliability test, transcribed 19 percent of the interviews, while C transcribed the remaining 75 percent of the interviews—we feel that it is meaningful to report C's transcription consistency as well as the agreement rate between C and G.

Seventeen postvocalic *r* words were included in the reliability test. C agreed with herself 98 percent of the time in her transcriptions of the 28 interviews: on eleven of the 17 words her agreement score is 100 percent; it is 88 percent on one word and above 90 percent on the rest. No linguistic pattern is discernible among the words on which she is inconsistent; further, the group of words for which she achieves 100 percent consistency includes both words with the lowest and with the highest R-scores of any in the group of 17. C therefore contributed no systematic bias to the data, and her absolute contribution to over-all error was quite small. G, however, did differ systematically from C. For 97 percent of all disagreements between the two people, C scored *r* where G did not.

Now the 17 words tested seemed to fall into two groups: twelve high-agreement words, whose agreement scores ranged from 79 percent to 95 percent, with an average of 88 percent; and five low-agreement words, whose agreement scores ranged from 27 percent to 57 percent, with an average of 43 percent. With one exception, *poor,* the low-agreement words were those in which the *r* appeared in a nonfinal syllable; with one exception, *thirty,* the high-agreement words had no syllable following the *r.* The high-agreement of *thirty* was undoubtedly due to its stressed vowel; words in which *r* is preceded by a high-central vowel are distinctive. They are commonly pronounced by most Americans with a particular type of constriction which extends over virtually the entire duration of the vowel. A characteristic *r*-color is thus lent to the vowel itself, affording transcribers pronunciation clues of maximal length. The performance of *poor* cannot be so easily explained; however, it is the only *r* word containing its vowel in the entire sentence-list.

We may project these results upon the study as follows: In the 76 postvocalic *r* words in the sentence-list, twelve, i.e., 16 percent, may be expected to be low-agreement words (eleven words which contained syllables following the postvocalic *r,* plus *poor*). We assume that these twelve words would, if tested, have the same average reliability score, 43 percent,

446   as the five of their type in the reliability test. We also assume that the remaining 84 percent of the postvocalic *r* words would, if tested, have the same average reliability score, 88 percent, as the twelve of their type in the reliability test. A weighted estimate of the R-score disagreement to be expected on the entire sentence-list is thus (.12 × 84%) + (.57 × 16%), or 19 percent. Since virtually all of the C-G disagreement was symtematic (i.e., 97 percent of such disagreements occurred when C scored R and G did not), we may assume that the R-scores of the 19 percent of respondents transcribed by G would have been, on the average, 19 percent higher had they been transcribed by C. Putting this in another way, if C were to retranscribe all of the material transcribed by herself and by G we might ex-

pect $\frac{(98 \times 75) + (81 \times 19)}{(75 + 19)}$ or 95 percent of the scores to be the same as they

are now.

     We may view the reliability data in another way. C is a native Midwesterner, who has spent most of her life in that area; G is a native North Carolinian who has spent most of his life in that state. C's speech is considerably higher R than G's. Both had advanced training in phonetics; both participated in the same drills, explicitly designed to prepare them for this research. It is most interesting to observe that the systematic perceptual differences which remained between them were in the same direction as their speech differences; no "overcompensation" occurred. Further, it is interesting to observe that an area of perceptual difficulty can be specified in linguistic terms—perception of postvocalic *r* pronunciations can be said to be affected by the syllable structure of the words involved.

RESULTS

     Before discussing the various distributions of R-scores within the community, and the social factors which underly them, we inspect variations in scores among the words which make up our test instruments. There are 76 postvocalic *r* words in the sentence-list; among these, the R-scores vary from 100 to 20. No two words of adjacent rank differ in R-score by more than six. There are 46 *r*-words in the word list; among these, R-scores vary from 100 to 30, and there is only one case of a score difference as great as eight between adjacently ranked words. Word ranks in the two situations are highly correlated (Spearman's rho = + .93).

     When the R-scores of various groups of words on the sentence-list are compared, we find the following mutually crosscutting effects. (1) Words containing postvocalic *r* in stressed syllables average higher scores than other words (61 vs. 43). (2) Words in which the *r* is followed by another syllable average higher scores than words in which the *r* is followed by a final consonant or consonant cluster, and these in turn average higher scores than words in which the *r* is at the end of the word (69 vs. 54 vs. 47). (3) Words in which the *r* is preceded by high-central vowels average 95; words with low-central vowels (both monophthongs and diphthongs) average 76; words with front vowels average 66; words with back vowels (including those with the vowel in *down*) average 47. The position of the word in the sentence is almost certainly also relevant; however, we have not yet disentangled this effect from speech lability.

These ranks of word categories are duplicated exactly by the word-list data, but in each case scores are higher in the word-list than in the sentence-list. Since rather large differences exist among the numbers of cases (N's) in the various categories, no individual tests of significance of difference were employed; rather, we accept our statements concerning these linguistic factors because the ranking rules found in the two sets of data are exactly the same. This event is in itself highly significant. Further, we take the fact that such rules can be found as an indicator both of the validity of postvocalic *r* as a variable suitable for sociolinguistic study and of the validity of our data collection and data-scoring procedures.

We noted in our discussion of reliability and in the material just presented that those words are distinctive in which the *r* is preceded by high-central vowels which are stressed, e.g., *her, thirty,* or *sermon.* The ten words which were of this type in the sentence-list, and the eight in the word-list all have very high R-scores; further, both in the Piedmont and in the relatively low-R Coastal Plain, these words show little variability from person to person. Therefore, we decided to ignore them in sociolinguistic analyses. Thus, in what follows, the respondent's R-scores are based upon the remaining 66 words in the sentence-list and upon the remaining 38 words in the word-list. The R-score ranges for words on these two test instruments are, then, 86 to 20, and 95 to 30 respectively. When averaged over this material, the community R-scores are 53 for the words in the sentence-list and 60 for the word-list.

The community lies near the eastern limit of the North Carolina Piedmont. Thus, it is roughly midway between the high-R western part of the State and the low-R coast. The two community R-scores can neither reasonably be called high-R nor low-R. We ask, therefore, is the community intermediate or mixed?

When respondents were classified according to R-scores, a distribution resulted which ranged from 0 to 100 for sentence data and also for the word-list data. Respondents thus showed the maximum possible range of R-scores. The frequency distributions on the graph suggest that *in neither*

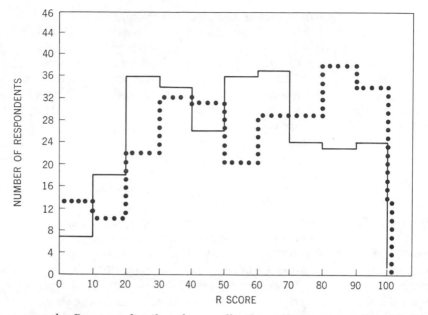

case are the R-scores distributed normally about their means. Considering
first the sentence-list scores; a chi square test of normality (using the
observed mean and standard deviation) showed that there was considerably less than one chance in a thousand that the observed frequencies
could have come from a normally distributed population. The same result
occurred for the word-list scores. Thus, the community cannot be called
a mid-R (intermediate) community. Given the appearance of the histo-
gram of Figure 1, which shows troughs near the mid-ranges, it is instead
reasonable to characterize the community as being linguistically mixed,
i.e., having at least two pronunciation norms in this community, a high-R
(*r*-pronouncing) and low-R (*r*-less) norm. However, to stop here would
be to present too simple a model. First, the troughs are shallow in both of
the curves. Second, the shapes of the two curves seem to differ from each
other, suggesting that, while there is more than one pronunciation norm
within the community, a change in the eliciting situation affects different
people differently.

To pursue these matters further, respondents were grouped into R-score
quintiles, as we show on Table 1; they were studied with respect to education, occupation, age, length of residence in the community, and sex. Also,
group R-scores (in this case the R-score is a mean) were computed for
people so categorized under each eliciting situation. Let us turn first to
relationships which occur in both eliciting situations between quintile
score and various social or demographic variables. Then we shall consider
group-score differences between the two eliciting situations.

Table 1   Quintile Distribution of Respondents by Use of Postvocalic r*

R Quintile	R Score Range	N	Per Cent
Sentence-List Scores			
4	79–100	53	20
3	61–78	53	20
2	43–60	56	21
1	28–42	52	19
0	0–27	53	20
TOTALS		267	100
Word-List Scores			
4	89–100	56	21
3	72–88	54	20
2	51–71	53	20
1	31–50	59	22
0	0–30	49	18
TOTALS		271	101

* Those transcriptions showing "no response" to one third or more of all postvocalic *r* words were eliminated from this and subsequent tabulations. A "no response" was recorded in cases where background noise or tape garbling obliterated the pronunciation, as well as in cases where the respondent uttered some word other than the one desired.

Tables 2 and 3 show, respectively, the frequency distributions within R-score quintiles tabulated separately by education and occupation categories and for sentence words and word-list words; Table 4 shows this R distribution against occupational prestige score categories[15] for sentence words only, the word-list having yielded near identical results. Table 2 shows that, in the highest education category, "any college," there are disproportionately many respondents in both the lowest and the highest R quintiles. In the lowest education category, "grade school or none," frequencies in the lowest and highest R quintiles are disproportionately low. Similarly, Table 3 shows overrepresentation of respondents in the highest and the lowest quintiles in the "nonmanual" category, and underrepresentation of respondents in these quintiles in the "manual" category. Last, considering respondents in terms of occupational prestige, Table 4 also displays this phenomenon. Thus, rather than linear relationships between R-scores and status, as measured in any of the above senses, we see curvi-

[15] The occupational prestige scores developed by Duncan are used here. See Otis Dudley Duncan, in Ira J. Reiss, Jr., *Occupations and Social Status,* New York: Free Press, 1961, pp. 263–275.

Table 2 *Postvocalic r and Level of Education*

| | Level of Education | | | | | | | | | |
| | Any College | | High School Graduate | | Some High School | | Grade School or None | | TOTALS | |
R Quintile	N	%	N	%	N	%	N	%	N	%
Sentence-List Scores										
High										
4	18	27	10	23	6	14	18	16	52*	20
3	8	12	7	16	8	18	30	27	53	20
2	12	18	9	20	12	27	23	21	56	21
1	9	14	13	30	8	18	22	20	52	20
Low 0	19	29	5	11	10	23	19	17	53	20
TOTALS	66	100	44	100	44	100	112	101	266	101
					$X^2 = 18.3, P < .12$					
Word-List Scores										
High										
4	25	30	11	20	8	18	16	14	55*	20
3	10	15	10	23	9	20	25	22	54	20
2	8	12	10	23	9	20	26	23	53	19
1	9	14	11	25	11	24	28	24	59	22
Low 0	19	29	2	5	8	18	20	17	49	18
TOTALS	66	100	44	101	45	100	115	100	270	99
					$X^2 = 21.3, P < .05$					

* Education not ascertained for one respondent.

450

linear relationships, in which high education and occupation are associated, respectively, with *both the highest and the lowest R-scores*. Both of the two pronunciation norms we have posited can thus be said to be socially sanctioned in the community: respondents highest by our various measures of status, are sharply polarized with respect to *r*-pronunciation habits.

Let us now view these tables from a somewhat different perspective. Let us consider respondents who arc in neither the highest nor the lowest R-score quintile. If the frequencies of the intermediate R-quintiles (i.e., 3, 2, and 1) are added together, for each social category, Tables 3 and 4 show that these sums are overrepresented, respectively, for manual workers (as expected) and for each of the two lower prestige categories. In the latter case, Table 4 suggests that intermediateness thus considered is an inverse function of social status, i.e., the lower the status the greater the proportion of intermediate-R people. Table 2 supports this idea if the scores for the two "high-school" categories are combined both in Parts A and B of the table, i.e., if the number of education categories is reduced to three: "any college," "any high-school," and "grade school or none." (In both parts of Table 2 and prior to such addition, high-school graduates had a higher proportion of people in the intermediate R-quintiles than did either adjacent educational category.) Thus, in addition to having found maximum polarization among respondents at the highest ends of the social scales considered, we now find maximum intermediateness among respondents at the lowest ends and "intermediate intermediateness" among respondents in the middle. And so if we wish to speak of "norm clarity," we can say that the two *r*-pronunciation norms posited above are held to more clearly by the people at the higher ends of the various social scales than by those at the lower ends. *R-norm clarity, or R-norm strength, rather than R-score, seems to be that which is linearly associated with social position.*

Data which are not shown indicate that all of these relationships hold even when we eliminate people born outside of the six-state region—the Carolinas, Kentucky, Tennessee, Virginia, and Maryland. The effects just described are not the outcomes of the migration into the community of highly educated Yankees and of natives of the Deep South.

Crosscutting the curvilinear relationship are two linear ones. Tables 5 and 6 summarize the distribution of respondents in each quintile by age and by length of residence in the community, respectively. Table 5 shows that older people are lower-R than younger people, both for sentence eliciting and for word-list eliciting. Table 6 shows that comparing people who have been residents in the community for ten years or less and those resident in the community for eleven years or more, the shorter term residents are the higher R. This effect persists when age of respondent is controlled: in each age-group, short-term residents are higher R than long-

Table 3   Postvocalic r and Occupation*

		Occupation					
R Quintile		Nonmanual		Manual		TOTALS	
		N	%	N	%	N	%
Sentence-List Scores							
High	4	22	26	27	16	49	20
	3	11	13	42	25	53	21
	2	17	20	34	21	51	20
	1	15	18	37	22	52	21
Low	0	20	24	25	15	45	18
TOTALS		85	101	165	99	250	100

$$X^2 = 9.47, P < .06$$

		N	%	N	%	N	%
Word-List Scores							
High	4	25	29	28	17	53	21
	3	16	19	38	22	54	21
	2	11	13	40	24	51	20
	1	16	19	41	24	57	22
Low	0	18	21	22	13	40	16
TOTALS		86	101	169	100	255	100

$$X^2 = 11.1, P < .05$$

* Unmarried women excluded. Married women are classified by their husbands' occupations.

Table 4   Postvocalic r and Prestige of Occupation*

		Occupational Prestige Score Category							
R-Quintile Sentence-List Scores		70 and Above		50–69		Below 50		TOTALS	
		N	%	N	%	N	%	N	%
High	4	20	27	16	16	12	16	48	19
	3	10	13	18	18	25	33	53	21
	2	10	13	24	24	17	23	51	20
	1	16	21	25	25	11	15	52	21
Low	0	19	25	16	16	10	13	45	18
TOTALS		75	99	99	99	75	100	249	99

$$X^2 = 19.3, P < .02$$

* Unmarried women excluded. Married women are classified by their husbands' occupations. The N here is one less than that shown on Table 3 because sufficient information for assigning an occupational prestige score was lacking for one respondent.

Table 5   Postvocalic r and Age

R Quintile		21–39 Years		40–59 Years		60 Years and Over		TOTALS	
		N	%	N	%	N	%	N	%
Sentence-List Scores									
High	4	28	27	18	16	7	15	53	20
	3	15	15	30	26	8	17	53	20
	2	23	23	26	22	7	15	56	21
	1	21	21	21	18	10	21	52	20
Low	0	15	15	21	18	16	33	52*	20
TOTALS		102	101	116	100	48	101	266	101

$$X^2 = 15.8, P < .05$$

R Quintile		21–39 Years		40–59 Years		60 Years and Over		TOTALS	
		N	%	N	%	N	%	N	%
Word-List Scores									
High	4	27	26	20	17	9	18	56	21
	3	22	21	24	21	8	16	54	20
	2	20	19	28	24	5	10	53	20
	1	2	21	29	25	8	16	59	22
Low	0	12	12	16	14	20	40	48*	18
TOTALS		103	99	117	101	50	100	270	101

$$X^2 = 24.8, P < .01$$

* Age not ascertained for one respondent.

term residents. Moreover, separate age distributions were tabulated using sentence data for respondents within each of the four extreme categories formed by education and R-quintile: "Quintile 4—some college," "Quintile 4—grade school or none," "Quintile O—some college," and "Quintile O—grade school or none." These data show that relationship between R and age obtains for *both* of the extreme education categories; in either case the average age of the Quintile 4 respondents was lower than the average age of the Quintile O respondents. However, using these sentence data, the difference between the average ages of respondents in the extreme quintiles was twice as great in the case of the college people than in the case of the grade-school people (the difference being 13.0 years and 6.3 years respectively). That younger people and shorter-term residents are more likely than older people and longer-term residents to pronounce *r* with constriction suggests, of course, that the community is experiencing transition. Since the national norm is clearly high-R, it is reasonable to assume that factors outside the community, rather than

454   *Table 6   Postvocalic r Length of Residence in Community*

		Length of Residence in Community					
	R Quintile	Ten Years or Less		More Than Ten Years		TOTALS	
		N	%	N	%	N	%
Sentence-List Scores							
High	4	23	40	30	14	53	20
	3	10	18	43	21	53	20
	2	6	11	49	23	55*	21
	1	11	19	41	20	52	20
Low	0	7	12	46	22	53	20
TOTALS		57	100	209	100	266	101

$$X^2 = 21.1, P < .001$$

Word-List Scores							
High	4	23	40	33	16	56	21
	3	8	14	46	22	54	20
	2	10	18	42	20	52*	19
	1	7	12	52	24	59	22
Low	0	9	16	40	19	49	18
TOTALS		57	100	213	101	270	100

$$X^2 = 18.0, P < .002$$

* Length of residence for one respondent not ascertained.

within, underlie this transition (e.g., not any rise in influence of the speech of some high-prestige inhabitants when compared to others). The suggestion that the community is in transition will now be discussed when we report score differences between the two eliciting situations.[16]

So far we have only reported certain effects which appear separately in each set of data. Let us now compare the two sets.

Linguists have on occasion characterized some speech performances as being more formal than others. Such characterizations, when they are

[16] Note that the community, though depicted on Kurath and McDavid's map as being reasonably near the Midland-South boundary, is in fact in their own Southern dialect area. They consider this area *r*-less. If we take the map as a reflection of the preponderant pronunciations in the community some 30 years ago (when their data were collected) rather than any methodological naiveté on their part, then we could consider the present community R-scores, and the status and age relations we have discussed, to be the outcomes of this transition toward the national norm.

not wholly *a priori,* are typically based either upon a social characterization of the speech situation[17] or upon the presence or absence of certain vocal qualifiers and certain features of intonation.[18] Of the various motives underlying the use of a term such as "formal speech," perhaps two are frequent: an attempt is either made to formulate some aspect of a speaker's view of his language, e.g., his concept of "correct" pronunciation; or an attempt is made to characterize the speaker's view of some social situation or social relation. Distinctions between "formal" and "informal" speech are then neither clear nor unambiguous. Nevertheless, we wish to consider differences between our sentence-list scores and our word-list scores in this context.

Now, linguists generally would agree that between conversation and reading aloud, the latter is the more likely to yield formal speech performances, having appropriate intonational characteristics and even having some distinctive pronunciations of vowels and consonants. Both our sets of data are reading data; nevertheless, of the two reading situations we expect the word-list responses to be "more formal" than those of the sentence-list. The reader should note that, in reading the sentences, respondents were at least unaware of the particular words whose pronunciation we should study, and at best were unaware of our interest in anything except the items used to fill in the blanks. We did not study the pronunciations of these items. On the other hand, there was no way that we could disguise, even from our least reflective respondents, the fact that their reading the word-list was an exercise in pronunciation. We attempted no such disguise; thus, while both situations were artificial and perhaps even disturbing, we attempted to present respondents with two situations which were disturbing in explicitly different ways. As well as we could manage it, respondents were invited to "worry" about their word-choices on the sentence-list and about their pronunciations on the word-list. No check has yet been made of differences in vocal qualifiers and intonations between the two situations except this: Impressionistically, the word-list pronunciations appear to be much slower than sentence-list word pronunciations.

There is certainly no way in which we might interpret pronunciation differences between the two eliciting situations in terms of attitudes toward social situations. However, we do choose to consider that if pronunciation differences between the two situations have any meaning apart from considerations of methodology, these differences must somehow reflect the speakers' attitudes toward "correct" pronunciations. Once

---

[17] For example, see John L. Fischer, "Social Influences in the Choice of a Linguistic Variant," *Word,* 14 (1958), pp. 47–56.

[18] See Labov, *op. cit.*

456   again, we remind the reader that the literature of linguistics is very far from compelling us to take this view.

As noted earlier, the community's R-score for word-list is higher than its R-score sentence-list (60 vs. 53). This difference is significant, i.e., t = 2.98, p < .01. The increase in R-score is net: of those 265 respondents for whom both sets of data are available, 188 increase, 68 decrease, and nine are constant in score from sentence-list to word-list. Not only do the increasers outnumber the decreasers, it is also the case that the average increase per person increasing is greater than the average decrease per person decreasing: 13.2 as against 7.3. Further, when respondents are grouped by sentence-list R-scores into "high-" "mid-," and "low-R" people, we find that although increasers outnumber decreasers in each of these groups, the high-R group has a disproportionate share of increasers while the low-R group has a disproportionate share of decreasers.

This broad comparison of the two sets of data adds credence to the propositions already offered. First, the difference between the R-scores of the two situations is significant, hence we have some basis for believing that different psycholinguistic factors underlie pronunciations in the two situations. Second, if we take word-list pronunciations as being more likely than sentence-list pronunciations to tap respondents' concepts of "correct" speech, i.e., if we describe the word-list as having a "speech-value intensification" effect, we can then see, in the net-increase in R-score, the presence of the outside, national *r*-pronouncing norm. Further, the disproportionate number of decreasers among sentence low-R people, and the disproportionate number of increasers among sentence high-R people is consonant with the notion that two separate *r*-norms exist in the community. The fact that the number of increasers is greater than the number of decreasers, and the fact that average increases per increaser exceed average decreases per decreaser remind us that for low-R people, the outside norm and the local *r*-less norm conflict while for high-R people the local and the outside norms are the same. Note that the results of these comparisons can be treated in an alternative fashion. If, instead of considering our statements about norms to be hypotheses, we had taken them as given, we could then interpret the comparisons as supporting the view that word-list pronunciations tap speakers' concepts of correct pronunciation. This alternative approach will not be pursued in this paper at all; to do so without considering data on pronunciation variables other than R would be foolish.

People differ in their tendencies to change in R-score according to certain social and demographic characteristics: age, length of residence in the community, occupation and education, and sex, all appear to be related to score differences between sentence-list and word-list. These relations appear both when score change values are studied and when proportions of increasers and decreasers are studied. Also, when the latter proportions are retabulated separately in terms of the demographic variables and for respondents classified into "high-," "mid-," and "low-R" groups (on the basis of sentence R-scores), the systematic effects which appear for the whole sample are sustained. Thus, in a gross sense, at least, the effects of nonlinguistic characteristics on changes in R-score are independent of the R-score itself.

The reader will recall the relation we have noted between sentence-list R-score and frequencies of score increase and decrease: The proportion of score increasers is greater among high-R people than among either mid- or low-R people; and the proportion of score decreasers is greater among low-R people than among either high- or mid-R people. When social and demographic variables are held constant, and proportions of increasers and decreasers in the various R-groups are compared in this way, we find that, while the relationship between R-score and change in R-score tends to hold, there are some anomalies. They are all of the following form: For one term of each of the variables, sex, occupation, and education (e.g., college respondents), score increasers are slightly more frequent proportionately among mid-R respondents than among high-R respondents; and, for the same term, score decreasers are proportionately slightly more frequent among high-R than mid-R respondents.

Specifically, the social and demographic factors show the following systematic effects. As we have noted above, the younger respondents tend to have higher R-scores than the older ones in both eliciting situations. Table 7 shows that younger informants also tend to increase in R-score from sentence-list to word-list more so than do the older ones. Consonant with this we find that respondents who increase in R-score have a lower average age, 44 (N = 188), than do respondents who decrease in R-score, 49 (N = 67). This average age difference occurs among respondents in all three sentence-score ranges; however, it is miniscule for mid-R respondents (one year) but higher for low- and high-R respondents (seven and eight years respectively). A somewhat surprising picture is presented when respondents are grouped by length of residence in the community. Newer residents had higher R-scores than did longer-term residents, in both eliciting situations; however, Table 7 shows that respondents living in the community for ten years or less showed a smaller tendency to increase on the word-list than did the older residents. Since the sentence R-score of the "newer residents" group was itself quite high, a "ceiling effect" severely restricts the net increase here; in fact, the newer residents' R-score for the word-list was the highest of all of the subgroup scores in the table.

Respondents in households headed by nonmanual workers or by workers in higher-prestige occupations increased in R-score from sentence-list to word-list more than did manual and lower-prestige respondents (Table 7). The R-scores for education subgroups in Table 7 suggest that respondents who were high school graduates but who did not attend college made

Table 7   R-Scores by Sentence and Word-List, and by Age, Length of Residence in Community, Occupation, Education, and Sex

	Sentence-List	Word-List	Net Increase
Age			
21–39 Years	56.6	65.1	8.5
40–59 Years	54.2	60.3	6.1
60 Years and Over	44.5	49.3	4.8
Length of Residence in Community			
Ten Years or Less	63.1	67.5	4.4
More than Ten Years	50.8	57.3	6.5
Occupation			
Nonmanual	52.8	62.4	9.6
Manual	54.0	60.2	6.2
Prestige of Occupation			
70 and Above	47.9	58.8	10.9
50–69	50.7	59.6	8.9
Below 50	56.5	61.1	4.6
Education			
Any College	52.7	58.9	6.2
High School Graduate	54.6	65.6	11.0
Some High School	50.0	57.0	7.0
Grade School or None	52.6	57.3	4.7
Sex			
Male	52.3	57.4	5.1
Female	52.9	61.1	8.2

an important contribution to this effect, having the highest net increase in R-score of any educational group (or indeed, of any subgroups shown in the table). Table 7 also shows that those with only a grade school education had the lowest net increase of all education categories (though not the lowest net increase of all subgroups in the table). When the respective frequencies of respondents who increased and who decreased are considered, we find that score increasers are overrepresented among nonmanuals in relation to the total sample and decreasers are overrepresented among manual workers. Considering education in this way we find that the high school graduates were almost always increasers, while the greatest proportion of score decreasers were found among grade school respondents. It is interesting to note that among respondents who attended college, decreasers were somewhat overrepresented. However, when college people were grouped by sentence-score range we found that this overrepresentation was localized among high-R and low-R respondents; increasers were overrepresented among mid-R college respondents.

Turning now to the sex variable, Table 7 shows that although there was no significant difference between males and females in sentence-list R scores, females showed a greater net increase than did males. When the numbers of respondents who increased and decreased were tabulated, females showed some overrepresentation of increasers and males some overrepresentation of decreasers. When such a tabulation was performed separately for respondents classified by sentence score as "high-," "mid-," or "low-R," this effect prevailed throughout.

The anomalies to which we have referred apply to nonmanuals, to college people, and to females. When frequencies of increasers and decreasers across the sentence R-score ranges are compared, we find that the mid-R respondents among these people have slightly more increasers proportionately than did high-R respondents, and high-R respondents have proportionately slightly more decreasers than mid-R respondents.

In summary, women, members of families headed by nonmanual workers or by those in prestigeful occupations, high school graduates who did not attend college, young persons, and long-term community residents all showed a disproportionate number of score increasers and higher net score increases than did the other respondents. Spurious results seem likely only in the case of length of residence, where the high sentence R-score (63.1) of shorter term residents precludes any appreciable increase in score.

We conclude the data presentation on speech variation and social organization in this community by considering only the large score differences (so far we have considered all score differences, regardless of their size). We compared occupations after having combined sentence-list and

Table 8   Postvocalic r Joint Quintile Scores on Sentence-List and Word-List by Occupation*

R Quintile for Sentence-Word		Occupation					
		Nonmanual		Manual		TOTALS	
		N	%	N	%	N	%
High	4–4	18	21	21	13	39	16
	3–3	5	6	19	12	24	10
	2–2	6	7	17	10	23	9
	1–1	8	9	22	13	30	12
Low	0–0	15	17	16	10	31	12
	Increasing	23	27	38	23	61	24
	Decreasing	11	13	31	19	42	17
	TOTALS	86	100	164	100	250	100

$$X^2 = 10.0, P < .12$$

* Unmarried women excluded. Married women are classified by their husbands' occupations.

460   word-list R-scores by classifying respondents into seven groups: Those whose scores were in the highest quintile, next highest quintile, etc. in *both* situations; those whose scores increased from sentence-list to word-list sufficiently to place them one quintile higher on the word-list distribution than on the sentence-list distribution ("increasing"); and those whose scores decreased sufficiently to place them one quintile lower on the word-list distribution than on the sentence-list distribution ("decreasing"). Table 8 shows that the binormal characterization of the community still holds; and, while in both occupational distributions the highest proportions of respondents fell into the increasing R-group, respondents from manual households appear more frequently in the decreasing R-group than do respondents from nonmanual households. This effect is highlighted by comparing proportions of increasers and decreasers within each of the two occupational categories: among the nonmanual respondents, these respective proportions are .27 and .13; among the manual respondents, the comparable figures are .23 and .19.

If we assume that the respondents' concepts of correct speech are also positive indicators of directions of linguistic change, we may see the community's march toward the national norm as spearheaded by women, young people, short-term residents of the community, and by those who are near but not quite at the top of the "white-collar" class. Instead of invoking the "spearhead" image, by which we imply that the community is composed of those who lead and those who lag in some single direction of change, we can of course ask whether a reference-group approach might not also apply. The latter view would suggest that women, young people, the newer residents, and higher status persons take the national *r*-norm as their speech model, while the linguistic behavior of males, older people, long-term residents, and blue-collar respondents is referred to a Southern prestige norm—the *r*-less pronunciations of the coastal plain—a thesis which is consonant with McDavid's.[19] We have no reason to take a position at this time. In either event, when the word-list—sentence-list score differences are used as predictors of change, there is strong suggestion that *r*-score distributions within the community will show a more linear relation to social stratification at some future time than is now the case. High-status people may come to be higher-R than low-status people.[20]

[19] McDavid, *op. cit.*

[20] Adding this speculation to that expressed in footnote 15 above, we would then get the following developmental sequence: a low-R community; a mixed-R community with both norms socially approved; a socially stratified, mixed-R community or a socially stratified, intermediate-R community; and, finally, a high-R community.

Breaking, Umlaut, and the Southern Drawl

James H. Sledd

There has not yet been advanced an analysis of American
English that fits all dialects. Professor James H. Sledd
has on many occasions pointed out that the current analyses
do not take into account the distinctive phonetic features
of Southern English. In this article he discusses a number of
these features, and points out what governs their
occurrence. The pronunciations on which he bases his
discussion can be found in large areas of the South. Dr. Sledd
is Professor of English at the University of Texas.

In 1955, in a review of the Trager-Smith *Outline of English Structure,*[1]
I made a first attempt at phonemicizing an old-fashioned dialect of Atlanta, Georgia, which did not seem to fit the over-all pattern of nine vow-

From *Language,* Vol. 42, Pt. I (1966) 18–41. Reprinted with the permission of the Linguistic
Society of America and James H. Sledd.

[1] *Lg.* 31.312–45 (1955).

462   els and three semivowels that Trager and Smith had proposed. Further
discussion followed at the First Texas Conference in 1956, where the
arguments for a tenth vowel were strengthened by Raven I. McDavid and
Sumner Ives; but even the rebellious, at that time, were still working
within the Smith and Trager framework, and when their arguments were
published in the proceedings of the Conference, they suffered because the
secretary who transcribed them had been unable to cope with so many
different dialects and because proofreading had been peccable. A tentative report on the Conference to the 1956 Linguistic Institute at Ann
Arbor was received with benevolent amusement, and ensuing debates
with myself and Hans Kurath appeared in later numbers of *Language*[2]
and in my *Short Introduction to English Grammar*.[3] Kurath has maintained
his outspoken skepticism of all Trageretic analyses in *The Pronunciation
of English in the Atlantic States*[4] and in *A Phonology and Prosody of
Modern English*.[5] Meanwhile Morris Halle and Noam Chomsky launched
their attack on "the taxonomic approach," and Chomsky suggested, at
the Fourth Texas Conference, that the phonetic features which seemed to
set the Atlanta dialect so distinctively apart are really predictable by low-
level rules in the morphophonemic component of a generative grammar,
so that the dialect's phonemic system is actually the same or much the
same as his, which in turn is much like the General American of Kenyon
and Knott's *Pronouncing Dictionary*.[6] If this is true, then the analysis in
A Short Introduction, which seemed to me in 1959 a departure from the
Trager-Smith system, was in fact an unintentional reduction to absurdity
of their still dominant bad principles; and Kurath's analysis, though
closer to The Truth, still recognizes unnecessary phonemes and is unsup-
ported by adequate theory. Chomsky invited me to contemplate these un-
flattering conclusions at MIT in the summer of 1962. The result is the
present paper, which owes a great deal to the continuing spiritual minis-
trations both of Chomsky and Halle and of my colleagues William B.
Rood Jr. and Harold Hungerford.

No one, I hope, will suspect my mentors of the light-mindedness and informality which characterize the discussion: any guilt is mine. The intention is, however, that the earnest and competent inquirer should be able
to translate my conclusions into MITesian lingo of distinctive features and
formally stated rules. The rules would appear in the third and last part of

[2] 33.111–22 (1957), 34.252–60 (1958).

[3] Chicago, 1959.

[4] Ann Arbor, 1961 (with Raven I. McDavid).

[5] Ann Arbor, 1964.

[6] Springfield, 1944.

the morphophonemics, so that my transcriptions belong in the no-man's-land between systematic phonemics and systematic phonetics. Hence they are enclosed neither in phonetic brackets nor phonemic slants, but within vigilant exclamation points; and on the occasions when I do refer to distinctive features, the context must indicate whether they are the binary features of phonemics or the graded features of phonetics. Quotations and citations from other works naturally follow the authors' usage of slants or brackets.

More particularly, I assume seven pairs of vowels which I am rashly calling tense and lax. The seven tense vowels are the !i! of *meet,* the !e! of *mate,* the !æ! of *bare,* the !u! of *boot,* the !o! of *boat,* the !ɔ̄! of *bought,* and the !ā! of *bar.* The first five are matched by lax !ɪ! in *mitt,* !ɛ! in *met,* !æ! in *mat,* !ʊ! in *put,* and !ʌ! in *mutt.* Lax !ɑ! is in *pot,* and lax !ɔ! is decorative and may be nice to keep in the house for British guests, though I have no immediate use for it myself. I call the first elements of the four diphthongs lax: !ɑɪ! in *flle,* !ɑʊ! in *foul,* !ɔɪ! in *foil,* and !ɪu! in *tune.* Only !ɑɪ! and !ɑʊ! are important to the argument.

Latent indignation unaroused by those assumptions may be visited on my nontechnical use of the term *glide,* which is prompted by the optimistic thought that the context should usually keep things fairly clear while I avoid hassles over consonantal and vocalic and pluses and minuses. Anyway, I recognize three glides, two that I call velar and one palatal. The velar glide !ʊ! is upward and backward toward high back round, as usual; the velar glide !ə! is centering; the palatal glide !r! is upward and forward toward unround high front; but—again as usual—the areas represented by the chosen letters include a considerable range of ending-points. I suppose it is useless to remind the indignant that in the context of this discussion the choice of alphabetic symbols is ultimately of no importance; and if these explanations will not suffice, I can only predict that catharsis will be complete when I sometimes use *preconsonantal* in reference to positions before Jakobsonian consonants, glides, and liquids—all three. The symbol !#!, I should add, is Chomskyite, not Trageretic: not double cross, but the boundaries in *hear#* and *hear#ing.*

As for the argument itself, it begins with Kurath's free mid-central vowel /ɜ/ as in *word,* which I think is neither /ɜ/ nor the !ʌr! sequence. The set of informal rules which closes this first section is expanded, at the end of the second, to apply to other developments involving preconsonantal and final !r!; and after announcing a belated conversion to the doctrine that the *r*-less dialects are *r*-ful, I next attempt to apply much the same rules to words with final and preconsonantal !l!. The most hubristic section defends the Anglo-Saxon heritage of the South by discovering that breaking and umlaut are vigorously alive in Modern English—and governed by the same rules that handle !l! and !r!. A final section reviews and

464   illustrates all the rules, restores the South to the Union by emphasizing that its differentness is only superficial, and repeats a number of exaggerated claims.

/ɜ/

       In Modern British and American English, words like *bird, earth, err, first, fur, work,* and *word* itself are pronounced in a good many different ways, as everybody knows. In the Received Pronunciation of British English, they have a long, unrounded, mid-central vowel without *r*-color, which Jones writes as [ə:] in his *Pronouncing Dictionary,*[7] Gimson as /ɜɪ/ in his *Pronunciation of English.*[8] In the English of Scotland and in some dialects of the north of England, according to Gimson, a pronunciation with [ɪ], [ɛ], [ʌ], or [ʊ] plus /r/ is used instead of [ɜ:]; and in southwestern English dialects one hears either the obscure vowel [ə] followed by a usually retroflex /r/ or else the obscure vowel with simultaneous retroflexion of the tongue, the well-known *r*-colored vowel of much American English.[9] In the United States, the situation is just as complicated. Kurath describes the most common variant as "a more or less 'constricted' mid-central [ɜʳ] sound, in which the tongue is withdrawn, humped up in the back, and laterally constricted. Not infrequently, there is an upglide with progressive constriction of the tongue."[10] Some American pronunciations, however, are phonetically *r*-less. In particular, they include various long mid-central vowels like that of RP, and a diphthong (Kurath's [ɜɨ]) which is popularly regarded as Brooklynese but has been reported from various other localities in the Atlantic states for three-quarters of a century. Though its origin is unexplained, it is so common in the up-country of the lower South that Kurath calls it dominant "from South Carolina westward." Despite such phonetic variety, he treats the mid-central vowel of RP and all the American variants as one and the same free vowel /ɜ/, whether the variants are retroflex or nonretroflex, constricted or unconstricted, monophthongal or diphthongal.
       Not every linguist has been as willing as Kurath to accept the consequences of univocalic analyses like his (or as unwilling to supply an explanatory theory). The phonetic manifestations of his postulated vowel differ widely—but without explanation—both within and between dialects; its acceptance forces the recognition of surprising word-structures,

[7] 11th ed.; London, 1956.

[8] London, 1962.

[9] Gimson 117.

[10] *Phonology* 120.

like /hɜ-i/ (*hurry*) in some American English; a certain amount of morphophonemic alternation becomes necessary, as in *furry* with /r/ but *fur* without it; the postulated vowel itself adds one to the roster of phonemes; and if that addition is made, the force of system may compel the addition of still other units, like Kurath's vowel /ɑ/ as in *car* and his semivowel /ə/ in words like *dear,* both of which he assumes for dialects where postvocalic /r/ has been 'lost as such'.[11] These last postulations are not only open to many of the same objections which can be made to Kurath's free mid-central vowel: they also create an appearance of greater structural difference between dialects than the fact of easy communication would suggest. Historians, finally, might think it significant that the free mid-central vowel, without an /r/, should appear only in words where /r/ historically did occur and where *r*-coloring is still heard in the speech of millions. The modern dialects show plainly that *r*-lessness in *bird* etc. is a late phonetic development from an earlier sequence [ər], which itself had resulted from the merging of three lax vowels before /r/ plus a consonant or before /r/ final.

In these circumstances, the obvious proposal has repeatedly been made —namely, to replace Kurath's free mid-central vowel with the sequence /ər/ as the basis for the dialectal variants. But Kurath's is not the only way to construct an overall pattern. One may also reject altogether any single underlying representation, whether /ɜ/ or /ər/ or anything else, and propose instead a whole set to match the variants, as Trager and Smith have done: /ər/, /əhr/, /əh/, /əy/, etc. The three questions which thus emerge are (1) whether to represent the variants individually or by some underlying form or forms from which they can be derived, (2) what underlying form or forms to postulate if derivation is attempted, and (3) by what precise phonetic rules to describe that derivation. Trager and Smith have chosen individual representation; Kurath has postulated a dubious underlying form; and no one, so far as I know, has even attempted to formulate phonetic rules. That attempt should make the previous questions easier to talk about.

For the northern British dialects which Gimson mentions, there is apparently no problem. Since they preserve the historical three-way distinction, a single representation, like /ɜ/ or /ər/, would only force a second listing of most of the relevant words in the rules that would divide them into their three groups. Hence, underlying forms with !er!, !ɪr!, and !ʊr! will have to be entered in the North Briton's lexicon and will emerge on the phonetic level generally unmodified by the operation of any rules. In a grammar of American English, on the other hand, three separate vowels in underlying forms cannot normally be assumed. In *work* (say), and *bird,*

---

11 Op. cit. 108, 81.

466 and *earth,* the vowels are alike, whatever they are, and the language affords the native speaker no cues for making a distinction, which would have no psychological reality even for the ingenious dialectologist. The familiar /ər/, in these circumstances, seems at first a plausible analysis. The difference between Scottish and American dialects, in the /ər/ words, would then be statable as the falling together of American lax vowels in the one lax vowel /ə/ before /r/ plus a consonant, liquid, glide, or major morpheme boundary.[12] The statement would be purely historical and would not enter into the description of any dialect.

Unfortunately for the advocates of single representations, whether /ər/ or Kurath's /ɜ/, it turns out that that statement actually is necessary, as a descriptive phonetic rule, for all of Kurath's and Gimson's dialects except only the northern British. The evidence is clear, though limited to a rather small group of words of which the noun *error* and the verb *to err* provide a good example. In the noun, [ɛr] (with retracted vowel) before a vowel matches Kurath's free mid-central in word-final in the verb; and since *hear* and *heard* are comparable to *bleed* and *bled, err* is comparable to *heard* and !ɛ! underlies *heard, err,* and *error*—all three. Parallels to *hear* and *heard* include *dear, dearth, inferior, infernal, superior, superlative,* while *error* and *err* are related as *clerical* to *clerk, deterrent* (sometimes with retracted [ɛ]) to *deter,* and *experiment* to *expert.* (I will not risk *eremite* and *hermit.*) Such pairs demand the rule for collapsing the distinctions among the lax vowels in the stated environments before !r!.

And the rule does not complicate the grammar. On the contrary, its incorporation into American and southern British grammars may really simplify them, since the rule allows some hundreds of words to be represented, before it operates, with nothing more definite than lax vowels, instead of particular lax vowels fully specified. So, because *err* happens to be paired with *error,* the grammar of an American dialect will specify !ɛ! as the underlying vowel in both words; but in *work* and *bird* and *earth,* since no such cue as *error* is available, a correct specification, and one sufficient for the phonetic rules, will be lax vowel only, without the full range of distinctive features. In this connection, therefore, northern British will differ from American English in two ways: it will distinguish dif-

---

[12] It seems necessary here to say !r! plus major morpheme boundary instead of !r! final, for inflected and derived forms of words with final !r! have been reshaped by analogy with the simplices: *carry* and *hurry* show that *starry* and *stirring* are not regularly developed. The analogy belongs to history, not description, which it awkwardly complicates. For example, between a tense vowel and intervocalic !r! in *hairy, boring,* and the like, one hears the same glide as in *hair* and *bore;* but the glide of *feel* does not appear in *feeling,* though the two liquids are governed generally by the same rules.

To say "word boundary" would confuse the absolute final of *star* with the medial !r! of *starry;* and to say "major" is necessary because the boundary in *error* is not the same as the boundary in *erring.*

ferent lax vowels before !r!, whether or not the !r! is prevocalic; and a
grammar for northern British will lack the suggested phonetic rule that
lax vowels in the stated environments fall together as !ʌ!. The phonetic
rules will operate quite satisfactorily without giving !ʌr! (more commonly
taken as /ər/) a place in the American lexicon.

For some southwestern British as described by Gimson, !ʌ! would itself
be phonetically adequate and no further rules of derivation would be
necessary; but divergent rules would split the other dialects into at least
two groups. The *r*-colored vowel of American English and of other southwestern British results from the application of a rule by which the articulation of !r! is anticipated in the sequences !ʌrC! and !ʌr#!, so that the
entire syllabic assumes the *r*-coloring; in other dialects the articulation is
not anticipated but perhaps delayed, for a glide develops between the !r!
and the syllabic peak. Glides of at least two kinds must be assumed. The
mid-central vowel of RP presupposes a schwa glide, which would be extended (as the articulation of the !r! failed altogether) and ultimately
absorbed into the stressed vowel, which would thus become long; but in
some kinds of Southern American, though the long vowel of *fur* presupposes schwa as the glide, the diphthong of *word* requires that the glide be
palatal, not velar. This bifurcation into syllabic !ʌ! plus velar glide and
syllabic !ʌ! plus palatal glide may be accounted for by a rule which dis-
tinguishes two varieties of !r!, with the palatal variety between stressed !ʌ!
and an immediately following consonant (and possibly elsewhere). In fact
such varieties of !r! have already been distinguished by American phoneticians. Arthur J. Bronstein, for example, describes the palatal variety as
follows: "In another common formation of /r/, the tongue tip remains
low, while the central part of the tongue bunches and is raised toward the
posterior section of the hard palate."[13] One might thus score a debating
point by noting that the machinery which the present hypothesis demands
is independently available.

The necessary sequence of descriptive phonetic rules may now be summarized more directly though still informally.

Rule A. In dialects other than northern British, lax vowels fall together
as !ʌ! before !r! plus consonant, liquid, glide, or major morpheme boundary. (No other rule applies to some southwestern British speech as Gimson describes it.)

Rule B. In some Southern American dialects, and in at least some
others, !r! becomes palatal between stressed !ʌ! and an immediately following consonant, glide, or liquid. The !r! of !ʌr#! remains velar.

Rule C. In dialects having the *r*-colored vowel, the articulation of the
!r! before a consonant, glide, liquid, or major boundary is anticipated so

---

[13] *The Pronunciation of American English* 116 (New York, 1960).

468   that the entire syllabic assumes *r*-coloring; in RP, in some varieties of Southern American, and in some other dialects the articulation is not anticipated but perhaps delayed, so that a glide develops after the syllabic peak—a palatal glide !r! before the palatal variety of !r!, a velar glide !ə! elsewhere. (This rule accounts for Kurath's "upglide with progressive constriction" in *r*-ful dialects and for the Trager-Smith sequence /əhr/.)

    Rule D. For phonetic accuracy in describing some dialects, one might wish, at this point, to give a rule that the syllabic !ʌ! remains or is somewhat lowered and retracted before the velar glide, but is somewhat raised and fronted before the palatal glide. (These differences are clearly audible, in the old-fashioned Atlanta speech with which I am most familiar, in *cur, her, purr* as opposed to *curt, hurt, pert.*)

    Rule E. In *r*-less dialects, the glides of Rule C are now extended in duration as the tongue fails to reach the position for *r*-coloring; that is, the *r*-less dialects become so by the vocalization of the !r! in absolute final and before a consonant, glide, or !l!. (The Brooklynese pronunciation, Trager-Smith /əy/, is explained in this way.)

    Rule F. The sequence !ʌə!, for the *r*-less becomes Gimson's [ɜ:] and Jones's [ə:] as the vowel absorbs the matching glide. (Hence RP, and Southern American *stir* and *stirred,* Trager-Smith /əh/, which does not rhyme with *bird* when *bird* has the palatal glide.)

    The mere statement of these six descriptive rules may be the strongest argument against both Kurath's /ɜ/ and the Trageretic miscellany of /əhr/, /əh/, /əy/, and the like. While preserving the underyling unity of English, it might be said, the rules not only represent but explain its superficial phonetic diversity, to which the Trager-Smith analysis only points and for which Kurath's free mid-central vowel is only a cover symbol. And the rules may have other advantages. They make the distribution of !r! more similar to that of its companion liquid !l!; they suggest the possibility of further simplification by the elimination of Kurath's vowel /ɑ/ in *car* and his semivowel /ə/ in *dear;* they relate description to history without confusing the two; by suggesting an answer to a particular historical riddle, they may cast some light on the dark souls of Brooklyn and South Carolina; and they offer one practical suggestion for the making of textbooks and pronouncing dictionaries—such books may be most useful internationally if they write *word* at least as abstractly as *ward* (or *wərd*)[14] and give the phonetic rules in their introductions, so that there will never be an embarrassing discrepancy between less abstract transcriptions and the individual teacher's pronunciations.

---

[14] The argument about identifying stressed [ʌ] with unstressed [ə] loses much of its interest when one characterizes the two by their distinctive features. The [ə] is simply the back reduction vowel as opposed to the front reduction vowel, but [ʌ] must be further specified as lax, noncompact, etc. The choice of an alphabetic writing is practical, not theoretical.

But exaggerated claims were to be saved for the conclusion. It is more   469
prudent to say that at least the rules cannot be rejected as "too complicated," for they add nothing to the complexity of the grammar. They all
have independent motivations. All of them, or their analogues, would
have to be stated even though English had no such word as *word*.

THE GHOSTLY SNARLS OF LITTERA CANINA

If *word* is usually !wV̆rd! and if *err* is !ɛr!, the *r*-ful consequences
for the *r*-less dialects must be accepted: Kurath's /ɑ/ and /ə/ must be
abandoned, and the liquid !r! will appear in the representations of such
words as *beer, beard, hear, hair, laird, lure, bore, board, war, ward, bar,
bard, fire,* and *our,* as well as *beery, hearing, boring,* and the like, where the
intervocalic !r! is regularly preserved though the development of the
vowels preceding it looks like analogy. Three principal phonetic rules will
be necessary for the *r*-less !r!—the first analogous to Rule C above, by
which the schwa glide develops between a vowel or diphthong, on the one
hand, and !r! plus consonant or plus major morpheme boundary on the
other; the second analogous to Rule E, by which preconsonantal and final
!r! is fully vocalized; the third analogous to Rule F, by which the glide is
optionally absorbed by back vowels except !ʊ!. These three rules alone
will account for a good many of the phonetic facts in a number of dialects.

Some modifications and extensions, however, are obviously desirable
before these rules and the previous set can be combined in a single sequence. Rule A above provides the first suggestion. When lax !ɪ!, !ɛ!, and
!ʊ! fall together as !ʌ! before !rC! and !r#!, no contrast remains with
tense !i!, !e!, and !u! in these environments; and in some dialects the
three tense vowels become phonetically lax themselves. In some old-
fashioned Georgia speech, for example, *err* is !ɛr! = [ʌː]; the vowels of
hair, bore, war, and *bar* are tense; but *beer* has lax !ɪ!, *here* lax !ɛ!, and
lure lax !ʊ!. Both the !ʊ! and the !u! of this dialect, it should be observed,
are noticeably fronted, so that clever people might make !i!, !e!, and
fronted !u! a plausible set in at least this respect, that none of them is fully
back (or grave). Their phonetic laxness, of course, does not determine
their phonemic representation. Apparently they are phonemically tense,
since they are tense phonetically in other dialects and since tenseness
must be assumed for alternations like *sincere, sincerity.* At some point,
therefore, a descriptive phonetic rule must specify the result of the historical phonetic change.

Another feature of some Southern American dialects suggests that the
scope of Rule B above should also be extended. Just as forms like *work*
show a palatal glide (/y/ for /r/ in the Trager-Smith system), so the same

470   glide may appear in *porch, scorch, gorge, march, large,* and *harsh.*[15] The explanations in the two cases are quite similar. For these dialects, that is, the palatal variety of !r! must be assumed not only between stressed !ʌ! and any following consonant but between tense !o!, !ɔ!, or !ā! and a following palatal. The palatal glide which accordingly develops is not absorbed by the preceding vowels. *Err* phonetically is long [ʌ:], and there may be no centering glide in words like *pork;* but *work* and *porch* keep their front glides after their back vowels.

Though this statement may later be made a little simpler, for the moment it may be allowed to stand while some of its consequences and relations are explored. In these Southern American dialects for which the palatal !r! in certain environments has here been assumed, the *larger* words have made a difficulty for phonemicists, particularly for the followers of Trager and Smith. A palatal glide of course appears in *Elijah* as well as in *larger,* yet *larger* and *Elijah* do not rhyme. The Trager-Smith transcriptional arsenal would give /ay/ for *Elijah,* but then only /ar/, /ahr/, or /ahy/ remains for *larger.* Within the Trager-Smith system, none of these writings is satisfactory. If /ar/ or /ahr/ is chosen, the system does not allow the student to explain why he assigns an upward and forward glide now to /r/ in *larger* and now to /y/ in *Elijah.* If on the other hand the choice is /ahy/, clusters of semivowels must be accepted freely after vowels as well as before them, the already large number of possible syllabic nuclei is much increased, and the suspicion grows that the system does not provide phonemic analyses at all but only an odd phonetic alphabet.

The representation !lārȷ̆#ər! is descriptively and historically much more plausible. Descriptive phonetic rules then make the first !r! palatal but leave the second velar; the palatal and velar glides develop in their respective positions; in both positions the !r! is fully vocalized; after the back vowel !ā! the front glide remains; but the schwa glide in the second syllable is absorbed, and a final rule then shortens the resulting long schwa in unstressed position. The difficulty vanishes with the abandonment of the Trager-Smith alphabet.

The word *Elijah,* with its !ɑɪ!, suggests the controversy about the tenth or Confederate vowel, for whose addition to the nine vowels of Trager and Smith I share the guilt. The argument began when it was pointed out that with only nine vowels it is impossible to write such common words as *fire,* since all the plausible front and central slots are already filled by *fear* /ih/ or /ɨh/, *here* /eh/, *fair* /æh/, *far* /ah/, and *fur* /əh/. No symbol remains for writing the vowel of *fire* or *wire,* in which Kurath and Mc-

---

[15] For a few such forms, see James B. McMillan, *Phonology of the Standard English of East Central Alabama* 57, 62, 93 (University of Chicago dissertation, 1946).

David's Atlanta synopsis shows a long, retracted, and raised [a] followed   **471**
by [ə], as opposed to the [ɑˑə] of *garden;*[16] and with more or less reluctance, the orthodox were thus obliged to shatter the symmetry of the nine-
vowel square.

An argument can be made out, however, for the representation of
Elijah simply with !ɑɪ! and of *fire* with !ɑɪr!, both of them contrasting
with the !ār! of *larger,* which has already been justified, and with !ɑʊr!
for *our,* which may conveniently be discussed in this connection. One relevant phonetic rule, though it would not apply directly to the three suggested underlying forms, is the familiar one for the difference in length of
vowels and of diphthongs before following voiced and voiceless sounds.
It may be phrased as the simple statement that vowels and diphthongs become somewhat shorter when they are followed by voiceless consonants.
The diphthongs of *fire, our,* and *Elijah* are therefore longer than those of
fight and *out,* to which the rule for shortening does apply.

Another of the relevant rules is also needed for more dialects than one
and is necessary, in much Southern American speech, to account for
other pronunciations than those of *Elijah, fire,* and *our.* The lax vowel
!a!, this rule asserts, is considerably fronted wherever it occurs before a
nonintrusive palatal or labiovelar glide—namely, before the !ɪ! and !ʊ!
that appear in words with Middle English tense /i/ and tense /u/. Thus
the same rule that fronts the first element of the Southerner's diphthong in
words like *out,* where the fronting is extreme,[17] will in addition help to
explain why *fire* and *far* do not rhyme "in the Piedmont of South Carolina
and adjoining parts of Georgia";[18] nor will *Elijah* rhyme with *larger* in
dialects where *larger* has its palatal glide, since in *larger* the glide intrudes
after a tense !ā! when the rule which strongly fronts the *lax* vowel !a!
before NON-intrusive glides has already operated. The !a! in the diphthong
!ɑɪ! in *fire* and *Elijah* is indeed the lax counterpart of the tense !ā! of *far*
and *larger,* but phonetically it differs also by its fronting.

When the two rules which have just been stated have applied, together
with the rules for final !r! in *r*-less dialects, the stressed syllabic of *Elijah*
will be !aˑɪ!, *fire* will be !faˑɪə!, and *our* !aˑʊə!, the first vowel fronted in
each diphthong, and each of the last two successive glides. For phonetic
accuracy, another rule for length or tempo must next be invoked. As
Kurath points out, diphthongs in words with Middle English tense /i/
and tense /u/ have fast and slow variants before following voiceless and
voiced sounds respectively in both the upper and the lower South.[19] In

---

[16] *PEAS* 100.

[17] Kurath, *Phonology* 106 f.

[18] *PEAS* 122.

[19] *PEAS* 19, 22.

472   some speech from the Georgia Piedmont, the rule seems to be that diphthongs as in *wide* and *loud,* which are temporally long, are produced by physically short, slow movements of the tongue, while diphthongs as in *white* and *lout,* which have been temporally shortened before voiceless consonants, are made with physically long, fast glides. The stressed syllable of *Elijah,* then, as actually pronounced, is [aˑɛ], and the first of the successive glides in *our* and *fire* must be regarded as similarly reduced in physical length. That fact helps to explain the last rule for words like *fire:* the nonintrusive palatal and velar glides disappear between the long, somewhat fronted !ɑˑ! and a following glide or unstressed vowel (in *our* only in connected speech). The approximate end-products of the derivations are *fire* [faˑə] and *our* [aˑə] or [aˑoə], which are strikingly similar to the transcriptions in the Atlanta synopsis in Kurath-McDavid.

    Though the Confederate vowel thus suffers filicide, the ridiculous suggestion should carefully be avoided that with more abstract underlying forms and ordered phonetic rules all phonological problems are now well along toward solution. On the contrary, the proposed rules have not been fitted into the total structure of the phonological component of a grammar; their extremely tentative ordering has been in part expository, not descriptive; and as yet they apply only to some more striking features of a few selected dialects, though their extension to related materials elsewhere (no doubt with modifications) is obviously necessary if the rules are to win any general acceptance. (So for at least twenty-five years in some advanced forms of RP, words like *tire, tower,* and *tar* have rhymed, plainly by the loss of the !ɪ! and !ʊ! from *tire* and *tower* and the subsequent absorption of the final !ə! into the stressed vowel; but the present rules do not exploit these parallels to developments in Southern American speech.) The rules, moreover, must offend all readers who wrongly ask them to do what grammars never do and to predict the unpredictable variability of real talk in mixed dialects. To take only one instance, *r*-lessness seems to be losing its old status in some parts of the American South, so that the same speaker may have some words regularly *r*-less, others regularly *r*-ful, and still others flopping back and forth; yet this vacillation does not appear in the rules, a sort of ideal pattern from which raw speech nearly always deviates more or less. The answer may not commend itself even to other students who are willing to try all things: without the rules for the impossibly ᴜɴmixed dialect, the objection itself could not be stated, and the field notes of the dialectologist would remain what they have too often been, an unintelligible barrenness.

    However that may be, the rules still have some advantages over competing analyses, of which none is beyond criticism. The abolition of the Confederate vowel is certainly an unmixed blessing; another stone on the grave of the postvocalic semivowel /h/ will not strike everyone as desecration; and the given arguments against /ɜ/, /ɑ/, and /ə̣/ at least deserve discussion. Other benefits too are imaginable. The principles of Trager and Smith, and the ideal of total accountability, were rarely taken in all seriousness, and the few halfhearted attempts to take them seriously led to unpromising complexities like my long and short diphthongs, as in *veer* [vɪə] (with retracted [ɪ]) but *via* [viə]. This contrast is better explained by assuming that *veer* is !vir! and applying the relevant phonetic rules. Other ingenious inventions turn out to be as illusory as the long diphthongs. The stressed "barred eye" for instance, with which Trager and Smith would have to corrupt good Southern *beer*—[bɪə] (with retracted [ɪ]) = /bɨh/—is no real English phoneme, nor is the fourth semivowel which they should logically accept in contrasts between length and a centering glide: the *r*-less !r! is a good way to separate words like *bare,* with tense !æ! and a centering glide, from oddities like the sheep's cry, *baa,* or like *pa* and *ma* with the vowel of *bad* in low-country South Carolina.[20] Where no solution is perfect, a less imperfect one should still be welcome.

Exaggeration, however, has got ahead of itself again. The rules which have so far been proposed, combined now in a single set, must speak for themselves as a conceivable alternative to the treatments of final and preconsonantal !r! by Kurath and by Trager and Smith. For simplicity and a minimum of security, the rules are here limited to certain dialects of the American South, principally to my old-fashioned variety of Atlanta speech, though some of the rules are much more widely applicable. Emphatically, their now descriptive ordering is tentative at several points.

Rule i. Lax !ɑ! is strongly fronted before !ɪ! and !ʊ! (the nonintrusive glides in words with ME tense /i/ and tense /u/).

Rule ii. Tense !u! and lax !ʊ! are fronted generally.

Rule iii. Lax vowels fall together as !ʌ! before !r! plus consonant, liquid, glide, or major morpheme boundary. (Cf. Rule A in the previous list.)

Rule iv. In the same environments, tense !i!, !e!, and fronted !u! become lax.

Rule v. Vowels and diphthongs are somewhat shortened before voiceless consonants.

Rule vi. !r! becomes palatal between stressed !ʌ! and an immediately following consonant, glide, or liquid and between !o!, !ɔ!, or !ɑ̄! and an immediately following palatal consonant. (Cf. Rule B in the previous list.)

Rule vii. Between any vowel or diphthong and a following !r! plus consonant, liquid, glide, or major boundary, a glide develops—a palatal glide

---

[20] *PEAS* 165.

474   before the palatal !r!, elsewhere a velar glide. (Cf. Rule C in the previous list.)

    Rule viii. Lax vowels move slightly toward the end positions for following glides. (Cf. Rule D in the previous list.)

    Rule ix. !r! vocalizes (optionally?) before a consonant, glide, or !l! and in absolute final. (Cf. Rule E in the previous list.)

    Rule x. Back vowels except fronted !ʊ! absorb following velar glides, with accompanying lengthening if the absorbing vowel is short. The absorption is obligatory for !ʌ!, optional for other vowels. (Cf. Rule F in the previous list.)

    Rule xi. Unstressed long vowels are shortened.

    Rule xii. The second elements of diphthongs as in *wide, loud, buy,* and *bough,* though temporally long, become physically short. (That is, the tongue takes a long time to move a short distance.)

    Rule xiii. The second element is lost from triphthongs as in *fire* and *our* (only in connected speech in *our*).

    Readers will hardly need the warning that these rules may be still further modified and rearranged as they are applied to more and more material.

!l!-PLAYING

    One minimal defense of the rules for the *r*-less !r! is that they seem to escape some difficulties in which other analyses are trapped: the rules can hardly raise more doubts than Kurath's /ɜ/, /ɑ/, and /ə/ or the Trager-Smith maneuvering with the semivowels /y/, /h/, and /w/. A much stronger defense has of course been suggested in the remark that the rules which abolish the phoneme /ɜ/ would be necessary even if the phoneme /ɜ/ had never been invented. That defense may now be elaborated, and first with examples involving the other liquid, !l!.

    Historians are of course familiar with the influence of !l! on preceding vowels and with the occasional vocalization of !l! itself, and scholars as different as Joseph Wright and Cabell Greet have independently described similar phenomena in living speech. In 1940, for example, N. M. Caffee reported both the development of glides and the subsequent vocalization of "Southern 'l' plus a consonant."[21] In some sections of the United States, Caffee said, "a glide is formed before *l* when it is preceded by any vowel"; and after the glide has intruded, *l* is optionally but frequently lost before *k,* occasionally lost before *m, b, f,* and *p*. "When the *l* is lost, the glide vowel originally preceding the *l* is extended to a complete vowel

---

[21] "Southern 'L' plus a consonant," *American Speech* 15.259–61.

sound and, as far as has been discovered, is invariably formed in the same manner. The back of the tongue is raised, no contact is made by the tip of the tongue, the sides of the tongue may or may not touch the upper teeth, and the back of the throat is constricted." Though the articulation is vocoidal, "the speakers themselves who have lost the *l* believe, however, that they form an *l;* and apparently the sound is heard as an *l,* even by those people who regularly have the normal lingual lateral continuant in all positions in their speech." Citing Greet, Kurath, Stanley, and Wright, Caffee reported the glides and the vocalization from British dialects, from New England, and from Virginia, South Carolina, Georgia, Mississippi, and east Texas.

A number of the forms with vocalization or only glides are particularly troublesome in a Trager-Smith analysis. For example, a good deal of morphophonemic alternation has to be accepted (*fill* /fɨhl/: *filling* /fɨlin/ etc.), clusters of postvocalic semivowels are again necessary (*feel* /fiyhl/ and the like), and at least one obvious contrast cannot be written at all, since *million* and *billion* keep their stressed vowels short after !l! has vocalized and so do not rhyme with *paeon* and *eon:* both pairs cannot be written with /iyə/. Such forms provide a test for the rules for *r*-less !r!, which might be expected to have their analogues for !l!.

It turns out that they do. Just as it is necessary to establish a palatal and a velar !r!, so clear !l! and dark !l! must be distinguished. Ideally the distinction should be made for all environments and made along a scale (distinctive features at the phonetic level need not be binary); but in some southern American speech !l! is obviously clear at least before and after palatal glides (*million, hellion, scallion; oil, vile*) and obviously dark at least before !r! (*Elroy*), before !w! (*Elwin*), and before any consonant (*silk, help, Alf, pelt, Elgin*). Final !l! is generally dark, though in the speech here described it is certainly clear after the palatal glide in the words like *oil* and *vile* (contrast the very dark !l! in *vial*).

These statements are sufficient for an admittedly tentative and incomplete account. After the rule that establishes the two !l!s, there must then follow the analogue to Rules vii and ix in the second list above: between any vowel or diphthong and a following dark !l! in the specified environments, a raised back glide develops; before clear !l! in the specified environments, the intrusive glide is palatal; and both !l!s next optionally vocalize in words like *million* and before labials and !k! (not !g!).[22] The products of these rules include a good many actually occurring forms. Front vowels before preconsonantal and final !l! are properly glided (*feel, field, fill, build,* etc.), while *feeling, failing* and the like are properly glide-

---

[22] There is no final -!lg!, and syllable-break hinders the vocalization. In a more precise statement, !g! might not need to be excepted. Cf. McMillan 18.

476   less (since analogy with the simplices did not operate as it did in *beery*); and !l! is sometimes vocalized in *billion, William, silk, milk, help, kelp, elm, helm, helve, Ralph, salve, valve, talcum, solve, revolve, bulb, gulf,* and *polka.*

Yet obvious inexactitudes remain, particularly after back vowels, where in actual speech no glides are heard, and in such words as *file, oil, owl,* and *billion,* where the rules seem wrong in predicting identical successive glides. Happily, the rules for *r*-less !r! again provide the needed analogies. The development of the schwa glide and the vocalization of !r! after the stressed lax vowel in *err* result in a single long vowel, [ʌː]; the similarly developed long vowel in *pattern* is shortened because unstressed. One would expect, therefore, that lax back vowels preceding the raised back glide before dark !l! would be pronounced quite long but without perceptible glide, which seems to be the case in *pull, gull, gulf,* and *doll,* and that the unstressed second syllables of *buckle, opal,* and the like would be the simple back reduction vowel, which also seems correct. Finally, if the model of *pattern* and *buckle* may serve for the identical successive glides, one should hear only one glide in *file, oil, owl,* and *billion,* and the tense back vowels should be heard simply as tense back vowels, since the syllabics of *fraud, load,* and *rood* are commonly up-gliding even without the following !l!. Observing the slight retraction of the vowels in *pill, bell,* and *pal,* one may conclude with some justice that Rules viii, x, and xi for !r! must be extended to apply to !l! and that the behavior of the two liquids and of vowels before them does indeed form a single pattern.

HUBRIS

If the defense of the rules for *r*-less !r! is strengthened by their applicability to !l!, the irresistible temptation is to push the rules as far as they will go. An enthusiastic yielder therefore suggests that the most striking phonetic pecularities of his kind of Atlanta talk, which has baffled him and others by its apparent complexity, can actually be traced to two very simple causes: first, the dialect has two reduction vowels, not just one; and second, two corresponding kinds of glide appear between its consonants and liquids and the syllabics that precede them. The behavior of !r! and !l! is only a special case of very general tendencies, and those tendencies (to defy Nemesis utterly) may be given their proper names of umlaut and of breaking. Even in speech, the South is distinguished by its Anglo-Saxon heritage.

The existence of the two reduction vowels, !ɪ! and !ə!, is obvious in a good many dialects of southern England and the United States. "All dialects of American English," according to Kurath and McDavid,[23] "have

23 *PEAS* 8 f.

a free vowel /ə/ that occurs only in unstressed syllables," and some also have /ɪ/, particularly "before /s, z, t, d, ǧ, č/".[24] Similar observations have been made from the very beginnings of American dialectology, professional and amateur. Among southern speakers, Grandgent reported "unaccented *I*" as strongly dominant in words like *palace, courage, fountain, orange, senate, Monday, naked, college, fishes, goodness, finest,* and *sonnet,*[25] and the keen amateur Joel Chandler Harris indicated the two unstressed vowels in his Uncle Remus stories.[26] More recent observers tell the same story, sometimes with a good deal of vehemence. From east central Alabama, J. B. McMillan coolly reports "two unstressed syllabic phonemes ..., /i/ and /ə/,"[27] and in her spirited discussion of "Southern standards,"[28] Katherine E. Wheatley records [ɪ] in syllabic plurals and in such words as *pocket, palace, goodness, naked, sonnet, rabbit, prelate, minute, poem, college, courage, usage, damage, manage, darkness, bucket,* and *honest.* With schwa-users in these words, Miss Wheatley is righteously vexed. The schwa, she says, is "vulgar," "unpleasant to the Southern ear," "extremely offensive"; and though there may be a good deal of vacillation among Southerners, even in the same word as pronounced by the same speaker, still the extent of agreement among the Cultured is perhaps more significant (in the face of Yankee scepticism): my own lists for old-fashioned Atlanta speech would coincide with Miss Wheatley's lists nine times in ten. Contrasting pairs, for the sake of the skeptical, are not hard to find. A few hours with informants from Georgia, Alabama, and Mississippi will certainly turn up the opposition in pairs like *pagan : chicken, minus : promise, ballot : salad, mattock : rustic, ballot : palate, Stella : belly, Duncan : dunking, gallus : necklace, ballast : Dallas,*[29] or in *chorus : iris, crocus : heiress, robot : cubit, stomach : garlic, mammoth : stinketh, Philip : tulip, Aaron : Reuben, seraph : sheriff, forehead : torrid, sofa : Sophy, mister : misty, comma : Commie, Willa : Willy* (pairs which have been successful with informants from Atlanta to Lubbock, Texas). The contrast is structurally of great importance.

The palatal and velar glides to match the contrasting unstressed vowels have already been seen in the discussions of !r! and !l!, but they are not limited to position before the liquids. Rather generally in the drawling South, the !ɪ! and !ə! appear under changing pitch between lax stressed vowels and following consonants, with the nature of the glide apparently

---

[24] Kurath, *Phonology* 123 f.; *PEAS* 8 f.

[25] *Dialect Notes* 1.319–23 (1894).

[26] Sumner Ives, "The Phonology of the Uncle Remus Stories," *Publications of the American Dialect Society* 22.29 (1954).

[27] Op. cit., 26, 67 f.

[28] *American Speech* 9.36–45 (1934).

[29] All taken from Oma Stanley, "The Speech of East Texas," *American Speech* 11.159–64 (1936).

478   determined in part by the consonants and in part by the vowels themselves; and their common appearance clearly sets off southern speech
from the speech (say) of New England. Kurath's synopses suggest the
three possibilities. Throughout the Atlantic States, his fieldworkers report, the vowel of *six* is generally unglided; *crib* has either no glide, as in
much of New England, or a schwa, with the schwa heavily predominant in
most of the South; while *bag* and the dissyllabic *ashes,* which most commonly show no glide in Synopses 3–91, are usually glided in the South,
where up-glides and centering glides compete. It is drawlers, then, who
favor the glides; and the glides' appearance, and their nature when they
do appear, depend both on the vowels and on the following consonants.

To make that statement usefully precise, however, is extremely difficult.
There is a great deal of individual and dialectal variation, and even within
relatively homogeneous areas not everything is always clear. In the first
place, the distinctions that I have assumed between lax and tense vowels,
short and long, are difficult to agree on. Is the checked vowel of words
like *college,* which Kurath describes as "rather short" above the fall line
in the lower South,[30] really to be considered lax or tense? What shall be
made of the low front vowel, which in the same area (Kurath says) is
"usually ... upgliding"? Is it a single vowel or a tense-lax pair (with the
tense vowel in words like *bare, half, glass,* and *aunt*); and if indeed it is
sometimes tense, is the upglide that commonly accompanies it a manifestation of the tenseness, or is it a glide intruding before the following
consonant? How, moreover, shall the consonants be grouped according
to the glides which they determine? In particular, do the dentals and
alveolars favor schwa glides or no glides at all? Or must one distinguish
still more finely, as between !t! and !s! and !n!? A pretended final answer
to these and similar questions would only provoke a justified disbelief.

In these circumstances, the answer which is here attempted for old-
fashioned Atlanta speech must be plainly labeled tentative, schematic,
and nonetheless quite venturesome. To avoid argument, Kurath's description of the correlation between checked vowels and the following preconsonantal glides will be repeated. "In the Lower South", he says, "the
checked high and mid vowels . . . are normally ingliding"; above the fall
line the low-front commonly has an upglide; and in the same area the
vowel of *crop* and *college* (here taken as lax) is "rather short." Without too
great inaccuracy, those values of the glide may be considered typical before dental and alveolar consonants, as in *pit, pet, put, putt, pot;* there no
glide is very clearly audible, so that with respect to glide-conditioning, the
dentals and alveolars as a group may be considered neutral. The labials,
on the other hand, seem to belong with velar !r! and dark !l!. An obvious

[30] *PEAS* 21.

glide of the schwa variety may be heard between them and the front vowels, and the apparent exception of words like *half* may be disposed of by treating the vowel there as tense (and similarly with such words as *path, grass,* and *can't*). The remaining consonants are the palatals, which condition the palatal glide (like palatal !r! and clear !l!), as might be expected. The !n! in words like *lunch* and *lunge* must be included among them, and probably !k! and !g! after front vowels; but [ŋ] should perhaps be classed with the alveolars as a cluster !ng!, and !k! and !g! after back vowels with the schwa-conditioners.

That classification fits the more obvious facts rather well. Given the inherent tendency of lax vowels to trail off toward the Ruhelage, one would expect the very easily audible schwa glide between the lax fronts and the labials; that such forms do occur widely in the South is a commonplace observation.[31] After back vowels, one would expect the contrasting palatal glide to be less obvious, though sometimes it does overcome both the inherent centralizing tendency in words like *bush, push, gush, hush, much, such,* and the shortness of lax !ɑ! in *wash, bosh, watch, dodge.*[32] Finally, one might expect the general centralizing drift of lax front vowels to be simply blocked by the influence of a following palatal, though occasional reports of a very high vowel in such words as *itch* and *inch* may indicate a genuine palatal glide.[33] The most common exceptions to all this, though not the only ones, are the upglides before the voiced alveolar stop in words like *bad* and *bed* and the apparent tensing of lax !æ! (which has already been mentioned) before final and preconsonantal voiceless spirants as in *half, path,* and *grass,* and sometimes before final and preconsonantal nasals as in *pan* and *aunt*. That tensing, or its consequences, are widely observable in both British and American dialects. Its phonetic manifestation, in a good deal of the lower South, is either length or an upward glide.

With so much by way of preparation, the phenomena of umlaut and breaking in some forms of Modern English may now be described in moderate detail. Both, it is here maintained, exist in modern dialects, and both should be investigated as possibilities (no more) in any dialect which has the two reduction vowels and the corresponding palatal and velar glides between stressed vowels and the following consonants or liquids. Surprisingly, though the glides which are part of breaking have been frequently observed, the full range of both developments has never been ex-

---

[31] McMillan, op. cit.; Robert Howren, "The Speech of Ocracoke, North Carolina", *American Speech* 37.163–75 (1962); etc.

[32] George P. Wilson, "Some Unrecorded Southern Vowels," *American Speech* 9.212 (1934); Howren 167; McMillan 44.

[33] McMillan, 49 n., citing Wilson 210.

480   plored; and hence the essential unity of the two processes with one another, with the influence of !r! and !l!, and with parallel developments
over the centuries from Old English to modern times—all these things
have been missed as well. A venturesome attempt may have this merit:
that it will either fail utterly or else brighten some dark corners of history
and description.

It is fairly easy to extend the partial account of breaking which has
already been given in the description of the glides before consonants and
liquids. Principally, the account must be extended (for lax vowels only) to
medial consonants and liquids as well as finals; and the point of departure
may be a kind of kittenish, female Southern speech in which pitch-
changes often occur within the stressed syllable of plurisyllabic words and
not between the syllables. Twenty years ago, Kenneth Pike remarked
briefly on the speech of a female "graduate student from Houma, Louisiana."[34] "Instead of using steps of pitch, or delaying the glide," Pike wrote,
"she tended to give a glide to the stressed syllable at the beginning of the
contour even when a stressed one appeared in the same contour with it."
Pike's example was the phrase *Northern part,* in which he marked his °3–2
pitch-change not on *part* but within the first syllable of *Northern.* He concluded by adopting the suggestion of C. M. Wise, that the southern drawl
is not primarily a matter of intonation but "rather a system of diphthongization, triphthongization and double diphthongization, affecting
vowels . . ."

Pike was both right and wrong about the drawl. Extensive off-gliding of
the vowels is indeed an obvious characteristic of southern speech, but the
placing of pitch changes within the stressed syllables of plurisyllabics
makes the gliding of the vowels easier to hear. Close listening to the kittenish female turns up a glide not only in words like *rib* but also in words
like *ribbon,* which she is likely to pronounce as something like [rɪəbən]
(with retracted [ɪ]). The same sort of thing, presumably, is what Wilson
describes[35] when he reports a schwa glide before the !l! in *balance, gallon,*
and *valentine* and a palatal glide before !š! in *bushel* and *cushion.* In the
description of less drawling kinds of Southern American, therefore, one
must first introduce the proper glides between lax vowels and medial as
well as final consonants and liquids, but must then add rules by which
these vowels absorb the medial glides but are somewhat assimilated to
them. Hence the thoroughly centralized stressed vowel of the less drawling
southern *ribbon,* which has often but wrongly been treated as a separate
phoneme, /ɨ/ not /i/. The vowel is centralized by the glide which it absorbs, so that the !ɪ! of *ribbon* is further back than that of *richer,* where the

---

[34] *The Intonation of American English* 105 f. (Ann Arbor, 1945).

[35] Op. cit. (*fn.* 32).

consonant is palatal not labial. One may hear similar contrasts in pairs like *picking : pippin, picker : ripper, pitcher : piffle, fickle : Philip, pickle : pillar, heckle : heron.*

Umlaut sometimes enhances the effects of breaking and sometimes reduces them, but it too is immediately explicable as the influence of a consonant or a liquid on a lax preceding vowel. An easy example is the contrast between *ribbing,* with the front reduction vowel in the unstressed syllable, and *ribbon,* with the schwa. In this pair, the greater centralization of the stressed vowel of *ribbon* cannot be explained by breaking, the explanation which serves for the moderate centralization in *pippin* as opposed to *picking.* The vowel of *ribbon* is more fully central than that of *ribbing* or *pippin,* yet the medial consonants in all three words are labials. The immediate explanation must be that the !b! of *ribbon* is even more conducive to the development of a schwa glide than the !b! of *ribbing* or the !p! of *pippin,* and the remote cause must lie in the difference between the reduction vowels, the !ə! of *ribbon* and the !ɪ! of *ribbing.*

That these affect their preceding consonants differently is not only plausible, historically and phonetically; it is also definitely suggested by certain statements in the literature. Arthur Norman, for example, reports clear !l! intervocalically before "mid-high or high front and central vowels, . . . as in *Dallas, . . . jelly, Nelly, pallet.*"[36] In umlauting dialects, the stressed vowels of these words will be more advanced than the stressed vowels of *ballast, bellow, seller,* or *ballot,* where the !l! is not so clear. Wheatley and Stanley[37] are even more revealing in their comment on the pronunciation of the name *Horace,* where the reduction vowel of their rebel informants was not !ə! but "centralized [ɪ] or [ɛ]." With all but one of their nine victims, Wheatley and Stanley write, "the stressed vowel was followed by a retroflex glide for which we use [letters with subscript circle] to show retroflexion, rather than [ɚ], because there is a distinct [ɪ] or [ɛ] quality to the glide which [ɚ] would not adequately represent. These pronunciations differ markedly from that heard in some Midwestern speech, where the word occurs as [hɔɚs]. The difference between the Southern and this Midwestern pronunciation is as marked in the glide as in the stressed vowel."

To understand the precise mechanism of umlaut, one needs only to add that in umlauting dialects the vowel of *Horace* is distinctly less retracted than the vowel of *horror.* The inherent qualities of the medial consonants and liquids are modified, that is, by the following reduction vowels; the glides which must be postulated before the consonants and liquids differ accordingly; and the lax stressed vowels which absorb the glides are in

---

[36] "A Southeast Texas Dialect Study", *Orbis,* 5.76 (1956).

[37] "Three Generations of East Texas Speech", *American Speech* 34.91 (1959).

482   turn retracted or advanced along a finely graded scale. Among the manifestations of the high front lax vowel !ɪ!, for example, one may find at least four degrees, and perhaps six, by combining the two series *picket, pick, picker* and *ripping, rip, ripper;* and along the low row a moderate ear can sometimes distinguish at least three degrees in *packet, parry, parrot.* An understanding of breaking and umlaut thus allows the prediction of finer phonetic detail than dialectologists have normally observed; for relevant data may escape the observer who has no hypothesis to guide his search through the brute mass of the merely given.

    Historians will see immediately that the phonetic rules which are here postulated for some contemporary southern American speech are strikingly similar to the rules for breaking and the umlauts in Old English, and phonologists will recognize the consequences for descriptive analysis (if other investigations confirm my data). Those consequences involve a good deal more than the explanation of particular oddities, though such explanation is also provided. To dispose quickly of a few quaint specimens, one may cite the remark of Joseph Sargent Hall[38] to the effect that the vowel of *hollow* is likely to be somewhat rounded or at least very far back, while the vowel of *holly* is usually unround and less retracted, or the comment of Argus Tresidder[39] that "*miracle* has a lowered vowel that often becomes [ɛ]," or the puzzlement of George P. Wilson[40] at the centralized vowels of *dinner, sinner, winner* and *better, letter, setter,* or the observation of Carroll Reed,[41] from a very different part of the country, that "the nuclear [il] of *milk* (and similar words) is strongly velarized," or the eyebrow-raising of Charles K. Thomas[42] at the retracted varieties of !ɪ! and !ɛ! before !r!, !l!, and the labials. Breaking and umlaut undoubtedly operate, to some degree, in many dialects, both of the Confederacy and of less civilized areas.

    But the time for quaintness in dialectology is long past, like the heyday of *lighthouse-keepers.* To observe the Alabaman's retracted vowels in words like *cripple, river, dinner, trestle, little, till, pillow,* and *children*[43] is useful indeed, but much more useful if such observation leads to consequences beyond itself. One consequence is that the refusal to accept two reduction vowels will merely lead, in some dialects, to a completely un-

---

[38] *The Phonetics of Great Smoky Mountain Speech* 28 (New York, 1942).

[39] "The Speech of the Shenandoah Valley," *American Speech* 12.284–88 (1937).

[40] Op. cit. (*fn.* 32) 211.

[41] "The Pronunciation of English in the State of Washington," *American Speech* 27.186–89 (1952).

[42] *An Introduction to the Phonetics of American English* 63, 75 (New York, 1958).

[43] McMillan, passim.

acceptable multiplication of lax stressed vowels. In the second member of each of the following pairs, umlauters will have a more retracted vowel than in the first—*cereal, mirror; jelly, mellow; parry, parrot; hopping, hopper; putty, putter; bully, buller*: yet without the two reduction vowels the difference is unpredictable, and six vowels must become twelve. Conccivably, that is a structural reason for Confederate indignation at Midwesterners who cannot pronounce *Horace* to suit a southern lady.

A more devastating consequence is one more dilemma for users of the Trager-Smith phonemic system. They are committed to the recognition of a high central vowel, /ɨ/, which McDavid[44] quite accurately observed in transcribing his *ribbon* as /rɨbən/ and his *ribbing* as /ribɨn/, though the alleged contrast is a transparent result of umlaut. A number of unanswerable questions now arise. For one, where does /i/ end and /ɨ/ begin on the scale of four to six degrees provided by *picket, pick, picker,* and *ripping, rip, ripper?* The influence of the front reduction vowel keeps the !ɪ! of *picket* fronter than it is in *pick,* while in *picker* the other reduction vowel causes backing; similarly, there are three degrees of frontness in *ripping, rip,* and *ripper;* and the vowel of *rip* is more centralized before the labial than the vowel of *pick* before the palatal. Again, if one phonemicizes the high central (whether or not he knows where he should write it), what defensible theory can save him from phonemicizing retracted /c/ in *heron* (vs. *herring*), retracted /æ/ in *parrot* (vs. *parry*), or fronted /u/, /a/, and /ə/ in *bushy, horrid,* and *hurry* (vs. *pusher, horror, furrow*)? To say that umlaut and breaking do not operate with perfect regularity only compounds the difficulty; for irregularity in the operation of the rules will only multiply the different shapes of taxonomic morphemes, which will already be distressingly numerous if *filling* (to repeat an instance) gives us /fil/, *fill* gives /fihl/ or /fɨhl/, and *filler* an indubitable /fɨl/. The seductive shapeliness of a system of nine vowels and three semivowels loses much of its attractiveness when once one faces the complications to which flirtation with the aging lady inevitably leads.

But hubris has gone far enough.

IN CALM OF MIND

Though it is not actually of the first importance that the bookkeeping should be correct in every detail, the argument of the preceding sections leads to the following combined set of partially ordered rules. The first seven are preliminary and need not be strictly ordered among themselves, though 3 must precede 4 and 4 precede 6, and though 1–7 must

---

[44] *Lg.* 26.330 *n.* 4 (1950).

484   precede the rest. With one or two exceptions, the ordering of those that follow and do the most work is essential but obvious. Together the rules repeat the assertion that the superficial phonetic complexity of old-fashioned Atlanta speech results very largely from the development of characteristic glides before consonants and liquids.

Rule 1. By processes unstated here, some vowels reduce to !ɪ!, others to !ə!.

Rule 2. Lax !ɑ! is strongly fronted before a glide as in *bite* and *bout.*

Rule 3. The tense and lax vowels !u! and !ʊ! are fronted generally.

Rule 4. Lax vowels fall together as !ʌ! before !r! plus consonant, liquid, glide, or major morpheme boundary.

Rule 5. Lax !æ! becomes tense before final and preconsonantal voiceless spirants as in *half, path,* and *grass* and (with unspecified limitations) before final and preconsonantal nasals.

Rule 6. Tense !i!, !e!, and fronted !u! become lax before !r! plus consonant, liquid, glide, or major boundary.

Rule 7. Vowels and diphthongs are somewhat shortened before voiceless consonants. (In the following derivations, the operation of this rule is tacitly assumed unless there is some special reason to call attention to it.)

Rule 8. Consonants and liquids in various environments are placed along a scale with three main divisions (sharp, flat, plain?). Specifically:

    a) Normally retroflex or velar !r! becomes palatal between stressed !ʌ! and an immediately following consonant, glide, or liquid between !o!, !ɔ!, or !ɑ̄! and a following palatal consonant. The !r! of !r#C! remains velar.

    b) Normally dark or velar !l! becomes palatal or clear before and after palatal glides.

    c) Normally velar !k! and !g! become palatal after front vowels.

    d) Plain (?) !n! becomes palatal (sharp?) before a palatal consonant or palatal glide.

    e) Medial consonants and liquids move toward the clear or dark ends of the scale according as they stand before the front or back reduction vowel (!ɪ! or !ə!). The rule does not apply to !r#V!.

Rule 9. Palatal or velar glides develop before consonants and liquids in certain positions. Specifically:

    a) Between any vowel or diphthong, on the one hand, and, on the other, a liquid which is either final or itself followed by a consonant, glide, or liquid, there develops a glide which is palatal before palatal !r! and clear !l!, otherwise velar. The velar glide also develops before !r! plus major boundary.

    b) Between any stressed lax vowel, and any prevocalic liquid (except !r#V!) or any consonant except a dental or alveolar whose neutrality has not been modified by Rule 8, there develops a glide which matches the position of the consonant or liquid on Rule 8's scale. The glides of 9b are distinct from those of 9a.

Rule 10. Stressed lax vowels move slightly toward the end positions for following glides of opposite quality—front toward back or back toward front.

Rule 11. The glides of 9a are extended in duration as the liquids vocalize in certain positions—!l! optionally, !r! perhaps optionally in today's changing social situation. Positions of vocalization for !r! are final and before consonants, glides, or !l! (not before !#V!); !l! vocalizes before labials and velars (not !g!), and between a stressed lax front vowel plus a palatal glide, on the left, and a palatal glide plus an unstressed vowel on the right.

Rule 12. Some glides are now absorbed by preceding vowels and diphthongs. Specifically:

a) The glides of 9b are absorbed before a medial consonant or liquid in a plurisyllable.

b) With the exception of fronted !ʊ! before !ə!, lax back vowels and tense !ā! absorb the velar glides of 9a and are thus lengthened. For !ā! before !ə!, the absorption is optional. In unstressed position, long vowels are shortened.

c) The tense back vowels except !ā! absorb velar glides without change. The absorption is optional and sporadic for !o! and !ɔ! before !ə!.

d) Two successive identical glides are reduced to one.

(The basic principle of b, c, and d is apparently the coalescence of matching vocoidal segments—to use Pike's term again. Conceivably, a simpler statement would relate Rules 6, 10, 12, and 14 (below) in a broader generalization having something to do with the rarity of triphthongs and the frequent neutralization of the tense-lax opposition before !r!.)

Rule 13. Before voiced sounds and, finally, the second elements of the diphthongs !ɑɪ! and !ɑʊ! (with first vowel fronted), though temporally long, become physically short.

Rule 14. From triphthongs as in *fire* and *our,* the second element is lost (only in connected speech in *our*).

Though many things must be wrong with this first effort to predict minute phonetic detail, yet a few examples will show that together the rules do account for a good many distinctive pronunciations in a believable way. The chosen examples are words that might all give some difficulty.

1) *bird* !bV̆rd!: lax vowel becomes !ʌ! (4); palatal !r! (8a); palatal glide (9a); vowel raised and fronted (10); !r! vocalizes (11): [bʌɪd] with raised and fronted [ʌ].

murder !mV̆rdər!: lax stressed vowel becomes !ʌ! (4); first !r! palatal-

486 ized (8a); palatal glide before first !r!, velar glide before second (9a); stressed vowel raised and fronted (10); both !r!'s vocalize (11); unstressed vowel absorbs following glide, lengthens, then shortens (12b): [mʌɪdə] with raised and fronted [ʌ].

stirred !stV̌r#d!: lax vowel becomes !ʌ! (4); velar glide (9a); !r! vocalizes (11); vowel absorbs glide and lengthens (12b): [stʌ:d].

2) *err* !ɛr!: vowel becomes !ʌ! (4); velar glide (9a); !r! vocalizes (11); vowel absorbs glide and lengthens (12b): [ʌ:].

erring !ɛr#ɪn!: stressed vowel becomes !ʌ! (4); velar glide (9a); stressed vowel absorbs glide and lengthens (12b): [ʌ:rɪn].

error !ɛrər!: velarity of !r! reinforced (8e); strongly velar glide before first !r!, velar glide before second (9b, 9a); stressed vowel retracted (10); final !r! vocalizes (11); stressed vowel absorbs following glide (12a); unstressed vowel absorbs following glide, lengthens, then shortens (12b): [ɛrə] with retracted [ɛ].

3) *star* !stɑr!: velar glide (9a); !r! vocalizes (11); !ā! optionally absorbs glide and lengthens (12b): [stɑˑə], [stɑ:].

starry !stɑr#ɪ!: velar glide (9a); !ā! optionally absorbs glide and lengthens (12b): [stɑˑərɪ], [stɑɪrɪ].

4) *dear* !dir!: !i! becomes !ɪ! (6); velar glide (9a); !ɪ! lowered and retracted (10); !r! vocalizes (11): [dɪə] with lowered and retracted [ɪ].

dearest !dir#ɪst!: !i! becomes !ɪ! (6); velar glide (9a); !ɪ! lowered and retracted (10): [dɪərɪst] with lowered and retracted [ɪ].

5) *porch* !porč!: palatal !r! (8a); palatal glide (9a); !r! vocalizes (11): [poɪč].

larger !!lārǰ#ər!: first !r! palatalized (8a); palatal glide before first !r!, velar glide before second (9a); stressed vowel unfronted because tense (10); both !r!s vocalize (11); unstressed vowel absorbs following glide, lengthens, then shortens (12b): [lɑˑɪǰə].

Elijah !əlaɪǰə!: lax !a! strongly fronted (2, 10); second element of diphthong physically shortened (13): [əlɑˑɛǰə] with fronted [ɑ].

6) *fire* !faɪr!: lax !a! strongly fronted (2, 10); velar glide before !r! (9a); !r! vocalizes (11); !ɪ! becomes physically short (13), then disappears (14): [fɑˑə] with fronted [ɑ].

our !aʊr!: lax !a! strongly fronted (2); velar glide before !r! (9a); !r! vocalizes (11); !ʊ! becomes physically short (13), then disappears in connected speech: [ɑˑoə], [ɑˑə] with fronted [ɑ].

7) *million* !mɪljən!: clear !!l! (8b); palatal glide before it (9a); !!l! optionally vocalizes (11); identical glides reduced to one (12d): [mijən]. (The predicted form with unvocalized !!l! is phonetically inaccurate in having a palatal glide before the liquid.)

oil !ɔɪl!: clear !!l! (8b); palatal glide before it (9a); identical glides reduced to one (12d): [ɔɪl].

vile !vaɪl!: !a! strongly fronted (2, 10); clear !!l! (8b); palatal glide before

it (9a); identical glides reduced to one (12d); !ɪ! physically shortened (13):
[vɑˑɛl] with fronted [ɑ].

vial !vɑɪəl!: !ɑ! strongly fronted (2, 10); velar glide in unstressed syllable (9a); unstressed vowel absorbs glide, lengthens, then shortens (12b); !ɪ! physically shortened (13) and then lost (14): [vɑˑəl] with fronted [ɑ].

8) *help* !hɛlp!: velar glide (9a); stressed vowel retracted (10); !l! optionally vocalized (11): [hɛu̯p], [hɛu̯lp] with retracted [ɛ]. (Note that the glide before !l! ends higher than the schwa glide before !r!.)

bulb !bʌlb!: velar glide (9a); !l! optionally vocalizes (11); glide absorbed and vowel lengthened (12): [bʌːb], [bʌˑlb].

polka !polkə!: velar glide (9a); !l! optionally vocalizes (11); glide absorbed (by 12c where !l! has vocalized, by 12d before retained !l! if tense !o! is upgliding): [pokə], [polkə].

talcum !tælkəm!: velar glide (9a); stressed vowel retracted (10); !l! optionally vocalizes (11): [tæu̯kəm], [tæu̯lkəm] with retracted [æ].

9) *picket* !pɪkɪt!: vowels very short (7); !k! palatal (8c, 8e); palatal glide before it (9b; but the effect is only to overcome the inherent centralizing of the lax vowel); stressed vowel very front (10); any glide absorbed (12a): [pɪkɪt].

pick !pɪk!: like *picket* but without so front a vowel, since 8e does not apply.

picker !pɪkər!: stressed vowel very short (7); !k! weakly velar (8e opposes 8c); velar glide in both syllables (9a, 9b); stressed vowel slightly retracted (10); !r! vocalized (11); glide before !k! absorbed (12a); unstressed vowel absorbs following glide, lengthens, then shortens (12b): [pɪkə] with retracted [ɪ].

ripping !rɪpɪn!: stressed vowel very short (7); gravity of !p! somewhat reduced (8e); weakly velar offglide (9b); stressed vowel slightly retracted (10); glide absorbed (12a): [rɪpɪn] with first [ɪ] retracted. (The rules seem accurate in predicting that the vowel of *ripping* is further back than those of *picket* and *pick;* but the equation with the vowel of *picker* is uncertain.)

rip !rɪp!: short vowel (7); velar glide (9b); vowel definitely retracted (10): [rɪəp] with retracted [ɪ]. (The retraction is greater than in *picker,* where the gravity of the !k! is reduced by 8c.)

ripper !rɪpər!: 8e reinforces the gravity of the !p!, so that the stressed vowel is more completely centralized than in *picker, ripping,* or *rip.*

10) *heckle* !hɛkəl!: stressed vowel short (7); !k! weakly velar (8e opposes 8c); velar glide in both syllables (9a, 9b); stressed vowel slightly retracted (10); glide before !k! absorbed (12a); unstressed vowel absorbs glide, lengthens, shortens (12b): [hɛkəl] with retracted [ɛ].

heron !hɛrən!: !r! strongly velar (8e); velar glide before it (9b); stressed vowel definitely retracted (10); glide absorbed (12a): [hɛrən] with retracted [ɛ]. (The rules accurately predict a more retracted vowel than in *heckle,* where 8c reduces the gravity of !k!.)

488   The proposed rules and their applications should now be clear enough for judgment, one extreme of which will certainly be instant dismissal as irresponsible ingenuity. That extreme will certainly be wrong; but how far wrong is another question. The most hastily lenient judge is sure to observe both the rash ambition and yet the incompleteness of an argument which imposes a sometimes minutely detailed pattern on speech behavior that may seem chaotic. More vigorously condemnatory judges will find out more inaccuracies even than have been confessed—for example, the failure to provide for umlaut through consonant clusters as in *whiskey* and *whisker* or (perhaps) through !r#! as in *hearing, hearer.* If amusement should be the majority response, in this case it will hardly be benevolent.

A good many stone-throwers, however, entertain improper guests in their own glass houses. If I am obliged to admit that the description in my *Short Introduction* was misguided, I must also say that I see no reason for anyone to defend any longer a high-central vowel phoneme /ɨ/, or /h/ as a semivowel, or Kurath's /ɜ/, /ɑ/, and /ə/. In Kurath's terms, perhaps there is a better argument for a tense low front than for a free mid-central —at least it would help to make sense of the very rapid upglides that become obvious when some southern pronunciations of *bare* and *pass* are played backwards on a tape: they have three vocoidal segments, so that Smith[45] transcribed an Alabaman's *chair* as /cay(y)ə/. In such forms the upglide may represent tenseness. Anyway, there is some excuse for a rashly novel exercise when the established analyses themselves have so many faults.

And the exercise suggests that there is something to be said for MITesian vowel-breeding. An amateur linguist-watcher is much impressed by the attempt to discover more abstract underlying forms than Kurath or Trager and Smith provide, and the phonetic rules are an illuminating device for comparing dialects. As a discovery procedure if nothing else, the attempt to write them compels one to take a general view of facts which are meaningless in isolation.

Since self-education is no excuse for publishing, and a distant follower derives no credit from those he follows, it might finally be said that the present paper makes one or two specific observations of some importance. Two reduction vowels, it maintains, are structurally necessary for some southern American dialects, where umlaut is a live phenomenon, along with breaking; and breaking and umlaut in turn are closely related to the parallel developments before the liquids !r! and !l!. The southern drawl and Brooklyn *woik* are boids of a feather—which is about the right note for an inconclusive conclusion.

[45] *Lg.* 28.147 (1952).

Vowel Nasality as a Sandhi-Form of the Morphemes -nt and -ing in Southern American

James B. McMillan

Professor McMillan describes the alternate pronunciations of the negative auxiliary verbs *aren't, can't, daren't, don't, mayn't, shan't, weren't, won't,* which occur in Southern English. In these forms the *nt* is often lost and the vowel nasalized. A somewhat similar situation exists in the case of the *-ing* of *going.* Professor McMillan is Chairman of the Department of English at the University of Alabama.

The published descriptions of present-day English phonology agree in recording vowel nasality as a non-distinctive feature which may occur

From *American Speech,* 14:120–123 (April, 1939). Reprinted with the permission of Columbia University Press and James B. McMillan.

490   with any vowel, particularly any vowel adjacent to a nasal consonant. Professor Daniel Jones comments as follows:

> It can be shown by experimental methods that slight nasalization of vowels occurs in English when nasal consonants follow. Such nasalization is, however, not sufficient to give to the vowels the characteristic nasal tamber.[1]

Of vowel nasality in American English Professor Krapp says:

> Nasalization of vowels is so general in American speech that it often passes unnoticed, and is often present in the speech of persons who are quite unaware of the fact. . . .[2]

Professor Kenyon remarks that "Nasalized vowels are regular in French, but are not ordinarily used in English."[3] A kymogram showing vowel nasality as a substitute for [nt] in *don't* has been published by Professor Willem Graff, but his comment is merely:

> A negligent pronunciation even produces a regular nasal vowel after dropping [n] entirely in a combination like 'I don't want to,' which often sounds [aɪdõwɔˑntu].[4]

Professor Bloomfield has noted that, in English, vowel nasalization often accompanies fatigue or relaxation,[5] and Professor Greet has noticed in the South that "The speech of the southern hills . . . is often nasal and high pitched."[6]

Investigation of vowel nasalization in Southern American indicates that general statements such as those cited above are valid for this dialect, and that in addition there are two specific occurrences of vowel nasality in SA in which the nasality performs a linguistic function.

In SA the phoneme [n] occurs initially, medially, and finally (as in *new, penny, pin*); in initial clusters with [s] (as in *sneak*); and in final clusters with [s, z, t, d, tʃ, dʒ, θ] (as in *hence, hens, ant, and, Hench, hinge, month*). In all these positions except the *nt* clusters the [n] is a tongue-point alveolar or tongue-point dental (or interdental) nasal consonant, with nasality of an adjacent vowel as a non-distinctive accompanying feature.

---

[1] Daniel Jones, *An Outline of English Phonetics* (New York: Dutton, 1934), p. 198.

[2] George P. Krapp, *The Pronunciation of Standard English in America* (New York: Oxford, 1919), p. 11.

[3] John S. Kenyon, *American Pronunciation* (Ann Arbor: Geo. Wahr, 1935, 6th ed., rev.), p. 50.

[4] Willem L. Graff, *Language and Languages* (New York: Appleton, 1932), pp. 34 and 60.

[5] Leonard Bloomfield, *Language* (New York: Holt, 1933), p. 96.

[6] William Cabell Greet, "Southern Speech," *Culture in the South,* ed. W. T. Couch (Chapel Hill: University of North Carolina Press, 1935), p. 614.

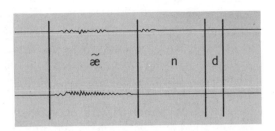

FIGURE 1. The word *and* as recorded on the kymograph. (All the kymograms accompanying this paper were made with mouthpiece and nasal olive; hence, the upper line represents nasal vibrations, and the lower line represents buccal vibrations.)

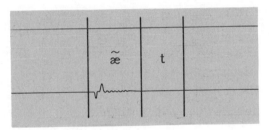

FIGURE 2. The word *ant*. It is plainly seen that the nasal resonance occurs only during the vowel resonance, not between the vowel and the final [t].

Such nasality is illustrated in a kymogram of the word *and* (Figure 1).[7] In the [nt] clusters the [n] tends to lose its character as a tongue-point consonant, and to appear simply as nasality of the preceding vowel (illustrated in Figure 2).

These facts do not indicate of course that, in SA, vowel nasality is a separate phoneme. In the circumstances described it is either (1) a nondistinctive acoustic feature of any vowel preceding [n], or (2) an acoustic feature which is a member of the [n] phoneme.

The conditions are somewhat different, however, in the nine negative auxiliary verb forms *aren't, ain't, daren't, don't, mayn't, shan't, weren't, won't,* and *can't* in which a vowel precedes the [nt]; in the articulation of these words the [t] is frequently omitted. When the form of the phoneme [n] in these words is nasality of the preceding vowel, and at the same time the [t] is omitted, the vowel nasality is an alternate phonetic form of the morpheme *-nt,* appearing as a sandhi feature.

---

[7] The kymograms accompanying this paper were made in the phonetics laboratory of the University of Chicago, where the author was studying under Professor C. E. Parmenter. The phonetic data presented herein are the author's first-hand observations, recorded principally in Alabama, but including subjects from Georgia, Mississippi, Tennessee, South Carolina, and Virginia. The kymograms, *which are purely illustrative,* are records of the author's own speech, which is that of east-central Alabama.

492   It is necessary to describe the vowel nasality thus, and not as a form of the phoneme [n], because words can be distinguished by the minimal opposition of vowel nasality and [n], and by the minimal opposition of the nasalized vowel and the corresponding pure oral vowel.

Since it can be demonstrated by paired sentences that the positives *are, can, dare, may, were* are not homophonic with the negatives *aren't, can't, daren't, mayn't,* and *weren't,* it cannot be said that the *-nt* is simply lost. Likewise, the words *won't* and *woe, don't* and *dough,* and (for some speakers) *can't* and *cane,* which would be pairs of homophones if the *-nt* were completely lost, are distinctive. In the following groups of sentences, the sentences within each group are, by actual test, distinctive to speakers of Southern American:[8]

1)   Don't set it.   [dõ sɛt ɪt]
2)   Doane set it.   [dõn sɛt ɪt]
3)   Doe set it.   [do sɛt ɪt]

1)   Phillis won't set him off.   [fɪlɪs wõ sɛt ɪm ɔf]
2)   Phillis' woe set him off.   [fɪlɪs wo sɛt ɪm ɔf]

1)   That coke ain't hot?   [ðæt kokẽɪ̃ hɑt]
2)   That cocaine hot?   [ðæt kokẽɪ̃n hɑt]

1)   No, can't set it down.   [no kẽɪ̃ sɛt ɪt daʊn]
2)   No, Caine set it down.   [no kẽɪ̃n sɛt ɪt daʊn]
3)   No, Kay set it down.   [no keɪ sɛt ɪt daʊn]

The sentences in the fourth group are *minimally* distinctive only for speakers who pronounce *can't* with the vowel of *rain;* for speakers who have here the vowel of *can* any pairing of *can* and *can't* will suffice.

To illustrate the occurrence of vowel nasality as a sandhi form of *-nt,* kymograms of one set of sentences are reproduced in Figures 3, 4, 5, 6. It must be understood, however, that the picture of the gross acoustic features provided by the kymograph must be interpreted by the operational test provided by the minimally contrasting pairs.

Vowel nasality also appears in SA as a phonetic form of the morpheme *-ing* under precisely limited conditions.

A common future tense construction is *going to* plus the infinitive form of the main verb. In American English generally the phrase *going to* is often reduced to [gʌnə] or [gonə]. These forms occur in SA, with an additional alternative [gõ] (which in the first person singular is often reduced to [õ], as in [aɪm õ du ɪt]).

---

[8] The I.P.A. symbols used in this article, except for the vowel nasality tilde, represent phonemes; it is not the author's purpose to present a "narrow" transcription.

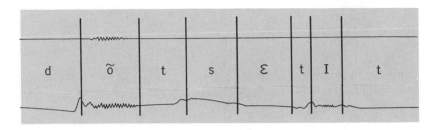

FIGURE 3. The sentence *Don't set it* [dõt sɛt ɪt]. Here the [t] of *don't* is carefully articulated. It can be seen that the phoneme [n] is not a separate consonant, but is nasality of the vowel; the nasal and buccal resonance are simultaneous. If the [n] were a tongue-point alveolar nasal consonant, there would be nasal vibrations between the end of [o] and the implosion of [t].

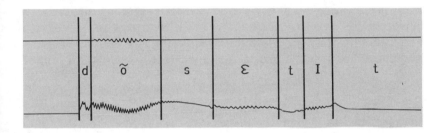

FIGURE 4. The sentence *Don't set it* articulated naturally, so that the [t] is omitted. Omitting the [t] of *don't* does not leave [dõn] (see Figure 5), but [dõ].

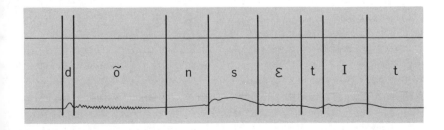

FIGURE 5. The sentence *Doane set it*. The word *Doane* here is distinguishable semantically from the word *don't* [dõ] as in Figure 4; hence the omission of [t] from *don't* does not leave [dõn]. Here the [n] is clearly a separate consonant occurring between [o] and the next phoneme.

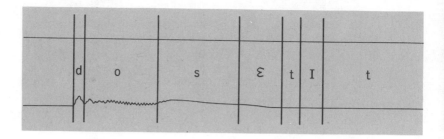

FIGURE 6. The sentence *Doe set it*. This sentence is presented to show that the omission of [t] from *don't* does not leave simply [do]. The forms [dõ] and [do] differ in meaning and in form; the formal difference is the feature [˜]; the difference in meaning demands that we describe the [˜] as a significant feature.

This variant [gõ] is limited to the future tense construction with *to* omitted; that is, the vowel nasality is not a free substitute for *-ing* as a verbal suffix, as [ɪn] is a free substitute for [ɪŋ]. A Southerner can say [aɪm gõ bi æt hom], and [aɪm goɪŋ hom]. He does not say* [aɪm goɪŋ bi æt hom] nor* [aɪm gõ hom].

When used thus, vowel nasality can be minimally paired with the form [ɪŋ], and hence the auxiliary *going* can be distinctively paired with the full verb *going*, as in following sentences: [a: ðeɪ gõ fæst] and [a: ðeɪ goɪŋ fæst]. (In the first sentence, *fast* is a verb; in the second, *fast* is an adverb.)

Kymograms of the two sentences (Figure 7 and 8) show the phonetic difference, which is the presence or absence of nasal vibrations between [go] and [fæst]. Vowel nasality is present in both; in the first it is the phonetic form of the morpheme *-ing;* in the second it is a non-distinctive feature accompanying [ŋ].

It is difficult to equate these facts with the evidence afforded by published transcriptions of SA speech, because of the different methodologies employed. In a few transcriptions of Virginia and North Carolina speech published recently in *American Speech,* the word *don't* appears as [doʊ], [ɾoʊ], [doũ], [do], [do⁺], [doʊn?], and [don]. If the speakers who have no remnant of [n] in *don't* do not make *don't* and *dough* homophones, or if the speakers who retain [n] do not make *don't* and *Doane* homophones, then it is evident that some features hitherto considered non-distinctive must be sandhi forms of the *-nt*. Obviously, further study is needed.

Finally, an interesting point in phonemics is raised. It seems clear that in SA there is a physical feature, vowel nasality, which is sometimes the form of a phoneme, and is at other times capable of being distinctively different from another form of the same phoneme. That is, vowel nasality

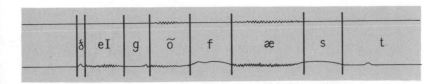

FIGURE 7. The sentence *(Are) they going (to) fast?* [ð eɪ gõ fæst]. The morpheme [ɪŋ] appears as nasality of the vowel [o].

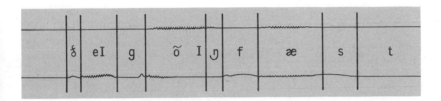

FIGURE 8. The sentence *(Are) they going fast?* [ðeɪ goɪŋ fæst]. In the full verb *going* the *-ing* appears as [ɪŋ]; it differs in meaning and form from the form [gõ] as in Figure 7.

can be the phoneme [n], and in different circumstances it can be paired minimally with another form of [n] with a corresponding semantic difference. This fact seems to support the conclusion that, although the phoneme may at times correspond to a physical reality, it must be, like any other scientific concept, a pure abstraction.

Selected Features of Speech: Black and White

Juanita V. Williamson

A great many articles have been written in the last decade about the speech of Negroes; many of them treat only a limited number of features. In this article, Professor Williamson looks at one description of selected features of the speech of Negroes and compares these with features of the speech of Whites.

There has been in recent years an increasing interest in the speech of American Negroes. Many of the journals, among them *American Speech* and the journals of the National Council of Teachers of English and of the National Education Association, have published at least one article which deals with their speech. The articles usually discuss a limited number of phonological and/or grammatical features which seem to set the speech of

From *CLA Journal,* Vol. XIII, No. 4 (June 1970), 420–423. Reprinted with permission of the College Language Association.

Negroes apart from that of other speakers of American English. One such article is Beryl Bailey's "Toward a New Perspective in Negro Dialectology" (*American Speech*, October 1965, pp. 171–177). In her article Professor Bailey analyzes selected structures found in the speech of Negroes: the absence of the copula (zero copula), the marked forms which are "past and future," the negation markers *ain't* and *don't*, and the treatment of *there* and "possessive *their*." One or more of these structures is usually included in most treatments of the grammar of the speech of Negroes.

Professor Bailey's analysis is based upon the speech of Dude, the narrator in Warren Miller's *The Cool World* (Boston, 1959). The rationale for using a fictional character as her informant rests upon the belief that "an author regularly packs his dialogue with those features which he knows to be the most distinctive in the dialect which his characters speak"

It is of interest to compare the four features of Dude's speech, which Professor Bailey discusses, with those of Paul Valentine, a klansman and the author of an article entitled "Look Out Liberals: Wallace Power Gonna Get You," which appeared in the Fall, 1968, issue of *Katallagete Be Reconciled*, the Journal of the Committee of Southern Churchmen (Nashville, Tennessee, pp. 34–37). An editorial note accompanying the article states that "Paul Valentine is the pseudonym of a Christian who has operated for years in the Southern Klan. He employs by choice the raw words of militant alienation." The article is written just as the author might have spoken it.

In Dude's speech, Professor Bailey points out that the zero copula, that is, the omission of the verb *be,* occurs before adjectives as in:

> I sure they aroun.
> You afraid of jail bait Big Man?

before nouns as in:

> She a big woman not skinny like my mother.
> He one of us all right.

before adverbs and prepositional phrases as in:

> I in a big hurry.
> Did you find out anything while you over in they territory?

after the filler subjects *there* and *it* as in:

> "It the truth." She say.
> They a lot of people on this street have Stomach Trouble.

In Valentine's speech the zero copula also occurs before adjectives and nouns, as may be seen in the following:

> Bobby, I think you right about that.

498

> You dumb and you crazy.
> I think that funny as hell.
> I say you hate and you violent. . .
> We just about the most stubborn, onery bunch of. . .
> They somethin else which we givin a whole lot a thought.
> He our mean and ugly bastard.[1]

There occurs several times before *is* in fairly emphatic, positive statements such as the following: "They is black niggers, yellow niggers, white niggers, and for all I know they is blue niggers somewhere."

The second feature Professor Bailey treats is the marked forms which are "past and future." She states that in Dude's speech it "appears that *was* is reserved for events that are completely in the past, while *been* extends from the past up to, and even including the present moment. *Be* is a simple future, with *gonna* the intentional future." The following are among the examples she gives to illustrate the use of these four forms:

> . . .you just end up scared like you was walkin down a empty street at night.
> . . .you was the sweetest baby so good.

> He bin inside too much.
> You been smokin without me?

> "You be back." Priest say lookin at me.
> "We be waiting for you." Little Flower say.
> Things gonna be a lot diffrent aroun here now Duke in command.
> I sure you gonna contribit some of you earned money to your mother.

Valentine uses *was, been, be,* and *gonna* in a like manner, as the following examples show:

> Now Bobby was able to carry four or five states for Barry.
> Bobby he was real strong for Goldwater.

> You been to college.
> You been stealin our country blind.
> You been forgettin about our problems.

> I be back and catch you next time.
> We still be rollin.
> I think it be close.
> I think it be a generation or more. . .[2]

---

[1] No adverbs or prepositions occur after the zero copula in "Look Out Liberals."

[2] *Be* occurs in another sense also in Valentine's speech, as may be seen in the following: "So Barry he be half Jewish."

We gonna do this because you not fit to run it.
We gonna let you live knowin what you done to the country.
I gonna agree with every thing you say. . .
You gonna whine and moan. . .
So George, he gonna have to cut hard. . .

The third feature of Dude's speech which Professor Bailey discusses is the use of *ain't* and *don't* as negation markers. She states that her analysis reveals that the "American Negro system has a curious deployment of the negative markers *don't* and *ain't. Ain't* is used consistently in non-verbal predications and before the tense markers," and this is also the form "preferred before the progressive *-in* form of the verb." She indicates that *don't* may be used in all other cases. The following are among the examples she gives:

> "I aint afraid of nothin."
> That piece aint been worth no fifteen dollas since you was a little boy Priest.
> He aint comin back.
> He aint gonna get no money out of it.
>
> I dont know why he done it.
> I dont care if they aint room for him.

Valentine uses *ain't* without any verbal form following it in the same manner that Dude uses it. It also occurs in his speech before the *-in/-ing* form of the verb. *Don't* is used in the same way Dude uses it:

> It ain't hardly a secret.
> It ain't quite so slick as ours.
> Some of you ain't gonna be able to live with that.
> We ain't kidding and we ain't quitting, we ain't turning back.
>
> It don't work that way.
> He don't tell folks what to do.

To support her fourth point, that in Dude's speech *there* and *their* occur as *they,* Professor Bailey lists the following examples:

> They must be over a 100 books in they apartment.
> They jus ain't no place in a gang for girls.
> Everybody look down at they feet.
> In the day time those places full of kids and they mothers.

In "Look Out Liberals," *there* occurs as *they* in the following:

> How come they is so many of us?
> They is black niggers. . .

500   Valentine's and Dude's speech patterns are noticeably similar. The question which arises, however, is that of whether the patterns Valentine uses in his article are representative of his speech and/or that of white speakers who live in the area where he lives, the South,[3] or whether what appears in his article is a mishmash he has created.

Since what has been dealt with up to this point is written material, it is of value to look at the dialogue found in fictional works written by authors who deal with the Southern scene and at the representations of Southern speech in articles and magazines. An examination of the dialogue found in William Faulkner's *Light in August,* "Spotted Horses," and *Sanctuary;*[4] Catherine Marshall's *Christy,*[5] Flannery O'Connor's "A Good Man Is Hard to Find," "The Life You Save May be Your Own," and "The Artificial Nigger";[6] John Steinbeck's *The Grapes of Wrath,*[7] Wilbur Daniel Steele's "How Beautiful With Shoes";[8] Percy Walker's *The Moviegoer,*[9] Robert Penn Warren's *All The King's Men* and "Blackberry Winter"[10] reveals that the four features discussed by Professor Bailey and found in Valentine's speech are used by some of the characters in these works.[11] Examples are given below.

Examples of the use of the zero copula:

"You mighty right it is." (*The Moviegoer,* p. 119)

"Name Lucynell Carter. . . ." ("The Life You Save May be Your Own," p. 498)

"Name Tom Shiftlet," he murmured. ("The Life You Save May Be Your Own," p. 498)

[3] The South here includes all of the states usually thought of as Southern, and whose governors belong to the Southern governors conference. Some of these states (or parts of them) are actually a part of the South Midland speech area.

[4] *Light in August,* Modern Library edition (New York, 1950); "Spotted Horses," in *The Faulkner Reader* (New York, 1954), pp. 434–482; *Sanctuary,* Vintage Book edition (New York, 1958).

[5] Avon edition (New York, 1967).

[6] "A Good Man Is Hard to Find," in *An Introduction to Literature,* ed. Sylvan Barrett et al. (Boston, 1967), pp. 281–294; "The Life You Save May Be Your Own," in *Literature,* ed. Walter Blair et al. (Chicago, 1959), pp. 497–505; "The Artificial Nigger," in *Short Fiction,* ed. James R. Frakes and Isadore Traschen (Englewood Cliffs, 1959), pp. 101–118.

[7] Bantam edition (New York, 1939).

[8] In *Literature, Form and Function,* ed. P. Albert Duhamel and Richard Hughes (Englewood Cliffs, 1965), pp. 429–439.

[9] New York, 1960.

[10] *All the King's Men* (New York, 1947); "Blackberry Winter," in *Literature, Form and Function,* ed. P. Albert Duhamel and Richard Hughes (Englewood Cliffs, 1965), pp. 419–429.

[11] Only the speech of white characters is given. Not all of the structures, of course, are found in any one of the works.

"You the chairman?" I asked the other fellow. (*All the King's Men,* p. 60)

"Six of us Holts in school." (*Christy,* p. 84)

"Mission house round the bend now," the old man said blithely. (*Christy,* p. 127)

"Settin chair over yan," he volunteered. (*Christy,* p. 162)

Examples of the use of *was, been, gonna,* and *be* (*Gon* occurs in some works instead of *gonna*):

"So they was Flem's horses." ("Spotted Horses," p. 467)

"They wasn't as advanced as we are." ("The Life You Save May Be Your Own," p. 500)

"It's nothing so sweet," Mr. Shiftlet continued, "as a boy's mother. My mother was a angel of God." ("The Life You Save May Be Your Own," p. 504)

"And I been a decent Baptist all my life, too." (*Sanctuary,* p. 258)

"We been here a long time without a girl." (*Grapes of Wrath,* p. 7)

"I been most everything." ("A Good Man Is Hard to Find," p. 291)

"I been rackin' my lungs out for you." ("How Beautiful With Shoes," p. 431)

"You been messing in politics a long time, Judge." (*All The King's Men,* p. 50)

"Time gonna come for some folks this year," another man said. ("Blackberry Winter," p. 425)

"You gonna git ice cream." (*The Grapes of Wrath,* p. 374)

"You gon behave yourself." (*The Moviegoer,* p. 134)

"We gon stay right here." (*The Moviegoer,* p. 134)

"Don't know himself where he be." (*Christy,* p. 98)

"That be a sealed bargain, fair and square . . ." (*Christy,* p. 85)

Examples of the use of *ain't* and *don't:*

"There ain't nobody there." ("How Beautiful With Shoes," p. 435)

"They ain't got nothing out of this trip." ("Spotted Horses," p. 438)

"That car ain't run in fifteen years," the old woman said. ("The Life You Save May Be Your Own," p. 498)

"Ain't nobody giving me money." (*The Moviegoer,* p. 96)

"You ain't been into my beer have you boy?" (*Sanctuary,* p. 245)

"Now ain't Mr. Duffy a card?" (*All the King's Men,* p. 17)

"You know, when this conscience business starts, ain't no telling where it'll stop . . ." (*All the King's Men,* p. 52)

"It ain't any of my bizness, I'm the sheriff." (*All the King's Men,* p. 59)

"It ain't no secret," he said. (*All the King's Men,* p. 60)

502

"How you know you ain't following the tracks in the wrong direction?" ("The Artificial Nigger," p. 112)

"Don't see good no more." (*Christy,* p. 176)

"Lucy don't favor drinking," Willie said quietly. (*All the King's Men,* p. 20)

"Even a fool gal don't have to come as far as . . ." (*Light in August,* p. 22)

Examples of the use of *they* for *there:*

"They's a looney loose out of Dayville Asylum . . ." ("How Beautiful With Shoes," p. 430)

"They was a big dance in Shawnee." (*The Grapes of Wrath,* p. 5)

"They was a guy paroled . . ." (*The Grapes of Wrath,* p. 22)

"They ain't no need to hurt her feelings." (*The Grapes of Wrath,* p. 369)

Mary Washington Cable in "Jesse Stuart's Writings Preserve a Passing Folk Idiom" (*Southern Folklore Quarterly,* Vol. XXVII, September, 1964, pp. 157–198), gives a list of vocabulary items which show the "range and depth of Stuart's grasp of his native folk speech." The following occurs in the list:

they: expletive, there. "I was afraid they would be trouble there."

The quoted speech in two Memphis, Tennessee, newspapers, *The Commercial Appeal* and the *Memphis Press-Scimitar;* in *The Best of Hillbilly,* a collection of articles from Jim Comstock's *West Virginia Hillbilly,* edited by Otto Whittaker (New York, 1969); and in three articles dealing with Southerners, "George Branch Kentucky," (*Look Magazine,* Dec. 2, 1969, pp. 49–67), "My Brother Lyndon," by Sam Houston Johnson (*Look Magazine,* March 4, 1969, pp. 25–33), and "The People of Cades Cove (Tennessee)," by William O. Douglas (*The National Geographic,* July, 1962, pp. 60–95) include some of the structures discussed in this paper. John Steinbeck in *Travels With Charley* (New York, 1965) records the speech of persons he talks with on his travels around the country. He visits several Southern states; several of the structures occur in his representation of Southern speech.

Examples of the use of the zero copula:

"Rails too thick." ("Cades Cove," p. 67)

"Only five families left." ("Cades Cove," p. 93)

"This your house," the reporter asked. (*The Commercial Appeal,* Dec. 3, 1968)

"You partial, coach?" (*Memphis Press-Scimitar,* June 5, 1969)

"Not many folks in the Cove." ("Cades Cove," p. 67)

Examples of the use of *was, been,* and *gonna:*

"I tuk a look and shore 'nuf that was a big rattler." ("Cades Cove," p. 63)

"They wasn't clean." (*Travels With Charley,* p. 223)

"Where you been, Nellie?" (*Travels With Charley,* p. 224)

"They been coming since dawn . . ." (*Travels With Charley,* p. 225)

"Where you been keeping yourself?" (*The Commercial Appeal,* Feb. 19, 1969)

". . . wuz it the way the squirrels been out early and . . .?" (*Hillbilly,* p. 166)

"He ain't gonna run against you." ("My Brother Lyndon," p. 57)

Examples of the use of *ain't* and *don't:*

"Ain't these cheerleaders something?" (*Travels With Charley,* p. 203)

"I just ain't used to this." ("George Branch Kentucky," p. 37)

"I ain't got no strength no more." ("George Branch Kentucky," p. 32)

"But it ain't such a bad road." (*Hillbilly,* p. 183)

"I don't know what's wrong with this country." ("George Branch Kentucky," p. 28)

"It don't beat normal." ("George Branch Kentucky," p. 29)

"She don't like snakes." ("Cades Cove," p. 66)

Examples of the use of *they* for *there:*

"They's no greater life on earth . . ." ("George Branch Kentucky," p. 28)

"They's a class that's livin' and a class what's daid and don't know it." ("George Branch Kentucky," p. 33)

"They's times I hurt so bad I don't even know whur I'm at." ("George Branch Kentucky," p. 33)

In a column, written by a Southerner, in which the activities of Mississippi are reported, an imaginary conversation between T. X. Payer and Capitol Observer, which takes place on the first floor of the Capitol (Jackson, Mississippi) is recorded (*The Commercial Appeal,* November 30, 1969). The conversation includes sentences that have no copula, no auxiliary, and in which *been* is the only verb:

Mr. C.O. went on, "You ever been in that place?" "You gettin' sarcastic," said C. O. "You some kind of lobbyist or something, who do you represent anyway?"

It is of interest to note what those trained to observe and record speech have written about these features. Fewer studies have been made of Southern speech than of the speech of other areas east of the Mississippi River. Those made deal primarily with the phonological features of the

504   region. Bits of information about some of the grammatical features dealt
with here can, however, be found in them. Some information can also be
found in studies which deal with the speech of other areas.

One of the major reference grammars sheds some light on the sentence
type which has no copula. George O. Curme in *Principles and Practices of
English Grammar* (New York, 1947, pp. 23, 106) states that this sentence
type is "quite common" in colloquial speech and gives the following
examples:

> Our sister dead!
> Everything in good order.

E. Bagby Atwood in *A Survey of Verb Forms in the Eastern United
States* (Ann Arbor, 1953, p. 26) shows that *have* is often missing in the
speech of many persons in the phrase "I (have) been thinking." He states
that "the /v/ is often lost through assimilation." Raven I. McDavid, Jr.
and Virginia G. McDavid point out in "Grammatical Differences in
the North Central States" (*American Speech*, February, 1960, pp. 5–19)
that this omission is common in the North Central States also. They say
that despite "the disapproval of handbooks and self constituted authorities certain forms occur everywhere in the speech of all social groups."
One of these is "I been thinking."[12]

Professor James McMillan in "Vowel Nasality as a Sandhi Form of the
Morphemes *-nt* and *-ing* in Southern American" (*American Speech*, April,
1939, pp. 120–123) describes the various forms of *going* which occur in
the speech of Southerners. Like other American English speakers they can
say *gonna* [gonə] or [gʌnə]. In addition they have a form [gõ] in which
the [o] is nasalized. "I'm going to do it" may be realized as "[a.m gõ] do
it." They have a third form [o] which occurs only with the first person
singular. Thus, "I'm going to do it" may also be realized as "[aˑmo] do it."
Carmelita Klipple in "The Speech of Spicewood, Texas" (*American
Speech*, October, 1945, pp. 187–191) shows that this form is also found
in Texas.

The negative form *ain't* is found in all sections of the United States. Its
wide use is attested to by the many articles that appear defending or
damning it. It is used to mean *am not, is not, are not, have not,* and *has not.*
Professor Archibald A. Hill, of the University of Texas, in "The Tainted
Ain't Once More" (*College English*, January, 1965, pp. 298–303) discusses
the long history of the form, points out that he uses it, and describes the
circumstances under which he does. Raven I. McDavid points out in "The
Position of the Charleston Dialect" (*The Publication of the American Di-*

---

[12] Since *was* is used in all varieties of American English in discussing events which are "completely in the past," no comments on *was* are given in this section of the paper.

alect Society, April, 1955, pp. 35–49) that *ain't* is used in colloquial speech   505
by the educated and socially prestigious in the South. McDavid and Mc-
David in the article referred to above also show that *ain't* and *hain't*
occur side by side as negatives of both *have* and *be* in the North Central
States.

Don't is a negative form used everywhere in all varieties of American
English. Its use as a third person singular present tense form is generally
frowned on by English teachers, but this usage is widespread. Kemp
Malone states in "Current English Forum" (*English Journal,* February,
1950, pp. 104–105) that he has "heard *don't* for *doesn't* innumerable times
from persons of good breeding and high cultivation. This form is well
established in English colloquial speech, and has been for years." He
states also that he has "heard it often in the mouths of highly educated
people (Ph.D.'s in English among them). . . ."E. Bagby Atwood in *A Survey of Verb Forms of the Eastern United States* (p. 28) shows that "he
don't" is used by both the educated and the uneducated. The evidence
shows that the use of *ain't* and *don't* by Americans is no "curious deployment;" it is rather just one of the patterns found in American English.

John Sargeant Hall, in the *Phonetics of the Great Smoky Mountains*
(*American Speech* Monograph, New York, 1942, p. 26), indicates that
there is pronounced as *they* in that region. He says that *there* often appears
as *they* [ðe] in such uses as, "They come a snow that day." Carmelita
Klipple shows also that *there* is pronounced as *they* in Texas: "*There* is
heard as *they* so often that apparently *they* has come to be used for *there.*"
She gives the example: "Are they a pencil on the table?"

Are the structures presently in use in the South? The following examples taken from my files on Southern speech show that they are. All of
them were recorded on tape or taken down in phonetic notation as the
speakers were talking.[13] All of the speakers are white; all of the material
has been gathered since 1967.

Examples of the use of the zero copula:

> You just beautiful. (*professor of English, Southern university*)
> Roger, you all excited. (*well-dressed shopper in a supermarket*)
> He mad. (*professor of English, Southern university*)
> They right over here. (*clerk in a department store*)
> Here your keys. (*clerk in a cleaning establishment*)
> You my buddy. (*man on a bus*)
> He over there. (*high-school English teacher*)
> We still on the Mid-South title. (*bank employee*)

---

[13] All of the material was recorded by the writer.

506   Y'all from Nashville and . . . (*Member, Tennessee legislature*)
They never anybody there. (*diner in a motel*)

In the film *William Faulkner* (available through the University of Mississippi), in which Faulkner himself is featured, Faulkner says to a resident of Oxford, "Gilbert, you lame."

Examples of the use of *was, been, be,* and *gonna:*

It was a colored guy there. (*housewife*)
You was on that route. (*bus driver*)
See how things was. (*ticket-seller in Knoxville bus station*)
I been sleeping with a pistol by my side. (*secretary, State university*)
I been south. (*clerk in a department store*)
First time I been in four hours. (*man in bus station*)
I been had it. (*bus driver*)
Thisn be all right. (*customer in department store*)
She be fifteen in November. (*man talking to a clerk in a department store*)
I be glad to help you. (*clerk in a department store*)
Think how cool you are and you be cool. (*customer in a department store*)
That be all? (*clerk in a supermarket*)

Examples of the use of *gonna*, [a·mo], [gõ]

We gonna lose a lot of manpower. (*university professor*)
You gonna hear the people. (*federal employee*)
[a·mo] try this one on. (*customer in a department store*)
[a·mo] run over here, while you get . . . (*customer in a department store*)
I hope this not [gõ] be true. (*member, men's service club*)
They [gõ] have a big moon day celebration. (*bus driver*)

Faulkner says, in the film mentioned above, "We [gõ] get the big one this time."

Examples of the use of *ain't* and *don't:*

They ain't doing no good. (*bus driver*)
I ain't [gõ] bring you nothin. (*clerk in a shoe store*)
I ain't fixed it. (*teen-ager on a bus*)
Naw I ain't out; you out. (*young girl telling a story*)
I don't wanta see no splashdown. (*clerk in a store*)
You don't want none. (*clerk talking to another clerk*)
She don't like it short. (*clerk talking to a customer*)
It don't look good. (*man in a bus station*)

Examples of the use of *they* for *there* and *their:*

> They's [ðez] been a controversy going on. (*high-school English teacher*)
>
> They's [ðez] enough difference. (*book company representative*)
>
> They [ðe] was a lot of people didn't know where they was at. (*retired airlines pilot*)
>
> They [ðe] was another guy making . . . (*bus driver*)
>
> . . . express they [ðe] feeling. (*book company representative*)
>
> They have they [ðe] religious convictions. (*high-school English teacher*)
>
> We hear they [ðe] idea. (*policeman*)
>
> In they [ðe] life . . . (*university professor*)

The above examples show that Valentine's representation is clearly no mishmash. Whether he himself uses these structures cannot, of course, be ascertained; they are, however, found in the Southern region, most certainly in Tennessee, Alabama, North Carolina, Georgia, Virginia, Kentucky, Texas, Mississippi—and even Missouri, a border state. There are examples in my files from all of these.

That the four features are found in Dude's speech is no surprise, for most Negroes, wherever they might live outside the South, migrated to that place from the South. And it should be no surprise that they carried their Southern language patterns with them.

part **6**

STUDIES
OF URBAN
DIALECTS

The Language
of the City

Raven I. McDavid, Jr.

The speech of urban centers has always been of interest
to linguists, but in recent years that interest has grown.
The migration of large numbers of persons from other speech
areas, particularly the rural South, to urban centers
has resulted in a more complex speech situation than
previously existed. Professor McDavid, who has written
a number of articles on the subject, discusses some of the
social and regional differences that affect the speech
of the city.

In a sense, to speak of the language of the city is a contradiction in
terms. There is no one voice for the city, any more than there is a single
type of urban personality. Nor, to be sure, is there much reason to speak
of *the* city: each city has its own set of characteristics—as anyone will
recognize who has changed jobs or residence from one community to
another. Chicago is not Cleveland; Greenville, South Carolina, is not

From *Midcontinent American Studies Journal,* Vol. 10, No. 1 (Spring, 1969). Reprinted with
the permission of *Midcontinent American Studies Journal* (University of Kansas) and Raven I.
McDavid, Jr.

512   Gary—nor is it Greenville, Texas. The function of a city is determined
by its location and its history; location and history and function in turn
determine what ethnic, religious, and social groups make up the population—and the relationships between these groups are responsible for
the varieties of language to be found in a city, the amount of prestige
assigned each variety and the kind and degree of difference among them.[1]
In a small midwestern town in the belt of Yankee settlements the only
overt social markers in language may be relatively slight differences in
grammar; in a comparable city in the South there will be significant
and more striking differences in pronunciation and grammar. In an older
city, particularly one with a relatively stable population, the differences
are likely to be well established by tradition and recognized by all groups;
in a newer city, or one with a great deal of recent immigration, the differences may not be so well agreed upon, and the new arrivals, or their
children, may even reject the traditional standards of the community as
represented by the old élite families.[2]

Those who have studied the rise of cities are in fair agreement that
with increasing importance and better transportation, a city will grow
in size and complexity and attract special groups to handle manufacturing, wholesale and retail trade, service industries, and the proliferation
of government services, including public education. Moreover, as cities
grow in size and complexity, they become increasingly dependent on this
outside world. Not only is this true of food—an American city may get
some of its milk supply from five hundred miles away—but of other
commodities as well. Chicago's steel mills and electrical system are both
dependent on soft coal mined far downstate. Likewise, no city out of its
own resources can fill all the jobs created as the economy expands; it
must lure workers from elsewhere—from smaller communities in its own
region, from other regions of the nation and from other nations. As the
groups are brought together in the relatively impersonal urban scene,
those of similar background will tend to live in the same neighborhood—
whether by choice or by design. But at work—and in going to and from
work—each person will come in contact with representatives of all kinds
of regional, ethnic and social groups. In the course of a day he will
hear all kinds of accents and evaluate their speakers, often most cruelly,
in the light of his past experiences. This has been true of urban communities of the last five thousand years, but the more rapid urbanization

[1] See Lee Pederson, *The Pronunciation of English in Chicago: Consonants and Vowels, Publica-
tion of the American Dialect Society,* 44 (1965), and William M. Austin and Raven I. McDavid,
Jr., eds., *Communication Barriers to the Culturally Deprived,* Cooperative Research Project 2107
(Chicago, 1966).

[2] For a dramatic change in attitudes toward certain features, see William Labov, *The Social
Stratification of English in New York City* (Washington, D.C., 1966).

of the United States and the development of faster means of transportation have recently juxtaposed more cultural groups, of more diverse background than ever before—with greater shock at difficulties in the way they communicate.

Speech, we must remember, never takes place without other behavior. The speakers stand in a physical relationship to each other, and in no two societies is this exactly the same. Edward Hall[3] and others have calculated that in the United States two men communicate most effectively when they stand about two feet apart; we become uncomfortable when another man comes closer to us—but Latin Americans cannot relax if they are more than a foot apart, and Arabs like to be close enough to smell each other's breaths. We may feel there's something wrong but not notice it specifically unless we are trained to observe it. In 1967, to my surprise, I felt vastly more at home in Helsinki than I had been in Bucharest or even in Prague, though my Swedish is subminimal and my Finnish non-existent; then I realized that Finns just don't like to crowd each other, even in department stores or when lining up for a trolley at rush hours. When I commented on this to Tauno Mustanoja, Professor of English at the University of Helsinki, he was surprised that I had noticed this so soon, and went on to say that this difference in comfortable space was one of the most noticeable differences the Finnish soldiers had found between themselves and their temporary German allies. Perhaps the reason that the Southern poor whites are the most difficult group to cope with in Northern cities is that they don't like to think of themselves as a group or get into organized crowds but prefer to go their ways as individuals.

In speaking we do not confine ourselves to the vocal tract but accompany ourselves with all kinds of body movements.[4] Sometimes the accompaniment is more significant than the overt words, as when we say "yes" but shake our heads. We often think that there is something sinister about the way the other person uses body movements in communication; to the American white Protestant, Italians and Levantines seem to gesticulate wildly, while Orientals are impassive. Still, despite my six generations of Upcountry South Carolina ancestry, some of my Northern friends have commented on my "Jewish" gestures; one of my childhood friends observed, perhaps more accurately, that some hand movements we both use are found nowhere else in America.

And even in our speech, the language itself is only a part. We frequently make up our minds about a person or a group on the strength of the accompanying orchestration of speech—loudness, tempo, rhythm,

---

[3] *The Silent Language* (New York, 1959); *The Hidden Dimension* (New York, 1965).

[4] Ray Birdwhistell, *An Introduction to Kinesics* (Louisville, Kentucky, 1954).

514   rasp, nasality and the like—before we hear clearly a single sentence they have uttered.[5] Those who speak a different language from our own—especially if their language is one we have learned painfully and imperfectly—always seem to talk fast; those who belong to groups we do not normally associate with always talk loud and with a pitch level unpleasantly high or unpleasantly low. The salient quality of hillbilly music is the strong accompanying nasality. Even occupations seem to induce peculiar vocal orchestrations. It is inconceivable that a Southern politician could campaign successfully in the back precincts without at least a simulation of a Bourbon baritone or without the throaty prolongation of what he thinks are his most important syllables, or that a Marine topkick could induce the proper *esprit de corps* in recruits without his rasp, or that a kindergarten teacher could convey the mystique of the public schools without the Miss Frances wheedle.

     With these differences existing in the behavior accompanying the use of language, it is no wonder that we find a wide range of differences in the way people use the English language. The Middle Western American—even though he is only a statistical abstraction—thinks the Englishman has a wider pitch range and a greater variety of speech tunes. The Southerner is likely to consider the speech of the Middle Westerner as monotonous, because it has a narrower range of pitch and stress than he is accustomed to. The Middle Westerner, in turn, thinks the Southerner has a "lazy drawl," though the actual tempo of Southern speech may be more rapid than his own, because the stressed syllables of Southern speech are relatively more heavily stressed and more prolonged. In compensation, the Southerner—like the Englishman—weakens and shortens the weak-stressed syllables, with accompanying neutralization of their vowels, so that *borrow* and *Wednesday* become /bárə/ and /wénzdiy/, with the final vowels of *sofa* and *happy* respectively; the Middle Westerner labels this as "slurring." But turning the coin again, the Middle Westerner often pronounces the final syllables of *borrow* and *Wednesday* with the full vowels of *go* and *day* respectively; the Southerner is likely to consider such pronunciations as affectation, if not the over-precise articulation of foreigners.

     We often notice that people in other groups have different pronunciations of vowels than our own. Differences in the pronunciations of consonants are less common. Nevertheless we do notice the "peculiar" sounds made by many New Yorkers (and by some speakers in other cities) when they pronounce /t, d, n, s, z, r, l/ with the tip of the tongue

---

[5] Robert E. Pittenger, Charles F. Hockett, and John J. Danehy, *The First Five Minutes* (Ithaca, New York, 1960); William M. Austin, "Some Social Aspects of Paralanguage," *Canadian Journal of Linguistics,* XI (1965–66), 31–39.

against their teeth instead of against the gums, which is the usual American fashion. It is quite evident that most Southerners have a different kind of /r/ and /l/ from what Chicagoans use in *borrow* and *Billy.* In the Upcountry of South Carolina we used to laugh at the peculiar vowels the Charlestonians had in *date* and *boat;* in recent years I have learned to tolerate the Northerner's amusement at my vowel in *all,* or the fact that the Northerner may interpret the Upcountry pronunciation of *oil* as his own pronunciation of *all.*[6] Americans from the Mississippi Valley have often commented about the very high vowels found along the Atlantic Seaboard, from New York to Baltimore, in such words as *bad* and *dog.* And what seems to have become a standard Southern pronunciation (though it is not my own), the use of a long vowel instead of a diphthong in *nice white rice* (as well as in *high rise,* where I do have it), has never ceased to bewilder unsophisticated Northerners, even to the barbarous assumption that Southerners confused *right* and *rat.*

But even more disturbing to us are the contrasts that our fellow speakers of English make where we don't make them and don't make where we do. I was twenty-five before I was aware that an educated person might not make a distinction between *do* and *due,* between *hoarse* and *horse,* between *merry* and *marry* and *Mary.*[7] I recall that even as a child I was irritated when a poet rhymed *hill* with the preposition *till;* I pronounced *hill* with the vowel of *hit,* but *till* with a vowel halfway between that of *hit* and that of *put.* Later I found myself a source of delight to my fellow linguists and of distress to my students because the vowel I have in *till* also occurs, in my speech, in such words as *dinner, sister, milk, mirror, scissors, ribbon, pillow,* to mention only a few; for me these words contrast with *sinner, system, silk, spirit, schism, ribbing, billow,* all of which have the vowel of *hit.* None of my Chicago-born students have such a contrast. Few of my students have my three-way contrast between *have, salve, halve,* or *had, sad, bad.*[8] No true-born Englishman has my contrast between *wails* and *whales;* no Charlestonian makes a distinction between the night *air*

---

[6] One cannot be reminded too often that "confusions" among *speakers* of a given dialect are usually confusions in the perception of *listeners* accustomed to other dialects. The Southerner makes a clear distinction between *all* and *oil;* the Middle Westerner is not accustomed to perceiving the kind of difference that the Southerner makes.

[7] All these differences are characteristic of the South and South Midland areas, from the Potomac and Kanawha south. Older speakers in the areas of early New England settlement distinguished *horse* (with the vowel of *law*) and *hoarse* (with the vowel of *low*), *merry* (with the vowel of *met*) and *marry* (with the vowel of *mat*) and *Mary* (with the vowel of *mate*), but these differences have disappeared as the Yankees moved west into upstate New York and the Great Lakes region.

[8] I have a short vowel in *have* and *had,* a higher and longer vowel in *salve* and *sad,* an upgliding diphthong in *halve* and *bad.*

516   and the ring in her *ear*. Despite decades of ridicule, some educated New Yorkers of the older generation still pronounce alike a *curl* of hair and a *coil* of rope. I was well over thirty when I learned that Pittsburghers and Bostonians did not distinguish *cot* and *caught, tot* and *taught, collar* and *caller*. It was my wife who apprised me that this homonymy was also found in Minneapolis; and later I found it in most of Canada and in parts of the Rocky Mountain area.[9] But even today some European observers, who know only British Received Pronunciation, refuse to believe that such homonymy can exist. Nevertheless, even if I have close to the maximum number of contrasts found among speakers of English, there are some which I lack; I do not have the peculiar "New England short *o*" of *coat, road* and *home*, which I have recorded in some of the smaller communities of Northern Illinois.

Needless to say, we do not always agree on which vowel or consonant we will use, even when we share the whole repertoire. North of Peoria one is likely to find *greasy* with /-s-/, further south with /-z-/; a person familiar with both pronunciations is likely to consider one more repulsive than the other—depending on which is his pronunciation at home. In metropolitan Chicago the natives of smaller suburban communities are likely to pronounce, *fog, hog, Chicago* with the vowel of *father;* in the city itself these words normally have the vowel of *law*. The words with derivatives of Middle English long *ō* have a wide variety of pronunciations today. My own pattern is unlikely to be duplicated by anyone native to the Chicago area:

/uw/ the vowel of *do*	/u/ the vowel of *foot*	/ə/ the vowel of *cut*
root	*coop*	*gums*
roof	*Cooper*	
food	*hoop*	
spoon	*soot*	
moon		
soon		

With *broom, room,* and *hoof,* I may have either the vowel of *do* or that of *foot*. Many Pennsylvanians rhyme *food* with *good;* many highly educated Southerners rhyme *soot* with *cut*. *Roof* with the vowel of *foot* is widespread in the area of New England settlement and some of the areas settled from Pennsylvania; *coop* with the vowel of *do* is almost universal north of the Kanawha River; *root* rhyming with *foot* is characteristic of Yankee settle-

---

[9] In some areas this vowel is unrounded, like the vowel Americans who distinguish these pairs usually have in *father;* in others it is rounded, like the usual vowel in *law*. The significance is that in these areas there is no contrast between such pairs as *cot* and *caught*.

ments. President Ruthven of the University of Michigan, an Iowan of Yankee descent, always said *gums* with the vowel of *do;* a former president of the American Academy of Physicians, a native of the belt of Yankee settlement in northern Illinois, consistently says *soon* with the vowel of *foot.*

We even show differences in our grammar. No one in South Carolina, however uneducated, would say *hadn't ought,* which is still current in educated Northern speech, nor would we say *sick to the stomach,* which in the North is almost universal. But many educated Southerners—and I include myself—find a place in conversation for *might could, used to could* and *used to didn't.* I have heard the basketball announcer for the Chicago *Tribune* become almost schizoid as he hesitated between *dived* and *dove* (with the vowel of *go*), and there seems to be no regional or social distinction between *kneeled* and *knelt.* Even *ain't*—a four-letter word still taboo in writing despite *Ulysses, Lady Chatterly* and Norman Mailer[10]— may be found in educated conversation, especially among the first families of Charleston. When we realize this, we can take calmly the diversity of names for the grass strip between sidewalk and street, the earthworm, the dragon fly or cottage cheese; the debate among New Englanders as to whether a doughnut should be made with yeast; or the fact that the New Orleans *poor boy* sandwich may be a *hoagy* as in Philadelphia, a *submarine* as in Boston, a *grinder* as in upstate New York or a *hero* as in New York City. Only in recent years have people outside learned that *clout* is our local Chicago name for political influence, a *Chinaman* is a dispenser of such influence, a *prairie* is a vacant lot and a *gangway* is a passage, usually covered, between two apartment buildings. I would not be surprised if these terms were unfamiliar to many who have grown up as close to the city as the DuPage Valley.

Yet if we are sometimes bewildered by the differences in American English, we should be comforted to learn that by European standards these differences are very small. We can notice, in fact, that not only are differences along the Atlantic Seaboard fewer and less sharp than one finds in the much shorter distance between Cumberland and Kent, but that differences diminish as we go west. We owe our relative uniformity of speech to several forces. First, the speakers of the more extreme varieties of British local speech were not the ones who migrated; most of the early settlers had already migrated, in Britain, from village to towns, especially to seaport towns. There was dialect mixture in all of the early

---

[10] In a review of Morton Bloomfield and Leonard Newmark, *A Linguistic Introduction to the History of English,* James H. Sledd observes sardonically that "the agonizing deappraisals of *Webster's Third New International* show that any red-blooded American would prefer incest to *ain't.*" *Language,* XL (1964), 473.

518 settlements—a situation repeated in the westward movement—so that what survived in each area was a compromise. There has always been a tradition of geographical mobility, epitomized in various ways by Daniel Boone, Sam Houston and Steinbeck's Joads. There has been an equal tradition of social mobility; except for Taft and the Roosevelts, no president of the United States since 1890 has come from an old family of social prestige and inherited wealth. There has been a tradition of industrialization—of substituting better tools and more intricate machinery, wherever possible, for human hands and muscle. The Yankee farmer was the son of a townsman—uninhibited by traditional English ways of farming but determined to make a good living. The curved American axhandle made it easier to clear the forests; the computer and scanner promise to make it easier to collect citations for dictionaries—though no technological development can eliminate the need for judgment. There has been a tradition of urbanization—of cities arising in response to opportunities for trade and providing in turn greater opportunities for industry and the arts alike; if we are aware of the open spaces of colonial America and the rugged strength of the frontiersman, we should be equally aware that in 1775 Philadelphia and Boston were the second and third most important cities under the British crown and that they provided the sophisticated citizen with most of the cultural advantages of his British counterpart. And finally, there has been a tradition of general education, beginning when the Northwest Ordinance provided that public schools be financed from the public lands, and proceeding through coeducation and the great state universities first established on a large scale in the Middle West but now found everywhere. All of these forces have combined—and are still combining—to replace local and even regional terms with commercial terms of national use, to eradicate the most noticeable non-standard grammatical features and even to reduce the differences between the pronunciation of one region and that of another.

Yet though these forces have reduced some of the regional differences in American English, they have not eliminated them. If cottage cheese is now a commercial product, so that only the older people are likely to remember *Dutch cheese, smearcase* or *clabber* cheese, the regional designations for the large complicated sandwich are becoming established, and the designations for the grass strip near the street seem to be fairly stable, and indeed often peculiarly local, as *tree belt* in Springfield, Massachusetts, *tree lawn* in Cleveland, and *devil strip* in Akron. Many of these differences are due to the nature of the original population: *pail* and *swill* were spread westward by New Englanders and York Staters, *bucket* and *slop* by Pennsylvanians and Southerners, in the same way that East Anglians brought to eastern New England the "broad *a*" and the loss of /-r/ in *barn*. Where Germans have settled, one may say *got awake;* in communities settled heavily by Scandinavians, one *cooks coffee.*

The routes of communication often stay the same, though the mode of transportation has changed; relatively few of these routes—the Mississippi is a notable exception—cross the major dialect boundaries. Even the monstrous expenditures for highways have not reduced the isolation of some of the more striking relic areas: the Maine coast, the eastern shore of Chesapeake Bay, the Outer Banks of North Carolina and parts of the Kentucky mountains are still off the beaten track; even in Illinois the tongue of land between the Illinois and the Mississippi has become accessible to metropolitan St. Louis only in the last few years. Since our system of public education is highly decentralized (in most ways, a source of strength, since it allows one community to learn from the successes or failures of another), the differences in taxable wealth make it possible for expenditures per pupil to be much less in Mississippi than in Illinois, even though Mississippi spends a far greater proportion of her tax revenues on education, so that libraries are far smaller and the best-trained teachers are tempted to go elsewhere; as a result, regional non-standard grammatical forms in Mississippi prove strikingly resistant to the influence of the classroom.

Because the nation is too large for any single center to establish its speech as a model of excellence—even if we had not had a number of stubbornly autonomous regional centers of culture from the beginning— we can expect to have a number of regional varieties of cultivated speech, unlike the situation in France or Spain or England. If some of the colonial centers no longer have the prestige they once had—Newport, Charleston and Savannah have certainly ceased to exert much influence on their neighbors—new centers have come into existence, such as Chicago and St. Louis, Atlanta and Nashville, Houston and Denver, Salt Lake City and San Francisco. It is certain that the differences among educated speech—always less than those among uneducated varieties—will become even less with the passing of time. But some differences will remain. And as corporations emulate the traditional policy of the army and the older policy of the Methodist Church, in shifting their executives around as they rise in the hierarchy,[11] we can be sure that any respectable suburban classroom will contain children speaking several varieties of cultivated American English. It behooves the teacher to recognize that in the long run one such variety is as good as another, and to make the diversity a

[11] For example, in early 1965 in Baton Rouge, I met the husband of one of my former students, a personnel scout for the Humble division of Jersey Standard, attached to the Baton Rouge office. Later that year he was transferred to Houston; in September, 1967, he was shifted to New York and to suburban living in New Canaan, Connecticut.

520   source of both more interesting instruction at present and greater cultural understanding in the future.

Social differences arise essentially in the same way as regional ones, through close association with those who speak one variety of the language, and remote association—or none—with those who speak other varieties. Standard or cultivated speech is such because it is used by those people who make the important decisions in the speech community. There is nothing sacred about any particular variety; what was once unacceptable becomes acceptable if its speakers rise to positions of economic and social prestige, and it may change under the influence of other speakers who come into the prestige group. After the Norman Conquest, Winchester yielded to London as the cultural center of the south of England, and by the end of the fourteenth century—despite some brilliant writers in the North—London English was so dominant that even a Yorkshireman like Wyclif had to use it in his writings. But London English did not remain static; under the influence of the rich wool merchants and others from the north of England, it replaced the *-th* of the present indicative third singular with *-s;* it replaced *be* as an indicative plural with *are;* it established *she* as the feminine nominative third person pronoun, and *they* and *their* and *them* as pronouns of the third person plural. And as we are well aware, every long vowel and diphthong of fourteenth-century London English has changed in pronunciation and some have fallen together, as the verb *see* /se:/ and the noun *sea* /sæ:/ have both become /siy/. For a more recent example we can take the rise in status of the Southern monophthongal /ay/ in *nice white rice:* as a boy I was taught that this was substandard, but it is now widely heard from educated Southerners.[12]

Social differences in language have always been with us, but in the contemporary American scene there are three forces which make for a different kind of situation from that which prevailed in older societies, more rural than ours. In such older societies, the social intervals in the speech of one community in a given country were likely to be about the same as those elsewhere. Migration was likely to be in terms of individuals, or at most of separate families, and the aspiring—or at least their children—had a fair chance of breaking into the group of standard speakers in their new home. Finally, there was no hard-and-fast segregation between wealthy and poor neighborhoods. To take myself once more as an example, though my parents lived half a block from the richest street

[12] This vowel, as in *right nice,* is characteristic of the upper Piedmont and mountain regions of the South. As the inhabitants of those regions acquire education and money, their speech acquires prestige; since they constitute the overwhelming majority of white Southerners, it is to be expected that their accents will prevail, like their votes, in the South of the future.

in town, we were the same distance from one of the Negro enclaves and not too far from immigrant and less affluent local whites. We all played together even though we didn't all go to school together; we were familiar with most of the local varieties of English and took their existence as a matter of course, assuming that the differences would grow less as more people became educated, and meanwhile delighting in the tunes and figures of speech each group of speakers used. For the most part we not only had the same sound system but—except for such shibboleths as *nice white rice*—the same pronunciations of the vowels and consonants; the differences were in distribution of sounds, in vocabulary and in grammar.

But in metropolitan areas there is now a different kind of situation. Some of this began long ago when—after the rise of the steamboat—immigrants from overseas, brought in to tend heavy industry, settled in ethnic neighborhoods under the watchful eye of their clergy and political leaders; with affluence, many of them left the old neighborhoods and entered into the dominant culture. Their consciousness was perhaps aggravated by the rampant xenophobia of World War I,[13] but the language tended to disappear. When German—a language used in urban and rural communities on all social levels—could be stigmatized, it is small wonder that the Slavic groups, usually peasants and often illiterate, should give up their language.

During my five-year stretch at Western Reserve, though at least half of my Cleveland students were of East European descent, less than one percent admitted knowing the languages of the countries from which their parents and grandparents had come. Culturally they have been deracinated. Immigrants from other parts of the United States, however, had usually followed the traditional pattern of individual movement, settling in a neighborhood according to their economic situation and mingling with those who were already there. Among Negroes[14] who were born in Chicago before 1900 there is essentially the same range of variation as there is among their white contemporaries.

But the situation changed when it became convenient to encourage heavy migration of unskilled labor from other parts—mostly rural areas

[13] In 1917 the Texas legislature abolished the teaching of German in all state institutions because (among other reasons) Eduard Prokosch, head of the German Department in the state university, had referred to English as a Low German dialect.

[14] The designation "Negro" is now rejected by many of the self-designated leaders, who prefer *Black;* however, for other members of the group, *Black* is still an offensive label. For various designations of ethnic groups in America, and the record of their acceptance or rejection, see H. L. Mencken, *The American Language* (one-volume abridged edition, New York, 1963), 367–389. As George Schuyler, the distinguished columnist for the Pittsburgh *Courier,* once said, it seems rather trivial to raise points of protocol about designations while those designated lack the right to participate fully in American society.

522 —of the United States. This became noticeable during World War I, when the migration from Europe was cut off; but even before then some companies had found it expedient to introduce Negroes and Southern whites as strikebreakers, to counter the influence of the unions among the recent arrivals from Europe. Like the immigrants from Europe, these new groups—and after them the Puerto Ricans and Mexicans—tended to come in blocks and settle in patterns like the old ethnic neighborhoods, but lacking their structured community life. (Mexicans and Puerto Ricans have had such a community structure, and in this way strikingly differed from Negroes and rural whites). The economic threat these groups posed to those who had arrived just before them—those from Southern and Eastern Europe—provoked hostility and fear, which was especially directed toward the more visible Negro: the bitterness between Negro and Hunky is an old story, which Rap Brown did not have to invent.[15] The demands for labor during World War II and the later mechanization of Southern agriculture accelerated the northward movement, and the Negro and poor white neighborhoods continued to spread—most noticeably the former. Nevertheless, although the newspapers have ignored the fact, Metropolitan Cleveland contains 200,000 Southern poor whites, most of them disadvantaged.

The very economic forces that led the poor Southerners north contributed to their problems after they arrived, except during times of unusually full employment, as in World War II. The South until very recently has been a region of unskilled labor;[16] the trend in all industry has been to upgrade the skills of labor and to transfer the unskilled work to machinery. With this trend increasing at the same time that migration from the South increased, employment opportunities for the unskilled tailed off, and with them the chance to participate in the well-advertised affluence of the community. Moreover, the Southern tradition of unskilled labor was paralleled by a regional inferiority in the educational system, especially in the schools available to the groups from which the northward migration was drawn. Thus the new arrivals from the South were at an added disadvantage where reading and mathematical skills were required. And in the South, finally, there has always been a wider difference between educated and uneducated speech than one finds in other regions. So what we have seen in the urban slums (especially in the North and West) is the establishment locally of strongly divergent varieties of non-standard English, with a larger proportion of non-standard

[15] Nor did he invent the pronunciation of *hunky* as *honky,* with the vowel of *law;* the analogous pronunciation of *hungry* is widely used in the rural South, without racial distinction.

[16] See Marshall R. Colbert, "Southern Economic Development: Some Research Accomplishments and Gaps," *Perspectives on the South,* Edgar T. Thompson, ed. (Durham, N.C., 1967), 17–32.

grammatical forms than one finds in uneducated Northern English, and with strikingly different features of pronunciation. And as the children of uneducated Mississippians and Alabamians grow up hearing at play such varieties of uneducated speech, they tend to perpetuate these varieties even when by chance they go to school alongside sizeable numbers of speakers of Northern types of English. In short we are now witnessing the establishment in our Northern cities of non-standard varieties of English that diverge sharply from the local standard.

Last, we are getting into a pattern of one-class neighborhoods, where we seldom know people of different social strata from our own. We have indicated the rise of such neighborhoods through negative forces—the inability of the poor to buy or rent alongside other groups. But such neighborhoods have also arisen from the ability and desire of the affluent to flock with their kind. The automobile, which (among its other deleterious social effects) isolates the individual traveler from all but his own kind, has accelerated the trend, and so have the corporations, through an insistence that executives live in a style and community befitting their income and status. So there has been an increasing flight from the city, and new bedroom suburbs spring up, with their inmates insulated not only from the city but from all those below or above a narrow economic range. In the ninety-odd major suburbs in northeastern Illinois, a survey about ten years ago worked out a clear pecking order from Kenilworth down to Robbins; as their income grows, there is a clearly defined drift of young executives from Mount Prospect to Barrington; and the turnover of property in Park Forest is nationally notorious.[17] Under these circumstances, not only are some of the more effective models of standard English removed from the city, but those who grow up using these models have no chance to hear at close range what other varieties of English are like and are confirmed in linguistic myths and sociological stereotypes of superiority and inferiority.

I shall not conclude by trying to instigate a crusade. In too many aspects of American life—in education no less than in foreign affairs— we have sounded too many trumpets to hasty action without looking into the possible consequences. But I think we can rationally conclude that the problems of dialect differences are highly complex, and that where— as is apparent with some groups in our cities—these differences interfere with participation in the benefits our society has to offer, we must somehow contrive to bridge these differences. But we must not try to bulldoze out of the way the habitual idiom of the home and neighborhood; what-

---

[17] For information on the local migrations of the upward-mobile in Metropolitan Chicago, I am indebted to Lee Pederson.

524 ever we do, for the short term, must be done by adding without taking away, by full appreciation of the fact that all dialects are acquired in the same way, that each is a part of the speaker's personality and that each is capable of expressing a wide range of experience. In the intermediate range, the success of any program of commingling widely diverse neighborhoods in a school will depend on how well the teachers understand the nature of dialects and impart this understanding to their students—particularly to those who up to now have had economic and social advantages. In the long run, the solution will come as more communities are opened to a greater variety of ethnic groups and social classes; it is apparently working in such a racially diverse middle-class neighborhood as Hyde Park in Chicago. The new developments in the outer suburbs, such as those which the Weston atomic reactor has already inaugurated in northern Illinois, are certain to bring to many communities a greater amount of population diversity than they now have. To produce stability, to reduce tensions rather than aggravate them, it is important that teachers and pupils, school board members and the public at large, realize the nature of diversity in language behavior, that aspect of behavior most closely identified with the human condition.

The Pronunciation of English in Metropolitan Chicago

Lee A. Pederson

Professor Pederson considers his study to be "an experiment
with the conventional apparatus of American dialectology."
He regards the classification of informants as the "most
clearly experimental aspect" of the study. In light of
these judgments, it seemed best to present most of the
section entitled "Preliminary Procedures" so that readers
could see the experimental aspects and the interdisciplinary
character of the procedures. Though it was difficult to
excerpt material in such a tightly knit study, a presentation
of Pederson's analysis of the pronunciation of the
segmental phonemes (vowels only) and two passages from
his conclusions were selected to highlight one sequential
analysis and two conclusions of high interest—the findings
on urban and exurban speech and on Negro and Caucasian
speech. Dr. Pederson is Professor of English at Emory
University and Director of the Gulf States (Atlas) Project.

526   *Introductory.* This experiment with the conventional apparatus of American dialectology was undertaken to analyze and describe the pronunciation of English in Metropolitan Chicago[1] in the light of recent historical developments. More specifically, this is an attempt to relate the speech of the rural and suburban satellites to the dialect of the urban center, to identify the speech characteristics of the social groups within this speech community, and to provide inventorial data for future research into the relationships of language and culture in Metropolitan Chicago.

The procedures of this survey are those developed and applied over the past eighty-five years by European and North American dialect geographers.[2] Each departure from traditional methodology is the extension of a well-established procedure; each modification is intended to meet the special problems of a metropolitan dialect survey.

The problems which complicated this survey are largely the result of recent developments, viz., urban centralization, mass education, highly developed systems of public—mostly commercial—communications, and social mobility.[3] These problems were approached with the following preliminary procedures: 1) a delimitation of the geographical area to correspond with the settlement and development of Greater Chicago, 2) the modification of worksheets to include items of the urban lexicon and to continue the investigation of relic pronunciations in and around the city, 3) the selection of informants to include as many records as possible of the social groups which comprise the native metropolitan population, 4) the incorporation of field records made by other trained investigators to expand the corpus and to gain insights into the peculiarities of local speech, and 5) the development of a check-list to investigate critical items of pronunciation on a broader scale than would be otherwise feasible.

The most clearly experimental aspect of this study, however, was the

From *Publication of the American Dialect Society,* No. 44 (November, 1965). Reprinted with the permission of the American Dialect Society, the University of Alabama Press, and Lee A. Pederson.

[1] In this study *Metropolitan Chicago* means the Illinois counties of Cook, DuPage, Kane, Lake, McHenry, and Will, as well as Lake County, Indiana.

[2] Basic statements of the principles and procedures of dialectology appear in the important German, French, Swiss, American, Scotch, and English works in the field, all of which are well known to the readers of *PADS* and several of which are listed in my fuller discussion, "The Pronunciation of English in Metropolitan Chicago: Vowels and Consonants" (University of Chicago diss., 1964). Also, "An Introductory Field Procedure in a Current Urban Survey," *Orbis* XI, No. 2 (1962), 465–69.

[3] For a good discussion of these problems and for the theoretical basis for the present study, see Raven I. McDavid, Jr., "The Second Round of Dialectology in North American English," *Journal of the Canadian Linguistic Association,* VI (Fall, 1960), 108–114.

classification of informants. In order to distinguish more carefully between those of similar education and social class, a rather elaborate scale of ranking is used to characterize informants on the basis of cultivation, occupation, source of income, type of residence, and dwelling area.

When these procedures were completed, five informants were reexamined to establish a phonemic basis for the phonological analysis.

.   .   .

Area Delimitation. A realistic survey of pronunciation in a metropolitan community should include the entire dialect area influenced by the speech of the urban center. Such area delimitation, of course, requires more investigation into regional and social dialects than can be practically managed by the same field worker who is responsible for the collection, analysis, and presentation of the data. For this reason the five recent studies of American urban speech which were undertaken as doctoral dissertations and which are based on the field work of the authors[4] were restricted to pronunciation within the respective city limits. Although each of these five investigations was made to deal with a particular set of problems and was justified by its contribution to dialectology, none of these can be properly regarded as metropolitan dialect geography.

The two works which most closely approximate an analysis of metropolitan speech are Mrs. Frank's survey of the pronunciation of the New York City Area[5] and Brengleman's broad study of spoken English in the Puget Sound Area.[6] Mrs. Frank's study demonstrates the possibility of using Atlas[7] records to determine the speech patterns in a metropolitan area: with the fieldwork already done by Guy S. Lowman, Jr., in New York City and in the New York counties of Westchester, Nassau, and Suffolk, as well as in the New Jersey counties of Middlesex, Union, Essex, Hudson, Bergen, and Passaic, Mrs. Frank had a rich corpus for the social dialect analysis of an important segment of the native population.[8] Brengleman's investigation traces the linguistic influence of the urban

[4] Allan Forbes Hubbell, *The Pronunciation of English in New York City* (New York, 1950); David DeCamp, "The Pronunciation of English in San Francisco" (University of California diss., 1953); Janet B. Sawyer, "A Dialect Study of San Antonio, Texas: A Bilingual Community" (University of Texas diss., 1957); Robert Ray Howren, "The Speech of Louisville, Kentucky" (Indiana University diss., 1958); Juanita V. Williamson, "A Phonological and Morphological Study of the Speech of the Negro of Memphis, Tennessee" (University of Michigan diss., 1961).

[5] Yakira Hagalili Frank, "The Speech of New York City" (University of Michigan diss., 1948).

[6] Frederick Brengleman, "American English Spoken in the Puget Sound Area of Washington" (University of Washington diss., 1957).

[7] Mrs. Frank's analysis is limited to the speech of native Caucasian informants of native parentage; see Frank, p. 11.

[8] The Linguistic Atlas of the United States and Canada; hereafter indicated as as LAUSC.

528   center, but this operation prevented his making an extensive analysis of the speech of Seattle itself. A survey like Brengleman's complements the kind of urban studies done by Hubbell in New York, DeCamp in San Francisco, and Howren in Louisville.

With these precedents available, area delimitation of Metropolitan Chicago was considered in terms of history and population distribution and was established on the basis of anthropological research already completed in northeastern Illinois by social scientists and linguistic geographers.

The most suitably organized and most nearly current socio-historical statement of the development of Metropolitan Chicago is the Northeastern Illinois Metropolitan Area Planning Commission's *A Social Geography of Metropolitan Chicago.*[9] Therein the settlement of Northeastern Illinois is considered in terms of these three major stages of development:

1. The Water Transportation Era (1840–1880) is characterized by the establishment of the processing and trading centers of Aurora, Elgin, Joliet, Lockport, and Waukegan. These centers developed as the percentage of improved farmland rose from less than 25 percent to more than 90 percent during the forty-year period. These phenomena are most closely related to the completion of the Illinois and Michigan Canal.[9]

2. The Railroad Era (1880–1920) is characterized by the establishment of the industrial suburbs of Cicero, Summit, Clearing, Blue Island, and the South Chicago-Gary-Hammond complex. This area developed around Chicago with the 130-mile arc of beltline railroads which reached from Porter, Indiana, out to Aurora and Elgin, and up to Waukegan. These activities were paced by the opening of the Mesabi Range in the '80s, the parallel development of the Southern Illinois Coal Fields, and the advent of Big Steel on the South Side.

3. The Automobile Era (1920–1960) is characterized by the establishment of the dormitory suburbs (i.e., residential communities, the citizens of which gain their income in the urban center), such as Glencoe, Mount Prospect, Elmhurst, Westmont, Midlothian, Phoenix, Forest Park, and Lansing. These have grown with the development of the expressway system which has facilitated population growth and expansion within the Cook County area. The dormitory suburbs have developed somewhat differently from the old Chicago suburbs of Hyde Park, Kenwood, Oak Park, Kenilworth, Wilmette, and Winnetka, all of which in 1960 had a greater degree of cultural stability and of socio-economic diversity than did the more recently established suburbs.

These three major phases of development in northeastern Illinois and

---

[9] *A Social Geography of Metropolitan Chicago: Trends and Characteristics of Municipalities in the Chicago Metropolitan Area* (Chicago, 1960), pp. 15–25. The NIMAPC has generously granted permission to use its research and its maps for this survey.

northwestern Indiana urbanized the eight-county area of more than 3700 square miles, approximately one and one half the size of Delaware.

A ring analysis is most useful in considering the areas, their social interrelations, and their historical and cultural development. The seventy-five communities of Chicago form the central city, and the metropolitan area forms four concentric rings around this core: the dormitory suburbs, the inner Cook County rectangle outside of Chicago, is Ring I; the inner suburban ring—DuPage, the rest of Cook, and the southern portion of Lake County, Illinois—is Ring II; the middle suburban ring—the urban townships of the outlying counties—is Ring III; the urban-rural peripheral ring—the outlying rural townships—is Ring IV.

Delimitation of area within the city itself is based on the seventy-five communities, which still have cultural and economic significance. As Wirth and Furez pointed out in 1938:

> The boundaries of the 75 local communities within the city limits were determined after a consideration of several factors indicative of their individual existence: 1) settlement, growth, and history; 2) local trade area; 3) distribution of membership and attendance of local institutions; and 4) natural and artificial barriers such as the Chicago River and its branches, elevated and other railroad lines, and parks and boulevards.[10]

These boundaries were determined in the late 1920s by the University of Chicago's Social Science Research Committee.[11] They are used in all City of Chicago publications and have general acceptance among the residents of the city.

The principal linguistic resources which were used in the delimitation of the Chicago Metropolitan Area were Shuy's investigation of the Northern-Midland dialect boundary in Illinois[12] and the field records on file in the Chicago office of the LAUSC. Both sources indicated the dialect of the Inland Northern Area prevailed across Northern Indiana and Northwestern Illinois. On the basis of this evidence the Chicago Area could be limited to the eastern tier of counties in Illinois—Lake, Cook, and Will—which Shuy had excluded from his survey and which the LAUSC had given only cursory treatment.[13] On the other hand, it seemed better to

[10] Louis Wirth and Margaret Furez (eds.), "Introduction," *Local Community Fact Book 1938* (Chicago, 1938) [unnumbered p. 12].

[11] The community areas of Chicago now number seventy-six to include the land annexed for the O'Hare International Airport. This community is excluded from the present survey because it is nonresidential.

[12] Roger W. Shuy, *The Northern-Midland Dialect Boundary in Illinois, PADS,* No. 38 (November, 1962).

[13] Several more records in these counties have since been done by Shuy, four of which are incorporated here in the phonological analysis.

530   extend the investigation over the seven counties because this area is certainly within the social and cultural dominion of the City of Chicago.

Informant Selection and Classification. The 136 informants whose speech is analyzed in this study include 135 natives of Metropolitan Chicago and one German immigrant, now age 86, who learned English in the city eighty-three years ago. These subjects are distinguished as primary and subsidiary informants. A *primary informant* is one whose speech was investigated on the basis of a 700-item questionnaire and whose speech was used as primary evidence in the phonological analysis. A *subsidiary informant* is one whose speech was investigated on the basis of a 67-item check-list and whose speech was used to support the primary evidence.

The thirty-eight primary informants and sixty-six subsidiary informants interviewed by the writer were not selected to match rigidly the population statistics of Metropolitan Chicago. Instead, the principle followed was to survey as many ethnic groups as possible and to represent these with primary informants. Then, within each ethnic group, pronunciation was investigated among members of as many different age groups, educational types, and social classes as were available for interview as primary or subsidiary informants. These criteria of selection must be considered in terms of the problems involved in obtaining representative informants.

As the survey was originally projected, twenty informants were to be selected within the city, five others from within the inner suburban ring (Ring I), and five others from the area covered by Rings II, III, and IV. In addition to these thirty, eight more informants were interviewed to investigate more carefully the pronunciation of English by members of certain age groups and social classes.

The population analysis provided in the NIMAPC's social geography was used as a guide in the selection of informants from the areas within Rings I–IV. Representatives of the German, Czech, Scotch, and Yankee farm communities were interviewed, as well as representatives of those suburban developments which have overlaid the previously rural areas. A tabulation of the NIMAPC's ranking of ninety urban places by selected socio-economic characteristics was used in the selection of informants in the suburbs of Chicago.[14]

In the City of Chicago, however, several sources were combined to de-

---

[14] Pederson (1964), p. 24. "Northeastern Illinois Metropolitan Area Planning Commission's Socio-Economic Ranking of 90 Urban Places of 2,500 or More in the 1950 Census." The selected social characteristics are 1) median school year completed, 2) percentage of white-collar workers, 3) median family income, 4) median value of homes, 5) median value of new home permits, and 6) per capita property valuation. Characteristics 1, 2, 3, and 4 are based on 1950 census reports, 5 is based on 1958 real estate reports, and 6 is based on 1957 real estate reports.

termine the range of the investigation. In 1961, a social map of the city was drawn, based on information received from the following sources: The City of Chicago's Department of City Planning, Commission on Human Relations, Fire Department, and Police Department; the Chicago *Tribune;* the Chicago *Sun-Times;* and the United States Department of Commerce Bureau of Census.[15] A version of that map is "A Social Map of Chicago."* The sources cited above were the principal guides in the composition of that map and in the selection of primary informants.

The ethnic composition of the seventy-five city communities includes four racial groups numbering over 25,000, nine other nonracial ethnic groups, and five rather clearly distinguished social classes. The Caucasian population of the city is generally found in wholly segregated communities. Three notable exceptions are Douglas (the Lake Meadows and Prairie Shores developments), Kenwood, and Hyde Park. The Negro area of Chicago includes the communities of East Garfield Park, Near West Side, North Lawndale, Fuller Park, Kenwood, Woodlawn, Chatham, Englewood, Great Grand Crossing, Grand Boulevard, New City, West Englewood, Roseland, Riverdale, and Douglas. The third group, the Mexicans and Puerto Ricans, are found in three major concentrations in the communities of Near West Side and Lower West Side, in the Back-of-the-Yards area of Bridgeport, and in the South Chicago and East Side communities on the far South Side. Puerto Ricans are also found in East and West Garfield Park, Near West Side, Near North Side, Lincoln Park, and Lake View. The Oriental population, the fourth racial group, is distributed over the city, with the only concentration being found in the old area of "Chinatown."

The major non-racial ethnic groups[16] of Chicago are concentrated as follows:

1. The Germans live in all communities with well-established racial segregation and especially along Lincoln Avenue in the North Side communities of West Ridge, Lincoln Square, and North Center.

2. The Irish live in all communities with well-established racial segregation and especially in the parish of St. Gabriel in northeast New City and across the South Side west of Ashland Avenue.

---

* All maps have been omitted. Eds.

[15] The first version of the social map is included in the prospectus for the present work, Raven I. McDavid, Jr., and Lee A. Pederson, *A Social Dialect Survey of Chicago* (Chicago, 1963).

[16] These groups include first and second generation descendants of European immigrants, as well as the economically unsuccessful descendants of those pioneers who settled Appalachia. The designations of communities are intended to indicate representative neighborhoods which are traditional concentrations of these older immigrant groups. The in-migrant from Appalachia settles where he can. First, second, and third generation descendants of the older groups are found in all parts of the city. Only the Negro is truly segregated in Chicago.

532   3. The Poles and Czechs live in the communities of Lincoln Square, South Chicago, Brighton Park, and Hegewisch and especially in the communities of West Town, Logan Square, and Avondale, the neighborhoods intersected by Milwaukee Avenue.

4. The Italians live in the communities of West Town, Montclare, Austin, South Chicago, East Side, and Hegewisch.

5. The Jews live in the communities of Rogers Park, Albany Park, Lincoln Square, and South Shore.

6. The Lithuanians live in the communities of Bridgeport and Chicago Lawn.

7. The Scandinavians live in all communities with well-established racial segregation and especially in the North Side communities of Uptown, Edison Park, Norwood Park, and Jefferson Park.

8. The Dutch live in the communities of Auburn Gresham and West Pullman.

9. The in-migrants from Appalachia, i.e., the "Southern Poor Whites," or "hillbillies," as they are popularly designated, share territory with Mexicans and Puerto Ricans in the communities of Near West Side and Lower West Side, in the Back-of-the-Yards area of Bridgeport, and in the South Chicago and East Side communities on the far southside. They are also settling in increasingly large numbers in the unimproved areas of Uptown, Lake View, and Near North Side, as well as in all of those communities intersected by Madison Street from the Loop west to Austin Boulevard.

The socio-economic classes of the Chicago Caucasian population establish the following residential pattern:

1. The lower class resides in those areas occupied by the Mexican, Puerto Rican, and Appalachian elements of the population, the southeastern edge of the city, and the periphery of the Negro areas.

2. The lower-middle class resides in those areas west of those occupied by the lower class, especially in the two large rectangles of the near southwest side of the city and the industrial districts of Clearing and the southeastern edge of the city—South Chicago, East Side, and Hegewisch.

3. The middle class resides in the segregated communities northwest and southwest of those occupied by the lower-middle class.

4. The upper-middle class resides in the communities which form the northern boundary of the city, in lakefront apartment areas—which cannot be distinguished on the social map because they are enveloped by Negroes on the South Side and by Mexicans, Puerto Ricans, and Appalachians on the North Side—and in the southwestern communities of Beverly and Morgan Park.

5. The upper class resides in the estates and apartments along the lakefront and in the communities of Forest Glen and Beverly.

It is assumed that a similar social stratification exists in the Negro community, but its class structure is not a part of this investigation. It was hard enough to find adult Negroes[17] who were natives of Chicago to represent the speech of several South Side communities.

The problem of finding representative informants within these communities was complicated by the mobility of the population, e.g., less than half of the population of Metropolitan Chicago lived in the same house in 1960 as in 1955.[18] To meet this problem, informants are identified with the communities in which they have spent most of their lives. The only exception is in the representation of the dormitory suburbs (Ring I), where most natives of these communities are either children or retired farmers. In order to represent the current speech of such communities, informants were selected who had lived in the dormitory suburbs for at least five years and who had been born in the Metropolitan Chicago area.

In addition to the records of the thirty-eight primary informants interviewed by the writer, seventeen more were included to expand the corpus of data and to provide representation of geographical areas and ethnic groups which were omitted in the survey. These fifty-five informants were then classified according to educational groups and ranked within each group on the basis of social class.

The criteria used to classify primary informants include an expanded version of the "Table of Informants by Types" in the *Handbook*[19] and the "Index of Status Characteristics" in *Social Class in America*.[20]

In the *Handbook*, informants are classified according to three basic types:

> Type I: Little formal education, little reading and restricted social contacts.
> Type II: Better formal education (usually high school) and /or wider reading and social contacts.

---

[17] All Negroes over age 50 who were interviewed for this survey have some Caucasian ancestry. This is not to suggest there are no full-blooded Negroes who are both over age 50 and natives of Chicago, but, rather, that none was found during the two years spent in this investigation. These informants of mixed racial ancestry are regarded here as Negroes on the basis of Gunnar Myrdal's findings: "The 'Negro race' is defined in America by the white people. Everybody having a *known* trace of Negro blood—no matter how far back it was acquired—is classified a Negro. No amount of white ancestry, except one hundred percent, will permit entrance to the white race." Arnold Rose, *The Negro in America* (Boston, 1956), p. 42.

[18] Pederson (1964), pp. 30–33. See Tables 2 and 3 for population statistics and socio-economic characteristics for the City of Chicago and suburbs.

[19] Hans Kurath et al., *Handbook of the Linguistic Geography of New England* (Washington, D.C., 1939).

[20] W. Lloyd Warner et al., *Social Class in America* (New York, 1960).

534

Type III: Superior education (usually college), cultured background, wide reading and/or extensive social contacts.[21]

Each informant is then classified according to age:

Type A: Aged and/or regarded by the fieldworker as oldfashioned.
Type B: Middle-aged or younger, and/or regarded by the fieldworker as more modern.[22]

Because the age factor is to be considered separately, it is removed from the general classification, and the three basic education types are expanded to include

Type 1. A superior level of education, indicating a college degree with formal or informal graduate-level studies or reading, and extensive social contacts.

Type 2. A high level of education, indicating a college degree with less post-graduate studies or readings and fewer social contacts than Type 1.

Type 3. A college degree, indicating exposure to four years of higher education.

Type 4. A superior high-school education, perhaps intellectually and culturally superior to Type 3, but heavily dependent on written authoritarian sources for vocabulary development and "preferred pronunciations."

Type 5. A good high-school education.

Type 6. A high-school education, indicating exposure to four years of secondary schooling.

Type 7. A superior elementary-school education, perhaps intellectually and culturally superior to Type 6, but characterized by uncultivated speech.

Type 8. A good elementary-school education.

Type 9. An alert uneducated informant.

Type 10. An uneducated informant.

The ranking of informants within each educational class is determined by four factors: 1) occupation, 2) source of income, 3) house type, and 4) dwelling area.[23] Each factor is rated on a seven-point scale, and each rating is then multiplied by the following weights:

Occupation   ×   4
Source of Income   ×   3

[21] Kurath, p. 44.

[22] *Ibid.*

[23] Warner, p. 41. These are used by Warner to make primary ratings which undergo considerable refinement, pp. 176–199. Class analysis in the present survey is restricted to the primary ratings.

House Type $\times$ 3
Dwelling Area $\times$ 2

The social equivalents of these products are as follows:

A. 12–17 Upper Class
B. 18–22 Upper Class probably, with some possibility of Upper-Middle Class
C. 23–24 Intermediate [*sic*]: either Upper or Upper-Middle Class
D. 25–33 Upper-Middle Class
E. 34–37 Indeterminate: either Upper-Middle or Lower-Middle Class
F. 38–50 Lower-Middle Class
G. 51–53 Indeterminate: either Lower-Middle or Upper-Lower Class
H. 54–62 Upper-Lower Class
J. 63–66 Indeterminate: either Upper-Lower or Lower-Lower Class
K. 67–79 Lower-Lower Class probably, with some possibility of Upper-Lower Class
L. 70–84 Lower-Lower Class[24]

The thirty-eight primary informants interviewed by the writer are rated by this system.[25] The remaining seventeen informants are evaluated A to L on the basis of the personal data sheets which accompany their field records.

.   .   .

Subsidiary informants were selected on the basis of age, race, and social class. The aim was to interview a large number of speakers under age 60 and to concentrate on Negroes and Caucasians of the middle and upper social classes, especially those under age 21.[26] Most of these informants were interviewed at high schools and places of business in the metropolitan area, an expedient which sacrificed the relaxed atmosphere of the home interview.

.   .   .

PHONOLOGICAL ANALYSIS

The Pronunciation of Segmental Phonemes. The segmental phonemes (the vowels and consonants) of the Chicago dialect were estab-

[24] *Ibid.*

[25] See Pederson (1964), "Appendix A," p. 195, for tabulation and rating of status characteristics for these thirty-eight primary informants.

[26] Only three primary informants are under age 21.

536   lished in terms of the definition enunciated by Bernard Bloch and George L. Trager: "A phoneme is a class of phonetically similar sounds, contrasting and mutually exclusive with all similar classes in the language."[27]

The phonemes established for this study were classified on the basis of contrast through minimal pairs. Five primary informants—# 18, 29, 30, 34, and 48—pronounced the words given below with complete phonemic agreement in thirteen of fourteen vowels and in all twenty-four consonants. The single exception is a matter of incidence, the alternation of /ɑ/ and /ɔ/, which is discussed later in this chapter. These informants are all Caucasians of the socio-economic middle class and upper-lower class (C-H) and of education types 3 to 8. They range in age from 17 to 86; two are male and three are female.

The vowel phonemes were established by testing vocoidal phones before voiced and voiceless stops, before voiced and voiceless fricatives, before laterals, and before tautosyllabic and heterosyllabic /r/. Although a unitary interpretation of vowel phonemes is adopted here, both unitary and binary analyses are satisfactory in describing the speech of these 136 Chicagoans because neither the low-front [a] nor the mid-central [ɜ] is phonemic in their dialect.

The fourteen vowel phonemes[28] of the Chicago dialect are:

/i/   as in *bead, beet, leave, leaf, feel*
/ɪ/   as in *bid, bit, live, riff, fill, beer, *beery*
/e/   as in *raid, bait, rave, safe, sail*
/ɛ/   as in *bed, bet, rev, ref, sell, bare, berry*
/æ/   as in *bad, bat, calve, laugh, pal*
/ə/   as in *bud, but, love, rough, dull, her, hurry*
/ɑ/   as in *rod, tot, *Raav, *Raphael, doll, bar, borrow*
/u/   as in *wooed, toot, groove, aloof, pool*
/ʊ/   as in *wood, put, pull, poor, puritan*
/o/   as in *road, tote, grove, loaf, pole, *hoar, hoary*
/ɔ/   as in *bawd, bought, Paul*
/ɑɪ/   as in *wide, bite, live, file, wire, wiry, life*
/ɑʊ/   as in *cloud, pout, owl, bow, bowery*
/ɔɪ/   as in *cloyed, *adroit, oil, boy, *Boyer*

The twenty-four consonant phonemes were established by testing con-

---

[27] Bernard Bloch and George L. Trager, *Outline of Linguistic Analysis* (Baltimore, 1942), p. 41.

[28] The phoneme /ɨ/ is excluded from this list because it does not occur in the speech of these five informants in any of the contexts listed below; but, because this phoneme is tentative in the speech of several other primary informants, it is to be noted here and discussed later. An asterisk indicates a form which could not be elicited from several of these five informants, who were subsequently asked to read the forms from the typewritten questionnaire.

toidal phones in initial position before /ɪl/, thereby establishing eighteen phonemes. The remaining six consonant phonemes were established with minimal pairs, in five instances /θ ð/ in *thigh* and *thy*, /n ŋ/ in *sin* and *sing*, and /z j/ in *zoo* and *you*, and with nonminimal /ǰ ž/ in *pledge* and *pleasure*.

The twenty-four consonant phonemes of the Chicago dialect are:

/p/	as in *pill, taps, tap*
/b/	as in *bill, tubs, tab*
/t/	as in *till, tots, tot*
/d/	as in *dill, lids, tad*
/k/	as in *kill, licks, tack*
/g/	as in *gill, tags, tag*
/m/	as in *mill, tams, tam*
/n/	as in **nil, tans, tan, sin*
/ŋ/	as in *sing*
/f/	as in *fill, *riffs, laugh*
/v/	as in *village, halves, have*
/θ/	as in *thigh, cloth*
/ð/	as in *thy, clothe*
/s/	as in *sill, task, lass*
/z/	as in *zeal, zoo, his*
/š/	as in *shill, hash*
/ž/	as in *Zsa Zsa, pleasure, azure*
/č/	as in *chill, hatch*
/ǰ/	as in *Jill, pledge, edge*
/h/	as in *hill*
/j/	as in *you*
/w/	as in *will*
/l/	as in *Lil, tills, till*
/r/	as in **rill, rears, rear*

The Pronunciation of Stressed Vowels. The vowel phonemes are classified here as checked vowels (which occur only before a consonant), free vowels (which occur before either a consonant or juncture), and vowels which occur before tautosyllabic or heterosyllabic /r/.

The six checked vowel phonemes which occur in the speech of all informants are /ɪ, ʊ, ɛ, ə, æ, ɑ/.

The /ɪ/ phoneme of *whip*,[29] *chimney, Michigan, Christmas, sycamore, minnows, Billy, rinses, fifth, six,* and *fist* occurs most frequently as [ɪ], an unrounded lower high-front monophthong. The nasalized monophthong

---

[29] All sample forms that appear in this section are of the 278 words and phrases which were used in the original phonological analysis.

538   [ɪ̄] is positionally restricted, occurring only with a contiguous nasal consonant as in *minnows, rinses,* and *Michigan.*

The centralized monophthongs [ɪ̈', ɪ̈, ɨ, ɨ̈] occur twenty-nine times in pronunciations of all the words listed above except *Billy* and *minnows.* These allophones are tentatively assigned here to the /ɪ/ phoneme because there is not evidence available to justify the establishment of a /ɨ/ phoneme,[30] but with these monophthongs occurring under primary stress in the speech of twelve informants it is necessary to consider the possibility of an additional phoneme.

The occurrence of the centralized monophthong is most frequent among the highly educated; seven of twelve informants who pronounce these phones under primary stress are Types 1 and 2: # 2, 3, 4, 5, 6, 10, and 11. Four of the remaining five are over age 60: # 22, 42, 45, and 47. The single exception is a 37-year-old Negro, #27.

The free variants of the /ɪ/ phoneme are [ĭ, ᵉɪ, ɪᵊ, ɪ̈ᵊ, ɪˋ, ɪˆ, ɪˇ, ɪᵋ, ɪ̈].

The /ʊ/ phoneme of *pull, push, hook, wood, soot, hoofs, roof, root, broom,* and *hoops* occurs most frequently as [ʊ], a rounded lower high-back monophthong. The shortened monophthong [ŭ] occurs sporadically in all these contexts except *hook* and *wood* in the speech of #4, 14, 20, 21, 26, 28, 29, 30, 31, 34, 35, 38, 41, 42, 43, 48, and 53. Only two of these, #4 and 14, are of educational types 1–3, and only two, #28 and 29, are of high social classes A–C.

The ingliding diphthongs [ʊᵊ, ʊˀᵊ, ʊˋᵊ, ŭᵊ] are prosodically and socially restricted. These diphthongs occur most frequently before front consonants [ʃ, t, f] as in *push, soot, hoof, roof,* and *root.* These allophones occur in the speech of eight highly educated informants: #1, 2, 3, 4, 6, 9, 10, and 12, and seven less educated informants, five of whom are over age 60: #19, 20, 22, 49, and 53. The exceptions are #27 and 32.

Other diphthongs [ʊᵘ, ʊˣ, ʊˀᵘ, ʊᵋˇ, ʊᵋ] and monophthongs [ʊˆ, ʊ', ɵ', ʊ·] are regarded as free variants.

The /ɛ/ phoneme of *bedroom, secretary, yesterday, genuine, yellow, chest, kettle, February, seven, ten,* and *deaf* occurs usually as [ɛ], an unrounded lower mid-front monophthong. The nasalized monphthong [ɛ̃] is positionally restricted, occurring only before the alveolar nasal [n] in *ten.* In this same context are found five of six occurrences of the rising diphthongs [ɛɨ, ɛᴵ]. The lengthened monophthong [ɛ·] occurs most frequently before the glottalized stop in *kettle,* usually [kɛ·ˀtɨ], without social, historical, or educational restriction. Free variants include the allophones [ɛˋ, ɛ̆, ɛˆ, ɛˇ, ɛ', ᴵɛ, ᵃⁱɛ, ᵁɛ, ɛᵋˋ, ɛˆᵒ].

The /ə/ phoneme of *brush* (noun), *brush* (verb), *touch* (verb), *mushroom,*

---

[30] Contrastive material which would have been useful here are such nonminimal pairs as *chill* and *children* or *just* (in *just a minute*) and *gist.* Unfortunately these were not elicited.

nothing, tusks, and *such* (in the context *such a nice day*) occurs most frequently as [ʌ], an unrounded lower mid-back monophthong. There is no clear pattern of distribution of the allophones [ɜˈ, əˆ, əˇ, əˀ, ʌˀ, ʌˇ, ʌˑ, ʌˑə, ʌ̃ə].

The /æ/ phoneme of *ashes, bag, January, asphalt, vacuum, casket, Matthew, raspberries, glass, pasture, swam, ladder,* and *rather* is usually [æ], an unrounded higher low-front monophthong. The centering diphthong [æə] and the retracting diphthong [æᶤ] are positionally restricted. Both upgliding diphthongs are most frequent before the velar consonants of *bag* and *vacuum.* The nasalized monophthong [æ̃] is positionally and socially restricted. The [æ̃] allophone occurs most frequently with a contiguous nasal, as in *January, Matthew,* and *swam,* but can be found sporadically in *rather, ladder, casket, afternoon, ashes,* and *vacuum,* as pronounced by #4, 15, 23, 30, 32, 39, and 47. Six of these seven informants belong to classes E–J. Only #4 is of the distinctly upper-middle class, D. The free variants of the /æ/ phoneme are [æˆ, æˇ, æˈ, aˆ, æˑ, æˀ, æˑ].

The /ɑ/ phoneme of *crop, college, hospital, want, vomit, palm, calm, Ma,* and *Pa*[31] occurs most frequently as [ɑ], an unrounded low-central monophthong. The centering diphthongs [ɑə, ɑˑə, ɑˀə, ɑˈə] are common before the bilabial nasals of *vomit, palm,* and *calm.* The nasalized monophthong [ɑ̃] occurs usually with a contiguous nasal, as in *vomit* and *Ma.* The backed monophthong [ɑˈ] occurs sporadically in all contexts except *Pa* in the speech of eleven informants. Six of these are over age 60: #7, 11, 31, 44, 46, and 49. Three of the four under age 35 are Negroes: #8, 9, and 41; the fourth is Puerto Rican, #35. All eleven are of social classes D–J. The free variants are [ɑˈ, ɑˑ].

The eight free vowels which occur in the speech of all informants are /i, u, e, o, ɔ, ɑɪ, ɑʊ, ɔɪ/.

The /i/ phoneme of *three, grease, either, yeast, wheelbarrow, wheat, theater, greasy, D[istrict], C[olumbia], teeth,* and *mosquito* is usually [ɪi], an upgliding diphthong. The free variants of the /i/ phoneme are [iˇ, iˈ, iˑ, iˀi, iˇi, iˆi, iˀi, iˇi, iᶦ, ɪi].[32]

The /u/ phoneme of *beautiful, music, roof, Tuesday, tube, new, suit, spoon, tooth, due, dues,* and *root* is usually [u], a rounded high-back vowel, or [ʊu], an upgliding diphthong. The positional variants are the diphthongs [ɪʊ, ᶦu, ᶦuᵘˇ, ᶦu, ɪˆu, ɪˇu], which occur most frequently after dentals

---

[31] The /ɑ/ phoneme (not to be confused with /a/, which would have low front allophones) is classified here as a checked vowel because its occurrence in open syllables is restricted to these family terms of affection and to a fairly predictable set of interjections—*ah, bah, hah,* and *ha-ha.*

[32] The unlengthened monophthongs [iˇ] and [iˈ] are designated as *short* to distinguish them from the lengthened monophthong [iˑ]. Elsewhere, the *Handbook* system is followed: "Vowels heard as neither distinctly long or distinctly short are not specially marked" (Kurath, p. 131).

540   in *Tuesday, due, dues,* and *tube,* and the centering diphthong [uᵊ], which occurs most frequently before the alveolar nasal in *spoon.*

The occurrence of the centralized allophones is most frequent among the highly educated. The allophones include the monophthongs [ʉ, ʉ›, ʉ‹, ʉˆ, ʉˁ, ʉˁ] and the members of the diphthongs and triphthongs [ʉᵊ, ʉᵘ, ʉˇᵘ, ʉˇʉ, ʉᵉu‹, ʉˀʉ›, ʉˀʉ›, ʉu, ɪʉ, ɪʉᵘ›, ˡʉˀʉ›, ɪʉˀʉ, ɪʉ›ʉ›] in *beautiful, music, Tuesday, tube, new, suit, spoon, tooth, due, dues,* and *root.* Informants #1, 2, 3, 4, 5, 10, 21, 28, and 38 pronounce the centralized allophone in at least seven of these eleven contexts. These include the five most highly educated, #1–5, as well as #10. Two of the remaining three, #21 and 28, are older Negroes. Thirteen informants have no instances of the centralized allophone in their pronunciation of these words; they are #7, 8, 17, 18, 29, 33, 36, 43, 46, 47, 50, 51, and 52. Eleven of these are over age 55; the exceptions are #8, a cultivated Negro of Lake County, Illinois, and #43, a Lithuanian bilingual. More than two-thirds of these informants, nine of thirteen, are Types 5–8.

Free variants of the /u/ phoneme include [uˑ, uˇᵊ, uˁuˁ, ŭ, ˡu, uˑᵊ, u̞, ˡˤu, ˡˀu].

The /e/ phoneme of *eight, April, bracelet, tomato, pail, vase, Pennsylvania, [New York] State, afraid,* and *egg* is usually pronounced [eɪ], an upgliding diphthong.[33] The monophthongs [e, eˇ] are socially restricted in that these occur with a high frequency in the speech of three informants, #15, 35, and 47, all of whom are bilinguals, Sicilian, Spanish, and German respectively. Free variants of the /e/ phoneme are [eᵋ, eᵊ, ɛe, eˇɪ, eɪ, eˇɪ, eˆɪ, eˀɪ, eɪ].

The /o/ phoneme of *ago, coat, post, yolk, shoulder, road, home, ghost,* and *won't* is usually an upgliding diphthong [oʊ].[34] The rounded mid-back monophthong [o] occurs with a high frequency in all of these contexts in the speech of #1, 3, 20, 21, 22, 37, 47, and 55. These informants are predominantly older and German or Yiddish bilinguals. Free variants of the /o/ phoneme are [ɵᵁ, ɵ‹ᵁ, oˤᵁ, oˤᵁ‹, o‹ᵁ‹, o‹ᵁˇ, o‹ᵁ‹, ɵ‹ʉ‹, oᵁ, oᵊ].

The /ɔ/ phoneme of *dog, moth, moths, strong, log, crawl, always, often, haunted, Washington,* and *daughter* is usually [ɔ], a slightly rounded higher low-back monophthong. The nasalized monophthong [ɔ̃] is a positional variant, occurring only with a contiguous nasal as in *moth, strong,* and *haunted.* The centering diphthongs [ɔᵊ, ɔˇᵊ, ɒˑᵊ, ɒᵊ] are also positionally restricted, occurring most frequently in monosyllabic utterances before velar consonants in *dog* and *log.*

The occurrence of the lower back vowel [ɒ] is sporadic and its analysis

---

[33] In P's early records the second member was frequently transcribed as [j] to indicate tenseness in closure. In S's records the /e/ phoneme in initial position is transcribed as a glottalized vowel [ˀe], as in *eight* and *April.*

[34] In P's early records this diphthong was erroneously transcribed as a lengthened monophthong [oˑ].

is complicated by the fact that transcription of low back vowels is frequently dependent on the "personal boundaries" of the field workers.[35] Although the variants of this vowel occur in all eleven of the contexts, only four informants pronounce it in four or more instances. These are two young and highly cultivated speakers, #2 and 6, and two informants of low educational types, #38 and 47; both of the latter are over age 60 and are German bilinguals.

The free variants of the /ɔ/ phoneme are [ɔˇ, ɔˋ, ɔˣ, ɔˇˈ, ɔˈ, ɒˆ, ɒˀ, ɒˋ, ɒˆˈ, ɒˈ].

The /ɑɪ/ phoneme of *nine, twice, library, Ohio, China, nice* (in the context *such a nice day*), and *viaduct* occurs most frequently as [ɑɨ], a "fast" upgliding diphthong, beginning in the low central position and gliding swiftly in the direction of [i].[36] The initial member of this diphthong occurs frequently as [a, aˈ, aˆ, aˀ, aˈ] in any of the seven contexts. The low front vowels occur most frequently in the speech of Negroes of all age groups, as recorded by M and P, and in the speech of young cultivated Caucasians, as recorded by M. The initial member is pronounced [ɑˈ], a lengthened low central vowel, with sporadic occurrence in the speech of seven informants, #5, 9, 25, 29, 35, 41, and 55, four of whom are Negroes. The vowels of the second member of this diphthong are [ɪ, ɪˈ, ɨ, ɨˋ, ɨⁱ]. These are all regarded as free variants because they occur in the speech of all types and groups of informants and in all of the seven contexts.

The /ɑʊ/ phoneme of *mountain, how* (in the context *how often?*), *county, houses, towel, fountain, mouth,* and *stout* is usually pronounced [ɑʊ], a "fast" upgliding diphthong. The initial member of this diphthong has the same range as the initial member of the /ɑɪ/ phoneme with a similar preponderance of fronted allophones among Negro and young Caucasian informants. The final member of the diphthong varies among informants without a discernible pattern of distribution.

The /ɔɪ/ phoneme of *oil, joint, Detroit, poisonous, joined,* and *boiled* is usually [ɔɨ], a "fast" upgliding diphthong, beginning as a lower mid-back rounded vowel and gliding to a lower high-central position. Variation among the initial element of this phoneme includes the range of the monophthongal allophones of /o/ and /ɔ/, i.e., [o, ɵ, oˇ, ɔˣ, ɔˇ, ɒ]. The second member of this diphthong has the same range as the second member of the /ɑɪ/ phoneme.

The Vowels before /r/. The occurrence of vowels before /r/ is treated separately because these vowels behave differently in this position than they do before other consonants.

---

[35] For disagreement in the treatment of low back vowels among the original field workers in New England, see Kurath, *Handbook,* pp. 126–127.

[36] In P's records this diphthong is frequently transcribed as [ɑi] or [ɑiʲ].

542   Two allophones of the /r/ phoneme occur after vowels. These are [ɚ], a constricted retroflex continuant, and [ə̣], a nonsyllabic continuant.

Although all fourteen stressed vowels occur before tautosyllabic /r/, most informants have only nine phonemic contrasts in this position: two front vowels /i/ or /ɪ/ and either /e/, /ɛ/, or /æ/; two central vowels /ə/ and /ɑ/, two back vowels /u/ or /ʊ/ and either /o/ or /ɔ/; and three diphthongs /ɑɪ, ɑʊ, ɔɪ/. Thirteen informants have ten phonemes before tautosyllabic /r/ with contrasting /ɔ/ and /o/ in *morning* and *mourning* or *horse* and *hoarse*. The number of phonemic contrasts is the same whether the phoneme /r/ is articulated as [ɚ] or [ə̣].

The /i/ phoneme of *ear* and *beard* is rare in Chicago speech. It occurs in the speech of only five informants, #5, 8, 31, 45, and 50. Only one, #5, pronounces this phoneme in both contexts, and he is a younger, highly cultivated Caucasian. Two of the others are rural residents of Ring IV, and two are Negroes. All of these instances occur before the constricted retroflex continuant. Among subsidiary informants, eleven of thirteen young Negroes have the /i/ phoneme in *pier,* all followed by the [ɚ] allophone. Only four of fifty-three Caucasian subsidiary informants pronounce the /i/ phoneme in *pier.*

The /ɪ/ phoneme of *ear* and *beard* is common in the speech of all types and classes except young Negro subsidiary informants, #54–66.

The /e/ phoneme of *care* and *scarce* occurs in the speech of only two informants, #8 and 46, a young cultivated Negro and an old uncultivated Caucasian, both interviewed by students. The /ɛ/ phoneme is usual in these contexts and is representative of speakers of all classes and types. The /æ/ phoneme in *care* and *scarce* is restricted to the speech of one old, uncultivated, Polish bilingual, #54. Her pronunciations are [kæɚ] and [skæˆɚs].

The /ə/ phoneme of *cur* and *sir* occurs in the speech of all informants.

The /ɑ/ phoneme occurs before tautosyllabic /r/ in *garbage* and *far* in the speech of all informants except those few who, here and elsewhere, alternate /ɔ/ and /ɑ/. This problem is taken up later in the chapter under *Incidence.*

The /u/ phoneme occurs before tautosyllabic /r/ in the pronunciation of *whore* /hur/ (instead of /hɔr/, /hor/, or /hʊr/) in the speech of ten informants, #16, 18, 29, 32, 35, 36, 40, 47, 48, and 54. All of these are of lower-class origins, and all consider the word indecent. The only occurrence of the /u/ phoneme in this context among subsidiary informants is in the speech of #51, a Type 7, age 49.[37]

[37] The staff workers for the Cognitive Environment Study at the University of Chicago deleted the word *whore* from the check-list used to interview subsidiary informants, #67–81. The acting superintendent at the New Trier High School deleted the word *whore* from the check-list used by this writer to interview subsidiary informants, #5–8.

Five subsidiary informants have the /u/ phoneme in *poor,* which was elicited as an item on the check-list. Four of these are Negroes over age 39, #68, 71, 76, and 77. The only Caucasian to pronounce /u/ in this context is #35, a highly cultivated college English teacher, age 43, who—the interviewer observed—was being facetious and articulating what he thought to be an elegant form.

The only word regularly elicited from primary informants to provide evidence of the /ʊ/ phoneme before tautosyllabic /r/ is *whore.* The seven informants who have /ʊ/ in *whore,* #15, 17, 22, 26, 34, 38, and 41, are all of lower-class origins, and all consider the word indecent.

The /o/ phoneme or the /ɔ/ phoneme of *four, door, mourning, morning, hoarse,* and *horse* occurs before tautosyllabic /r/. The incidence of these vowels is discussed later in this chapter.

The phonemes /aɪ, aʊ, ɔɪ/ of *fire, ours,* and *Boyer,* respectively, have the same ranges of allophones before tautosyllabic /r/ as they do before other consonants.

Before heterosyllabic /r/ most informants contrast nine vowels: /ɪ, ɛ, ə, ɑ, ʊ, ɔ, aɪ, aʊ, ɔɪ/. Three informants with contrasting /e/ and /ɛ/ in *Mary* and *merry* and eleven other informants with contrasting /ɛ/ and /æ/ in *merry* and *married* have ten vowel phonemes in this position.

The /ɪ/ phoneme of *diphtheria, stirrup,* and *syrup* is usually pronounced as [ɪ]. These vowels [ɪ', ɪ², ɪ², ɪ˞] occur in the speech of highly cultivated and younger informants, #2, 5, and 10, and eight older and less cultivated informants (Types 5–9), #34, 37, 45, 49, 50, 51, 52, and 53. Again, there is no evidence of the high-central vowel with phonemic status.

The /e/ phoneme of *Mary* and *dairy* occurs in the speech of three highly cultivated informants, #3 [dᵉeəɹii], 7 [meˡəɹɪ], and [deˡɹɪ], and 16 [mᵉeəi˙] and [deəiʲ]. One young Negro subsidiary informant, #66, also pronounces /e/ in *Mary* [ɪne˙əɹɪ].

The /ɛ/ phoneme of *Mary, dairy, cherry, merry, married,* and *wheelbarrow* is usually pronounced as [ɛ]. The nasalized monophthong [ɛ̃] occurs sporadically after the bilabial nasal [m] of *Mary* and *married,* but there are no instances of the nasalized monophthong in *merry.*

The /æ/ phoneme of *married* and *wheelbarrow* occurs in the speech of twenty-six informants as [æ] in free variation with the other allophones of this unit, which have been listed above. These occurrences of /æ/ before heterosyllabic /r/ alternate with /ɛ/, which is more common in this position. Eight informants have the /æ/ phoneme in both words; these include all three young Negro informants, #8, 9, and 41, two younger and highly cultivated Caucasians, #3 and 12, and three less cultivated Caucasians over age 55, #36, 40, and 46. Eleven informants have the /æ/ phoneme in *married;* these include four highly cultivated Caucasians, #4, 6, 11, and 13, three of whom are under age 45, five less

544   cultivated Caucasian informants over age 45, #23, 32, 47, 53, and 54, and two Negro informants over age 45, #21 and 28. Seven informants have /æ/ in *wheelbarrow;* these include three highly cultivated Caucasian informants, #1, 5, and 10, two of whom are under age 45, two less cultivated Caucasian informants over age 45, #44 and 45, and two Negro informants, #27 and 55.

The /ə/ phoneme of *furrow, worry, stirrup,* and *syrup* is usually pronounced as [ɚ]. Free variants include [ɜ, ɜ', ʌˈ, ʌˆ, ʌ, ᵋɚ, ˡɚ, ³ɚ].

The /ɑ/ phoneme of *tomorrow* and *borrow* is usually pronounced [ɑ]. Free variants include [ɑ‹, ɑˀ, ɑᵊ, ɑˈ, ɑ›, ã]. The nasalized monophthong is pronounced in *borrow* by an old Polish bilingual, #54.

The /ɔ/ phoneme of *tomorrow* and *borrow* occurs in the speech of sixteen informants as [ɔ] or as [ɔˀ, ɔˬ, ɔˠ, ᶾᵊ, ᴅ, ᴅ›]. Five informants, #6, 21, 40, 49, and 53, four of whom range in age from 79 to 87, have the /ɔ/ phoneme in both words. Three of these five are Types 7–9; the exceptions are #6, a highly cultivated Caucasian female, age 33, and #21, a Negro Type 4, age 85. Five of eight informants who pronounce /ɔ/ in *tomorrow* are over age 45, #1, 17, 22, 32, and 53; the exceptions include #9, a highly cultivated Negro, age 34, and two very young Caucasian females, #24 and 30. The three occurrences of /ɔ/ in *borrow* are restricted to the speech of two Caucasians over age 45, #29 and 47, and one highly cultivated Caucasian, #12.

The /o/ phoneme is recorded once in *borrow* in the speech of a very old Caucasian informant of Wheaton (Ring III) as [oˀ].

The phonemes /u, ʊ, ɑɪ, ɑʊ, ɔɪ/ were not investigated systematically before heterosyllabic /r/. In the preliminary phonemic analysis, which was described earlier, three of these phonemes occurred in this position. The /ʊ/ phoneme of *puritan,* the /ɑɪ/ phoneme of *wiry,* and the /ɑʊ/ phoneme of *bowery* occurred with the same range of allophones as did these phonemes before other consonants.

The Vowels of Weakly Stressed Syllables. The six phonemes /i, ɪ, e, u, o, ə/ occur in weakly stressed syllables in the speech of all informants.

The /i/ phoneme of *three* and *creek* occurs also in weakly stressed syllables as in *Indiana* /ìndĭǽnɘ̌/, *diphtheria* /dìpθírĭjɘ̌/ or, less frequently, /dìfθírĭjɘ̌/, and *thirty* /θɘ́rtĭ/. When deliberately, i.e., carefully, pronounced, all of these instances of /i/ with weak stress occur frequently with tertiary stress.

The/ɪ/ phoneme of *whip* and *chimney* occurs also in weakly stressed syllables, as in *sausage, sandwich* (usually tertiary stress), and *bucket.* This phoneme is usually pronounced [ɨ] under weak stress in all sequences recorded for this survey.

The /e/ phoneme of *eight* and *tomato* occurs in weakly stressed syllables, as in *yesterday* and *Tuesday* (frequently tertiary stress in both instances).

The /u/ phoneme of *Tuesday* and *beautiful* occurs in weakly stressed syllables, as in *mushroom* (frequently tertiary stress) and *genuine,* usually pronounced as a shortened monophthong [ŭ].

The /o/ phoneme of *ago* and *coat* occurs in weakly stressed syllables, as in *swallow* and *tomorrow,* usually as a diphthong [oᵁ].

The /ə/ phoneme of *bucket* and *stomach* occurs in weakly stressed syllables, as in *hospital* /háspɪtʒl/ and *Illinois* /ɪlʒnɔ́ɪ/, usually as [ə].

A seventh vowel phoneme /ɔ/, that of *foggy* and *dog,* occurs occasionally in weakly stressed syllables, as in *asphalt* (usually tertiary stress).[38]

.   .   .

CONCLUSION

The phonological analysis indicates that the speech of all 136 informants can be described within a single phonemic system. The vowel and consonant phonemes established in the preliminary analysis . . . are a satisfactory framework for the phonology of the seven-county area, as represented in the data of this survey. The following summary of the regional and social differences within this system includes a comparison of urban and extraurban speech, the distinctions between Negro and Caucasian speech, and the speech characteristics of significant age, education, and social groups. Finally, the implications of these findings are related to the kinds of further investigation which are needed to complete the description of pronunciation of English in Metropolitan Chicago.

Urban and Extraurban Speech. Because of the high percentage of Caucasian Chicagoans who have moved into the suburbs, especially those of Ring I, it is impossible to make any distinction between the speech of the city and speech of the inner suburbs which is based simply on the criterion of geography. The only meaningful regional distinction found in the present survey and analysis is based on contrasts between urban and extraurban speech. Urban speech includes the representative informants of the City of Chicago and the inner suburbs of Ring I. Extraurban speech includes the representative informants of the outer suburban and rural areas of Rings II, III, and IV.

Features of extraurban speech which seem to be distinctive include such Midland and Southern forms as:

a. /i/ for /ɪ/ in *beard, ear,* and *pier*

b. /ɛ/ for /ɪ/ in *chimney, rinses,* and *since*

---

[38] "The Pronunciation of Consonant Phonemes" is omitted. Professor Pederson found that "The same consonant phonemes occur in the native speech of Metropolitan Chicago as in other dialects of American English." Eds.

c.   /ə/ for /ɪ/ in the weakly stressed second syllable of *vomit* and *jaundice*
d.   /u/ for /ʊ/ in *root* and *roof*
e.   /ɔ/ for /ɑ/ in *crop, wasp,* and *on*
f.   /o/ for /ɔ/ in *hoarse* and *mourning*
g.   /ɪ/ for /ə/ in weakly stressed second syllable of *beautiful, kettle, faucet,* and *mountain*
h.   /hw/ for /w/ in *wheat, whip,* and *wheelbarrow*
j.   /ju/ for /u/ in *Tuesday, news,* and *dues*

and such old-fashioned Midland or North Central forms as:

a.   /ɑ/ for /ɔ/ in *frost, fog, foggy, hog,* and *log*
b.   /u/ for /ə/ in *gums*
c.   /ɪ/ for /i/ in *creek*
d.   /ə/ for /ʊ/ in *soot*
e.   /ɑɪ/ for /ɪ/ in the third syllable of *genuine*
f.   /ə/ for /ɪ/ in *syrup*
g.   /ɑ/ for /ɔ/ in *jaundice*
h.   /n/ for /m/ in the final syllable of *mushroom* (/məšrun/ or /məšərun/)
j.   /i/ for /ji/ in *yeast*

All nine Midland forms, however, occur in the speech of young urban Negroes, most of whom are of Midland or Southern ancestry. Similarly, all nine old-fashioned forms occur in the speech of old urban Caucasians. Such co-occurrence makes impossible any clear distinction between urban and extraurban speech on the basis of these eighteen items.

Seven features of urban speech which seem to be distinctive include:

a.   [e] for [eᵉ] or [eˡ] in *eight* and *April*
b.   /ʊ/ for /u/ in *room* and *broom*
c.   /ʊ/ for /ɔ/ in *whore*
d.   /u/ for /ɔ/ in *whore*
e.   /t/ for /θ/ in *moth, thrashed,* and *with*
f.   /d/ for /ð/ in *either, mother,* and *father*
g.   /n/ for /ŋk/ in *precinct*

Of these features b and g occur only in the speech of Caucasian and Negro informants of lower-class origins, and c and d occur only in the speech of Caucasian informants of lower-class origins. Features a, e, and f occur only in the speech of distinctive cultural groups, all members of which are (with the exception of the Irish) bilingual. Since only one informant from a distinctive cultural group of recent immigration was found and investigated in the extraurban area (Primary Informant #19), no satisfactory evidence is available to establish regional dialects within the Metropolitan Chicago area.

Negro and Caucasian Speech. The speech of the Negro in Metropolitan Chicago is characterized by the range of its variation in both pronunciation and alternation of phonemes. Few of these features, however, occur exclusively in Negro speech. The difference between Negro and Caucasian speech exists in the separate patterns of distribution and in the frequency of occurrence of those features. The non-exclusive features of Negro speech are used by most young Negroes, irrespective of education or social class; whereas, in Caucasian speech, these features correlate closely with age, education, social class, and regional ancestry.

Exclusive of forms occurring only once or twice, such as /ɔ/ for /ɛ/ in *whcelbarrow* and /e/ for /ɛ/ in *Mary*, the distinctive features in the speech of the native Negro in Metropolitan Chicago include:

1. Phonetic differences:

   a. [ɑ'] for [ɑ] in *Ma* and *Pa*
   b. [ʉ] for [u] in *beautiful, Tuesday, news,* etc.
   c. [ɑˑɪ] for [ɑɪ] in *nine, twice, nice,* etc.
   d. [aɪ] for [ɑɪ] in *nine, twice, nice,* etc.
   e. [aʊ] for [ɑʊ] in *how, mountain, fountain,* etc.
   f. [t] for [t] or [ɾ] in *fountain* and *mountain*
   g. [t] for [ʔt] or [tʔ] in *fountain* and *mountain*
   h. [ɾ] for [r] in *three*
   j. [ə] for [ɚ] in the weakly stressed syllable of *yesterday, father,* and *afternoon*
   k. [ə̣] for [ɚ] in the stressed syllable of *door, four, mourning,* etc.

2. Phonemic differences:

   a. /ɪ/ for /ɛ/ in *ten, genuine,* and *Pennsylvania*
   b. /ɛ/ for /ɪ/ in *chimney, rinses,* and *since*
   c. /i/ for /ɪ/ in *beard, ear,* and *pier*
   d. /ə/ for /ɪ/ in *syrup*
   e. /u/ for /ʊ/ in *poor*
   f. /æ/ for /ɛ/ in *married* and *wheelbarrow*
   g. /ɑ/ for /ɛ/ in *wheelbarrow*
   h. /ɑ/ for /ɔ/ in *moth*
   j. /ɑ/ for /ɔ/ in *fog, foggy, hog,* and *log*
   k. /ɔ/ for /ɑ/ in *crop* and *on*
   m. /o/ for /ɔ/ in *hoarse* and *mourning*
   n. /ɔ/ for /ɑ/ in *palm*
   o. /ɔ/ for /ɑ/ in *borrow* and *tomorrow*

548

p.	/ɑ/ for /ɔ/ in *water* and *Washington*
q.	/ɔ/ for /ɑ/ in *want* and *wasp*
r.	/ɔ/ for /ɑ/ in *watch*
s.	/ɑ/ for /ɔ/ in *jaundice*
t.	/ɑ/ for /ɔ/ in *sausage*
u.	/u/ for /ʊ/ in *root* and *roof*
v.	/ju/ for /u/ in *Tuesday, news,* and *dues*
w.	/hw/ for /w/ in *wheat, whip,* and *wheelbarrow*
x.	/ə/ for /ʊ/ in *soot*
y.	/ɑ/ for /ɔ/ in *Chicago*
z.	/ɑɪ/ for /ɪ/ in the third syllable of *genuine*
aa.	/ɛ/ for /ɪ/ in the first syllable of *Illinois*
bb.	/ə/ for /ɪ/ in the weakly stressed second syllable of *vomit* and *jaundice*
cc.	/ɪ/ for /ə/ in the weakly stressed second syllable of *beautiful, kettle, faucet,* and *mountain*
dd.	/ə/ (excrescent) in *O'Hare* /ohɛrə/
ee.	/n/ for /m/ in the final syllable of *mushroom* /məšrun/ or /məšərun/
ff.	/n/ for /ŋk/ in *precinct*
gg.	/i/ for /ji/ in *yeast*
hh.	/z/ for /s/ in *grease* and *greasy*
jj.	/ɑ/ for /æ/ in *aunt*
kk.	/ɔ/ for /ɑ/ in *God*
mm.	/ʊ/ for /u/ in *room* and *broom*
nn.	/t/ for /d/ in *kettle*

Of these features, only 1. f, g, h and 2. h, nn occur exclusively in Negro speech. With the exception of 2. e—which occurs in the speech of only one Caucasian—the remaining features are shared with the following groups:

A. Those of low social class and education types: 1. a, b, c, k and 2. b, d, f, j, o, q, r, s, t, u, v, x, z, aa, dd, ff, gg, mm

B. Residents of Rings II, III, and IV: 2. b, c, d, j, k, m, q, s, u, v, w, x, z, bb, cc, ee, gg

C. Those of Midland-born parents: 1. b, j, k, and 2. d, f, h, m, o, r, w, z, aa, hh

D. Those under age 40 and highly educated: 1. b, d, e, and 2. f, m, w, bb, mm

E. High-school students: 2. b, g, n, r

F. Those over age 40 and highly-educated: 2. f, j, o, u

H. Protestants: 2. kk

J. Old Jewish residents of Hyde Park: 2. jj

The Pronunciation of English in San Francisco

David DeCamp

In the introduction to his study, Professor DeCamp states
that the speech of San Francisco is "a mixture composed
of so many parts New England, so many parts New York,
etc., for the eastern United States were the linguistically
genitive region for California as well as for the inland
states." In the study he discusses the sound system of the
city and relates it to that of eastern areas. The study is
based on complete field interviews of twenty-five
long-time residents of San Francisco, all conducted by
Professor DeCamp. The study is in four parts. Part I
presents the method and classification of informants, both
of which are based on those of the *Linguistic Atlas*
procedures. Part II deals with "The Social and Historical
Context of San Francisco Speech." These two parts
appeared in *Orbis* (7:372–391) for June, 1958. Part III,
"The Phonemes of San Francisco Speech," and Part IV,
"San Francisco Pronunciation in its Social and Historical

Context," are reprinted here almost in their entirety.
Dr. DeCamp is Professor of Linguistics at the University
of Texas.

The Phonemes of San Francisco Speech. The phonemes of San Francisco speech include eleven vowels, three semivowels, twenty-one consonants, four levels of pitch, and at least three degrees of stress. The data were insufficient for analysis of juncture phenomena. All field records were transcribed in the phonetic alphabet of the Linguistic Atlas of the United States and Canada, as described by Bernard Bloch in the *Handbook of the Linguistic Geography of New England,* pp. 122–146. Unfortunately, this alphabet recognizes only three degrees of stress, for secondary and tertiary stress are probably phonemically distinct in San Francisco as in most dialects of American English. Four degrees of stress would indeed have been difficult to distinguish in the field, as Bloch points out. However, if such data were available, the range of apparently free variation in vowels might have been better explained as centralization under reduced stress.

In previous American linguistic atlases, intonation was recorded only for a few isolated words, primarily animal calls and habitual forms of affirmation and negation. In San Francisco, intonation was recorded for a larger corpus, including all questions elicited from the informants. Kenneth L. Pike's system of transcription[1] was used, recognizing four relative levels of pitch (1. high, 2. higher-mid, 3. lower-mid, and 4. low). As in most American dialects, the normal intonation contour for declarative sentences in San Francisco is 3-2-4 (i.e., the intonation level progresses approximately from lower-mid to higher-mid on the last stressed syllable of the sentence, then falls to low pitch). San Franciscans strongly favor this 3-2-4 contour also for content questions (requests for information other than a yes-or-no answer; e.g., *Who taught you that?*) and prefer such rising contours as 3–2, 2–4–3, and 2–1 for non-content questions (e.g., *Am I going to get some?*). Out of 273 transcriptions of content questions, only twenty occur with rising intonation.[2] Conversely, out of 115 transcriptions of non-content questions, only twenty-five occur with falling contour. The cultivated speech of Type III informants is noticeably more consistent in this preference than is that of Types I and II.

From *Orbis,* Bulletin International de Documentation Linguistique, 8:54–77 (January, 1959). Reprinted with the permission of A. J. Windekens, Directeur, Centre International de Dialectologie Générale, and David DeCamp.

[1] Kenneth L. Pike, *The Intonation of American English,* Ann Arbor, 1946.

[2] These twenty include six transcriptions of the conventionalized personal greeting *How are you?* and nine of the question *Who taught you that?* which was frequently misinterpreted by informants as involving a reproachful accusation.

The semivowel and consonant phonemes of San Franciscan speech differ from other American dialects in only a few particulars. The following brief sketch will therefore suffice. The phonemic norms are as follows:

/y/ [j], /r/ [r], /w/ [w], /p/ [p], /t/ [t], /c/ [tʃ], /k/ [k], /b/ [b], /d/ [d], /j/ [dʒ], /g/ [g], /f/ [f], /θ/ [θ], /s/ [s], /š/ [ʃ], /h/ [h], /v/ [v], /ð/ [ð], /z/ [z], /ž/ [ʒ], /m/ [m], /n/ [n], /ŋ/ [ŋ], /l/ [l].

Fortis stops and spirants are normally voiceless; lenis stops and spirants are normally voiced, although voiceless lenis and voiced fortis varieties occasionally occur; e.g., *houses,* /ˈhaʊzəz/, [ˈhaᵁzəz], [ˈhaᵁz̦əz̦]; *seventy,* /ˈsɛvənti/, [ˈsɛvə̃nti], [sɛvə̃n̦ti]. Before nasal consonants, both fortis and lenis stops are frequently nasally released; /t/ is also frequently laterally released before /l/. In syllable-final position, all stops are commonly articulated by some informants with glottal stricture, occasionally with simultaneous glottal closure. In the speech of Type I informants, [ʔ] is a common allophone of /t/ in syllable-final position or before /n/ or /l/; e.g., *bottle,* /ˈbatəl/, [ˈbaɾəł], [ˈbatł], [ˈbaʔł]; *coat,* /kot/, [koᵁt], [koᵁʔ]. A transcription of [ʔ] also occurs rarely where one would expect [p] or [k]; e.g., *chipmunk,* [ˈtʃɪʔˌmʌŋk]. Although this [ʔ] varies freely with [p] and [pʔ], it has been interpreted here as an allophone of /t/. The word *chipmunk* thus occurs as /ˈcɪpˌmoŋk/, [ˈtʃɪpˌmʌŋk], and as /ˈcɪtˌməŋk/, [ˈtʃɪʔˌmʌŋk]. Intervocalically or in the intervocalic clusters /nt/ and /rt/, /t/ is commonly voiceless flap [ɾ] or voiceless stop [t]. [ɾ] is more frequent in conversational forms, [t] in deliberate and forced forms; e.g., *twenty,* /ˈtwenti/, [ˈtwɛ̃ⁿti], [ˈtwɛ̃ɾi]; *forty,* /ˈforti/, [ˈfɑˑɾi], [ˈfɑˑti]. Both /t/ and /d/ are post-dental in clusters with /θ/ and /ð/, otherwise alveolar.

Before /f/, /m/ is commonly labiodental [ɱ]; e.g., *grandfather,* /ˈgræmˌfaðər/, [ˈgræɱˌfaðɚ]. Presumably, /n/ is similarly post-dental in clusters with /θ/, but words containing such clusters were lacking in the worksheets. Before /y/, /n/ is commonly [n], but occasionally palatalized [ɲ]; e.g., *onions,* /ˈənyənz/, [ˈʌnjə̃nz], [ˈʌɲjə̃nz]. In syllables under weak stress, the sequences /əm/, /ən/, /əŋ/, and /əl/ are commonly either [əm], [ən], [əŋ], and [əł], or syllabic [m̩], [n̩], [ŋ̩], and [ł̩]; e.g., *button,* /ˈbətən/, [ˈbʌʔn̩]. Before clusters of nasal plus homorganic consonant and in weak-stressed syllables containing a nasal, vowels are commonly nasalized for most informants. In such homorganic clusters, the nasal consonant is commonly weakly articulated, occasionally zero. In the latter case, /m/, /n/, or /ŋ/ has been written to indicate the "color" of articulation; i.e., the approach to, but not contact with, bilabial, alveolar, or velar points of articulation; e.g., *climbed,* /klaɪmd/, [klã̄ⁱmd], [klã̄ⁱᵐd]; or /klaɪnd/, [klã̄ⁱⁿd].

In syllable-initial or post-initial positions, /l/ is the relatively "clear" (i.e., weakly velarized) [l]; in syllable-final or pre-final position, it is the

552 "dark" distinctly velarized [ɫ].³ The sequence /ʊl/ is commonly [ʉɫ], [ʊʻɫ], or syllabic [ɫ̩]; e.g., *bull,* /bʊl/, [bʉɫ], [bʊʻɫ], [bɫ̩]. After /w/, this syllabic /l/ is commonly rounded to [ɫ̩]; e.g., *wool,* /wʊl/, [wʉɫ], [wɫ̩]. In syllables under weak stress, the sequence /əl/ is commonly [əɫ] or syllabic [ɫ̩]; e.g., *bottle,* /ˈbatəl/, [ˈbɑɾəɫ], [ˈbatɫ̩].

In the clusters /hw/ and /hy/, which occur in the speech of most informants, the semivowels are occasionally voiceless. Usually, however, they are at least partially voiced; e.g., *whip,* /hwɪp/, [hwɪʼp], [hw̥ɪʼp], [w̥ɪʼp]. In these clusters, the /h/ (by definition the whispered counterpart of a following vowel or semivowel) represents that portion of the sequence which precedes the onset of voicing.

/r/ has several allophones. As the second member of the cluster /θr/, it is either a strongly retroflex or weakly trilled [r] or, occasionally, an alveolar flap [ɾ]. Otherwise in syllable-initial or post-initial position, /r/ is strongly retroflex alveolar, occasionally weakly trilled by some Type I informants. The phonemic sequence /ər/ is a syllabic [ɚ] or [ə], with the retroflexion usually stronger in stressed syllables than in unstressed. This sequence is frequently rounded to [ɚ] or [ə] following /w/, in such words as *worm.*⁴ Following vowels other than /ə/, /r/ is commonly non-syllabic [ɚ], occasionally non-syllabic [ə]; e.g., *barn,* /barn/, [bɑɚn], [bɑən].

The eleven vowels and their phonemic norms are as follows: /i/ [iⁱ], /ɪ/ [ɪ], /e/ [eⁱ], /ɛ/ [ɛ], /æ/ [æ], /a/ [ɑ], /u/ [uᵘ], /ʊ/ [ʊ], /o/ [oᵘ], /ɔ/ [ɑ], /ə/ [ʌ]. These and their diphthongal combinations comprise the syllabic nuclei of San Francisco speech. /i/, /e/, /u/, and /o/ are tense; other vowels are comparatively lax. Centralized allophones are usually less tense than the phonemic norms. Centralized allophones of all vowels are common under reduced stress. Centralized allophones of /ɪ/ and /ʊ/ occur also before /r/ and /l/. Lowered and occasionally centralized allophones of tense vowels occur before /r/. Tense vowels under primary stress usually contain an upward glide which is frequently absent under reduced stress.⁵

³ [l] occurs rarely in pre-final position in affected or deliberate responses; e.g., *milk,* /mɪlk/, [mɪ²ɫk], [mɪlk].

⁴ The asymmetrical analysis illustrated by the pair *bull* and *burr,* /bʊl/ and /bər/, [bɫ̩] and [bɚ], seems objectionable but unavoidable. *Burr* is in contrast with *boor,* /bʊr/, [bʉɚ]; hence the syllabic /r/ cannot be written /ʊr/. Conversely, *bull* contrasts with *bulge,* /bəlj/, [bʌɫdʒ]; hence the syllabic /l/ cannot be written /əl/ unless /ə/ and /ʌ/ are recognized as separate phonemes. The alternative would be to accept Kenneth L. Pike's phoneme of syllabicity (*Phonemics,* pp. 140–141) and write *bull* and *burr* as /bl̩/ and /br̩/. For such transcriptions as [θəti] in the "*r*-dropping" subdialect of San Francisco, see the discussion of /ə/ below.

⁵ Because of these glides, a widely accepted alternative analysis would segmentalize [iⁱ], [eⁱ], [uᵘ], and [oᵘ] into /iy/, /ey/, /uw/, and /ow/ and would interpret [ɪ], [ɛ], [ʊ], and [ɑ] as /i/,

As one would expect, there is a great deal of apparently free variation   **553** in the allophones of vowels. Furthermore, the twenty-five informants differed in the phonetic range of the phonemes. Consequently, the field records contain a great variety of transcriptions for each phoneme. The following description of the "normal" allophones for each significant phonetic environment is only a summary statement, based on extensive counts of the relative frequency of allophones for each informant and for the dialect as a whole. Most of this variation is merely minor differences in the position of articulation or in the degree of length and lip rounding.[6]

/e/, /u/, /o/. This interpretation is inadvisable for San Francisco for two reasons. First, /i/ only rarely consists of [ɪ] plus a glide; the onset of the vowel of *beet* is normally considerably higher than the vowel of *bit*. Second, tense vowels without glides are more common under reduced stress and are occasional even under primary stress. Any segmental analysis would require the theoretically objectionable proviso that postvocalic /y/ and /w/ have zero allophones which predominate under reduced stress and which vary freely with [i̥] and [u̥] in all environments. For a segmental analysis of tense vowels into vowel plus consonant, see G. L. Trager and Henry Lee Smith, *An Outline of English Structure*. For a segmental analysis into vowel plus vowel, see Morris Swadesh, "On the Analysis of English Syllabics," *Language* (1947) 23. 137–150. The unit vowel analysis of American English has recently been defended by Hans Kurath, "The Binary Interpretation of English Vowels: A Critique," *Language* (1957) 33. 111–122.

[6] For this analysis, a master chart was made for each informant. Each master chart consisted of the conventional phonetic vowel quadrilateral in large scale on 22-by-30-inch paper. A basic group of 259 forms were selected as representing all the common vowel phones in all principal phonetic environments. The transcriptions of each informant's pronunciation of these 259 forms were entered on his master chart, each transcription being written on the chart at that point of the vowel quadrilateral representing the point of articulation of the vowel of the transcription (more than one entry was made for transcriptions with more than one vowel). About a hundred entries were then added to each chart in order to include examples of all phones used by each informant in as many environments as possible. The result was a two-dimensional representation of each informant's vowel phones. As the entire forms, rather than just the vowels, were entered, phonetic environments were apparent, complementary distribution could be determined directly from the charts, and phonemic boundaries could be tentatively drawn. No additional charting was required for most phones; for those whose phonemic affinities were still unclear, reference was made to the remainder of the data in the field records, excepting only animal calls and interjections, which often deviate from the normal phonemic pattern. As the points of articulation were similarly located on each chart, the charts could be compared to determine the differences between informants in the number and distribution of allophones and in the "placement" of phonemes. A running count was then made of a considerable sample of the data, in some cases all of the data, in order to determine the relative frequency of the apparently free variants within each significant phonetic environment. A phone constituting ten percent or less of the occurrences in its phonetic environment was considered "rare" for that informant; a phone constituting eleven to thirty percent of occurrences was considered "occasional," and a phone constituting more than thirty percent was considered "common." Frequency for San Francisco was calculated by the following method. A value of four points was given to a phone for common occurrence in the speech of one informant, two points for occasional occurrence, and one point for rare occurrence. A phone

554   The phoneme /i/ under weak stress is commonly [ɨ] or [i'], although the more fronted [i] also occurs in very deliberate speech. Before /r/, /i/ is commonly [ɪˆ] or [iˇ], with [iⁱ] and [ɪ] the extremes of the range. Under secondary stress it is [i], though sometimes centralized as far as [ɨ]. Under primary stress, /i/ is commonly [iⁱ], occasionally only [i]. Transcriptions such as [ɪⁱ], which would justify a segmental analysis into /iy/ are rare.

The phoneme /ɪ/ under weak stress is commonly [ǂ]. Before /l/ or /r/, it is centralized and sometimes lowered to [ɪ'], [ǂ], or [ɪ²]; e.g., *syrup*, /'sɪrɪp/, ['sɪ'ɚǂp], ['sǂɚǂp], or ['sɪ²ɚǂp].[7] Centralization (but not lowering) is also common after /w/. Under secondary and primary stress, /ɪ/ is commonly [ɪ].

The phoneme /e/ rarely occurs under weak stress or before /r/ in San Francisco. Under secondary or primary stress, it is [eⁱ], although allophones without perceptible glide occur occasionally. Rarely is the onset as low as [ɛ].

The phoneme /ɛ/ is commonly [ɛǂ] before /g/, with an offglide which is more central and lower than that found in /e/. /ɛ/ occurs occasionally under weak stress (although perhaps the limitations of the phonetic alpha-

was considered "common" for San Francisco if it totaled more than thirty out of the possible hundred points and was common in the data for five or more informants; e.g., [i'] is used commonly as weak-stressed /i/ by fourteen informants, occasionally by eight informants, and rarely by one informant; its point value is therefore seventy-three and it was duly labeled as "common." Similarly, a phone was considered "occasional" for San Francisco if it totaled between eleven and thirty points and either was common in the data for one or more informants or was occasional in the data for five or more informants. A phone was considered "rare" if it totaled less than eleven points. This brief summary lists only the common allophones, with some indication of the range of less common variants.

[7] Note that in the interpretation of vowels before /r/ and in certain other points, this analysis requires the recognition of overlapping phonemes; i.e., [I] before /r/ is an allophore of /i/, but otherwise [I] is an allophone of /ɪ/. The variants of /i/, /e/, and /æ/ before /r/ and, to a lesser extent, /u/ and /o/ before /r/ may be considered macrophonemes; i.e., the phonetic range of the allophones followed by /r/ is greater than that of the allophones not followed by /r/, so that, for example, /ir/ and /ɪr/ may be mutually exclusive, likewise /is/ and /ɪs/, but /ir/ and /ɪs/ may overlap. This interpretation has been considered necessary despite certain theoretical objections to such procedure which have been voiced by Bernard Bloch, "Phonemic Overlapping," *American Speech* (1941) 16. 278–284. High front vowels before /r/ in English are a classic illustration of phonemic neutralization, for [ɪˆ] and [iˇ] are the most frequent phones, with [ɪ] and [iⁱ] representing the extremes of the distribution. If one chooses to follow American phonemic practice and combine these phones with one of the adjacent vowel phonemes, then /i/ is preferable to /ɪ/ for two reasons. First, higher variants are favored in slow and deliberate articulation; thus interpretation as /ir/ does less violence to the speaker's naive interpretation of his language. Second, interpretation of [ɪˆɚ] and [iˇɚ] as /ir/ permits one to interpret such sequences as [ǂɚ], [ɪ'ɚ], and [ɪ²ɚ] as /ɪr/. For many San Franciscans, the first syllable of *stirrups* is homophonous with neither *steer* nor *stir*. An alternative solution would be a high central vowel phoneme /ɨ/.

bet obscure a tertiary stress here), with centralized allophones of [ε'] or even [ə']. Under primary and secondary stress, it is normally [ε]. There is no evidence of the neutralization of /ɪ/ and /ε/ before nasals which is so common in some parts of the western United States; pairs like *pin* and *pen*, *him* and *hem*, are always contrastive.

The phoneme /æ/ rarely occurs under weak stress. Before /r/, /æ/ is commonly raised to [æˆ] or even [εˇ], though [æ] is also common, especially in more deliberate enunciation. Under primary and secondary stress, [æ] is normal, though allophones with an upward and centering glide occasionally occur before /g/.

The phoneme /a/ is normally [ɑ], though a raised allophone of [ɐ] is heard in the rare occurrences under weak stress.

The phoneme /u/ rarely occurs under weak stress or before /r/. Under primary and secondary stress it is [uᵘ] or [u], with the glide occuring more frequently under primary stress. The back vowels /u/, /ʊ/, and /o/ generally parallel the front vowels /i/, /ɪ/, and /e/ in the distribution of centralized and glide allophones.

The phoneme /ʊ/ is commonly centralized to [ʉ] or [ʊ'] under weak stress or before /r/ or /l/. As has been mentioned above, the sequence /ʊl/ may be [ʉɫ] or [ʊ'ɫ] or may be simply a syllabic [ɫ]. Under primary or secondary stress, /ʊ/ is normally [ʊ].

The phoneme /o/ is rare before /r/, occurring consistently in the speech of only one informant. Centralized allophones occur under weak stress in such words as *widow* and *tomorrow*. Otherwise /o/ is commonly [oᵘ], though allophones without the glide are also frequent under secondary stress.

The phoneme /ɔ/ has a wider phonetic range than any other phoneme. Though the most frequent allophone is the low back unrounded [ɑ], other allophones in apparently free variation range as far forward as [ɑ‹] and as high as [ɔ]. Various degrees of lip rounding occasionally occur, with rare occurrences of even the extreme overrounded [ʊ]. It is curious that lip rounding of this phoneme is more common among the three Negro informants. These almost entirely avoided the completely unrounded variants and used the strongly rounded variants with about twice the frequency of the other informants. Some informants tend to favor fronted allophones like [ɑ‹] and [ɑ›] (especially in such words as *hogs* and *foggy*, which contain /a/ in some American dialects, /ɔ/ in others) so that the /a/-/ɔ/ contrast is partially obscured. Questioned after the interviews were completed, some informants were able to hear a contrast between [ɑ] and [ɑ] or [ɔ], but they were unsure which alternative was closest to their own intermediate pronunciation of [ɑ']. In parts of the western United States (Utah, for example), /a/ and /ɔ/ have fallen together into one phoneme, usually with a wide phonetic range. In cer-

556   tain other western areas, including parts of Washington, this coalescence is not complete, for /a/ and /ɔ/ still contrast in some words; however, many words occur with [ɑ], [ɒ], [ɔ], and various intermediate variants all in free variation. Some speakers there are unable to hear this contrast in *knotty-naughty* yet they clearly perceive it in *cot-caught.* Clearly the coalescence of /a/ and /ɔ/ is a phonemic change which is now moving into the Pacific Northwest. It is possible that the peculiar use of fronted allophones of /ɔ/ is an indication that this coalescence is beginning in San Francisco. The ever-increasing number of migrants to San Francisco from other western states seems to support this hypothesis. The entire subject needs further investigation.

The phoneme /ə/ under weak stress is [ə]. Under primary and secondary stress it is [ʌ]. The tautosyllabic sequence /ər/ is a syllabic [ɚ]. The sequences /əm/, /ən/, /əŋ/, and /əl/ may also indicate a syllabic consonant.

All vowels except /e/, /u/, and /o/ occur commonly before /r/. All vowels occur under primary and secondary stress, but only /i/, /ɪ/, /ə/, and /o/ occur commonly under weak stress. Several diphthongal combinations occur, although only /aɪ/, /ɔɪ/, /aʊ/, and /ɪu/ are common. The second element in a diphthong may be /ɪ/, /ʊ/, /u/, or /ə/, normally with the centralized allophones [ᵻ], [ʊˋ], [uˋ], [ə]. The syllabicity of /ɪu/ is about equally divided; the relatively infrequent transcriptions such as ['hjuᵘmɚ] for *humor* have been analyzed here as /yu/. /ɪu/ varies with /u/ in many words, with /ɪu/ less commonly used, though generally considered the more elegant variant in San Francisco. All other diphthongs are distinctly "falling" types, with the peak of syllabicity on the first element. The diphthong /ɔɪ/ [ɜᵻ] is used by most of the Type I informants in certain words in which informants of Types II and III use /ər/. This pronunciation, often popularly labeled "New York" or "Brooklynese," is very nearly in complementary distribution with /ər/, for /ɔɪ/ occurs almost exclusively before voiceless fortis consonants. For example, the words *heard* and *nurse* are /hərd/ and /nərs/ for informant 17, but are /hərd/ and /nəɪs/ for informant 8. A series of diphthongs such as /aə/, /iə/, /ɛə/, /ɔə/, etc., are also common in the speech of informant 20, rare in the speech of a few others, as the result of the loss of postvocalic /r/.

Reduction of consonant clusters, assimilation, and epenthesis are not so common in San Francisco as in many American dialects. Syllable initial clusters are generally unaffected by these processes. Very complex final clusters tend to be simplified, usually by the elimination of the post-final phoneme; e.g., *sixth* is /sɪkstθ/ in careful speech, but is often /sɪkst/ or even /sɪks/ in conversation. Total assimilation of /t/ to /s/ is common, but assimilation of other stops to /s/, as is common in Southern and South Midland dialects, is rare; e.g., /fɪss/ is common for *fists,* but

/wass/ or /wɔss/ for *wasps* and /hɔss/ for *husks* are rare. When followed by a non-homorganic stop, a nasal consonant is frequently assimilated in point of articulation, although sometimes an epenthetic stop occurs instead; e.g., *climbed* occurs as /klaɪnd/ or as /klaɪmbd/, rarely as /klaɪmd/. /s/ and /z/ are commonly palatalized to /š/ and /ž/ by a following /y/; e.g., *this year* /ˌðɪš'šir/, *here is your* /ˌhɪržər/.

San Francisco Pronunciation in Its Social and Historical Context. San Francisco speech is the product of the complex settlement history and social structure of the city. Consequently, the complexity and variety of its linguistic structure are to be expected. Any set of data which indicated uniformity in the speech of twenty-five San Franciscans would be immediately suspect.

Variations in San Francisco pronunciation may be classified in three ways, according to whether they are 1) variations within the speech of a single informant or differences between informants, 2) structural or non-structural variations, and 3) phonemic or sub-phonemic variations. Phonemic variations are apparent in differing phonemic transcriptions for equivalent utterances, whereas sub-phonemic differences are reflected only in the description of the allophones and their distribution; e.g., the difference between /fag/ and /fɔg/ for *fog* is phonemic, whereas the difference between [fɑg] and [fu·g] for /fag/ is sub-phonemic. Differences affecting the number or the system of distribution of phonemes or allophones are structural; e.g., variation between /o/ and /ɔ/ as the vowel of *hoarse, porch, mourning,* etc., indicates whether /o/ occurs before /r/ and is therefore structural. Differences which involve only the choice of one phoneme or phone from a group of free variants are non-structural; e.g., variation between /fag/ and /fɔg/ for *fog* and variation between [fɑg] and [fɑ·g] for /fag/.

Variations within the speech of individual informants reflect similar differences between informants in San Francisco. For example, in three occurrences of *wash,* nineteen informants consistently used /wɔš/, two informants (10 and 12) consistently /waš/, and four informants (1, 8, 22, and 25) both /wɔš/ and /waš/. The inconsistency of these four informants is undoubtedly the result of the conflicting influences of the two forms they had heard. Much of this kind of variation consists of alternation of /a/ and /ɔ/ and of weak-stressed /ɪ/ and /ə/; e.g., /'sɛvɪn/ and /'sɛvən/ for *seven.* Such variation between /i/ and /ɪ/ and between /u/ and /ʊ/ is rare, with marked preference for one of the two forms; e.g., informant 25 used both /krik/ and /krɪk/ for *creek,* informants 2 and 19 used /krɪk/ but corrected their responses to /krik/, while all other informants used only /krik/. Under weak stress, /o/ occasionally varies with /ə/; e.g., /'yɛlo/ and /'yɛlə/.

Structural variations within an idiolect are considered by some linguists

558   as a contradiction in terms and therefore impossible. Fries and Pike,[8] however, have convincingly shown how two or more differing phonemic systems can coexist in the speech of one speaker. Low-front vowel phones in the area of [a] were recorded frequently for informants 15 and 16, rarely for informants 3, 7, 9, 11, 13, 14, 17, 18, 21, 22, 23, and 24. These vowel phones occurred in the words *calve, Nevada, patio, plaza, rather,* and *salmon* and in certain words in which the vowel is followed by a fortis spirant or by a cluster of /n/ plus consonant; i.e. the so-called "ask-words": *calf, pass, bath, dance, aunt,* etc. No single informant used the low vowels in all of these words (18, for example, used [a] in *France* but [æ] in *dance*).

Rigid structuralist procedure would require recognition of three separate phonemes, /æ/, /a/, and /ɑ/. However, one would not recognize a rounded-front vowel phoneme in the English of a person who pronounced *jeu d'esprit* after the French fashion. Similarly [ant] for *aunt* and [kaf] for *calf* are inter-dialectal loan words and, like many foreign loan words, are at variance with the phonology of the borrowing dialect. For some San Franciscans one must recognize the coexistence of San Francisco and other phonemic systems, in this instance Eastern New England. For these twelve informants, [a] is a point of articulation which is rarely used, which has certain affinities with both /æ/ and /a/, but which is an allophone of neither of these phonemes; rather it belongs to a phoneme in an alien system. New England culture has considerable prestige value in San Francisco. Many San Franciscans proudly trace their ancestry to New England families. Hyper-urbanism occasionally occurs in the extension of [a] to words in which [æ] is the New England usage; e.g., informant 13 used [kaˑf] for *calf* but [ˌhavə'kæf] for *have a calf.* The use of [a] in *salmon* is probably by analogy with *calf* and *half.* In *Nevada, patio, plaza* and *rather,* [a] is a compromise articulation between the two variants [æ] and [ɑ]. These words occur with both /æ/ and /a/, and a few speakers resolve the conflict between these alternant phonemes by the use of the intermediate extra-phonemic [a].

Compromise rather than choice between alternant phonemes other than /a/ and /æ/ also occurs. For example, *catch* occurs commonly as [kɛtʃ], /kɛc/, or as [kætʃ], /kæc/, but it is also occasionally [kæˆtʃ] and [kɛˇtʃ]. As the phones [æˆ] and [ɛˇ] are both extremely rare except when followed by /r/, one may conclude that in [ɛˇ] the articulation of /ɛ/ is attracted in the direction of /æ/, and in [æˆ] the articulation of /æ/ is attracted in the direction of /ɛ/. Similarly, *threshed* occurs as [θrɛʃt], /θrɛšt/, as [θræʃt], /θræšt/, and as the intermediate [θræˆʃt].

---

[8] C. C. Fries and Kenneth L. Pike, "Coexistent Phonemic Systems," *Language* (1949) 25. 29–50.

Some informants are also inconsistent in the distribution of phonemes.
Again rigid structuralist procedure demands a clearcut decision: Does
/o/, for example, ever occur before /r/ or does it not? Some linguists
settle such problems of distribution on the basis of a single example, just
as they hold that every phone that is not prosodically conditioned or
freely varying must be recognized as a phoneme. Such a procedure, however, can obscure the complex linguistic and social structure underlying
the data. For example, the sequence /or/ as in *hoarse* occurred commonly
only in the speech of informant 20; it occurred in from one to five words
in that of informants 7, 9, 14, 16, 21, 23, and 24. In the course of the interview sessions, seventeen informants (1, 2, 3, 5, 6, 7, 8, 10, 11, 12, 13, 17, 18,
19, 20, 22, and 25) were also tested on their ability to hear a distinction
between /or/ and /ɔr/. Of this group, eight informants (6, 10, 12, 13, 17,
19, 22, and 25) were easily able to distinguish such pairs as *hoarse-horse*
and *mourning-morning* and insisted that these words were not comparable to such homophonic pairs as *sale-sail* and *weighed-wade;* yet these
eight informants pronounced *hoarse, horse, mourning,* and *morning* all
with the same vowel, /ɔ/. That is, the /or/-/ɔr/ distinction has a psychological reality for these speakers which is not indicated in the phonetic
transcriptions. Similarly the initial cluster /hw/ was perceived but not
pronounced by informants 5 and 19; they pronounced *whether-weather*
and *which-witch* identically but could hear the /hw/-/w/ distinction and
believed that they were pronouncing it. Finally, eight informants (2, 5, 6,
8, 10, 17, 20, and 25) pronounced both *Mary* and *merry* as /'mɛri/ but
were able to hear and identify the distinction between /'meri/, *Mary,* and
/'mɛri/, *merry*. Furthermore, informants 12, 19, and 22 used /er/ in *chair,*
but were not able to hear the *Mary-merry* distinction.

It is obvious that /or/, /er/, /hw/, and such pronunciations as [kæˇf]
for *calf* and [kæˆtʃ] for *catch* are in a state of transition in San Francisco.
The distribution of these features by age groups is not sufficiently conclusive to warrant predictions as to whether they will become more or less
frequent in future years. It is significant that the occurrence of such transitional features is affected by homophonic conflicts. /or/ in the speech of
several informants, for example, is confined to words in which it is in contrast with /ɔr/ in otherwise identical forms. Informant 7 normally uses
/hɔrs/ for *hoarse* and /'mɔrnɪŋ/ for *mourning,* but when any misunderstanding arises from the homophonic conflict with *horse* and *morning* she
uses /'hors/ and /'mornɪŋ/. Similarly ⌊a⌋ is more frequent in *aunt* than in
can't. Many speakers use [ānt] or [ãnt] in order to distinguish *aunt* from
ant, but they reject [kānt] or [kãnt] as a hyperurbanism.

The research of the Linguistic Atlas of the United States has indicated
four major dialect areas in the Eastern United States: Northern, North
Midland, South Midland, and Southern. The boundaries of these four

560

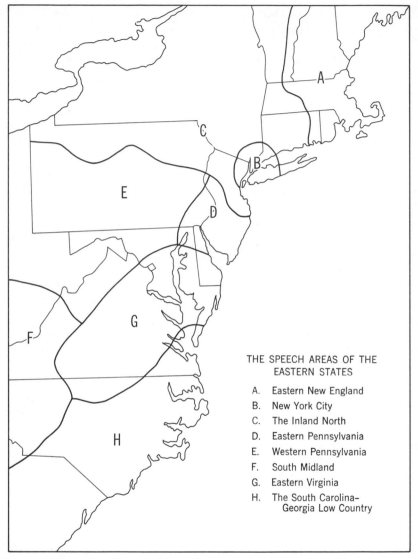

THE SPEECH AREAS OF THE
EASTERN STATES

A. Eastern New England
B. New York City
C. The Inland North
D. Eastern Pennsylvania
E. Western Pennsylvania
F. South Midland
G. Eastern Virginia
H. The South Carolina–
    Georgia Low Country

Based on maps in Hans Kurath, *A Word Geography of the Eastern United States,* Ann Arbor, 1959.

areas have been tentatively determined for some distance inland on the basis of the lexical data from the atlas; and the data on pronunciation, mostly still unpublished, seem to corroborate them. These areas can be subdivided so as to produce eight subdialects, indicated in the following tabulations by the letters A to H in this manner: A, Eastern New England; B, New York City; C, the Inland North; D, Eastern Pennsylvania; E,

Western Pennsylvania; F, South Midland; G, Eastern Virginia; and H,   561
the South Carolina-Georgia Low Country. For comparing the pronunciation in San Francisco with that in these eight areas, the following forty-
six test words have been selected.[9]

1–3. The use of /o/ in *hoarse, mourning,* and *porch,* respectively, defines
areas AFGH; /ɔ/ is used in these words in areas BCDE. /o/ is used in
hoarse by seven informants (7, 9, 14, 20, 21, 23, 24). /o/ is used in *mourn-*
ing by five informants (7, 9, 16, 20, 24). /o/ is used in *porch* only by informant 20.

4–5. The use of /e/ in *Mary* and *dairy* defines area ABGH; /ɛ/ is
used in areas CDEF. /e/ is used in *Mary* by seven informants (7, 9, 13, 14,
15, 16, 24). /e/ is used in *dairy* by six informants (3, 4, 7, 9, 15, 16).

6–8. The use of /ɛ/ in *married, barrel,* and *carried* defines area C; /æ/
is used in all other areas. None of the informants use /ɛ/ in *married* or
carried. Only informant 12 used /ɛ/ in *barrel.*

9–11. The use of /ɔ/ in *hogs, log,* and *fog* defines areas AEF; /a/ is
used in area BCDGH. Note that /a/ and /ɔ/ are not phonemically
distinct in parts of area E, but the articulation of these words there corresponds phonetically to the San Francisco /ɔ/. /ɔ/ is used in *hogs* by
eighteen informants (all except 2, 7, 8, 10, 14, 17, 19). /ɔ/ is used in *log*
and *fog* by twenty-one informants (all except 7, 8, 15, 19).

12. The use of /a/ in stressed *on,* as in *put it on,* defines areas BCD; /ɔ/
is used in areas ADEFGH; i.e., both /a/ and /ɔ/ are used in *on* in area
D. /a/ is used by sixteen informants (all except 4, 9, 13, 15, 16, 18, 21,
23, 24).

13–14. The use of /z/ in *greasy* and in the verb *grease* defines areas
EFGH; /s/ is used in areas ABCDE. /z/ is used in *greasy* by six inform-

[9] These test words for Eastern American dialects have been selected after consulting and attempting to reconcile many varied and often conflicting sources of information, including the
Linguistic Atlas of New England; E. Bagby Atwood, "Outline of the Principal Speech Areas of
the Eastern United States;" Mrs. Y. H. Frank, *The Speech of New York City;* A. F. Hubbell,
The Pronunciation of English in New York City; C. K. Thomas, *An Introduction to the Phonetics
of American English;* John S. Kenyon, *American Pronunciation;* and John S. Kenyon and
Thomas A. Knott, *A Pronouncing Dictionary of American English.* The data of the atlases of
the Middle and South Atlantic States and of the North Central States are not yet published and
were not directly consulted, although Atwood's privately mimeographed "Outline" is based
on these data. The distribution of the words has in general been confirmed in a recent article
by Raven I. McDavid, Jr., and Virginia G. McDavid, *Orbis* 5 (1956) 349–386. In selecting more
than one word for certain pronunciation characteristics (e.g., *hoarse, mourning,* and *porch,* all
illustrating the occurrence of /o/ before /r/), an attempt has been made to "weight" features
which appear to be structurally more significant in determining the differences between
dialects. That is, the occurrence of /o/ before /r/ in an entire series of words seems more
significant than the occurrence of /ɛ/ in the one word *afraid.* A different selection of pronunciation features and a different system of weighting would, of course, produce different results.

562 ants (1, 3, 7, 10, 12, 20). /z/ is used in the verb *grease* only by informants 10 and 20.

15–16. The use of [a] or similar low vowels in *calf* and *dance* defines areas AG; [æ] is used in areas BCDEFGH. [a] is used in *calf* by nine informants (3, 7, 9, 13, 15, 16, 17, 21, 22). [a] is used in *dance* only by informants 13 and 16.

17–18. The use of diphthongs /ɪu/ or /yu/ in *due* and *Tuesday* defines areas CFGH; /u/ is used in areas ABCDE. Diphthongs are used in *due* by four informants (7, 14, 23, 24). Diphthongs are used in *Tuesday* by ten informants (7, 9, 13, 15, 16, 17, 18, 19, 21, 22).

19–20. The use of /r/ in *barn* and *horse* defines areas CDEF; /ə/ or a lengthened vowel is used in areas ABGH. /r/ is used in *barn* by twenty-two informants (all except 5, 16, 24). /r/ is used in *horse* by twenty-three informants (all except 4 and 20).

21–22. The use of /r/ in *water* and *oysters* defines areas CDE. /r/ is used in *water* by twenty-four informants (all except 20). /r/ is used in *oysters* by twenty informants (all except 9, 10, 15, 16, 20).

23–24. The use of intrusive final /r/ in *law* (as in *law and order*) and in *sofa* defines areas AB; pronunciation of these words without the final /r/ is used in areas BCDEFGH. In area B the use of this /r/ is characteristic of less educated speakers. /r/ is used in *law* by four informants (2, 3, 5, 8). /r/ is used in *sofa* by six informants (1, 2, 3, 5, 8, 9); six other informants (4, 6, 7, 11, 19, 25) did not use the word *sofa* at all and so did not provide comparable data.

25–26. The use of diphthong /əɪ/ in *nurse* and *purse* defines area B. /əɪ/ is used in both words by six informants (2, 3, 5, 8, 9, 10).

27. The use of [ʔ] in *bottle* defines area B. This glottal allophone is used by nine informants (2, 3, 4, 5, 7, 8, 9, 10, 25).

28–29. The use of initial /w/ in *whip* and *wheel* defines areas ABDH; /hw/ is used in areas ACEFG. Within area A, /w/ is common along the coast of Maine and New Hampshire; elsewhere in the area /hw/ predominates. /w/ is initial in *whip* for seven informants (4, 5, 8, 9, 19, 23, 24). /w/ is initial in *wheel* for seven informants (4, 5, 8, 9, 19, 22, 24).

30. The use of /ɔ/ in *oranges* defines areas ACEF; /a/ is used in areas ABDFGH. /ɔ/ is used by twenty-two informants (all except 7, 8, 17).

31. The use of /ɛ/ in *afraid* defines area G; /e/ is used in all other areas. No comparable data for informant 15. The other twenty-four informants all used /e/, never /ɛ/.

32. The use of /mɪz/, /'mɪzɪz/, or /'mɪzəz/ for *Mrs.* (as in *Mrs. Brown*) defines areas FGH; /'mɪsɪz/ or /'mɪsəz/ is used in areas ABCDEF. The "Southern" forms without /s/ are used only by informants 20 and 25.

33–34. The use of /ʊ/ in *bulge* and *bulk* defines areas FGH; /ə/ is used in areas ABCDE. /ʊ/ is used in *bulge* by three informants (9, 20, 25). /ʊ/ is used in *bulk* only by informants 9 and 20.

35–36. The use of /a/ in *wash* and *wasps* defines areas ABCD; /ɔ/ is
used in areas AEFGH. /a/ is used in *wash* by four informants (1, 10, 20, 22). /a/ is used in *wasps* by thirteen informants (1, 3, 5, 6, 7, 10, 11, 12, 17, 18, 19, 20, 25; no comparable data for informant 2).

37. The use of /ss/ in *wasps* defines areas FGH; /sps/ is used in areas ABCDE. The assimilated /ss/ is used only by informants 4 and 20; no comparable data for informant 2.

38–40. The use of /əʊ/ in *house* and *out* and the use of /æʊ/ or similar fronted diphthongs in *houses* define areas GH. None of the informants use these pronunciations.

41. The use of [æʊ] or similar diphthongs in *mountain* defines areas AFGH. These fronted diphthongs were used in *mountain* by three informants (12, 19, 20).

42–43. The use of /ɔ/ in *crop* and *God* defines areas AEH; /a/ is used in areas BCDFG. /ɔ/ is used in *crop* by five informants (9, 14, 15, 19, 24). /ɔ/ is used in *God* by six informants (9, 13, 15, 16, 23, 24).

44. The use of /u/ in *drought* defines area E. None of the informants used this pronunciation; no comparable data for informants 2, 6, 8, 15, 16, 17.

45–46. The use of weak-stressed /ə/ in *bracelet* and *haunted* defines areas DEF; /ɪ/ is used in areas ABCGH. None of the informants used /ə/ in *bracelet*. Only informant 10 used /ə/ in *haunted*.

This list indicates that pronunciations with similar geographical range in the eastern United States are not always treated alike in San Francisco. For example, /hɔrs/ for *hoarse* outnumbers /pɔrc/ for *porch* by seven to one, possibly because of the homophonic conflict with *horse* (/hɔrs/). /'grizi/ for *greasy* outnumbers /griz/ for the verb *grease* by six to two. The extra-phonemic [a] in *calf* outnumbers [a] in *dance* by nine to two.

Of the forty-six words in the list, twenty indicate area A, twelve B, thirteen C, eleven D, fifteen E, twenty F, twenty G, and twenty-one H. Percentages may be derived from the total number of responses indicating each area which were used by each informant and the number of such responses which the informant might have used. For example, informant 2 used pronunciations indicating area A in five of the test words; he used an entirely different (and therefore not comparable) word in place of one other which might have indicated area A. Thus he used five out of nineteen, or 26 percent of his potential responses indicating A. Similarly he used six out of eleven, or 55 percent of the pronunciations indicating area B. On the basis of these percentages, the eight eastern dialect areas can be ranked for each informant in order of greatest similarity. The results of these computations appear in Table I.

This method of calculation provides an index of the relative degree of similarity of each area to the individual informants, subject, of course,

564   *Table I*

Informant Number	Percent used of possible responses								Rank order
	A	B	C	D	E	F	G	H	
1	35	33	62	64	60	35	5	5	DCEAFBGH
2	26	55	50	50	50	26	0	0	BCDEAFGH
3	45	67	54	55	60	35	15	10	BEDCAFGH
4	37	36	31	45	47	30	10	19	EDABCFHG
5	45	75	46	64	47	25	0	10	BDECAFHG
6	26	18	54	55	57	30	0	0	EDCFABGH
7	32	45	62	55	33	35	40	33	CDBGFEHA
8	20	67	38	64	29	10	0	10	BDCEAFHG
9	70	67	38	45	60	55	40	52	ABEFHDGC
10	25	50	54	64	60	40	10	10	DECBFAGH
11	26	18	54	55	53	30	0	0	DCEFABGH
12	30	17	62	55	60	40	10	10	CEDFABGH
13	40	8	46	36	60	35	20	14	ECADFGHB
14	30	17	54	45	53	35	15	19	CEDFAHBG
15	35	17	38	27	50	25	21	24	ECADFHGB
16	50	17	31	18	50	35	32	24	AEFGCHDB
17	20	17	54	55	43	25	10	5	DCEFABGH
18	25	8	54	45	53	35	5	5	CEDFABGH
19	32	36	62	73	40	35	10	24	DCEBFAHG
20	50	25	38	36	47	75	50	48	FAGHECDB
21	30	0	46	36	53	40	15	10	ECFDAGHB
22	35	25	62	64	53	35	10	10	DCEAFBGH
23	35	8	46	45	60	40	10	19	ECDFAHGB
24	55	25	38	45	60	40	20	38	EADFCHBG
25	26	27	54	55	53	35	5	5	DCEFBAGH

to the reliability of the San Francisco sampling, to the accuracy of the geographic range assigned to the criteria for the eastern dialect areas, and to the effects of arbitrarily choosing these forty-six pronunciations. A number of the criteria are indications of similarity with two or more non-adjacent areas; /e/ in *Mary,* for example, indicates similarity with areas ABGH (New England, New York, and Southern). Consequently, non-adjacent areas occasionally rank almost equally in this tabulation. From a purely descriptive viewpoint, this is entirely acceptable. However, further interpretation can be based on historical and biographical data. For example, informant 20 is a Negro who, although born in San Francisco, associates almost entirely with Negroes who have recently migrated from the South Midland and Southern areas (FGH). The ranking of areas

FAGH as most similar to her is descriptively an accurate measure of her resemblance to eastern dialects, for in such features as the use of /o/ in *hoarse, mourning,* and *porch,* she indeed resembles area A (New England) as well as areas FGH. However, the hypothesis that she acquired these features as the result of South Midland and Southern influence rather than New England influence seems sound. If New England resemblances in features also defining South Midland were discounted, the ranking of areas would be FGHECDBA.

Indeed the speech of informant 20 is strikingly different from that of the other two Negro informants (10 and 25). These two men were reared and educated in districts which were predominantly non-Negro. They have associated primarily with whites or with Negroes who have lived in San Francisco for a generation or more. Though informant 10 now lives on the fringe of the Negro district and informant 25, a chiropodist, has many Negro clients, they have been less influenced by recent South and South Midland migrants. Though informant 10 had only elementary education and informant 25 had postgraduate professional training, their speech is far more similar to each other and to San Francisco in general than to informant 20. The aberrant speech of informant 20 reveals how influential a Negro district can be, even in a city which has never had a rigid color barrier.

Informant 20 is by no means the only informant for whom correlations are possible between the biographical data and this ranking of dialect areas according to similarity. The parents and grandparents of informant 1 were all born and raised in New Jersey; area D (Eastern Pennsylvania and Southern New Jersey) ranks highest in similarity to his speech. As a child, he frequently visited relatives from Iowa and North Dakota; area C (the Inland North) is second in similarity. The parents of informant 16 were born and raised in Eastern New England; area A ranks highest in similarity to her speech. The father of informant 23 was from Indiana; areas EC (Inland Midland and Inland North) are the highest ranking.

By totaling the numbers of actual and of potential responses indicating various dialect areas, one obtains figures from which similar percentages can be calculated for various groups of the informants and for the city as a whole. The results of these calculations are as follows:

	A	B	C	D	E	F	G	H	Rank
Type I (infs. 1–10)	36	52	49	56	50	32	12	15	DBECAFHG
Type II (infs. 11–20)	34	18	49	45	51	36	17	17	ECDFABGH
Type III (infs. 21–25)	36	17	49	49	56	38	12	16	ECDFABHG
San Francisco total	35	31	49	50	52	35	12	16	EDCAFBHG

The similarities of San Francisco speech, as thus tabulated, are predominately with Northern and North Midland areas. This correlates well

566 with the settlement history. Migrants from Missouri, Kentucky, Arkansas, Oklahoma, and Texas (i.e., area F), so important in the settlement of the state of California as a whole, and migrants from the South (areas GH) were numerically insignificant in the settlement and later growth of San Francisco. Areas GH consistently rank lowest in linguistic similarity to San Francisco, and area F is similar only to the aberrent informant 20. In early years, New Yorkers predominated in San Francisco, constituting 34 percent of the interstate migrants resident in the city in 1870. This is reflected in the speech of Type I informants, which is strikingly similar to that of New York City (area B). The importance of the Inland North Midland and Inland Northern areas (E and C), especially in the speech of Types II and III informants, reflects the westward but consistently northern movement of the center of emigration to San Francisco in recent years. More than 40 percent of the interstate migrants resident in the city in 1940 came from the Midwest, especially the Great Lakes area. Today even casual visitors to San Francisco remark on the similarity to the speech of Chicago, Toledo, and Cleveland.

The table also indicates strong linguistic similarities to the speech of Eastern Pennsylvania (area D). This requires special comment, for Philadelphians have never been numerous in San Francisco. The explanation lies in the San Franciscan prejudice against all Southern and South Midland characteristics. So-called "*r*-dropping" is particularly a shibboleth, commonly stigmatized as an "Okie habit," though it is more characteristic of New England and New York City than of the South Midland. I know of one child, recently brought from New York, whose teacher referred her to a school clinic for speech defects simply because she failed to produce sufficient postvocalic retroflexion. The occasional *r*-dropping of certain older speakers, such as informant 16, can unquestionably be traced to New England origins, yet these speakers are ashamed of their "Southernisms." Informant 16, for example, shows conscious pride in her carefully cultivated New England "broad α," extending it even to the point of hyperurbanism, yet she tries hard to "sound the r" in *barn* and *water* and is embarrassed by her occasional lapses. Probably as a result of the similarity to Southern and South Midland as well as to New England and New York, *r*-dropping has become rare in San Francisco. This circumstance decreases the similarity to the speech of the North Atlantic areas AB and increases the similarity to area D, for this area (Eastern Pennsylvania) is characterized by the retention of postvocalic /r/. Tied characteristics (i.e., features which are characteristic of more than one area, sometimes of noncontiguous areas) are involved in any correlation of American dialects; they may at times even be a factor in the formation of a new dialect. Just as informant 20, by favoring certain Southern and South Midland pronunciations, accidentally increased her similarity to New England pronunciations, so many other, more typical San Franciscans, by consciously avoiding these same Southern and South Midland pronunciations, accidentally diminish their similarity to New England speech.

Why is the early settlement from the North Atlantic states reflected more strongly in the speech of Type I informants, while Types II and III more strongly reflect the later migrations from the Midwest? For one thing, Type I represents generally an older group (median age 68) than Types II and III (median age 46) and is therefore probably more conservative. However, the only consistent difference between the types is in level of education. It has long been held that vulgate speech is more conservative than that of cultivated speakers. In San Francisco we find differences which were once only geographical in distribution becoming distributed according to social class. Curiously enough, the social prestige of these linguistic features is often inconsistent with the attitude toward the areas of the eastern United States. San Franciscans highly respect New England and New York. However, a San Franciscan whose family background is characterized by education and financial security is likely to use pronunciation similar to that of the Great Lakes area and avoid New England and New York pronunciations, even though he may proudly trace his family history to New England or New York. Conversely, an economically and educationally less privileged San Franciscan's parents may have come from the Midwest or have been foreign born, yet his pronunciation may be noticeably more similar to New England and New York than is that of his more privileged fellow citizen.

There is a tradition in San Francisco that there is a "Mission Dialect" characteristic of Irish Catholics born south of Market Street. These persons are said to "talk like Brooklynites." There is some basis to this myth. Calculating the similarities with eastern dialect areas by the same method as for Types I, II, and III, the following ranking of areas and percentages are derived for a sub-group consisting of informants 2, 3, 5, and 8: B 66, D 58, C 47, E 47, A 34, F 24, H 7, and G 4 percent. Area B is the highest ranking area in similarity to each of these four informants and to no other informant. These informants all use [ʔ] in *bottle* and use /əɪ/ rather than /ər/ before fortis consonants (/nəɪs/ for *nurse,* etc.), two features popularly termed "Brooklynese." Furthermore, these four informants all have Irish family backgrounds and all were born and raised south of Market Street. Informants 7 and 15, however, also have Irish backgrounds; informant 7 was born and informant 15 born and raised south of Market Street; yet informant 7 has only a few of these dialect features characteristic of informants 2, 3, 5, and 8. Informant 15 has virtually none of them, area B ranking lowest of the eight areas in similarity to her speech. Conversely, some of these dialect features also occur in the speech of informant 9, who was born and raised south of

568   Market Street but in a German-Jewish home, and of informant 10, a Negro born and raised north of Market Street! One may therefore conclude that a sub-type of speech exists in San Francisco with remarkable similarities to the uncultivated speech of New York City, that some Irish Catholics born south of Market Street do speak this sub-dialect, but that the definition of the distribution of this form of speech is far more complex and requires further study.

      .   .   .

      Foreign language influences on San Francisco pronunciation are difficult to assess but are probably not great. A linguistic substratum is of course apparent in the pronunciation of many first-generation immigrants, but alien features are generally missing from the English pronunciation of speakers whose parents were born in the United States, even though many are still bilingual. Even recent loan words are generally Americanized. Italian has contributed a number of words for foods; yet *ravioli,* for example, is heard both with the vowel /a/ and with /æ/, even in Italian restaurants. The informants strongly prefer *rodeo* and *coyote* with second-syllable stress (i.e. /rə'deo/ and /ˌkaɪ'yoti/), and some mimic with contempt the "Okie" pronunciations /'rodio/ and /'kaɪˌyot/. Yet most of them (21 out 25) preferred /'pætio/ to the more nearly Spanish /'patio/. The almost universal San Franciscan pronunciation /ˌlæ'su/ for *lasso,* opposed to the more general American /'læso/, may reflect British influence. /ˌlæ'su/ is also heard in Seattle, and it is possible that this and other linguistic features (e.g., the use of the word *chesterfield*) which are common to western Washington, western Oregon, and northern California, but comparatively rare elsewhere, may define an area of British influence, reflecting either the speech of earlier English immigrants to the area or cultural diffusion southward from Canada. Data to confirm or deny these conjectures, however, are insufficient pending the completion of the research of David W. Reed in California and Nevada and of Carroll Reed in the Pacific Northwest.

      In summary, then, the pronunciation of English in San Francisco is distinctly similar to that of the Northern and North Midland dialects of the eastern United States. The speech of less educated informants is more similar to the coastal varieties of Northern and North Midland speech, preserving much of the character of the speech brought to San Francisco by early migrants from that area. Younger and more cultivated speakers have more affinities with the Inland North and Inland North Midland areas, from which more of San Francisco's population have come in recent decades. Some pronunciations are characteristic of one or more of the educational groups, although some speakers with only elementary education are linguistically more similar to high school graduates and vice versa. The speech of Negro informants is apparently characterized by a more prominent rounding of the vowel /ɔ/ and by certain affinities with South Midland and Southern speech, although the latter are generally absent from the speech of those Negroes who have had little association with recent migrants from the South. A sub-dialect, popularly called the "Mission Dialect," has striking similarities to the speech of New York City. It is spoken by some, but by no means all, persons of Irish Catholic background whose childhood was spent south of Market Street, although some of its characteristics also occur in the speech of persons with widely different backgrounds. Many pronunciations, however, characterize only individual informants, and correlations are often possible between such ideolectal features and the biographical data on the informant. Both structural and non-structural differences, both phonemic and sub-phonemic, occur between informants and even within the speech of a single informant. The result is a complexity of linguistic pattern equal to that of the city's population history.

Several general principles of dialectology seem to be indicated: First, the influence of the community tends to outweigh the influence of the home in the shaping of a child's speech. Second, the influence of a subcommunity, such as a Negro district, may be stronger than that of the community as a whole. Third, the linguistic influence of early settlers in an area tends to be far greater than that of later immigrants. Fourth, even if early settlers are overwhelmed by great numbers of later immigrants of different provenience, their speech may be preserved in a subdialect. Fifth, the speech of older and less educated persons is more likely to be conservative; that of the younger and more cultivated tends to be more affected by alien influences. Sixth, linguistic differences which are geographically distributed in one area may be socially distributed in another; i.e., the same linguistic feature may define an area dialect in the eastern United States but may define a class dialect within San Francisco. Finally, speakers are likely to avoid pronunciations thought to be characteristic of areas against which there is local prejudice, and, conversely, to cultivate pronunciations thought to be characteristic of areas with high prestige; although these attitudes are likely to be inconsistent, they are of great importance in the formation of dialects.

The Speech
of San Antonio, Texas

Janet B. Sawyer

In San Antonio, as in many of the urban centers of the
Southwest, there are large numbers of people whose first
language is Spanish. In the following article, Professor Sawyer
discusses selected features of the speech of the "Anglos" and
"Latins" and comments on the effect that English and Spanish
have had on each other in San Antonio. She has published
a longer article, also based on her dissertation materials,
in *Texas Studies in Bilingualism,* edited by Glenn Gilbert
(Walter de Gruyter & Co., Berlin). Dr. Sawyer is Associate
Professor of Linguistics, California State College at
Long Beach.

According to the theory of linguistic substrata in its simple form, the
presence of bilinguals in a language community, *A*, in whose speech there
is interference of a foreign language, *B*, opens the gate to the influence of
the foreign language *B* upon *A*. In historical linguistics certain changes in
languages which have otherwise not been explained have led scholars to
assume substratum influence even where there was no independent

This article was originally published under the title "Aloofness from Spanish Influence in
Texas English" in *Word* Vol. 15, No. 2 (August, 1959) 270–281. Reprinted with the permission
of the International Linguistic Association and Janet B. Sawyer.

evidence for such substrata. In a sociologically more refined form of the theory[1] it is held that the mere existence of foreign speakers does not necessarily lead to permanent foreign influence on the language; such influence will only be exerted under sociocultural conditions favorable to the foreign sector.

It has long been realized that of the two main forms of bilingualism in the United States—"immigrant" and "colonial"[2]—the immigrant type does *not* represent conditions favorable to substratum formation. The English of such communities is never noticeably affected in phonology, morphology or syntax, although a few words from the immigrant language may be added to the regional lexicon. It is, on the contrary, the immigrant language that is subjected to many changes in structure as a result of extensive borrowing from English before being completely displaced as the native language of succeeding generations of speakers. The immigrant language usually declines in usefulness as more and more speakers learn English, and, in the final stage, it disappears entirely. Such bilingualism is a static, one-way affair, always moving from the immigrant language to English, and this is the factor which explains the undisturbed state of English in such communities.

But is the situation different in the other type of bilingual situation, where a "colonial" language is in contact with English? Consider the case of Spanish-English contact in Texas. In a city like San Antonio, Spanish is the first language of almost half the population. It was spoken by the first permanent settlers brought in by the colonial government from the Canary Islands. Spanish was still the language of the three Texas outposts when the first English-speaking settlers arrived in 1821. When the real flood of immigration began to fill the territory in 1865, over twenty-seven percent of the settlers were from Mexico, and since 1910 the volume of Mexican immigration has steadily increased.

Unlike the typical immigrants who form a small cultural island cut off from their home culture, the Spanish speakers represent an extension of Mexican culture thrusting far north into Texas. Maintaining constant contact with their homeland, the people retain their Mexican peasant culture in the life of the family, neighborhood, church, and even generally in their occupations; the American state government makes its only effort toward acculturation within the schools, handicapped by the fact that the Spanish-speaking community regards segregation for language training as a form of discrimination.

Nothing, it seems, could differ more from the typical case of American

[1] See Uriel Weinreich, *Languages in Contact,* New York, 1953, and "Linguistic Convergence in Immigrant America," *Georgetown University Monograph Series on Language and Linguistics* No. 7 (1954), 40–49, where further literature is cited (p. 43).

[2] The terms are taken from Einar Haugen, *Bilingualism in the Americas: A Bibliography and Research Guide* (*Publication of the American Dialect Society,* No. 26), 1956, pp. 19–32.

572   immigrant bilingualism. And yet it turns out that the linguistic effects of this contact are the familiar ones. A recent study[3] showed that the characteristic deviations of the San Antonio dialect from other forms of American English *cannot* be attributed to Spanish influence. In fact, it even appeared that such Spanish loan words as are current in San Antonio English are not local borrowings from Spanish, but entered the language by other routes. In other words, despite the presence of extensive bilingualism and despite sociocultural conditions which are, on the surface, more favorable to the foreign group than in immigrant-English contacts, no evidence for substratum formation could be found. A possible explanation for this "paradox" is discussed on page 581.

In this study, seven native speakers of English, termed *Anglos* according to local usage, and seven native speakers of Spanish, termed *Latins* for this investigation, were interviewed in San Antonio. The informants were all permanent residents of San Antonio of the second generation, varying in age, education, occupation and economic status. The seven Anglo informants spoke very little if any Spanish, but the seven Latin informants all spoke English with varying degrees of skill although language ability had not been made a requirement for their selection.

The seven Latin informants were further classified as either *bilingual* or *unilingual* in English. Four were sufficiently skilled to be called Latin *bilinguals;* they were *L6* and *L7*, two young male college students; *L1*, female, 74, a retired seamstress; and *L4*, female, a middle-aged housewife who had often worked as a saleslady. The other three informants: *L2*, female, 53, a midwife; *L3*, male 46, a gardener; and *L5*, female, 41, an actress—were classified as *unilinguals* since they had an intensification of the "errors" caused by conflicts between the structures of Spanish and English. In addition, the unilingual informants were reluctant to speak English although they could read and understand it. Their English was markedly passive in contrast to the ease with which the bilingual speakers expressed themselves in their second language.

The workbook used in this dialect survey was a revised version by Dr. E. Bagby Atwood, of the University of Texas, of the workbook used in the Eastern Survey.[4] (Dr. Atwood is conducting a linguistic survey of Texas and the surrounding areas of the Southwest.) All interviews were taped to minimize transcription errors, and supplementary reading material was recorded as an additional check on formal and informal levels of speech.

[3] The author's unpublished doctoral dissertation, "A Dialect Study of San Antonio, Texas: A Bilingual Community," University of Texas, 1957; Microfilm Publication No. 25, 178.

[4] Hans Kurath and Bernard Bloch, *The Linguistic Atlas of New England,* 3 vols., 6 parts, Providence, 1939–1943.

A COMPARISON OF THE PHONOLOGICAL STRUCTURES OF ANGLO AND LATIN ENGLISH

Anglo English Phonology

In interpreting the features of the speech of any region of the inland United States, dialect geographers rely on the work done in the East by Hans Kurath and other linguists.[5] By correlating data on settlement in the East with facts of local settlement history, one can chart the influence of various cultural streams in a new community. Accurate information of Texas migration according to counties for the years 1865–1880 is provided in a study by Homer Lee Kerr.[6] The following table shows the sources of immigrant families arriving in Bexar County (where San Antonio is located) during those years:

Population Arrivals[7] (415 families)	Percentage
Arkansas	2.9
Alabama	1.9
Mississippi	3.4
Tennessee	2.2
Missouri	4.6
Louisiana	8.9
Georgia	1.4
Illinois	2.2
Kentucky	1.0
Kansas	2.4
Indiana	1.7
South Carolina	1.2
Virginia	1.7
North Carolina	.2
Mexico	28.4
Germany	8.4
Scattering	27.0

As outlined in Kurath's *Word Geography,* there are three large dialect

---

[5] In addition to the *Linguistic Atlas,* see Hans Kurath and Bernard Bloch and others, *Handbook of the Linguistic Geography of New England,* Providence, 1939–1943; and Kurath, *A Word Geography of the Eastern United States,* Ann Arbor, 1949.

[6] "Migration into Texas, 1865–1880," unpublished University of Texas Dissertation, 1953.

[7] *Ibid.,* pp. 93–94. The order of states expresses their rank as contributors of immigrants for the entire state; Arkansas ranks first because it contributed the most families during 1865–1880 throughout Texas.

574   areas in the East: Northern, Midland and Southern—with sub-dialects within each large area. Immigrants to Bexar County came predominantly from either the Midland or the Southern dialect divisions. Excluding the foreign immigrant groups, we find that 44 percent of the families emigrated from Louisiana, Alabama, Mississippi, and Georgia. These states are part of the Southern dialect area; the Southern slave culture and economy prevail in those regions. The inland states, Arkansas, Tennessee, Missouri, Illinois, Kentucky, Indiana, and Kansas, where Midland, and the sub-dialect, South Midland, prevail, contributed 47 percent of the Anglo settlers. (Emigrants from Virginia, North Carolina, and South Carolina have been purposely excluded since the eastern half of each state is within the Southern dialect area while the western half is South Midland.)

Since Midland and South Midland dialect speakers were slightly in the majority in Bexar County during the critical settlement years, it might be expected that their speech type would predominate in San Antonio. An alternate possibility, since the two groups were so nearly equal numerically, would be the blending or leveling of distinctive features in each dialect, producing a new dialect type. But neither of these possibilities was realized. Southern pronunciation features predominate in the speech of all the older San Antonio informants, indicating that the Southern dialect enjoyed a superior, or "prestige," status in San Antonio during the early settlement years. The further fact that these Southern features are also regular in the speech of the young, well-educated informants indicates that the South still enjoys the same prestige position at the present time.[8]

Pronunciation features believed to be Southern[9] which were characteristic of Anglo speech in San Antonio are the following:

a) DIPHTHONGAL /ɔ/.[10] The phones [ɔʷ] and [ɔº][11] occur in the speech of all informants in such words as *saw, fog,* and *brought.* How-

---

[8] Many of the socially prominent families of San Antonio send their children to Virginia to finishing school. Politically, Texas conforms to the rest of the "solid Democratic South," at least on the state and local levels.

[9] The actual extent of these features in the Gulf States area has not as yet been completely established. After the publication of Hans Kurath and Raven McDavid's forthcoming book on pronunciation, *and* after fuller observations have been made in the Gulf States, the distribution of these features will no doubt be demonstrated more clearly.

[10] The phonetic transcription used is in general conformity with that applied to the East. However, whenever possible, the symbols used will be equated with the Trager–Smith system: George L. Trager and Henry Lee Smith, *An Outline of English Structure* (*Studies in Linguistics,* Occasional Papers, No. 3), Norman, Oklahoma, 1951.

[11] Trager–Smith /ɔw/.

ever, this diphthongization seems a more regular feature of the speech of the older informants.

b) MONOPHTHONGAL /a/.[12] This phoneme occurs as a single vowel in *five, night*, in place of the diphthong /aɪ/[13] in the speech of all Anglo informants, but is most regular in the speech of the younger well-educated informants.

c) LOSS OF RETROFLEXION. The three older informants, including one Negro, had "loss" of /r/ after vowels regularly. Those of middle age have such loss of retroflexion half the time or less. At the other end of the scale were the two young educated informants who never showed such loss. Their speech was characterized by full retroflexion. (This is the one Midland feature which seems to be gaining in influence.)

d) PALATALIZATION IN *Tuesday, new*. This feature is of regular occurrence in the speech of all the Anglo informants.

e) /ɪ/[14] IN CERTAIN UNSTRESSED SYLLABLES. /ɪ/ in the form of [ɨ] is of regular occurrence in the speech of all Anglo informants in the weakly stressed syllables of *haunted, fitted, Dallas*, and *Texas*.

Several pronunciation features of irregular or undetermined extent in the South and the South Midland are also regular in San Antonio speech:

f) /æu/[15] INSTEAD OF THE LOW CENTRAL DIPHTHONG /ɑu/[16] IN *cow, house*, etc. This feature is common in the speech of all informants. It alternates with the lower phone [aʊ] in the speech of *A1* and *A5*.

g) /ɔr/~/or/ DISTINCTION. The distinction between *horse, forty*, and *morning* where /ɔr/ occurs, and *hoarse, fourteen*, and *mourning* where /or/ occurs, is apparently maintained in the speech of all the informants.

h) LOSS OF /ɪ/~/ɛ/[17] DISTINCTION BEFORE /n/ AND /m/. In *pin* and *pen*, this distinction is completely lost for at least four informants: *N* (an elderly Negro), *A1, A4*, and *A6*, and seems partially lost for the others.

Some of the individual words which show variant pronunciations in different regions of the East are:

[12] This vowel, a low front sound, is not provided for by Trager–Smith, and it was the subject of much discussion at the Linguistics Conference at the University of Texas in 1956. Professor J. H. Sledd, now at the University of California at Berkeley, presented contrasts in his particular Southern dialect which necessitated the addition of a tenth vowel.

[13] Trager–Smith /ay/.

[14] Trager–Smith /i/.

[15] Trager–Smith /æw/.

[16] Trager–Smith /aw/.

[17] Trager-Smith /e/.

576   *i*) *Grease* (verb) and *greasy* (adjective). These words have /s/ in the North and /z/ in most of the Midland and the entire South. Among the San Antonian informants there was general conformity to Southern usage. /z/ occurred in *grease* and *greasy*. (However, /s/ occurred in *grease job* [*A1, A4*]. This item was not attested by the other informants.)[18]

     j) *Roots*. /ʊ/[19] occurs in this word throughout the North; /u/[20] is general in the South. In San Antonio all the Anglo informants had /u/ in this word.

     k) *Hog, frog, fog*. The phoneme /ɑ/ occurred in a slightly back, rounded phone [ɒ] for all informants except *A5*. This is a Southern prestige pronunciation which occurs in the Coastal South and Inland North.

Latin English Phonology

     In preparation for the study of bilingual Latin speech, samples of the Spanish dialect of each Latin informant were recorded. These records were compared with those of Spanish students who had come to study at the University of Texas from various parts of Mexico and the rest of the Spanish-speaking world. It was found that the Spanish of the San Antonio Latin informants conformed to that of Mexican Spanish in its segmental phonemes, so the structure of Mexican Spanish will be used for comparative purposes in the discussion that follows.[21]

     Studies of immigration into Texas from Mexico[22] readily justify such an analysis. Most of the influx of Mexicans entered the area after the passage of the Reclamation Act in 1902. This law provided Federal funds for the construction of large-scale irrigation and reclamation projects. In 1900 Texas had only 71,062 Mexican immigrants; in 1930 there were 683,681. The immigration since then has increased even more rapidly.[23]

[18] E. Bagby Atwood, "*Grease and Greasy:* A Study of Geographical Variation," *University of Texas Studies in English* XXIX (1950), 249–259.

[19] Trager–Smith /u/.

[20] Trager–Smith /uw/.

[21] Harold V. King, "Outline of Mexican Spanish Phonology," *Studies in Linguistics* X (1952), pp. 51–62.

[22] See Carey McWilliams, *North from Mexico,* New York, 1949; Charles Marden, *Minorities in American Society,* New York, 1952; and Manuel Gamio, *Mexican Immigration to the United States,* Chicago, 1930.

[23] Articles by officials of the Mexican government printed in *La Prensa,* the Spanish-language newspaper of San Antonio, during the years 1956–1957, expressed concern over the exodus of the Mexican laboring and farming populations.

The Latin informants interviewed for this survey were the second-generation products of the migration which occurred at the turn of the century.
A comparison between Anglo and Latin English follows.

a) DIPHTHONGAL /ɔ/. This did not occur in either bilingual or
unilingual Latin English. The Spanish phones [o] and [o·] occurred
commonly in unilingual speech. [ɔ] was the phone for some of the
bilingual Latins.

b) MONOPHTHONGAL /a/. Only one bilingual speaker, *L6*, had the
phone [a·] characteristic of all the Anglo informants' English. Common
phones for the others were [ɑɪ] or [ɑ+y]. The balanced diphthong [ɑi]
occurs in Spanish.

c) LOSS OF RETROFLEXION. The unilinguals showed interference with
Spanish, transferring the strongly trilled /r̄/ or the single flap /r/.
(These are separate phonemes in Spanish.) The bilingual informants,
L6 and *L7*, produced the full retroflexion of the younger Anglo informants, their speech models. *L4* usually transferred the Spanish phones
into English. Only the 74-year-old seamstress, *L1*, occasionally had a
slight loss of retroflexion. At an earlier period, when her English speech
habits were formed, loss of retroflexion was apparently more common
in San Antonio English.

d) PALATALIZATION IN *Tuesday, new*. This feature occurred only in
the speech of *L6*.

e) /ɪ/ IN CERTAIN UNSTRESSED SYLLABLES. This feature occurs only
in the speech of *L6* and *L7*. Since /ɪ/ and /ə/ do not occur as phonemes
in Spanish, neither sound, common in unstressed syllables in various
dialects of American English, occurred in the speech of the unilingual
Latins. The phone they used was [i], similar to /i/ in English structure.

f) /æʊ/ IN *cow, house,* etc. This sequence, [æʊ], did not occur at all
in Latin English. [aʊ] did occur in the speech of the two younger bilinguals. All the other informants used [ɑʊ], the low central phone
similar to the Spanish balanced diphthong as in *baúl*. [æ] does not occur
either as a phoneme or allophone in Mexican Spanish.

g) /ɔr/~/or/ DISTINCTION. Since [ɔ] and [o] occur as allophones of
/o/ in Mexican Spanish, it is not surprising that the phonemes /ɔ/, /o/,
occurring in contrast in *horse : hoarse* in most Anglo speech, did not
do so in the English of any of the Latin informants. The contrast is
not of high frequency in English.

h) LOSS OF /ɪ/~/ɛ/ BEFORE THE NASALS. This loss of contrast occurred several times in the speech of *L6, L7* and *L4*, three of the bilinguals. The unilinguals had difficulty achieving /ɪ/~/ɛ/~/i/ contrasts
at all times, so no pertinent conclusion can be made from the random
occurrences of [ɪ] or [ɛ] before nasals in their speech.

578   *i) Grease* AND *greasy.* All the Latin informants except *L4* and *L6* used /s/ instead of /z/ in these words. This is the pattern for /s/ in Mexican Spanish. (See below for further discussion of this feature.)

j) Roots—/ʊ/ OR /u/? Mexican Spanish has only one high back vowel phoneme /u/ which is similar to English /u/. Thus Spanish structure coincides here with the regional variant typical of San Antonio English. All Latin informants used [u] in *roots,* but the unilinguals also used [u] in such words as *good, bull,* and *wool,* illustrating the force of the Spanish pattern in their speech.

k) Hog, frog, fog. These words occurred with the phones [o], [oᵘ], or [oˑ] in unilingual speech, and in the speech of bilinguals, *L1* and *L4.* [ɔˑ] occurred in *fog* for the bilinguals *L6* and *L7.*

Although other details might have been included to give a more complete description, this brief comparison illustrates the trend of the whole corpus. Seldom did the Latin unilinguals conform to the particular features of regional speech. When they did, a feature of their first language, Spanish, was a contributing factor. On the other hand, they experienced difficulty mastering vowel contrasts such as /ɪ/~/i/; /ʊ/~/u/; and in learning new phonemes such as /æ/ and /ə/. Consonant phonemes such as /š/, /č/ and /ǰ/ caused considerable difficulty; voiced consonants were frequently devoiced before juncture.

Such errors did not occur in the speech of the bilingual Latins. The most difficult pattern for them (and also for the unilinguals) was the distribution of /s/ and /z/ in English. Even in the English speech of *L6,* the most persistent feature of "accent" was the occurrence of [s] or [z̦] (fortis, weakly voiced), in final position where [z] (lenis, voiced) always occurred in Anglo English.[24]

The only suprasegmental feature of Anglo English that could be analyzed from the collected materials was that of stress—specifically, the compound-noun superfix which was either /´ + ˆ/ or /´ + ` /. The first pattern, with a strong secondary stress on the form which follows the plus juncture, seems to be particularly characteristic of Texas speech. Thus: *ápple + trêe* or *ápple + trèe.* The bilingual Latins generally achieved the English pattern although a strong, primary stress often occurred both before and after / + /: *ápple + trée.* However, the unilingual Latins trans-

---

[24] /z/ is not a phoneme in Spanish. It occurs only as [z], an allophone of /s/ when a voiced consonant follows without intervening / + / juncture. Thus the phrase *twice better,* an aberrant form in unilingual Latin English, was [twɑɪzbɛɾɚ], but *twice* before juncture occurred as [twɑɪs]. The fact that /s/ in Spanish and /s/~/z/ in English have morphemic status as plural suffixes and as members of verb paradigms may help explain the persistence of this feature of interference in bilingual English.

ferred the stress pattern characteristic of the adjective-noun phrase in
Spanish: *àpple trée, glòw-wórm* or *hàngóver.*[25]

In sum, the foregoing evidence shows that regional pronunciation variants in San Antonio English cannot be explained as features occurring in
Latin bilingual speech and transmitted through them into the speech of
the Anglo community. The situation is quite the reverse. San Antonio
regional English is the model toward which the Latin bilinguals strive;
and as they increase in skill, they eliminate points of interference with
their first language and come closer to the speech of the Anglo community.

GRAMMAR AND LEXICON OF ANGLO AND LATIN ENGLISH IN SAN ANTONIO

Only a few items of morphology such as variant verb forms
and pronoun usage are treated in the workbook. But even this limited
corpus revealed the wide gap between Anglo and Latin English. While
standard forms of written English were known by all but the oldest uneducated Anglo informants, *A1* and *A4*, standard regional variants were
still preferred.[26]

But the Latin usage ranged from that of *L2,* who used present tense
verbs almost entirely: "I sit yesterday," to a considerable proficiency with
standard written forms by *L6* and *L7.* These educated bilinguals were
very careful to conform to standard usage, and frequently commented on
the fact that they changed a given form either because a certain teacher
preferred another, or because another form occurred in standard textbooks. So the Latin bilinguals tended to deviate from Anglo regional
speech. For example, *ought to/ought not to* is a Southern pattern while in
the North the negative is either *hadn't ought to,* or the substitute form
should not.[27] Most of the Anglos used *ought not to;* all Latin informants
except *L6* and *L2* used *should not. L6* used *hadn't ought to* and *L2* used the
aberrant form *don't suppose to do it.*

---

[25] The English stress contrast between *whîte hóuse* and *White Hòuse* cannot be similarly sig-
naled in Spanish, so this pattern was a difficult one.

[26] All Anglo informants used *dived* (past tense form of *dive*). This is the form used in the Mid-
land and South. Yet bilingual *L6* used *dove,* apparently unaware that it is a Northern form.
For analysis of verb forms in the East, consult E. Bagby Atwood, *A Survey of Verb Forms in the
Eastern U.S.,* Ann Arbor, 1953.

[27] See Atwood, *Verb Forms,* p. 33.

580   The same separation between the linguistic behavior of the two groups occurred on the lexical level. The bilingual Latins either scrupulously avoided Spanish words, even those commonly used by the Anglos,[28] or they stipulated that since the words were Spanish, they would use one pronunciation when speaking to Anglos and another when speaking to Latins.[29]

On the other hand, the younger Anglo informants were usually unaware of the fact that such words as *canyon* and *lariat* were Spanish since they had been completely assimilated as had the numerous place names of the area; and *all* Spanish ranching and cattle-raising terms suffered the same fate as other rural words in this area. They were generally known only by the informants over seventy, and were gradually dying out in San Antonio speech. No evidence was obtained in the workbook materials to show that any recent borrowings had been made from Spanish by the Anglo informants.

Regional vocabulary typical of Anglo speech, however, was generally unknown to even the bilingual Latin informants because old dialect words, brought by the pioneers and cherished as an intimate reflection of Southern tradition and regional culture, were transmitted orally within the Anglo community from parent to child, seldom appearing in standard dictionaries. Thus the Latins, who learned their English either in school or at work, apparently never heard such terms. *Light bread* (white bread), *clabber* (soured, thickened milk), and *corn shucks* were unknown to the Latin informants. Instead a Northern variant which was more common in print might be familiar to them. For example, the Latin bilinguals used the terms *corn husk* and *wish bone* rather than *corn shuck* and *pulley bone*, common in the lexicon of the Anglo informants. Other terms unfamiliar to the Latins, yet typical of the Anglo speech, were *Christmas Gift!* (a greeting on Christmas morning), *snap beans* (in other regions, *green beans* or *string beans*), and *French harp* (*harmonica*).

Thus there is no evidence that Latin bilinguals have been a source for the transmission of Spanish words into English. In fact, they seemed to be more or less isolated from the Anglo speech community since they did not know the local vocabulary, and were hardly in a position to exert any influence upon regional English.

---

[28] This was characteristic behavior for the unilinguals and two of the bilinguals, *L3* and *L4*. They rejected such words as: *corral, lariat, morral, remuda, bronco, arroyo, canyon, burro, plaze, frijoles, partera, llano*, all of which are known and used by the oldest Anglo informants, indicating the fact that they were early borrowings. Even *melon* and *gallery* were rejected because of similar forms in Spanish although they probably did not come into English from that language.

[29] This pattern was characteristic of the English of *L6* and *L7*. For example, *corral*: English [kərǽl], Spanish [koɾál].

EVALUATION OF LINGUISTIC FINDINGS 581

The linguistic evidence reveals that English in San Antonio has not been affected by Spanish in phonology, morphology or syntax; and although a number of Spanish words are found in the speech of the oldest informants, they are words of extensive spread throughout the Southwest, so that we find no evidence that Spanish contact in San Antonio is even responsible for additions to the lexicon of San Antonio English.

However, the presence of Spanish word borrowings which are still used by the oldest informants seems to indicate that at an earlier time there was a different bilingual situation in the area. Apparently in the earlier period, the Spanish-speaking population of San Antonio enjoyed a somewhat equal status with the Anglo settlers. Historical evidence of frequent intermarriage between the Spanish and "Yankee" colonists, cooperation in fighting for freedom from Mexico, transmission of superior Spanish knowledge of mining and ranching to settlers from the United States, indicates that in the early days Spanish settlers had prestige status. At that time, apparently Spanish was a "colonial" language, although at present it has been demoted to "immigrant" status.

The dialect survey supports the hypothesis that there have been two separate stages of bilingual contact in San Antonio, since the Anglo informants distinguished two groups of Spanish-speaking San Antonians. The first group seems to be descended from the "colonial" culture; and it enjoys preferential treatment by the Anglos, who explained that these people were "white-skinned," "more dignified," "on a higher economic level," or "descendants of the original Canary Islanders." People who identified themselves with this group refused to participate as Spanish-speaking informants for the survey, explaining that they didn't speak Spanish any more. It is true that at least the younger members of the group speak English as a first language, and all of them share the prejudiced attitude of the Anglo community toward the second group of Spanish-speaking immigrants.

This group, which composes almost 50 percent of the population of San Antonio, is composed of the Mexican farmers and laborers who began to enter Texas in the early 1900's. Although they speak the same language as the "colonial" Spanish group, in all else—culture, education, economic status—they were very different. The Anglo informants expressed their prejudice toward this second group (which is so highly valued as cheap labor) by such terms as: "uneducated," "dark-skinned," "undignified," "bad Mexicans," "greasers," "wetbacks," "Tex-Mex," "pilaus," "brownies," "pepper bellies," "bean bandits," and "peons." These derogatory nicknames illustrate the low prestige status of this second group from which the Latin informants were second-generation descendants.

582   The fact that we are dealing with the second stage of a language contact clarifies the apparently paradoxical situation. At present the sociocultural conditions are not favorable to linguistic borrowing from Spanish to English because Spanish now has "immigrant" status comparable to that of foreign languages in other immigrant communities in the United States.

A Phonological and Morphological Study of the Speech of the Negro of Memphis, Tennessee

Juanita V. Williamson

Few systematic studies of the speech of the Negro have been made. Professor Williamson's study of the speech of the Negro of Memphis, Tennessee, is one of these. For her study she used the short worksheets of the Linguistic Atlas. Twenty-four informants ranging in age from twenty-seven to eighty-four were interviewed. They were classified as Type I, those with less than an eighth-grade education; Type II, those with a high-school education; Type III, those with a college education. They were further classified as Type A, above sixty-five years old; Type B, between forty-five and sixty-five; and Type C, less than forty-five. Professor Williamson shows that on the phonological level the distinguishing features of the speech of the Negro of Memphis are to be found primarily on the subphonemic

584   level and in the incidence of the phonemes. The
phonemic system does not differ greatly from other
varieties found in the South. On the morphological level
there are differences between the speech of the better-
educated and the less well educated. Chapter VI,
"Morphology," is reprinted here.

MORPHOLOGY

The short work sheets of the Linguistic Atlas of the United
States and Canada, used in this investigation, do not provide material for
a complete morphological description. Their primary purpose is to provide a body of material for a description of the pronunciation of the informant and "selected features of his vocabulary and grammar."[1] For
only a few nouns are both the singular and plural forms included. No
possessive forms are included. A number of the pronouns occur in the
materials, as do a number of the verbs. All forms of a given verb, however,
are not included. The following description, therefore, is limited to comments on the noun, the pronoun, and the verb.

The plural of nouns is formed, generally, as it is in American cultivated
speech. The /-ɪz/ allomorph is added to bases which end in /s, š, č, z, ž, ǰ/,
as in *ashes, dishes.* The /-z/ allomorph is added to bases which end in a
vowel or a voiced consonant, except /z, ž, ǰ/, as in *boys, hogs, bristles.* The
/-s/ allomorph is added to bases which end in a voiceless consonant, except /s, š, č/, as in *parents, hoops, posts.* For a limited number of nouns the
final consonant of the base may or may not be changed before the plural
morpheme is added, as in *hoofs, troughs, moths.*

One noun, *ox,* forms its plural by adding /-ən/. Another group form
the plural by changing the vowel of the base, as in *teeth.* For another
group the singular and plural forms are identical, as in *sheep.*

Nouns whose singular forms end in /-st/ or /-sp/, as in *post, wasp,*
show some variation in the formation of the plural, especially in the
speech of type I and II informants. Informants who do not have a final
/t/ in *post,* form the plural by lengthening the final /s/ of the base form,
[posˑ], /poss/, the final /s/ being the plural allomorph /-s/; by adding
/-ɪz/; or by adding the final /t/. Informants 1-C II, 6-C I have the plural
/posˑ/; 18-B I, /posɪz/; 10-B II, 20-A II, /post/. Five, four of whom are

From *Publication of the American Dialect Society,* No. 50 (November, 1968) 32–45. Reprinted
with the permission of the American Dialect Society and the University of Alabama Press.
[1] Hans Kurath, *Handbook,* p. 48.

type I, add /-ɪz/ to the base form, /postɪz/. Two, 8-C III, 11-B I, who have the singular form /post/, have the plural form /poss/. For six, five type II and one type I, the plural form has the same shape as the singular, /post/. Five, four of whom are type III, have the plural /posts/.

For *wasp*, the plural of which is not included in the work sheets, but which was given by eight informants, the situation is approximately the same. Two informants, 3-C I, 9-C II, who have the singular /wɔs/, add the /-ɪz/ allomorph, /wɔsɪz/. 22-A I has /wɔss/. Three, 7-C III, 11-B I, 15-B II, have /wɔsps/. For two, 10-B II, 19-B II, the singular and plural forms have the same shape, /wɔs, wɔsp/.

The plural of *hoof* is usually /hʊfs/. Eighteen of the twenty informants for whom responses were recorded have this form. Two, 7-C III, 12-C III, have /hʊvz/.

The plural of *trough* is usually /trɔfs/. Eighteen of the twenty-two informants for whom responses were recorded have this form. Four, 4-C II, 12-B III, 19-B II, 20-A II, have /trɔvz/.

The plural of *moth* is usually /mɔθs/. Fifteen of the twenty-four informants have this form. Nine, four young, four middle-aged and one older, have /mɔðz/.

For all of the informants the plural of *house* is /haʊzɪz/.

For all of the informants the plural of *tooth* is /tiθ/.

For *ox,* nine of the fourteen informants for whom responses were recorded have the plural form /ɑksən/. Five, all type I, form the plural differently. Informant 22-A I has the plural /ɑksɪz/. 3-C I has /ɑksənz/. Three, 5-C I, 17-B I, 24-A I, have /ɑks/.

The term *sheep* does not occur in the work sheets, but it was given by five informants for *ram.* Four, 4-C II, 9-C II, 16-B I, 19-B II, have the plural /šip/. One, 5-C I, has /šips/.

The informants generally use the pronoun forms current in cultivated speech: *I, me, mine; you, yours; we, us, ours; he, him, his; she, her, hers; they, them, theirs.* The plural form *you-all* alternates with the plural *you.* Most of the informants seem to use the two plural forms interchangeably. Informant 21-A III has only the *you* plural.

Informant 18-C I has the form /maɪnz/ for *mine.*

Themselves usually occurs as /ðɪmsɛlvz/. Two type I informants, however, 6-C I, 17-B I, have /ðesɛlvz/.

The forms *ourn, hisn, hern, yourn, theirn* do not occur in the materials.

Their are four inflected forms of the verb, the third person singular present tense, the past tense, the past participle and the present participle.

The third singular is generally formed as it is in cultivated speech. The /-ɪz/ allomorph of the third singular morpheme is added to bases which end in /s, š, č, z, ž, ǰ/, as in *rinses.* The /-z/ allomorph is added to bases which end in a vowel or a voiced consonant, except /z, ž, ǰ/, as in *favors.*

586   The /-s/ allomorph is added to bases which end in a voiceless consonant, except /s, š, č/, as in *makes, costs.*

Some variation occurs frequently in the speech of the type I informants, less frequently in that of type II. For the third singular of *cost,* five informants, four type I, one type II, have /kɔs/. Nine, three type I, five type II, one type III, 21-A III, have /kɔst/. One, 15-B II, has /kɔstɪz/. Six, two type I, three type II, and one type III, 14-B III, have /kɔss/. Three type III, 7-C III, 8-C III, 12-B III, have /kɔsts/.

For the third singular of *rinse,* sixteen, five type I, nine type II, two type III, have the uninflected form, /rɪnts/. Eight, four type I, one type II, three type III, have /rɪntsɪz/.

Four type I informants, 5-C I, 6-C I, 18-B I, 22-A I, frequently use the uninflected form for the third singular. The inflected form is often used for the first and second person form, singular and plural. Such forms as *I wants, I carries, she do, you needs, we has* occur frequently in their recorded free conversation.

The past tense is usually formed by adding one of the allomorphs /-ɪd, -d, -t/ to the base form of the verb or by changing the vowel of the base form. The allomorph /-ɪd/ is added to bases which end in /t/ or /d/, as in *fitted, sweated.*[2] The allomorph /-d/ is added to bases which end in a vowel or a voiced consonant, except /d/, as in *joined, raised.* The allomorph /-t/ is added to bases which end in a voiceless consonant, except /t/, as in *waked.*

Not all of the informants add /-ɪd/ to *fit* and *sweat* to form the past tense. For *fit* fourteen have the uninflected form, /fɪt/. Nine, three type I, four type II, one type III, have /fɪtɪd/. One, 1-C II, has both forms.

For the past tense of *sweat*[3] four of the ten informants for whom responses were recorded have the uninflected form, /swɛt/. Six have /swɛtɪd/.

The past tense of the following verbs, included in the work sheets, is formed in cultivated speech by changing the vowel of the base form: *throw, grow, drink, shrink, swim, drive, freeze, rise, see, eat, catch, fight, teach, run, sit, take.*

The type III informants usually have the forms used in cultivated speech. Type I informants frequently, and type II informants less frequently have other forms. In the following discussion the forms which differ from those which are used in cultivated speech are commented on.

[2] Very few verbs which form the past tense by adding /-ɪd(-ed), -d, -t/ to the base form are included in the work sheets. Most of the verbs included form the past tense by changing the vowel of the base form.

[3] Several informants have another term. They felt that *sweat* was not proper and should not be used.

For the past tense of *throw* two of the eight type I informants for whom responses were recorded, 3-C I, 22-A I, have /θrod/.

For the past tense of *grow* five of the eight type I informants,[4] 5-C I, 6-C I, 17-B I, 22-A I, 24-A I, have /grod/. One type II, 4-C II, also has this form. 18-B I has /gron/.

For the past tense of *drink* two of the eight type I informants, 1-C I, 3-C I, have /drɪŋkt/. One type I, 1-C I, has /dræŋkt/.

For the past tense of *shrink* three of the seven type 1, 3-C I, 5-C I, 24-A I, and three of the six type II informants, 1-C II, 10-B II, 15-B II, have /šrɪŋkt/. Five, two type I, 11-B I, 16-B I, and three type II, 9-C II, 19-B II, 23-A II, have /šrʌŋk/. Two type I informants, 17-B I, 18-B I, have /šrɪŋk/.

For the past tense of *swim* three of the eight type I informants, 5-C I, 6-C I, 22-A I, and three of the ten type II, 4-C II, 13-B II, 20-A II, have /swɪmd/. 5-C I has /swɪm/.

For the past tense of *drive* one of the seven type I informants, 3-C I, has /drovd/.

For the past tense of *freeze* one of the nine type I informants, 24-A I, has /frozən/.

For the past tense of *rise* one of the nine type I informants, 22-A I, has /rɪz/.

For the past tense of *see* one of the nine type I informants, 3-C I, has /sin/ and /sɔ/. 6-C I has /sɔ/, /sin/, and /sid/.

For the past tense of *eat,* one of the eight type I informants, 24-A I, and one of the ten type II, 4-C II, have /it/. 22-A has /ɛt/.

For the past tense of *run* one of the seven type I informants, 18-B I, has /rʌn/.

For the past tense of *sit* one of the six type I informants, 5-C I, has /sɑt/. 6-C I has /sɛt/.

For the past tense of *take* four of the nine type I informants, 3-C I, 6-C I, 22-A I, 24-A I, have /tekən/.

For the past tense of *catch, fight, teach* all of the informants have the forms used in cultivated speech, /kɔt, fɔt, tɔt/.

Each of the verbs *dream, kneel, dive, wake* has two past tense forms which are used in cultivated speech, /drimd, drɪmpt; nild, nɛlt; daɪvd, dov; wekt, wok/. A majority of the informants have the forms /drimd, nild, daɪvd, wekt/.

For the past tense of *dream* nineteen of the twenty-two informants

---

[4] The total number of informants of any type for whom responses were recorded are given in this way. There are nine type I informants, ten type II, five type III. Not always could a desired term be elicited from an informant for several reasons. Sometimes he used other terms. Sometimes he was unsure of the "right" term and would not respond.

588   have /drimd/. Two of the ten type II informants, 14-B II, 18-B II, have /drimpt/. 4-C II has /drim/.

For the past tense of *kneel* seven of the twenty informants, five of whom are type II, two, type III, have /nɛlt/.

For the past tense of *dive,* twenty-one of the twenty-three informants have /daɪvd/. 10-B II and 14-B III have /dov/.

For the past tense of *wake* eighteen of the twenty-two informants have /wok/. Three, 12-B III, 13-B II, 21-A III, have /wekt/. 5-C I has both forms.

For a large number of verbs the past participle form is identical with that of the past tense. The past participles of a small number are formed by changing the vowel of the base, by adding /-n, -ən/ to the base or by changing the vowel and adding /-n, -ən/.

For the past participles of *climb* and *raise,* all of the informants have /klaɪmd, rezd/. For the past participle of *drown* two of the nine type I informants, 16-B I, 22-A I, and two of the ten type II, 1-C II, 2-C II, have /draʊndɪd/. 9-C II has the uninflected form /draʊn/.

The past participles of the following verbs, included in the work sheets, are formed by changing the vowel of the base, by adding /-n, -ən/ or by doing both: *grow, drink, bite, drive, ride, write, tear, wear, take.* Type III informants usually have the forms used in cultivated speech. Type I informants, frequently, and type II less frequently, have other forms. In the following discussion only forms differing from those used in cultivated speech are commented on.

For the past participle of *grow* one of the nine type I informants, 18-B I, has both /gro/ and /gron/.

For the past participle of *drink* three of the nine type I informants, 3-C I, 18-B I, 22-A I, and one of the nine type II informants, 1-C II, have /drɪŋkt/. Two type I, 5-C I, 6-C I, have /dræŋkt/. One type I, 11-B I, three type II, 2-C II, 9-C II, 20-A II, and two of the five type III, 14-B III, 21-A III, have /dræŋk/. One type I, 18-B I, has /drɪŋk/.

For the past participle of *bite* four of the nine type I informants, 5-C I, 6-C I, 22-A I, 24-A I, and one of the ten type II informants, 1-C II, have /bɪt/. 20-B II has both /bɪt/ and /bɪtən/.

For the past participle of *drive* four of the eight type I informants, 6-C I, 11-B I, 18-B I, 24-A I, have /drov/. 22-A I had /drɪv/.

For the past participle of *ride* five of the nine type I informants, 5-C I, 16-B I, 17-B I, 18-B I, 24-A I, and two of the type II, 2-C II, 9-C II, have /rod/. One type I, 11-B I, has both /rod/ and /rɪdən/. One type I, 22-A I, has /rɪd/. 6-C has /rɪd/ and /rod/.

For the past participle of *write* two of the nine type I informants, 17-B I, 24-A I, and one of the ten type II, 4-C II, have /rot/. 1-C II has both /rot/ and /rɪtən/.

For the past participle of *tear* two of the nine type I informants, 6-C I, 17-B I, and one of the nine type II, 13-B II, have /to/ or /tɔə̣/.

For the past participle of *wear* one of the seven type I informants, 6-C I, has /wo/.

For the past participle of *take* two of the nine type I informants, 16-B I, 18-B I, and three of the type II, 4-C II, 13-B II, 19-B II, have /tʊk/.

Three type I informants use *done* with the past participle instead of *have*. 6-C I has *done* in the phrase, *they done fought,* 5-C I in *you done got back,* and 18-B I in *I done heard.*

The present participle suffix *-ing* for most of the informants has only one allomorph, /-ɪn/. For the majority of the type III informants it has two allomorphs, /-ɪŋ, -ɪn/. /-ɪŋ/ occurs in the speech of informants 7-C III, 12-B III, 21-A III in careful pronunciation, and when words are pronounced in isolation, /sɪŋɪŋ, læfɪŋ/. In context, in phrases, as in *Am I going to get some,* /-ɪŋ~-ɪn/ in *going.* Type I and II informants seldom have /-ɪŋ/ here.

It is of interest to compare the verb forms discussed in this study with those included in *A Survey of Verb Forms in the Eastern United States,* by E. Bagby Atwood.[5] Atwood examined the approximately 1,400 field records of the Linguistic Atlas. Thirty-three of the informants in the South Atlantic States were Negroes. Most were older persons; in Virginia, for example, they were more than seventy years old. Of the twelve interviewed by Raven I. McDavid, Jr., in Georgia, North Carolina, and South Carolina, three were classed as educated. The twenty-one interviewed by Guy S. Loman were all classed as illiterate or uneducated. Atwood did not attempt to include the usage of Negro informants in the main body of his discussion, although he often commented on it.[6] The comments do not include enough material for a comparison. For the white informants he uses the classification of the Linguistic Atlas. The classification used in this study is also based on that classification. It is possible, therefore, to compare his findings on the verb forms used by white informants of the Eastern United States with those of this study. In the comparison which follows, the forms found in Atwood's study[7] are given first, then those found in the materials of this study.

For the third singular of *cost,* the inflection with /-s/ is universal in the M.A.S. (Middle Atlantic States) and dominant in the S.A.S. (South Atlantic States). No data is available on New England. Phonetic reduc-

---

[5] E. Bagby Atwood, *A Survey of Verb Forms in the Eastern United States* (Ann Arbor: University of Michigan Press, 1953).

[6] *Ibid.,* p. 1, n. 4.

[7] *Ibid.,* pp. 6–34.

590   tions such as [-sᵗs, -ss, sˢ, -s] are extremely common everywhere, but especially in the S.A.S. (South Atlantic States). A variant /kɔstəz/ occurs sporadically, as does /kɔsəz/. In this study the same phonetic reductions occur. Five informants have /kɔs/, six, /kɔss/. The uninflected form occurs in one-third of the type I, one-half of the type II and one-fifth of the type III responses. One type II has /kɔstɪz/. /kɔsəz/ does not occur.

For the third singular of *rinse,* the inflected form with /-ɪz/ is predominant everywhere. The uninflected form occurs sporadically. In this study sixteen of the twenty-two informants have the uninflected form. The inflected form is used by most of the type III informants.

For the past tense of *fit,* two forms, /fɪtɪd/ and /fɪt/, are current. In areas where one form predominates in other types, it dominates in cultured speech also. In this study fourteen of the twenty-four informants have /fɪt/, nine, /fɪtɪd/. One has both forms.

For the past tense of *sweat,* the uninflected form is almost the only form in the Northern area. The inflected form is more frequent as one moves southward. There is no difference between the types in the use of these forms. In this study four of the ten informants for whom responses were recorded have /swɛt/, six have /swɛtɪd/.

For the past tense of *throw,* /θru/ occurs in all areas and among all groups. /θrod/ occurs in all parts of the East. It is primarily a type I form, but occurs sporadically in type II speech. /θro, θron/ also occur sporadically. In this study, one-fourth of the type I informants use /θrod/. No type II or III informant has this form. /θro, θron/ do not occur in this study.

For the past tense of *grow,* /gru/ occurs in all areas and among all types. It is the form used in cultivated speech. /grod/ occurs primarily in type I speech. Its occurrence in the various areas is anywhere from one-fourth to over nine-tenths. In this study five-eighths of the type I informants use /grod/. No type II or III informant has this form. One type I informant has /gron/.

For the past tense of *drink,* /dræŋk/ predominates in all classes, except in a few specified areas. /drɪŋkt/ is primarily a type I form, but also occurs in type II speech. It occurs more frequently in the Southern area than elsewhere. In some Southern areas it is the only form used by type I informants. /dræŋkt/ occurs sporadically. In this study the type II and III informants have /dræŋk/. One-fourth of the type I informants have /drɪŋkt/. One has /dræŋkt/.

For the past tense of *shrink,* /šrʌŋk/ predominates among all types in all areas. In New England one-half of those who use cultivated speech have this form. Three-fourths of the informants in the M.A.S. and S.A.S. use it. /šræŋk/ occurs sporadically, more frequently in cultivated speech than in other types. Several other forms such as /šrɪŋkt, šrɪŋk, šræŋkt/

also occur. In this study three-sevenths of the type I and one-half of the type II use /šrıŋkt/. Two-sevenths of the type I have /šrıŋk/. The type III informants have /šræŋk/.

For the past tense of *swim,* /swæm/ is universal in cultivated speech. It predominates in all types in parts of New England, New York, and New Jersey. It is used by type II informants everywhere. /swʌm/ occurs in the speech of the older informants in New England. It predominates in the speech of type I informants in the M.A.S. and S.A.S. /swımd/ occurs sporadically everywhere, more frequently in the South than in the North. In this study about one-third of the type I and three-tenths of the type II informants have /swımd/. One type I has /swım/. All of the type III informants have /swæm/.

For the past tense of *drive,* /drov/ is the predominant form in all classes in all areas. /drıv/ occurs with fair frequency in type I speech. /drʌv, druv, draıv, draıvd/ occur sporadically. In this study /drov/ is used by all except one informant. One type I informant has /drovd/.

For the past tense of *freeze,* /froz/ is almost the only form used outside the South. In the South the most frequently used variants are /frizd, frozd/, both of which are primarily used by type I informants. Other variants, which occur sporadically, are /frız, frɛz, frozən, frizən/. In this study /froz/ is used by all of the informants except one; one type I informant has /frozən/.

For the past tense of *rise,* /roz/ is fairly current in all areas. The most frequent variant is /rız/, which occurs chiefly in the speech of type I informants. It occurs more frequently in the South than in other areas, it being the dominant form used by type I informants in this area. /raızd, raız, rezd/ occur sporadically. In this study /roz/ is used by all of the informants except one. One type I informant has /rız/.

For the past tense of *see,* /sɔ/ is the form used in cultivated speech. /si/ is the most common variant in New England; it is used by type I and II informants. It occurs also with fair frequency in all other areas. /sin/ occurs sporadically in New England; it is the predominant type I form in the Midland area and much of the South. Type II informants use it almost as frequently as do type I. /sid/ frequently occurs in all areas of the South in the speech of type I informants. In this study all of the type II and III informants have /sɔ/. One type I informant has /sin/ and /sɔ/; one has /sin/, /sid/, and /sɔ/; one has /sin/ and /sid/.

For the past tense of *eat,* /et/ is the dominant form in cultivated speech and is fairly common in type II speech. From one-half to three-fourths of the type I informants have /ɛt, it/. In this study one older type I informant has /it/, one older type II, /ɛt/. All other informants have /et/.

For the past tense of *run,* /ræn/ occurs generally in cultivated speech. South of the Potomac and east of the Merrimack the usual form is /rʌn/

592 for all except those who use cultivated speech. In this study one type I informant has /rʌn/. All other informants have /ræn/.

For the past tense of *sit,* /sæt/ occurs with fair frequency everywhere. /sɪt/ occurs in the various areas in the speech of the type I and II informants. /sɛt/ also occurs. /sɑt/ occurs with fair frequency in the S.A.S., less frequently elsewhere. In this study one type I informant has /sɑt/, one, /sɛt/. All others have /sæt/.

For the past tense of *take,* /tʊk/ is universal in cultivated speech and in type I and II speech as far south as the Pennsylvania-Maryland border. South of this line /tʊk/ is the dominant form in type II speech; it occurs to some degree in that of type I. /tekən/ occurs with fair frequency in the Midland, more frequently in the South. It occurs in both type I and II speech. Other forms which occur sporadically are /tʌk, tekənd/. In this study four-ninths of the type I informants have /tekən/. All other informants have /tʊk/.

For the past tense of *catch,* /kɔt/ is the form most frequently used by all types. Type I informants also use /kɛčt/. /kɑč/ occurs sporadically. In this study all of the informants have /kɔt/.

For the past tense of *fight,* /fɔt/ is the form used in cultivated speech in the M.A.S. and the S.A.S. No data is available for New England. In the speech of type I and II informants other forms occur. /fɪt/ occurs in type I speech in the northern section of the M.A.S. It occurs in type I and II speech as one goes southward. /faʊt/ also occurs. In this study all of the informants have /fɔt/.

For the past tense of *teach,* those who use this verb (many use *learn,* instead) almost always have /tɔt/. /tɪčt/ occurs sporadically in type I and II speech. In this study all of the informants have /tɔt/.

For the past tense of *dream,* /drɛmpt/ is the form most used in all areas. But in all areas a large number of informants of all types use /drimd/. In the S.A.S., wherever both forms occur, the more modern informants have /drimd/. Cultivated usage is in these areas evenly divided. Other forms such as /drim, dræmp, drʌmp/ occur sporadically. In this study nineteen of the twenty-two informants have /drimd/. One type II has /drim/.

For the past tense of *kneel,* /nɛlt/ is the dominant form in all areas; it is the form used by most of those who use cultivated speech. /nild/ is used frequently in the South, but not as frequently as /nɛlt/. In this study thirteen of the twenty informants have /nild/. Two of the three type III informants and five of the ten type II have /nɛlt/.

For the past tense of *dive,* /dov/ is the dominant form in New England, New York, parts of Pennsylvania, and New Jersey. In a section in Pennsylvania and along the upper Ohio /daɪvd/ and /dov/ occur about equally. In the other sections of the M.A.S. and in the S.A.S., /daɪvd/

is the dominant form. /dɪv, dʌv/ occur sporadically. In this study twenty-one of the twenty-three informants have /daɪvd/. Two have /dov/.

For the past tense of *wake,* /wok/ is the most common form in all areas. /wekt/ occurs with fair frequency in parts of New England. It is fairly common in the South. In this study eighteen of the twenty-two informants have /wʊk/. Three have /wekt/; one has both forms.

For the past participle of *climb,* in New England, the only area in which it was recorded, /klaɪmd/ is universal in cultivated speech. In other types, several variant forms occur. Where /klɪm, klʌm, klom/ occur as past tense forms, they are likely to occur as past participle forms. In this study all of the informants have /klaɪmd/.

For the past participle of *drown,* /draʊnd/ predominates in cultivated speech and in that of type II informants. One-fourth to nine-tenths of the type I informants in the various areas use /draʊndɪd/. In this study two-ninths of the type I and one-fifth of the type II informants have /draʊndɪd/. One type II informant has /draʊn/. All other informants have /draʊnd/.

For the past participle of *grow,* which was recorded only in New England, /gron/ is used by all of those who have /gru/ as a past tense form and by almost half of those who have /grod/. In this study one type I informant who has the past tense form /gron/ has both /gro/ and /gron/ for the past participle. All other informants have /gron/.

For the past participle of *drink,* a very large number of speakers have the same form as they have for the past tense. Those who have /dræŋk/ for the past tense usually have the past participle /drʌŋk/. Those who have the past tense /drʌŋk/, usually have the past participle /drʌŋk/. The /dræŋk—drʌŋk/ past tense-past participle combination occurs in all areas but is not common. In New England half of the cultivated speakers use it, in the M.A.S., about one-third. In the S.A.S. it predominates in cultivated speech but has almost no currency in other types. Among other past participle forms which occur sporadically arc /drɪŋkt, drɪŋkən, dræŋkən/. In this study the two informants who have /drɪŋkt/ as a past tense form also have it as a past participle. The one who has /dræŋkt/ as a past tense form, has it as a past participle, also. A little less than half of the informants, ten of the twenty-three, have the /dræŋk —drʌŋk/ combination. Three-fifths of the type III informants have it, but only one-fifth of the type I do.

For the past participle of *bite,* /bɪtən/ is the dominant form used in cultivated speech. In New England only, it is the form used by a majority of all the speakers. Elsewhere /bɪt/ is the form used most frequently by type I speakers, a little less frequently by type II. In this study all of the type III informants have /bɪtən/. Four-ninths of the type I informants and one-tenth of the type II have /bɪt/.

594   For the past participle of *drive*, /drɪvən/ is the form used by the majority of speakers in the northern area. As one moves southward, it becomes
less and less frequent. In North Carolina two-thirds of the speakers have
other forms. Leveling of the past tense and past participle forms is common. Most of the type I informants have /drov/; from one-third to one-
half use this form. Among other forms which occur are /drɪv, drov/. In
this study one-half of the type I informants have /drov/. One older
type I informant has /drɪv/. All other informants have /drɪvən/.

For the past participle of *ride*, /rɪdən/ is universal in cultivated speech.
It occurs with some frequency in type II speech. /rod/ occurs more frequently in type I speech. /rɪd/ occurs sporadically among the older type I
informants in the Northern area, more frequently among all type I
speakers in the South. In this study all of the type III informants have
/rɪdən/. Five-ninths of the type I informants and one-fifth of the type II
have /rod/. One older type I informant has /rɪd/. One young informant
has /rod/ and /rɪdən/, one /rɪd/ and /rod/.

For the past participle of *write*, /rɪtən/ is the most frequently used
form in cultivated speech; it occurs in other types much less frequently.
/rot/ is used by one-half of the type I informants in New England; elsewhere from three-fifths of the type I informants in New York to nine-
tenths in North Carolina use it. It also occurs frequently in type II speech.
/rɪt/ occurs sporadically. In this study two-ninths of the type I and
one-tenth of the type II informants have /rot/. One type I informant has
/rot/ and /rɪtən/. All other informants have /rɪtən/.

For the past participle of *tear*, /tɔrn/ is about universal in cultivated
speech. /tɔr/ or /tor/ also occurs in the other types to varying degrees.
In the M.A.S. it is used by most of the type I informants; in the S.A.S.
it is used by most of the type I and II informants. In this study two-ninths
of the type I and one-ninth of the type II informants have /toə, to/. All
of the type III informants have /tɔən, toən/.

For the past participle of *wear*, /wɔrn, worn/ is the dominant form in
parts of New England, New York, and New Jersey. Elsewhere it is dominant in cultivated speech but not in the speech of type I and II informants. /wɔr, wor/ occur in the M.A.S. and S.A.S. in the speech of from
two-thirds to more than nine-tenths of the type I informants. It is used
sporadically by type II informants. In this study one type I informant
has /wo/. All other informants have /wɔən, woən/.

For the past participle of *take*, /tekən/ is the most commonly used
form. /tʊk/ occurs sporadically. The forms /tʌk, tekənd, tʊkən/ also
occur sporadically. In this study two-ninths of the type I and three-tenths
of the type II informants have /tʊk/. All other informants have /tekən/.

For the present participle ending two forms are current, /-ɪŋ/ and
/-ɪn, -ən/. In general, /-ɪŋ/ is used in cultivated speech, /-ɪn, -ən/ in

other types. In some areas, chiefly Northern, /-ɪŋ/ and /-ɪn/ occur with about equal frequency in type I and II speech. In the S.A.S., where both forms are acceptable, /-ɪŋ/ and /-ɪn/ occur with about equal frequency in cultivated speech. In this study type I and II informants have /-ɪn/. Type III informants have /-ɪŋ/ in careful speech.

In general, the type I and II informants of this study use the same forms as the type I and II informants of Atwood's study. The type I informants of this study, however, use the uninflected form for the third singular somewhat more frequently than do those of Atwood's study.

The type III informants of this study use the same forms as the type III informants of Atwood's study.

The Position
of the Charleston
Dialect

Raven I. McDavid, Jr.

Charleston, South Carolina is a focal point from which
speech forms have spread to the surrounding region. The
dialect spoken in the Charleston area is recognized, by those
who have heard it, as noticeably different from the speech
of other areas of South Carolina. Professor McDavid, in this
article, describes a number of the distinctive phonological,
grammatical, and lexical features of this dialect.

The position of one dialect within a speech community may often be
appraised intelligently by the layman, who recognizes that beyond a
certain swamp or mountain the inhabitants talk differently. Many times,
too, the layman may have a fair understanding of the ways in which that
particular dialect differs from his own; he will notice the unfamiliar
words or grammatical constructions, and may even be able to mimic pas-
sably well the pronunciation and intonation. The interest of the amateur

From *Publication of the American Dialect Society*. No. 23:35–49 (April, 1955). Reprinted
with the permission of the American Dialect Society. University of Alabama Press, and
Raven I. McDavid, Jr.

in the strange details of neighboring dialects is often invaluable in suggesting where dialect boundaries may occur and which communities might most profitably be investigated.

Beyond this, however, the work of the lay observer needs at least consultation with the professional. Even though the layman may be well aware of the ways in which his county's speech differs most noticeably from that of an adjacent county, he ordinarily cannot evaluate the position of either dialect in reference to the whole body of American English. For instance, the average white Southerner may use the term *jackleg preacher* freely as a gloss for such more local terms as *chair-backer, stump-knocker, table-tapper,* and *yard-ax*—designations for a part-time voluntary preacher, normally without formal seminary training and generally with a low degree of competence. To the native speaker from other regions, however, *yard-ax* and *jack-leg* are equally strange, so that the Southerner speaking to a non-Southern audience must define in detail either *yard-ax* or *jack-leg.* Conversely, a low-country South Carolina term like *haycock* or *mouth organ* may sound exotic to the man from the up-country but turn out to be the prevailing term north of the Potomac.

In other words, in identifying and characterizing a dialect it is necessary not only to indicate some of the more characteristic words, forms, and pronunciations in that area, but also to point out what other areas also share these features. To do this, the assistance of the trained scholar is necessary, whether he conducts the investigation himself or merely supplies advice for the lay investigator.

The Charleston area is an excellent example of a dialect area which is easily identified by the lay observer but whose position with reference to other dialect areas of American English cannot be indicated without reference to systematic evidence gathered from other parts of the eastern United States. For our purposes, we will define the Charleston area as that dialect area of the South Atlantic coast whose center and main cultural focus is the port of Charleston. Its limits do not turn out to be the same for all features; in fact, these features seem to group themselves into three major geographical patterns, to be defined later. But all seem to center around the city of Charleston and seem to owe their persistence to settlement through that city or later cultural radiation from it.

The distinctiveness of the Charleston dialect has been long recognized by up-country South Carolinians. If someone from the Charleston area attends college at an inland institution or runs for state political office, he is readily identified, and his speech is often mimicked by his colleagues. This mimicry usually is confined to an imitation of the Charlestonian pronunciation of /e, o/ as in *date* and *boat,* to distortion of the [əu] diphthong in *out* toward [u], and to the replacement of /æ/ with /a/, especially in *Battery.*

598   Scholarly attention was first directed toward Charleston speech in a paper by Sylvester Primer, then of the College of Charleston, delivered at the Modern Language Association of America in 1887, and published in three different journals under the title "Charleston Provincialisms."[1] Ignoring vocabulary and grammar, he summarized the characteristics of Charleston pronunciation as follows:

(*a*) homonymy of *fear* and *fair, ear* and *air.*
(*b*) /e/ in *again.*
(*c*) /æ/ in *pa, ma;* also in *calm, palm, psalm,* etc.
(*d*) distinction of *morning/mourning, horse/hoarse,* etc.
(*e*) /o/ in *poor;* also in *to.*
(*f*) a tendency for /ʌ/ to replace /ʊ/ in *book, put, pull, pudding*
(*g*) coalescence of /v/ and /w/, with resulting homonymy of *wail* and *veil,* etc.
(*h*) simplification of initial /hw/ to /w/[2]
(*i*) /č/ retained in *pasture,* which remained distinct from *pastor*
(*j*) postvocalic /r/ as [ə] or length, in *war, hard,* etc.
(*k*) initial /kj, gj/ (or palatalized /k, g/) in stressed syllables, as in *car, garden, girl*
(*l*) /θ/ in *with*

However, this pioneer work—one of the first attempts to describe the speech of an American community—was not followed up. The economic blight which struck Southern educational institutions following the Confederate War greatly restricted the opportunities for research in such newer disciplines as linguistics, which only recently has won the attention of Southern universities and Southern scholars.

Neither the observations of the lay observer nor Primer's list takes into account the totality of the dialect in its relationships with other dialects. For such a complete picture it is necessary to have (a) a summary of the historical and cultural features that might make for a sharply differen-

---

[1] *American Journal of Philology,* IX (1888), 198–213; *Transactions of the Modern Language Association; Phonetische Studien.* "[Primer] was born in Wisconsin in 1842, but removed to New York as a child. He served in the Civil War as a cavalryman under Sheridan and Custer and was wounded at Antietam. After the war he took to language studies at Harvard, Leipzig, Göttingen and Strassburg, and in 1895 was given a Ph.D. by the last-named. From 1891 to his death in 1913 he was professor of Germanic languages at the University of Texas." Mencken, *The American Language,* Supplement II (New York, 1948), p. 213.

Is it possible that Primer's concern with German made him unable to perceive the most striking feature of Charleston pronunciation, the pure vowels and in-gliding diphthongs in *date* and *boat?*

[2] See Raven I. McDavid, Jr. and Virginia G. McDavid, "*h* before Semivowels in the Eastern United States," *Language,* XXVIII (1952), 41–61.

tiated dialect; (b) comparable data for several classes of speakers over a wide area. The first of these has been provided by the research of many historians; the second by the field records of the Linguistic Atlas of the United States and Canada.

Both historical and socio-cultural forces suggest that distinctive speech-forms would develop in the Charleston area.

Historical evidence indicates a sharp difference between the earliest settlers of coastal and inland areas in South Carolina and adjacent parts of Georgia.

The tidewater area was settled first as mercantile plantations, with a quasi-feudal structure. The first settlers appear to have been predominantly from southern England, though their precise origins have not been worked out. The original mercantile and planter groups were reinforced fairly early by Huguenots and Sephardic Jews; both of these increments were strongest in the immediate neighborhood of Charleston and in the Santee Delta around Georgetown. From early in the colonial period there has been a small but steady amount of direct migration from other countries, particularly Ireland and Germany; as with other American cities, the peak of Irish and German migration was reached about 1850. The importation of Negro slaves as a labor force for indigo and rice plantations began rather early, reaching a peak about 1800; although the slave trade was prohibited by law in 1820, illicit slave-running continued till the eve of the Confederate War. Large numbers of Negroes were settled on islands and necks of land; partly through peonage, partly through lack of training for anything except agriculture, these Negro groups continued relatively undisturbed until far into the twentieth century. In the last thirty years, northern capitalists have bought up many abandoned plantations as winter homes, and many northern artists and writers have established studios in Charleston or neighboring communities.

Inland South Carolina, on the other hand, was settled by two distinct movements, in neither of which the tidewater plantation settlements played a prominent part. The coastal plain, from Conway and Queensboro near the North Carolina line to Ft. Moore on the Savannah, was planted with frontier townships designed as military outposts to protect the tidewater settlements; north of the Santee the townships were settled predominantly by Ulster Scots and Welsh Baptists, south of the Santee by Germans and German-Swiss. As a rule, the first settlers of each of these townships were recruited and transported in a body to their new homes, generally but not always by way of Charleston. The Piedmont and mountain areas were settled by two southwestward movements, one of English, Irish, and Ulster Scots from the Virginia Piedmont, the other

600   of Ulster Scots and Pennsylvania Germans by way of the Shenandoah Valley; the documentary evidence does not always distinguish between these two movements.[3]

Over this rather diverse population the city of Charleston early established economic and cultural domination that has hardly been challenged down to the present day. A colonial capital and until the end of the eighteenth century the most important city south of Philadelphia, Charleston exerted over South Carolina and Georgia an influence equaled in the South only by that of New Orleans in the lower Mississippi Valley. During the colonial period it was the center of the Indian trade, both with the Cherokees in the Southern Appalachians and with the Creeks and Choctaws in the Gulf States. It was the port through which the Carolina plantation owners generally bought and sold, and the business center through which they financed their operations; as plantation agriculture and cotton culture spread inland, the financial domination of Charleston was extended over the entire state. Even the economic changes of the last century have not destroyed this dominant financial position; until fairly recently it was easy for demagogues to rally the voters of the inland counties by appealing to their hatred of Charleston bankers and brokers.

The early feudal pattern of Charleston society has been perpetuated in the form of a select social upper class, based primarily on ancestry and connections, secondarily on education and cultural experience, and to a relatively minor degree on wealth. This group has always maintained close relationships with similar groups in Boston, New York, and other coast cities; it has also maintained a tradition of close relationships with English society, derived from the fact that down to the Confederate War it was common for planters and merchants to send their sons to the English universities and to the Inns of Court. The exclusiveness of this group has meant relatively high prestige in inland communities for all Charlestonians, whether of the Charleston elite or not. The elite of many inland communities stemmed originally from low-country planters who removed their families from the coast during the summer malaria season, a group later reinforced by refugees during the Confederate War.[4] In other communities the earliest banks and business houses were organized by Charlestonians. Finally, the fact that the College of Charleston has remained a small institution, offering free education in a liberal arts curriculum to a selected student body, supports the tradition of social status based on family and culture rather than on wealth.

[3] See Robert Lee Meriwether, *The Expansion of South Carolina 1729–1765* (Kingsport, Tenn., 1940).

[4] See Julian J. Petty, *The Growth and Distribution of Population in South Carolina*, Bulletin No. 11, State Planning Board (Columbia, S. C., 1943).

It is thus evident that speech-forms which became established in Charleston would tend to spread inland in South Carolina and adjacent parts of Georgia and North Carolina, regardless of whether they were favored in other parts of the South. Many speech forms current in Charleston not only are dominant in the coastal plain but are found in the South Carolina Piedmont, particularly in the speech of educated informants. Occasionally, as with *batteau* "rowboat" and the general Southern *carry one home* "escort, as from a party," they have even spread into the mountains of western North Carolina.

The analysis of the Charleston dialect in this paper is based on the field records of the Linguistic Atlas of the United States and Canada, inaugurated in 1930 by the American Council of Learned Societies.

The Atlantic Seaboard collection of the Linguistic Atlas comprise nearly 1500 field records, so that one is able to determine not only what speech forms occur in a given area but how one area compares with the others. The area of Charleston influence has been especially well studied, with 136 field interviews from South Carolina, 75 from eastern Georgia, and 7 from northeastern Florida. From the city of Charleston itself there are 11 interviews (9 white, 2 Negro), a greater number than from any other Atlantic Seaboard community except New York City.[5] Thus there is adequate evidence for determining the complex interrelationships among the various local speech-types as well as among the various social levels of speech.

Each field record represents an average of about 8 hours of oral interviewing, in a conversation situation, in an effort to get the natural responses of a native informant, well-rooted in his community, for about 800 items of everyday speech. These items concern details of pronunciation, such as *horse, hoop, wheelbarrow, greasy;* details of grammar such as *I dove,* or *div,* or *dived;* details of vocabulary, such as the name for the common worm used in fishing.

Each bit of evidence may be plotted on a map of the area for which we have data. When it is found within a sharply defined area, one may draw a line called an *isogloss,* to indicate the boundaries of the area in which this form occurs. Where several isoglosses tend to coincide, we conclude we have a *dialect boundary.* If the speech forms of a given area seem to be spreading into other areas, it is called a *focal area;* an area whose local speech forms are disappearing is a *relic area;* an area with few local peculiarities but subject to influence from several directions is a *transition area* or *graded area.*[6]

---

[5] Of the field records from this area, 189 were made by Raven I. McDavid, Jr., 28 by Guy S. Lowman, Jr., and one by Bernard Bloch.

[6] For more detailed discussion of the history, methods, and aims of linguistic geography, see Sever Pop, *La Dialectologie* (Louvain, 1950).

602   It is clear that the key to the speech patterns of the Carolinas and Georgia is the preëminent position of Charleston. The Ulster Scots and Germans of the coastal plain have left scarcely a trace on the patterns of South Carolina speech. The transfer of the state capital to Columbia (about 1800) and the industrialization of the Piedmont since Reconstruction have not yet been reflected in the spread of Columbia or Piedmont speech forms, except insofar as they coincide with the forms of cultivated Charleston speech.

To determine the characteristics of Charleston speech we must return to the three geographical patterns in which Charleston speech forms occur. Here we must be careful to exclude certain classes of forms which occur not only in the area around Charleston but in wider areas as well:

(*a*) Forms characteristic of urban and cultured speech almost everywhere, such as /č/ in *pasture.*

(*b*) Forms characteristic of the Midland and South, such as *bucket* or /ɔ/ in *on.*[7]

(*c*) Forms characteristic of the South Midland and South, as *disremember, theirselves, hisself, corn shucks,* /z/ in *greasy,* or /o/ in *poor.*

(*d*) Forms characteristic of the entire South, such as *all two, all both,* "both," *more prettier, Confederate War, haunts* /hænts/ "ghosts," and *carry one home* "to escort."

As previously suggested, Charleston speech-forms are distributed in three basic geographic patterns. The first of these is that of Carolina coastal speech forms that are restricted to a narrow strip of the coastal plain in North Carolina (where there was no dominant coastal center) but in South Carolina have spread inland at least to the neighborhood of Columbia and often to the cities of the Piedmont. The northern limit of these forms is sometimes the Neuse River, sometimes the Virginia Capes, and occasionally the Delmarva peninsula. In Georgia these forms normally spread throughout the coastal plain. For these items Charleston usage differs from that of the Virginia Piedmont focal area.

Pronunciation:

/iu/ occasionally in *puke, music, dues, new,* etc. (Also in New England settlement area, especially in old-fashioned speech.)

[7] As in Kurath's *Word Geography* and Atwood's *Survey of Verb Forms,* the term *North* designates New England, the Hudson Valley and their derivative settlements: *North Midland,* Pennsylvania and Northern West Virginia; *South Midland,* the Shenandoah Valley and the Southern Appalachians; *Southern,* the plantation settlements from Chesapeake Bay to Northern Florida, plus their immediate derivatives.

/o/ in *wounded* (very old-fashioned)
/ʌ/ in *bulge, bulk* (also North and North Midland)
/-b/ in *coop* /kʊb/
/war-, wor-/ in *walnut* (also Delmarva and South Midland)

Grammar:

he) *belongs to be* (careful
church will be over) *time I get there.* (Also upstate New York)
I) *ran up with* (him
I) *ran across* (him
In addition *them boys* "those" is heavily predominant; the Virginia
    Piedmont favors *them there boys.*

Vocabulary:

mosquito hawk "dragon fly"
press peach "clingstone" (not in the cities of Charleston or Beaufort)
beast "bull"
troughs, water troughs "gutters"
hay pile "haycock"
take) *a milling of corn* (to be ground
corn dodger "dumpling"
breakfast strip "bacon"
clearstone peach "freestone"
earthworm (book word elsewhere)
whicker "whinny" (also Maine and Southeast New England)
piazza "porch" (also New England)
spider "frying pan (also Northern).

The second pattern is that of forms which have spread inland from
coastal ports and plantation areas. Such forms occur near the coast in
the Cape Fear Valley of North Carolina, but in South Carolina push
inland at least to the fall line communities of Cheraw, Camden, Columbia,
and Augusta; in Georgia they sometimes spread throughout the coastal
plain, more often are confined to the Tidewater plantation areas around
Savannah, Darien, Brunswick, and St. Mary's. These forms may or may
not occur in the communities of northeastern Florida. Forms in this
group often occur in the Virginia Piedmont as well; when this happens,
as with *crocus sack,* occurrences in the South Carolina Piedmont may
have spread from either focus or both.

604   **Pronunciation:**

/ɔ/ in *watch, wash*[8]

/ʊ/ in *room, broom,* along with /u/. (/ʊ/ dominant in Northeast New England, Eastern Virginia, and the Buffalo-Rochester area)[9]

/-rʊm/ in *mushroom* (also Chesapeake Bay, Eastern New England)

No linking /r/ in *your aunt*

Centered beginning of /ai, au/ [əi, əu] before voiceless consonants, as in *knife, ice, out, house* (also Eastern Virginia and Canada)

/ɪ/ in unstressed syllables in *funnel, mountain* (also Eastern Virginia and Eastern New England)

[eˑ, eˑə, oˑ, oˑə] in *take, boat,* etc. [eˑ, oˑ] also in Pennsylvania German area[10]

/-jə/ in *nephew* (also Eastern Virginia)

/mʌs-/ in *mushmelons* (also Eastern Virginia)

[a] in *pasture, hammer, Saturday* (also Eastern Virginia and Eastern New England). Old and receding

/-stɪd/ in *instead* (also New England and upstate New York)

/bɪ'kʌz/ *because* (also Northern)

[nlɛs] *unless*

Palatalized /k, g/ in *car, garden, girl,* etc. (also Eastern Virginia)

/w/ in *whip, wheelbarrow, whetrock* (also Northeastern New England, Hudson Valley, Eastern Penna.)

/-r/ as [ə] or length in *beard, barn, born* (also Eastern Virginia, New York City, Eastern New England)

/ɔ/ as well as /a/ in *pot, crop, borrow, orange,* etc.

/ʊ, u/ in *won't* (also Hudson Valley, Chesapeake Bay, Nantucket, and Martha's Vineyard)

/θ/ in *without* (also Chesapeake Bay, Midland)

Grammar:

/dov/ along with *dived.* /dov/ is dominant in the North, occurs alongside *dived* in Pennsylvania

used to didn't

sweat (preterit). As common as *sweated*

---

[8] For the low back vowels, see the forthcoming University of Michigan dissertation of Thomas Wetmore.

[9] For the vowels in *room, hoop,* etc. see the forthcoming University of Michigan dissertation of Miss Helen Wong. Also Raven I. McDavid, Jr., "Derivatives of Middle English ō in the South Atlantic Area," *Quarterly Journal of Speech,* XXXV (1949), 496–504.

[10] For the vowels in *date* and *boat* see the forthcoming University of Michigan dissertation of Walter S. Avis.

swim (preterit). Old-fashioned (also Virginia Piedmont)
et (preterit). Even in cultured speech (also New England and other
    Coastal points, and Southern England)
he was) *dogbit*. Not in culture centers (also South Midland)
he did it) *purpose* (rare; also New England, New York State)
he was) *named for* (his uncle (also Eastern New England)
he fell) *off of* (the horse (also South Midland)
he fell) *out the bed* (also Eastern Virginia)
he isn't) *home* (also New York State and Delaware Valley)
two) *yokes* (of oxen (also Virginia Piedmont)
towards (also Virginia Piedmont)
ran acrost (also North Midland)
he do. Old-fashioned (also Eastern Virginia)
40) *bushel* (also North Midland)
wait on "wait for" (also Midland)

Besides these grammatical forms, certain others are far more common
in South Carolina than elsewhere:

he's not) *as tall as me.*
I'm not) *as tall as him.*
you can do it) *better than me.*
Me and you (can do it.
Me and him (are going.
Omission of the nominative relative: *he's the man owns the orchard.*
Omission of the genitive relative: *there's a boy his father is rich.*

Vocabulary:

a little piece (also Midland)
cherry kernel "seed" (also Delmarva)
armful of wood (also North, North Midland)
coal hod (also New England, Chesapeake Bay)
turnip greens (also North, North Midland)
mutton corn "green corn" (also Northeast Florida)
cooter "turtle"
candlefly, candlebug "moth"
done worked (also Eastern Virginia). Spread into South Midland.
sick on the stomach (also Pennsylvania German area, including central
    North Carolina)
creep "crawl" (also Northern)
he was) *up in* (Hartford (also Southern New England, upstate New York,
    New York City, Philadelphia, Eastern Virginia, widespread in South
    Carolina, Georgia)

606   *savannah* "grassland" (rare in Georgia and not in immediate Charleston
        area)
    batteau "rowboat" (spread into North Carolina, also in Chesapeake Bay
        and Delaware Bay)
    snake fence "rail fence" (sporadic elsewhere)
    cornhouse "crib" (also Eastern Virginia)
    pinder "peanut"
    crokersack (also Eastern Virginia, Martha's Vineyard)
    buckra "white man"
    curds "cottage cheese" (also Chesapeake Bay)
    bloody-noun "bullfrog"
    sivvy beans, sewee beans "lima beans"
    mouth organ "harmonica" (also Northern, North Midland)

These first two groups of forms attest to the importance of Charleston as a *focal area* from which linguistic forms have spread. For the third group of forms one must consider Charleston and its cultural dependencies as a *relic area,* in which generally old-fashioned forms are confined to a relatively narrow strip of coast. Some of these forms follow the coastal rice plantation area from Georgetown to the Florida line; others stop at the Savannah River. Inland, they rarely go beyond the area of rice plantations, though a few are found as far up the Santee as the neighborhood of Columbia. Sometimes a form, such as *hall* "living room," is not found in the seaport towns but only in the more old-fashioned speech of the surrounding country.

Pronunciation:

/æ/ in *tomatoes* (also Northern)
/u/ alongside /ju/ in *tube, due, new,* etc. (normal in North Midland, Hudson Valley; dominant in rest of North)
/ɪ/ in *creek* (also North, North Midland)
/vez/ "vase" (sporadic along coast, common in Canada)
/nɛvjə/ "nephew" (sporadic along the coast, common in Canada)
[a, ɑ] in *glass* (also Eastern New England)
/ʊ/ in *cooter*
/e/ in *again* (also Hudson Valley, Eastern New England)
/o/ in *to*
Only one front vowel phoneme before /r/: *fair* rimes with *fear, air* rimes with *ear,* etc.
/æ/ in *pa, ma*
/æ/ in *palm, calm,* etc., even in cultured speech (old-fashioned elsewhere)

Grammar:

see (preterit). Rare (also in Eastern Virginia and North)
a little way (down the road; *a long way* (to go. Especially in Charleston
    and Beaufort; in metropolitan areas of other regions

Vocabulary:

hall "living room" (rare)
fatwood "lightwood" (from Georgetown to Northeastern Florida)
cornbarn (rare elsewhere)
joggling board "springboard anchored at both ends"
haycock (uncommon) (also North, North Midland)
pinto "coffin" (chiefly Negro)
worm fence (also North Midland)
wagon pole (also Northern, Chesapeake Bay)
goober "peanut"
ashbread "ashcake"
whetseed "whetstone" (also Albemarle Sound)
yard-ax, table-tapper "unskilled preacher"
awendaw "spoonbread"
groundnuts "peanuts" (receding). (To the St. Mary's River; also in Phila-
    delphia area and British English)
bush colt, bush child "bastard"
(marsh) tacky "small half-wild horse"
groomsman "best man" (rare in Virginia)
squinch owl, skrinch owl "screech owl"

    Cutting across the three geographical patterns, certain social patterns
must be recognized in the speech of this area. The most striking of these
patterns is the pronunciation of postvocalic /-r/ in such words as *beard,
barn, four.* Contrary to tradition, a strongly constricted /-r/ is often
found in folk speech, not only of the mountains and the cotton-mill villages but also of the sand hills and the low-country pine barrens. However, constriction is less strong in younger speakers than in older, in
urban speakers than in rural, in cultured speakers than in uneducated;
so that the social appraisal of this feature is needed to balance the
geographical.[11]

[11] For the status of postvocalic /r/, see the forthcoming University of Michigan dissertation
by Robert Van Riper. See also Raven I. McDavid, Jr., "Post-Vocalic /-r/ in South Carolina:
a Social Analysis," *American Speech,* XXIII (1948), 194–203.

608   In other details, too, urbanization is affecting the speech of the Charleston area just as it affects that of other regions. Two details will illustrate this: (1) *hall* "living room" is a relic surviving only in rural communities around Charleston and Georgetown; (2) although *press peach* "clingstone" is the dominant term in the coastal plain from the Virginia capes south, and is common in both Georgetown and Savannah, it was not recorded from a single informant in either Charleston or Beaufort.

Negro speech, in general, seems to have the same speech forms as white speech. The lexical contributions of the Negro to the Charleston vocabulary are found in Turner's *Africanisms in the Gullah Dialect* and have been identified by various reviewers.[12] A list of Gullah vocabulary elements with likely African origins is as follows:

> *bloodynoun* "bullfrog"
> *buckra* "white man"
> *bush child, bush colt* "bastard"
> *cooter* "turtle"
> *cush* "mush"
> *da* "colored nurse"
> *goober* "peanut" (more common in the Virginia Piedmont than in South Carolina)
> *hu-hu owl* "hoot owl"
> *joggling board*
> *pinder* "peanut"
> *pinto* "coffin"
> *tacky* "horse"
> *titta* "sister"
> *tote* "carry" (general Southern, also Western North Carolina and Western Pennsylvania)
> *yard-ax, table-tapper* "unskilled preacher"

Some of these forms, like *cooter, pinder,* and *tote,* are used widely by white speakers without any suspicion of their African background; others like *pinto* and *hard-ax,* are used by whites as conscious Negroisms. But all are known to whites.

Grammatically, the most old-fashioned Negro speech shows a lack of inflection in both noun and verb (*I have drive, a pair of shaft*) and /(j)ʊnə/ as the second person plural pronoun, and uses *for* /fə/ rather than *to* or *for to* with the infinitive of purpose, as *he come over for tell me.* Phonolog-

[12] See Raven I. McDavid, Jr., review of Turner's *Africanisms in the Gullah Dialect,* in *Language,* XXVI (1950), 323–333; Raven I. McDavid, Jr. and Virginia G. McDavid, "The Relationship of the Speech of American Negroes to the Speech of Whites," *American Speech,* XXVI (1951), 3–17. The status of Africanisms in white speech of the South Atlantic states was discussed by Raven I. McDavid, Jr. in an unpublished paper before the Present-Day English Group (English XIII) of the Modern Language Association at Boston in 1952.

ically, old-fashioned Negro speech does not contrast /v/ and /w/, has (along with the speech of the North and North Midland) /s/ rather than /z/ in *grease, greasy,* and lacks an /æ/ phoneme. The noticeable differences in intonation patterns await further investigation.

Few of these speech forms of the Charleston area occur only in that area, notably the in-gliding [e·ə], [o·ə] and such lexical items as *pinder, cooter, mutton corn, sivvy beans,* and *savannah.* The rest are shared with other speech areas of the Atlantic Seaboard; sometimes with the Midland as /-θ-/ in *without,* sometimes with Eastern Virginia as *corn house, croker sack* and the centered beginning in [əut, nəif], sometimes with New York City, as /wunt/, sometimes with the Boston area as *piazza.* In the early periods of settlement and expansion from the coast, dialect mixture must have been the norm rather than the exception. It is not surprising, then, that the same speech form (whether in pronunciation, grammar, or vocabulary) may crop up in widely separated areas along the coast, and that the identification of dialect areas is less a matter of individual traits than the combinations in which traits appear. As Primer concluded his article: "I must again caution all not to understand the above observations on the peculiarities of Charleston pronunciation [or grammar, or vocabulary] as applying to Charleston alone. The peculiar circumstances under which the whole country was settled would exclude any monopoly of sound [or inflection, or word] by any one place." It is not surprising that some of his "Charleston provincialisms" turn out to be rather widespread, or that investigation has revealed other items which give Charleston speech its individuality, even in the South.

The Pronunciation of English in Boston, Massachusetts: Vowels and Consonants

Robert L. Parslow

Boston is the focal area for the Eastern New England dialect, a dialect distinctly different from that of the rest of New England. In his study, Professor Parslow undertook to "describe the salient features of this important dialect, to relate this to other dialects, and to determine the structural changes that have occurred in the dialect during the present century."

The raw material, obtained in fieldwork throughout the greater Boston area, included the records of thirty informants responding to a battery of 110 test sentences designed to elicit all the phonological segments of the dialect. The informants, selected to represent a cross-section of the metropolitan population, were not aware that pronunciation was being sampled; they were under the impression that it was a study only of regional vocabulary. This arrangement reduced informants' consciousness of phonology to a minimum.

Professor Parslow's investigation disclosed three subdialects
within the city of Boston. Since this finding should be of
considerable interest, Chapter VI, which describes these
subdialects, is reprinted there. Also included to indicate
the scope of the study is the Conclusion, which reviews
several matters, among them the phonological congruence
of Boston English with other American English dialects
and recent phonological changes in the Boston dialect.
The Conclusion also suggests directions for future
research. Dr. Parslow is Professor of Linguistics at the
University of Pittsburgh.

At least three subdialects of Boston English may be identified on phonological bases; the lexical evidence in this investigation likewise supports
a trichotomy.

Subdialect *A* prevails in the region and typifies most levels of society
outside the central area.

Subdialect *B* (for "Brahmin," let us say) is characteristic of a small
minority of upper-class speakers, representatives of a durable local
aristocracy. Although this group constitutes primarily a vertical, societal
division, certain topographical sites such as Beacon Hill, Back Bay, and
Milton, have long been associated with it.

Type *B* should not be confused with any dialect variety of a larger
"cultivated" class, that is, of a body of well-educated, often economically
solvent persons of some prestige in the community. A comparison of informants 2 and 3 will demonstrate the difference. The former is a member
of an eminent Brahmin family; nonetheless, his higher education lasted
a year only, his present social mobility is restricted, his income is modest.
The latter, informant 3, finished Harvard, attended MIT, is prominent in
financial and commercial activity and in society. The two informants
speak respectively subdialects *B* and *A*.

Subdialect *C* (which may safely stand for "Central") occupies those
contiguous sections at the center of the metropolis: South Boston, East
Boston, Charlestown, South Cambridge, to name a few.

Subdialect *C* is the only one of these three which can be confined
within reliable boundaries. Type *A* certainly extends beyond the pre-
scribed limits of investigation into a larger Eastern New England zone.
Type *B* will extend to whatever colonies its speakers inhabit in New England, notwithstanding the primacy of Boston as its hub.

The possibility of identifying additional subdialect areas is enticing,
most of all in the southwest quadrant of Greater Boston, where retro-

From "The Pronunciation of English in Boston, Massachusetts: Vowels and Consonants,"
unpubl. diss. (The University of Michigan, 1967). Printed with the permission of Robert L.
Parslow.

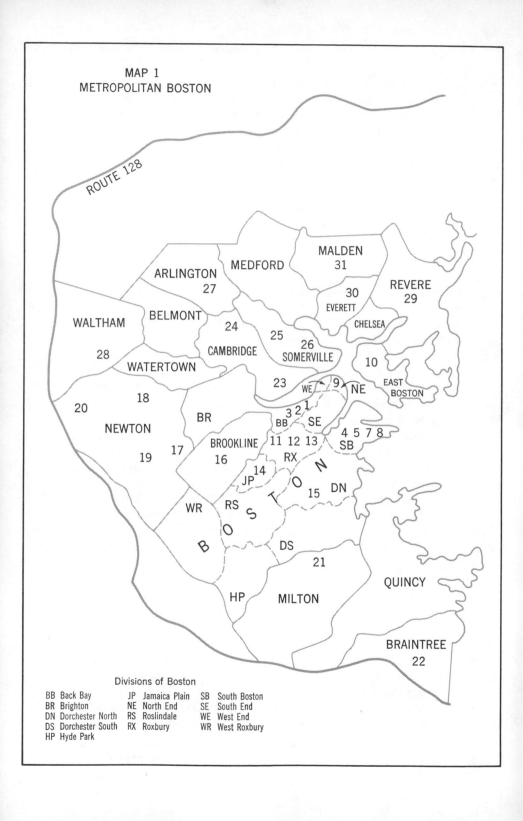

MAP 1
METROPOLITAN BOSTON

ROUTE 128

MALDEN
31

ARLINGTON
27

MEDFORD

REVERE
29

30
EVERETT

WALTHAM

BELMONT

24

CHELSEA

28

WATERTOWN

CAMBRIDGE

25

26
SOMERVILLE

10

23

20

18

NEWTON

BR

19   17

BROOKLINE

16

WE   9   NE

3 2 1

BB   SE

11 12 13

RX

EAST
BOSTON

4 5 7 8
SB

14
JP

B   O   S   T   O   N

15   DN

WR   RS

DS

21

HP   MILTON

QUINCY

BRAINTREE
22

Divisions of Boston

BB Back Bay   JP Jamaica Plain   SB South Boston
BR Brighton   NE North End   SE South End
DN Dorchester North   RS Roslindale   WE West End
DS Dorchester South   RX Roxbury   WR West Roxbury
HP Hyde Park

flexion occurs in the vocalic nucleus of *dog*, where linking /r/ is rare even in phrases like *ginger ale*. However, in spite of the distinctiveness of these items, they are fewer in number than those chosen to separate dialect types *A, B,* and *C*.

Few of the informants from Boston are completely *r*-less, that is to say, without an occasional postvocalic *r*-sound that is not involved in sandhi. A few informants—19, 21, and 22 specifically—produce *r*-timbred vocoids regularly. The presence of *r* in these idiolects does not require the identification of another, fourth subdialect; the *r*-sounds are simply refinements of the determined phonemic structures of types *A, B,* or *C*. These *r*-sounds may necessitate a revision of phonotactics: a familiar pair of homophones. *Weston* and *western,* both transcribable as /wéstərn/ for most speakers, become heterophonic wherever *r* is utilized. In this case the phonemic interpretation might be /wéstan/ for the name of the town.

Subdialect A

Since Type A is general in Greater Boston and environs, its description is the burden of this entire work. Therefore no delineation of Type A is necessary; where A differs from B and C, the contrasts are noted.

Subdialect B

The following phonology is unique to subdialect B:

1. The vocoid of *glass* is [a], opposed to the [æ] of *sap* and *bag* and the [ɑ] of *half, aunts,* and *past*. [On . . . the interpretation of this [ɑ], see the notes to Chapter III, "Vowel Phonemes."]

2. *Ago, home,* and other words phonemicized with /ow/ may contain a diphthong whose first element is a fronted vocoid, [ɐu], resembling a familiar Southern British pronunciation.

3. *Four* is pronounced ['fɔwə], phonemicized /fówər/. (*Sure* is similarly /šúwər/ in Type B, but this pronunciation is shared by one-fourth of the Boston informants.)

Although the feature occurs sporadically throughout the metropolis, nowhere is /iw/ common except within subdialect *B,* as [ɪu] or [ɨu] in *suit, new,* and *due*.

Subdialect C

Characteristic of more than half the informants within the central area but of less than one-fourth outside the central area are the following:

614   1. *Washed* has [ɒ], where Type *A* uses [ɑ]. (Map 2)

2. [ɐ] occurs as the first element of the nucleus in *joint, ice.* For Type *A*, these usually contain [a].

3. Sequences like *law and order* exhibit a linking /r/ between the first and second words. (Map 3)

4. The initial contoid of the stressed second syllable of *potatoes* is a flap [ɾ]. (Map 4)

5. Loam is pronounced /luwm/ *versus* the /lowm/ of Type *A*. (Map 5)

6. *Chimney* has /l/ as the initial contoid of its second syllable. (Map 6)

7. The unstressed syllables of *library* and *strawberry* are the same, [bri] /briy/.

The central area shares these features with the northern urban and suburban regions:

1. Monophthongal [i] is frequent for /iy/ in closed syllables, as in *cheese* and *cream.* (Map 7)

2. The medial contoid of *bottles* (and less often of *battle* and *kettle*) is [ʔ]. (Map 8)

The maps on the next pages chart the occurrence of most of these features in this subdialect. A distinct symbol identifies a feature for the informant corresponding to an adjacent number.

.   .   .

THE CORRESPONDENCE OF BOSTON ENGLISH TO OTHER DIALECTS

The phonemic structure of Boston English, insofar as this structure identifies all unit phonemes with broad functional capacity and with open adaptability to new sequences in new morphemes, does not differ from that of other Northern dialects. The single phonemic item of Boston speech that does not have an equivalent in most other dialects is the "short *o*," /ə/, which is, however, of severely limited distribution in the lexicon, operant for a small minority of speakers, and unquestionably on the verge of extinction (or surviving as a conscious anomalous relic).

The set of basic oppositions shared by the vowel systems of the several dialects would not be deranged by the positing of an /ɨ/ phoneme for any one. Indeed, the probable load limitations for /ɨ/ in any one dialect are similar to those of /ə/ in Boston speech. . . .

The consistent phonemic structure runs through the various subdialects of Boston. The peculiarities of a given subdialect are matters of allophonic distribution or of tactical fluctuations among the phonemes.

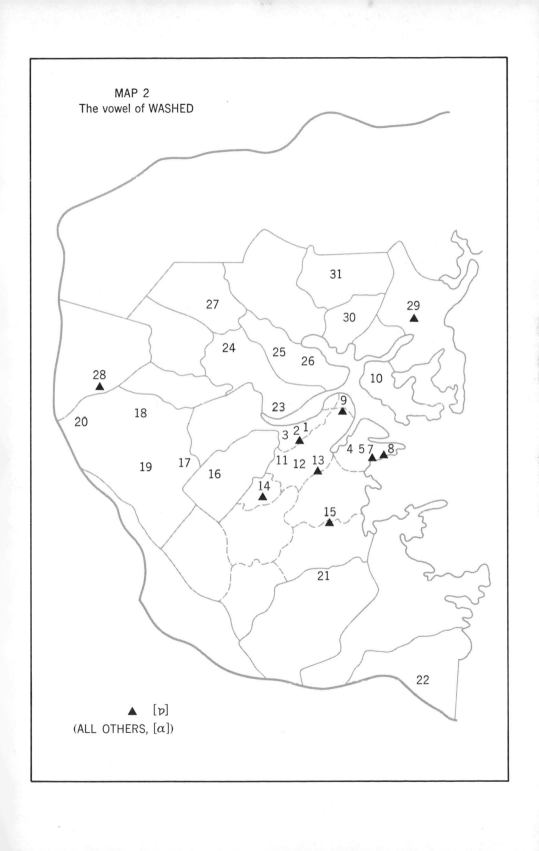

MAP 2
The vowel of WASHED

27

31

24

29

30

25

28

26

23

10

20

18

9

3 2 1

4 5 7 8

11 12 13

19 17

16

14

15

21

22

▲ [ɒ]
(ALL OTHERS, [ɑ])

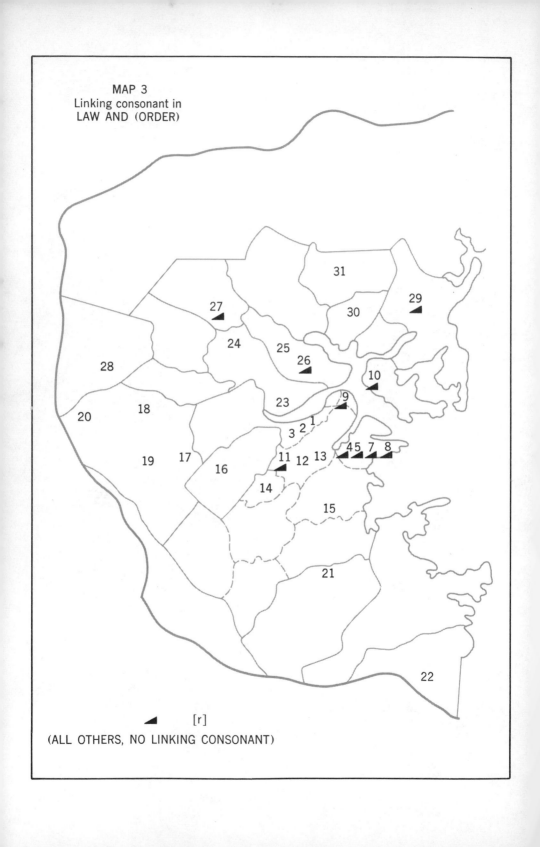

MAP 3
Linking consonant in
LAW AND (ORDER)

27

31

29

30

24   25

26

28

10

23   9

18   1

20   3 2

19   17   16   11 12 13   4 5 7 8

14

15

21

22

▲   [r]
(ALL OTHERS, NO LINKING CONSONANT)

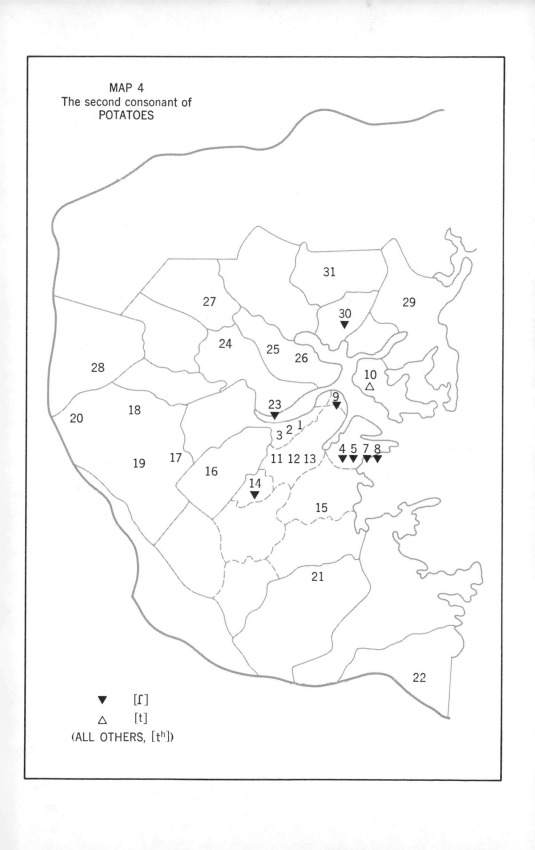

MAP 4
The second consonant of
POTATOES

27

31

29

24

25

26

30 ▼

28

10
△

18

23 ▼

9
▼

20

3 2 1

4 5 7 8
▼ ▼ ▼ ▼

19

17

16

11 12 13

14
▼

15

21

22

▼   [ɾ]
△   [t]
(ALL OTHERS, [tʰ])

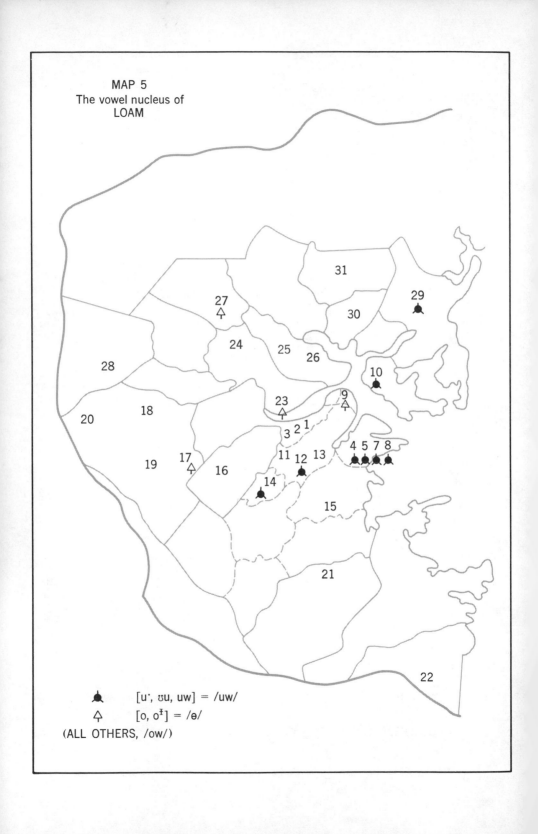

MAP 5
The vowel nucleus of
LOAM

[u·, ʊu, uw] = /uw/

[o, oᵻ] = /ɵ/

(ALL OTHERS, /ow/)

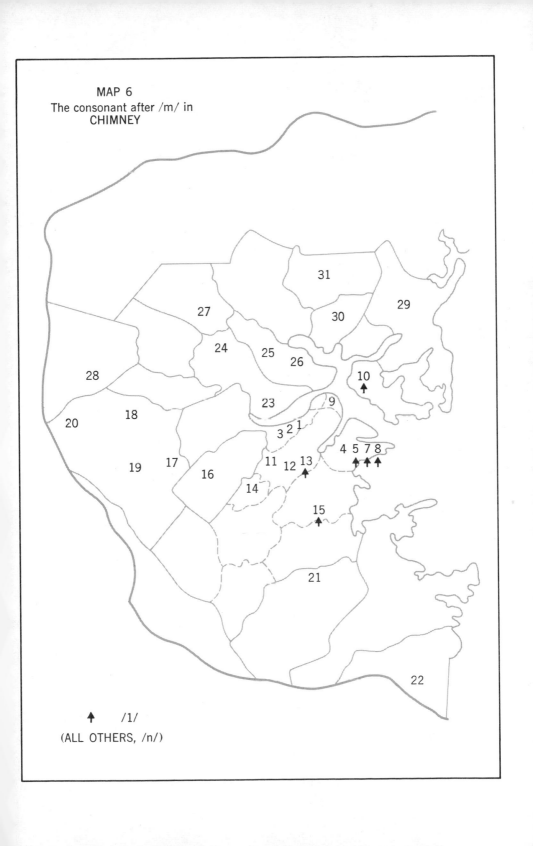

MAP 6
The consonant after /m/ in
CHIMNEY

↑   /1/
(ALL OTHERS, /n/)

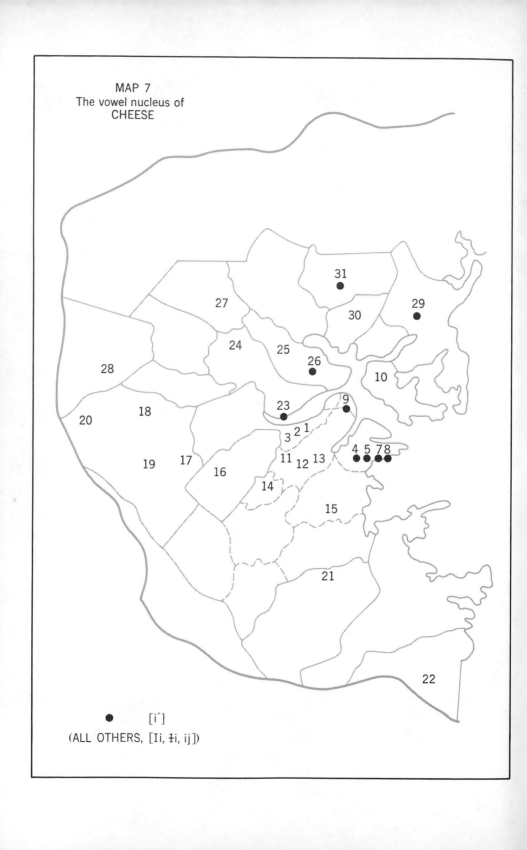

MAP 7
The vowel nucleus of
CHEESE

●   [iˑ]
(ALL OTHERS, [Ii, ɨi, ij])

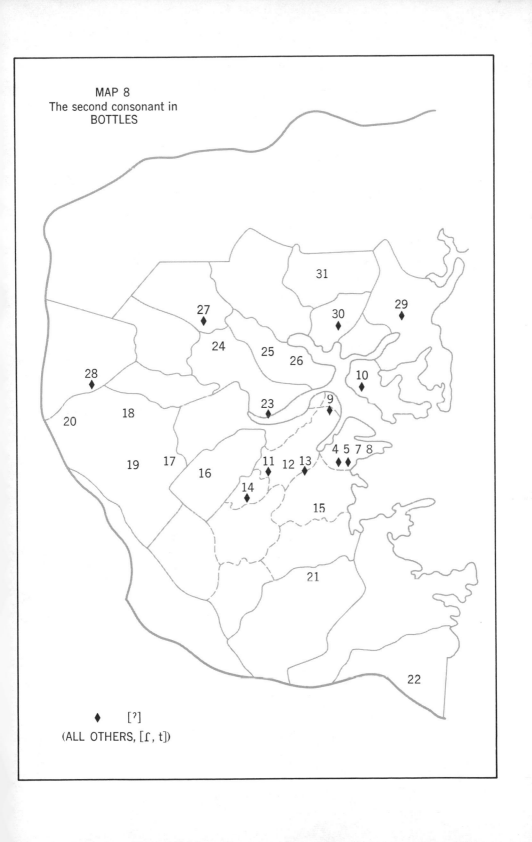

MAP 8
The second consonant in
BOTTLES

♦ [ʔ]
(ALL OTHERS, [ɾ, t])

622   **RECENT PHONOLOGICAL CHANGES IN THE BOSTON DIALECT**

Of all present phonological developments in the Boston dialect, the most apparent is the re-introduction of *r*-timbre in vocalic nuclei. Although earlier records fail to provide a scientifically reliable indication of the extent of *r*-lessness in the coastal dialects of the United States, it is safe to assume a general lack of constricted nuclei in Boston speech at the beginning of this century (just as it is not difficult to assume an opposite state of affairs for Cape Ann and Marblehead to the north). Oddly enough, Grandgent has little to say of positive comparative value about vowels with this feature; his relative silence may emphasize a universal acknowledgment in parentheses to suggest its limited frequency.[1]

.   .   .

Comparison of Boston informants in the LANE[2] and the present study demonstrates a steady progression to *r*-timbre for all regions and social levels. Of five LANE informants only one produced a constricted stressed vowel in *girl* and *thirty;* in this study the contemporaries of the *Atlas* speakers had even less constriction, but there was a fourfold increase in the frequency of this feature between the middle-aged and younger generations.

A similar, though more restrained, tendency to *r*-timbre is observable in diphthongal sequences such as the nuclei of *hear, care, shore,* and *poor.*

Noted by Grandgent, again with no hint of frequency, is the intrusive-*r* phenomenon (present in *Shah of Persia* and *raw oysters,* and other phrases).[3] Only the cultivated youngest informant of the *Atlas* Boston group linked the adjacent vowels of *law and order* and *Ma, I* with an *r.* The present evidence indicates a successive increase and decrease in this feature, probably within the past forty years; there is a persuasive correlation between the decline of linking-*r* and the increase in frequency of *r*-nuclei.

The emergence after stressed single vowels of glides, either as additions to allophony or as phonemes, may be traced from Grandgent's record,

---

[1] The set of vowels above differs from the 3x3 schema of Smith and Trager at several points. The S–T "barred *i*" phoneme, /ɨ/, cannot be isolated for these Boston informants: all [ɨ] or [ɪ] phones may be assigned to either /i/ or /ə/ phonemes (*vide* their location on this chapter's charts). The present /o/ is generally identical to the S–T /ɔ/. The S–T /o/, on the other hand, equates to /ɵ/ in this study. Since /ɵ/ is so rare, considerable phonemic economy is effected for most speakers by employing /o/, already required in the diphthong /ow/, for the low-back vowel.

[2] Kurath, Bloch, et al. *Linguistic Atlas of New England,* 3 vols. in 6 parts. Providence: Brown University Press, 1939–43.

[3] Grandgent, *Old and New,* 42.

through the *Atlas,* and to the present. The New England "short *o,*" phonemically /ɵ/, is the major casualty of this tendency toward diphthongization. Grandgent claims /ɵ/ in at least fifty words for urban speakers;[4] the *Atlas* has /ɵ/ regularly as characteristic in at least a dozen words. Among the thirty individuals contributing to this text the occurrences of /ɵ/ are rare and sporadic.

All of the earlier collections locate the vowel of *past, glass,* and *grass* in more central positions, as [a] or [ɑ]. The present pronunciation is increasingly (if frequencies for age-groups are compared) a more forward [æ]: one-half of the more recent informants use this phone, and thus the phoneme /æ/, for these words.

Grandgent and the *Atlas* concur in the divided usage for *sue, due,* and *duty:*[5] for both sources a high-front element, /i/ or /y/, is present in no more than half the occurrences. Among the younger informants of this study only four produce either glide in one or more words of this type.

There remain several aspects of Boston phonology worthy of future attention.

Despite its evanescence, the /ɵ/ phoneme may have a lingering vitality directly related to the speaker's style of discourse—a premise that the somewhat fixed approach of this paper could not test. Research in depth on social dialects could ascertain the conditions under which this /ɵ/ persists as well as the conditions which favor the use of such localisms as [ɪn] for *-ing* in cultivated speech.

The possibility of identifying additional subdialects within the metropolis could be investigated; the presence of several unique features for Newton informants suggests that more refined elicitations could discover other local characteristics.

The correlation of some dialect differences with ethnic backgrounds could perhaps be proved for Boston by more specialized field techniques.

In the course of the present study it was observed that the glottal stop allophone, [ʔ], of /t/ was most common among persons of Irish descent. The temptation to associate these particulars is subdued by the consideration that the glottal allophone of Boston is articulatorily distant from the analogous allophone of the Irish dialects of English, a dental [t̪]. On the other hand, the flap allophone, [ɾ], of /t/ observed in the central region's pronunciation of *potatoes* (the consonant of the stressed syllable), is close in articulation and auditory effect to [t̪].

The interpreter of these data is faced with a dilemma: The same techniques of analysis applied to both the [ʔ] and [ɾ] phones lead to similar conclusions on the provenience of the sounds, but the historical correla-

[4] *Ibid.,* 132.

[5] *Ibid.,* 135–6.

624 tion of [ɾ] and [t̪] is reasonable in phonetic terms, that of [ʔ] and [t̪] far from reasonable.

Subdialect C, in which this [ʔ] and [ɾ] allophony is prevalent, is the vernacular of the central region of Boston and therefore of an "Irish" majority. But there is no conclusive evidence, as the foregoing problem suggests, that these particular features are anything else than coincidental with the ethnic composition.

One phonological item which might appear related to ethnic background is *r*-timbre for allophones of /r/ since most languages with an analog to /r/ in their phonology effect it with strong contoidal segments. On present evidence the verdict must be "not proven"—constriction for *r*-timbre occurs principally for informants: No. 12, descended from many generations of local Yankee stock; No. 19, on the father's side, long-time Yankees, on the mother's, Ohioans; No. 21, of East European Jewish parentage; No. 29, a first generation American of Italian descent.

Restricted field work of the present sort cannot provide adequate proof of ethnic-grading. It is doubtful that any sample of less than several hundred informants would give proper assurance that dialect differences are related to the influences of foreign language or dialect or of foreign culture. In a city where many neighborhoods are ethnic ghettoes, self-imposed or otherwise, a population sample of thirty will never be able to distinguish regional from ethnic groupings.

Let's Take Another Look at New York City Speech

Arthur J. Bronstein

New York City has one of the most complex speech
situations in the United States. In this article, Professor
Bronstein is concerned with the information that one should
have if he is to understand its complexity. This information
should include both geographical and sociological facts.
Arthur Bronstein is Professor of Speech and Linguistics
at Lehman College. Among his many publications
arc *The Pronunciation of American English* (1961) and
Vowels and Diphthongs of Nineteenth Century America (1949).

The speech of the city of New York and its environs has been the subject of a reasonable number of studies, some carefully descriptive, some
carelessly so, some completely prescriptive, some concerned only with
substandard forms. Some studies are based on impressions of early
twentieth-century New York speech and, as such, are somewhat out of
date now. Some, though based on a narrow sampling of this highly com-

From *American Speech,* Vol. 37 (February, 1962) 13–26. Reprinted with the permission of
Columbia University Press.

626   plicated speech area, have contributed to a clearer picture of the speech of the city of New York. Isolating certain common forms in the speech of those who use a less-cultivated variety seems to have been a common method of describing this dialect, hardly a thorough approach to an analysis of the functional varieties of the language used in this socially complex area.

The bibliographical items of concern to anyone interested in understanding the phonological varieties of New York City speech should include at least those noted below.[1] Hubbell's study, now twelve years old, was based primarily on an investigation of the speech of thirty native New Yorkers. In addition, the recordings of nine other New Yorkers who had served as Linguistic Atlas informants and the recordings of the speech of many Columbia University freshmen were available to him. His analysis is still the most thorough one available. Thomas's findings are based on an analysis of the speech patterns of thousands of speakers, among whom were many natives of the city of New York. A large number had been interviewed face to face. Others recorded on tape. Thomas's sources make the largest collection of raw data in any one place, and his careful analyses are very useful to the student of linguistic geography. Yakira Frank's dissertation was based on the speech of forty-six Linguistic Atlas informants. It too provides carefully analyzed information to the interested reader. These three sources are the basic ones for anyone interested in this dialect area. Interestingly enough, they are not in complete agreement on all points—nor could they have been—since their primary sources were all different, an additional support to the obvious contention that the speech of this heavily populated and highly complex area is still in need of much careful study.

[1] Allan F. Hubbell, *The Pronunciation of English in New York City* (New York, 1950); Yakira H. Frank, "The Speech of New York City," (dissertation; University of Michigan, 1948); Charles K. Thomas, "The New York City Area," pp. 219–222 and *passim,* and "Regional Variations in American Pronunciation," pp. 191–215, in *The Phonetics of American English* (2d ed.; New York, 1958); Claude M. Wise, "Speech of New York City: Standard and Substandard," in *Applied Phonetics* (Englewood Cliffs, N.J., 1957), pp. 280–292; and Marshall D. Berger, review of *Applied Phonetics, American Speech,* XXXIV (1959), 116–119. A copy of Hans Kurath and Raven I. McDavid, Jr., *The Pronunciation of English in the Atlantic States* (Ann Arbor, Mich., 1961), arrived just before the typescript of this article was forwarded to the editor. This long-awaited volume is based on the collection of the Linguistic Atlas of the Eastern United States. Even a rapid perusal indicates the necessity of including the book in any list of sources that treat current American-English pronunciation. Special references to the speech of metropolitan New York appear on pages 14–15 and throughout the discussions in Chapter 3, "The Regional and Social Dissemination of the Diaphones of Stressed Vowels," pp. 101–113; in Chapter 4, "The Consonant /r/ and the Vowels before /r~ə/," pp. 115–127; and in Chapter 5, "Regional and Social Differences in the Incidence of Vowels and Consonants," pp. 129–179.

It is not my intention to present still another descriptive analysis of the   627
speech of the city of New York, or of a part thereof. Rather, I wish to discuss briefly four general items of information which I believe should be
useful to those who desire to know more about this speech community:

1. The New York City speech area is a clearly separate dialect area;
the evidence does not support authors who continue to place it in the
"Eastern" or "New England" dialect areas.

2. This dialect area, like others, is understood better when the data
about its geographical confines, and the social and economic forces that
combine the city's adjacent geographic areas into a single speech community, have been studied. Such recently gathered data are now available,
and they lend support to the already posited premise that New York City
is an integral part of a larger metropolitan region, of which most of the
city is the geographic, social, and economic core. Nor is there reason to
assume that the speech community involved does not reflect almost the
very same boundaries. The dialect area of the New York City speech
community goes beyond the confines of the five boroughs which comprise the civic entity which is the largest city in the country.

It should be clear that synchronic analyses of the linguistic data need
not make reference to other cultural and social aspects of the community
under investigation. Such data, when available, do not explain the linguistic data. Along with the evidence supplied by the dialectologist, they
merely add to an understanding of the area being investigated.

3. Substandard and "foreignized" speech forms heard in New York
City and its environs are not, as is too often assumed by too many, the
speech most commonly heard in New York City.

4. Certain conclusions about New York City speech, commonly found
in texts used in many of the schools, are hardly warranted by the facts of
usage known to many who work in the area. What are considered and
taught as substandard forms are often common to the speech of educated
speakers in that area. The evidence does not always warrant the appellation "questionable," "careless," or "substandard" applied to many typical
forms of New York City speech.

It is not consistent with the facts of usage to continue to place New
York City speech in the same category with that of Bangor, Boston, Portland, Providence, and New Haven, as is still done in certain speech and
phonetics texts, including some published within the past few years.[2] The

---

[2] See, for example, Wise, *op. cit.,* p. 280 and *passim* pp. 221–238; C. E. Kantner and R. West,
Phonetics (rev. ed.; New York, 1960), p. 291; L. Sarrett, W. T. Foster, and A. J. Sarrett, *Basic
Principles of Speech* (3d. ed.; Boston, 1958), p. 232; E E. White, *Practical Speech Fundamentals*
(New York, 1960), p. 172; J. Carrell and W. R. Tiffany, *Phonetics* (New York, 1960), pp. 5,
274–275.

628   Linguistic Atlas studies do divide the Eastern seaboard area into the
        Northern, Midland, and Southern major dialect belts, with metropolitan
        New York City as a *separate* Northern subarea.[3] Although this division is
        based on an analysis of word usage rather than pronunciation, Kurath
        did note at the time that "features of pronunciation and of grammar seem
        to exhibit regional distributions that resemble the dissemination of words
        very closely."[4] No other single metropolitan area, regardless of size, is
        separated from the surrounding regional areas. (The six Northern
        subareas are noted as northeastern New England, southeastern and
        southwestern New England, the inland North, the Hudson Valley, and
        metropolitan New York City.) C. K. Thomas probably has been the most
        outspoken critic of the notion that New York City speech belongs in the
        same category with the speech of the New England–Atlantic seaboard
        area, starting with his "Pronunciation in Downstate New York."[5] He
        continued the discussion in "The Place of New York City in American
        Linguistic Geography."[6] The second edition of his *Phonetics of American
        English* continues the designation of New York City as a separate area.
        Hubbell, whose work clearly established the separateness of New York
        City speech, calls the "eastern type of pronunciation that included the
        speech both of New York City and eastern New England . . . an elocu-
        tionist's fiction."[7] He states in his previously cited work:

> The city and its suburbs must . . . be considered a separate area in the
> linguistic geography of the country. The term "Eastern American"
> should either not be used at all or should be restricted in its application
> to the region east of the Connecticut.[8]

Exclusive of some few who may still believe that the "best New York
City speech" belongs to those who sound like the native New Englanders
of the Beacon Hill section of Boston, New Yorkers who are cognizant of
the facts of usage in the city as well as those of the coastal area north
of it find it hard to disagree with these conclusions.

The presence of New England patterns of speech in the New York
area is, of course, not to be denied. Available migration data indicate

---

[3] Hans Kurath, *A Word Geography of the Eastern United States* (Ann Arbor, Mich., 1949),
Fig. 3.

[4] *Ibid.,* p. 12. The same speech areas that appeared in the earlier *Word Geography* are repeated
in the Kurath-McDavid *Pronunciation of English in the Atlantic States.* Map 2 continues to
show metropolitan New York as a separate subarea of the Northern speech area.

[5] *American Speech,* XXVII (1942), 30–41, 149–157.

[6] *Quarterly Journal of Speech,* XXXIII (1947), 314–320.

[7] Hubbell, *op. cit.,* p. 1.

[8] *Ibid.,* p. 3.

that New England did contribute the largest number of white lifetime migrants to the state of New York. These migrants came, however, before 1900. After 1900, the largest number of in-migrants came from the Mid-Atlantic states. For example, in 1949–1950, out of a total of 156,790 in-migrants, New Jersey and Pennsylvania contributed 20,000 each, while California, Florida, Massachusetts, and Connecticut contributed 10,000 each. These make up 52.6 percent of the total. The remaining 47.4 percent came from all the other states. It is interesting to note in passing that the South Atlantic states have always contributed more than half of the in-migrants of nonwhites to New York State. Most of the in-migrants to the state settle in New York City.[9]

Perhaps a quick review of certain pertinent geographic and sociological evidence, as reported in sources and studies published within the last few years,[10] should be made, in order to provide a clearer picture of what is meant when one talks today about the New York City speech community. Such evidence is useful in providing necessary background for the understanding of the nature of the area that houses the people who comprise this speech community. W. Nelson Francis succinctly defines the term *dialect* as "the variety of language spoken by the members of a single homogeneous speech-community," in his *The Structure of American English*.[11] Later in the same text Raven I. McDavid, Jr., describes the same term somewhat more cautiously as "a variety of a language . . . set off (more or less sharply) from other varieties by (more or less clear) features of pronunciation, grammar, or vocabulary."[12] The question is,

---

[9] The cited figures are taken from Charles E. Ramsey and Walfred A. Anderson, "Migration of the New York State Population," Bulletin No. 929, New York State College of Agriculture (Ithaca, N. Y., 1958).

[10] See Walfred A. Anderson, "Characteristics of New York State Population," Bulletin No. 925, New York State College of Agriculture (Ithaca, N. Y., 1958); *The Statistical Guide for New York City* (1959), edited by Cecilia Winkler for the Department of Commerce and Public Events of the City of New York; and especially the results of the recently conducted New York metropolitan region study. This regional survey culminated in a series of specialized studies edited by Max Hall. Those available at the time of preparing this article were: Oscar Handlin, *The Newcomers: Negroes and Puerto Ricans in a Changing Metropolis* (1959); Martin Segal, *Wages in the Metropolis: Their Influence on the Location of Industries in the New York Region* (1960); Benjamin Chinitz, *Freight and the Metropolis: the Impact of America's Transport Revolution on the New York Region* (1960); Sidney M. Robbins and Nestor E. Terleckyj, with the collaboration of Ira O. Scott, Jr., *Money Metropolis: a Locational Study of Financial Activities in the New York Region* (1960); Roy W. Helfgott, W. Eric Gustafson, and James M. Hund, *Made in New York: Case Studies in Metropolitan Manufacturing* (1959); Raymond Vernon, *Metropolis 1985* (1960); Edgar M. Hoover and Raymond Vernon, *Anatomy of a Metropolis* (1959).

[11] (New York, 1958), p. 43.

[12] p. 480.

630   of course, how homogeneous this speech community really is. The sociological evidence clearly points to the conclusion that it is one of the most complex in the nation. A survey of the complexities of this single region does, however, lead to the conclusion that it is not a homogeneous one sociologically, yet it is bound together strongly into a single sociological entity by economic, cultural, and social ties.

The dialect spoken by the people of this region is considered a single linguistic entity, despite the many phonological varieties one can hear for certain phonemic forms in different parts of the region and at different levels of the social scale. It is the dialect used and understood by all those who live there, except perhaps the few linguistically (and socially) isolated foreign groups, such as the new in-migrants from Puerto Rico. These statements are not meant to imply that the region described below does not possess many subdialects and subdialect areas. One can, and does, hear numerous features of the language not heard consistently everywhere else in that region, and, as one approaches the outer fringes of the metropolitan area, many of the significant features of this dialect disappear. The thought has occurred more than once to investigators of New York City speech (if not to the nonspecialist who manages to spend his days in different sections of the city and its environs) that this region is hardly a "single homogeneous speech community." Perhaps such a conclusion is warranted. But on the basis of available data, more and different evidence than we now have would be required before one could draw this conclusion. If certain linguistic features do occur more frequently in Forest Hills or Astoria (Queens) than they do in Williamsburg (Brooklyn) or in Washington Heights (Manhattan), the available evidence does not warrant the drawing of a bundle of isoglossal lines separating any of these geographic areas from others in the metropolitan region. Despite the different features, the metropolitan New York area can be considered a single speech community.

Five or six decades ago, it might have suited the purpose of the sociologist, if not the linguist studying speech patterns, to consider the four main boroughs as comprising the metropolitan region of the city. Today, the metropolitan area of New York City, like many other urban areas, has spilled into the surrounding countryside, engulfing cities and communities which had their own economic and cultural centers. The island of Manhattan has now become the central point of a rather large geographic area, probably best thought of as a core and two encircling rings, as noted in the Hoover-Vernon analysis cited above. The core, or innermost part of the region, contains the greatest number of dwelling units and jobs. Employment is densest in the core, as is the population concentration. Both become progressively less dense as one moves from the core to the periphery of the region. The three zones of the metropolitan region contain twenty-two counties, with an estimated population, as of 1956, of 15,375,000 and, as of March 15 of that year, a total of 6,699,800 jobs.

The core contains five counties: New York (Manhattan), Bronx, Kings (Brooklyn), Queens, and Hudson, the last in the state of New Jersey. This core has grown in population from approximately four million at the beginning of the century to approximately eight million today. To it, on each working day of that year, hundreds of thousands of commuters arrive each morning (and depart therefrom each evening). It is estimated that approximately 87,000 arrive from Westchester County to the north of the city, 132,000 from Nassau and Suffolk counties to the east, and 151,000 from the New Jersey counties to the west.[13] Puerto Ricans comprise one-sixth of the inhabitants of Manhattan and one twentieth of the remainder of the core. New York City (the boroughs of Manhattan, Bronx, Brooklyn, Queens, and Richmond) contains 80 percent of the Puerto Ricans of the entire United States. The core houses 50 percent of the population of the entire metropolitan region.

The inner part of this core, Manhattan and adjacent parts of the surrounding counties, is peopled by a large mass of bottom-income, unskilled, manual, and service workers, including what our sociologist colleagues call the "disadvantaged" (those who use what we might recognize as the least cultivated variety of New York speech)—plus the wealthy, mainly childless people who work at professional and executive tasks (those who use what we know to be a well-educated, urbanized, social dialect of the region). Younger families with children, who could afford to do so, have tended to move out to suburban areas. Lower income families have remained.

The seven counties immediately surrounding the core of the metropolitan area are called the inner ring. This ring contains three New York State counties (Nassau, Richmond, and Westchester) and four New Jersey counties (Essex, Union, Bergen, and Passaic). These seven counties house approximately 30 percent of the total metropolitan region. They are the region's suburbia, containing such well-known communities as Great Neck, Levittown, Scarsdale, Rye, and Summit. In this region are located many large plants and industrial concerns which, because of space requirements, the local tax picture, and zoning laws, find these areas quite convenient. The inner ring provides 24 percent of the jobs of the entire region, comparatively little obsolete housing, and more living space for its residents. The average number of people per acre is 14, as compared to 114 per acre in the core.

In the outermost parts of the core and in the most urbanized parts

---

[13] These figures are based on available commuter reports for 1955.

632   of the inner ring, the population falls into the middle-income bracket. As one moves farther out into the inner ring, there is a gradual rise in income level and a rising proportion of households with children. At the edges of the inner ring (and at the inner edges of the outer ring) there are many more upper-income families. From the beginning of the century, the inner ring has grown from one million to over three and a half million people.

The outer ring of the region is its exurbia. It contains four New York counties (Suffolk, Putnam, Rockland, and Dutchess), five New Jersey counties (Monmouth, Middlesex, Somerset, Morris, and Orange), and Fairfield County in Connecticut. Only a few daily commuters come into the center of the core from this region. Its per capita income is lower than that of the inner ring. It has grown from 750,000 people at the beginning of this century to about 2,500,000 today. It contains a few fox-hunting clubs (in Somerset, Morris, and Suffolk counties), heavily industrialized Bridgeport in Fairfield County, many small homesteads, and large rural areas. Although not altogether of the metropolitan area, yet economically tied to it, the outer ring is becoming more closely linked with the inner ring and the core because of the new highways—the New York Thruway, the New England Thruway, the Merritt, Garden State, and Taconic parkways, and the Long Island Expressway. Perhaps within a generation this outer ring will lose much of its rural character. The dialect features common to the New York City core and to the more urbanized parts of the inner ring seem to dissipate and, in some instances, disappear before the outer ring is reached, although no clear dividing line is drawn easily.

The social complexities of this large region cannot be reviewed here. A few highlights must suffice. This regional community is the center of the garment industry, the printing industry, the publishing field, and the country's varied financial activities. It contains a leading shipping port on the Hudson and East rivers, along with the many industries connected therewith. The New York metropolitan region is the country's largest retail outlet and the leading center for theater, music, and the visual arts. It is the home of three of the country's largest airports: Newark, La Guardia, and Kennedy. It is the center of international diplomacy and a tourist mecca for the country at large. The restaurants and night clubs of the city region, many of them world famous, are counted in the thousands. New York City boasts of many fine museums, art galleries, and recital halls, more than are found anywhere else in the country. Thirty-three colleges and universities are in this metropolitan region.

All these industries, cultural pursuits, business, economic, and social activities attract many thousands to the core each day and evening. They come from different sections to other sections of the core, as well as from the inner and outer rings of the metropolitan region. The social, industrial, economic, and cultural life of the three areas is closely knit.

Neither substandard nor foreignized speech forms are typical of most speakers of the New York metropolitan area, despite impressions to the contrary that may be gained from a study of some speech improvement texts and brochures used in the schools of the city, in the 1920s and since. These sources were written by teachers of speech in the New York City area.[14] They resulted from the teachers' needs for materials and guidance in eradicating traces of speech which they considered substandard or foreign. Perhaps it should be noted that, regardless of attitudes of narrowness and rigidity toward language usage that derive from a strongly prescriptive approach to our language that many teachers are wont to take, the efforts of the New York City speech teachers did, and do, stem from a sincere desire to eradicate the traces of "uncultivated," "careless," or "slovenly" speech found in the patterns of many of the schoolchildren.

Speech work had begun as a special and separate area in the New York City public schools by the end of the first quarter of the century. As in many other school systems, what became the speech field had been a part of English departments. "Oral English" had become an activity that English teachers knew to be a valuable aspect of their discipline. The greatest felt need was for guidance and work in remedial English, both oral and written. As a result, speech work, requiring teachers with specialized orientation and training, came into being. The Board of Examiners scheduled special examinations for speech-improvement teachers in the elementary schools, where teachers worked under the jurisdiction of a special Bureau of Speech Improvement, with headquarters at the Board. Examinations for high-school teachers of speech were also scheduled, and successful candidates holding this special license were assigned to individual high schools. In many instances these teachers worked in departments of English where no separate speech department existed. (Such is still the situation in some New York City schools. In December, 1960, there were twenty-four speech departments and eighty-four English departments in the New York City high schools.)

Perhaps somewhat more than elsewhere in the United States, the habits of speech which were considered uncultivated could be associated with a rather large group or class of speakers. Not all native-born speakers of native-born parents use the same phonetic patterns, especially when there is wide divergence in education, occupation, and family back-

[14] Such as Grace A. McCullough and Agnes V. Birmingham, *Correcting Speech Defects and Foreign Accent* (New York, 1925); Margaret P. McLean, *Good American Speech* (New York, 1928); Letitia Raubicheck, *Voice and Speech Problems* (New York, 1932); and Ruth Manser, *Speech Correction on the Contract Plan* (New York, 1935).

634   ground. Whereas laborers, farm hands, lawyers, and bankers in Nebraska and Utah might differ in syntactic or vocabulary usages, but not greatly in pronunciation, New York's construction workers, cab drivers, and soda jerks are known to use many words, grammatical constructions, *and* pronunciations quite uncommon to the speech of the professors, the downtown bankers and investment counselors, and the midtown executives. The differences in pronunciation that may be heard in different social groups in New York City have been noted before[15] and undoubtedly account for the comparative ease with which one can find mention and discussion of certain of these forms in almost all speech texts. The difference is not so great as that between speakers in metropolitan London who use Received Pronunciation and those who use Cockney dialect. Nor are the differences between the social groups and their language patterns to be compared with the divergences found in the speech of many socially isolated American Negroes whose speech patterns differ from those of others in the same geographic area.[16]

The less-cultivated speaker of New York City can and does walk on the same side of the street and ride in the same part of the bus, and can eat in the same restaurants, as does his better-educated neighbor. If he lives in the same community with somewhat more fortunate persons, as occurs in many suburban areas, he attends the same neighborhood motion picture theaters and worships in the same churches and temples. In the inner-ring areas, his contact with his better-educated neighbors is closer than it is in the core, where the residential neighborhoods tend to be restricted to homogeneous social groups. In general, however, his social contacts remain almost completely within his own social group, unless and until the educational system, or perhaps chance, permits him the opportunity to climb the social ladder.

The reason for the concern by the school system with language patterns other than English is seen when we check the census figures of the New York City area since the early part of this century. The generalization that foreign-speaking immigrants tend to have very little influence on the phonetic and phonemic patterns of native inhabitants is well known. Questioning whether this generalization holds true for the peculiar situation existing in New York City is not uncommon, but no real evidence has come forth that seriously contradicts the generalization.

The immigrant groups came to New York City in vast numbers. The new arrival was not the stranger among many natives, fairly rapidly absorbed. Rather, he remained geographically and socially isolated

[15] See, for example, Hubbell, *op. cit.,* pp. 4–5.

[16] See Raven I. McDavid, Jr., and Virginia Glenn McDavid, "The Relationship of the Speech of American Negroes to the Speech of Whites," *American Speech,* XXVI (1951), 3–17.

among other immigrants, many from his own native country, if not from the same general section of his native land. He worked and lived next to his boyhood friend from Europe, dated the immigrant girl who spoke his native tongue, and spoke to his children in the foreign language or in a "broken English," while they answered him in the language of their own birth. He was a member of a foreign-language-speaking society or fellowship group. He attended plays, ate in restaurants, and shopped in stores at each of which the language heard and used was that of his native land. This heavy concentration of immigrants in their own native language areas was found throughout the city: the Germans in Yorkville and later in the midtown West Side sections of Manhattan; the Norwegians near the Fort Hamilton section of Brooklyn; the Russians on the lower East Side of Manhattan, in the east Bronx, and in the Williamsburg section of Brooklyn; the Italians on the lower East Side, off Canal Street, in Greenwich Village, downtown Brooklyn, and in the Bensonhurst and Bath Beach sections of the same borough; the Chinese near the Bowery, south of Canal Street; the Romanians, Irish, Armenians, Hungarians, and, presently, the Puerto Ricans in their own neighborhoods of the city. The in-migrant Negroes from the South concentrated in their neighborhoods too, in all the boroughs, the largest concentration being the Harlem section in uptown Manhattan, north of 110th Street.

Some pertinent census figures are noted in the accompanying tables. The 1910 figures show a total population of a little over five million in the five boroughs, of which almost one and a half million came from homes in which both parents were foreign-born. The 1930 figures do not reflect much of a change (see Tables 1 and 2). Of the five-borough total population of 6,935,500, there were 4,310,000 native whites, 325,500 native Negro, and 2,300,000 foreign born. Thirty-three percent of the city's population was foreign born at this time.

By 1950, New York City had a total population of 7,892,795 people, with 70 percent, or 1,700,000, of the state's foreign-born population. The foreign-born had decreased by 600,000 since the 1930 census, and most of them were aging people. (The median age of all native whites was

Table 1. Census Figures for New York City (in Round Numbers)

County	1910	1930	1950
Kings	1,634,000	2,568,000	2,738,000
New York	2,763,000	1,864,000	1,960,000
Queens	284,000	1,088,000	1,551,000
Richmond	86,000	152,500	192,000
Bronx	431,000	1,263,000	1,451,000
Totals	5,198,000	6,935,500	7,892,000

Table 2. *Foreign-Born Population Living in New York City*
(in Round Numbers)

County	1930	1940	1950
Kings	900,000	760,000	(not
New York	640,000	540,000	available
Queens	270,000	275,000	by
Richmond	40,000	35,000	borough)
Bronx	450,000	460,000	
Totals	2,300,000	2,070,000	1,700,000

28.9 years, while the median age of all foreign-born was 54.2 years, with only 1.5 percent of the foreign born less than fifteen years old.) The pertinent 1960 census figures were not available when this article was being prepared, but one figure, published in the local press in October, 1960, is of importance: New York City is the largest Puerto Rican city in the world. Of its more than 8,000,000 people, 753,000 are Puerto Rican. San Juan has only 500,000 people!

Native-born children of these in-migrants were surrounded by language patterns of American English spoken in the schools, heard over the radio (once that medium became part of the culture), at the local motion picture theater, and on the streets of their neighborhood. In their homes they heard another language, and even if they could not speak the foreign tongue, they could understand it and, under pressure, could talk to their aunts and uncles in simple phrases of that language. The constant pressure of the foreign-language influence was bound to have some effect on the English-speaking habits of the child, especially if, as often happened, the first language learned was the non-native one. As the child moved into his own play group, the influence lessened. When he entered school, it lessened further. If he continued into higher education and moved away from the parental neighborhood to other sections of the city and country, still fewer traces remained after a while. English was his only tongue, the foreign one recurring only at those sporadic intervals when he returned to visit the family. This is not meant to deny the continued existence of earlier speech patterns, native to the home environment, in the speech of some of the city's officials, fairly high-ranking members of the judiciary, professors in the city's schools, and others who reached the upper levels of the social structure from rather modest beginnings.

The speech of the foreign-born in New York City is a part of the total picture of the speech of the area. It is not one of the dialects of American English, and judging from all the evidence we have, it has had no effect on the dialect spoken by the natives of New York, except to enlarge the vocabulary of the latter with a certain number of expressions native to many languages. Speech with foreign forms is the concern of the public-school teachers whose students possess such patterns, and the speech-improvement teachers probably assume the greatest burden here. It is not too difficult to see why the New York City school system was, and is, so concerned with the speech habits of non-native speakers of American English.

Of the many patterns of New York City dialect that have been associated with substandard or uneducated speech, many sources mention certain forms that are actually quite common in educated speech. Some of these are so common that a continued "substandard" label should be seriously questioned. Still other patterns, considered common to the speech in other dialect areas of the country but not typical of New York City, actually seem to be common enough to warrant their inclusion in the over-all pattern of the area.

In an attempt to verify some of these impressions, I examined the records of approximately 200 entering freshmen at Queens College, randomly selected from each entering class of between 800 and 1,000 students for the five years between 1947 and 1952. These students had been interviewed by members of the Department of Speech for speech placement purposes, each interview lasting approximately ten minutes. In order to substantiate these reactions with a further check, I studied the records of sophomore and junior students who had been interviewed for acceptance in the teacher-training program. The interviewers were members of the department who had not interviewed these students during their freshman year. These latter records were examined for the four years 1952 through 1955. In both instances, interviewers had noted what they considered as variations from normal, educated, colloquial speech. In addition, I have been keeping notes on the speech of students enrolled in one section of the Department's freshman course, each semester since 1947 (approximately thirty-six students per year). These three sources provide evidence that questions some commonly held impressions about the speech of the metropolitan area. These impressions are presented with the understanding that further study is needed to substantiate their typicalness. Such verification will need to be based on the speech of more carefully selected informants from widely scattered parts of the metropolitan area.

Over 90 percent of the students who attend Queens College are residents of Queens County. Almost all come from the middle-class level of the social structure. Many come from families which, soon after the end of the Second World War moved to Queens from Brooklyn, Manhattan, and the Bronx.

1. Final and preconsonantal /r/, as in *here* and *charm,* is used more

638   widely in the New York City area than seems to be reported in the literature. As noted in the previously cited works by Hubbell and Thomas, complete consistency in the use of this sound is not present. But the impression is growing that perhaps as many educated speakers use it, with reasonable consistency, as do not. Perhaps Thomas's statement that New York City speech is "characterized by a frequent, but by no means universal, loss of /r/ in the final and preconsonantal positions . . ."[17] does not seem to hold now, unless one understands this to mean that both the loss and the presence of final and preconsonantal /r/ are almost equally frequent.

    2. The use of [ɛɪ/ɛə] for [eɪ] before /l/ is a common variant, as in *hail, daily,* and *sailor.* Hubbell notes this as occurring on the "uncultivated and intermediate levels";[18] Wise, as a substandard form.[19] Actually, few of the student informants retain [eɪ] for both words of these pairs: *say—sailor; may—mail; bake—bail.* The pairs *dairy—daily, airing—ailing* differ only in the intervocalic consonant. (Some of my colleagues in the city insist that these variants appear on the socially intermediate levels and are not, as yet, common to more cultivated New York City speech. Others are equally convinced that such variant forms are not uncommon to colloquial, cultivated speech.)

    3. A raised sound for the /æ/ in words like *ask, hand,* and *crab* has been noted many times (especially by G. L. Trager in papers published in *American Speech,* 1929–1930, 1934, 1940, and by Hubbell in his study on New York City speech). The complex situation in which this variant may appear need not be detailed here, but there is little doubt that three forms, [ɛə, æ⁺ə, æ], exist in free variation in words of this type in the New York City dialect of American English. Although the schools, from the early years, may try to prevent the widespread usage of a raised sound, the variations continue, quite commonly, in the speech of many educated speakers. Although consistent use of [ɛə] for [æ], with hardly any occurrence of [æ], appears in uncultivated speech, there is mounting evidence of the widespread use of [ɛə], [æ⁺], or [æ⁺ə] in educated speech in the New York City area. These variants do not appear in all words with /æ/. Such words as the "*ask* words" and others like *bad, bag, cash, badge,* and *salve* will continue the raised form, but one never hears such variants in *Alice, Africa, shack, cap, batch,* and *mathematics.* Nor does the tense and strongly nasalized form appear in cultivated speech.

    4. [ɑɪ] for [aɪ], as in *time* and *pie,* with the first element being the sound of the vowel in *calm* and *got,* is more widely used in New York City

[17] *Phonetics of American English,* p. 219.

[18] p. 75.

[19] p. 282.

than is assumed. Suggested avoidance of the still farther back [ɒɪ] has been noted many times in various texts and brochures. The strong pressures to avoid the retracted sound [ɒɪ] may have given many the impression that only the forward [aɪ] allophone is the cultivated New York City form. Actually, [aɪ] and [ɑɪ] vary freely in this dialect, and many educated New Yorkers rarely use the [aɪ] variant, the [ɑɪ] form being their principal member of this phoneme.

5. The use of an "added *r*" in such phrases as *idea-r-of* and *sofa-r-is* is a frequent form in educated speech in New York City. Few speech texts permit it the label of acceptability. Thomas indicates that "most speakers in the area in which intrusive /r/ is frequent regard it as substandard."[20] Sticking to the facts of usage, he does not label it himself. Hubbell notes that there are "many among the cultivated who pronounce in this fashion."[21] Kurath and McDavid report in their *Pronunciation of English in the Atlantic States* that the incidence of this "intrusive" /r/ occurs in about one third of the responses in Eastern New England. They add that:

> Cultured speakers use it as freely as the other social groups (e.g., in Providence, Newport, Plymouth, Boston, Portland). In Metropolitan New York it occurs with slightly greater frequency, but seems to be avoided by cultured informants (only two in nine offered it).[22]

The actual incidence of this added /r/ is not known. Many educated speakers seem to use it and many avoid it. It is certainly more common in substandard usage than in cultured speech. Far too many speakers in the New York City area use this added /r/ to deny its existence as part of educated speech. Regardless of attitudes toward its usage, and the continued counseling against it over the years, the facts of usage do not deny its presence in the pronunciation of many educated speakers.

This article has tried to present certain items of information about New York City and its speech in order to add to the impressions commonly held about this socially and linguistically complex area. No single study has been completed that answers all the questions one can raise about this region and its speech. Surely no single study can.

[20] p. 197.

[21] p. 47.

[22] p. 172.

The Effect of Social Mobility on Linguistic Behavior

William Labov

Professor Labov is well known for his studies of New York City speech, which relate linguistic behavior and socio-economic status. This approach is generally known as the sociolinguistic approach. (See Haver C. Currie's analysis on page 39 in this volume.) In this article Professor Labov shows the relation of linguistic behavior and social mobility in New York City. William Labov is Professor of Linguistics, Columbia University.

Previous investigations of sociolinguistic structure in New York City included quantitative study of five variables of the sound system.[1] These

This article was originally published in *Sociological Inquiry,* Vol. 36, No. 2 (Spring, 1966) 186–203. Reprinted with the permission of *Sociological Inquiry.*

[1] William Labov, "Phonological Correlates of Social Stratification," in John J. Gumperz and Dell Hymes, editors, *The Ethnography of Communication* (*American Anthropologist,* Special Publication, volume 66, number 6, part 2), pp. 164–176. A complete report is given in *The Social Stratification of English in New York City,* Columbia University, 1964: dissertation to be

variables displayed a regular structure of social and stylistic stratification, in which linguistic behavior was closely correlated with productive indicators of socioeconomic status. Patterns of sociolinguistic stratification will be analyzed further in the present paper by considering the added dimension of social mobility. Each sociolinguistic stratum will be differentiated into subgroups according to the speakers' histories of social mobility. It will then be possible to determine which of the subgroups represents the modal tendency of sociolinguistic behavior within each class and to ask whether a second form of stratification exists within each class which is based on social mobility. Finally, sociolinguistic stratification will be reexamined in terms of the added information on social mobility, so that further light may be shed on the question of how such stratification is maintained.

SOCIAL MOBILITY IN THE MECHANISM OF A RURAL SOUND CHANGE

Before considering the New York City situation, it is worth noting that social mobility was found to play an important part in the mechanism of linguistic change in an earlier study of the island of Martha's Vineyard.[2] The linguistic variable studied was the centralization of the diphthongs /ay/ and /aw/ in words such as *right, ride, my, about,* and *down.* This sound change was unusual because of its complex distribution over several ethnic groups, occupational groups, and age categories of the island population, and also because increased centralization departed from the recessive character of this feature to be found in many American dialects. The overall social significance of this sound change was its association with a positive orientation toward Martha's Vineyard. Those who laid claim to native status as Vineyarders showed the greatest centralization, while those who were excluded from this status, or who abandoned their claims to pursue a career on the mainland, would show no centralization of these vowels.

Thus the complexity of the distribution of this sound change can be attributed to the phenomenon of social mobility. The older generation of Yankee fishermen who initiated the change had behind them a history

---

published by the Center for Applied Linguistics, Washington, D. C. Cf. also "Reflections of Social Processes in Linguistic Structures," to appear in Joshua A. Fishman, editor, *A Reader in the Sociology of Language,* The Hague: Mouton, and "Hypercorrection by the Lower Middle Class as a Factor in Linguistic Change," appearing in William Bright, editor, *Sociolinguistics,* The Hague: Mouton, 1966.

[2] William Labov, "The Social Motivation of a Sound Change," *Word,* 19 (December, 1963), pp. 273–306.

642 of downward social movement. Under economic and social pressures, they had retreated from their grandfathers' positions as ship captains and landed proprietors to become small-boat lobstermen and small-scale contractors. The younger Yankee Vineyarders split into two groups: one moved up and out, to college on the mainland and to urban occupations; the other remained on the island at a lower economic level. The latter showed strong centralization, the former none at all. The strongest centralization was shown by the few who abandoned their mainland careers and reasserted their claims to island status.[3]

A simpler pattern of upward social mobility was shown by the large Portuguese ethnic group. The older Portuguese were hardly considered Vineyarders at all by the Yankees; they occupied the lowest socioeconomic level on the island and showed almost no centralization. The younger generations of Portuguese moved up to positions vacated by Yankees and began to appear as merchants, aldermen, and contractors; centralization became increasingly strong in this group.

The small group of Gay Head Indians had been suffering from steady attrition of economic and social position ever since they were deprived of reservation status in 1870.[4] In the last several decades they have reasserted their Indian identity and claimed the elementary social services and rights to which they are entitled as citizens. As with the Portuguese, we find the younger Gay Head Indians increasing centralization, in most cases surpassing the Yankee islanders.

It is thus clear that the complexity of linguistic change reflected a complex set of underlying social movements, and linguistic change could not be understood without analyzing patterns of social mobility on the island. On the other hand, linguistic data added further confirmation to our social analysis, and illuminated features that might otherwise have escaped notice. Furthermore, linguistic data were shown to facilitate the recognition of similar phenomena in diverse settings.

THE LOWER EAST SIDE SURVEY

The 1963–1964 investigation of the sociolinguistic structure of New York City was designed to study a similar problem of complex

[3] This is the pattern termed *hypercorrection*, which appears below in the discussion of New York City speech as an important element in the mechanism of linguistic change.

[4] The Governor of Massachusetts terminated the reservation status of Gay Head in 1870, on the ground that the inhabitants were no longer Indians as the result of intermarriage with Negroes. They were thus given the normal privileges of citizens, including the payment of taxes, and lost most of the land which had traditionally belonged to the community. Details are given in William Labov, "The Social History of a Sound Change," Columbia University M.A. essay, 1963.

distribution.[5] Previous descriptions of New York City English had reported a very wide range of variation in the sound system—a variation
so extensive that the concept of language as a structured, integrated
system began to seem meaningless.

Exploratory interviews suggested that one reason for this fluctuation
is that the linguistic behavior of New Yorkers varies with their socioeconomic position. This independent variable was controlled and studied
through the selection of a stratified random sample of adult, native
English speakers from the Lower East Side. The sample was one that
had been constructed for Mobilization of Youth in 1961 in a survey of
social attitudes and aspirations.

Socioeconomic information on these subjects was, therefore, already
available; and the population had been classified on the basis of this
data into ten socioeconomic strata by MFY analysts. The 988 adults
interviewed by MFY represented a population of 100,000. From this
sample, 312 native speakers of English were randomly selected.[6] Over
the intervening two years, 117 had moved or died, leaving a target sample
of 195. Linguistic information was obtained from 158 subjects; the most
detailed interviews were completed with 122 subjects.

The interview was designed to analyze another major dimension of
variation, that of contextual style as it is governed by the immediate
context of discourse, the topic, and the attitudes of speaker and listener.
This dimension was systematically studied through interview techniques
which elicited a wide range of styles in a partly predictable manner.[7] At
one extreme of the stylistic range is *casual* or *spontaneous speech,* which
approximates the language used in everyday family situations. The main
bulk of the interview, however, is in *careful speech,* which is appropriate
to an interview situation.[8] At the more formal end are *reading style,* the
pronunciation of individual words, and the contrasting *minimal pairs,*
where the speaker's attention is focused directly on the phonological
variable.

[5] This survey was carried out by the author and Mr. Michael Kac of Haverford College.
Reports are given in the references of footnote 1.

[6] About one third of the population were recent arrivals from Puerto Rico, and included no
native speakers of English. Of the total native speakers of English, 100 percent of the socioeconomic groups 0–2 and 6–9 were selected, and 67 percent of groups 3–5.

[7] The primary problem is one of eliciting casual or spontaneous speech in an interview situation for which careful speech is socially defined as appropriate. Techniques for overcoming
this dilemma are discussed in Labov, "Phonological Correlates of Social Stratification," *op. cit.*

[8] No attempt is made to isolate speech styles by impressionistic means. The style used in
answering interview questions is used as a reference point, and other styles are defined by
contrastive cues: specifically, the occurrence of one or more contrastive "channel" cues in a
set of predetermined interview situations.

644   Five phonological variables were selected for quantitative study. Each occurrence of each attribute in the tape-recorded interview was rated on a codified scale which represented the possible range of articulatory variation. The mean value of these ratings for a given stylistic context in any one interview is the basic datum for further analysis—the value of the variable for that person and that style.

The simplest case is that of the variable (r),[9] representing the occurrence of a consonantal (r) in final and pre-consonantal position: in *beard, beer, guard, car, board,* and *bore,* but not in *red, berry,* or *four o'clock.* The index here is the percentage of occurrences of constricted [r] among all occurrences of (r).

Table 1 displays the typical complex of regularities which characterize

Table 1   Mean (r) Values by Contextual Style and Socioeconomic Class for Subjects Raised in New York City Who Yielded Full Interviews

Contextual Style	0–2 Lower Class	3–5 Working Class	6–8 Lower Middle Class	9 Upper Middle Class
Casual Speech	02.5	04.0	04.0	19.0
Careful Speech	10.5	12.5	20.5	32.0
Reading Style	14.5	21.0	27.0	37.0
Word Lists	23.5	35.0	61.0	47.0
Minimal Pairs	49.5	55.0	77.5	60.0

the social and stylistic stratification of the variables—in this case, the variable (r). The socioeconomic classes represent subdivisions of the aforementioned ten-point index developed by Mobilization for Youth, which was based upon three equally weighted indicators of productive status: occupation of the breadwinner, education of the subject, and family income (adjusted for family size).[10] The pattern of social stratification is generally preserved for each style,[11] and similar patterns of stylistic stratification are preserved for each group. Thus although New Yorkers

[9] In the notation used here, (r) represents a linguistic variable, defined by the existence of ordered covariation with other linguistic or extralinguistic variables; (r-1) represents a particular value of a variable in one instance; (r)-22 represents a mean index value for a set of instances. Square brackets, as in [r], enclose phonetic notation and italic *r* indicates the unit of spelling.

[10] For further details and the rationale behind this approach as developed by John Michael of MFY, see *The Social Stratification of English in New York City, op. cit. Education of the subject,* as an indicator, gave results equivalent to *education of the male head of the household.*

[11] In casual speech, all New Yorkers except upper middle class speakers are essentially *r*-less; the small figures here show no significant differences.

are quite finely differentiated by their use of (r),[12] they also appear to be quite similar in the direction of their stylistic shifts with respect to (r).

One major deviation from this pattern appears in the behavior of the lower middle class,[13] which surpasses the upper middle class in the use of (r) in the more formal contexts. This crossover pattern is not idiosyncratic here: it reappears in similar structures for other variables which, like (r), represent a linguistic change in progress.[14] This "hypercorrect" behavior seems to characterize the second highest status group, given its extreme range over the contextual scale. The native speech pattern used by almost all children growing up in the city is rejected whenever attention is paid to the speech process, and the pattern used by an exterior reference group is substituted.

There is considerable agreement among native New Yorkers in their unconscious evaluation of the phonological variables. A subjective response test described in earlier reports[15] was designed to isolate such unconscious reactions to particular variables. There was often remarkable uniformity of response to this test. All forty-two New York subjects in the 18–39 age group responded to this test in a manner which clearly indicated recognition of the prestige status of (r), although no such agreement was found in the responses of older people or out-of-towners. Such unanimity in the evaluation of (r) is parallel to the uniform direction of stylistic shift in the use of (r): both patterns indicate that normative behavior may be more consistent than actual performance. Indeed, it seems preferable to define the New York City speech community as a group with similar evaluative norms in regard to language, rather than similar patterns of speech performance.

The evidence of (r) is reinforced by the data for the other four main variables. In all five cases, a regular structure of social and stylistic variation was found; the degree of regularity was such that groups as small as four or five subjects fitted into the matrix in a predictable manner. Table

[12] This is an example of *fine stratification,* in which it appears that almost any fine subdivision of the socioeconomic scale will be reflected in a corresponding stratification of (r). The case of (dh), discussed below, is the opposing type of *sharp stratification.*

[13] Such "class" terms are employed informally to represent the objective divisions of the MFY scale as indicated in the tables. See "Hypercorrection by the Lower Middle Class . . ," cited above, for a detailed discussion of this crossover pattern.

[14] These variables are: (eh), the height of the vowel in *bad, ask, dance,* etc., and (oh), the height of the vowel in *law, coffee, talk, bore,* etc.

[15] Cf. *The Social Stratification of English in New York City, op. cit.,* Chapter 11. The subjects listened to 22 sentences on a test tape, and rated the speakers on a scale of occupational suitability ranging from television announcer to factory worker. A particular variable was concentrated in a given sentence, and the listener's unconscious reaction to that variable was determined by comparing his rating of that sentence to his rating of the same speaker in a "zero" sentence which contained none of the variables in question.

646   *Table 2   Mean (dh) Values by Contextual Style and Socioeconomic Class*
for Subjects Raised in New York City Who Yielded Full Interviews

Contextual Style	0–2 Lower Class	3–5 Working Class	6–8 Lower Middle Class	9 Upper Middle Class
Casual Speech	79	64	30	22
Careful Speech	52	45	19	7
Reading Style	49	34	12	5

2 shows the pattern of social and stylistic variation for (dh), the initial consonant of *this, then, the,* etc. The (dh) index is built on a scale which rates the prestige form, the fricative [ð], as (dh-l); the affricate [dð] as (dh-2); and the most stigmatized form, the stop [d] as (dh-3). The numerical average of all ratings multiplied by 100 gives the numerical scale used in Table 2.[16] The higher the (dh) index, the greater the percentage of nonstandard, nonprestige forms. This is a case of relatively sharp stratification of the population into two major groups, with lower class and working class at the top, and middle class groups near the bottom of the scale. No crossover pattern is found for this relatively stable linguistic variable. Again we find that great differentials in the speech performance of New Yorkers are accompanied by high agreement in their directions of stylistic shift and in their subjective reactions. Two other variables which represented changes in progress yielded the same results and, in addition, the hypercorrect pattern of the lower middle class.

The results which have been shown are based on data for 81 subjects raised in New York City. The 37 informants who were raised outside New York City showed similar patterns for variables which are general throughout the country, but no pattern at all for variables specific to New York City. The 35 informants who were briefly interviewed by anonymous methods, a sample of the refusers and nonrespondents, provided similar results in the context of careful speech.

SOCIAL MOBILITY ON THE LOWER EAST SIDE

Socioeconomic classification of the Lower East Side subjects is based on characteristics they acquired at different times in their lives.

[16] The scale is adjusted by subtracting 100 points, so that consistent use of the prestige form [ð] is rated as (dh)-100. The values given for the upper middle class exclude one speaker with a highly idiosyncratic use of (dh-3), initial [f] for (th), and other speech characteristics which specifically prevented from him pursuing an academic career. This case is discussed in detail in *The Social Stratification of English in New York City, op. cit.,* Chapter 8. With the values of this individual included, the upper middle class figures are (dh)-29, 15.5, 14.5.

Educational level is the earliest, occupations reflect decisions made somewhat later in life, and incomes reflect only present status. In many cases, income by itself would be a poor measure of status—in the case of a college student, for example, who has a high expectation of upward social mobility, or that of a plumber with a sixth grade education, who may retain behavior more characteristic of the working class than of the middle class despite his high income level. These cases of "status incongruence" are not always resolved by the equal weighting of the three indicators in the socioeconomic index. More regular correlations existed between phonological variables and socioeconomic status once analysis was restricted only to where there was status congruence among the three indicators.

The members of any one class also differ among themselves in characteristics which antedate the three SES indicators. One would expect that the status of the family of origin and their own earliest occupations, would provide social experience which would in turn be reflected in linguistic behavior. Lower middle class speakers with a history of upward social mobility should indeed be different than speakers whose parents were members of the same social class and who themselves had always maintained middle class status. The first, most obvious hypothesis would be that such "steady" middle class speakers would exemplify the norms of middle class society more completely than upwardly mobile speakers who grew up in a working-class environment. One would expect members of the "upward" group to show erratic behavior and inconsistent performance, because they had not been trained in middle class linguistic norms early enough to have internalized them. Therefore, the structure of social and stylistic stratification would appear most clearly if we considered only the "steady" groups with a history of two generations of membership in the same class.

This reasoning fails to take into account the specific structure of New York City society, especially the fact that upward social mobility is normal, even normative, for the middle class groups. The subdivision of class groups along the additional dimension of social mobility does indeed clarify our view of sociolinguistic stratification, but in precisely the opposite manner from that suggested above.

MEASURES OF SOCIAL MOBILITY

The original survey of the Lower East Side carried out by Mobilization for Youth provides two data that can serve as measures of social mobility: (1) the occupation of the subject's father, and (2) the first

648   occupation of the subject after leaving school. Combining these two measures provides an overall measure of social mobility.

Ideally, one would prefer a status history which made use of all three indicators of the SES scale. But the income levels and educational attainments of parents are difficult to ascertain, unreliable at best, and hard to calibrate against today's standards. Occupational data are more reliable, more comparable, and provide a fair measure of social mobility to use in conjunction with the current SES index. The categories by which occupations were recorded follow Census Bureau's practices with minor deviations. For the study of social mobility, it is useful to establish the following four levels:

Level	Occupations
1	Professionals, semiprofessionals, proprietors or managers of large and medium businesses
2	Proprietors or managers of small businesses, clerical, sales, or kindred workers
3	Craftsmen, foremen, or kindred workers
4	Operatives or kindred workers, service workers, laborers

It might have been possible to use seven categories, following the census in separating proprietors from clerical workers and operatives from service workers and laborers. But in the Lower East Side, small businessmen were chiefly shopkeepers; thus, it was more realistic to group them with clerical workers. Among the three lowest occupational groups, it would be difficult to assert that operatives performing semi-skilled work in a factory at minimum wages should be ranked higher than policemen, firemen, nurses aides, or other service workers. Furthermore, the status of laborer was more common fifty years ago and approximately equivalent to that of factory operative today. It would also be difficult to maintain that an operative had risen in the social scale because his father had been a laborer. When studying social mobility, therefore, it seems appropriate to refrain from making distinctions among these three occupational groups. The resulting types of social mobility are the following:

Mobility	Occupational History
Upward [U]	Father's occupational level or earliest occupational level lower than present level, and neither higher than present
Steady [S]	Father's occupational level and earliest occupational level same as present level
Downward [D]	Father's occupational level or earliest occupational level higher than present level, and neither lower than present
Up and Down [UD]	Earliest (or earlier) occupational level higher than father's occupational level, and also higher than present level

A fifth possible type, "Down and Up," does not appear to any noticeable degree.[17] Additional information about the subject's present status was used to correct his formal reply to the question about current occupation. Some subjects had not worked for many years, depending entirely on welfare and living under poor conditions at a bare subsistence level; their occupations of record were no longer relevant. Unless it was known that their parents had also lived under these same conditions, they were considered downwardly mobile. Married women yielded a further datum: husband's occupation in addition to last occupation of record. The former is taken as the primary datum. In almost every such case there was no difference between last occupation and earliest occupation; consequently no new types occurred.

SOCIAL DISTRIBUTION OF MOBILITY TYPES

The top portion of Table 3 shows the distribution of mobility types among those informants whose linguistic behavior has been exhibited in Tables 1 and 2. Reliable social mobility data were available for 74 of the 81 subjects.

The "Upward and Downward" type has no immediate value for the analysis, since the eight cases are distributed among four small cells. Furthermore, the "UD" class is not a consistent type. Some are women who had held white-collar jobs but married working-class men; others are people who had followed a normal upward path but who were subsequently disabled, blinded, or addicted to drink or drugs.

The three principal mobility types, "U," "S," and "D," form a three-by-four matrix considered together with the four SES groups. The "U" cell for the lower class and the "D" cell for the upper middle class are empty by definition. The only other empty cell is the "S" category within the upper middle class. The absence of a steady segment of the upper middle class is a reflection of the particular social history of the Lower East Side. It is a port of entry for immigrants and a place of nurture for those on the way up, but normally not a permanent home for children of upper middle class parents.[18]

---

[17] It would be difficult to detect such a pattern from the information we have on most subjects. It is not unusual for a person's first job to be relatively low ranking, as a temporary expedient in his upward career. It would be necessary to show that this first occupation did not imply future advancement to establish a "Down and Up" class.

[18] A number of the subjects were raised in other parts of New York City, and there is reason to think that this characterization is generally true for the city as a whole.

650   The middle of Table 3 shows the distribution of mobility types for all adult informants who were raised in New York City, including those interviewed by brief, anonymous methods. The distribution is approximately the same for these 99 subjects as for the basic set of 74. A somewhat different distribution appears in the lower part of the table, which enumerates types among all adult subjects, including those raised outside of New York City. It is apparent that the "Up-and-Down" type is much more heavily represented among the out-of-town informants than for New Yorkers; this category appears as 22 percent of the total compared with eleven percent in other parts of the table. Two "steady" upper middle class persons also appear among the subjects from out-of-town.

Table 3   Distribution of Social Mobility Types

		Socioeconomic Class				
Subjects	Mobility Type	0–2 Lower Class	3–5 Working Class	6–8 Lower Middle Class	9 Upper Middle Class	All Classes
All subjects	U	0	5	12	9	26
raised in New	S	9	13	4	0	26
York City who	D	9	4	1	0	14
yielded full	UD	1	3	3	1	8
interviews						
	ALL TYPES	19	24	21	10	74
All Subjects	U	0	9	15	12	36
raised in	S	10	14	6	0	30
New York City	D	13	7	2	0	22
	UD	2	5	3	1	11
	ALL TYPES	25	35	26	13	99
All subjects	U	0	11	19	13	43
	S	17	19	9	2	47
	D	13	10	2	0	25
	UD	10	12	9	2	33
	ALL TYPES	40	52	39	17	148

THE EFFECT OF SOCIAL MOBILITY ON LINGUISTIC VARIABLES

The most extensive and reliable data are available for the 74 subjects at the top of Table 3. The association between mobility type and linguistic behavior will first be examined within this group, using the larger samples for corroboration wherever possible. There are four comparisons which can be made within class groups: (1) between "D" and "S" in the lower class, (2) between "U" and "S" in the working class, (3) between "S" and "D" in the working class, and (4) between "U" and "S" in the lower middle class.

Table 4 shows the relation of (r) to mobility types for 66 native New York City informants interviewed at length who were of the "U," "S,"

Table 4   Distribution of Mean (r) Values by Contextual Style, Socioeconomic Class, and Mobility Type for Subjects Raised in New York City Who Yielded Full Interviews

		Socioeconomic Class				
Contextual Style	Mobility Type	0–2 Lower Class	3–5 Working Class	6–8 Lower Middle Class	9 Upper Middle Class	All Classes
Casual Speech	U	*	12	4	18	10
	S	4	2	7	*	4
	D	2	5	*	*	3
	ALL TYPES	3	6	5	18	
Careful Speech	U	*	17	23	34	26
	S	14	8	20	*	12
	D	3	15	*	*	7
	ALL TYPES	8	12	22	34	
Reading Style	U	*	23	29	35	29
	S	17	16	21	*	16
	D	4	26	*	*	12
	ALL TYPES	10	19	27	34	
Word Lists	U	*	58	62	49	57
	S	40	27	48	*	37
	D	11	45	*	*	26
	ALL TYPES	28	37	58	49	
Minimal Pairs	U	*	72	72	57	67
	S	70	46	54	*	56
	D	31	70	33	*	44
	ALL TYPES	53	57	68	57	

* No cases of this type.

652   and "D" types. The table gives the distribution of mean (r) values for each mobility type within each socioeconomic class under each of five contextual styles, from casual speech to minimal pairs. In each socio-economic class regular association may be seen between mobility type and the use of (r). Among lower class subjects the "S" class used the prestige form [r] considerably more than did the "D" type. The lower class "D's" show a minimum tendency to use [r] in careful speech, just as they show the least recognition of the prestige value of [r] in subjective response tests.[19] The "U" group shows by far the highest (r) values among working class subjects and the "S" group the lowest. It is perhaps surprising to find that the working class "D's" do not show the lowest (r) indexes; for all five styles "D" is intermediate between "U" and "S." Two considerations may be relevant here. First, there is good reason to believe that the working class is the chief exponent of a value system opposed to that of the middle class. This does not prevent overt endorsement of middle class values, as shown in subjective reaction tests; but underlying opposition in their covert values could produce that extreme stratification in speech actually used which is characteristic of New York City. The lower class, by way of contrast, does not participate as actively in this system of dual sociolinguistic norms—a system exemplified most clearly in the generalization that those who have the highest incidence of a stigmatized feature are most sensitive to its use by others.

The second consideration concerns an apparent difference in the composition of the two "D" groups. Most members of the lower class "D" group seemed to be less intelligent than average, were slower in their speech, and misunderstood questions more often. From their references to successful, upwardly mobile brothers and sisters it could be seen that they frequently deviate from their own family pattern. On the other hand, there appears to be no such psychological correlate of downward mobility in the working class. Broad social and economic forces seem to account for the inability to maintain middle class status. The fact that a majority of the working class "D's" are Negroes is consistent with this observation.

The working class "U" shows a surprisingly high set of (r) scores, almost equal to that of the lower middle class "U." In actual fact, these persons are members of an upper stratum of the working class, having higher occupational skills than most of the "S" group.

The lower middle class "U's" show the archetypal pattern of *hypercorrection* in the use of (r). As compared to the smaller lower middle class "S" group, the "U" group shows a much wider range of (r) usage shifting from near zero in casual speech to 72 in the most formal contextual style. Both the "U's" among the working class and those in the lower middle

---

[19] See Table 9.

class show this hypercorrect pattern, going beyond the upper middle class standard in their more formal speech. Therefore, we can infer that the shift to the hypercorrect pattern is more characteristic of upward mobility than of membership in any particular socioeconomic group.[20]

Because these comparisons involve small numbers, in most cases the figures are not conclusive for any one variable under any one style.[21] But repeating the comparison, under many styles and for several variables, yields strong confirmation that these differences are indeed among linguistic characteristics of the subjects. We can further investigate the question whether these subjects are characteristic of the population by considering an extended sample—one which includes the briefly interviewed and anonymous *r*-less regions, where *r* is not pronounced in the vernacular of casual speech when it is in final or preconsonantal positions. Thus, this group includes a large number of Negro subjects who were born in the South. Table 5 shows the distribution of (r) for the careful

Table 5   Distribution of Mean (r) Values by Socioeconomic Class and Mobility Type for Careful Speech of All Subjects

Mobility Type	Socioeconomic Class				
	0–2 Lower Class	3–5 Working Class	6–8 Lower Middle Class	9 Upper Middle Class	All Classes
U	*	11	25	37	26
S	08	07	18	*	09
D	03	12	*	*	07
ALL TYPES	06	09	23	37	

* No cases of this type.

speech of 99 subjects.

In general, this table shows an increase in association with mobility, the larger differences occurring in the middle class groups and the smaller

[20] This suggestion is generalized to include linguistic stratification as a whole in New York City in the concluding section of this paper. For the role of hypercorrection in linguistic change, see "Hypercorrection by the Lower Middle Class as a Factor in Linguistic Change," *op. cit.*

[21] A large portion of the difference between the "U" and "S" groups is due to a single member of the "S" group whose (dh) values are quite high. This subject is a plumber whose high income raises his objective socioeconomic index to the level of the lower middle class group—an example of status incongruence. Without his values, the "S" group shows considerably lower average (dh).

654 ones in the two lower groups. The "D" working class is here at a level with the "U" group; this hints at the special position of the Negro subjects, for whom objective socioeconomic position and social mobility may not be accurate indexes of participation in the cultural norms of middle class society.

Comparable data are shown on Table 6 for the (dh) variable, the form of the first consonant in *the, then, these,* etc. This variable differs from (r) in that it is not an instance of linguistic change in progress; therefore, a hypercorrect "crossover" pattern was not expected. Only three contextual styles are used for this variable. In the lower middle class group, there is a sharp difference between the "U" and "S" subsets, the "S" group showing much freer use of the stigmatized form and the "U" group holding much closer to the upper middle class norm. A similar contrast exists between "U" and "S" in the working class. The working class "D's," shown in careful speech only, occupy the same intermediate position as with (r). Finally the situation appears to be somewhat irregular in the lower class group. Though the "D" type has a higher (dh) index

Table 6   *Mean (dh) Values by Contextual Style, Socioeconomic Class, and Mobility Type for Subjects Raised in New York City Who Yielded Full Interviews*

Contextual Style	Mobility Type	Socioeconomic Class				
		0–2 Lower Class	3–5 Working Class	6–8 Lower Middle Class	9 Upper Middle Class	All Classes
Casual Speech	U	*	27	17	28	23
	S	63	80	50	*	70
	D	83	*	*	*	83
	ALL TYPES	72	68	30	28	
Careful Speech	U	*	27	9	8	12
	S	52	62	38	*	55
	D	44	40	*	*	43
	ALL TYPES	48	51	19	8	
Reading Style	U	*	17	6	6	8
	S	26	52	29	*	40
	D	69	*	*	*	69
	ALL TYPES	43	42	12	6	

* No cases of this type.

in casual speech, as expected, the situation is reversed during careful speech. As in all of these tables, the most realistic and accurate view is a vertical one across styles. The "S" group conforms to the most general social norms by showing a regular downward trend in the (dh) index with increasing formality of style, but the "D" group shows lack of participation in these norms through failure to display such a regular pattern of stylistic variation.

Table 7 shows the distribution of (dh) in an enlarged sample of all 107 subjects tested under conditions of careful speech. Similar results obtain. In this case, the differences within the lower class seem to dis-

Table 7   Mean (dh) Values by Socioeconomic Class and Mobility Types in Careful Speech for All Subjects

	Socioeconomic Class				
Mobility Type	0–2 Lower Class	3–5 Working Class	6–8 Lower Middle Class	9 Upper Middle Class	All Classes
U		38	12	10	18
S	47	55	21	*	43
D	46	34	*	*	41
ALL TYPES	46	45	23	10	

* No cases of this type.

appear, while the other differences are maintained. Again, we see that downwardly mobile members of the working class do not show a linguistic pattern that corresponds to its objective socioeconomic position.

Table 8 shows the related variable, (th), an index for the form of the first consonant in *thing, three,* etc.[22] The pattern is approximately that of Table 6, with the following characteristics:

1) The lower class "D's" do not follow a regular pattern of stylistic stratification, while the "S's" do.

2) The working class "U's" are more like the lower middle class than they are like the working class "S's," the latter showing a high incidence of nonstandard (th) forms. Again the "D" group is intermediate rather than being lower.

[22] This consonant is phonologically parallel to (dh), and uses the same three-point scale of fricative (th-1), the prestige form; affricate (th-2), the intermediate form, and stop (th-3), the stigmatized form. The (th) variants are voiceless, while (dh) is voiced.

656   *Table 8   Mean (th) Values by Contextual Style, Socioeconomic Class, and Mobility Type for Subjects Raised in New York City Who Yielded Full Interviews*

| | | Socioeconomic Class | | | | |
Contextual Style	Mobility Type	0–2 Lower Class	3–5 Working Class	6–8 Lower Middle Class	9 Upper Middle Class	All Classes
Casual Speech	U	*	*	26	9	19
	S	97	95	35	*	82
	D	65	*	*	*	60
	ALL TYPES	80	78	29	9	
Careful Speech	U	*	19	18	8	6
	S	65	84	39	*	53
	D	68	43	*	*	60
	ALL TYPES	66	61	22	8	
Reading Style	U	*	14	6	2	5
	S	20	35	28	*	30
	D	80	*	*	*	48
	ALL TYPES	46	25	11	2	

* No cases of this type.

3) The lower middle class "U" group shows a much lower (th) index than does the "S" group, and a much lower percentage of nonstandard forms.

RESPONSES TO SUBJECTIVE EVALUATION TESTS BY MOBILITY TYPE

The high rate of agreement in recognizing middle class norms of careful speech is reflected by three different kinds of data from the Lower East Side survey: by regular patterns of stylistic stratification, by responses to subjective reaction tests, and by answers to direct questions about values associated with language. In all of these sources we found confirmation of the following scheme:

1) The highest degree of uniformity in the endorsement of these norms, and the most extreme values, appear in the second highest status group.

2) More moderate values are shown by the highest status group.

3) Least recognition of middle class values regarding language occurs   657
in the lowest status group. For many types of data, there is sharp separation in this respect between the lowest class and all of the others.

Table 9 shows the responses to the subjective reaction tests for (r)
and (dh)[23] for those adults who were raised in New York City and pro-

Table 9   Subjective Evaluations of (r) and (dh) by Socioeconomic Class and Mobility Type for Subjects Raised in New York City Who Yielded Full Interviews

	Socioeconomic Class				
Mobility Type	0–2 Lower Class	3–5 Working Class	6–8 Lower Middle Class	9 Upper Middle Class	All Classes
Ratio of (r)-Positive Response					
U	*	2/5	11/12	6/8	19/25
S	4/8	8/13	2/4	*	14/25
D	1/7	2/3	*	*	3/10
ALL TYPES	5/15	12/21	13/16	6/8	
Ratio of (dh)-Positive Response					
U	6/8	5/5	10/11	8/9	29/33
S	6/8	11/13	3/4	*	20/25
D	3/7	2/4	*	*	5/11
ALL TYPES	15/23	19/22	13/15	8/9	

* No cases of this type.

vided complete interviews. In the case of (r), we can see that the data
parallel its actual use in Table 4. Eleven out of twelve of the lower middle
class "U" group responded in a way which indicates that they recognized
the prestige of (r). No differentiation appears within the working class,
but in the lower class it seems clear that the "D" group is practically
outside the value system which governs the behavior of the other subgroups. Only one out of seven of the lower class "D's" showed an
(r)-positive response.

In the case of (dh) there is an even closer parallel with speech data
(see Table 5). Again, the lower middle class "U" group shows the highest
percentage of agreement, though not significantly higher than "U's" in

23 The subjective response test for (dh) is actually a joint response to (dh) and (th).

658   the upper middle class. The working class also shows a high degree of agreement about the value of this variable, the "U" group more consistently so, however, than the "S" group. The only significant deviation from a (dh)-sensitive response was found in the lower class "D" group —and this it will be recalled, was the only group which did not follow a regular pattern of stylistic stratification.

CONCLUSIONS AND FURTHER IMPLICATIONS

That English in the Lower East Side is socially stratified may be regarded as confirmed by a large body of evidence. Confidence in these findings is provided by many sets of correlations and cross checks within the survey as well as by independent corroboration in another survey of a completely different type.[24] The findings on the relation of mobility type to socioeconomic status and linguistic behavior of sample subjects have been described. Whether the small cells of the sample are typical of those found in the population as a whole is difficult to state with complete confidence. The conclusions of this paper must therefore be considered as hypotheses which are subject to further confirmation.

The most striking finding of this discussion is that a group of speakers with a past history of upward mobility is more apt to resemble the next higher socioeconomic group in their linguistic behavior than the one with which they are currently associated. Despite the fact that these speakers may be expected to show traces of their class origins by retaining behavior patterns of the next lower class group, we find exactly the reverse. This finding is consistent with the view that linguistic behavior reflects participation in a set of norms which are widely recognized through all (or almost all) segments of the community. This observation may be specified as follows:

1) Upwardly mobile persons adopt the norms of an exterior reference group—as a rule, the norms of the next higher group with which they are in contact.[25]

2) A group which shows a past history of social stability tends to be governed more by its own linguistic norms—more precisely, to achieve a balance in which own and external norms are reflected in fairly consistent performance, without a wide range of style shifting.

3) A downward mobile category deviates in its nonacceptance of the normative patterns which other segments recognize. Here we are speaking

[24] See Chapter 3 of *The Social Stratification of English in New York City, op. cit.,* for a discussion of the survey of New York City department stores.

[25] It appears that relatively few speakers are directly influenced by the speech patterns heard on radio and television. Some type of personal contact seems to be required as a rule.

of a set of individuals who deviate from the principal subgroup in which they were raised. This finding does not apply to an entire group, such as the Negro subjects, who were downwardly mobile through broad social factors almost independently of their own behavior.

It has been suggested in previous studies that a speech community can be defined as a group of speakers who have a common set of values regarding language. We might amplify this suggestion by saying that, in an urban society linguistic stratification is the direct reflection of underlying sets of social values, rather than sets of habits which are produced by close contact and are differentiated by discontinuities in the communication system.

In a large city like New York, we cannot explain the differential spread of a linguistic trait in terms of differential density in the communication network. Everyone is exposed to the prestige patterns of radio and television. If a person borrows a prestige element from an exterior group, it is reasonable to say that this act symbolizes more than his recognition of the values of that group; it symbolizes the adoption of at least some of these values as critical for his own behavior. This act is characteristic of an upwardly mobile person. Thus most New Yorkers can agree in deciding on the type of speech appropriate for high-ranking occupations; but this does not mean that such recognition results in the same range of behavior for all. For many New Yorkers the application of such middle class values would appear limited by conflict with other values—namely, the value system symbolized by their group's vernacular from early adolescence onward. Upwardly mobile individuals show the maximum tendency to apply the values of an external reference group to their own behavior. As a result we find that mobility types offer as good a basis as socioeconomic position or better for stratifying New York City speech. The vertical totals on the right of Tables 4 through 8 compare favorably with the horizontal totals[26] in terms of identifying discrete levels. The difference in reference group behavior reflected in mobility types may therefore be viewed as an intervening variable between social and linguistic stratification.

This line of reasoning applies to a relatively open society where such reference group behavior can bring about changes in objective socioeconomic position. The situation is quite different for groups that have limited opportunities for mobility, such as the Negro group in New York City; and linguistic behavior must be analyzed along other dimensions.

---

[26] These totals for mobility classes and socioeconomic classes include small cells such as "D" lower middle class, which are not shown independently in the tables.

APPENDICES

Selected Dissertation Abstracts

The purpose of this section is threefold: to acquaint readers with research not represented in this collection; to assist readers in furthering their own research as speedily as possible; and to encourage further research in regional and social American dialects.

With the publication of volume XXX, number I, *Dissertation Abstracts* became *Dissertation Abstracts International.* The editors wish to express their appreciation in particular to Mrs. Patricia Colling, Editor, Periodical Publications, and to University Microfilms, Ann Arbor, Michigan, for permission to reprint these abstracts.

THE NATIVE AMERICAN ENGLISH SPOKEN IN THE PUGET SOUND AREA[1]

Frederick H. Brengelman, Ph.D.
University of Washington, 1957

The Puget Sound area is closely unified by geography, economy, and culture. It has, at the same time, a heterogeneous population which has been dominated at different times by migrants from New England, the inland northern United

1 L. C. Card No. Mic 58-1073

664   States, and the central states. Important proportions of the population of the area have also come from the British Empire and northern Europe. A study of the language of the area should thus be expected to provide valuable evidence for conclusions about the effects of migration and mixture on a developing common language.

The present study has attempted to carry out the following objectives:

1) To describe the actual pronunciation of English in the Sound area.

2) To determine its relationship to other regional dialects, particularly those of the eastern United States.

3) To describe differences between the dialects of the aged and young, the rural and urban, and the educated and uneducated, and to compare these differences with those reported from various sections of the eastern United States.

4) To discover by means of these comparisons what factors have been most important in establishing the dialect features of the Puget Sound area.

The data used for the study were the phonetic transcriptions of interviews of thirty life-long residents of Puget Sound towns and rural areas. The interviews were made as part of the research for the *Linguistic Atlas of the Pacific Northwest.* Each record contains about 600 items (words and sentences), many of which have lexical and morphological as well as phonological significance. Separate tabulations were made of the three kinds of data in each record. These formed the basis for a phonemic analysis and a number of comparisons between the dialects of the local social classes and between those of this area and the East. The morphological and lexical data were compared with those relating to phonology to determine whether they would support the conclusions reached with respect to regional and cultural dialect relationships.

The evidence collected for this study suggests the following general conclusions about the development of a common language in this region:

1) Vocabulary and pronunciation have been established here by the predominant settlement groups, namely those from the northern and north midland areas of the United States, rather than by the groups who made the first settlements in the area, the Canadians and New Englanders. As a result of heavier Northern settlement west of the Sound, the speech of that area is more consistently Northern than that of the east side.

2) Regional forms have often been replaced by national ones, specifically in those instances where a great deal of speech variation existed among settlers of the area. This applies to vocabulary, grammar, and the pronunciations of particular words, but not to the phonetic system.

3) The shifting economic and social status of newcomers to the area has apparently resulted in a blurring of linguistic class boundaries. Here there are fewer differences between the dialects of the cultured and uncultured, the rich and poor, and the rural and urban than in areas having a more stable population. The speech of the aged is, however, distinguished from that of the young by differences in the phonemic system, in pronunciation, and in vocabulary.   225 pages. $2.95

A WORD GEOGRAPHY OF CALIFORNIA AND NEVADA[1]

Elizabeth Sweet Bright, Ph.D.
University of California, Berkeley, 1967

Based on the 300 field records of the *Linguistic Atlas of the Pacific Coast,* this study is an investigation into the extent to which the interaction of geographical and historical forces can be discerned in the common speech. The vocabulary taken from the records consists of words used by 15 percent or more of the informants, and words which, although perhaps used by a smaller percentage, exhibited special distribution patterns.

After a brief geographical and historical summary, nineteen patterns of distribution are shown, fifteen particularly concerned with California and four with Nevada. For each pattern there are an isogloss map, a chart showing the density of distribution by geographic areas, and the list of words that make up each pattern. The twentieth map in the group is a composite of the first fifteen (which also show Nevada occurrences); this map shows the highest concentration of usage of words found in special distribution to be in the Sacramento Valley and northern Nevada. Low percentages of usage are found along the north border and in the central and south coastal area of California, and in southeastern Nevada. The patterns reflect historical migratory routes, concentration in areas of the gold rush and the Comstock lode, the relative importance of San Francisco and Los Angeles as centers of influence, and the slow rate of spread to areas isolated from the main migratory paths.

Grammatical forms are treated in a separate section because of the difficulty of eliciting natural responses. Usually the standard form was in general distribution, with one substandard form appearing in minor distribution. Only twenty-seven forms fit any of the above-mentioned distribution patterns.

In the discussion of loan words, those from Spanish are separated from those of other languages. An isogloss of Spanish usage shows a close relation between the occurrence of words used with Spanish pronunciation and the areas of Spanish settlement which generally coincided with the central and south coastal area. Americanizations occurred mainly along the paths of northern migration and in the parts affected by the Gold Rush. Of the loan words from other languages, Indian words were found generally in Nevada, European borrowings in California.

Folk terms are included because of interest in their origins and the folk myths connected with them, even though generally the percentage of usage was low and distribution is not significant.

Relation to studies of a similar nature made in the East, the Great Lakes region, Colorado, Texas, and Washington State is shown in three tables: Table I, terms in common with the East and combinations of the East and others; Table II, terms in common with regions other than the East; Table III, terms found only in California-Nevada. As a rule, items found in general use in the East were found

[1] Order No. 68-10,289

666 to be general elsewhere. Words that may be typical of the West, the Pacific Coast, and the California-Nevada regions are suggested.

The general conclusions are:

1) Words in general use in other parts of the country continued in general use in this region unless strong competition occurred as a result of other influences.

2) While geographic barriers have influenced the flow of speech forms, they have not prevented it when a strong incentive was present.

3) The rate of the process of language change and the direction of language flow have been directly affected by major changes in the social, political, and economic forces of the region.

A complete listing of the vocabulary and a selected bibliography are included in the appendix.   Microfilm $4.55; Xerography $16.00.   365 pages.

THE SPEECH OF TERRE HAUTE: A HOOSIER DIALECT STUDY[1]

Marvin Dale Carmony, Ph.D.
Indiana University, 1965

This study, the first detailed analysis of the dialect of an Indiana community, uses the framework of the *Linguistic Atlas* to ascertain and describe the speech of Terre Haute. A city admirably suited for linguistic investigation, Terre Haute was founded in 1816, the year that Indiana achieved statehood; it is located on two migration routes, the Wabash River and the National Road, the latter long looked upon as a dialect boundary marker; it is the industrial and cultural center of the Wabash Valley; its settlement and cultural history set it somewhat apart from the other cities in the area.

The basic material of this study consists of *Linguistic Atlas* interviews conducted by the writer, involving more than one hundred hours of tape-recorded conversations with sixteen white and Negro informants who have lived in or near Terre Haute all of their lives (14) or since early childhood (2), and who are representative of various age groups and social classes.

The introduction deals primarily with the settlement history of Terre Haute. Chapter I, concerned in part with the regional composition of the vocabulary, consists chiefly of a topical survey of Terre Haute usage, using Kurath's *Word Geography* as a framework. Chapter II concerns the pronunciation of English in Terre Haute; in it the phonemic inventory is established, the principal allophones are discussed, and the incidence of vowels and consonants is described, with Kurath and McDavid's *Pronunciation* and James Whitcomb Riley's dialect poetry providing points of reference. Chapter III is a brief consideration of the salient grammatical features of the dialect, using Atwood's monograph as a partial framework. Appendix A consists of forty-four maps, showing the place of a number of Terre Haute features of speech in an Indiana setting. Based on 140 spectograms, Appendix B is devoted to an instrumental analysis of a supplementary Terre Haute informant's vowels. Appendix C provides pertinent details on the lives of the informants.

[1] Order No. 66–1428

This study indicates, in brief, that (1) the vocabulary of Terre Haute is essentially **667** Midland, with a strong admixture of Northern and North Midland words, as well as a sizeable proportion of Southern words; (2) the pronunciation of Terre Haute, like its vocabulary, clearly reflects the city's settlement and cultural history, the prestige dialect of today stemming from the prestigious and dominant Yankee element of yesterday, while "inferior" speech of the community is that containing the most substantial number of South Midland features; (3) the degree of both social stratification and racial segregation is considerable, judging from the number of lexical, phonological, and grammatical features with social and ethnic connotations.

The interesting possibility that the Wabash River marks a slight bundle of isoglosses between Terre Haute and West Terre Haute is a matter for further study.

Microfilm $3.10; Xerography $10.80. 240 pages.

THE DIALECT VOCABULARY OF THE OHIO RIVER VALLEY: A SURVEY OF THE DISTRIBUTION OF SELECTED VOCABULARY FORMS IN AN AREA OF COMPLEX SETTLEMENT HISTORY. (VOLUMES I–III).[1]

Robert Ford Dakin, Ph.D.
University of Michigan, 1966

Chairman: James W. Downer

This is a study of the distribution of the variant forms of 205 words and expressions used by residents of the Ohio River Valley. The 254 county study area includes the sections of Ohio, Indiana, and Illinois between the Ohio River and the National Road and the entire state of Kentucky. The linguistic data are from the unedited field records made for the proposed *Linguistic Atlas of the North Central States*. Data from 207 records provide evidence of the usage of 246 primary and auxiliary informants.

The study has three general purposes. The first is to present a synchronic description of the areal distribution of variant usages and to identify subsidiary dialect areas. The second is to describe differences in the vocabulary of speakers of different age, sex, education, occupation, and socioeconomic status. The third purpose is to provide a diachronic description of the vocabulary and to trace the historical bases and development of the dialect in various sections.

Part I introduces the Ohio Valley as a region of secondary settlement of particular interest to students of American dialectology. A resumé of the known dialect areas of the Eastern United States is provided, and the historical and geographical relationships of the study area to these seaboard areas are described. Chapters are devoted to the physical environment, the chronology and character of the settlement, and to certain aspects of the later development of the study area.

[1] Order No. 66–14,505

668   Another chapter describes the North Central States survey and discusses problems inherent in the use and interpretation of the *Atlas* field records. This chapter also describes the methods of charting and recording the data for the study and for preparing the word maps and tables which are included.

Part II first presents discussions of the variants recorded for the 205 items studied. Each includes a description of the areal distribution of the variants and, if the evidence permits, a description of their social distribution. When possible, evidence of changing usage is also reported.

Part II treats more generally the historical development of the vocabulary and its present status. Tables show the distribution in the study area of terms characteristic of dialect areas on the seaboard and textual discussion and maps present the subsidiary dialect areas of the Ohio Valley Midland. Part II includes 17 tables and 158 illustrative maps.

The evidence supports a number of conclusions. This region of secondary settlement belongs to the Midland speech area. Although focal areas are evident and leveling has occurred, the vocabulary reflects the complexity of the original settlement which was the major force in establishing the dialect. With a few striking exceptions, the common usages can be readily traced to Eastern Midland origins, but differences in the incidence of usage and the exceptions indicate that the Ohio Valley Midland is not simply an extension of the Seaboard Midland. The oldest layer of usage reflects the predominance of the Southern element in most of the Valley and the major dialect boundary sets off a South Midland section. The region between the Ohio River and the National Road is a complex transition area between this South Midland section and an assumed extension of the North Midland. These areas are further divided into five major subsidiary areas and eighteen minor ones. The latter are not all equally well defined. The evidence does not permit as positive statements about social distribution nor about the influence of foreign languages. Tentative conclusions regarding variant usages attributable to difference in social class and sex can be made, however, and German-speaking immigrants were evidently influential in establishing the common use of certain words.

Microfilm $14.95; Xerography $53.40. 1187 pages.

FEATURES OF NEW ENGLAND RUSTIC PRONUNCIATION IN JAMES RUSSELL LOWELL'S BIGLOW PAPERS[1]

James Walker Downer, Ph.D.
University of Michigan, 1958

This study seeks to analyze and identify features of pronunciation in Lowell's *Biglow Papers* by the use of features of pronunciation in present-day rustic dialects in New England. The assumption underlying the study and determining the method followed is that conservative rural speech of certain parts of New England

[1] L.C. Card No. Mic 58-7708

has preserved features which were present in Lowell's day and in the area of New England which he knew well: Cambridge and Middlesex County, Massachusetts.

The body of evidence which makes this study possible is that contained in *The Linguistic Atlas of New England*[2] and the *Handbook of the Linguistic Geography of New England*,[3] which present an extensive treatment of original settlement and later population growth and movement in New England communities, along with close phonetic recordings of the speech of over 700 speakers carefully selected and classified as to age, social position, and education.

The area of New England most likely to have preserved archaic features of pronunciation is Northeastern Massachusetts, New Hampshire, and Maine. Within this broad area, the speech of northern Middlesex County, Massachusetts, and the Merrimack Valley in New Hampshire is likely to be closest in phonemic system to rural Middlesex speech of the early nineteenth century.

To determine what Lowell represented as significant about Middlesex Yankee pronunciation, it is necessary to find what is contrastive between rustic speech and cultured speech in modern New England. We assume these contrasts to be a sound basis for determining the differences between nineteenth century rustic speech and Lowell's own cultured speech. Analysis of the speech of six old-fashioned rustic informants in Middlesex County, Massachusetts, and the Merrimack Valley in New Hampshire and of two cultured speakers in the same area has shown no differences in the inventory of phonemes, a few differences in the pronunciation of phonemes, a few in the frequency of occurrence of phonemes, and some in the conditions of occurrence of phonemes. More striking are the differences in incidence of phonemes in words.

Interpretation of Lowell's unconventional spellings requires analysis of the relation between spelling symbols—graphemes—and phonemes. The base of this analysis must be the correlation between the graphemes of conventional spelling and the phonemes of cultured speech. Then the contrasts between conventional spelling and the unconventional spellings can be matched with the contrasts between cultured speech and rustic speech.

With the results of the spelling analysis it is possible to turn to what Lowell was actually trying to show as significant about rustic Yankee speech. Classification of Lowell's misspelled words and checking with *Linguistic Atlas* evidence reveals that Lowell indicated principally differences in incidence of phonemes and perhaps suggested a few differences in pronunciation of phonemes. In representing incidence of phonemes Lowell has been on the whole accurate. He has certainly been extensive. His characterization of the dialect primarily by incidence of phoneme, is successful, suggesting to the informed reader the actual sounds, the intonation, the rhythm, and the cadence of rustic Yankee speech.   Microfilm $4.70; Xerox $15.80.   368 pages.

[2] Hans Kurath and Bernard Block (ed.), *The Linguistic Atlas of New England* (3 vols. in 6 parts: Providence, Rhode Island: Brown University, 1939–1942)

[3] Hans Kurath and others, *Handbook of the Linguistic Geography of New England* (Providence, Rhode Island: Brown University, 1939)

A WORD GEOGRAPHY OF MISSOURI[1]

Rachel Bernice Faries, Ph.D.
University of Missouri, Columbia, 1967

Supervisor: George Blocker Pace

The purpose of this study is to discover existing affiliations between the speech of Missouri and the dialects of the Eastern United States. The method employed has been to collect data from a large number of native Missourians and to compare these findings with the data in Hans Kurath's *A Word Geography of the Eastern United States.*

It is generally agreed that the most important single factor determining the type of speech used in an area is settlement history. A study of the settlement history of Missouri was made. This study reveals that the state was primarily settled by two distinct waves of migration from the Eastern States, one wave from the South and South Midland dialect areas and the other from the North and North Midland. But the history of the state's settlement could not show which wave of migration was the more influential, or indeed whether either wave had left an influence still detectable. Settlement history alone obviously cannot provide the answer.

The actual usage of seven hundred Missouri informants is, therefore, carefully examined in order to determine which of four possibilities prevails: (1) that Missouri is a speech area wholly distinct in its own right, with no resemblance to those of the Eastern States; (2) that it is divided into separate speech areas, some of which may resemble those of the Eastern States; (3) that it exhibits a rather equal blending of the dialects of all the Eastern areas; or (4) that it resembles primarily the speech of one or two of the Eastern speech areas.

In order to assure reliability and uniformity, the informants were all native-born Missourians, aged sixty-five or older, who were lifelong residents of their communities and who were, in the main, not highly educated. In addition, the informants were selected from the older, relatively rural communities (of less than 5,000 population) since these would presumably be more representative than the newer or more urban ones. Each of the informants completed a checklist of 124 separate items containing most of the expressions discussed by Kurath.

The responses of the informants were tabulated by hand and organized into meaningful tables and maps. The tabulations supplied the necessary information for an item-by-item comparison of the frequency of usage and the distribution of dialect terms in Missouri with those of the Eastern areas, the purpose of this comparison being, as said, to determine the existing relationship between Missouri speech and that of the Eastern areas discussed by Kurath.

The actual determination of the relationship is based on a series of analyses of the number, the frequency, and the kind of dialect expressions used in Missouri as well as various comparisons with the Eastern areas. The relationships appear to be unambiguous: Missouri dialect, so far as the data presented in this study indicate, has a strong Midland base; it is more akin to the South than to the North; a recurrent

[1] Order No. 68–3604

pattern of isoglosses marks off the Ozark Highland and its contingent areas, but as 671 subareas within the general Midland orientation of the state as a whole, not as something separate from that.

This conclusion relates to the settlement history as follows: so far as vocabulary is concerned, the first wave of settlement, that from what are now the South and Midland dialect areas, seems to have set the pattern. Included in the dissertation are 128 maps charting the geographically limited dialect expressions. The principal internal patterns evident in these maps are presented on ten isogloss figures. A copy of the checklist used is also included.

Microfilm $4.45; Xerography $15.75. 348 pages.

BACKGROUND AND PRELIMINARY SURVEY OF THE LINGUISTIC GEOGRAPHY OF ALABAMA. (VOLUMES I AND II).[1]

Virginia Oden Foscue, Ph.D.
University of Wisconsin, 1966

Supervisor: Professor Frederic G. Cassidy

The purpose of this study was to lay the foundation for an investigation of the speech in Alabama according to the methods developed in Europe and the United States. First a study of the settlement history was made, and then from it the places which have been of greatest significance in the development of the area and which would provide informants who are representative of the various population groups were determined. From each of the twenty-five places chosen, at least two informants suggested by the farm agents from each county were selected.

In almost all communities both were natives of the area, one over sixty who had had less than a high-school education and who had traveled little, and one between forty and sixty who had had a high-school education and more outside experience. In the two largest cities, one additional informant who had had more education and still more outside experience was chosen.

Each of the informants was mailed a checklist of 147 vocabulary items similar to the one developed by Alva L. Davis under the direction of Hans Kurath at the University of Michigan in 1948. The material thus obtained was then digested in order to determine (1) the geographical distribution of these terms in Alabama, (2) whenever possible the origin of these terms in the light of their distribution in Alabama, (3) the social distribution according to age and education, and (4) any dialect trends.

The study consists of five chapters. The first contains a statement of the problem and a brief discussion of the methods of linguistic geography, the second is an account of the settlement of Alabama, the third is a discussion of the procedures used in this study, the fourth is an analysis of the geographical distribution of terms, and the fifth is an analysis of the social distribution of terms. Four appendices are also included: The first contains maps of all the items, the second is a table showing the

[1] Order No. 66–7646

social distribution of items according to age, the third is a table showing the social distribution of items according to education, and the fourth is a list of all responses.

The result of the analysis was that three general conclusions could be drawn:

1) A boundary between the South Midland and the Southern dialect areas, a projection of the line established in the East, exists in Alabama. Isoglosses for twenty-three items were used to determine this line, which is essentially the same as that proposed in a previous study.

2) The analysis of dialect variants correlated with age and education indicates that Midland and Northern influence on vocabulary is increasing. This is shown by the fact that the older and less well-educated informants predominantly use the Southern terms and by the fact that the middle-aged and better educated use mainly Midland and Northern expressions.

3) The analysis of the social distribution of the items also indicates that national terms are replacing regional expressions. This is shown by the fact that the younger and less well-educated informants use fewer regional terms than do the older and less well-educated informants.   Microfilm $6.25; Xerography $22.30.   491 pages.

THE REPRESENTATION OF NEGRO DIALECT IN CHARLES W. CHESNUTT'S *THE CONJURE WOMAN*[1]

Charles William Foster, Ph.D.
University of Alabama, 1968

This dissertation is an analysis and an examination of the dialect of the North Carolina Negro as represented by Charles W. Chesnutt in his collection of dialect tales, *The Conjure Woman.*

An analysis such as this is facilitated by the field records for the *Linguistic Atlas of the South Atlantic States.*[2] The field records provide close transcriptions, made in the 1930's, of aged, uneducated Negro and white residents of the area around Fayetteville, North Carolina (the setting of *The Conjure Woman*). These speakers have been carefully classified, for *Atlas* purposes, by age, education, and social rank.

An essential step in a study of this sort is the determination of the author's dialect as nearly as possible. Through the use of *Atlas* field records of three cultured informants of the Cape Fear—Peedee River valleys, it is possible to reach a relatively accurate phonemic conclusion in this respect. Such a determination serves two purposes: (1) it allows for the interpretation of dialectal respellings using the author's "eye-dialect" as a key; (2) it provides a set of bases for assumptions as to what the author might have considered truly dialectal and what dialectal terms or pronunciations he might have omitted because, having these features in his own speech, he did not consider them dialectal.

[1] Order No. 69–6541

[2] These field records are presently stored at the University of Chicago; they provided the bases for observations made in *The Pronunciation of English in the Atlantic States,* by Hans Kurath and Raven I. McDavid, Jr. (Ann Arbor, Michigan, 1961). Dr. McDavid kindly granted permission to use the field records for the present study.

Since an author's re-spellings are often based on an assumed correlation between graphemes or grapheme clusters and certain phonemes, it is necessary to investigate the extent of grapheme-phoneme correlation in English. This has been done in this study using several of the accepted high-frequency word lists available today. On the basis of this correlation, it can be demonstrated that Chesnutt depends to a great extent on the reader's analogical extension of phoneme-grapheme correlation into words with which he is not familiar.

The author's phonology and the correlation of phonemes and graphemes having been determined, the next step is to check the author's representation of dialectal pronunciations against actual phonetic records of speakers from the same area. Five field records were used for this correlation, for a dialect character's speech is likely to be representative rather than individual. The author's veracity is further checked by a correlation of verb forms in *The Conjure Woman* with the same forms in the five *Atlas* field records.

This study indicates that Chesnutt deals primarily with incidence of phonemes in his dialectal respellings, the phoneme inventory being the same for Type I and Type II speakers of the same geographical provenience in the *Atlas* records. It also indicates, through a historical study of the pronunciations recorded, that Chesnutt was not utilizing Americanisms or strange pronunciations with an eye solely to their potential humorous effect, and that the phonological features of the speech of Uncle Julius can be shown to have existed in England early enough to preclude the possibility of their origination in North America.

To be regarded as authentic, the representation of dialect should record characteristics which are relatively limited, both geographically and socially. Using the distributional maps of the *Atlas,* it is possible to delineate areas of concentration for certain forms, and to use lines limiting these areas of concentration to delimit the dialect in question rather markedly. Using, for example, dialectal pronunciations of *hoof, took, hearth, yonder, crop,* and *melon,* one finds that the area in which *all* of the pronunciations occur as cited by Chesnutt in the speech of Uncle Julius is limited to a relatively small area around Fayetteville, North Carolina.

The conclusion of this study, then, is that Chesnutt was remarkably accurate in his representation of the dialect of the area which corresponds roughly to that delineated in *Atlas* studies as the Cape Fear—Peedee River Corridor. He does not exploit dialect for its own sake, but depends on its accurate use for additional depth of character development in Uncle Julius.   M $3.35; X $11.70.   258 pages.

THE SPEECH OF NEW YORK CITY[1]

Yakira Hagalili Frank, Ph.D.
University of Michigan, 1949

The purpose of this study is to analyze and to describe the pronunciation of English in New York City. Features common to all types of speakers as well as social differences and age differences in speech are treated and discussed.

[1] Library of Congress Card Number Mic A48-312 (Publication No. 1103)

674   The study is based upon records of the Linguistic Atlas of the United States. These records consist of phonetic transcriptions of approximately 800 items made of the speech of forty-six informants in New York City and in the Metropolitan area, including Suffolk, Nassau, and Westchester Counties in New York, and Middlesex, Union, Hudson, Essex, Bergen, and Passaic Counties in New Jersey.

Before an analysis of the social differences or age differences in speech was undertaken, a study of the phonemic system was made. On the basis of a preliminary survey, lists of words taken from the Linguistic Atlas were selected to illustrate each phoneme, the number of words used depending on several factors. If only one major variant occurred, few words were used. However, if it became necessary to resolve a phonemic problem, or to establish the spread of a variant, geographically or socially, all possible instances were used.

Variations in the pronunciation of the phonemes are positional or prosodic; or they are correlated with social classes, age groups, or individuals; or else they can be explained historically as the result of dialect mixture, either within a family, or a city, or along the boundary of two speech areas.

Uneducated speech and cultivated speech are characterized by distinct features of pronunciation. Older middle class informants frequently agree with the uneducated, whereas the younger may adopt features of cultivated speech. Certain variants are, nevertheless, common to all age groups and social classes. There is also evidence of the borrowing of upper class features by middle class; and, less frequently, by lower class speakers. Cultured speakers, particularly cultured women, educated in finishing schools, adopt Standard British English subphonemic (and phonemic) features.

Differences in the incidence of phonemes, whether systematic (i.e., confined to particular environments or to a limited number of morphemes) or individual (i.e., confined to one morpheme) are readily noticed, imitated, and acquired. They are, therefore, the clearest indicators of regional and social differences in pronunciation.

The coalescence of the historical phonemes as in *bird* and *Boyd,* a feature confined almost entirely to New York City, is characteristic of the speech of the uneducated and of the older middle class informants. Most of the cultured and the youngest of the middle class informants retain the historical contrast. The usage of others is, however, very unsettled. This is not surprising in view of the complex population, the constant mingling of the social classes, and the strong influence of the schools.

Another feature that sets off New York City from most of the surrounding New England settlement areas is the difference in the treatment of the vowel phonemes before tautosyllabic and intersyllabic /r/. Hudson County and parts of Middlesex and Bergen counties in New Jersey, and southern Westchester County and Nassau County in New York agree with New York City in this respect.

Microfilm $2.22.   177 pages

LANGUAGE DIFFERENCES AMONG UPPER- AND LOWER-CLASS NEGRO AND WHITE EIGHTH-GRADERS IN EAST CENTRAL ALABAMA[1]

Richard Layton Graves, Ph.D.
Florida State University, 1967

Major Professor: Dwight L. Burton

The purpose of this study was to identify language differences among four groups of eighth-grade students in east-central Alabama: (1) upper-class white, (2) upper-class Negro, (3) lower-class white, and (4) lower-class Negro.

There were twenty students in each group. Subjects were selected on the basis of the educational level and the occupation of their parents.

All subjects wrote in three forty-five minute sessions on three topics selected by the investigator. Each subject also participated in an eight-minute interview which was recorded and transcribed. The mean number of words produced in writing was 665.02 and in speech was 667.43.

The analysis of the materials was twofold: (1) the analysis of indexes of syntactic complexity, and (2) the analysis of selected usage items. The first is based on investigations by Kellogg W. Hunt and by Roy C. O'Donnell and extends their findings to include the dimension of social class. The second is based on the work of linguists such as Fries, Atwood, Bryant, and others.

Upper-class students produced in both written and spoken language a significantly larger number of words and had significantly longer T-units than did lower-class subjects. These findings are consistent with those of Hunt and O'Donnell. In written language, upper-class students produced significantly longer clauses, but not a larger number of clauses per T-unit. In spoken language, upper-class students did produce a significantly greater number of clauses per T-unit, but these clauses were not significantly longer than those of lower-class subjects.

In the usage analysis, two tendencies were observed. In spoken language, there was frequently a large difference between the low production of upper-class subjects and the high of lower-class subjects. In written language, there was often a regular progression in which the production of each group approximately doubled the preceding group.

The usage analysis revealed the following findings:

1) The singular subject with an uninflected verb occurred primarily among lower-class Negro students.

2) The singular subject with *don't* appeared only in lower-class language.

3) Lower-class subjects had a higher frequency of occurrence of the present tense form for the nonpresent.

4) Lower-class Negro subjects used in oral language *be* as a substitute for *is, are, was, were,* or *am,* and omitted the linking verb a significantly greater number of times than did the other groups.

---

[1] Order No. 68-2917

676   5) *Ain't* occurred only in the spoken language of lower-class Negro and white children.

6) Lower-class subjects used a significantly higher frequency of occurrence of *me* as one element of a compound subject.

7) Eight of the nine occurrences of *them* as a demonstrative adjective appeared in the lower-class.

8) All groups used *-ly*-less adverbials, though white subjects had a significantly greater frequency of occurrence of the adverbial *real*. *Good* as an adverbial was characteristic of lower-class luaage. The loss of the *-s* adverbial *sometimes* was characteristic of lower-class students.

9) Lower-class Negro students had a higher frequency of omitted plural noun inflections than did all other groups combined.

10) Lower-class subjects had a significantly greater frequency of occurrence of double negatives.   Microfilm $3.00; Xerography $7.00.   150 pages.

A COMPARISON ON A PHONETIC BASIS
OF THE TWO CHIEF LANGUAGES
OF THE AMERICAS, ENGLISH AND SPANISH[1]

Louise Gurren, Ph.D.
New York University, 1955

Chairman: Professor Dorothy Mulgrave

English and Spanish are the two chief languages of the Americas. As these languages were brought from the mother country during the periods of exploration and colonization of the New World, each one followed a similar pattern of development. One evidence of this is the fact that both English and Spanish in the New World have phonetic survivals, or archaisms, from pronunciations that date back to the time of their importation into the Americas. According to authorities, all these archaisms may be found today in the mother country.

Another characteristic of English and Spanish in the Americas is a strong tendency toward uniformity. Philologists in the field of these two languages, such as Bello, Cuervo, Lenz, Alonzo, and Navarro in Hispano-America; Webster, Worcester, Lounsbury, Krapp, Tilly, and Pyles in the United States, agree that, although spoken in the much wider territory of the New World, each language is more uniform in usage in the Americas than in the country of its origin. They cite, for example, the more extreme dialects prevalent in the British Isles and in Spain.

In this comparative study of English and Spanish pronunciation, the phonetic structure of these languages has been analyzed as follows: formation of sounds according to point and manner of articulation; lengthening of sounds; degree and location of stress on single words and in groups of words; syllable division in words and in groups of words; breadth or thought groups; intonation. In order to repre-

---

[1] Publication No. 13,612

sent visually as accurately as possible the pronunciation of each language, narrow transcription of the International Phonetic Alphabet and Klinghardt's and Navarro's intonation markings have been used.

Some of the differences in the formation of sounds are due to the fact that English and Spanish belong to different subdivisions of the Indo-European family of languages. English, Germanic in origin, uses the alveolar point of articulation for the sounds *t* and *d*, while Spanish, Latin in origin, uses the dental point of articulation for these sounds. A difference in manner of articulation of the sounds *p*, *t*, and *k*, also due to difference in family origin, is the aspiration of these sounds before a vowel in English and the lack of aspiration of these sounds before vowels in Spanish.

Another difference in manner of articulation of sound in English and Spanish stems from the fact that while certain English vowels, diphthongs, and consonants may be lengthened, all Spanish vowels and consonants are short. There are also fundamental differences in syllable division in groups of words in the two languages. English rarely carries over the last consonant of a word to the next word when that word begins with a vowel. In Spanish, on the other hand, the carryover is a fundamental characteristic of the sound structure of the language.

Location of stress on a syllable in a word in English follows no rule, nor is the location of the stress indicated in the spelling of the word. In Spanish there are rules for the location of stress on syllables in a word; if a word does not follow the rule, the stress is indicated in the spelling.

The length of intonation groups in English and Spanish is somewhat similar, since both languages in this respect fall between the lengthy groupings of Italian and the very short grouping of French.

This study points out in detail the phonetic differences and similarities in the two languages by analyzing and comparing single sounds, words, groups of words, and intonation. All these phonetic elements are brought together in the final chapter, which contains original phonetic transcriptions of a pertinent quotation from a famous writer in each language. 253 pages. $3.16. Mic 55-547

PRESSURES FOR DIALECT CHANGE IN HOCKING COUNTY, OHIO[1]

James Walter Hartman, Ph.D.
University of Michigan, 1966

Chairman: James W. Downer

This study, using items drawn from the worksheets of the Linguistic Atlas of the United States and Canada, attempts to show the dialectal relationship among three generations of native speakers of Hocking County, Ohio. Located in southeastern Ohio, Hocking County is relatively isolated and somewhat conservative culturally. Little immigration or other significant population changes have taken

[1] Order No. 66-14,529

678   place since the nineteenth century. This stability of population, coupled with a settlement history which shows a mixture of peoples from diverse parts of the United States, makes Hocking County nearly ideal for comparing internal changes in competing dialect items from one generation to the next.

A personal interview, using a prepared questionnaire, was conducted with each of the twenty native informants who were selected on the bases of age, place of residence, and amount of schooling. The three generations, twelve to forty, forty to sixty, and above sixty, comprise a more complete sampling than the *Atlas* materials, thus allowing more detailed conclusions to be drawn.

This study reveals the following about dialect change in Hocking County:

1) Of the competing items discussed, 83 percent of them are undergoing some kind of change. That is, 17 percent of the competing items retain a stable relation to each other throughout all three generations.

2) Semantically, food, animal, and other rural terms are receding with the strongest changes taking place between the middle and young age groups.

3) Folk pronunciations begin receding (at least) with the oldest generation. Local pronunciations start to change in the middle group.

4) Grammatical items change at a nearly constant rate between generations with Northern forms replacing Midland forms (with one exception).

Hocking County dialect is a composite of Eastern forms which, through the influence of historical, linguistic, and social pressures, is undergoing its own kind of standardization. As regional variations are often the innovative forms, this standardization is not a simple replacement of dialect forms with national standards.

Geographically, the old settlement centers of the county still reflect the speech of the early settlers. The east is Southern, the west, Pennsylvanian, the center a mixture of the two, and the city has, in addition, some Northern showings. The topographical and economic conditions of the county have influenced the speech of the county by virtue of the nature of the settlers attracted to various sections.

The study roughly supports Kurath's inclusion of southeastern Ohio in his area eleven, a North Midland area. However, it reveals a much more complex picture than indicated in earlier studies.

The status of any item may be seen in detail through biographical sketches of the informants, maps of the area, the questionnaire used, and an appendix with basic data.   Microfilm $3.00; Xerography $7.80.   168 pages.

THE REPRESENTATION OF GULLAH-INFLUENCED DIALECT IN TWENTIETH CENTURY SOUTH CAROLINA PROSE: 1922–1930[1]

Ann Sullivan Haskell, Ph.D.
University of Pennsylvania, 1964

Supervisor: Professor Harold S. Stine

Analyses of American dialect representation have been made before, most notably by George P. Krapp in his *English Language in America* (1925). Since that time, however, there has been research that disproved the theory of dialect by which Krapp conducted his analysis. The investigations of the *Linguistic Atlas* have provided records of actual speech by which the authenticity of dialect representation in literature may be determined.

In this study the dialect in works by Ambrose Gonzales, Julia Peterkin, Marcellus S. Whaley, E. C. L. Adams, Samuel Stoney, and Gertrude Shelby was examined. All of these authors attempted to represent the speech of lower-class Negroes of the South Carolina Coastal Plain, and all of this dialect literature was produced within the period of 1922–1930.

This analysis was based on Sumner A. Ives' "A Theory of Literary Dialect," *Tulane Studies in English,* II (1950), 137–182. Ives' method was devised for the analysis of the work of a single author, however, and modifications were made to accommodate the representation by several authors.

The phonology of the South Carolina dialect group was analyzed by grouping together respellings which implied like phonemes. The resultant groups of sounds were checked against the records of Type I South Carolina informants in the *Linguistic Atlas* files. When a phonological feature could not be checked in the field records of the *Atlas,* it was sought in one of the *Atlas*-based studies, such as E. Bagby Atwood's *A Survey of Verb Forms in the Eastern United States* (Ann Arbor, 1953), Hans Kurath's *A Word Geography of the Eastern United States* (Ann Arbor, 1949), Hans Kurath and Raven I. McDavid, Jr.'s *The Pronunciation of English in the Atlantic States* (Ann Arbor, 1961), and Sumner A. Ives' *The Phonology of the Uncle Remus Stories,* PADS, No. 22 (1954). Further, all phonological features were checked in the publications on Gullah dialect by Lorenzo Dow Turner, principally his *Africanisms in the Gullah Dialect* (Chicago, 1949). Only the records of actual speech as recorded by professional linguists were considered in this aspect of the study.

Lexical items in the written dialect were initially checked against the records of the *Linguistic Atlas, Atlas*-based material, and Turner's works. Subsequently other sources were checked, proceeding from the most geographically restricted—such as regional wordlists—to general works on American English dialect.

Summaries were made and conclusions reached concerning the dialect representation of the area as a whole, and of the individual authors. The degrees of Gullah influence in the different authors' works were stated. In general, the dialect presented

[1] Order No. 64-10,382

by this group of writers was found to represent an honest effort to produce a spoken language, within the limitations imposed by the orthographical system. However, the dissemination of specific terms among writers in comparison to their actual employment in the spoken language frequently showed remarkable differences. Hence, a literary tradition for this area with an accompanying dialect standard can readily be ascertained.   Microfilm $3.60; Xerography $16.20.   280 pages.

A PHONOLOGICAL ANALYSIS OF THE SPEECH OF HAYS COUNTY, TEXAS[1]

Betty Ruth Heard, Ph.D.
Louisiana State University and Agricultural
and Mechanical College, 1969

Supervisor: Professor J. Donald Ragsdale

The purpose of this study was to describe and analyze the phonology of the speech of the people of Hays County, Texas. Although the major emphasis of this study was phonological, some attention was devoted to a survey of selected lexical items.

The problem was to determine the following: (1) the phonological characteristics of the speech of Hays County, Texas; (2) the patterns suggested by differing speech usage at several levels of age and education; (3) the possibility of pronunciation or vocabulary isoglosses within the County.

The conduct of the stages of the study proceeded in the following manner. First, a study of the history and settlement patterns of the County determined that most of the pre-Civil War immigrants came from or through the Southern states, but most of the post-Civil War immigrants came from Missouri, Tennessee, or Arkansas. Second, a questionnaire was compiled for the interviews. Third, from each community, representative Hays County residents of varied age, education, and occupation were chosen. Fourth, thirty-three interviews yielded twenty-seven usable tape recordings. Fifth, the workbooks were transcribed phonetically. Sixth, the phonology of the speech of Hays County was described, and selected lexical items were discussed.

The dialect of Hays County was mixed. Features more characteristic of Northern and Midland pronunciation predominated. For example, postvocalic [r] and unstressed syllabic [ɚ] were retained in words like *door* and *father*. [ɝ] appeared in words like *thirty*. Monophthongal checked vowels [ɪ, ʊ, ɛ, ʌ, æ] were used in words like *whip, wood, red, sun, sack*. Other Northern or Midland sound patterns were the use of [u] in *two;* [ɔ] in *law, orange, fog;* [aʊ] (with a low-front quality) in *cow;* [ɪ] in *ear, rinse;* [ʊ] in *poor;* [ɛ] in both *merry* and *Mary, deaf, yellow;* [o] as the unstressed vowel in *yellow* and infrequent use of [r] in *wash*.

Features of Southern pronunciation that occurred were usually restricted to posi-

[1] Order No. 69-17,110

tional allophones or choice of a sound within *one* word. Examples were the use of [eɪ] before the voiced velar [g] in *egg* and the use of [z] in *greasy*.

A large number of characteristically General Southern words influenced the vocabulary of the County. For instance, use of *pallet,* (corn) *shucks, pully bone, light bread,* (horse) *lot,* and *whetrock* was widespread. The survey of lexical items also revealed several terms apparently somewhat restricted to the central Texas area and Hays County. They were *cedar chopper* (poor white trash), *Jew Pudding* (a Christmas strudel), and *Roosevelt* or *Hoover willows.* Some of the terms used more often or only with informants over sixty were *mantelboard, mantelpiece, wardrobe, bakery bread,* (cherry) *kernel, clingstone* peach, *shirtwaist, widow woman, French harp, a right smart, tolerable,* etc. Some of the words highly homogeneous among many informants were *seven-thirty, downpour, drouth, norther, mantel, andirons, kindling, backlog, gutters, couch, pallet, skillet, shucks, light bread, soda water, freestone* peach, *tank* (pond), *dinner* at noon, *supper* at night. Some of the words used by a majority of or only by German informants were *shelf* (mantel), *bakery bread, sour milk, Sleif-steine* (grindstone), *not normal* (bastard), *Katzenmusik* (shivaree), *Stinkkatze* (skunk), *rain worm* (earthworm), *Tante Meier* (outhouse). Spanish words that occurred in a very limited currency were *grullo* (ash-colored horse), *mott* (clump of trees), *arroyo* (dry stream bed), *sendero* (canyon), *remuda* (herd), *caballero* (cowboy), *bronco* (wild horse), and *mecate* (rope).

Hays County settlers may have brought both an "r" dialect and a Southern vocabulary with them. Dialect studies of the inland states and of surrounding counties must be made before Hays County could be called a transitional area.

M $3.95; X $13.95. 308 pages.

A DIALECT STUDY OF
FAULKNER COUNTY, ARKANSAS[1]

Patricia Joanne Hoff, Ph.D.
Louisiana State University and Agricultural
 and Mechanical College, 1968

Supervisor: Professor Claude L. Shaver

The purpose of this study is to determine the speech characteristics of the people of Faulkner County, Arkansas.

First, a study was made of the history of Faulkner County in order to determine influences on immigration into the area. Most of the people came from the Southern states, particularly Tennessee.

Second, thirty informants were interviewed and the responses recorded. Two of these tapes were not usable; consequently twenty-eight informants were used in the study. The responses were transcribed into phonetic symbols and a description was given of the dialect. Although the study is primarily a descriptive phonological

[1] Order No. 68-10,745

682   study, certain lexical items were examined and comparisons, primarily with Southern, Mountain, and Midland speech, were made.

The speech of Faulkner County has similarities with Southern, Mountain and Midland speech along with great differences from all three. The great diversity in pronunciation and in the use of lexical items suggests that Faulkner County may be a transitional area. Among the evidence to support this is the following: (1) In words such as *ma* and *pa,* either the Midland pronunciation [ɔ] or the Southern [ɑ] may be used by the same individual. (2) The Southern [ɔ] in *water* does not occur; but the Southern [ɑ] is predominant in *wash.* (3) The Southern diphthongization of vowels and the Southern and Mountain monophthongization of [aɪ] are predominant; but the loss of [r] does not occur. (4) The Northern terms *brook, pail, quite* (spry) and (cherry) *pit* are common. (5) The Southern and Midland terms *lightbread, clabbered, shuck, pallet, snack, pulley bone, snakedoctor,* etc., are all common; whereas the Southern terms *tote, turn of wood, fritters, Confederate War,* etc., and the Southern Midland terms *milkgap, blinds, a little piece,* etc., are either infrequent or nonexistent. Further studies need to be made in the areas around Faulkner County before the evidence will be clear. There are suggestions that isoglosses appear; but the evidence suggests they may be a result of the few informants used and the small geographical area studied.

There is evidence to show that certain pronunciations and terms are dying out. These include: (1) [æ] in *care, chair, stamp* (one's foot); [ɪ] in cherry syrup; [ɛ] in *syrup, shut;* [i] in *drain;* [ɚ] in *heart, tushes, widow;* [ju] in *new due, Tuesday;* [æʊ] in *wound; loafbread; lunch* (for snack); *skeeter hawk; devil's horse; fritters; Confederate War; tap; stob; firedogs; fire irons; stinging lizard; fireboard;* etc.

In most instances there is no difference in pronunciation or terminology between the educated informants or those from Conway, the county seat of Faulkner County, and other informants. In a few instances the educated or those from Conway did not use pronunciations or terminology of other speakers. These include: (1) *loafbread;* (2) *lunch* (snack); (3) *skeeter hawk;* (4) *devil's horse;* (5) *stinging lizard;* (6) *low* (moo); (7) *frying pan;* (8) *sty;* (9) *hog lot;* (10) rounding of the vowel in *sun, brush, gums, judge, shut, touch;* (11) voicing of the fricative in *nephew;* (12) [i] in *drain* and (13) [r] in *wash.*

Until further evidence is available it can be said tentatively that (1) Faulkner County seems to be a transitional area with influences of Southern, Mountain, and Midland speech; (2) certain terms are dying out; (3) in most instances the educated informants and the informants from Conway use the same pronunciations and terminology that is used by other informants; (4) the indications of possible isoglosses will probably not be valid as other studies are completed.

Microfilm $3.65; Xerography $12.85.   282 pages.

THE SPEECH OF LOUISVILLE, KENTUCKY[1]   683

Robert Ray Howren, Jr., Ph.D.
Indiana University, 1958

The chief foreign sources of the population of Louisville have been Germany and Ireland, especially the former; the principal sources of native white American population of the city have been the South Atlantic and Middle Atlantic States (before the middle of the nineteenth century) and the North Central States (since the mid-nineteenth century). The Negro population, on the other hand, has been drawn largely from the South Central States. This study undertakes, through the analysis of some thirty-five hours of tape-recorded conversation with fifteen carefully selected native white and Negro residents of various ages and widely differing backgrounds, to describe the lexicon and phonology of the dialect which has emerged from this mingling of linguistic streams, and to comment somewhat less extensively on salient features of the morphology and syntax.

The vocabulary of Louisville speech is chiefly North Midland in character, and would seem to differ significantly from that of other Kentucky dialects in this respect. The vocabulary has, nevertheless, a strong South Midland flavor. We may say that the lexicon of Louisville speech is composed, roughly, of one part Southern words, three parts Northern words, and five parts Midland words. Considerable levelling of dialectal features may be observed, however, as a result of urbanization.

The prosodic features of the dialect are described in terms of three degrees of stress, four junctures, and four pitch-levels. Certain aspects of suprasegmental phenomena are treated in some detail: (1) the allophones of major stress and the lexical distribution of stress patterns; (2) the allophones and distribution of microjuncture; (3) the allophones and distribution of the macrojunctures; and (4) the intonation contours and their variants.

The major portion of the study is devoted to a detailed description of the segmental phonology, which is, for white informants, characteristic of the South Midland area, and, for the Negro informants, basically Southern rather than South Midland. An examination of some regional patterns in the lexical distribution of phonemes reveals an overwhelming predominance of patterns typical of the Midland area in general, with a slight admixture of Southern features.

The study concludes with an examination of some miscellaneous features of the morphology and syntax which might prove significant for differentiating the speech of Louisville from that of other areas. Chief among the morphological items studied are the tense forms of fifty-seven strong verbs, which show a heavy influence from the combined Midland-Southern area, with very little influence from the Southern area alone. The social distribution of these tense forms is also studied, and, as in the vocabulary, the levelling effect of urban life is seen in the relatively large proportion of standard forms in general usage. On the whole, the Midland and Southern dialects combined are found to be not only the greatest contributors to Louisville tense forms, but by far the most important influence on the morphology and syntax in general.   Microfilm $2.75; Xerox $9.60.   211 pages.

[1] L.C. Card No. Mic 58-2918

684

AN ANALYSIS OF CERTAIN COLORADO ATLAS FIELD RECORDS WITH REGARD TO SETTLEMENT HISTORY AND OTHER FACTORS[1]

Elizabeth Hope Jackson, Ph.D.
University of Colorado, 1956

Supervisor: Professor Marjorie M. Kimmerle

This study attempts to answer two questions raised in connection with the first editing and analysis of responses for the Colorado survey of the *Linguistic Atlas of the United States:* Does settlement history materially affect the dialect vocabulary of Colorado? How else can differences in usage be accounted for?

In search of answers I dealt with vocabulary materials in responses from the 21 oldest informants in eastern Colorado—those over 60 at the time of the field interviews in 1950-1951. These represented 16 communities of the survey, selected for such reasons as location, early establishment, or settlement history. The material fell into two parts: expressions for terms discussed in Kurath's *Word Geography of the Eastern United States,* basic to all *Atlas* studies since its publication in 1949; items of state and regional significance added to the standard *Atlas* questionnaire to check cultural, topographical, climatic, and economic influences on dialect vocabulary in this region.

Information was also gathered from United States census records for 1870 and 1880 and the unique semidecennial state census of 1885, all of which added record of place of parents' birth to the customary statistics concerning an individual's age, occupation, place of birth, etc. The information thus gathered, together with facts about life in the region, especially between the years 1870 and 1885, provided a background for analyzing the *Atlas* responses in the light of the period in which these older eastern Colorado informants were acquiring their speech habits and within which there was enormous population growth. Three major strains built up a complex population in these years: people from the Northeast and its settlements in the upper Midwest, from the Middle and South Atlantic States and their South-Central and Midwestern settlements, and from various foreign stock, including indigenous Spanish-speaking Spanish-Americans in the southern counties.

Results of this correlation support certain tentative conclusions about the dialect vocabulary of Colorado. To some extent, responses tended to pattern, but they also showed many inconsistencies. Both tendencies are explained largely by the following findings.

Most of eastern Colorado is a notable transition area due to blending of native speech elements from the East and some foreign influence in the first years of Anglo-American settlement. Except for a relatively minor Spanish-American influence, the large flow of non-English-speaking peoples has had no appreciable influence. The British-English influence cannot be assessed until *Atlas* projects in the British Isles and Canada are completed. In some places, settlement history has determined some

[1] Publication No. 22,611

consistency of choice as to a community's use of Eastern regionalisms; in other 685
places of similar backgrounds, other phenomena—contiguity, proximity, or accessibility for communication have overruled original speech tendencies. In still other places, sharply contrasted regional usages have survived side by side, with no predominance reflected by the *Atlas* survey. Denver appears to be a focal center because of its original favorable location and its continual development as a trade, social, cultural, and political influence. Midland is the principal source of eastern Colorado dialect, a conclusion based on responses and borne out by the history of migration to Eastern secondary settlements in the East from which many Colorado settlers came and the history of direct migration into Colorado from Midland areas. Local, areal, or regional peculiarities of topography, soil, climate, and special human activity have determined the use of some terms here that are not current in the Eastern United States.

Thus settlement history has materially affected eastern Colorado dialect and differences are due mainly to the transition character and peculiar conditions of the area. 435 pages. $5.55. Mic 58–4695

THE SPEECH OF THE CENTRAL COAST OF NORTH CAROLINA: THE CARTERET COUNTY VERSION OF THE BANKS "BROGUE"[1]

Hilda Jaffe, Ph.D.
Michigan State University, 1966

Along the central coast of North Carolina, on the long lines of sand reefs called the Outer Banks and on the extreme fringes of the mainland, a variety of American English is spoken which differs radically from its nearest neighbors. Some of its characteristics are still perceptible fifteen to twenty miles inland, but from then on it rapidly fades out. This dialect is a result of the pattern of settlement of the coastal country. The coastal fringes, ideally suited to those who make their living from the sea, were in the main settled by such people in the first half of the eighteenth century, and where they settled they stayed. Predominantly English by descent, they or their immediate ancestors had come first to other colonies—New England, Maryland, Virginia—before moving on to North Carolina. Later settlers moved in behind them, leaving them virtually undisturbed until encroachments began in the early part of the twentieth century.

In pronunciation the dialect is surprisingly unlike the general speech of the rest of eastern North Carolina. Two features are immediately notable: The first is a marked retroflection of postvocalic /r/, very striking in a region where "r-less" speech is universal. The second is the treatment of the diphthong /aɪ/. Unlike the speech farther inland, which has [aɨ] before voiceless and [a.] before voiced consonants, the dialect has only one allophone, [âɨ]. Newspaper feature writers usually render this as "oy," writing "hoy toyde" for *high tide.* This is misleading, since the diphthong does not rhyme with *boy,* but is a good indication of the effect of the allo-

[1] Order No. 66–8467

686 phone on an unaccustomed ear. Other phonetic features of the dialect are a fronting of the vowels /u/, /ʌ/, and /ʊ/, and /o/ is usually [əʊ]. There are other lesser phonetic features as well. Certain features, however, the dialect does share with the rest of eastern North Carolina: Final stops are generally unreleased; final [-ŋ] in participles is [-n] more often than not; some speakers have [sr] for initial [šr]; and the plural form of the pronoun *you* is commonly *you-all* or *y'all*.

The data for the study was collected by means of the Linguistic Atlas worksheets for the South Atlantic states, administered to twelve informants. Because of the overwhelming reluctance of the people of these isolated communities to be interviewed at all, interviews were made by local residents using a tape-recorder. Because of this same reluctance, length of interview time was reduced by having the informant go through the worksheets, item by item, while the interviewer stood by to give explanations as necessary. The method proved to be successful. Very few of our informants were concerned about notions of "correctness," and did not hesitate to phrase their responses in nonstandard forms even when the worksheet item was worded in the standard form. Further, they were not self-conscious about pronunciation. Thus the method gave excellent results for the phonetic data, very good results for the vocabulary items, and some usable results for most of the grammatical items.

For the reader's convenience in comparing this dialect with the findings already published for the Atlantic states, selection and ordering of examples and discussions follow closely that in *The Pronunciation of English in the Atlantic States*[2] and in *A Survey of Verb Forms in the Eastern United States,*[3] with close cross-references to those volumes. Microfilm $3.00; Xerography $5.60. 113 pages.

A PHONOLOGICAL STUDY OF ENGLISH AS SPOKEN BY PUERTO RICANS CONTRASTED WITH PUERTO RICAN SPANISH AND AMERICAN ENGLISH[1]

Morgan Emory Jones, Ph.D.
University of Michigan, 1962

The primary purpose of this study is to describe the sounds and sound system of Puerto Rican Hybrid English, a second language or one spoken with a "foreign accent." The secondary purposes are (1) to contrast this English with Puerto Rican Spanish and American English, which are respectively the first and target languages of the speakers, and (2) to describe the sociocultural circumstances surrounding the acquistion and use of Puerto Rican Hybrid English, i.e. who speaks it, when it is spoken, and how it is learned.

The English described is the "dialect" spoken by adult natives of Puerto Rico.

---

[1] Order No. 63–375

[2] Hans Kurath and Raven I. McDavid, Jr. (Ann Arbor: The University of Michigan Press, 1961).

[3] E. Bagby Atwood (Ann Arbor: The University of Michigan Press, 1953).

This English is differentiated from that of North American immigrants to Puerto Rico and from that of North American progeny brought up in Puerto Rico. It is not a pidgin or Creole language but a hybrid dialect, a cross between Puerto Rican Spanish and American English.

To begin with, two questionnaires were constructed and proved. (These appear in the dissertation as appendixes.) Then, thirty-seven of the most populous municipalities of the island were canvassed for Puerto Ricans who spoke English more than any others. Four hundred forty-five were found, many of whom spoke English daily at home and at work, and the first questionnaire was administered to them. It measured the amount of English learned from North Americans before adolescence and the amount of English the subjects spoke in their daily lives.

Next, a second interview was held for the twenty-seven who spoke the most English and yet had not learned much of it from North Americans before adolescence. In this interview, answers to the second questionnaire gave a profile of each informant—his history, occupation, social standing, and personal characteristics—and responses to the *Pictorial Linguistic Interview Manual,* which were tape-recorded, furnished the corpus for the linguistic description.

In the dissertation, there is an account of the Puerto Rican culture, with emphasis on the place of English, and a history of English in Puerto Rico, especially in the schools. Brief descriptions of the phonology of Puerto Rican Spanish (partly original) and of American English (not original) are included as precise entities with which to contrast Puerto Rican Hybrid English.

The twenty-seven informants spoke English with twelve different segmental inventories, the number of phonemes ranging from twenty-five as in Puerto Rican Spanish to thirty-five as in American English. Out of diversity, a single phonology was synthesized according to majority usage. The synthesis has twenty-one consonants, eight vowels, four pitches, four stresses, and four junctures.

The suprasegmentals and rhythm are usually like those of American English. The distribution of segmentals resembles the American English distribution much more than it does the Puerto Rican Spanish; yet the segmental inventory is more like the Puerto Rican Spanish inventory than like the American English. As in Puerto Rican Spanish, stress reduction is not accompanied by vowel change. And there is an elaborate morphophonemic system modeled after a similar though rudimentary system in Puerto Rican Spanish and a similar though subphonemic system in American English. Altogether, the phonology of Puerto Rican Hybrid English is about 30 percent like that of Puerto Rican Spanish and 70 percent like that of American English.

Conclusions reached are:

1) The difference in accent between Puerto Rican Hybrid English and American English lies more in the differences in the phonetic shape and distribution of phonemes than in the differences in phonemic inventory.

2) Puerto Ricans can communicate very satisfactorily with North Americans in an English "dialect" which has a Spanish phonemic inventory if the phonetic shape and occurrence of the phonemes are numerically similar to those of the American English diaphones (phonemic counterparts) and if enunciation, voice quality, fluency, vocabulary, and the like are acceptable.

Microfilm $4.45; Xerox $15.75.   348 pages.

A STUDY OF THE INFLUENCE OF ENGLISH ON THE SPANISH OF PUERTO RICANS IN JERSEY CITY, NEW JERSEY[1]

Charles William Kreidler, Ph.D.
University of Michigan, 1958

The purpose of this study is to discover the amount and nature of change in the Spanish dialect of a group of Puerto Ricans as a result of their exposure to English in the mainland community in which they have settled. The importance of this study in the much-neglected field of interlanguage influences derives, aside from the recentness of the particular contact situation under investigation, from the attention given to the structural implications of language borrowing. The theoretical considerations involved draw largely from the recent works of Haugen, Weinreich, and others, whose writings are summarized.

The linguistic material studied consists of 228 forms of English origin elicited from thirty informants in response to a prepared questionnaire. Informants were chosen to give adequate representation of groupings according to age, length of residence in the continental United States, and comparative degree of exposure to English through employment, social contacts, and cultural media.

A sketch is given of the sociocultural background of the language-contact situation. Jersey City, a community in the heart of the world's largest urban agglomeration, is characterized by a high degree of industrialization, ethnic heterogeneity, and population saturation. The Puerto Ricans who settle there bring with them the results of American cultural influence in political and economic spheres already received in their island home, but retain Hispanic mores in family and social life. The consequent group solidarity largely hinders acquisition of fluency in English through social contacts outside the migrant colony. For the adult, employment is the prime locus of exposure to English.

A phonemic analysis of Puerto Rican Spanish shows five vowels, eighteen consonants, and two degrees of stress. Vowels occur initially, medially, and finally in isolable forms, alone and in clusters. Consonants are comparatively restricted in final occurrence and in the possibility of occurrence in clusters. In contrast, the Metropolitan New York dialect of English possesses twenty-one vowel and diphthong units, twenty-four consonants and four degrees of stress. The borrowing of English forms occasions innovations of two sorts in the phonemic structure of the Spanish dialect under study: Certain consonants occur in new environments and a new consonant, /š/, is added to the inventory of phonemes.

Morphemic analysis of Puerto Rican Spanish reveals ten form classes. Borrowings from English are assigned to five of these classes in the following proportions: nouns 81 percent, verbs 7 percent, adjectives 6 percent, interjections 4 percent and adverbs 2 percent. Forms borrowed as nouns receive the usual Spanish inflection for number and are assigned to a gender category. In general, the assignment of gender correlates with the natural sex of the referent; when the referent is inanimate, the noun is

[1] L. C. Card No. Mic 58–3691

most commonly assigned to the masculine gender. Forms borrowed as verbs are 689 mostly assigned to the largest inflectional category of Spanish regular verbs. Forms borrowed as adjectives do not show the inflections for gender and number characteristic of this Spanish form class.

The findings of this study give some support to three general conclusions: 1) In a situation of language contact, borrowed forms in use by the more nearly monolingual members of the borrowing group show greater adaptation to the phonemic structure of the receiving language than do forms in use only by the more nearly bilingual members of the group; 2) in the adapting of foreign linguistic forms to the structural norms of the receiving language, there is greater likelihood of the occurrence of a native phoneme in a new position than of the borrowing of a new phoneme; 3) when a phoneme is borrowed into a language, its introduction may have been facilitated by the existence of a corresponding "hole in the phonemic pattern" of the receiving language.　　　　Microfilm $2.50; Xerox $8.60.　190 pages.

THE LINGUISTIC GEOGRAPHY OF EASTERN MONTANA[1]

Thomas Joseph O'Hare, Ph.D.
University of Texas, 1964

Supervising Professor: Rudolph C. Troike

During the summer of 1963, eighteen field interviews were conducted by the writer in the state of Montana, using the short worksheets that were originally compiled for the *Linguistic Atlas of the United States* and later revised for the *Linguistic Atlas of the Upper Midwest* by Harold B. Allen with additions from the vocabulary worksheets used by E. Bagby Atwood in his survey of Texas. From a consideration of their roles in the settlement history of the state, as well as their present economic positions and their geographical locations, nine eastern Montana communities (ten informants) were selected to serve as representatives of the speech of that area. Two western communities (two informants) were selected on the same criteria, to serve as a basis for comparison and as points of preliminary investigation for future studies.

Items of vocabulary that showed any differentiation among the informants are presented in a chapter dealing with the word geography of eastern Montana, chiefly on maps (93) which show their geographical distribution. An additional twelve maps present outer limits of some of these geographical distributions. Two separate bundles of isoglosses emerge, which intersect at the point of heaviest concentration, dividing the area into northern and southern on the one hand and eastern and western on the other.

The state was settled mostly by immigrants from the Northern and Midland dialectal areas and their westward extensions through the states of the West North Central Census Division. Analysis of vocabulary items collected in the interviews

[1] Order No. 64-11,823

690 shows that terms which are generally distributed throughout the states of the Atlantic Coast enjoy widespread usage in Montana. Of the terms which have restricted distributions in the East, those that are restricted to all or to parts of the North and Midlands are much more common in Montana than terms that are restricted to the South, most of which are rare or unknown in Montana.

Significant pronunciation features in Montana are analyzed within the framework adopted for the Atlantic Coast material (vocalic nuclei in selected key words). Although no major phonemic differences are apparent from the material recorded in the interviews, some allophonic differences appear, mainly in the area of the low-central, low-back and mid-back vowels.

The questionnaire that was used in the survey is included in the final chapter.
Microfilm $3.25; Xerography $11.25.   249 pages.

THE DIALECT OF NORTHWESTERN OHIO: A STUDY OF A TRANSITION AREA[1]

Edward Earle Potter, Ph.D.
University of Michigan, 1955

This study of speech patterns in six counties of northwestern Ohio is based on responses given to a mail questionnaire by sixty informants. The questionnaire dealt only with vocabulary items and asked the informant to choose the terms which he regularly used for approximately one hundred folk concepts. The vocabulary items thus collected were studied to determine these four things: (1) the geographical distribution of the terms in the six counties, (2) the origin of the terms in the light of their dissemination in the East, (3) the social distribution of the terms according to age, occupation, and education; and (4) any dialect trends.

A chapter is devoted to each of the following: (1) an account of the settlement and growth of northwestern Ohio, (2) a full description of the linguistic materials and informants used by the study, (3) an analysis of the vocabulary items according to their geographical distribution and to their origins in the Eastern United States, (4) an analysis of each of the terms in the light of its dissemination in various age, occupation, and education groups; and (5) a statement of the conclusions which appear to be warranted by the analysis. Two appendices are also included. Appendix I has a map for each of the one hundred concepts to show at a glance in which counties the various terms appear. In Appendix II each of the concepts is shown in its distribution, by county, through each of the six social groupings.

The result of the analysis was that five general conclusions could be drawn. First, the area appears to be moving toward more general use of Midland rather than Northern terms. This is suggested by the fact that the percentage of Northern terms declines from the high point of 30 percent for old people to only 17 percent for both the middle-aged and the young; and it is further evidenced by the fact that the

[1] Publication No. 12,635

Northern terms are commonest among the least educated people. Both youth and education favor the Midland dialect.

Second, the data confirm the observation made by many linguists that the least-educated people tend to be more conservative than the better-educated people. Educated people appear to be more ready to accept terms outside of their own dialects.

Third, it was found that occupation is considerably less important than age or education in shaping the common, everyday vocabulary.

Fourth, the kind of item that is subject to the most confused usage is one having some connection with edibles. All instances of mixed Northern and Midland usage were in this category except one.

Fifth, and finally, the study offers further evidence of the reliability of the mail questionnaire as a means of collecting information about matters of vocabulary, because it confirms previous findings that the major isogloss between Northern and Midland areas cuts through the waist of the six counties in the northwestern corner of Ohio.   388 pages. $4.85.   MicA 55-2153

LINGUISTIC RESEARCH IN AMERICAN UNIVERSITIES: DISSERTATIONS AND INFLUENCES FROM 1900 TO 1964[1]

Phillip Roland Rutherford, Ph.D.
East Texas State University, 1966

Adviser: Dr. Fred A. Tarpley

The purposes of this dissertation are fourfold: to compile a bibliography of all dissertations in linguistics and language from 1900 to 1964, to trace the influence of certain major American linguistic publications on the dissertations, to discover which institutions appeared to be interested in which areas of linguistics and language, and to determine certain trends in linguistics and language that the bibliography seemed to indicate.

The 1640 linguistic and language dissertation titles that were collected is the data source on which the study is based. To determine the influences on the writing of the dissertations, the years between 1900 and 1964 are divided into five periods— 1900 to 1930, 1930 to 1940, 1940 to 1950, 1950 to 1960, and 1960 to 1964—each of which becomes the basis for a chapter. In each chapter other than the first, a major American linguistics publication is reviewed and summarized, along with quotations from many eminent linguists as to the publication's impact on linguistics. For the first chapter, Holger Pederson's *The Discovery of Language* is investigated to discover the linguistic interests of the nineteenth century which could be expected to continue into the early twentieth. In each of the succeeding periods, Leonard

[1] Order No. 67-1535

692 Bloomfield's *Language,* Charles C. Fries' *American English Grammar,* George L. Trager and Henry Lee Smith's *Outline of English Structure,* and Noam Chomsky's *Syntactic Structures* are used respectively. Immediately following the review in each chapter is the dissertation bibliography for the period, divided into approximately forty subject categories. After the bibliography occurs a subject and language listing, subdivided to show the various institutions that contributed dissertations to that section and how many they contributed. Percentages are calculated on each of the major divisions and the subdivisions to determine the entry's relative importance to the period. Commentaries are then presented on the degree of influence the publication for that period seems to have, the trends which seem to be evident for that period, and the institutions which are especially interested in certain areas of linguistics or certain languages listed in that period. In the concluding chapter is given a set of tables, category and language, created from the listings in the five chapters, showing the relative importance of each category and each language to the sixty-four year period and to the individual institution.

While it is difficult to accurately ascertain the influences exerted by the publications on the writing of the dissertations, the trends of linguistics through the sixty-four year period are relatively easy to discern. Certain institutions are more active than others in producing linguistic and language dissertations and frequently concentrate on one or a few areas of linguistics or on one or a few languages.

Of the many conclusions which could be drawn from the study, these seem the most worthy of noting: Certain influences of the publications can be determined by observing the bibliography; "parts of speech" study has declined markedly in the past sixty-four years; the study of phonology, dialects, comparative linguistics, language structure, and morphology increases substantially during the period; few dissertations using American Indian languages as subjects were written prior to 1950; internationl tension seems to cause emphasis to be placed on certain language areas; the study of the classical languages increased through the 1930–1940 period, then declined rapidly; and Columbia University, Harvard University, the University of Michigan, and the University of Pennsylvania have been the most active in producing linguistic and language dissertations.

Microfilm $7.95; Xerography $28.15.   628 pages.

PUERTO RICAN-ENGLISH PHONOTACTICS[1]

Mercedes de los Ángeles Sáez, Ph.D.
University of Texas, 1962

Supervisor: E. Bagby Atwood

The primary concern of this study is to present the order characteristics of the phonemes and the recurrences of certain arrangements of phonemes in English compared with Puerto Rican Spanish.

[1] Order No. 62-2569

This study is based on the spoken language. The data was gathered from twenty-two informants, who were born, raised, and educated in Puerto Rico. Questionnaires were used which were graded according to two considerations: (a) the vocabulary which the informants were more familiar with, and (b) their proficiency in the language.

1) This study shows that there are five vowel phonemes and seventeen consonant phonemes in Puerto Rican Spanish.
2) The particular dialect of Spanish spoken in Puerto Rico is characterized as follows:
   a. The "seseo"
   b. The "yeísmo"
   c. Aspirated /h/ instead of /j/
   d. Velar [ŋ] in place of final /n/
   e. Aspirated /h/ in place of syllable-final and word-final /s/
   f. Velar /rr/
   g. Frequency of initial /ñ/ in uneducated speech
   h. /l/ instead of final /r/ in uneducated speech
3) The Puerto Rican learner of English, at all levels, has difficulty in producing and recognizing the following:
   a. Vowels: [i, ɪ, æ, ə, u, ʊ, ɔ, o]
   b. Consonants:
      (1) In initial position: [p', t', k', ð]
      (2) In initial position, the semivowel [w], in the word *wood*
      (3) In initial and medial position, [š], in the words *show* and *machine*
      (4) In all positions: [v, θ, z, j, s]
      (5) In final position: [-m, -n, -d, -t]
4) English consonant clusters, especially final clusters, present a major difficulty, since a very large number of these clusters do not occur in Spanish.

This study throws light on a number of problems related to the teaching and learning of English in Puerto Rico and which for many years have been controversial issues. The following conclusions can be drawn from this study:

1) The difficulties encountered by a Puerto Rican while learning English may be summed up as being the result of:
   a. Differences in the number of phonemes and contrasts
   b. Difference in the permissible sequences
   c. Differences in the phonetic expression of "similar" contrasts.
2) The teaching and learning of English in Puerto Rico has to be on the basis that English is a second language.
3) The first years of training in the second language should be conducted orally and after the student has some mastery of his native vernacular.
4) If the learning of the second language is to be efficient and profitable, the model used must be a good one, and effective practice in the difficult areas must be given. Microfilm $2.75; Xerox $7.40. 157 pages.

PHONOLOGY AND MORPHOLOGY OF
AN AMERICAN-ENGLISH DIALECT[1]

Mary Dorothea Sleator, Ph.D.
Indiana University, 1957

This analysis of a sample of the speech of a native speaker of English consists of a treatment of phonology, inflection, and phrase morphophonemics. The informant was a 70-year-old lady, a native of Southern Indiana. The corpus, 14 hours of recorded material, includes interviews held for the *Linguistic Atlas,* as well as ordinary conversation and other specially elicited responses. Because of the size of the corpus and the form of presentation of the analysis, the study is regarded not as a complete grammar of the dialect or a complete treatment of those levels with which it deals, but rather as a first step in the creation of a grammar.

The theory underlying the study is that presented by Chomsky in *Syntactic Structures:* The goal of linguistic theory is to provide an evaluation procedure for grammars, not a discovery procedure. A grammar, although based on observations of utterance tokens, is a model which generates grammatical utterances and hence consists of various levels of representation, with rules for deriving sequences on one level from sequences on another.

The phonemic transcription developed in Chapter 1, "Phonology," contains segmental and nonsegmental elements. Members of the former class are: tense vowels and vowel sequences /i e u o ɔ ai æʊ ɔi/, lax vowels /ɪ ɛ æ u ʌ a/, reduced vowel /ə/; consonants /p t k c b d g j f θ s š v ð z ž m n ŋ l r w y h/. Nonsegmental elements are: / / accent (on syllable following space, contrasting with absence of accent), /'/ stress (indicating prominent syllable or syllables in a phrase), /-/ internal juncture (occurs only before unaccented syllables and only contrastively), /|/ phrase marker, /‖/ utterance marker, /√/ continuative contour, and /=/ final contour (contours occur with markers and have morphemic as well as phonemic status). Allophones and consonant clusters are listed. The phonological treatment is not based on systematic spectrographic analysis, but correlations with spectrographic findings are shown for the vowel system. Inconsistency, redundancy, nongrammatical character, and failure to be supported by spectrographic evidence are considered bases for rejecting other systems of nonsegmental features.

In Chapter 2, "Inflection," three major and two minor inflectional classes are established: Verbs, whose paradigm consists of the forms {V}, {V} + {-ing}, {V} + {-Z'''}, {V} + {-D'}, {V} + (-D''); nouns, with subclasses {N} and {D} (demonstratives), whose paradigms consist of the forms {N}, {N} + {-Z'} and {D}, {D} + {-Z'}; adjectives, whose paradigm consists of the forms {A}, {A} + {-er} and {A} + {-est}; auxiliaries {have} and {do} followed by inflectional morphemes {-Z'''} and {-D'}; and modals, followed by {-D'}. Stems ending in /s/ + stop are added to those followed by the /-ɪd/ representation of {-D'} or {-D''}. Rules for deriving the phonemic shape of phonologically unpredictable sequences of {V} + {-D'}, {-D''} are given by examples representing each inflectional class

---

[1] Publication No. 24,571

(46 classes). The morphophoneme /Z/ requires four rules in derivation of sequences of {V} + {-Z'''}, {N} + {-Z'} and {-Z''} in addition to the usual three. There are nine classes of irregular nouns. {-er} and {-est} have phonologically predictable /O/ alternants; there are six irregularly inflected adjectives. A partial list of nouns, and a complete list of verbs and adjectives are included.

Chapter 3, "Phrase Morphophonemics," provides rules for the derivation of the phonemic shapes of members of the class personal pronouns, {P}; {P} + {-Z''} (possessive marker); and *noun phrase* + {-Z''}. In addition, rules for reduced forms and consonant alternation and loss are given to provide for most of the nongrammatical variation in phonemic shape.

Appendices consist of eleven pages of transcription from the corpus; vowel charts; and a discussion of the phonemic status of pitches, in which it is maintained that as used in current analyses they are not distinctive at the grammatical level.

151 pages. $2.00. Mic 58-321

EARLY NORTH CAROLINA PRONUNCIATION[1]

Edward Almand Stephenson, Ph.D.
University of North Carolina, 1958

Supervisor: Norman E. Eliason

The primary purpose of this study is to reconstruct the sounds of North Carolina speech in the eighteenth century and to determine the pronunciation of as many individual words as the evidence will permit. The achievement of these aims is sought by analysis of occasional spellings gathered from 165 collections of North Carolina manuscripts, preserved in the Southern Historical Collection of the University of North Carolina library.

The historical approach is used. The words are classified according to their Middle English forms; the sounds are viewed within the frame of reference of the transition from Middle English to Modern English; and a rationale is offered for every significant pronunciation indicated by the spellings. The study also provides a generous sampling of parallels between North Carolina pronunciations and those of other dialects, British and American. These comparisons serve to suggest the mixed character of North Carolina speech in the eighteenth century and to throw some light on its origins.

Examination of the treatment of consonants, which is first undertaken, reveals a considerable variety of forms, with several pronunciations of the same word often contending for supremacy. North Carolinians of the period, even cultivated persons, often dropped and added or voiced and unvoiced consonants in a way that would be considered slipshod today. Hypercorrect pronunciations, as seen in *linning* "linen," are also evident. A loss of postvocalic /r/ was in progress, but the direction of spread is not apparent.

The stressed vowels are next considered. The main affiliations of early North Carolina speech in this respect prove to have been with seventeenth-century British

[1] L.C. Card No. Mic 59-57

Standard English, although occasional influences of British regional dialects are detectable in the spellings. The sound of the vowel phonemes were no doubt in most instances much the same as they are today in North Carolina, but in the use of certain phonemes in certain words or classes of words a considerable amount of redistribution, both social and geographical, has evidently occurred since the eighteenth century. And some pronunciations then used have passed out of existence or survive only as relic forms in isolated areas, such as those indicated by the spellings *clark, marchant,* and the like. Again, diverse methods of pronouncing particular words can be inferred from the spellings.

In the selection of unstressed vowels, which are taken up last, North Carolinians in the eighteenth century had already established, or very nearly so, the present Southern modes of pronunciation in initial and final syllables, breaking away from British practice in this matter. Some aphetic forms (initially) and some hypercorrect forms (finally) were also used. In medial syllables, where American English has now standardized [ə] between consonants, both [ə] and [i] were competing actively in North Carolina. Examples of syncope and syneresis, moreover, abound in the manuscripts.

The present cleavage in pronunciation between the eastern and western parts of the state had not developed in the eighteenth century, or was only incipient. The picture that emerges from the spellings is one of marked diversity in both parts of the state with neither section having any characteristics that conspicuously distinguish it from the other. Furthermore, when the North Carolina spellings are compared with those in seventeenth-century Massachusetts town records, a similar inference must be drawn. Both states exhibit great diversity, with the same variations cropping up again and again. There were colonial modes of pronunciation, but as yet no distinctly Southern dialect.   Microfilm $4.05; Xerox $13.80.   316 pages.

NEW ENGLAND PRONUNCIATION BEFORE 1700[1]

Herbert Karl Tjossem, Ph.D.
Yale University, 1956

By applying the principles of historical phonology to the rhymes and spellings of early American poets, it is possible to discover something about the pronunciation of colo-English in its relation to the language of seventeenth-century England and to later American speech. With some general exceptions, the linguistic situation in New England before 1700 as reflected in the writings of the poets does not seem to have differed greatly from that of the present day. Although the pronunciation of Middle English ẹ wavers between [ệɪ] and [iɪ]. *oi* frequently appears as [əi] and the Middle English long vowels have more often been shortened than in present Standard English, the most striking difference is in the great number of variant pronunciations which analysis of the rhymes shows to have been in use. Many of these are Middle English doublet forms and can be found in the recom-

[1] Order No. 68-731

mendations of the orthoepists of the period, some have survived in English dialects,
others, particularly words with shortened Middle English ǫ, have remained one of
the distinguishing marks of New England speech. Comparison of the New England
writers' practices with those of Spenser and Shakespeare shows that the colonists
frequently followed a rhyming tradition already established and that they did not
often rhyme incorrectly by seventeenth century standards

Microfilm $3.30; Xerography $11.70.   256 pages.

A COMPARATIVE STUDY OF REGIONAL TERMS COMMON TO THE TWIN CITIES AND THE EASTERN UNITED STATES[1]

Robert Hickman Weber, Ph.D.
University of Minnesota, 1964

Adviser: Harold B. Allen

The purpose of this study is to describe that portion of the vocabulary
of the Twin Cities for which there is an Eastern geographical distribution defined
by Kurath in *A Word Geography of the Eastern United States* or Atwood in *A Survey
of Verb Forms in the Eastern United States*. The basic materials of the study are the
fifty field records of the *Linguistic Atlas of the Upper Midwest* for all of Minnesota
except the Twin Cities and Duluth, and twenty-seven records from Twin City
informants.

Chapter I sketches the settlement history of the Twin Cities and the background
of the informants. Chapters II and III present, for lexical items and verb forms, the
statistics of Twin City and rural Minnesota use, type by type, of all the significantly
distributed items mentioned by Kurath and by Atwood. In Chapter IV, these data
are examined and conclusions drawn from them.

The Eastern dialect areas that have in reasonably frequent use terms which also
appear in the Twin Cities were identified and the number of terms which the Twin
Cities have in common with each area was calculated. On the basis of the greatest
number of common terms, the Twin City vocabulary is most like that of Southern
New England, but this similarity is only slightly greater than it is to the vocabulary
of the remainder of the North. Similarity to Twin City vocabulary decreases in
almost regular tiers toward the south. In many items the Twin City informants prefer
generally distributed terms over regional ones. Among the predominant responses
to the 120 items, the general terms used in preference to available regional ones
outnumber the regional terms from any one of the Eastern areas.

Many of the terms studied are used with distinctly different frequencies by Type I
and Type II informants, but there is no strong evidence of a change in regional
preference. There is, however, some indication that the Type II's are using slightly
fewer terms with Southern and South Midland distributions than do the Type I's.

Few terms used in the Twin Cities have exclusively Northern or exclusively non-

[1] Order No. 65-165

698   Northern distribution, but the limited evidence indicates that the non-Northern terms are not confined to the speech of informants with non-Northern background. The background of the informants seems to have little effect on their use of these non-Northern terms.

Examination of that part of the vocabulary not used by both Twin City informants and other Minnesota informants indicates that the Twin City informants use significantly fewer terms in their responses than do the rural respondents. The vocabularies of both groups show slight but strongest similarity to the vocabularies of the same areas: Northeastern New England, Western Midland, and the Middle South. Twin City use of verbs adheres more closely to textbook standard and at the same time shows more of a tendency to evade difficult choices of verb form than does the rural use.

Although the Twin Cities have a large population with close foreign background, there is effectively no evidence of foreign-language influence in this sample of the vocabulary of the Twin City informants, even those with the foreign-language background.   Microfilm $2.75; Xerography $6.80.   145 pages.

PHONOLOGICAL STYLES IN ENGLISH: A STRATIFICATIONAL APPROACH[1]

Rose-Marie Olga Weber, Ph.D.
Cornell University, 1965

The choices available to a single speaker for pronouncing given constructions of a pronoun or interrogative word and verb phrase such as *He would not have* are described in terms of the stratificational model of generative grammar. This model posits four strata of linguistic structure, the sememic, the lexemic, the morphemic, and the phonemic, which are related to one another by realizational rules. Units on the sememic stratum, where the continuum that we may call experience is quantized into linguistic structure, are transduced by rules to elements on the lexemic stratum, the phrase structure of the language. Lexemic units are realized into strings of morphons, the elements on the morphemic stratum, which manifest the deeper phonological structure of the language. Morphons are in turn realized into units on the phonemic stratum, the ultimate phonological components such as stopness and nasality. A language is thus viewed as a coding device by which experience is transduced into another kind of reality: sound.

Within the limits of this study, phonemic variants are defined as stylistic variations if they are realizations of a single lexeme in a set of given environments which differ from one another only in the presence of a lexeme of style. The terms for these lexemes, namely, formal, semiformal, colloquial, and informal, reflect social situations in which the ultimate phonological realizations into speech would be appropriate.

To exemplify the usefulness of the model for describing phonological variants

[1] Order No. 66–68

and to demonstrate the kinds of variation in the active control of a single speaker, subject pronouns or interrogative words in construction with verb phrases were analyzed. Forms of auxiliaries *do, have,* and *be* and the modal auxiliaries *can, could, will, would, shall, should, may, must,* and *might,* and all the various arrangements of these with inflection, a lexical verb, and *not* comprise the verb phrases. Lexomorphemic rules, by which lexemes are realized into morphons, provide for stylistic variants on the morphemic stratum, e.g., formal /wud/, semiformal and colloquial /wɪd/ and informal /Ð/ in *I would* (*'d*) *go.* Morphophonemic rules, by which morphons are realized into phonemes or bundles of phonons, also provide for stylistically varying realizations, e.g., morphon /Ð/ as phonemic stops /g/ and /b/ in some informal environments, and /ɪd/ and /d/ elsewhere, including other styles.

The problem of analyzing styles and presenting them within a unified description of a language, and the ways in which linguists have attempted to meet the problems are reviewed. Finally, the relevance of style to investigations of the history and function of language in culture are briefly discussed.

Microfilm $3.00; Xerography $6.40.   135 pages.

Symbols Used for the Vowels

The symbols used in the phonetic transcriptions (enclosed in brackets) in most of the articles are those of the IPA. The vowels are presented in the following chart, which shows the tongue position of the vowels and their relation to each other:

Some of the studies, in addition, have another symbol [ɑ], which represents a low-back vowel between [ɑ] and [ɒ].

The phonemic symbolization is not the same in all of the studies. Those based on the materials of the *Linguistic Atlas* use the IPA symbolization, with some modification. Some of the other studies also use this symbolization. Some use the Trager-Smith system. The following chart shows most of the vowels of American English as they are generally symbolized by the two systems. Not all of the keywords are, however, pronounced the same way in all dialects.

Keyword	IPA	Trager-Smith	701
peat	i	iy	
pit	ɪ	i	
pate	e	ey	
pet	ɛ	e	
pat	æ	æ	
boot	u	uw	
put	ʊ	u	
boat	o	ow	
bought	ɔ	ɔ,oh	
cup	ʌ	ə	
above	ə	ə	
fur	ɜ	ə,ɨ	
father	ɑ	a	
tight	aɪ	ay	
out	aʊ	aw	
boy	ɔɪ	ɔy	

A Selected
Bibliography

BOOKS

Allen, Harold B., ed. *Readings in Applied Linguistics.* 2nd ed. New York: Appleton-Century-Crofts, 1964.

Atwood, E. Bagby. *A Survey of Verb Forms in the Eastern United States.* Ann Arbor: University of Michigan Press, 1953.

————. *The Regional Vocabulary of Texas.* Austin: University of Texas Press, 1962.

Baugh, Albert C. *A History of the English Language.* 2nd ed. New York: Appleton-Century-Crofts, 1957.

Bloomfield, Leonard. *Language.* New York: Holt, Rinehart and Winston, 1933.

Bronstein, Arthur J. *The Pronunciation of American English: An Introduction to Phonetics.* New York: Appleton-Century-Crofts, 1960.

Brooks, Cleanth, Jr. *The Relation of the Alabama-Georgia Dialect to the Provincial Dialects of Great Britain.* Baton Rouge: Louisiana State University Press, 1935.

Bryant, Margaret M. *Current American Usage.* New York: Funk and Wagnalls, 1962.

Francis, Winthrop Nelson. *The Structure of American English.* (Chapter IX "The Dialects of American English," written by Raven I. McDavid, Jr.) New York: Ronald Press, 1958.

Fries, Charles C. *American English Grammar* (NCTE Monograph, No. 10). New York: Appleton-Century-Crofts, 1940.

Gimson, A. C. *An Introduction to the Pronunciation of English.* London: Edward Arnold, 1962.

Hall, Joseph S. *The Phonetics of Great Smoky Mountain Speech* (*American Speech Monographs*) New York: Kings Crown Press, 1942.

Haugen, Einar. *The Norwegian Language in America: A Study in Bilingual Behavior.*   703
Philadelphia: University of Pennsylvania Press, 1953.

Hill, Archibald Anderson. *Introduction to Linguistic Structures: From Sound to Sentence in English.* New York: Harcourt, Brace & World, 1958.

Hubbell, Allan F. *The Pronunciation of English in New York City.* New York: Kings Crown Press, 1950.

Jespersen, Otto. *Growth and Structure of the English Language,* 9th ed. Oxford: B. Blackwell, 1956.

Joos, Martin, *The English Verb: Form and Meanings.* Madison: University of Wisconsin Press, 1964.

Kenyon, John Samuel. *American Pronunciation: A Textbook of Phonetics for Students of English,* 8th ed. Ann Arbor: George Wahr, 1940.

_____, and Thomas A. Knott. *A Pronouncing Dictionary of American English.* Springfield, Mass.: G. & C. Merriam, 1953.

Krapp, George Phillip. *The English Language in America,* 2 vols. New York: Century Company, 1925.

_____. *The Pronunciation of Standard English in America.* New York: Oxford University Press, 1919.

Kurath, Hans. *Handbook of the Linguistic Geography of New England.* Providence: Brown University Press, 1939.

_____. *A Phonology and Prosody of Modern English.* Ann Arbor: University of Michigan Press, 1964.

_____. *A Word Geography of the United States.* Ann Arbor: University of Michigan Press, 1949.

_____, Bernard Bloch, and others. *Linguistic Atlas of New England,* 3 vols. in 6 parts. Providence: Brown University Press, 1939–1943.

_____, and Raven I. McDavid, Jr. *The Pronunciation of English in the Atlantic States.* Ann Arbor: University of Michigan Press, 1961.

Labov, William. *The Social Stratification of English in New York City.* Washington, D.C.: Center of Applied Linguistics, 1966.

Lloyd, Donald J., and Harry R. Warfel. *American English in Its Cultural Setting.* New York: Alfred A. Knopf, 1957.

Marckwardt, Albert H. *American English.* New York: Oxford University Press, 1958.

Mencken, H. L. *The American Language: The Fourth Edition and the Two Supplements.* Abridged and ed. Raven I. McDavid, Jr. New York: Alfred A. Knopf, 1963.

Orton, Harold, and Eugen Dieth. *Survey of English Dialects.* Leeds: E. J. Arnold and Son, 1962.

Pyles, Thomas. *Words and Ways of American English.* New York: Random House, 1952.

Reed, Carroll E., and Lester W. Seifert. *A Linguistic Atlas of Pennsylvania German.* Marburg-an-der-Lahn, 1954.

Shuy, Roger W. *The Northern-Midland Dialect Boundary in Illinois.* Publication of the American Dialect Society, No. 38. University, Alabama: The University of Alabama, 1962.

704 Stanley, Oma. *The Speech of East Texas (American Speech Monograph* No. 2). New York: Columbia University Press, 1937.

Thomas, Charles Kenneth. *An Introduction to the Phonetics of American English.* 2nd ed. New York: Ronald Press, 1958.

Trager, George Leonard, and Henry Lee Smith, Jr. *An Outline of English Structure.* (Studies in Linguistics, Occasional Papers, no. 3). Washington, D.C.: American Council of Learned Societies, 1957.

Turner, Lorenzo D. *Africanisms in the Gullah Dialects.* Chicago: University of Chicago Press, 1949.

Wise, Claude Merton. *Applied Phonetics.* Englewood Cliffs: Prentice-Hall, 1957.

ARTICLES

Allen, Harold B. "Canadian-American Speech Difference Along the Middle Border," *Journal of the Canadian Linguistic Association,* V, (Spring, 1959), 17–24.

_____. "Minor Dialect Areas of the Upper Midwest," *Publication of the American Dialect Society,* No. 30 (November, 1958), 3–16.

_____. "On Accepting Participial Drank," *College English* XVIII, (February, 1957), 283–285.

_____. "The Linguistic Atlases: Our New Resource," *The English Journal,* XLV, (April, 1956), 188–194.

Atwood, E. B. "A Preliminary Report on Texas Word Geography," *Orbis,* II, (January, 1953), 61–66.

Babington, Mima, and E. Bagby Atwood. "Lexical Usage in Southern Louisiana," *Publications of the American Dialect Society,* No. 36 (November, 1961), 1–24.

Barrows, S. T. "Watch, Water, Wash," *American Speech,* IV (April, 1929), 301–302.

Berrey, Lester V. "Southern Mountain Dialect," *American Speech,* XV (1940), 45–54.

Cassidy, Frederic G. "On Collecting American Dialect," *American Speech,* XXIII (1948), 185–193.

_____. "Some New England Words in Wisconsin," *Language,* XVII (October-December, 1941), 324–339.

Clough, W. O. "Some Wyoming Speech Patterns," *American Speech,* XXIX (February, 1954), 28–35.

Davis, Alva L., and Raven I. McDavid, Jr. "Shivaree: An Example of Cultural Diffusion," *American Speech,* XXIV (1949), 249–255.

Dobbins, Austin C. "The Language of the Cultivated," *College English,* XVIII (October, 1956), 46–47.

Duckert, Audrey R. "The Linguistic Atlas of New England Revisited," *Publication of the American Dialect Society,* No. 39 (April, 1963), 8–15.

Dunbar, Gary S. "A Southern Geographical Word List," *American Speech,* XXXVI (December, 1961), 293–296.

Greet, William Cabell. "A Phonographic Expedition to Williamsburg, Virginia," *American Speech,* VI, (February, 1931), 161–172.

_____. "Southern Speech," *Culture in the South,* Chapel Hill: University of North Carolina Press, (1934), 594–615.

Hankey, Clyde T. "Semantic Features and Eastern Relics in Colorado Dialect," *American Speech,* XXXVI (December, 1961), 266–270.

Hubbell, Allan. "The Phonemic Analysis of Unstressed Vowels," *American Speech,* XXV (May, 1950), 105–111.

Ives, Sumner. "Pronunciation of *Can't* in the Eastern States," *American Speech,* XXVIII, 149–157.

Johnson, T. Earle. "Nasality in Southern Speech," *Southern Speech Journal,* XVII (September, 1951), 30–39.

Kurath, Hans. "Dialect Areas, Settlement Areas and Cultural Areas in the United States," *The Cultural Approach to History,* ed. C. F. Ware. New York: Columbia University Press, (1940), 331–351.

_____. "Linguistic Regionalism," Chapter X of *Regionalism in America,* ed. Merrill Jenson. Madison: University of Wisconsin Press, (1952).

Labov, William. "The Social Motivation of a Sound Change," *Word* XIX (December, 1963), 273–309.

Lehmann, W. P. "A Note on the Change of American English /t/," *American Speech,* XXVIII (December, 1953), 270–275.

Marckwardt, Albert H. "Folk Speech in Indiana and Adjacent States," *Indiana History Bulletin,* IV (1940), 120–140.

_____. "Middle English *o* in the American English of the Great Lakes Area," *Papers of the Michigan Acad.,* XXVI (1941), 561–571.

_____. "Principal and Subsidiary Areas in the North-Central States," *Publication of the American Dialect Society,* No. 27 (April, 1957), 3–15.

McDavid, Raven I. Jr. "Oughtn't and Hadn't Ought," *College English* XIV (May, 1953), 472–473.

_____. "Some Social Differences in Pronunciation," *Language Learning,* IV (1952–1953), 102–116.

_____. "The Pronunciation of *Catch,*" *College English* XIV (February, 1953), 290–291.

_____ and Virginia Glenn McDavid. "The Relationship of the Speech of American Negroes to the Speech of Whites," *American Speech* XXVI (February, 1951).

McDowell, Tremaine. "The Use of Negro Dialect by Harriet Beecher Stowe," *American Speech,* VI (June, 1931), 322–326.

Miller, Virginia R. "Present-Day Use of the Broad *a* in Eastern Massachusetts," *Speech Monographs,* XX (November, 1953), 235–246.

Mills, R. V. "Oregon Speechways," *American Speech,* XXV (May, 1950), 81–90.

Moore, Rayburn S. "Thomas Dunn English, A Forgotten Contributor to the Development of Negro Dialect Verse in the 1870's," *American Literature,* XXXIII (March, 1961), 72–75.

Owens, Bess Alice. "Folk Speech of the Cumberlands," *American Speech,* (December, 1931).

Penzl, Herbert. "The Vowel-Phonemes in *Father, Man, Dance* in Dictionaries and New England Speech," *Journal of English and German Philology,* XXXIX No. 1 (January, 1940), 13–32.

706   Read, Allen Walker. "The Speech of Negroes in Colonial America," *The Journal of Negro History,* XXIV (July, 1939), 247–258.

Reed, Carroll E. "The Pronunciation of English in the Pacific Northwest," *Language,* XXXVII (October-December, 1961), 559-564.

Sawyer, Janet B. "Social Aspects of Bilingualism in San Antonio, Texas," *Publication of the American Dialect Society,* No. 41 (April, 1964), 7–14.

Stephenson, Edward A. "Beginnings of the Loss of Postvocalic /r/ in North Carolina," *Journal of English Linguistics,* II (March, 1968), 57–77.

Thomas, Charles K. "Recent Discussion of Standardization in American Pronunciation," *Quarterly Journal of Speech Education* XIII (November, 1927), 442–457.

Wise, Claude M. "The Southern American Diphthong [aɪ]," *Southern Speech Journal* XIX (May, 1954), 304–312.

Wood, Gordon R. "An Atlas Survey of the Interior South (U.S.A.)," *Orbis,* IX (January, 1960), 7–12.

———. "Word Distribution in the Interior South," *Publication of the American Dialect Society,* No. 35 (April, 1961), 1–16.